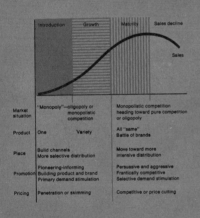

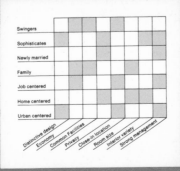

Marketing strategy planning requires judgment and research because every "market" can be conceived as a grid with many submarkets (see page 122).

Basic marketing: A managerial approach

Basic
marketing:
A managerial
approach

E. JEROME McCARTHY Ph.D.

Professor of Marketing   Michigan State University

Fifth Edition   1975

Richard D. Irwin, Inc.   Homewood, Illinois   60430

Irwin-Dorsey International   Arundel, Sussex   BN189AB
Irwin-Dorsey Limited   Georgetown, Ontario   L7G 4B3

Photo credits

Section 1, page 1: Bruce Davidson, Magnum
    pages 1&2 (red): Charles Harbutt, Magnum
    page 2 (top): Bob Henriques, Magnum
    page 2 (bottom): Sepp Seitz, Magnum

Section 2, page 1: Charles Harbutt, Magnum
    pages 1&2 (red): Charles Harbutt, Magnum
    page 2 (top): Inger McCabe, Rapho Guillumette
    page 2 (bottom left): Burk Uzzle, Magnum
    page 2 (bottom right): Erich Hartmann, Magnum

Section 3, page 1: Esaias Baitel, Rapho Guillumette
    pages 1&2 (red): Charles Harbutt, Magnum
    page 2 (top): Bruce Davidson, Magnum
    page 2 (bottom): Campbell Soup Company

Section 4, page 1: Esaias Baitel, Rapho Guillumette
    pages 1&2 (red): Bruce Roberts, Rapho Guillumette
    page 2 (top): Alex Webb, Magnum
    page 2 (bottom): Leonard Freed, Magnum

Section 5, page 1: Burk Uzzle, Magnum
    pages 1&2 (red): Burk Uzzle, Magnum
    page 2 (top): Bob S. Smith, Rapho Guillumette
    page 2 (bottom): Bob Combs, Rapho Guillumette

Fifth Edition

First Printing, January 1975
Second Printing, June 1975
Third Printing, December 1975
Fourth Printing, January 1976
Fifth Printing, March 1976
Sixth Printing, August 1976
Seventh Printing, January 1977
Eighth Printing, June 1977

ISBN 0-256-01567-8
Library of Congress Catalog Card No. 74-82928

Printed in the United States of America

Preface

■ This text is designed for use in an introductory course in marketing, either in schools with one or two marketing courses or in the larger business schools with a full complement of marketing courses.

All business students should be introduced to the basic problems and practices in marketing management. At the same time, it is clearly wishful thinking to assume that a student can be taught all there is to know about marketing in one or two courses. And it is just as clear that, even in larger schools with a range of marketing courses, less than one third of all business students become marketing majors.

This text, then, is an attempt to meet the needs of the majority of beginning marketing students who are taking their first and perhaps only course in marketing. It tries to give the student an understanding and a feel for the marketing manager's job, and the world in which the job must be performed.

Admittedly, this text does not offer a complete and detailed description of all possible problems or solutions in the marketing area. But it does offer a broad and necessary understanding of marketing problems, giving the student a foundation for investigating more comprehensive references. A student must see the whole picture before the details can be appreciated.

As a basic introductory text, *Basic Marketing* differs considerably from other works. First, it is designed to facilitate learning—in other words it is intended to be a learning aid, helping the student and instructor to accomplish specific behavioral objectives (which are listed separately in the *Teacher's Manual*). Second, it has a logical flow from chapter to chapter, taking an integrated, analytical approach to both macro- and micro-marketing problems. Third, it has a distinct and consistent focus throughout the text. While the text material, of course, is similar to that found in many other texts, the focus definitely is not. We will be primarily concerned with micro-marketing – that is, we will see marketing through the manager's eyes because that manager can affect the performance of both the individual firm and the macro-marketing system.

Marketing strategy planning, including designing a marketing mix (but not day-to-day implementation), is stressed to give the student the big-picture view of micro-marketing. This planning takes place within a dynamic social and political environment which affects the macro-marketing system, however; therefore, the effect of the environment on the macro-marketing system (and vice versa) is given extensive treatment.

The first chapter begins with a review of the many criticisms of marketing – of both macro- and micro-marketing. These criticisms lead logically to consideration of the nature of the two views of marketing and the evolution of thinking about marketing and marketing systems. The importance of understanding the macro-marketing system is stressed, while emphasizing that changes in our macro system are likely to come from the actions of individual consumer/voters and businesses. This sets the stage for the transition to a focus on the actions and potential contributions of business people and, in particular, marketing managers.

Following the introductory chapter, the vital role of marketing management in the operation of a firm and the macro-marketing system is stressed. The focus upon satisfying varying target markets on a market grid is emphasized especially. Then, the characteristics and buying habits of target customers – both final consumers in the United States and world markets, and intermediate customers, such as businesses, farmers, and governments – are described.

Next, based on the behavior of target markets and the company's own objectives, a marketing mix is developed out of four ingredients called the four Ps: Product, Place (that is, channels and institutions), Promotion, and Price. These sections comprise the bulk of the text and are concerned with developing the "right" Product and making it available at the "right" Place with the "right" Promotion and the "right" Price, to satisfy target customers and still meet the objectives of the business.

These materials are presented in an integrated, analytical way so that there is a logical, cumulative development of the student's thinking. After a final discussion on integrating the four Ps and controlling the marketing process, we return to a consideration of how efficient the marketing process is, and especially to the question "Does marketing cost too much?" Here we return to the many criticisms of marketing and evaluate the effectiveness of both micro- and macro-level marketing, considering whether any changes are needed. This final analysis is important because marketing people must be concerned about their impact on the economy and how they can help our system work more effectively.

Some textbooks treat currently "hot" topics such as "social responsibility," "consumerism," and "multinational marketing" as the basis for separate chapters. That is not done in this text. Instead, they are treated in their appropriate place within the integrated whole. Multinational marketing, for example, is treated not only in the early chapters and in Chapter 10, but also throughout the text in recognition of American businesses' growing interest and involvement in the world market. Technical details are not emphasized. The multinational emphasis merely provides perspective and shows the universal applicability of the principles and approaches presented throughout the text. Similarly, "social responsibility" and "consumerism" materials are not only treated at the beginning and end of the text, but also are woven into the text to emphasize that marketing managers must be continually concerned with, and work within, their environment. Isolating such materials in a separate chapter would lead to an unfortunate "compartmentalization" of ideas, when, in fact, a marketing manager must give continual consideration to these issues.

It is hoped that, in this framework, marketing will be looked upon by more students as a useful, fascinating, and a very necessary function in our American economy.

This material can be studied in a number of ways. *One*, the text material can be supplemented by lectures and class discussion of the text material and perhaps additional readings. A separate *Readings in Basic Marketing* has been prepared to provide additional complementary materials. *Two*, understanding of the text material can be enhanced by discussion of conventional questions and problems; further, a separate *Learning Aid* has been developed to offer additional opportunities to obtain a deeper understanding of the material. This *Learning Aid* includes not only exercises but also true-false and multiple choice questions (with answers). *Three*, thought-provoking questions included at the end of the chapters can be used to encourage the student to investigate the marketing process and organize an individual way of thinking about it. Some of the questions and exercises in the *Learning Aid* also can be used to implement this third approach.

The text is organized so that any of the approaches or any combination of them can be used, depending upon the time available and the objectives of the instructor. All are compatible. However, at least experimentation with the third approach is highly recommended. It is not only educationally sound, but can be fun too, for both the student and the instructor. The thinking behind this third approach is elaborated upon in the following paragraphs.

I reevaluated my approach to teaching beginning marketing when some educators made some interesting observations. Dr. J. S. Bruner, at Harvard, found that a child learned more geography when given a map and asked to predict where the biggest cities *should be*, rather than by straight memorization of where they actually are. Other educators had success using similar methods, such as asking children to "invent" multiplication as a short cut to addition.

Trying to apply these ideas using conventional marketing texts was difficult, however, since most of the "answers" were given early – sometimes in the first chapter or two. Thus it was not possible to have the student read the text and still develop individual ideas as the text moved along.

This text works differently. It assumes that the student comes to the beginning marketing course with some experience – if nothing else, as a consumer – and ability to project what "should be" or "probably will be" on the basis of this prior knowledge. Certainly the student's vocabulary, in the sense of conventional marketing terms and definitions, will be lacking. But the nature of these terms and especially the functions which are provided by the various firms can be anticipated.

It is for this reason – that the student should be encouraged to "think ahead" – that this text deliberately avoids introducing certain concepts and definitions before they are needed. Precise definitions of wholesaling and retailing, for example, are delayed until midway in the book, when the entire area of where and how goods should be made available is considered.

When all the details are not presented early, then creative thought can be encouraged by the questions following each chapter. These questions encourage the student to think ahead and develop what "ought to be," and then subsequent chapters present commonly accepted definitions and methods of operation. For example, following the introductory chapters, customers – both intermediate customers and final customers – are analyzed. The questions here encourage the student to think about the kind of products these customers *might like,* the kinds of shopping behavior they *would exhibit,* where the goods *should be made available,* and how they *should be priced and promoted.*

In the Product area, after the student has had a chance to roughly categorize the products which will be available, the conventional terms are introduced and past experience is organized.

The questions at the end of the Product chapters ask how these products should be made available. After a try at this, the conventional definitions and institutional material on wholesaling and retailing are introduced in the Place area; and so on.

This approach follows in sequence four basic steps in psychological learning theory:

1. Motivation.
2. Investigation.
3. Organization.
4. Utilization.

The first few chapters attempt to motivate the student by encouraging interest in the subject and indicating how important marketing and marketing management are to the operation of a whole economy. The questions at the end of the early chapters encourage independent investigation. Then subsequent chapters provide the commonly accepted organization.

In the middle chapters, the approach is to alternate between Steps 2 and 3 — from investigation to organization and then to further investigation, building upon the material previously organized. The cases at the end of the text or the many caselets in the *Learning Aid* can be used to encourage the student to utilize the thinking done in the investigation and organization stages. Ideally, some cases or caselets should be tried during and at the end of the course to "set" the material and give the student a chance to utilize the fruits of independent thinking. This completes the learning cycle. By the end of the course, the student should be better prepared to move on to a subsequent case analysis course in marketing or other management areas.

As indicated earlier, this third approach need not be used — the first two can be used quite satisfactorily. But I have thoroughly enjoyed teaching the course since experimenting with its use. Most students feel they know quite a bit about marketing when they come into this course. When the entire course is "high spotted" in the first few chapters, it becomes difficult to maintain interest in "old stuff." If, instead, the instructor and text encourage organization and use of experience and common sense to almost "write" the book, the student becomes involved. Many even enjoy the course. And this is one of my major objectives for these teaching materials.

To facilitate student understanding, important new concepts are given special treatment. They appear either in the headings, or in italics in the body of the text. They are also listed separately in the *Learning Aid*. Hopefully, this will help the student note important concepts and facilitate review before examinations.

Finally, feedback — from both students and instructors — is encouraged. It is our intention to prepare the best teaching materials we can. Learning should not only be fun but should accomplish specific objectives. Any suggestions for improving the learning process in the marketing area will be greatly appreciated.

December 1974   E. JEROME McCARTHY

acknowledgments

This book is a result of the blending of my experiences in business, at Northwestern University, Michigan State University, and the Universities of Minnesota, Oregon, and Notre Dame. Many people, too numerous to mention, have had an influence on this text. My colleagues at the University of Notre Dame had a profound effect on my thinking during the years we were developing a beginning course emphasizing marketing management. The original edition of this text grew out of this work. To all of them, and especially the many students who suggested case materials and have criticized and made comments about all of the editions, I am most grateful.

Helpful criticisms and comments were made on either the original edition or the revised editions by the following professors: Harry Lipson of the University of Alabama, William Stanton of the University of Colorado, Phillip McVey of the University of Nebraska, Edwin H. Lewis of the University of Minnesota, William T. Kelley of the Wharton School of Finance and Commerce, Louis Stern of Wayne State University, Henry Gomez of New York University, Walter Gross of the University of Georgia, David Revzan of the University of California, R. A. Klages of the State University of New York at Albany, Fred Kniffen of the University of Connecticut, Guy R. Banville of Kent State University, Steven J. Shaw of the University of South Carolina, John F. Grashof of Temple University, and Andrew A. Brogowicz and Eric S. Stein of the University of Illinois, Chicago Circle.

I am especially indebted to Professor Yusaku Furuhashi of the University of Notre Dame for reading several versions of all revised editions and counseling on the multinational marketing emphasis.

Others who have been especially helpful include Professors Ferdinand Mauser at Wayne State University, Gerald Albaum at the University of Oregon, Joseph Siebert and John Maggard at Miami University, Karl Reyer at Louisiana State University, George Schwartz and James Wiek at the University of Massachusetts, James D. Taylor of State University of South Dakota, G. J. Eberhart of Indiana State University, William G. Panschar of Indiana University, Noel B. Zabriskie at the University of Maryland, Alan Kelman at Michigan State University, and Keith Humphries at the University of Denver.

Mary Kollat, Durward Humes, Kenneth Wylie, and Don M. Smith provided invaluable editorial assistance and many fresh ideas.

Last, but not least, I must thank my wife, Joanne, for considerable patience, advice, and assistance, and finally for proofreading under typically chaotic conditions. Our children Mary and Tom helped in this final effort, too. To all of these persons and the many publishers who graciously granted permission to use their material, I am deeply grateful. Responsibility for any errors or omissions is certainly mine, but the book would not have been possible without the assistance of many others.

E. J. McC.

Contents

Contents

Contents

Part one

Introduction to marketing

All modern-day businesses must direct the flow of goods and services

Marketing begins with
the customer . . . determines
what products . . . what prices . . .
where and how sold . . .

that satisfies some customers in order to earn the right
to operate in our marketing system

1

Marketing's role in society

■ The market-directed U.S. economy has provided us with the highest standard of living of any nation in the world. This has come about for a variety of reasons, but the efforts of businessmen to satisfy consumer's needs has been an important factor. Market-oriented firms have aggressively competed with each other, trying to better satisfy consumers. Sometimes these efforts have been costly. Some critics have asked whether this marketing effort is really necessary. Does it cost too much? Is it truly useful to society?

Marketing activity is especially susceptible to criticism because the public sees its "end products" every day. There's nothing like a pocketbook issue for getting the average consumer stirred up.

Typical complaints include:

Distribution costs are just too high.
Product quality is terrible. They don't build things like they used to.
Packaging and labeling are often confusing.
Too many middlemen are adding to the cost and raising our prices.
Easy consumer credit is forcing people to buy.
All those model changes are just window dressing to exploit the consumer.
Marketing makes men materialistic—motivates them toward the 'almighty dollar' instead of social needs.
Greedy businessmen create monopolies which restrict output and employment.
The big incomes go to the smart promoters—the manipulators.

In recognition of the depth of some consumer complaints, the President of the United States appointed an "Assistant for Consumer Affairs." Many states have similar agencies. Then there are the independent consumer-oriented groups such as "Nader's Raiders." Individual politicians thrive on taking pot shots at business. Marketing makes a good "bad guy."

Other people feel that marketing is overrated, that it doesn't have to be so costly or complicated. Their attitude is reflected in Emerson's old adage: "If a man . . . make a better mouse trap . . . the world will beat a path to his door!" A good product, in other words, is all you need to succeed in business. Make that better product and the customers will find you.

The mousetrap theory probably was not true in Emerson's time, and it certainly is not true today. In modern economies, the grass grows high on the path to the Better Mousetrap Factory — if the new mousetrap is *not* properly marketed.

Today, the design and the production of a good product are only two of the many vital steps. A producer (or a wholesaler or a retailer) must continually study his customers' needs and preferences. He may have to advertise his product and arrange for transporting and warehousing. And, of course, he must offer it for sale.

The modern-day firm must design a production and marketing system — a total system — which satisfies some consumer needs. This process can be complex and sometimes very expensive. But are all the criticisms of marketing justified?

To be fairly judged, marketing must be clearly understood. Our study of marketing will begin with a look at the two levels of marketing — the *macro* level and the *micro* level. Individual businessmen work at the micro level but must be aware that they are part of the macro-marketing system. Then we will go on to see how various marketing systems have evolved and explore the role marketing plays in our economy. Finally, we will define the concept of marketing, explain the thrust of this book, and examine why an understanding of marketing is so important.

Marketing systems exist at two levels

■ A brief review of the complaints against marketing suggests that there are basically two levels of criticism. One level is concerned with the overall role of marketing and the performance of the entire economic system. The second level of criticism is directed to the activities of individual firms. If we are to understand these two types of criticism, we must learn to evaluate marketing systems at the macro level and the micro level.

Macro-
versus
micro-
marketing

■ *Macro-marketing* looks at the economy's entire marketing system to see how it operates and how efficient and fair it is. *Micro-marketing,* on the other hand, examines individual firms within the economic system, to see how they operate or how they should function.

The kinds of problems handled at each level and the methods of analysis are quite different, so it is important that a clear distinction be made. We will begin by discussing the macro-marketing concept and then go on to an analysis of micro-marketing. The latter will be emphasized in the bulk of the text. Along the way, the impact of individual businesses on the whole economy will be explored because individual firms must operate within the macro environment.

At the end of the course, we will return to the macro concept and to the many criticisms of marketing. We will then take a look at how effectively the marketing process operates and what opportunities there are for improvement.

Now, let's take a look at the macro — or "big-picture" — view of marketing.

Macro-marketing takes a big-picture view

■ All economies — whether state-run or market-directed — must have a *marketing system* — i.e., a system for ensuring that goods and services are produced and distributed. This means that some kind of mechanism, along with appropriate institutions, must be developed to decide: *what* and *how much* is to be produced and distributed *by whom, when* and *to whom. How* the decisions are made may vary from country to country, but the macro-level objectives are basically similar: to create goods and services and make them available when and where they are needed — to improve consumers well-being, i.e., their standard of living.

Producers and consumers make an economy

■ It is very useful (although greatly oversimplified) to think of an economy as consisting of producers and consumers. Actually, most people function in both roles. As a *producer* one is primarily concerned with his income, since this is his claim against the output of the economy. As a *consumer,* on the other hand, he is concerned with what his income will buy. These two roles are inherent in any economy, but they can lead to difficulties since what is "good" for some producers may not be so "good" for other consumers.[1]

A market-directed economy runs itself

■ The bulk of the U.S. economy (and most Western economies) is *market-directed*, that is, directed by the market mechanism which relies on a multitude of individual micro-level decisions, in both producing and consuming units. Each decision may be small in scope, but collectively they determine the macro-level decisions for the whole economy.

In a pure market-directed economy, people, as consumers, determine a society's production decisions when they make their consumption choices in the marketplace. In this sense, they decide what is to be produced, and by whom. Thus, ideally, the control of the economy is completely democratic, with dispersion of power throughout the economy.

Further, in a pure market-directed economy, people have free choice in finding work that is satisfying to them. Therefore, a market-directed economy enables people to decide for themselves both their role as producers and consumers. Ideally, no one is forced to take a job or buy goods or services he does not want. But he must find something "good" to do if he is to have a claim against the output of this system.

Price is a measure of value

To fully appreciate how a market-directed economy works, it is important to understand the role of market price. The prices of consumer goods and services serve roughly as a measure of their social importance. If consumers are willing to pay the market prices, apparently they feel they are getting at least their money's worth. Similarly, the cost of resources is a rough measure of the value of the resources used in the production of these goods and services. In a market-directed economy, both the prices in the production sector (for resources) and in the consumption sector (for products and services) fluctuate to allocate resources and distribute income in the light of the preferences of consumers. The end result is an equilibrium of demand and supply for all products and resources, and the coordination of the economic activity of many people and institutions.

The interaction among various people and institutions in a market-directed economy is shown in a highly simplified manner in Figure 1–1. Here we see that consumers offer their resources in the factor market (human resources as well as land and capital) for use in producing goods and/or services by business firms. (A firm is defined broadly to include any producing entity which acts as a unit, from a farm family to a large industrial corporation.)

These firms, in turn, make payments to people for use of these resources. These people, then, in their role as consumers can take these payments into the product market to buy finished goods and services. Their monies are exchanged for goods and services, and then flow to the business firms which are able to continue hiring and buying factors for further production.

Such a system requires continual flows within the system to keep it going. Ideally, the participants have enough information to make wise decisions with respect both to where they offer their resources for sale and what they buy.

Government is included in this diagram to show that a democratic society may assign the supervision of the system to the government. Since proper functioning of a market-directed system depends on continual, smooth flows throughout the system, the government is expected to ensure that the market system continues to work properly. In an effort to protect the rights and freedoms of all, the government will presumably set rules to ensure that: property is protected, contracts are enforced, individuals are not exploited, no group monopolizes the factor market or the product market, the various factors are compensated at competitive levels, and producers do, in fact, deliver the kind and quality of goods they claim to be offering.

Figure 1-1
A market-directed economy

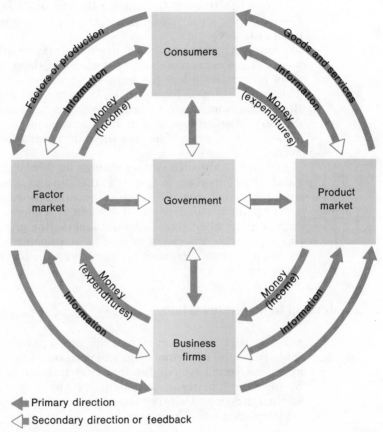

Primary direction

Secondary direction or feedback

Source: Adapted from Y. H. Furuhashi and E. J. McCarthy, *Social Issues of Marketing in the American Economy* (Columbus, Ohio: Grid, Inc., 1971), p. 5.

Basic economic utilities of a marketing system

■ If all works well, we have a dynamic system that is flexible enough to make continual adjustment to new technological developments and consumer needs. Such a market-directed system provides for the four basic utilities isolated by economists—*time, place, possession,* and *form* utility. In other words, it arranges for producing and having goods available *when* and *where* they are wanted, and then completing the sales transaction to provide possession utility.

Satisfying the four basic utilities

Many people take the four basic utilities for granted. It seems simple. If I have the money, I can purchase the product. However, it just doesn't work that way. Only when a product possessing form utility is conveniently there *when* the consumer needs it, can he plunk down his money and enjoy possession utility. For example, how much satisfaction would a Chicago consumer derive from owning a pound of coffee beans in Brazil? How happy would a co-ed be if her date brought her a certificate showing that she owned one orchid in Hawaii? Or consider the value of tire chains at the factory during a snowstorm, or electric fans in the warehouse during a heat wave.

From a macro point of view, producers may be willing to supply products and consumers may be demanding them, yet no transactions take place unless the buyers and sellers get together. The Chicago consumer, for example, doesn't want coffee beans in Brazil, she wants a jar of instant coffee in her house, *now*. Here, the job of marketing is to match supply capabilities to the demand of potential consumers, moving the right goods wherever they are needed.

Our market-directed system ensures that these utilities are provided. It is important to note that this process is not unique to a market-directed system. These same utilities would have to be provided for in another way if a planned economic system were employed. In other words, the macro-marketing process would still be required, but instead of relying on an impersonal marketplace, the basic economic decisions would have to be handled by central planners.

Markets develop to facilitate exchange

■ So far we have presumed that the various producing units will "automatically" come into being and perform effectively as part of a macro-marketing system. But they have freedom of choice, too, so we must get a better understanding of why they would choose to do what they do and why our seemingly complicated production and distribution system has evolved.

**Speciali-
zation
demanded a
central
market**

■ Begin by asking why central markets have developed. Suppose a group of five families found that each has some special skill for producing some item. After meeting basic subsistence needs, each family might decide to specialize. This decision would be very practical. It is easier for one family to make two pots and another to make two baskets than it is for either to make one pot and one basket. Specialization makes labor more efficient and more productive.

If these five families specialize in one product apiece, they will have to trade with each other. As Figure 1–2 shows, it would take the five families ten separate trips and exchanges to obtain some of each of the products. If the families live near each other, the exchange process would be relatively simple. But if they are far apart, travel back and forth will be time-consuming. And who would do the traveling and when?

Faced with this problem, the families can agree to come to a central market and trade on a certain day. Then, each family would need to make only one trip into the market to trade with all the others, reducing the total number of trips to five. The reason for

Figure 1–2
Ten exchanges required when central market not used

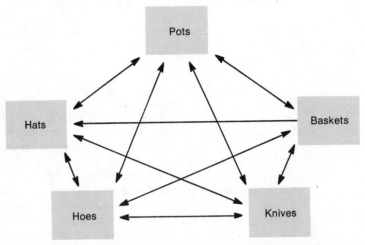

Source: Wroe Alderson, "Factors Governing the Development of Marketing Channels," in
Richard M. Clewett, ed., *Marketing Channels for Manufactured Products* (Homewood, Ill..
Richard D. Irwin, Inc., 1954), p. 7.

the development of central markets is clear. They facilitated exchange, left more time for production, and also served as social gatherings.

Modern economies are well beyond this simple example, but the principle still holds. The fundamental purpose of markets is to facilitate exchange and allow greater time for production or other activities, including leisure.

Money system speeds trading

■ But while a central meeting place would simplify exchange, all of the individual bartering transactions would still take much time. Bartering takes another party who wants what you have and vice versa. Each trader must find others who have products of approximately equal value. After trading with one group, a family might find itself with a collection of hats, knives, and pots, and then it would have to find others who were willing to trade for these products.

A money system would change all of this. A seller would merely find a buyer who can either use or sell his product, negotiate the price, and be free to spend his money to buy whatever he wants.

Specialists facilitate trade even more

■ Even though a money system simplifies the trading, considerable time and effort are needed to complete all transactions among the families. And once they were using money, each family head might have to open (and pay for) a stall at the market, while other family members shopped at other parts of the market.

Enter the middleman

■ The exchange process can be facilitated by the appearance of a dealer who is willing to trade with the families for *all* of their surpluses in exchange for what they need (see Figure 1–3).

In our simple example, using the services of a dealer at a central market, the ten exchanges needed previously are now reduced to five. Such a dealer would make a charge for this service, but if the time saved were considerable, each family might have more time for production at home and visiting at the market. Each family could specialize in production and let the dealer specialize in trading.

Such dealers, offering permanent trading facilities, are known today as wholesalers and retailers. The advantages of working with a dealer become substantial as the number of producers and customers, their distance apart, and the number and variety of competing products increase. That is why there are so many wholesalers and retailers in more complex economies.

Marketing functions needed at macro and micro levels

■ At both the macro and the micro levels of marketing, we find the same basic marketing functions – buying, selling, transporting, storing, grading, financing, risk-taking, and market information. It will be helpful to explain these basic functions and how they serve as a foundation for our approach to marketing.

Buying and selling

■ *Buying and selling* involve what is called the exchange process. The *buying* function is directed to the search for, and evaluation of, products and services. For middlemen, this means a search for the products that will appeal to their customers. The *selling* function involves promoting the product and would include the use of personal selling, and advertising and other mass selling methods. This is the best-known, and some people feel the only, function of marketing.

Transporting and storing

■ The functions of *transporting* and *storing* involve the handling and movement of goods. These are the major activities of many marketing institutions, especially warehouses, transportation agencies, wholesalers, and some retailers.

Grading, financing, and risk-taking

■ *Grading, financing, risk-taking*, and *market information* assist other functions. *Grading* is dividing the product into the most attractive and useful quantities, thus aiding the storing and selling functions. *Financing* facilitates the exchange of money for goods and provides the credit necessary for storing. *Risk-taking* is inherent in any business activity – because the future is uncertain. One of management's jobs is to measure and control the risk.

Figure 1–3
Only five exchanges required when dealer in central market is used

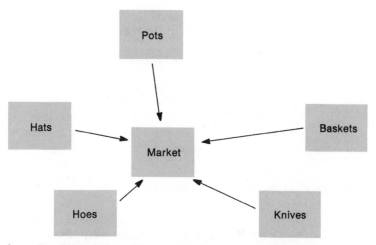

Source: Wroe Alderson, "Factors Governing the Development of Marketing Channels," in Richard M. Clewett, ed., *Marketing Channels for Manufactured Products* (Homewood, Ill.: Richard D. Irwin, Inc. 1954), p. 7.

Market information

■ The *market information* function, including collecting, analyzing, and disseminating data, provides the feedback activity that is needed in any system. Without current information, the manager will probably rely on old information—and last year's facts may prove to be the basis of this year's mistakes.

Functions can't be eliminated

■ From a macro point of view, no matter how simple or how complex the marketing process is, all the functions of marketing must be performed by someone. If a manager were trying to improve the efficiency of a system, he would attempt to provide these functions with maximum efficiency. In some cases, this might require combining various middlemen into a larger system. In such a system a farmer, for example, would permit a wholesaler to pick up his products at the farm, haul them into town, grade them according to recognized standards, carry the financial burden until they are sold, and throughout this period, take the risk that they can be sold. If this job is complicated, one wholesaler may not be willing to handle all these activities, and two or more wholesalers may become involved.

The important fact is that even if the farmer were to do all of this himself, *none* of the functions could be skipped. He would still have to grade the products on his own farm, store them until needed, and transport them into town. He would have to finance his own activities and bear any risk of price fluctuations or quality deterioration. In either situation, he would feel obligated to watch the newspaper or listen to the radio for market information on prices, supplies, and weather conditions.

Note that in a planned economy the central planners would have to try to be sure that all of these functions were provided by someone at the right time and place since all of these functions must be provided regardless of the kind of economy. This helps explain why there are frequent breakdowns in more sophisticated planned economies.

From a macro point of view, we can see that these basic marketing functions must be performed by someone.

An extremely important question at the micro level, then, is who does what and for how much. We will discuss these matters in more detail later. Now, it is important to note that an efficient macro-marketing system does not just happen. It is the result of considerable decision making.

Who makes decisions in an economy?

The decision is yours

■ In a market-directed society, producers and consumers make their own decisions. No consumer is forced to buy any goods or services except those which society insists are essential. Schools, police, national defense, public health, and food inspection are considered essential services. These are provided by the community, and citizens are taxed to pay for them. Similarly, producers are given the role of satisfying consumers. They are free to engage in whatever activities they want, subject to the rules and taxes imposed upon them by government (i.e., by "consumers" as voters). If they do their job well—if, through sound decision making, they satisfy enough customers—they will make a profit, and stay in business and grow. But a profit, survival and growth are not guaranteed.

Such a system can continue moving without the bureaucratic controls that go along with central planning. Whenever a new need arises, an opportunity is created for some profit-minded businessman. Thus, all market needs which can be served profitably will produce businessmen to meet the need.

The decision is the central planners'

■ In planned economies, on the other hand, central planners attempt to make the producers' decisions. The consumers may have some freedom of choice as it is more difficult to control some sectors. Open marketplaces may be permitted. As long as the economy is simple and the variety of goods is small, this approach may work fairly well. However, as economies become more complex, central planning becomes more difficult and may even break down.

There are some guidelines

■ Even in a market-directed economy, we usually find that the government (following the wishes of its consumer citizens) establishes some guidelines for how the system is to work. There are no completely pure market-directed economies operating at this time. The American economy is essentially, but not totally, market-directed. The federal government, for example, controls interest rates and the supply of money. Further, it sets import and export restrictions, alternately restricts and stimulates the agricultural sector, controls prices and wages on occasion, and so on. Basically, however, our system relies on a market-directed economy, with modifications.

All decisions are not always good ones

Lack of information and/or training may hurt

■ Are all the decisions of producers and consumers "good?" We generally assume so because presumably the individual decision makers are making decisions in their own self-interest – maximizing their own welfare as they see it at the time of the decisions. Unfortunately, however, it seems likely that not all decisions are "good." Some consumers and producers may not have all the information they should have before making a decision and/or such information may be difficult or impossible for them to obtain. Or, they may not even know how to make good decisions – that is, they were never trained or were poorly trained to be consumers and producers.

Some of the criticisms of our macro-marketing system probably result from the fact that some producers and/or consumers are making poor decisions. And some of our legislation is designed to improve this decision making or to help producers and/or consumers avoid poor decisions. For example, school attendance is required for young consumers, and health and safety regulations are designed to protect everyone as both producers and consumers.

Some marketers concerned with social marketing

■ Allowing individual consumers and producers to make their own "selfish" decisions may lead to the relative impoverishment of offerings which some people feel are "desirable." For example, there may be "excessive" interest in automobiles, sporting equipment, and homes and home furnishings while the purchase of concert or symphony tickets, books, or even higher education may be neglected. Further, the elementary needs of the poor, for example for better food and housing, may be neglected because they do not have enough income to be an attractive market. At the same time, producers may neglect the secondary or long-run impacts of some of their decisions. While trying to produce better products, for example, they may also pollute the area around their factories.

Such imperfections in our market-directed system have interested a variety of critics and concerned businessmen. Some even see the need for a separate area of study called *social marketing.*[2]

Keeping our system running effectively is certainly a vital matter and alleged deficiencies and efforts to remedy them will be discussed as we move through the text.

"Patching up" our system is not a trivial matter, however, because very often what would appear to be good for one part of the macro system may, at the same time, be bad for another. For example, trying to protect many small businessmen from the impact of competition might actually cause an increase in prices and, therefore, be less desirable for consumers. Similarly, attempting to protect consumers might not always work to their advantage, at least as they saw it. For example, legislation requiring a *completely safe* automobile would probably mean the elimination of the automobile as we know it today.

Compromises may be necessary to handle macro-micro dilemma

■ The unfortunate fact that there may have to be some compromises in the development and running of a macro-marketing system has been called the *macro-micro dilemma*. Basically, the dilemma is that what is "good" for some may be "bad" for others.[3]

This means that there are not always obvious "right" answers that everyone will agree upon with respect to building or patching up a macro-marketing system. This topic will be taken up again in Chapter 30 when we return to an evaluation of how our macro-marketing system is working — that is, after we have had a chance to develop a deeper understanding of how and why consumers and producers think and behave the way they do.

Improving the macro-marketing process can be aided by improving business decision making. In this text we will emphasize the micro view of marketing since individual businessmen can and do make a difference in our economy. A great deal depends on how well they do their jobs (make decisions) and how efficiently they manage their businesses. We will examine in depth how business firms can better meet customers' needs and, in the aggregate, make the macro-marketing system work better. We will not spend much time on how present firms work, but will focus on *why* they do what they do and how they might do it better. Ultimately, you should be able to understand the *why* of present marketing efforts, *how* they might be improved, and *how* you can contribute to the marketing process in the future.

Evolution of consumer-oriented economies and customer-oriented companies

■ In a modern economy, marketing plays an extremely vital role. But it has not always been so important or complex. If we define marketing as a process of getting goods from producers to consumers (a simplified definition), it is obvious that relatively little marketing was done in ancient Egypt, for example, or in feudal Europe. Even today, a marketing structure far less complex than that in the United States operates in many parts of Asia, Africa, and Latin America.

To understand why marketing is so important to modern societies, it will be fruitful to look at the development of economic systems, with primary emphasis on Western civilization.

From subsistence to money economies

■ The life of early man, scratching as he did for an existence, could truly be described as *subsistence living*. Yet there are still many parts of the world that have not advanced much beyond this level of living. Such peoples still raise and consume almost everything they produce, living without money and sharing both the output and the work of their communities. In India, for example, approximately 85 percent of the population lives in villages that still operate on a partially communal basis. There is little need there for selling.[4]

In some economies, specialization in production took place at an early stage. About 2100 B.C., the Code of Hammurabi was set down to help regulate the highly developed society that had grown up on the fertile river valleys of the Tigris and the Euphrates. Trade flourished, and these communities rose above the subsistence level because of (1) specialization in production and distribution and (2) an assurance that this specialization would work. That is, artisans were willing to leave the self-sufficient farm economy when they were fairly sure of being fed out of the food production of others. Trade also continued to grow whenever there was political stability — especially during the long period when the Romans ruled the Mediterranean area and controlled its commerce.[5]

Trade between nations dried up when Rome's power was broken. Western Europe moved into feudalism. Basically, feudalism was a return to an almost self-sufficient economy in which each family or manor grew and made what it needed. Eventually, however, the feudal manors began to come out of their isolation. At first, small weekly markets were developed. These markets — from perhaps 5 to 15 miles apart — were close enough to travel to and from in one day.

Slowly, as towns grew, these market meetings became more frequent until they became daily events. Eventually, a town would build a market hall to protect the sellers and buyers from the weather. Retail shops and warehouses developed so that the produce and wares did not have to be hauled back and forth to the farms each day.

This was a natural evolution of retail markets in the interior of Western Europe. The Middle East and the Mediterranean seacoast cities had gone through these stages many centuries before. As soon as there was a sufficient surplus for trading beyond the town boundaries, wholesale markets in nonperishable commodities went through an evolution similar to that of the retail markets.

Industrialization forces more emphasis on marketing

■ During the Middle Ages, the roots of organized industry and specialization of labor were implanted. With the greater demand for goods, the old retail-handicraft method was no longer adequate. In the small village, journeymen and apprentices could produce goods that satisfied local preferences. But the great variety in design and quality was not satisfactory for large-scale trading in other areas. More standardized products were needed, and in larger quantities.

These needs were met by wholesale handicraftsmen, who supplied specifications and materials to workers paid by the piece. They were similar to some of our present subcontractors or small independent manufacturers, although their work usually was done in the homes of the workers.

In this system of production, workers became more dependent on production for the market. This work was profitable to the workers *as long as the goods were sold.* When the system did not function because of wars, famine, or other reasons, there was a natural reversion to village self-sufficiency.

Starting about 1700, the Industrial Revolution and the growth of the factory system increased productivity. Both new and old commodities were produced at lower prices. This offered new opportunities for trade, but it also meant that markets had to be found to absorb the greater output.

Adam Smith's *Wealth of Nations,* published in 1776, encouraged the development of free and unrestricted trade. Yet, in spite of the revived interest in trade, much of Europe's trading of this period took place—and, in fact, still takes place—in the original markets developed in the Middle Ages.

Development in the United States

■ The development of trade in the United States parallels that of the Middle East and Europe. Some of the very early trade in America, especially in the southern colonies, was conducted by European trading companies operating under charters from their governments. Some of the early colonies were actually trading settlements established to gain a foothold in the New World. These colonies were supposed to provide a market for Europe's finished products and a source of raw materials for the mother country.

As settlers moved west, however, there was less and less dependence on England. As long as the majority of finished products came from Europe, the import-export firms pretty much controlled trading. But finished-goods production in the United States began to increase after the Revolutionary War and during and after the War of 1812, when imports declined. The canning industry, for example, developed during this period, and the meat-packing industry was started in 1818 in Cincinnati.

The ports, the railroads, the discount houses

■ Even before the development of a substantial American finished-goods industry, many of the larger retailers in the seacoast cities began buying from importers in large lots and servicing the smaller retailers, especially inland. Many of these large retailers switched entirely to wholesaling in the early 1800s.

These early wholesale centers usually were in waterfront towns, since transportation was still tied to the rivers, lakes, and oceans. By 1850, most of the major wholesale centers were well-established centers that have maintained their importance through the years, such as New York, Philadelphia, Baltimore, Boston, New Orleans, Detroit, Chicago, and the river towns of Pittsburgh, Cincinnati, Louisville, and St. Louis.[6]

The growth of railroads also opened new markets. After the Civil War, the number of manufacturing establishments grew rapidly, but the established wholesalers and retailers, while providing outlets for the many small farmers and manufacturers, easily dominated distribution. In the late 1800s, many manufacturers became dissatisfied with their distribution arrangements because they found that they could produce more goods than existing retailers and wholesalers wanted. Some manufacturers, discovering the value of aggressive sales and advertising efforts, began sending out their own salesmen and branding and advertising their products.

Some retailers also responded to this outpouring of goods. Abandoning the general store approach of the day, they began to specialize in various types of goods. Stores grew larger and larger. Today, we find a great variety of specialists in retailing, from small shops catering to special tastes to large discount houses offering lower prices to the masses.

The productivity of the American economy continued to grow at the rate of about 3 percent annually. Many progressive manufacturers sensed that more and more consumers were able to satisfy their basic needs and have something left for luxuries. They began to cater to the mass market rather than just the "carriage trade." In the early 1900s, for example, automobiles were already an important part of the American economy.

From the production era to the marketing era

■ In recent years, an increasing number of producers, wholesalers, and retailers have recognized the importance of marketing. These companies have traveled the long evolutionary road from the days when the basic consideration was producing or stocking products. Now they focus their attention on the customer and try to integrate the company's total effort toward satisfying him.

Identifying the following four orientations should help clarify this evolution: (1) production or product, (2) sales, (3) marketing department, and (4) marketing company.

Seldom has the story of this evolution been put so clearly and candidly as by R. T. Keith, a top executive of Pillsbury, Inc., a manufacturer of flour, cake mixes, and animal feeds.

Keith admitted that the marketing concept had been a long time coming for his company. Pillsbury was formed in 1869. It continued until about 1930 in what Keith called the *production era*. This was a period when their products were relatively scarce, and the most important function of the company was production. Beginning in 1930, the company went into the *sales era*. It became conscious of the fact that it had to go out and get customers and that its dealers had other sources of supply. Promotion of the available products became extremely important, both to middlemen and for attracting their customers' customers.

The sales era continued until about 1950. By then, Pillsbury had developed new cake mixes, and the sales of these products were growing so rapidly that a coordinator became necessary to organize the efforts of production, research, procurement, and sales. As Pillsbury faced up to this task, Keith pointed out, the sales era was replaced by the *marketing department era*. This meant a heavy emphasis on short-run policy planning.

The advertising department and the sales promotion department were dissolved into the one coordinating policy-making body. Obtaining people who were effective at short-run marketing policy making was difficult. Experienced men were relatively scarce. This led to a three- to four-year development period during which some of the marketing department's short-range planning was not fully effective. These marketing men were maturing, however, and learning how to translate ideas into products and products into profits.

In a relatively few years, Pillsbury had developed men with a marketing management approach, and in 1958, according to Keith, the company went into a new era – the *marketing company era.* Now, in addition to short-run marketing planning, the total company effort is guided by the marketing concept, that is, that all the firm's activities should be organized to satisfy its customers. Long-range as well as short-range planning is involved. Pillsbury's marketing specialists now look and plan three to ten years ahead.[7]

Much more is said about the marketing concept in the next chapter, but it is important to note here that the marketing concept is well accepted in many progressive companies.

What is marketing?

■ We have deliberately avoided defining "marketing" until now, to allow you to develop some tentative definitions of your own.

From the historical discussion, for example, you may have based your definition upon the exchange of surplus commodities. This certainly would have been appropriate for past times.

Or your tentative definition may have stressed the exchange of goods in a production-oriented economy. Such a definition would emphasize the production of goods by a family or a business, and the exchange of those goods for other goods they were less able to produce for themselves.

A more modern definition, in tune with greatly expanded productive capacity, might emphasize the adaptation of production facilities to the market. Specifically, marketing might be defined as the response of businessmen to consumer demands through adjustments in production capabilities. Adjusting production capabilities would refer to the coordination of production, accounting, finance, and marketing in the light of the changing needs of consumers who are affluent enough to have varied buying choices.

Or, recognizing the growing interest in consumerism and the performance of our marketing system, you might have developed a definition which emphasized macro-marketing concerns, such as:

Marketing is concerned with designing an efficient (in terms of use of resources) and fair (in terms of distribution of output to all parties involved) system which will direct an economy's flow of goods and services from producers to consumers and ac-

complish the objectives of the society. We will make more use of this definition in Chapter 30, when we return to a macro-level discussion.

As the marketing manager knows, marketing directs!

■ For a more active view of marketing, however, we are going to look at it from the marketing manager's viewpoint — that is, the micro-level viewpoint.

The marketing manager is concerned with directing specific functions and activities (which encompass several functions). In this sense, the definition that emphasizes the need to adjust production capabilities might be too general. The marketing manager is concerned with specific activities, and he works toward specific results.

Within this micro-level framework, we can define marketing in the following way:

Marketing is the performance of business activities which direct the flow of goods and services from producer to consumer or user in order to satisfy customers and accomplish the company's objectives.

So that the student will realize the full importance and scope of micro-level marketing, let's examine the meaning of this definition by discussing its components.

Are the activities of product development, product design, packaging, credit and collection, transportation, warehousing, and price setting included in "marketing?"

There is little doubt that personal selling and advertising are marketing activities, and many business executives would limit the scope of marketing to them. They feel that the job of marketing is to "get rid of" the product which has been produced and priced by the production, accounting, and finance executives. This narrow view of marketing should obviously be rejected.

When we define marketing as those activities which *direct* the flow of goods and services, we mean just that: direct.

Marketing should begin with the customer, not with the production process. Marketing and not production should determine what products are to be made — including decisions about product development, design, and packaging; what prices are to be charged — credit and collection policies; and where and how the products are to be advertised and sold.

This does not mean that marketing should take over the traditional production, accounting, and financial activities, but merely that it provide direction for these activities.

After all, the purpose of business is to satisfy customer needs through the sale of products or services. It is *not* to supply products or services which *might* sell.

A factory can make products, and wholesalers and retailers can stock an assortment of goods, but it takes coordination of all the activities of a particular business to create profitable sales. In other words, we should see marketing as the coordinating force of the "total system" which is the business itself.

Why study marketing?

Businesses must be "customer-oriented"	■ In our economy of abundance, businesses *must* cater to their customers. They cannot simply wait until customers "beat a path" to their doors, because most of us can get along quite well without the product offered by any particular manufacturer, wholesaler, or retailer. We need clothing, for example, but we do not need a particular clothing manufacturer's product. The same is true of food, house furnishings, automobiles, sports equipment, and most other consumer goods. Likewise, manufacturers usually have several sources of supply for the components incorporated into their products.
Almost half the consumer's dollar for marketing	■ A good share of the consumer's dollar goes for marketing activities.[8] Professor R. Cox estimated that 41.7 percent of this dollar is consumed by distribution activities. Other analysts, using other methods, have calculated figures up to 58.9 percent. Professor P. D. Converse estimated that the cost of marketing for 1929 through 1948 varied from 48 to 50.5 percent of the consumer's dollar.
	An activity of this size and importance certainly requires study.
Greater job opportunity	■ An equally important reason for a college student to study marketing is the availability of many interesting and rewarding jobs in this area. Even more important, marketing offers opportunities for rapid growth and advancement. A careful study of marketing will give the student a better idea about business and where the best opportunities lie for a career.
	In marketing, the compensation on the way up is very attractive. Although some marketing jobs offer lower starting salaries than other jobs, after five years the average earnings of those who started in marketing have matched or bettered those of other business groups (see Table 1–1).
Marketing encourages innovation and growth	■ There is an even more fundamental reason for studying marketing. Without sales, there can be no business. Marketing is a stimulus that encourages innovation. Research effort and investment money are attracted when customers are willing to pay for a new product or service. When sales and profits justify it, companies press on to further innovations and improvements. In recent years, industries that have followed this pattern include business machines and electronics.
	In general, where a well-organized market economy is operating, there are opportunities for new investment, and the level of business activity, employment, and so on, is high. But when marketing activities are neglected, the result is often slower growth or even stagnation.
	Further, without an effective marketing system, the less developed countries may be doomed to what Professor Nurkse has called *a vicious circle of poverty*.[9] By this, he means that no one will

Table 1-1
Average monthly salaries for those starting out in selected fields

Field	Five years after graduation
Engineering	$1,213
Accounting	$1,193
Sales-marketing	$1,175
General business	$1,114

Source: Frank S. Endicott, "Trends in Employment of College and University Graduates in Business and Industry," (Evanston, Ill.: Northwestern University, 1973), p. 6.

leave his subsistence way of life to produce for the market, because there is no market for any goods he might produce. And there are no buyers, because everyone else is engaged in producing for his own needs. Marketing institutions can provide the dynamic element for breaking this vicious circle.

In this sense, a study of marketing systems will not only improve our understanding of our present and future institutions but will also throw light on the problems of the less developed economies. A knowledge of these economies will be increasingly important as our interest in the rest of the world grows.

One management expert holds that marketing is the key to the growth of less developed countries. He states this idea as follows:

> Marketing occupies a critical role in respect to the development of such "growth areas." Indeed, marketing is the most important "multiplier" of such developments. It is in itself in every one of these areas, the least developed, the most backward part of the economic system. Its development, above all others, makes possible economic integration and the fullest utilization of whatever assets and productive capacity an economy already possesses. It mobilizes latent economic energy. It contributes to the greatest needs: that for the rapid development of entrepreneurs and managers, and at the same time it may be the easiest area of managerial work to get going.[10]

Conclusion

■ Marketing has its critics—both at the macro and the micro levels. Some of the complaints are justified; some are based primarily on theory or perhaps a few unfortunate run-ins with unscrupulous businessmen or exposures to offensive advertising. And some criticism is based on naïveté (or ignorance). Some consumers believe that marketing is a basically simple process of moving a finished product to an eager consumer. Farmers, especially, hold this idea.

They look at marketing as a process for bringing their potatoes, tomatoes, eggs, and so on, into town where they are suddenly marked way up by monopolistic distributors.

Some of the complaints ring true, but the student should not base his own conclusions on limited information. It's a good idea to take a thorough look at the facts and try to understand the problems, practices, and objectives of those being criticized before reaching a judgment.

Before trying to reach any conclusions, let's proceed with our analysis of marketing, recognizing that any economy requires a marketing system—and the more complex the economy, the more complex the marketing system may have to be. In this text, we will take the viewpoint of marketing managers to give you a better understanding of marketing systems and processes. Thus, the primary focus will be on the micro view of marketing.

As we proceed, the role of marketing management will be emphasized. However, running a strong second in emphasis will be an evaluation of the impact of consumer behavior and the firm's actions on the economy.

At the end of the course, we will return to an evaluation of how well the macro-marketing process is working and can work in the future. This macro view is highly important because if consumers (and voters) decide that the process is not working well, they might decide to adopt some other system. There is no guarantee that the present system will be allowed to continue indefinitely; there is no mandate from heaven for business firms to operate the way they do. Each firm must continue to earn the right to operate as part of the marketing process. It is only through the long-run satisfaction and acceptance of consumers that marketing management can justify its role in a market-directed system.

In more direct terms, even though central planners probably could not manage our economy (or any advanced economy) very efficiently, if the consumers and/or voters became disenchanted with the present system, they could opt for a centrally planned system, or at least a substantial modification of the present system. Some consumer-protection advocates, for example, have suggested that government standards should be established for new products. The logical next step would be specifying the price and perhaps even the quantities which could be produced and sold. Finally, bureaucrats would be running the economy. This could happen in any market-directed economy if producers do not meet the needs and demands of the consumer-voters.

questions and problems

1 It is fairly easy to see why people do not beat a path to the mousetrap manufacturer's door, but would they be similarly indifferent if some food processor developed a revolutionary new food product which would provide all necessary nutrients in small pills for about $100 per year per person?

2 Some critics feel that marketing costs too much. If this is true, who gets this "too much"? Be specific.

3 Distinguish between macro- and micro-marketing. Then explain how they are inter-related, if they are.

4 What costs are included in marketing costs? Which of these do you feel might be eliminated? How would our economy be changed if it were illegal to incur any marketing costs?

5 Identify a "central market" in your own city and explain how it facilitates exchange.

6 Discuss the nature of marketing in a socialist economy. Would the functions which must be provided and the development of wholesaling and retailing systems be any different?

7 Explain in your own words what the macro-micro dilemma is. Then present a new example.

8 Contrast the importance of a market orientation for individual business firms in primitive economic systems and modern economies.

9 Explain, in your own words, why the emphasis in this text will be on micro-marketing.

10 Why is the satisfaction of consumers apparently considered of equal importance with satisfying the firm's objectives in the text's definition of micro-marketing?

11 Describe a recent purchase you have made and indicate why that particular product was available at a store, and, in particular, at that store.

notes

[1] Most of this section has been adapted from Y. H. Furuhashi and E. J. McCarthy. *Social Issues of Marketing in the American Economy* (Columbus, Ohio: Grid, Inc., 1971), pp. 4–5; see also: J. F. Grashof and A. Kelman, *Introduction to Macro Marketing* (Columbus, Ohio: Grid, Inc., 1973).

[2] See, for example, William Lazer and Eugene J. Kelley, *Social Marketing: Perspectives and Viewpoints* (Homewood, Ill.: Richard D. Irwin, Inc., 1973, 505 pp.); William Lazer, "Marketing's Changing Social Relationship," *Journal of Marketing*, January 1969, pp. 3–9; Daniel J. Sweeney, "Marketing: Management Technology or Social Process?" *Journal of Marketing*, October 1972, pp. 3–10; and Philip Kotler and Gerald Zaltman, "Social Marketing: An Approach to Planned Social Change," *Journal of Marketing*, July 1971, pp. 3–12.

[3] Furuhashi and McCarthy, *Social Issues of Marketing*, p. 6.

[4] Ralph Westfall and Harper W. Boyd, Jr., "Marketing in India," *Journal of Marketing*, October 1960, pp. 11–15.

[5] Herbert Heaton, *Economic History of Europe* (New York: Harper & Bros., 1948).

[6] T. N. Beckman and N. H. Engle, *Wholesaling—Principles and Practices*, rev. ed. (New York: Ronald Press Co., 1951), chap. 5.

[7] Robert J. Keith, "The Marketing Revolution," *Journal of Marketing*, January 1960, pp. 35–38.

[8] Reavis Cox, *Distribution in a High-Level Economy* (Englewood Cliffs, N.J.: Prentice-Hall, Inc., 1965), p. 149; Paul W. Stewart and J. Frederick Dewhurst, *Does Distribution Cost Too Much?* (New York: Twentieth Century Fund, 1939), pp. 117–18.

[9] Ragnar Nurkse, *Problems of Capital Formation in Underdeveloped Countries* (Oxford: Basil Blackwell, 1953), p. 4.

[10] Peter F. Drucker, "Marketing and Economic Development," *Journal of Marketing* 22 (January 1958), p. 253. Reprinted from the *Journal of Marketing*, national quarterly publication of the American Marketing Association.

2

Marketing's role within the firm

■ Marketing and marketing management play important roles in our society and in our business firms. As we saw in the previous chapter, marketing (the micro view) is concerned with those business activities which direct the flow of goods and services from producers to consumers. This occurs to satisfy the needs of consumers and accomplish either the economy's (the macro view) or the company's (the micro view) objectives.

Through the eyes of the marketing manager

■ To arrive at a better understanding of both macro- and micro-level marketing, we are going to study it from the point of view of the marketing manager – the man who makes the crucial company marketing decisions. In this chapter, we will look at the nature of the marketing function within a firm. We will also consider the importance of marketing strategy planning to the success of individual business firms and, in the aggregate, to the effective operation of the macro-marketing system.

The marketing concept – a new view of business

■ Modern management has evolved from a production-oriented to a sales-oriented and finally to a marketing-oriented view of business. The Pillsbury story in Chapter 1 was an outstanding example of this, but the same sort of evolution in thinking and organization has occurred in many companies.[1]

What is the marketing concept?

■ The marketing concept says that a firm should focus all of its efforts on satisfying its customers, at a profit. This is really a new philosophy of business, replacing a production-oriented philosophy which focused on organizing a firm's resources to make products and *then* selling them. The marketing concept calls for reorienting the firm's ways of doing things. Instead of trying to get customers to buy what the firm has produced, a marketing-oriented firm would try to sell what the customers want.

The underlying principle of the marketing concept is that a firm should seek to meet the needs of customers, at a profit, rather than placing its main emphasis on its own internal activities and utilization of its resources. These latter factors are also important, of course, but those who believe in the marketing concept feel that customers' needs should be the firm's primary focus and that resources should be organized to satisfy those needs.

Three basic elements are implied in the definition of the marketing concept:

1. A customer orientation.
2. An integrated company effort.
3. Profit, rather than just sales, as a goal of the firm.

Implementing the marketing concept, therefore, might require three related changes:

1. A change in management attitudes.
2. A change in the firm's organization structure.
3. A change in its management methods and procedures.

Changes in all three areas would probably be required if the firm really wanted to adopt the marketing concept; otherwise it would only be paying lip service to the idea.

A production orientation is a major obstacle

■ Give the customer what he needs—this may seem so obvious and logical that it is difficult to understand why the marketing concept is considered such a breakthrough. However, people haven't always done the logical and obvious. In a typical company, production men thought mainly about getting the product out. Accountants were only interested in balancing the books. Financial people were absorbed in the company's cash position. And salesmen were mainly concerned with getting orders. No one was particularly concerned with whether the whole system made sense. As long as the company made a profit, each department went merrily on its independent way, "doing its own thing." Unfortunately, they still do in the majority of companies today.

This typical lack of a unifying focus is called production orientation. But to be fair to production men, it also is seen in sales-oriented salesmen, advertising-oriented admen, finance-oriented finance men, and so on. We will use "production orientation" to cover all such myopic orientations.

Typical firms have overlapping, conflicting interests

■ The difference between production orientation and marketing orientation in a company can be grasped better by considering the typical conflicts of interest which develop in production-oriented businesses. The typical executive in a production-oriented firm comes to view the company's operation from his own vantage point. He looks at the rest of the business as working around *him*. He often expects the other executives to adjust themselves to his plans and activities.

It should be a "sharing" situation

■ Ideally, these executives should work together because the output from one department may be the input to another one. For example, most manufacturers have departments such as sales, accounting, and production. Larger firms have even more departments. These departments are necessary because there are efficiencies in specialization. But the production department, for example, should use inputs from the sales department to decide how much and when to produce, even though this may inhibit its own independence.

Unfortunately, it's more of a "hands-off" situation

■ Managers in production-oriented firms may erect fences around their domains, as seen in Figure 2–1a. Such businesses do not operate as a system. Rather, each department runs its own affairs for its own benefit. There may be coordinating committees to try to get them to work together, but usually each department head comes to such meetings with the idea of protecting his own interests (without seeming to appear too obstinate!)

Work together . . . do a better job

■ In a firm which has accepted the marketing concept, however, the fences tend to come down. There are still departments to be sure, but the total system's effort is guided by what customers want and what the firm can deliver, rather than what the various departments would like to do.

In such an environment, it might be more realistic to view the business as a box with both an internal and an external sector (see Figure 2–1b). Here, there are some internal departments primarily concerned with affairs inside the firm, such as production, accounting, and research and development (R&D). And there are external departments primarily concerned with outsiders, including sales, advertising, and sales promotion. Finally, there are departments that must be concerned with both the internal and the external sectors, such as warehousing, shipping, purchasing, finance, and personnel. The efforts of all of these departments are directed to satisfying some market needs—at a profit.

The marketing concept points the way

■ General Electric was the pacesetter in the movement toward a marketing orientation. As GE saw it, a logical implementation of the marketing concept would provide a systematic approach to managing the marketing process in any business, large or small.

This approach (1) ensures that the manager knows what and

Figure 2–1a
A business as a box (most departments
have high fences)

Figure 2–1b
Total system view of a business
(implementing marketing concept; still
have departments but all guided by what
customer wants)

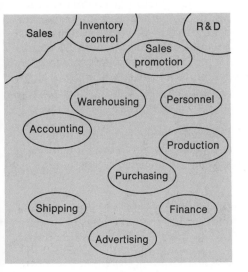

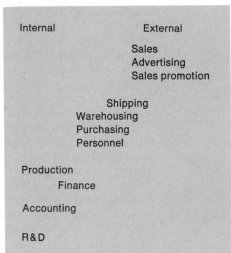

where his markets are; (2) provides effective customer and product
service; (3) puts the right product at the right place at the right
price; (4) sells to the greatest possible number of customers through
the most efficient sales and distribution channels; and (5) supports
the product adequately with advertising and sales promotion.[2]
This approach keys on the customer but also requires that all
marketing activities focus on specific company objectives – profit,
sales volume, and market share targets.

Where the marketing concept has been wholeheartedly accepted
and implemented, it has led to substantial changes in the operation
and often to significantly better results.

**Computers
ease the way**

■ The move toward the marketing concept has been aided in
larger companies by an important technological development – the
computer. Departmental or functional "empires" may have been
necessary when the flows of information between and among departments were slow. Now, however, with the growing use of data
processing equipment, we see that the traditional departmental
approach is not only unnecessary but may be quite inefficient.
Furthermore, when the whole business is seen as a system, tasks
that formerly seemed to require considerable management judgment can now be assumed by computers.

General Electric's system illustrates the possibilities of electronic
data processing. It demonstrates why an internal business system

should be seen as a system, crossing traditional functional lines wherever necessary.

Ask the computer, wait 15 seconds

■ General Electric has developed a computer-oriented system that ties together its widely dispersed manufacturing and distribution facilities. This computer system links together 65 customer service centers (sales offices) located in 49 states, 18 distribution warehouses in 11 states, and 40 product departments with 53 manufacturing plants in 21 states. If, for example, a customer wanted to place an order for a truckload of lamps *on the condition that shipment be made promptly,* he could call one of the GE local sales offices and place his order tentatively, assuming that GE could, in fact, meet his conditions.

If the customer telephoned the order to the local sales office, the salesman there could enter the required data into the GE computer system while the buyer was still on the phone. The computer system then would check to see if GE wanted to sell to this particular buyer (a credit check) and if the item were in stock at a convenient location. If the answer to both questions were yes, the computer would (*a*) issue an order to ship, (*b*) bill the customer, (*c*) update the inventory records, (*d*) generate the records that are reviewed periodically so that orders are issued automatically to factories to replenish inventory at the various distribution points, and (*e*) relay the message back to the GE salesman that the customer's order is on the way. And all of this would take less than 15 seconds!

No mourning for the passing of boundaries

■ The speed of this system is remarkable—but the most remarkable achievement is the integration of the system. What this means is that the computer now does a number of jobs that were formerly handled by separate departmental or line operations. These include credit checking, inventory control, production scheduling, shipping control, billing, order entry procedure, and all the bookkeeping that formerly kept many clerks busy.

This system also allows random inquiry for specific management information, and it regularly produces special reports for management.

Clearly, then, the traditional functional departmental boundaries make little sense in such an integrated system.[3]

Marketing concept forces a sense of mission and integrated effort

■ The marketing concept says that all of a firm's efforts should be focused on satisfying its customers, at a profit. This relatively innocent sounding concept is really very powerful if taken seriously, because it forces the company (1) to think through what it is doing, and why, and then (2) to develop a plan for accomplishing its objectives. And, as we have seen, it encourages an integrated effort to achieve these objectives.

To illustrate, we can compare a very successful application of the marketing concept with an unsuccessful management effort. The Ford Motor Co. Mustang "sports" car *was* designed according to the marketing concept. Considerable marketing research was done *before* the product was designed or the marketing strategy developed. The strategy finally adopted took into consideration consumer research and company resources and objectives.[4] The outstanding success of the Mustang is well known.

Ford's earlier experience with the ill-fated Edsel is another story. While there was considerable consumer research on the Edsel, it tended to focus on promotional possibilities, because the automobile design itself and the basic marketing strategy were already fixed. Even though consumers expressed little enthusiasm for those parts of the plan to which they were exposed, their attitudes were not permitted to alter the basic plan. The research had come too late and was not used to help direct the whole effort.[5]

It's easy to slip into a production orientation

■ It is very easy to slip into a production-oriented way of thinking. In fact, this is probably the most logical way of running a business if one thinks in terms of his own personal needs, rather than those of his customers. Producers, for example, might prefer to emphasize long production runs of easy-to-produce products. And retailers might prefer only daytime weekday hours, avoiding nights, Saturdays, and Sundays. Various differences in outlook between production-oriented and marketing-oriented businessmen are presented in Figure 2–2.

Marketing concept useful for nonprofit organizations too

■ Most of this book will focus on how to apply the marketing concept in a specific business firm—be it a manufacturer, farmer, miner, wholesaler, or retailer—selling goods *or* services. Our primary focus will be on business firms which typically have some kind of a profit orientation.

But the same general principles can be applied directly to nonprofit organizations. All that must be changed are the objectives against which alternative plans are measured. The Red Cross, art museums, and governmental agencies are all seeking to satisfy some consumer groups, and most of the ideas and principles are directly applicable.[6]

How far should marketing concept go?

■ Recently a new viewpoint has been added. Growing problems with resource shortages and ecological damage to the environment have created a new awareness. Some marketing men are asking whether they really should try to satisfy *all* consumer needs. This is a very difficult issue to handle because there are no definite guidelines. But socially responsible businessmen must be concerned with this issue and we will consider it in various places, and especially in Chapter 30. For now, we will just assume that *responsible* implementation of the marketing concept will not lead to socially irresponsible activities.

Figure 2–2
Some differences in outlook between adopters of the marketing concept and the typical production-oriented businessmen

Marketing orientation	Attitudes and procedures	Production orientation
Customer needs determine company plans	← Attitudes toward customers →	They should be glad we exist, trying to cut costs and bring out better products
Company makes what it can sell	← Product offering →	Company sells what it can make
To determine customer needs and how well company is satisfying them	← Role of marketing research →	To determine customer reaction, if used at all
Focus on locating new opportunities	← Interest in innovation →	Focus is on technology and cost-cutting
A critical objective	← Importance of profit →	A residual, what's left after all costs are covered
Seen as a customer service	← Role of customer credit →	Seen as a necessary evil
Designed for customer convenience and as a selling tool	← Role of packaging →	Seen merely as protection for the product
Set with customer requirements and costs in mind	← Inventory levels →	Set with production requirements in mind
Seen as a customer service	← Transportation arrangements →	Seen as an extension of production and storage activities, with emphasis on cost minimization
Need-satisfying benefits of products and services	← Focus of advertising →	Product features and quality, maybe how products are made
Help the customer to buy if the product fits his needs, while coordinating with rest of firm—including production, inventory control, advertising, etc.	← Role of sales force →	Sell the customer, don't worry about coordination with other promotion efforts or rest of firm

Source: Adapted from R. F. Vizza, T. E. Chambers, and E. J. Cook, *Adoption of the Marketing Concept—Fact or Fiction?* (New York: Sales Executives Club of New York, Inc., 1967), pp. 13–15.

Organizing to implement the marketing concept

Pointing the company toward its goal

■ The first and most important step in applying the marketing concept is a wholehearted commitment to a customer orientation. Without acceptance of this concept, at least by top management, any change in the organizational structure will be purely mechanical. Such a commitment has been likened to a magnet applied to the bottom of a piece of paper sprinkled with iron filings: "The force of the magnet orients all of the filings toward the common point."[7]

Some organization structure helps

■ After top management has accepted the marketing concept, some formal reorganization usually is desirable. The product planning function often is under the production or engineering departments; pricing is under the finance or accounting departments; and both sales and advertising often are separate departments. Sales forecasting and budgeting frequently is done in a separate department, or by the finance or accounting departments.

All of these activities involve the customer and should properly be under the direction and control of the marketing manager. The marketing manager normally should report directly to top management along with the heads of production, engineering, finance, and accounting. The exact arrangement of the marketing management department depends somewhat on the needs of a particular company and the personalities involved. Organization charts showing the structure in one company before and after adoption of the marketing concept are shown in Figure 2–3.

Who should organize and run the total system?

■ Top management is responsible for developing and running a total system of action, which is designed to meet the needs of target customers. Ideally, the whole company becomes customer-oriented, and all the company departments pull together to reach its objectives. We will still have departments, because there are advantages in job specialization. But the former battles to protect "empire" boundaries are reduced because the total system is (or should be) supreme. To be sure, there may be disagreements over strategy. The production department might question whether the consumer really does want, and is willing to pay for, products which are practically custom-made. But rather than resort to an internal power struggle, a marketing-oriented system would do some marketing research, perhaps run some market tests, and calculate potential costs and company (not departmental) profits for alternate strategies. Then it would decide what is best for the firm, not just what is best for the strongest department or coalition of departments.

In such a system, the marketing manager would help develop this total system attitude within his firm. He must work regularly with the external system as well as the internal system and is in an ideal position to keep the system working. In a sense, he is a coordinator and integrator—as well as a liaison man between the customers and the executives in his own company.

Figure 2–3
One company's organization chart before and after acceptance
of the marketing concept

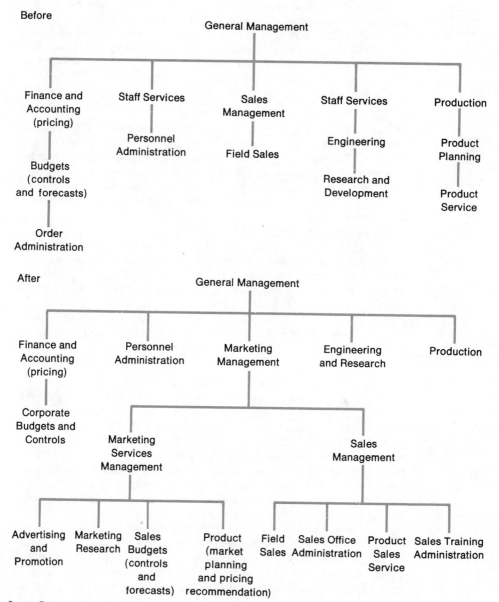

■ Many marketing managers probably will come from the ranks of sales management because they are more likely to be familiar with target customers. But this is not always the case. Some sales managers would make poor marketing managers because of allegiance to personal selling and their unwavering loyalty to the sales force. Similarly, an advertising manager may be so advertising-oriented that he believes almost any difficulty can be overcome with a larger advertising budget. Production managers, research and development engineers, and accounting and finance experts as well may be hindered by this sort of myopia.

Theoretically, at least, the marketing manager and the prospective marketing-oriented president could come from any specialty. In one cosmetic company, as might be expected in this type of business, the advertising and sales promotion manager gradually assumed major planning and coordinating responsibilities. In another firm, however, which produced highly technical custom-built products, the production manager was the leader in the move toward the application of the marketing concept.

The most important consideration is that the prospective marketing manager and top manager accept the marketing concept.

The management job in marketing

Hitting the
target
customer
■ The marketing manager's job consists of trying to meet the needs of a particular group of customers (the target group) with a particular good or service. Out of the almost infinite number of products offered to the consumer, the marketing manager wants to be sure that *his product* will succeed. How can he do this?

First, the marketing manager is a manager. It should be helpful, therefore, to look closely at the role of any manager.

Nature of
the manage-
ment job
■ Management generally has three basic tasks:

1. To set up a general plan or strategy for the business.
2. To direct the execution of this plan.
3. To evaluate, analyze, and control the plan in actual operation.

For simplicity, this might be condensed to planning, execution, and control. The three-cornered diagram in Figure 2–4 shows the interrelation of these three basic tasks. The relationship of the control and planning jobs is extremely important, since the feedback of information often leads to changes in the general plan or even a totally new plan. Thus the management job is *continuous*.

The *marketing* manager's job, then, consists of these basic management responsibilities. First, the marketing executive must evolve a plan—or as we will call it, a "marketing strategy"—aimed at a given group of customers. How this group is selected will be discussed in Chapter 4 and beyond. The development of a market-

Figure 2–4
The management job (given the company's objectives
and present resources)

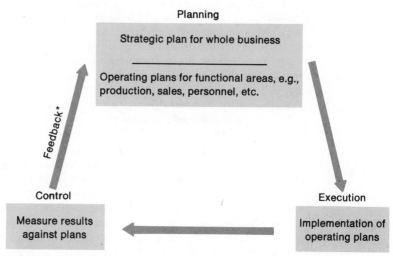

* In the form of information concerning results of management planning.

ing strategy is of primary importance. Without a well-defined master plan, there are no guidelines for execution or control.

Only after the basic strategy is developed can management concern itself with the implementation of that strategy (personnel selection, salary administration, dealer selection, commission rates, and so on). Implementation may, in fact, absorb a greater part of the manager's time, but it is not the major concern here. Detailed study of execution decisions must be left for your advanced work, after you have seen the "big picture," that is, when you have learned about planning marketing strategy.

We will emphasize control, too, since it provides the feedback that leads to the modification of marketing strategies. The tools most frequently used by the marketing manager to exert this control are electronic data processing, marketing research, and accounting.

All marketing jobs require planning and control

■ At first, it might appear that the planning and control responsibilities are only of concern to top management of large companies. This is not true. Even the smallest farmer, retailer, or wholesaler must plan his strategy.

Similarly, every salesman, however limited his territory or department, also must have a plan of attack. He may not have complete freedom, because of the master strategy already outlined for him, but he usually has some latitude. He develops his own special strategy in the light of his abilities and the problems of his particular area.

What is a marketing strategy?

■ We have used the words "marketing strategy" rather casually thus far, but now it is desirable to define them formally. A marketing strategy consists of two distinct and yet interrelated parts:

1. *A target market* – A fairly homogeneous group of customers to whom a company wishes to appeal.
2. *A marketing mix* – the controllable variables which the company combines in order to satisfy this target group.

The central role of the target customers can be seen in Figure 2–6 where the customer Ⓒ is in the center of the diagram surrounded by the controllable variables, which we call the marketing mix. A typical mix would include some product or service offered at a price, probably with some promotion to tell potential customers about the availability of the offering.

Mass marketing is *not* target marketing

■ A marketing strategy focuses on *some* target customers, with a view to developing a more satisfying and profitable marketing mix – one that will give the firm a differential advantage over its competitors. This is a logical application of the marketing concept. We will call this market-oriented approach to micro marketing: *target marketing,* to distinguish it from *mass marketing* – the typical production-oriented approach.

It is important to see that target marketing is not limited to small market segments, only fairly homogeneous ones. The "mass market" may be fairly homogeneous in some cases and the target marketer will deliberately aim at it.

In mass marketing, on the other hand, there is no clear focus. Mass marketers just naïvely assume that "everyone" is similar and will want what they offer. No attempt is made to define what *some* customers might want. Rather, everyone is considered a potential customer. See Figure 2–5.

Hereafter, the words *strategy planning* will refer to "marketing strategy planning" and in particular *target marketing,* since we will emphasize only the market-oriented approach.

Strategy planning takes place within a framework

■ A marketing manager's strategy planning does not take place in a vacuum. Instead, he works with his controllable variables within a framework which involves many uncontrollable variables which he must consider even though he cannot control them. Figure 2–6 illustrates the framework within which the typical marketing manager must operate. Included are the cultural and social environment, political and legal environment, economic environment, existing competitive business situation, and resources and objectives of the firm. These uncontrollable variables are considered in more detail in Chapters 3 and 5, but clearly, the framework within which the marketing manager operates will have a bearing on his strategy planning.

Figure 2–5
Target marketer and mass marketer have different views
of the market

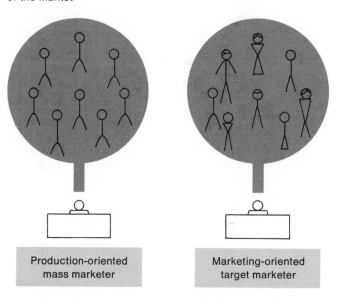

Production-oriented
mass marketer

Marketing-oriented
target marketer

Two levels of strategic planning might be desirable

■ Depending on how large and how well organized a firm is, it might be helpful to think of needing two levels of strategic planning—first, for the whole company and, second, for each department (including the marketing department). The top level would focus on companywide objectives, top management's view of its mission, and what it could do with its resources. This could lead to a *corporate* strategic plan. The second level, then, would get into more detail about each department's part in accomplishing the corporate plan. All of these would have to fit together, of course, if the firm is to work as an integrated whole.

We will not get into such detail in this text, but it is important to see that the marketing department's plan is not the whole corporate plan. On the other hand, it is clear that a good corporate plan should be market-oriented. And to the extent that the corporate plan is simply the sum of the various department plans, then the marketing department's strategic plan may set the tone and direction for the whole company.

Strategic planning is still largely an art, with firms doing varying amounts of planning. (Actually, most do very little, failing even to make their objectives explicit.) So we will not discuss two-level planning. Our emphasis will be on market-oriented strategic planning, with more attention to the marketing department's special areas of interest.

Figure 2–6
Marketing manager's framework

Importance of marketing strategy planning

■ Most of our emphasis will be on the planning phase of the marketing manager's job, for a very good reason. The "one-time" planning decisions—the critical decisions that determine what business the company is in and the general strategy it will follow—may be more important than has been realized. In fact, an extremely good plan might be badly implemented and still be profitable, while a poor but well-executed plan can lose money. The several case histories that follow illustrate the importance of planning and show why we are going to be emphasizing strategy planning throughout this text.

General Foods study and General Foods hypothesis

■ A basic study of the retail grocery industry for General Foods was designed to reveal why some retail grocery stores were more profitable than others. The study began with an extensive evaluation of traditional internal company operating data such as turnover per square foot, and the like. This turned out to be of little help, but when the study shifted its focus to each company's planning decisions, new insights *were* developed. It became clear that original strategy decisions about (1) where a grocery store was placed in relation to competition and (2) how large it was compared to competition, were related to the profitability of individual stores.[8]

Within this framework, an analysis of operating effectiveness made sense. It was clear that some well-managed stores were doomed to poor profitability because of the initial planning decision. Conversely, some well-placed stores were doing very well, almost in spite of their operating management.

This leads to what we will call the *General Foods hypothesis:* Good strategy planning may be more important to the profitable operation of a business than good execution and control.

Gamble-Skogmo sought small-town markets

■ A practical application of this hypothesis can be seen in Gamble-Skogmo's successful effort to place relatively *large* discount stores in small midwestern towns. Importantly, this strategy reversed a general tendency for discounters to stay close to larger cities and markets. When asked why he was moving into small towns, the president of Gamble-Skogmo answered: "If you're first, you're apt to be alone. Most of the towns we're in won't take two stores of that size."[9]

Sears, Roebuck sought its own market

■ The General Foods hypothesis also helps to explain Sears, Roebuck's success since World War II. While other large retailers were concentrating downtown, Sears developed a new strategy – the development of stores with their own parking facilities in outlying and suburban areas where the population was growing fast. Some conventional retailers predicted dire results for Sears' new plan. But the company knew what it was doing. Sears placed its new units away from competition, provided ample parking space, and then built stores so large and well stocked that the customer could do all her shopping under one roof.

In short, instead of trying to meet competition head on, Sears developed a strategy for reaching some target markets that had not previously been completely satisfied. At the same time, the market itself was shifting to those outlying areas.

Henry Ford's strategy worked

■ Henry Ford is remembered for his development of the mass production techniques that *enabled* a car to be produced for the mass market. His own recollection of his approach, however, suggests that mass production developed *because* of his basic strategy decision to build a car the mass market could buy. That is, he decided to depart from the then common practice of building cars for the wealthy, the sports drivers, and other specialty buyers, and to produce a car that would appeal to the majority of potential buyers. Ford felt that the low price necessary to appeal to so many buyers would stimulate the new production methods that would make the price possible.

As Henry saw it, the company set "a price so low as to force everybody in the place to the highest point of efficiency. The low price makes everybody dig for profits. We make more discoveries concerning manufacturing and selling under this forced method than by any method of leisurely investigation."[10]

Certainly, production innovations were required to implement Ford's mass-market strategy. But in terms of current thinking about marketing, it appears that the really critical decision was the initial market-oriented decision that there was a market for millions of cars in the $500 price range. Much of what followed was merely implementation.

General Motors found a better strategy

■ A great deal has been written about how and why General Motors has been such a spectacular success, but the focus has tended to be on its method of organization and financial arrangements. In his published memoirs, Alfred P. Sloan, Jr., the man who helped develop and guide General Motors Corp. to its position of dominance, adds new insights into General Motors' success. He claims that in the early stage of the reorganization of General Motors, he made only three really basic decisions. These concerned organization, financial controls, and product (product line). The balance of his tenure in the job was concerned with implementing those basic decisions. One of these three basic decisions was what we would call a marketing decision.

In the 1920s, Henry Ford, following his very successful strategy introduced many years earlier, was still offering a "mass-market" automobile in "any color you want as long as it's black."

Mr. Sloan and General Motors sensed that there was room for a new strategy. Their basic decision was to add new colors and styling, even if this required raising prices. They also hit upon the idea of looking at the market as having several segments (based on price and model types), and then offering a full line of cars with entries at the top of each of these price ranges. They planned to appeal to quality-conscious consumers, always offering good values.

Mr. Sloan acknowledges that the strategy was not immediately successful and that there were many who felt that other strategies should be followed. But he persisted, and it is to this basic decision that Sloan gives credit for eventual success, even more than to the years of implementation.

As is now well known, General Motors persisted with its plan through the 1920s and slowly caught up with the unyielding Ford. Finally, in May 1927, Ford closed down his assembly line and had to switch his own strategy to meet the new competition. He stopped producing the long-successful Model T and introduced the Model A. But General Motors already was well on its way to the commanding market position it now holds.[11]

General Motors and the replacement parts market

■ Thus far we have focused on success stories. But a failure may help demonstrate the General Foods hypothesis even more effectively. We have shown that General Motors' success was due, in great part, to a market-oriented decision. But it is important to note that while General Motors was successfully capturing a giant share of the automobile market, it was neglecting another very important market—the automobile replacement parts market. To be sure, parts were supplied—they had to be. But in those early days, supplying parts was viewed by the auto makers more as a supplemental service than an important business in itself. As a result, the market was left to many smaller suppliers, who were willing to move into this profitable market.

Even today, General Motors does not have the commanding position in the replacement parts and service market that it has in the car market. In other words, Mr. Sloan's successful strategy was concerned with automobiles, not with the broader concept of personal transportation and keeping the cars moving.

More emphasis on service

Only recently has more attention been paid to providing service. And this refocusing on the customer's needs has had a beneficial effect on the organization according to a GM vice president commenting on a new manufacturer-dealer service program. "The whole program is motivating the entire organization on the need for customer satisfaction. We are now coming out publicly and putting a little more onus on ourselves. We have got to turn the service thing around and we already see a definite improvement."[12]

Strategy planning needed by non-marketing people too

■ Clearly, good strategy planning can help ensure a firm's success, while at the same time satisfying consumers and, therefore, contributing to more effective operation of our macro-marketing system.

While strategy planning is helpful to marketing people, it is also important to recognize that it is vitally needed by accountants, production and personnel people, and all other specialists. A strategic plan lets everybody in the firm know what "ball park" they are playing in and what mission they are seeking to accomplish. In other words, it gives direction to the whole business effort. Further, it enables them to proceed with clarity. An accountant cannot set budgets if there is no plan, except perhaps mechanically projecting last year's budget. Similarly, a financial officer cannot project cash needs without some notion of expected sales to some customers and the costs which are associated with satisfying them. Also, the personnel department needs to know what kinds of tasks the firm must accomplish before it can hire and train personnel. And, obviously, the purchasing and production departments need to know how much, of what, is to be produced before they can make their plans.

We will use the term "marketing manager" for editorial convenience, but really, when we are talking about marketing strategy planning, we are talking about the planning which a market-oriented manager should do when developing a firm's strategic guidelines. This kind of thinking should be done, or at least understood, by everyone in an organization who is responsible for planning his own or other people's responsibilities—and this means even the lowest level salesman or production supervisor.

Innovative strategy planning needed for competitive survival and dynamic growth

■ Another reason for focusing on strategy planning is that in our increasingly competitive markets, good strategy planning is needed just for survival. The standardized products which production-oriented people like to turn out in quantity often are not profitable anymore in head-on competition with similar products. Even competent execution of poor or obsolete strategies can lead to poor results.

Too many businesses are worried about maintaining or increasing their share of their *current* market, rather than trying to find new markets or expanding the current market. *They are essentially competitive rather than innovative* – getting by with yesterday's strategies, *not* creating more effective and satisfying ones. This accounts in part for the declining profit rates we see in some industries and firms.

Although investments in plant and equipment have been growing, it appears that profits no longer can be bought simply by spending more money on hardware. Moreover, domestic and foreign competition threatens those who do not create more satisfying goods and services. New markets, new customers, new ways of doing things must be found if companies are to operate profitably in the future and contribute to the operation of our macro-marketing system.

Focus on the "new" rather than the "now"

■ The importance of aggressive, imaginative marketing strategy planning was discussed with respect to the General Foods hypothesis. There we saw that it may be desirable to pay less attention to finding ways to use a company's present resources – a typical production-oriented approach – and pay more attention to locating wholly new market opportunities which may obsolete the firm's own or competitors' strategies. By looking for "breakthrough opportunities" a company may expand its horizon and find profit possibilities which might otherwise be missed.

Tap unsatisfied markets – for breakthrough opportunities

Research in the watch industry, for instance, showed that there were three distinct groups of watch customers but that only one was being catered to by present strategies.

Consumers in the first two groups were primarily motivated by economic factors. The first group wanted to pay the lowest price possible for a watch that worked reasonably well. Consumers in the second segment were willing to pay higher prices for product features that added longer life, greater durability and accuracy, or more attractive styling. Consumers in the third segment, on the other hand, were turned on by emotional values. They usually purchased a watch as a gift and wanted it to have symbolic or sentimental value.

The research showed that 23 percent of the market was in the first segment — the low-price buyers; 46 percent was in the second — those who want durability and general excellence; and 31 percent was in the third segment — those who buy a symbol for some important occasion. It was clear that the better known watch companies were aiming at the third segment almost exclusively. They produced primarily expensive watches and stressed the symbolic appeal in advertising. Their promotion was heavily concentrated in the gift-buying seasons of Christmas and graduation time. Jewelry stores were the distribution outlets.

This commonly accepted strategy of the major watch companies left the first two segments unsatisfied. But then the U.S. Time Co. successfully filled this void with its "Timex" watches. This strategy has made the U.S. Time Co. the world's largest watch company.[13]

It is interesting to note that the major companies had been trying to compete with lower priced foreign competition, but all competitors were using essentially the same marketing mixes. U.S. Time completely upset the watch industry, both foreign and domestic, by not only offering a good product (with a one-year unconditional guarantee) at a lower price but also by using new channels of distribution. Its watches are widely available in department stores, drugstores, discount houses, and nearly any other retail outlet which will carry them.

Such drastic shifts in strategy may be startling to the conventional production-oriented businessman. But they are becoming much more frequent in industries where some or all of the firms have accepted the marketing concept. Such new marketing strategies often cannot be met by competitors through a simple price cut. In effect, the innovators carve out their own market. This search for unsatisfied target markets is not only socially desirable, since it can offer new and better values to consumers, but absolutely necessary for survival in a marketing-oriented age.

Conclusion

■ Marketing's role within a marketing-oriented firm is to provide an integrative force. The marketing concept provides direction. It stresses that the firm's efforts should be focused on satisfying *some* customer groups (target marketing), at a profit, rather than preoccupation with the firm's own internal affairs and naïve reliance on mass marketing.

Production-oriented firms tend to lose sight of their mission and turn inward instead. Often the various departments within such a firm let their natural conflict of interests lead to the building of "fences" around their respective domains. Then, even coordinating committees may be frustrated trying to redirect the firm's efforts.

Wholehearted acceptance of the marketing concept probably will lead to new organizational arrangements. But the really critical matter is acceptance by top management of the marketing concept.

Without this, new arrangements would only be paying lip service to the idea of implementing the marketing concept.

The job of marketing management is one of continuous planning, execution, and control. The marketing manager must select target customers and design marketing mixes for them. But that is only the beginning of his task. He also must see that each strategy works successfully. If it does not, he must modify this strategy during the execution stage, or develop a new one.

The importance of marketing strategy planning was stressed in this chapter because good planning may be far more important than execution and control. The vital importance of good strategy planning was emphasized both for marketing and nonmarketing people. A strategic plan provides direction not only for the marketing department, but for the whole firm—it is vital in setting budgets, projecting cash flows, hiring personnel, and even deciding what to buy and/or make, and when.

Further, we saw that innovative strategy planning is needed not only for survival in our increasingly competitive marketplaces, but also to ensure the proper functioning of our macro-marketing system. Clearly, marketing strategy planning is an important topic and this is why it will be our major focus in this text.

questions and problems

1 Define the marketing concept in your own words, and then explain why the notion of profit is usually included in this definition.

2 Define the marketing concept in your own words, and then suggest how acceptance of this concept might affect the organization and operation of your college.

3 Distinguish between "production orientation" and "marketing orientation," illustrating with local examples.

4 Explain why a firm should view its internal activities as part of a "total system of action." Illustrate your answer for (a) a large grocery products manufacturer, (b) a plumbing wholesaler, and (c) a department store chain.

5 Does the acceptance of the marketing concept almost require that a firm view itself as a "total system of action"?

6 Distinguish clearly between a marketing strategy and a marketing mix. Use an example.

7 Distinguish clearly between mass marketing and target marketing. Use an example.

8 Explain the General Foods hypothesis. What is its relevance to marketing?

9 Provide a specific illustration of why marketing strategy planning is important for all businessmen, not just those in the marketing department.

notes

[1] For further discussion on this, see Bernard J. LaLonde and Edward J. Morrison, "Marketing Management Concepts Yesterday and Today," *Journal of Marketing,* January 1967, pp. 9–13; Robert F. Vizza, Thomas E. Chambers, and Edward J. Cook, *Adoption of the Marketing Concept—Fact or Fiction?* (New York: Sales Executive Club of New York, Inc., 1967), 128 pp.; and C. P. McNamara, "The Present Status of the Marketing Concept," *Journal of Marketing,* January 1972, pp. 50–57.

[2] Adapted from Edward S. McKay, "How to Plan and Set Up Your Marketing Program," *A Blueprint for an Effective Marketing Program* (Marketing Series No. 91

44

[New York: American Management Association, Inc., 1954]), p. 15.

[3] For more details on this system, see Clint DeGabriell, "Design Criteria for an On-Line Nation-Wide Order Processing System," *Disc File Applications* (Detroit: American Data Processing, Inc., 1964), pp. 71–75.

[4] Talk by George Brown, Director of Marketing Research, Ford Motor Co., at Tri-State Marketing Teachers Meeting, May 8, 1965.

[5] Talk given by Paul Lazarsfeld at the University of Notre Dame in 1964.

[6] William A. Mindak and H. Malcolm Bybee, "Marketing's Application to Fund Raising," *Journal of Marketing*, July 1971, pp. 13–18; Philip Kotler, "A Generic Concept of Marketing," *Journal of Marketing*, April 1972, pp. 46–54; and Benson P. Shapiro, "Marketing for Nonprofit Organizations," *Harvard Business Review*, September–October 1973, pp. 123–32.

[7] Robert E. Ringle, "The Marketing Concept in the Defense Industry," *Marketing Digest* (Southern California Chapter of American Marketing Association, June 1961), p. 28.

[8] *McKinsey–General Foods Study* (New York: General Foods Corp., 1963).

[9] "Small Town Greets the Discounters," *Business Week*, October 3, 1964, pp. 90–96.

[10] Henry Ford, *My Life and Work* (New York: Doubleday, Page & Co., 1923), pp. 146–47. See also Theodore Levitt, "Marketing Myopia," *Harvard Business Review*, July–August 1960, p. 45.

[11] Alfred P. Sloan, Jr., *My Years with General Motors* (New York: MacFadden Books, 1965), Introduction, chap. 4, and chap. 9.

[12] "Service is first in GM planning, says Chev head," *Boston Sunday Globe*, August 26, 1973, p. A-77.)

[13] Daniel Yankelovich, "Psychological Market Segmentation," in Jack Z. Sissors (ed.), *Some Bold New Theories of Advertising in Marketing* (Evanston, Ill.: Northwestern University, Jack Z. Sissors, 1963), pp. 23–25.

Demand and competition as seen by the marketing manager

■ The marketing manager has the job of trying to find an economic match between what his firm can offer and what some potential customers will want—what we have called marketing strategy planning. This is a challenging job because from a macro viewpoint, consumers have a wide variety of heterogeneous demands and many potential sources of supply. The role of individual businesses is to satisfy these varying demands. Each firm is expected to find some niche in the system, doing something useful to justify its existence as part of the macro system.

From the firm's viewpoint, just assuring survival means that it should seek some *differential advantage* over its competitors. And it is up to the marketing manager to help the firm find this differential advantage. In this job, he must work with the controllable variables while, at the same time, trying to understand and anticipate the likely future impact of the various uncontrollable variables.

In this chapter we will consider one of the uncontrollable variables—the *existing business situation*, in possible target markets—before going on in the next chapter to discuss how the marketing manager goes about his marketing strategy planning. This chapter is somewhat theoretical, but it is basic to an understanding of the job of the marketing manager.

A good marketing manager does not always "win" in the marketplace, because consumers' attitudes and competitive market conditions are continually changing. Nevertheless, understanding the nature of demand and competition in alternative markets and having a feel for where he is likely to find better and even *break-through opportunities* (highly profitable and hard-to-copy opportunities), will increase his chances for success.

Products and markets as seen by customers and potential customers

Economists
provide
useful
insights

■ How *potential customers* (not the firm) see the good or service that a firm is offering has an important bearing on how much they are willing to pay for it, where it should be made available, and how eager they are to obtain it, if at all. In other words, it has a very direct bearing on marketing strategy planning.

Economists have been concerned with these basic problems for some time and their analytical tools can be quite helpful in summarizing how customers view products and, in turn, how markets behave. The economic concepts reviewed in the following pages will be very helpful in deepening our understanding of the marketing manager's job.

Economists
see individual
customers
choosing
among
alternatives

■ Economics is sometimes called the "dismal" science because it shows that customers simply cannot buy everything they want. Since most customers have a limited income over any period of time, they must balance their needs and the costs of various products.

Economists usually assume that a customer has a fairly definite set of preferences. When he is given a set of alternatives, it is assumed that he evaluates these alternatives in terms of whether they will make him feel better (or worse) or in some way improve (or change) his situation.

But what exactly is the nature of the customer's desire for a particular product?

Usually the argument is presented in terms of the extra utility he can obtain by buying more of a particular product or how much utility would be lost were he to have less of the product. (Students who wish further discussion of this approach should refer to *indifference curve analysis* in any standard economics text.)

Utility is a conceptual framework. It may be easier to grasp this idea if we examine what happens when the price of one of the customer's usual purchases changes.

The law of
diminishing
demand

■ Suppose that a consumer were buying potatoes in 10-pound bags at the same time he bought other foods, such as meat and vegetables. If the consumer is basically interested in purchasing a certain amount of foodstuffs and the price of potatoes drops, it seems reasonable to expect that he will switch some of his food money to potatoes and away from some other foods. But if the price of potatoes rose, you would expect our consumer to buy fewer potatoes and more of other foods.

The general interaction of price and quantity illustrated by this example has been called the *law of diminishing demand*. This

Table 3-1
Demand schedule for potatoes

	Price of potatoes per bag P (1)	Quantity demanded (bags per month) Q (2)	Total revenue per month $P \times Q = TR$ $(1) \times (2) = (3)$
A	$0.80	8,000,000	$6,400,000
B	0.65	9,000,000	
C	0.50	11,000,000	5,500,000
D	0.35	14,000,000	
E	0.20	19,000,000	

law holds that *if the price of a commodity is raised, a smaller quantity will be demanded; conversely, if the price of a commodity is lowered, a greater quantity will be demanded.*

A group of customers makes a market

■ When our hypothetical consumers are considered as a group, we have what is called a "market." It seems reasonable that many consumers in a market will behave in a similar way – that is, if price declines, the total quantity demanded will increase, and if the price rises, the quantity demanded will decrease. Empirical data supports this reasoning, especially for broad product categories, or commodities such as potatoes.

The relationship between price and quantity demanded in a market is illustrated in Table 3–1. It is an example of what economists call a *demand schedule.* It should be noted that as the price decreases, the quantity demanded increases. In the third column, total dollar sales or *total revenue* of the potato market is shown. Notice, however, that as prices go lower, the total *unit volume increases,* yet the *total revenue decreases.* It is suggested that you fill in the missing blanks and observe the behavior of total revenue – an important figure for the marketing manager. We will explain what you should have noticed, and why, a little later.

The demand curve – usually down-sloping

■ If your sole interest is seeing at which price customers would be willing to pay the greatest total revenue, the demand schedule may be adequate. But in our subsequent analysis, it will help to think in terms of a "picture" of the relationship between price and quantity. When the demand schedule is graphed, the resulting curve is called a *demand curve.* Figure 3–1 shows the demand curve for potatoes, actually a plotting of the demand schedule. It shows how many potatoes would be demanded by potential customers at various possible prices. This is known as a *downsloping demand curve.*

Most demand curves have this downsloping appearance. It

Figure 3-1
Demand curve for potatoes (10-pound bags)

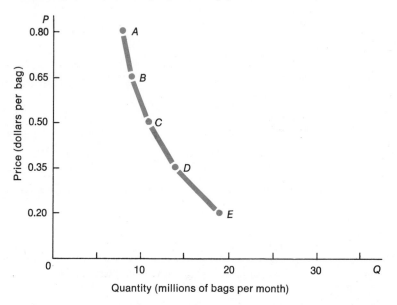

merely indicates that if prices were decreased, the quantity that customers would demand would increase.

Note that the demand curve only shows how customers would react to various prices. Usually, in a market, we see only one price at a time, not all of these prices. The curve, however, shows what quantities will be sold, depending upon what price is set. It would seem that most businessmen would like to see the price set at a point where the resulting revenue was large.

Before discussing this, however, we should consider the demand schedule and curve for another commodity to get a more complete picture of what is involved in demand-curve analysis.

Refrigerator demand curve looks different

■ A different demand schedule is the one for refrigerators shown in Table 3-2. Column 3 shows the total revenue that would be obtained at various possible prices and quantities. Again, as the price of refrigerators goes down, the quantity demanded goes up. But here, contrary to the potato example, total revenue increases—at least until the price drops to $150.

Every market has demand curve, for some time period

■ These general demand relationships are characteristic of all products, but each product has its own demand schedule and curve *in each potential market*, no matter how small the market. In other words, a particular demand curve has meaning only with reference to a particular market. We can think of product demand curves for individuals, regions, and even countries. And the time period covered really should be specified, although this is often neglected as we think implicitly of monthly or yearly periods.

Table 3-2
Demand schedule for refrigerators

	Price per refrigerator P (1)	Quantity de- manded per year Q (2)	Total revenue per year $P \times Q = TR$ (1) $\times$ (2) = (3)
A	$300	20,000	$ 6,000,000
B	250	70,000	17,500,000
C	200	130,000	26,000,000
D	150	210,000	31,500,000
E	100	310,000	31,000,000

The difference between elastic and inelastic

■ The demand curve for refrigerators (see Figure 3-2) is down-sloping, but note that it is flatter than the curve for potatoes. It is quite important that we understand what this flatness means.

We will consider the flatness in terms of total revenue, since this is what interests businessmen.*

When you filled in the total revenue column for potatoes, you should have noticed that total revenue would decrease continually if the price were reduced. This looks undesirable from a business-man's point of view, and illustrates what is known as *inelastic demand*. This means that although the quantity demanded would increase if the price were decreased, the quantity demanded would not "stretch" enough—that is, it is not elastic enough—to increase total revenue.

In contrast, the quantity of refrigerators demanded would stretch enough—at least for a while—to increase total revenue as prices were dropped. *This part* of the refrigerator demand curve is an example of *elastic demand*.

Note that if the refrigerator price were dropped from $150 to $100, total revenue would *decrease*. It can be said, therefore, that when the price is less than $150, demand is inelastic—that is, total revenue would decrease if price were lowered.

Thus, *elasticity* can be defined in terms of changes in total revenue. *If total revenue would increase if price were lowered, then demand is said to be elastic. If total revenue would decrease if price were lowered, then demand is said to be inelastic.*

Total revenue may decrease if prices are raised!

A point that is often missed in discussions of demand is what happens when prices are raised instead of lowered. In an elastic

---

* Strictly speaking, two curves should not be compared for flatness if the graph scales are different, but for current purposes we will do so to illustrate the idea of "elasticity of demand." Actually, it would be more correct to compare two curves for one commodity—on the same graph. Then, both the shape of the demand curve and its position on the graph would be important.

Figure 3–2
Demand curve for refrigerators

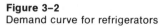
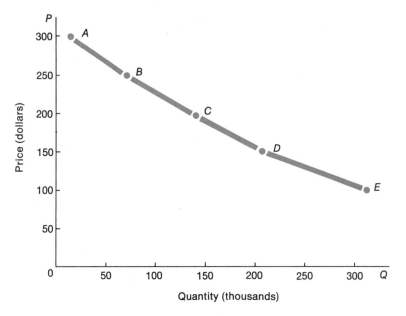

demand situation, total revenue will *decrease* if the price is *raised,* while in an inelastic demand situation, total revenue would *increase* if the price is *raised.* If total revenue remains the same when prices change, then we have a special case known as *unitary elasticity of demand.*

The possibility of raising price and increasing revenue at the same time should be of special interest to businessmen. This only occurs if the demand curve is inelastic. If this were the case, it would obviously be an attractive situation. Total revenue would increase if price were raised, but costs probably would not increase and might actually go down.

The ways total revenue changes as prices are raised are illustrated graphically in Figure 3–3. Here, total revenue is conceived of as the rectangular area formed by a price and its related quantity.

P_1 is the original price here, and the total potential revenue associated with this original price is shown by the area with the diagonal lines slanted down from the left. The total revenue area associated with the new price, P_2, is shaded, with lines running diagonally upward from the left. In both cases, there is some overlap, so the important areas are those with only a single shading. Note that in the lefthand figure, where demand is elastic, the revenue added when price is increased is less than the revenue lost (compare only the single-shaded areas). When demand is inelastic, however, only a small single-shaded revenue area is given up for a much larger one when price is raised.

Figure 3–3
Changes in total revenue as prices are increased

When demand is elastic, a price
increase decreases total revenue

When demand is inelastic, a price
increase increases total revenue

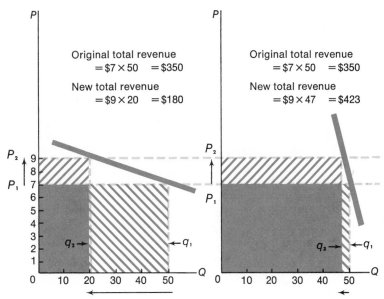

Original total revenue
$= \$7 \times 50 \quad = \$350$

New total revenue
$= \$9 \times 20 \quad = \$180$

Original total revenue
$= \$7 \times 50 \quad = \$350$

New total revenue
$= \$9 \times 47 \quad = \$423$

**An entire
curve is *not*
elastic or
inelastic**

■ It is important to note that it is *improper to refer to a whole demand curve as elastic or inelastic.* Rather, elasticity for a particular curve refers to the change in total revenue between two
points on a curve and not along the entire curve. The change from
elasticity to inelasticity can be seen in the refrigerator example.
Generally, however, adjacent points are either elastic or inelastic,
so it is common to refer to a whole curve by the degree of elasticity
of the curve in the price range that normally is of interest – the
relevant range.

**Demand
elasticities
influenced by
availability of
substitutes
and urgency
of need**

■ At first, it may be difficult to visualize why one product should
have an elastic and another an inelastic demand. Many factors,
such as the availability of substitutes, the importance of the item in
the customer's budget, and the urgency of the customer's need and
its relation to other needs influence demand for a particular product. By examining one of these factors, the availability of substitutes, we should better understand why demand elasticities vary.

Substitutes are goods or services that offer a choice or an alternative to the buyer. The greater the number of good substitutes available, the greater will be the elasticity of demand, the term "good"
here referring to the degree of similarity or homogeneity that
customers see. If they see the products as extremely different or
heterogeneous, then a particular need cannot be satisfied by easily

Figure 3–4
Demand curve for hamburger (a product with many substitutes)

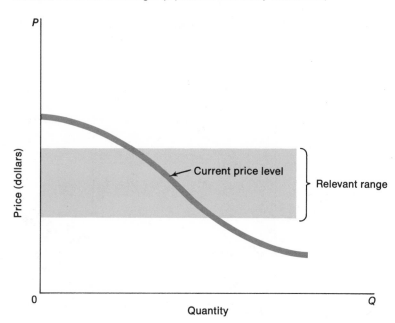

exchanging them, and the demand for the most satisfactory product may be quite inelastic.

As an example, if the price of hamburger is lowered (and other prices stand constant), the quantity demanded will increase considerably as will total revenue. The reason is that not only will regular hamburger users buy more hamburger, but those consumers who formerly bought hot dogs, steaks, or bacon probably will buy hamburger too. But if the price of hamburger rose, the quantity demanded would decrease, perhaps sharply. Consumers would still purchase some hamburger, depending on how much the price had risen, their individual tastes, and what their guests expect (see Figure 3-4).

In contrast to a product which has many "substitutes," such as hamburger, consider a commodity with few or no substitutes. Its demand curve will tend to be inelastic. Salt is a good example. Salt is needed to flavor food. Yet no one person or family uses great quantities of salt. And even with price changes *within a reasonable range,* it is not likely that the quantity of salt purchased would change much. Of course, if the price dropped to an extremely low level, manufacturers might buy more, say, for low-cost filler (Figure 3-5). Or, if the price rose to a staggering figure, many people would have to do without. But these extremes are outside the relevant range.

Figure 3–5
Demand curve for salt (a product with few substitutes)

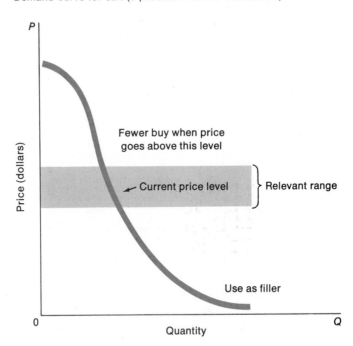

Product markets as seen by suppliers

■ Demand curves are introduced in this chapter because the degree of elasticity of demand is a characteristic of a specific product in a particular market for a particular time period. It summarizes how potential customers feel about the product, and especially, whether there are substitutes for the product.

Economists' thinking on demand provides an insight into product-market situations. But to obtain a fuller understanding, we must continue this economic analysis.

Customers may want some product, but if suppliers are not willing to supply it, then there is no market. So we will study the economist's analysis of supply and then bring analysis of supply and demand together for a more complete understanding of product-marketing situations.

Economists often use the kind of analysis we are discussing here to explain pricing in the marketplace. This is *not* our intention. Here we are interested in product markets and the interaction of customers and potential suppliers. The discussion in this chapter does *not* explain how individual firms set prices or should set prices. That will come in Chapters 23–25.

Table 3–3
Supply schedule for potatoes

	Possible market price per 10-lb. bag	Number of bags sellers will supply per month at each possible market price
A	$0.80	17,000,000
B	0.65	14,000,000
C	0.50	11,000,000
D	0.35	8,000,000
E	0.20	3,000,000

Note: This supply curve is for a month to emphasize that farmers might have some control over when they delivered their potatoes. There would be a different curve for each month.

Supply curves reflect supplier thinking

■ Generally speaking, suppliers' costs have a bearing on the quantity of products they are willing to offer in the market during any period. In other words, their costs affect their supply schedules and supply curves. While a demand curve shows the quantity of goods customers would be willing to buy at various prices, a *supply curve* shows the quantity of goods that will be supplied at various possible prices by all of the suppliers together (if we are thinking of a total market) or one supplier (if we are thinking of a single firm's situation). Eventually, only one quantity of goods will be offered and purchased, and so a supply curve is really a hypothetical description of what would be offered at various prices. It is, however, a very important curve. Together with a demand curve, it summarizes the attitudes and probable behavior of buyers and sellers with respect to a particular product in a particular market.

Some supply curves are vertical

■ We usually assume that supply curves tend to slope upwards, that is, suppliers will be willing to offer greater quantities at higher prices. If a product's market price is very high, it seems only reasonable that producers will be anxious to produce more of the product and even put workers on overtime or perhaps hire additional workers in order to increase the quantity they can offer. To go further, it seems likely that producers of other products will switch their productive resources (farms, factories, men, or retail facilities) to the product that is in great demand.

Contrariwise, if a very low price is being offered for a particular commodity, it's reasonable to expect that producers will switch to other products, reducing supply. A supply schedule (Table 3–3) and a supply curve (Figure 3–6) for potatoes illustrate these ideas. This supply curve shows how many potatoes would be produced and offered for sale at each possible market price in a given month.

Figure 3–6
Supply curve for potatoes (10-pound bags)

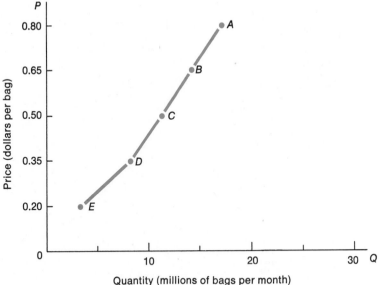

In the very short run (say, over a few hours, a day, or a week), a supplier may not be able to increase the supply at all. In this situation, we should see a vertical supply curve. This situation is frequently of practical significance in the market for fresh produce. Fresh strawberries, for example, continue to deteriorate, and a supplier must sell them quickly – preferably at a higher price – but in any event, he must sell them. For less perishable commodities, he may set a minimum price floor and, if necessary, store his goods until market conditions are more favorable.

If the product is a service, it may not be easy to expand the supply in the short run, and there is no way to inventory it either. Additional barbers or medical doctors are not quickly trained and licensed, and they only have so much time to give each day. When the day is done, the unused "supply" is lost. Further, the prospect of much higher prices in the near future cannot readily expand the supply of many services. A good play, or an "in" restaurant or nightclub may be similarly limited in the amount of product it can offer at a particular time.

Elasticity of supply

■ The term *elasticity* also is used to describe supply curves. An extremely steep or almost vertical supply curve, often found in the short run, is called *inelastic* because the quantity supplied does not stretch much (if at all) if the price is raised. A flatter curve is called *elastic* because it does stretch more. A slightly upsloping supply curve is characteristic of longer run market situations.

56

Figure 3–7
Equilibrium of supply and demand for potatoes

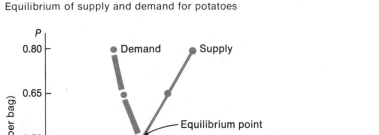

Given more time, suppliers have a chance to adjust their offerings and competitors may enter or leave the market.

Demand and supply interaction establishes the size of the market and price level

■ We have treated market demand and supply forces separately. Now we must bring them together to show their interaction. The *intersection* of these two forces determines the size of the market and the market price, at which point the market is said to be in *equilibrium*.

The intersection of demand and supply is illustrated for the potato data discussed above. The demand curve for potatoes is now graphed against the supply curve presented in Figure 3–6 (see Figure 3–7).

In this potato market, the demand is inelastic; the total revenue of all the potato producers would be greater at higher prices. But the market price is at the *equilibrium point*, where the quantity and the price that sellers are willing to offer are equal to the quantity and price that buyers are willing to accept. The 50 cent equilibrium price for potatoes yields a smaller *total revenue* to potato producers than would a higher price. This lower equilibrium price comes about because the many producers are willing to supply enough potatoes at the lower price. *Demand is not the sole determiner of price level. Cost also must be considered, via the supply curve.*

Figure 3–8
Some important dimensions regarding product-market competition

Important dimensions \ Types of situations	Pure competition	Oligopoly	Monopolistic competition	Monopoly
Uniqueness of each firm's product	None	None	Some	Unique
Number of competitors	Many	Few	Few to many	None
Size of competitors (compared to size of market)	Small	Large	Large to small	None
Elasticity of demand facing firm	Completely elastic	Kinked demand curve (elastic and inelastic)	Either	Either
Elasticity of industry demand	Either	Inelastic	Either	Either
Control of price by firm	None	Some (with care)	Some	Complete

Nature of product-market situations

■ The elasticity of demand and supply and the interaction of demand and supply curves help explain the nature of competition a marketing manager is likely to experience in various product-market situations. We will emphasize three kinds of market situations: pure competition, oligopoly, and monopolistic competition. A fourth type, called monopoly, is encountered so infrequently that it will not be treated separately. Usually, monopolies are controlled by local, state, or federal authorities. Where they are not, they can be treated as monopolistic competition, since monopolies are simply an extreme case of monopolistic competition.

Understanding these product-market situations is quite important because the freedom of a marketing manager (i.e., his control over price) is considerably reduced in some situations. The important dimensions regarding these situations are summarized in Figure 3–8.

When competition is pure, many competitors offer about the same thing

■ *Pure competition* develops in markets characterized by many buyers and many sellers offering very similar or homogeneous products. It is assumed here that all buyers and sellers have full knowledge of the market forces and that there is ease of entry for buyers and sellers – that is, new firms have little difficulty starting up in business and new customers can easily come into the market. This is more or less true in the potato industry, which is why we would call it a pure competition situation.

In pure competition, we find something like a perfectly flat demand curve for a particular firm. Although the potato industry as a whole has a downsloping demand curve, each individual potato

producer has a demand curve that is perfectly flat at the going
market price – the equilibrium price.

To explain this in more concrete terms, let's look at the demand
curve for the individual potato producer. Assume that the equilibrium price for the industry is 50 cents. This means he can sell as
many potatoes as he chooses at 50 cents. The quantity he and all of
his fellow producers choose to sell makes up the supply curve; but
acting alone, he can do almost anything he wants to do.

If this individual farmer raises $1/_{10,000}$th of the quantity offered
in the market, for example, it is obvious that there will be little impact on the market whether he goes out of business or doubles his
production.

The reason his demand curve is assumed to be flat in this example is that the farmer probably could not sell any potatoes above the
market price, and there is no point in selling below 50 cents. (The
subject of deciding the best quantity to offer is discussed in Chapters 24 and 25, where we cover pricing and output decisions.)

The relation between the industry demand-curve situation and
the demand curve facing the individual farmer in pure competition
is shown in Figure 3–9.

Not many markets can be characterized as purely competitive
where the competitors are facing a perfectly elastic demand curve.
But there are enough markets with some of these characteristics to
allow us to talk about extremely competitive situations in which the
marketing manager may have to accept the going price.

Squeeze on the orange growers

Florida orange growers, for example, have essentially homogeneous products, and they have little control over price. When
there is a very large supply, prices drop rapidly and are beyond the
producers' control. When supplies are short, the reverse happens.
The 1967 crop was 50 percent larger than the 1966 crop, and most
operators sold their oranges below their costs. Oranges "on the tree"
cost 75 cents a box to grow and sold for $1.25 in 1966. In 1967, they
were selling for 35 cents a box. Supply turned around in 1968, however, and oranges were selling for $2.40–$2.60 a box.[1]

Similar situations are found with many agricultural commodities, and farmers often seek government help to "save" them from
pure competition, especially if the industry demand is inelastic,
as it often is. Agricultural parity programs are designed in part for
this purpose, usually working to increase price by reducing supply.
In 1961, the cling peach growers in California voted to destroy part
of their crop in an effort to raise the market price.[2]

Nor are such highly competitive situations restricted to agriculture. In any field where many competitors sell essentially homogeneous products – such as chemicals, plastics, lumber, coal, printing, and laundry services – the demand curve seen by *each producer* tends to be flat. Assuming no collusion among the firms,
there is a tendency for each firm to expand production – and the
action of all producers forces down the market price.

Industries tend to become more competitive – that is, move

Figure 3–9
Interaction of demand and supply in the potato industry and resulting
demand curve facing individual potato producers

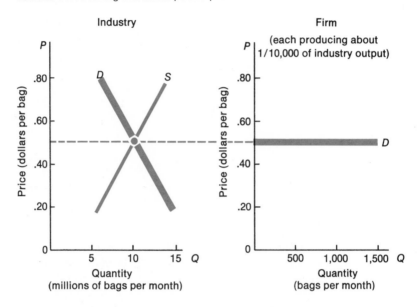

Industry

Firm

(each producing about
1/10,000 of industry output)

toward pure competition. More competitors enter the market, the
supply is increased, and the current equilibrium price is pushed
downward. This tends to force profits down until some competitors
are eliminated. Economists describe the final equilibrium position
as that point at which there are no entrepreneurial profits, only
sufficient return to keep the present competitors in the business.

On the way to this final equilibrium position, competition may
become so vigorous that companies may actually lose money as the
price goes below the equilibrium level and some firms are driven
out of the market. It may take some time, moreover, before the industry price moves up to the equilibrium level so the remaining
companies can survive. At the economist's final equilibrium point,
however, none of the firms make a profit! They just cover all their
costs.

**When
competition is
oligopolistic**

■ Not all industries or product-markets move toward pure competition. Some become oligopolies.[3]

Few competitors offering about the same thing

Oligopoly situations are special market situations which develop
when a market has:

1. Essentially homogeneous products, such as basic industrial
    chemicals or gasoline.
2. Relatively few sellers, or a few large firms and perhaps many
    smaller ones who follow the lead of the larger ones.
3. Fairly inelastic *industry* demand.

Figure 3–10
Oligopoly – kinked demand curve – situation

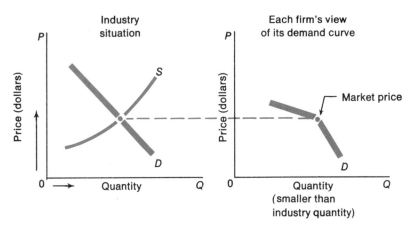

The demand curve for each firm is particularly interesting in an oligopoly situation. Although the industry demand curve can be inelastic throughout the relevant range, the demand curve facing each individual oligopolistic competitor looks "kinked," as shown in Figure 3–10. The current market price is at the kink.

There is a "market price," as in pure competition, because the competing firms must watch each other carefully. Each marketing manager must expect that raising his own price above the market for such a homogeneous product would cause a substantial loss of sales. His demand curve would be relatively flat above the market price, since few, if any, competitors would follow his price increase. But if he lowers his price, he must expect competitors to follow. Therefore, given inelastic industry demand, his own demand curve would be inelastic at lower prices. Since lowering prices along such a curve is clearly an unprofitable move, he probably should not do so. That is, he should leave his price at the kink – the market price.

Actually, however, there are price fluctuations (in particular, price cutting) in oligopolistic markets. Sometimes this is due to "overeager" firms who do not understand the product-market situation. In other cases, substantial increases in demand or supply will change the basic nature of the situation and lead to price cutting. Sometimes the price cuts are drastic, such as Du Pont's "Dacron" price cut of 25 percent on one occasion. This was caused, in part, by production capacity that already exceeded demand and that was scheduled for further expansion.[4]

Price wars are sometimes initiated

A common example of price fluctuations can be seen in retail gasoline marketing, at a major city intersection or along a busy highway where there are several obvious competitors. Apparently enough final consumers think of gasoline as homogeneous to create oligopoly conditions, and oligopoly-type "price wars" are common. These usually start when some gasoline discounter successfully attracts "too much" business, perhaps by price cutting one cent a gallon below his usual price. The war proceeds for a time, until one of the dealers calls a meeting and suggests that they all "get a little sense." Sometimes these price wars will end immediately after such a meeting, with prices returning to a "reasonable and proper" level.

As in pure competition, oligopolists face a long-run trend toward an equilibrium level where profits are driven toward zero. Along the way, a marketing manager would tend to try to avoid price competition, relying more on the other elements in his marketing mix. This is an extremely difficult job, however, because if all of the potential customers view the products as essentially similar, how can he obtain some differential advantage for his firm?

When competition is monopolistic

■ From the above discussion it is easy to see why firms would want to avoid pure-competition or oligopolistic situations. Clearly, a market in which they have more control would be preferable.

Different products may lead to different "industries"

To avoid such competitive situations, aggressive marketing managers seek to develop a differentiated or heterogeneous product (in the eyes of some consumers, not just the firm). If these efforts are extremely successful, the firm becomes, in effect, the "industry" for this product. More typically, target customers recognize the product as different and the firm does not have to share *this* industry demand with *all* competitors. Such a market situation is called *monopolistic competition.*

Substitutes provide competition

The term *monopolistic* indicates that the firm is attempting to attain its own little monopoly, but the term *competition* means that there is still a competitive situation. The extremely vigorous — even cutthroat — competition of the purely competitive market is reduced, although there are still somewhat similar products (substitutes) to provide competition for the monopolistic competitor.

In monopolistic competition, the firm has its own downsloping demand curve, but the shape of the curve depends somewhat on competitors' actions. Each monopolistic competitor has freedom, but not complete freedom, in his own little "industry."

Judging elasticity is helpful in strategy planning

■ Since the firm in monopolistic competition has its own downsloping demand curve, it must make a conscious price decision as part of its marketing mix. Here, the elasticity of the firm's own demand curve becomes extremely relevant. If it is highly inelastic, the firm may decide to raise prices to increase total revenue. But if demand is highly elastic, this may indicate many competitors with acceptable substitutes, and the company should focus on developing a more differentiated marketing mix.

Why are some products offered in pure competition?

■ Why would anyone compete in essentially profitless pure competition? The usual explanation is that the firm was either already in the industry, or enters without knowing what is happening or is going to happen, and then must stick it out until its resources are depleted.

Production-oriented people seem more likely to make such a mistake than the market-oriented businessman. Avoiding pure competition seems advisable, and certainly fits with our emphasis on trying to develop unique marketing strategies.

Pure competition cannot always be avoided

■ Despite their desire to avoid pure-competition conditions, however, some firms find that (at least for part of their operation) they cannot do so. In some cases, production processes make this inevitable. For instance, in the chemical industry, caustic soda is produced as a by-product in the production of more profitable chlorine. At one time, the supply of caustic soda was so great that it was being dumped as waste into the Gulf of Mexico. Obviously, this large supply had a depressing influence on the price (to say nothing about the water)!

Some industries appear to be almost purely competitive, yet new firms keep entering, replacing the casualties, possibly because they might not have more attractive alternatives and can at least earn a living in the industry. Examples of such industries include small retailing and wholesaling, especially in less developed economies. Modern farmers continually attempt to shift their production to more profitable crops, but since there are many thousands of other farmers making similar choices, almost pure competition is inevitable.

Competition leads to standardization efforts

■ A marketing manager caught in oligopoly or nearly pure competition may, and often does, encourage or participate in an industry standardization program to reduce the variety of products he has to offer and thereby reduce his costs.

Standards may be based upon quantitative factors, such as weight per volume, or ingredients or performance. Standards also may be based on a variety of qualitative factors such as ripeness, color, flavor, taste, and texture.

Generally, quantitative standards are preferred because of ease of measurement. But for many products, strictly quantitative measures are not enough. Raw materials for paint manufacturing, for example, defy complete description, so paint buyers often specify "the same as the last satisfactory shipment" on purchase orders.

Standard-
ization also
facilitates
marketing
process

■ Standardization has been called a "facilitating" function, since it frequently simplifies trade. Uniform quality and a reduction in the number of grades make buying and selling easier, more economical, and frequently save time. Comparison between the selling prices of competitors is facilitated, and sales by sample or description become feasible.

For agricultural commodities, the use of standard grades facilitates sorting. Commodities can then be traded like quality-controlled manufactured products. Standardized grades permit the use of published market statistics and promote the development of a more competitive market. For the consumer, standardization may lower prices.

Approaches for developing better strategies

■ Product standardization efforts may make sense if it is obvious that the firm has to remain close to or in pure competition or oligopoly. But, if it can be had, monopolistic competition is certainly a more attractive alternative. The key to achieving monopolistic competition is to have a better marketing strategy.

There are two basic ways to develop better strategies: market segmentation and marketing mix differentiation.[5]

Market segmentation is the process of isolating smaller, more homogeneous market segments within a market for the purpose of selecting one or more target markets and developing a unique marketing mix to satisfy the needs of each. The target markets probably will contain the least satisfied people in the general market area. Unsatisfied here means that not all of their needs were being completely fulfilled, although they may have had a variety of offerings to choose from.

Marketing mix differentiation on the other hand, is the process of attempting to differentiate a firm's marketing mix from the mixes of other firms competing for the same target market.

A target marketer would probably try market segmentation first, while a mass marketer would move directly to differentiation. A successful segmenter, however, may attract competition and be forced into differentiation. These ideas are illustrated in Figure 3–11 and explained more fully below.

Mix
differentia-
tion tries to
satisfy the
whole
market
"pretty well"

■ Mix differentiation seeks to direct consumer demand toward one manufacturer's or middleman's offering even though it may be quite similar to the competitors' offerings.

In other words, the firm tries to shift its own demand curve to the right.

This approach, which often stresses promotion, also may involve physical product changes, including new packages or brands, new features, new flavors, or new novelties slipped into the box.

Even if physical changes are made, the intention is not to focus on smaller markets but to improve the company's position in the

Figure 3–11
How a target marketer and a mass marketer see a market and compete over time

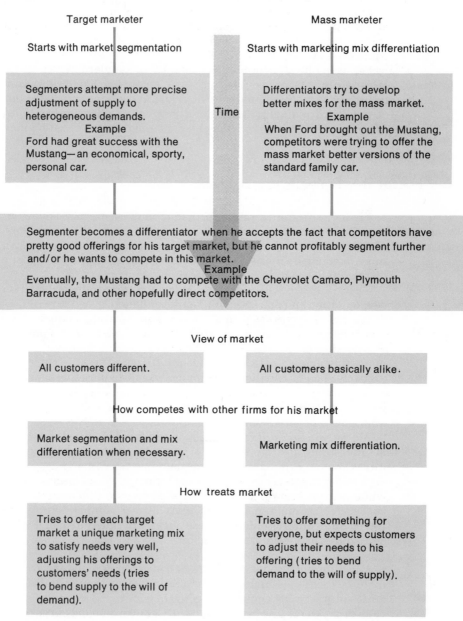

Target marketer	Mass marketer
Starts with market segmentation	Starts with marketing mix differentiation

Time

Segmenters attempt more precise adjustment of supply to heterogeneous demands.
Example
Ford had great success with the Mustang—an economical, sporty, personal car.

Differentiators try to develop better mixes for the mass market.
Example
When Ford brought out the Mustang, competitors were trying to offer the mass market better versions of the standard family car.

Segmenter becomes a differentiator when he accepts the fact that competitors have pretty good offerings for his target market, but he cannot profitably segment further and/or he wants to compete in this market.
Example
Eventually, the Mustang had to compete with the Chevrolet Camaro, Plymouth Barracuda, and other hopefully direct competitors.

View of market

All customers different.

All customers basically alike.

How competes with other firms for his market

Market segmentation and mix differentiation when necessary.

Marketing mix differentiation.

How treats market

Tries to offer each target market a unique marketing mix to satisfy needs very well, adjusting his offerings to customers' needs (tries to bend supply to the will of demand).

Tries to offer something for everyone, but expects customers to adjust their needs to his offering (tries to bend demand to the will of supply).

whole market. The aim is to differentiate but not to become so unique that general appeal is lost. The theory here is that a firm should offer a better homogeneous product rather than a unique heterogeneous product desired by fewer consumers.

Some firms use promotion heavily in their differentiation efforts because actual differences among competing products may be minor—but these minor differences, nevertheless, may be very important to some customers.

Some differences exist mainly in the eye of the beholder. If a woman truly believes that one cosmetic is more suited to her personality, she will use it. But different customers have different needs. Some women may be concerned with cleanliness, others with beauty, and others with glamour. A single cosmetic advertisement might appeal to all of them, but for different reasons. So, rather than trying to segment this market, the firm would try to cater to all of the different needs at the same time. If they are not too different, this may not only be possible but economically sensible for the firm.

Mix differentiation is employed for most widely advertised products appealing to mass audiences—products such as soaps, cosmetics, foods, and automobiles. It also is seen in the industrial area, where firms try to meet generally accepted specifications but with improved products and mixes.

With differentiation you want to be different—but not so different that you narrow your markets, excluding some customers. You may not satisfy anyone better than competitors can, but you hope your general appeal will be satisfying enough to a sufficient number of people to prove profitable.

Market segmentation tries to satisfy a part (or parts) of the market "very well"

■ With market segmentation, we attempt to develop a different marketing mix(es) to satisfy customers in only a part (or parts) of the market. Here, more drastic changes, perhaps even in the physical product, may be made to appeal to smaller target markets. The result may be achievement of more inelastic demand curves in whatever target markets are selected.

A market segmentation approach recognizes that there may be different demand curves in different parts of the market. This is because there are different customer needs in various parts of the market—a basic assumption for target marketers. Instead of assuming, like a mass marketer, that any market consists of a fairly homogeneous set of customers, a segmenter would tend to presume that there were subsets which might be catered to with different mixes. These different market segments would likely have different demand curves, as illustrated in Figure 3–12. Presumably, focusing on one or some of these smaller markets would provide greater satisfaction to customers and, therefore, provide greater profit and security for the marketing manager and his firm.

Although a differentiator might attempt to satisfy a lot of people "pretty well," a segmenter would attempt to satisfy a smaller number of people "very well." If done well, total sales would be greater with the same effort, because the market penetration in the chosen target market(s) would likely be much higher.

Smaller markets do not necessarily mean smaller sales

It is extremely important to note that when a target marketer takes the market segmentation approach, he is *not* settling for a smaller sales potential. Instead, he is focusing his efforts on a

Figure 3–12
There may be different demand curves in different market segments

Differentiator sees the "market"
with one aggregate demand
curve

Segmenter sees the "market"
with one demand curve for *each*
market segment

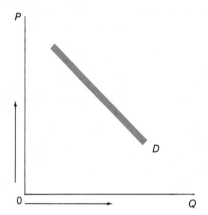

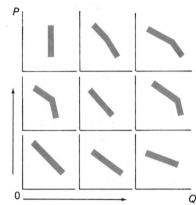

smaller market(s) but fully expects to get a much larger share of that market(s). In the process, his total sales may be larger and, even better, he may have almost a monopoly hold on his target market(s).

Market segmentation may enable a firm to move itself away from pure competition or oligopoly into monopolistic competition. For example, the Wolverine World Wide Co. came out with "Hush-Puppies," a casual, split-pigskin shoe, that enabled it to move into the extremely competitive U.S. shoe market with spectacular success while conventional small shoe manufacturers were existing in almost pure competition.[6]

The highly profitable operation of Volvo illustrates the possibility of successful market segmentation in a fiercely competitive international market. Volvo has stressed long life and performance in its cars and has not tried to compete head-on with the large producers aiming at the mass market. Similarly, Magnavox has fared well in the competitive U.S. television industry by aiming at the top of the market, not the whole market. Zenith, appealing to the quality- and reliability-conscious, at several price levels, also has done well.

Market segmentation combined with mix differentiation

■ Even if a firm attempts market segmentation, it probably will find that one or more competitors will quickly follow. Then it will have to shift emphasis to differentiation.

The automobile industry has developed many different kinds of cars to appeal to different target markets. But the various companies and divisions within companies have quickly copied each other. Sometimes the car builders frankly admit that one car was designed to compete directly with another — for example, Chevrolet's Camaro with Ford's Mustang. Then the competitive focus tends to shift to minor differences in features, trim, and accessories, together with psychological perceptions of the different products, styles, and brand names.

Even if a marketing manager preferred to apply market segmentation, the extreme competition that most firms find in the marketplace might force him to use differentiation along with market segmentation.

It's the intent that counts

■ It often is difficult for an outsider to tell which approach a firm is pursuing. What one firm would recognize as one market, another might see as many markets and systematically design products and marketing mixes to satisfy only some of them. Which firm wins would depend on how the market(s) respond(s) to the competing mixes. If there really are differences which are correctly identified and satisfied, then the (perhaps more costly) market segmentation effort may be more profitable. But if the whole market really is more or less homogeneous, then the differentiation efforts may be just as successful, perhaps at lower cost.

Given our present knowledge of consumer behavior, moving directly to differentiation may be the safe path. But it will lead one into fairly direct competition from others following the same course. Safety may be purchased at the price of the attractive profits which usually accompany marketing breakthroughs. This "safe" route seems to be the one instinctively chosen by the production-oriented businessman, and then he wonders why his markets are so competitive!

Conclusion

■ A good marketing manager should be an expert on markets and the potential competition he will face in various markets. He must continually study and interpret the uncontrollable environment for his firm.

The economist's traditional demand and supply analysis provides us with useful tools for analyzing the nature of demand and product-market situations. It is important that you master the concepts of a demand curve and demand elasticity and their relationship to the various product-market situations. A good marketer would try to avoid pure competition or oligopoly in favor of monopolistic competition — where he offers something different and achieves some differential advantage over his competition.

In an effort to achieve a monopolistic competition situation, a target marketer may use either market segmentation or marketing mix differentiation. Market segmentation focuses on smaller, more homogeneous target markets with the intention of developing more satisfying marketing mixes for those markets. Mix differentiation, on the other hand, is concerned with differentiating a firm's mix from competitors' mixes for a particular market. The two approaches are not incompatible, because competitors usually follow a firm's successful market segmentation efforts, and even a target marketer may have to resort to mix differentiation.

Following either approach, a target marketer may be able to achieve a relatively inelastic demand curve in one or more market segments. He may operate more profitably than the many production-oriented mass marketers that typically focus on lowering costs rather than satisfying customers' needs and end up in or near profitless pure competition. In the process, he also plays a vital role in the macro-marketing process—attempting to match heterogeneous demands and supplies in order to better satisfy consumers.

questions and problems

1 Explain in your own words how economists look at markets and arrive at the "law of diminishing demand."

2 Explain what a demand curve is and why it is usually downsloping.

3 What is the length of life of the typical demand curve? Illustrate your answer.

4 If the general market demand for men's shoes is fairly elastic, how does the demand for men's dress shoes compare to it? How does the demand curve for women's shoes compare to the demand curve for men's shoes?

5 If the demand for fountain pens were inelastic above and below the present price, should the price be raised? Why or why not?

6 If the demand for steak is highly elastic below the present price, should the price be lowered?

7 Discuss what factors lead to inelastic demand and supply curves. Are they likely to be found together in the same situation?

8 If a manufacturer's well-known product is sold at the same price by many retailers in the same community, is this an example of pure competition? When a community has many small grocery stores, are they in pure competition? What characteristics are really needed in order to have a purely competitive market?

9 Distinguish between marketing mix differentiation and market segmentation. Which policy is being followed if cold cream is offered in a new, more distinctively shaped jar? Which, if only the label is changed to gold foil for distinctiveness?

10 List three products which are sold in purely competitive markets and three in monopolistically competitive markets. Now list three products for which the sellers seem to be using marketing mix differentiation and three more where they appear to be using market segmentation. Do any of these products have anything in common? Can any generalizations be made about the relation between these approaches and product-market situations?

notes

[1] *Business Week,* May 13, 1967, p. 187; "Orange Crush," *Time,* January 27, 1967, p. 67; and "Oranges Start Coming Up Roses," *Business Week,* May 4, 1968, pp. 127–30; see also "Flood of Florida Orange Juice Threatened," *The Wall Street Journal,* November 16, 1970, p. 20; "Reassessing the Impact of Gasoline Prices," *Business Week,* July 27, 1974, pp. 58–59; and "What Went Wrong With Beef Prices," *Business Week,* April 13, 1974, pp. 64–68.

[2] *Wall Street Journal,* July 9, 1962, p. 2.

[3] There are several types of oligopoly, including differentiated and undifferentiated. Such details are beyond our scope. We will only treat the most typical type—undifferentiated oligopoly.

[4] *Business Week,* June 24, 1967, p. 85.

[5] For the original discussion on this topic, see Wendell R. Smith, "Product Differentiation and Market Segmentation as Alternative Marketing Strategies," *Journal of Marketing,* July 1956, pp. 3–8. Marketing mix differentiation is similar to his product differentiation.

[6] "This Little Pigskin Went to Market," *Business Week,* December 7, 1963, pp. 48–50.

4

Overview of marketing strategy planning

■ Marketing strategy planning is clearly vital to a firm's profitability and long-run survival. This chapter presents an overview of what marketing strategy planning is about and how a marketing manager would go about it effectively.

Marketing strategy planning leads to a master plan

■ Good marketing strategy planning provides the guidelines for all of a company's activities and it consists of only two distinct but interrelated jobs:

1. Selecting a target market.
2. Developing the most appropriate marketing mix for the target market.

These ideas were discussed briefly in Chapter 2 when the marketing manager's framework and basic responsibilities were discussed.

Both jobs must be done together

■ It is important to stress—*it cannot be overemphasized*—that these two steps are interrelated. A marketing manager cannot do one step and then another. Both steps must be done together because it is strategies which must be evaluated against the company's objectives—not alternative target markets or alternative marketing mixes. One cannot compare alternative target markets without considering their economic potential and whether the firm can profitably serve them. Similarly, alternative marketing mixes cannot be evaluated unless some target markets are also coupled with them. (Of course, the same target market could be considered for alternative mixes—but then we would still be comparing alternative strategies.)

Selecting target markets

■ Production-oriented businessmen do not concern themselves with selecting target markets. They simply assume that there is a large "mass market" eagerly waiting out there for their product or service.

Market-oriented businessmen, on the other hand, practice target marketing. They recognize that potential customers do have different demands and that different marketing mixes may be required for alternative target markets. Such a marketing manager would select his market segments.

Market grids help select target markets

■ When a market-oriented man looks at potential target markets, he realizes that what is often considered as one market may actually be many smaller, more homogeneous markets. An analytical approach to market segmentation would certainly be useful here. The market grid approach provides such a technique.

The *market grid concept* pictures a market as a box that is cross-hatched like a checkerboard or grid, on the basis of relevant *market* characteristics. Each square in the large box represents a smaller, more homogeneous market (see Figure 4–1). Keep in mind that only potential customers are considered within the market grid that we draw.[1] On a grid concerned with men's clothing needs, for example, only characteristics pertaining to men would be considered. Children and women generally are not potential customers in this market. They could be indicated in a little area below the potential markets, perhaps surrounded by a dotted line as shown in Figure 4–1. But for practical purposes, such groups are not part of the potential market, and hereafter the dotted area will not be shown.

An example—the market grid for refrigeration

The refrigeration market is an excellent illustration for the market grid concept. Remember that in the following analysis we are talking about customers and their needs, not products that might satisfy them or that the company can produce. This is why we will discuss "refrigera*tion*" rather than "refrigera*tors*."

Many consumers and businesses need refrigeration. It is used in homes, stores, institutions, and many other places, as shown in Figure 4–2. These customers do not all want the same product, nor are they equally accessible to the manufacturer. Some of these customer groups, indicated by the grid boxes, might be satisfied by electric refrigeration, while others would prefer gas refrigeration. Some would require large walk-in coolers and others would need compact units. Picnickers would prefer a small ice chest. Actually,

Figure 4–1
Market grid for a product — need area

		Potential target markets		

All others

to show all of the possible variations on a market grid would require more breakdowns than those in Figure 4–2.

In a more detailed breakdown, in Figure 4–3, the eastern food store market (shown with a large "X" in Figure 4–2) is analyzed. The food stores are listed by types: fruit and vegetable, dairy, fish, meat, and full-line grocery stores. These stores are of varying sizes, and this also may have a bearing on the type of refrigeration desired.

SIZE OF MARKET GRID BOXES NOT IMPORTANT INITIALLY The exact size of the markets represented by the boxes in Figures 4–2 and 4–3 need not concern us in this preliminary stage. Actually, it might take considerable market research to determine the potential sales volume in each of these boxes. But, by developing a grid like this, the marketing manager is alerted to the existence of smaller, individualized markets. Perhaps many of these little markets can be satisfied by a single product. Before assuming this, however, it would pay to take a closer look, perhaps with some formal market research, to determine which if any of the many smaller markets can be merged and treated alike. This analysis is important, since *each unique target market requires a separate marketing mix.*

When the marketing manager first constructs a market grid, each box can reflect what he feels is the volume represented by each market. In Figure 4–3, for example, the boxes for small stores are drawn larger than for the medium and large stores because there are many more small stores. This should be done with care, however, because the manager's notions about the market may reflect past, not present or future conditions.

EACH LITTLE MARKET DIFFERENT Each of the small markets within the larger refrigeration market shown in Figure 4–2 represents a homogeneous group of potential customers with special

Figure 4–2
Market grid for refrigeration

Region / Place of use	East	Midwest	South	Mountain	Pacific
Home					
Food stores	✕				
Wholesalers					
Restaurants					
Hospitals					
Schools					
Military reservations					
Business offices					
Other institutions					
Trailers					
Picnics					
Planes					
Trains					
Ships					

needs. But some of these groups may be quite similar to others, and one manufacturer (or middleman) may try to satisfy several groups of customers or perhaps a whole row or column in the grid at the same time. In this particular case, it is unlikely that one manufacturer would cater to a whole column represented in Figure 4–2, since the products desired would be quite different. Yet, it is entirely feasible for some of the larger consumer refrigerator manufacturers to sell successfully to the "Home" row in Figure 4–2, as Westinghouse, General Electric, and others do. And middlemen who can obtain their goods from various producers certainly have considerable freedom in deciding which groups to serve.

The same market might be served with different products, too. Gas and electric refrigerators of various types and sizes, and even

Figure 4–3
Market grid for refrigeration in eastern food store market

Size ／ Type	Large stores	Medium stores	Small stores
Fruit and vegetables			
Dairy			
Fish			
Meat			
Full-line groceries			

old-fashioned iceboxes in some areas, would be suitable for the "Home" groups shown in Figure 4–2. This acceptability of substitutes will affect the competitive situation, of course.

Customer dimensions should be used in splitting a grid

■ Keep in mind that a market grid defines the characteristics and needs of *potential customers* for the type of product or service being considered—*not* the characteristics of present or possible products. This forces us to reject the typical production-oriented approach to defining markets in terms of the products the customers buy. For example, we would have to reject the traditional production-oriented approach used in the automobile industry, with its splitting of markets into compacts, foreign cars, low-price, medium-price, and luxury cars.

It's no easy task

There is no magic formula for selecting the *right* grid dimensions. Rather, painstaking and systematic analysis of the thinking and characteristics of potential customers is required, while keeping in mind the company's own capabilities and objectives (to avoid excessive blue-sky thinking about markets that might be "nice," but impossible to serve). Insight may be aided by marketing research, but ultimately management judgment may have to enter, because this is an extremely important matter.

Selecting grid dimensions, and the resulting implications for marketing mix planning are illustrated and discussed further in this chapter. Then grid analysis is treated in more detail in Chapters 6 through 11. It is important to note here, however, that this is *not* just a simple, mechanical process. Different dimensions may even be needed for different parts of the same market grid, as will be illustrated later in the chapter. Marketing managers should be careful in gridding. Sloppy or too casual gridding can easily lead to bad strategies.

Flexible view of grids needed

■ The lack of profit potential in some target markets helps explain why some customers are poorly serviced or dissatisfied with the products available to them. Or sometimes, due to changing consumer preferences, a new market has developed and has not yet been recognized. These grid boxes should not be seen as static markets, since they are in a constant state of flux.

A firm may find that the market it serves or would like to serve has customers in many boxes, although they may not all be adjacent to each other on the grid drawing. This is especially likely if a large market is broken down geographically and then further subdivided. Even these differences may be important, however. The customers in various geographical markets — say, New York, Los Angeles, and Paris — may require different methods of distribution and, at the very least, will necessitate different wholesalers and retailers. Thus *each market grid box may require a unique marketing mix and should be thought of as a separate market.*

Developing marketing mixes

Many routes to the customer's satisfaction

■ Developing a marketing mix must be an integral part of selecting a target market. That is, all the elements of a marketing strategy must be set simultaneously.

There are a large number of possible ways to satisfy the needs of target customers. A product can have many different characteristics, colors, and appearances. The package can be of various sizes, colors, or material; the brand names and trademarks can be changed; services and returned-goods privileges can be adjusted; various advertising media (newspapers, magazines, radio, television, billboards) may be used; a company's own salesmen and perhaps other sales specialists can be employed. Different prices can be charged; cash discounts and markups can be changed; a higher caliber of salesman may be hired or a different type of distributor may be used; intensity of sales effort may be varied from one locality to another; credit policies may be adjusted; and so on.

Each of these approaches can have many shades of differences, making the number of possible marketing mixes extremely large. With so many variables available, the question becomes: Is there any way of simplifying the selection of marketing mixes? And the answer is "yes."

**The four
"Ps" make
up a
marketing
mix**

■ An analysis of the problems that face both large and small companies shows that it is possible to reduce the number of variables in the marketing mix to four basic ones:

Product
Place
Promotion
Price

It may help to think of the four major ingredients of a marketing mix as the "four Ps." Figure 4–4 emphasizes their interrelationship and their focus on customer Ⓒ.

This text includes a set of chapters on each of the four Ps, but for the present, each will be discussed briefly in the following paragraphs.

**Product—
the right one
for the target**

■ The product area is concerned with developing the right "product" for the target market. This product may involve a physical product and/or some combination of services. The crux of the matter in the product area is to develop something which will satisfy some customers' needs.

Most of this text will be concerned with tangible products, but the principles in most cases also apply to services. It is important to keep this in mind, since the service side of our economy is growing. It is also important to see the product concept as including services, because it is too easy to become overly occupied with producing and selling tangible products. Too many production-oriented people fall into this trap and neglect important opportunities for satisfying needs in other ways. Automobile manufacturers and dealers, for example, lost out in the rental car business when they focused exclusively on selling physical products.

Under *Product,* we will cover problems which are concerned with developing and managing a product line. We will be concerned with designing, packaging, and branding new products. We will also consider the characteristics of various kinds of products with a view toward developing generalizations about product classes so that we will be able to develop whole marketing mixes more quickly. The product area is only one of the four Ps, but how potential customers view the Product will have an immediate bearing on the development of the rest of the marketing mix. This is why Product is studied first. In the end, however, all of the four Ps must be set together. Chapters 12 to 15 will get us started in the Product area, and then we can move on to the other three Ps, building on a solid foundation.

**Place—
reaching the
target**

■ A product is not much good to a customer if it is not available when and where he wants it. We must consider where, when, and by whom the goods and services are to be offered for sale.

Goods and services do not flow from producers to consumers automatically. They move through channels of distribution where a great deal of marketing work is done. Channel members may or

Figure 4–4
A marketing strategy

may not handle the goods. Some may own them and transfer title, while others do neither. Some may provide return and repair services, while also storing and transporting them. And others may be primarily concerned with transmitting money and information. In other words, a number of things besides goods flows through a channel, both ways.

Any sequence of marketing institutions, from producer to final user or consumer, including any number of (or perhaps no) middlemen is called a *channel of distribution.* Marketing managers must work in and through such channels, and so our study of Place will be very important to marketing strategy planning.

Sometimes a channel system is quite simple (short), perhaps running directly from a producer to the final user or consumer. Often it is much more complex (long). In Figure 4–5, four basic channels for consumer goods are presented: (1) direct from manufacturer or producer to consumer, (2) to a retailer, (3) through a wholesaler and then a retailer, and (4) through two levels of wholesalers (who provide a different set of marketing functions) to a retailer and then to a final consumer. These four channels only suggest the possibilities. Actually, there are many different kinds of retailers and wholesalers, who will expand the number of possible channels.

Several different channels might be used

A marketing manager may have many different target markets in mind, and this might require him to use several channels *at the same time* to reach the different parts of his market grid. Each channel system should be thought of as a different entity and may be part of, or require, a different marketing mix.

The many possible channel variations and the problems that they can cause a marketing manager are discussed in Chapters

Figure 4–5
Four possible (basic) channels of distribution for consumer goods

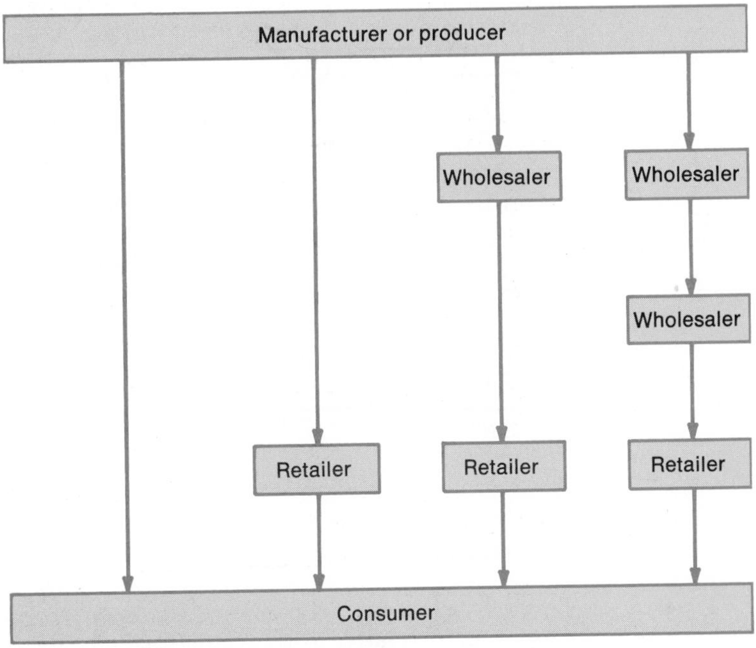

16–19. At that time, we will also consider the role that transportation and storage agencies play in the distribution of goods and services.

In summary, *Place* will be concerned with all of the problems, functions, and institutions involved in *getting the right product to the target market*.

Promotion— telling and selling the customer

■ The third P, *Promotion*, is discussed in Chapters 20–22. It is concerned with any method that *communicates to the target market* about the right product to be sold in the right place at the right price. Promotion includes personal selling, mass selling, and sales promotion. All are complementary methods of communicating with customers, and it is the marketing manager's job to develop the most effective blend of these alternative methods.

Personal selling—flexibility is the biggest asset

Personal selling involves *direct face-to-face relationships between sellers and potential customers*. A salesman is often a very important part of a marketing mix because he can adapt the company's marketing mix to the needs and circumstances of each little target market and, in the extreme, to each potential customer. Moreover, face-to-face selling provides an immediate feedback, which helps the salesman to adapt effectively. Salesmen are included in most marketing mixes, but their services come at a price.

Sometimes personal selling is very expensive and it is desirable to supplement this effort with mass selling and sales promotion.

Mass selling—reaching millions at a price or even free

Mass selling is designed to *communicate with large numbers of customers at the same time.* Obviously, such a method has less flexibility than personal selling, which can use *immediate* feedback to adjust the presentation for *each* prospect. When the target market is large and dispersed, however, mass selling may be much less expensive than personal selling.

Advertising is the main form of mass selling. *Advertising is any paid form of nonpersonal presentation of ideas, goods, or services, by an identified sponsor.* It involves the use of such media as:

Magazines and newspapers.
Radio and television.
Outdoor posters, signs, sky writing, and so on.
Novelties.
Direct mail.
Signs on stores, in buses, and so on.

Advertising must be paid for by the advertiser. There is, however, another form of mass selling which is "free," and that is *publicity.*

Effective publicity and public relations efforts can contribute to mass selling at relatively low cost. In some cases, it can be more effective than advertising. Advertising expenditures may be used primarily to create a favorable climate for publicity. Trade magazines, for instance, may write or carry articles featuring the products of regular advertisers. And this publicity may generate far more inquiries than the company's advertising. Such mass selling efforts may become increasingly important as more attention is focused on smaller and more clearly defined target markets.

Sales promotion—it tries to complement

Sales promotion specialists complement the efforts of salesmen and advertising men. *Sales promotion* refers to specific activities (such as point-of-purchase displays, booklets, and leaflets, direct mailings, and so on) which can make both personal and mass selling more effective, by coordinating and supplementing both efforts.

Sales promotion personnel may design and arrange for distribution of novelties, point-of-purchase material and premiums, store signs, catalogs, directory references, and circulars. They may assist in the development of displays, sales demonstrations, and trade-show exhibits. It is difficult to generalize about sales promotion efforts because they are custom-designed and nonrecurring. They can be very effective, but making them work is a learned skill and not a sideline for amateurs. Consequently, specialists in sales promotion have developed within companies and as consulting firms. Nevertheless, it would be the job of the marketing manager to specify what kind of promotion effort he wanted, and this might include assigning a complementary role to sales promotion.

■ While the marketing manager is developing the right product, place, and promotion, he also must decide on the right *price*—one that will round out his marketing mix and make it as attractive as possible. In setting the price, he must consider the nature of competition in his target market as well as the existing practices on markups, discounts, and terms of sale. He also must consider legal restrictions affecting prices.

We casually referred to "market price" and "equilibrium price" in the last chapter but, in fact, it is not so easy to define price in real-life situations. Price has many dimensions. For example, if you were offered a current model Ford station wagon for $1,000, would this be a good price for an automobile that normally sells for over $3,000? Or, if you were offered a 21-inch television set for $100 when they normally sell for $200, would this be a good buy?

In each case, the first reaction might be an enthusiastic "Yes!" But wait a minute. It might be wiser to investigate further. The $1,000 for the Ford station wagon might be the price of a wreck worth only a few hundred dollars at the scrap yard. And the $100 for the TV set might be a reasonable price for all of its components in a parts bin at the factory. If you wanted these assembled, you would have to pay $25 extra. If you were interested in buying the cabinet, it might be an additional $25. And if you wanted a quality guarantee, there might be an added charge of $50.

The price equation: Price equals something

These examples emphasize that when a price is quoted, it is related to *some* assortment of goods and/or services. *Any transaction in our modern economy can be thought of as an exchange of money—the money being the price—for Something.*

This *Something* can be a physical product in various stages of completion, with or without the services normally provided; with or without quality guarantees, and so on. And this "product" may or may not be conveniently available to you.

If the product is made available to channel members instead of final consumers or users, the price should be set so that each channel member has a chance to cover his costs and make a profit when he sells it at a higher price.

The nature and extent of this *Something* will determine the amount of money to be exchanged. Some consumers may pay list price, while others may obtain significant discounts or allowances because something is *not* provided. The possible variations are summarized in Figure 4–6 for consumers or users and in Figure 4–7 for channel members. Some of these variations will be discussed more fully in the pricing chapters, but here it should be clear that price is a multidimensional variable. Also, it is important to note that not everyone gets merely his money's worth in a sales transaction. Presumably, a transaction takes place *only* if both buyer and seller feel they will be better off after the sale.

Some consumers get a surplus

The price we are talking about is an equilibrium price related to demand and supply forces. You will recall that the demand curve

Figure 4–6
Price as seen by consumers or users

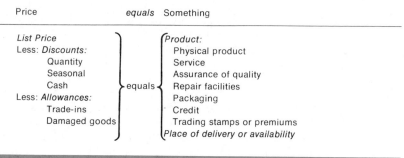

| Price | *equals* | Something |

that we discussed in Chapter 3 was generally downsloping and that some of the demand curve was above the equilibrium price. This is simply a graphic way of showing that *some* customers would be willing to pay more than the equilibrium price if they had to. In effect, some of them are getting a "bargain" by being able to buy at the equilibrium price. Economists have traditionally called these bargains the *consumer surplus.* It is important to see that there is such a surplus, because some business critics naïvely assume that consumers do badly in any business transaction. In fact, a sale only takes place if the consumer feels she is at least "getting her money's worth" and as we see here some would be willing to pay much more than the market price.

While price is only a part of a marketing mix, it is what the customer must pay if he is satisfied with the firm's marketing mix. Obviously, therefore, price is an important area for the marketing manager. Without customer acceptance of his price, all of his planning efforts will be wasted.

Chapters 23–25 will be concerned with determining the "right" price to move the right product to the right place with the right promotion for the target market.

Relative importance of four Ps

■ *All* four Ps, we have seen, are essential to the marketing mix. In fact, they are interdependent. But is any one of them more important than the others? Generally speaking, the answer is no. When a marketing mix is selected, all decisions about the Ps should be made at the same time. That is why the four Ps are arranged around the customer Ⓒ in a circle to indicate that they are coequal.

Some sequence is needed in our discussion, however, and the following one has logical advantages. We develop a *Product* that we feel will satisfy the target customers. Then we find a way (*Place*) to reach our target customers. *Promotion* tells the target customers about the availability of the product that has been designed for them. Then the *Price* is established in the light of expected customer reaction to the total offering.

Figure 4–7
Price as seen by channel members

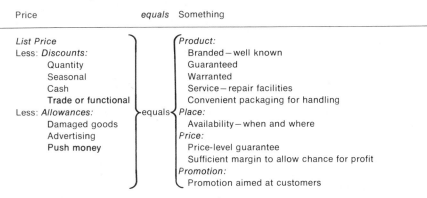

Price   *equals*   Something

List Price		*Product:*
Less: *Discounts:*		Branded — well known
Quantity		Guaranteed
Seasonal		Warranted
Cash		Service — repair facilities
Trade or functional		Convenient packaging for handling
Less: *Allowances:*	equals	*Place:*
Damaged goods		Availability — when and where
Advertising		*Price:*
Push money		Price-level guarantee
		Sufficient margin to allow chance for profit
		Promotion:
		Promotion aimed at customers

Strategy sets details of implementation

■ The needs of a target market virtually determine the nature of the marketing mix. Understanding the close interrelationship of market needs and the marketing mix is important, since it has a bearing on how the market gridding process is developed and the kinds of questions we ask about potential customers and their needs.

The objective of the gridding process is to find homogeneous sets of potential customers with needs which can be satisfied with the same marketing mix. And if the needs of potential target markets are fully spelled out, then logical marketing mixes follow quickly. Such target market descriptions, however, may require imaginative combining of several market grid dimensions to more clearly summarize the needs and preferences, and maybe attitudes, of the people in each market grid box. Further, it would be helpful in estimating the size of each potential market if at least one of the relevant dimensions were linked to demographic characteristics for which we already have data, such as age, sex, income, geographic area, and so on.

Ideally, the grid box dimensions should be complete enough to guide marketing mix planning, within the constraints of the uncontrollable variables. More is said about planning the four Ps in subsequent chapters, but Table 4–1, showing some kinds of dimension characteristics and their probable effect on marketing decisions, provides some perspective for what follows. Ideally, we would be able to describe any market grid box in terms of all three types of dimensions and these dimensions in turn would help us to develop more appealing marketing mixes.

These ideas can be seen more clearly with an example in the home-decorating market.

Table 4–1

Potential market grid dimensions	May affect these decision areas
1. Geographical location and other demographic characteristics of potential customers.	Affects size of *Target Markets* (economic potential) and *Place* (where products should be made available) and *Promotion* (where and to whom to advertise).
2. Behavioral needs, attitudes, and how present and potential goods or services fit into customers' consumption patterns.	Affects *Product* (design, packaging, length or width of product line) and *Promotion* (what potential customers need and want to know about the product offering, and what appeals should be used).
3. Urgency to get need satisfied and desire and willingness to compare and shop.	Affects *Place* (how directly products are distributed from producer to consumer, how extensively they are made available, and the level of service needed) and *Price* (how much potential customers are willing to pay).

A British paint manufacturer looks at the home-decorating market

■ The experience of a paint manufacturer in England who followed the approach discussed above illustrates the strategic planning process and how basic "one-time" decisions determine subsequent implementation details.

First, this paint manufacturer's marketing manager interviewed many potential customers and analyzed the various needs for the products he could offer. By combining several categories of customer needs and some available demographic data, he came up with the view of the market shown in Figure 4–8. In the following description of these markets, note that useful marketing mixes come to mind immediately.

There turned out to be a large mass market representing about 60 percent of the potential for all kinds of paint products. The manufacturer did not give much consideration to this market because he was not a large producer and he did not want to compete directly with the many companies already in the market. The other four markets, which he placed in the four corners of a market grid simply to show that they were different markets, were entitled Helpless Housewife, Handy Helper, Crafty Craftsman, and Cost-Conscious Couple.

The Helpless Housewife, the manufacturer found out, really did

Figure 4–8
A market grid for the home-decorating market
(paint area), in England

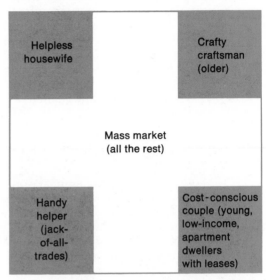

Helpless housewife		Crafty craftsman (older)
	Mass market (all the rest)	
Handy helper (jack- of-all- trades)		Cost-conscious couple (young, low-income, apartment dwellers with leases)

The "Helpless Housewife" describes a segment of the
English market as seen by this marketing manager. In
the U.S. there appears to be a "Helpless Homeowner"
market (male and female) which is not fully satisfied
with the typical "paint store." Some large paint manufacturers and retailers are now trying to cater to this
market.

not know much about home decorating or specific products. She
needed a helpful paint dealer who could supply not only paint and
other supplies but also considerable advice. And the dealer who sold
her the paint would want it to be of fairly good quality so that she
would be satisfied with the results.

The Handy Helper was a jack-of-all-trades who knew a great deal
about paint and painting. He wanted a good-quality product and was
satisfied to buy from an old-fashioned hardware store or lumberyard, which sells primarily to men. Similarly, the Crafty Crafstman
was willing to buy from a retailer who would *not* attract female
customers. In fact, this older man didn't want to buy paint at all,
but pigments, oils, and other ingredients to mix his own paint.

Finally, the Cost-Conscious Couple was young, had low income,
and leased an apartment. In England, an apartment dweller with
a lease must paint the apartment during the course of the lease.
This is an important factor for at least some tenants as they choose
their paint. If you were a young apartment dweller with limited
income, what sort of paint would you want? Some couples in
England, the manufacturer discovered, do not want very good
paint! In fact, something not much better than whitewash would
do fine.

The paint manufacturer decided to cater to the "Cost-Conscious Couple" with a marketing mix flowing logically from the description of that market. That is, knowing what he did about their relevant dimensions, he offered them a low-quality paint (Product), made it available in lower income apartment neighborhoods (Place), geared his price-oriented promotion to these areas (Promotion), and, of course, offered an attractive low price (Price). The manufacturer has been extremely successful with this strategy, giving his customers what they really want, even though the product is of low quality.

Differentiating between strategy and tactics

■ Our primary emphasis in this text is on strategy planning, but it should also be pointed out that a lot more than strategy planning is involved in successful marketing. Strategies work out as planned only when they are effectively carried out, and many decisions have to be made during these implementation efforts. These decisions are concerned with *tactics*.

Tactical decisions can enhance the basic strategy

■ Tactical decisions should be made within the guidelines set down during strategy planning. Product policies, place policies, and so on, are established as part of strategy planning. Then, tactical decisions within these policies probably will be necessary while carrying out the basic strategy. It is important to realize, however, that as long as these tactical decisions stay within these guidelines, no change is being made in the basic strategy. If tactical decisions do not produce the desired results, however, it may be necessary to reevaluate the whole strategy decision rather than just "redoubling the effort" in a tactical decision area.

It's easier to see the difference between strategy level policies and tactics if we illustrate these ideas using our paint manufacturer as an example. Possible four-P or basic strategy policies are shown in the left-hand column in Table 4–2, and likely tactical decisions are shown in the right-hand column.

It should be clear that some tactical decisions are made regularly, even daily, and such decisions should not be confused with strategic ones. Certainly, a great deal of effort can be involved in these tactical decisions, and they might take up a good part of the time of a sales manager, advertising manager, and others. But they are not the strategic changes which will be our primary concern. In subsequent chapters, we will discuss the policies which provide the guidelines for such tactical changes. You should be alert to the importance of such guidelines, recognizing, however, that additional thought and effort are required to put such policies into effect. These details of implementation are the subject of advanced texts and courses in marketing.

Table 4–2
Relation of strategic policies to tactical decisions for paint manufacturer

Strategic policies	Likely tactical decisions
Product—Carry as limited a line of colors and sizes as will satisfy the target market prospects.	Add, change, or drop colors and/or can sizes as customer tastes and preferences dictate.
Place—Try to obtain distribution in every conceivable retail outlet which will handle this type of paint product in the areas where the target customers live or buy.	If a new retailer opens for business in these market areas, immediately solicit his order.
Promotion—Promote the "low price" and "satisfactory quality" to meet the needs of the market's prospects.	Regularly change the point-of-purchase and advertising copy to produce a "fresh" image. Media changes may be necessary also. Salesmen have to be trained, motivated, etc.
Price—Maintain a low "one-price" policy without "specials" or other promotional deals.	If paint companies in other markets cut prices, do not follow.

Specifying and selecting among strategies

Making choices is not easy

■ This text is concerned with developing and evaluating marketing strategies—primarily the analysis of target markets and the four Ps.

The framework may appear simple enough, but the task of making choices within this framework is fairly complex. For one thing, each of the four Ps has many potential variations, making the number of possible marketing mixes very large. For example, if there were 10 variations in each of the variables (10 prices, 10 products, etc.) there would be 10,000 possible marketing mixes. Yet ten is a very small number of variations for each of these variables, and as the number of variations increases, the number of possible mixes increases geometrically.

But it can be done

■ It is obvious that no human mind is capable of accurately evaluating all possible mixes, but progressive elimination of the least desirable can reduce the problem to manageable proportions. And, fortunately, there are many combinations, not just a single combination, that can succeed. If competition is not too keen, just a "better" marketing mix may be quite successful even though it is nowhere near the "best."

Furthermore, some marketing strategies are obviously inferior, and by the end of the text you will be able to spot these fairly quickly. Some strategies, on the other hand, are obviously better than others. These, too, you should be able to spot by the end of the text. It is these strategies which can be singled out for more careful analysis, developing more precise estimates of the probable effectiveness of each marketing mix and the probable financial success, given the resources which would have to be committed.

If the firm is profit oriented, then possible strategies can be compared in terms of profit or return on investment or whatever objective the company is seeking. Sometimes, unfortunately, the likely outcomes of alternative strategies cannot be specified quite as clearly as would be required for a numerical comparison. Then, managerial judgment must come into play. Or, sometimes, financial considerations are not the main objective of the firm. In this case, the evaluation of strategies may have to be even more subjective. More will be said about this in Chapter 27.

It is important to note that the selection among possible strategies may be greatly simplified if the marketing manager has deliberately sought to develop breakthrough opportunities. In other words, if he has attempted to develop distinctly new strategies catering to previously unsatisfied market needs, then these strategies may be clearly so superior to competitors' strategies or others the company is considering that the choice will be simple. From both a firm and a macro point of view, it would seem that the search for such opportunities would be desirable and strongly encouraged.

Conclusion

■ Good marketing strategy planning is vital to a firm's success in our competitive marketplace. It also can contribute to making our macro-marketing system more effective.

Marketing strategy planning requires the simultaneous selection of a target market and the development of an appropriate marketing mix for this target market. It is extremely important that these two jobs be seen as interrelated. *They are not sequential.*

Target customer groups can be divided and subdivided almost without end. Market grids can be used to segment potential markets. Then, possible marketing mixes can be considered for each of the grid boxes to evaluate their potential. Some may be likely markets. Others may actually subdivide into several markets, each requiring different mixes. And still others may not be worth bothering about when expense is weighed against potential profit.

To limit the problem of choosing a marketing mix, without oversimplifying the problem, we settled on the four Ps – Product, Place, Promotion, and Price – to identify the main decision areas of the marketing manager. The problem, in brief, is to satisfy our target customers with the *right* product, available in the *right* place, promoted in the *right* way, and available at the *right* price.

questions and problems

1 Explain why it is desirable to define target markets and market grids in terms of *people's* needs rather than product characteristics. Further, explain why considerable ingenuity may be needed to develop market grids.

2 Why is the customer placed in the center of the four Ps in the text diagram of a marketing strategy? Explain, using a specific example from your own experience.

3 Explain, in your own words, what each of the four Ps involves.

4 Evaluate the text's contention that "a marketing strategy sets the details of implementation."

5 Distinguish between strategy and tactics, illustrating for a local retailer.

6 Develop a market grid for footwear in general, using as many customer needs and other characteristics as seem appropriate. Then discuss the many types and qualities of footwear which might appeal to the customers in your market grid boxes. Do not attempt to collect data.

7 Develop a market grid for the "automobile" market, using several customer-related dimensions—*not* product characteristics. Show where you are on the grid. Then, consider the products which are now available in the light of your breakdown and see if you can identify any unsatisfied target markets. Might they offer any substantial potential? Is your "ideal" available? Should it be?

8 Outline a marketing strategy for each of the following new products:
a. A radically new design for a haircomb.
b. A new fishing reel.
c. A new "wonder drug."
d. A new industrial stapling machine.

notes

[1] The general term *market grid* should be credited to Professor J. R. Malone, College of Business Administration, University of Notre Dame.

5

Uncontrollable variables affect marketing management

■ The marketing manager does not work in a vacuum. He must consider much more than the four Ps and choosing target markets. As we noted in Chapter 2 (see Figure 2-6), the uncontrollable variables he must work with fall into the following categories:

1. Cultural and social environment.
2. Political and legal environment.
3. Economic environment.
4. Existing business structure.
5. Resources and objectives of the firm.

In the long run, the marketing manager's actions may affect some or all of these variables.

These variables are increasingly important in our dynamic national and world environment. How they add to the complexity and challenge of marketing management will be seen in this chapter. We will not discuss the "existing business structure," however, because we have already discussed the nature of competition in Chapter 3 and more detail on the number and types of competitors is presented in later chapters. What competitors can and are likely to do is a major concern of this text.

Cultural and social environment

■ The cultural and social environment is beyond the control of the marketing manager—in the short run, at least. It is concerned with how and why people live and behave as they do. There are many changing dimensions in this variable and the speed and directions of change are difficult to predict. But this variable is still extremely important because it has a direct impact on customer thinking and buying behavior.

Since customer behavior is given extensive treatment in Chapters 7–10, we will only present a few examples here to emphasize the possible impact of this variable on marketing strategy planning.

The American "melting pot" is not homogenized

■ Americans are often stereotyped as a friendly people, but actually this varies by regions. People on the West Coast, for example, tend to be more open and, at least superficially, more friendly. This is, in part, because many have moved west to find a new life and have left behind the more tradition-bound social structures of the smaller towns of the Midwest and the East. People on the West Coast also seem more willing to travel great distances. Some Californians, for example, thought nothing of driving several hundred miles on a weekend, (before the energy crisis). This had an effect on the location of retail facilities and loyalty to particular stores.

Cultural differences are also exhibited in different regions and within urban areas. Take eating habits, for example. Biscuits and hushpuppies are much more popular in the South, and Mexican food has long been favored in the Southwest. Within large metropolitan cities, we still find national and religious pockets that represent separate markets for some goods and services. Large midwestern and eastern metropolitan areas often have distinct neighborhoods of Irish, Italians, Poles, Jews, Puerto Ricans, and blacks. These urban areas have newspapers, radio stations, restaurants, grocery stores, and record shops which cater specifically to these culturally defined markets.

Work and growth are important to some

■ Besides differences in consumption behavior, we also must take into account cultural attitudes towards life and work, which are a reflection of religious, ethical, and moral values. It is evident that national attitudes have an effect on a country's rate of growth and the direction of its development.[1]

The American culture tends to encourage and reward hard work and achievement, while other societies seem less concerned about what they feel are materialistic values. Americans are willing to work, but they also expect material rewards. This has led our economy into a preoccupation with growth and producing and distributing goods and services. Much of our analysis of the U.S. market will be within this cultural framework.

In some other societies, on the other hand, far greater stress is placed on leisure and the enjoyment of life. More holidays are built into the working year. The output of such economies may not be quite as high as it could be, but the people may not feel that they are suffering because of this lower physical output.

What quality of life do we want?

It is possible that some cultural and social changes may be taking place or may be forced upon Americans. The current interest in the "quality of life" suggests a desire for less materialistic solutions and, in time, we may learn to satisfy our needs in different ways. Or, the energy crisis may force us to readjust our thinking about how to meet our needs. Our way of satisfying needs has consumed huge quantities of energy and it is obvious that some changes will be needed.

Regarding the possibility of changing the cultural environment, it is important to recognize that changes in basic attitudes come slowly. An individual firm could not hope to encourage big changes in the short run. Instead, it should identify these attitudes and work within these constraints in the short run, while making long-run plans.

Sometimes, however, strong outside forces, such as the energy crisis, riots, or boycotts, may force more rapid changes in the cultural and social environment, or, on the other hand, may precipitate clashes between this environment and the political and economic environments.

Political environment

■ As the role of business grows in our society, the attitudes and reactions of the people, social critics, and governments become increasingly important to the marketing manager. In our discussion, we will separate political and legal questions, although in practice this separation is hard to maintain. A change in political environment often leads to changes in the legal environment or the administration of existing laws.

Consumerism cannot be ignored

■ Some social critics will never be satisfied, but others merely voice the growing frustration of some consumers with the quality and safety of products being offered by business. Consumer advocate Ralph Nader, for example, has done much to focus and organize consumer concern and to bring about the passage of specific legislation. His best seller, *Unsafe at Any Speed,* may have forced General Motors to remove its Corvair from the market. Nader is credited with the passage of major federal legislation designed to improve safety in automobiles, and to police the processing and distribution of some food products. And in this political environment, existing regulatory agencies may become much more aggressive. The Food and Drug Administration, for example, has been taking a tougher posture and banning some products for safety reasons, while requiring more informative labels on foods and drugs, and even warnings on products that have not been adequately tested for safety.[2]

Some of the complaints against business are certainly justified and unscrupulous practices have long been deplored by conscientious businessmen and exposed by Better Business Bureaus. Similarly, government agenices and regulatory bodies also act to police and correct many of these abuses.

But a new, more militant mood seems to have developed among

people. As the well-known business consultant, Peter Drucker, wrote: "We have been a very patient people by and large. Now people are fed up, and I do not blame them."[3] Some businessmen have recognized the new mood and are doing something about it. But more criticism can be expected, both in the United States and abroad.

This means that the marketing manager, as well as top management, will have to give serious consideration to consumer attitudes in marketing planning. The alternative could be pretty drastic. Court settlements for defective products could rise substantially. A Utah family was awarded $450,000 when it was decided that the Ford Bronco was an "inherently dangerous" vehicle which was, in part, the cause of a fatal accident.[4] Such an award against a small company could wipe it out. For a larger company, moreover, it opens the door to additional suits. Clearly, more attention must be paid to product design and safety in our political environment.

Nationalism can be limiting also

■ Strong sentiments of nationality may also affect the work of some marketing managers. These feelings can inhibit sales or even block marketing activity in some areas. Oil and copper mining firms have felt such pressures in recent years, for example, in Latin America, Africa, and the Middle East.

To whom the firms could sell, and how much, have been dictated by national interests. The Arab restriction of oil shipments to those friendly to Israel is probably the outstanding example in recent years. But the "Buy American" policy in many government contracts reflects similar attitudes in the United States. Similarly, Philippine businessmen have tried to drive "excessively aggressive" Chinese merchants out of the Philippines. And Africans have driven Indian merchants out of their countries.

Countries may choose to issue guidelines to foreign firms, as Canada did recently to encourage "good corporate behavior." These guidelines sometimes are supplemented with new laws or the threat of legislation. Laws were passed recently in Canada, for example, to restrict the flow of U.S. advertising and culture via television into the Canadian market. British Columbia banned cigarette and liquor ads in all media—including the U.S. press.[5] And Thailand recently passed laws restricting the kinds of businesses which foreigners can engage in and the kinds of jobs they can hold.[6]

Such guidelines can be extremely important in both domestic and international business, because often businesses must get permission to operate. In some political environments, this is only a routine formality; in others, a lot of red tape is involved and personal influence is sometimes necessary.

Political environment may offer new opportunities

■ The political environment is not always a negative variable. Governments may decide that encouraging business and opening markets are constructive steps for their people. Japan recently opened its market more to foreign investors and competitors.[7] The United States and other highly developed countries may give industrial development a boost in Latin America, Africa, and Asia by allowing manufactured goods from those areas to be imported duty-free.[8]

Within the United States, special programs and financial inducements have been developed to encourage urban redevelopment, employment and training of hard-core unemployed, and minority enterprises. State and local governments also try to attract and hold businesses, sometimes with tax incentives.

Some businessmen have become very successful by studying the political environment and developing strategies which use these political opportunities.

Legal environment

U.S. legislative developments: encouraging competition

■ American economic and legislative thinking has been based on the assumption that competition among many small firms will guide the economy with an "invisible hand." This idea became popular after the publication of Adam Smith's *Wealth of Nations* in 1776. Great Britain accepted this idea during the 1800s, in principle at least, and it was enshrined in common law there and in the United States. According to this concept, attempts to restrain or limit trade were held to be against the public interest and unenforceable. Practices tending to fix prices, limit markets, or in any other way control trade were considered undesirable.

This laissez-faire approach did not last long in Great Britain. But Americans have been especially reluctant to give up Adam Smith's free enterprise ideal. After the Civil War, however, industries began to grow larger, and some were consolidated into trusts, cartels, and monopolies by wealthy tycoons who were often called "robber barons." This led to a restraint of competition and hardships for smaller producers and consumers. As a result, there was a movement—especially among midwestern farmers—to curb monopolists.

Beginning in 1890, a series of laws were passed that were basically *antimonopoly or procompetition.* The names and dates of these laws are shown in Table 5–1.

The *Sherman Act* was aimed primarily at monopolists, or *conspiracies* to monopolize or restrain trade. The Clayton Act had the same intent, but was more specific. And the *Federal Trade Commission (FTC) Act* set up the Federal Trade Commission as a continuing body to serve as a watchdog for the public and to supplement the Justice Department's efforts to enforce the nations' laws affecting business. The FTC was to be concerned with "unfair methods of competition."

Besides supplementing the Sherman Act, the *Clayton Act* was aimed at several specific practices which the more general prohibitions of the Sherman Act did not cover—or did so in a manner that created confusion and ambiguities. The Clayton Act specifically tackled such practices as geographical price discrimination by manufacturers, exclusive dealer arrangements that limit a buyer's

Table 5–1
Outline of federal legislation affecting competition in marketing

	Antimonopoly (procompetition)	Anticompetition	Antispecific practices
1890	Sherman Act		
1914	Clayton Act Federal Trade Commission Act		Clayton Act
1936	Robinson-Patman Act	Robinson-Patman Act	Robinson-Patman Act
1937		Miller-Tydings Act	
1938			Wheeler-Lea Amendment
1950			Antimerger Act
1952		McGuire Act	

choice of suppliers, and tying contracts (contracts requiring that some goods have to be purchased in combination with others that the company controls, even if the former can be obtained more cheaply elsewhere). The intention of all this legislation was to protect and encourage competition, and to discourage monopolies.

The hardships of the depression of the 1930s, however, convinced many businessmen that too much competition had disadvantages. The pendulum swung the other way, and some of the resulting legislation was basically *anticompetition,* although it reads like the earlier procompetition legislation. The *Robinson-Patman Act* of 1936 was aimed at price discrimination and price cutting, especially that involving large price-competitive chains, such as A&P, which were hurting small competitors. Previous legislation had been directed at manufacturers, but the new threat was to small middlemen from the large-chain middlemen. Therefore, although the law was supposedly concerned with avoiding injury to "competition," it was often interpreted by the FTC and the courts to mean prohibiting injury to "competitors," especially small retailers. More is said about this in Chapter 23, when the impact of legislation on pricing is discussed.

Similarly, competitors were protected when price fixing was permitted by the *Miller-Tydings Act,* which was passed in 1937 and strengthened in 1952 by the *McGuire Act.* This legislation specifically exempted certain price fixers from the basic antitrust legislation, and reflected price-cutting problems for both brand name manufacturers and for small retailers during the depression. It allows a manufacturer or wholesaler to sign a price-fixing contract with retailers, in states permitting such contracts. (See Chapter 23 for more details.)

The *Wheeler-Lea Amendment* to the FTC Act, passed in 1938, started a new trend—protection of the consumer. Under this law, unscrupulous advertisers were singled out. These firms had escaped prosecution under the earlier laws, which were concerned with injury to competition rather than the impact on individual consumers. Now it was possible to prosecute for deceptive advertising or sales practices without having to show that competition had been restricted. Such prosecutions have occupied much of the Federal Trade Commission's time and effort in the past two decades. The FTC regularly holds hearings and issues "cease and desist" orders against companies using deceptive practices. The companies can either obey these orders or appeal them to federal courts.

The *Antimerger Act* of 1950, an amendment to the Clayton Act, is designed to make it easier for the FTC to regulate those mergers which might substantially lessen competition. The application of this law has led to tighter control over mergers, especially those which involve one firm buying out its competitors or those firms above or below it in a channel system. The issue generally is whether the merger will reduce competition in a market area. But this antimerger concept has now expanded to include acquisitions of noncompetitive firms by larger firms that might make it more difficult for the existing competitors to survive. Procter & Gamble, for example, was required to sell Clorox because of the fear of P&G's marketing power.[9]

Let the seller beware

■ Traditional economic thinking with respect to buyer-seller relations is *Let the buyer beware,* although some consumer protections are built into English and U.S. common law. A seller must tell the truth (if asked a direct question), fulfill contracts, and stand behind his product (to some reasonable extent). But beyond this, it is expected that vigorous competition in the marketplace will protect consumers, as long as they are wary.

Within this framework, the procompetition thrust of the antitrust laws is understandable. And the intention of both the Federal Trade Commission and the Justice Department has generally been to maintain competition in the marketplace.

But court interpretations and the growing success of the consumerism movement suggests that the ultimate criterion may be to protect the consumer, rather than to protect competition or competitors. Production-oriented businessmen and their "letter-of-the-law" advisors may find this new trend frustrating, but nevertheless they will have to adapt to the political and legal environment just as they have to learn to live with other uncontrollable variables.

This growing concern for the consumer may have a special impact on manufacturers. They now are increasingly held liable for any injury their product causes—even injury caused by users' carelessness. Recently, for example, a manufacturer was held liable for damages that occurred when one of his vacuum cleaners was plugged into a 220-volt circuit and blew up. The label clearly stated that the product was to be used in 115-volt outlets, but the court concluded that the manufacturer failed to warn the customer that the consequences of plugging the unit into anything hotter would be disastrous.[10]

The law and marketing mix planning

■ The evolution of economic and business law in the United States has been sketched above, and specific application to the four Ps will be presented in subsequent chapters. To round out our discussion here, it will be helpful for you to know what the government must prove to obtain a conviction under each of the major laws and which of the four Ps have been most affected by each law. Figure 5–1 provides such a summary, with a phrase following each of the laws to indicate what must be proved to obtain a conviction.

It is interesting to note how the wording of the laws leans progressively to the side of the consumer. And given the new emphasis on letting the seller beware, it is likely that future interpretations of the FTC and courts will be even more in favor of consumers.

Prosecution is a serious matter—one can go to jail

Business is subject to both criminal and civil laws. Many business activities are regulated by civil laws, and penalties are limited to blocking or forcing certain actions, together with fines. Where criminal law applies, jail sentences can be imposed.

This is an important point to understand. Some business executives have gone to jail or received suspended jail sentences in recent years because they violated the criminal law provisions of antitrust legislation. Jail sentences are a relatively recent development and have added a new note of seriousness to the political and legal environment.

Laws about specific matters

■ Over the years, there have been a number of acts which have been designed to eliminate or regulate specific business practices. Probably the one most vigorously debated was the *Pure Food and Drug Act* of 1906, which was designed to prohibit the adulteration and misbranding of foods and drugs in interstate commerce. Colorful exposes[11] of meat-packing practices in the Chicago stockyards fanned consumer interest in this act. Some loopholes in the original act were corrected in the 1938 Food, Drug, and Cosmetic Act. And the law was further tightened in 1962. Among other things, the law prohibits the shipment of unsanitary and poisonous food products and requires extensive testing of drugs. The *Food and Drug Administration* attempts to police manufacturers of these products and to confiscate products which violate its regulations. It has drawn up regulations on branding and requires that food shipped in interstate commerce contain labels which correctly describe the ingredients.

A variety of other acts have been designed to be in the consumers' interest. There are laws concerning the labeling and/or prohibition of products made of wool, furs, and flammable fabrics. And "truth-in-lending" legislation requires disclosure of the interest rates being charged for loans and credit. An act which was particularly damaging to the advertising industry was the Public Health Cigarette Smoking Act which restricted tobacco advertising

Figure 5–1
Focus (mostly prohibitions) of federal laws on four Ps

	Product	Place	Promotion	Price
Sherman Act (1890) Monopoly or conspiracy in restraint of trade	Monopoly or conspiracy to control a product	Monopoly or conspiracy to control distribution channels		Monopoly or conspiracy to control prices
Clayton Act (1914) Substantially lessen competition	Forcing sale of some products with others —tying contracts	Exclusive dealing contracts (limiting buyers' sources)		Price discrimination by manufacturers, especially basing point systems
Federal Trade Commission Act (1914) Unfair methods of competition		Unfair policies	Deceptive ads	Deceptive pricing
Robinson-Patman Act (1936) Tends to injure competition		Prohibits paying allowances to "direct" buyers in lieu of middlemen costs (brokerage charges)	Prohibits "fake" advertising allowances or discrimination in help offered	Prohibits price discrimination on goods of "like grade and quality" without cost justification, and quality discounts limited
Wheeler-Lea Amendment (1938) Unfair or deceptive practices	Deceptive packaging or branding		Deceptive ads or selling claims	Deceptive pricing
Antimerger Act (1950) Lessen competition	Buying competitors	Buying producers or distributors		
Miller-Tydings (1937) and *McGuire Acts* (1952) Price-cutting retailers can be prosecuted				Manufacturers or wholesalers can fix prices at retail level, in states which permit it

on TV and radio after January 1, 1971.[12] And the Consumer Product Safety Act of 1972 is likely to lead to more interest in product design and production quality control.[13]

State and local regulations

■ In addition to federal legislation which affects interstate commerce, marketers must be aware of state and local laws which concern intrastate commerce. Here legal advice and/or extensive knowledge of community or state politics is even more important. Some laws, for example, impose such harsh penalties that local prosecutors are reluctant to enforce them. For practical purposes, these particular laws are inoperative.

There are state and city laws regulating minimum prices and the setting of prices (to be discussed in Chapter 23); regulations for starting up a business (licenses, examinations, and even tax payments); and in some communities, regulations prohibiting certain activities, such as door-to-door selling or selling on Sundays or during evenings.

Some states have regulations about movement or importation of agricultural commodities, ostensibly to protect product quality or to prevent the spread of animal or crop diseases. Some of these, of course, are justifiable, but others are simply a device to enable local producers to obtain higher prices. This has been especially true with respect to milk, some citrus products, and wine. This is also true of the buy-local and buy-American provisions of some government contracts.

Know the laws, follow the courts

■ Because legislation must be interpreted by the courts, students should carefully study both legislative developments and the tenor of thinking of the courts. Often laws are vaguely phrased by legislators to convey intent but not specific detail. It is then up to the courts and administrative bodies to spell out the details. And good legal assistance is needed to keep up with these details.

If business students and businessmen had a better understanding of the intent of the makers and interpreters of the laws — legislators and jurists — there would be less conflict between business and government and fewer embarrassing mistakes. With such an understanding, businessmen might come to accept the political-legal environment as simply another framework within which business must function and develop its marketing strategies. After all, it is the consumers, through their governmental representatives, who determine the kind of economic system they want.[14]

Economic environment

National income changes make a difference

■ An otherwise good marketing strategy may fail if a country goes through a depression or rapid business decline. For this reason, the marketing manager cannot ignore macroeconomics — the analysis of national income and the whole economic environment.

During the U.S. recession of 1969–70, some firms were hurt badly while those offering lower priced goods did very well. Retailers such as Kresge, J. C. Penney, and Woolworth had sales gains, as did sellers of used cars, camping equipment, wedding gown *rental* services, and fabric for making one's own clothes. In contrast, the gloom in the lumber and home-building industry was severe.[15]

Economic dislocations can spread

■ It should be noted that when economic conditions for a particular industry or country turn sour, their impact may be far-reaching. The growing shortage of energy sources may cause severe dislocations in the petrochemical industries – some plastics manufacturers may find their costs rising so rapidly that they are priced out of many markets. Similarly, the manufacturers of large automobiles saw major declines in their sales in 1973 and 1974 as gasoline prices rose. These changes may require substantial product and production line changes. And the dislocations may be even greater in a country such as Japan which is almost wholly dependent on others for raw materials, including energy sources.[16]

Inflation can change mixes

■ Inflation is a major factor in many economies, and the marketing manager has a big job keeping up with it, especially with respect to pricing. In South America, inflation has become almost a way of life, and it's a fairly big problem in the United States. Latin countries have experienced far more spectacular inflation, however, and it has profoundly influenced their economic thinking. Most people there now assume that prices will always go up, and they buy and sell accordingly. This behavior, of course, adds fuel to the inflationary fires. Some Latin countries have had from 25 to 100 percent inflation per year for many years. In contrast, the 6 to 10 percent level reached in the late 1960s and early 1970s in the United States was small. Nevertheless, this U.S. rate properly caused great anxiety about whether inflation was out of control and led to restrictive monetary policies which did reduce income and employment.

Obviously, the marketing manager has a big stake in the economic environment. In contrast to the legal and cultural environments, economic conditions change continuously; they can move rapidly up or down, requiring tactical and even strategic responses.

Technological developments offer new opportunities

■ Underlying any economic environment is the *technological base*, which affects the way the resources of the economy are converted to output. In tradition-bound societies, relatively little technology may be used, and the output may be correspondingly small. In modern economies, on the other hand, aggressive competitors tend to copy the best methods quickly and continually seek better ways of doing things.

Spectacular advances in technology have been made in the last 30 years. This is due in part to our newfound interest in and support of research and development. More technological developments probably can be expected. Some of these certainly will affect marketing, just as previous ones have had their impact.

The modern automobile, for example, has enabled farmers to come to town and urban people to go wherever they want, thereby destroying the local "monopolies" of some retailers and wholesalers. Modern trucks and airplanes have opened up many new markets and permitted production for national or international markets, with resulting competition and benefits for consumers. Electronic developments have permitted mass promotion via radio, TV, and telephone thereby reducing the relative importance of other media. And, in time, we may be able to shop in the home with a combination TV-computer system, eliminating the need for some retailers and wholesalers.

Computers have also permitted more sophisticated planning and control of businesses. Electronic equipment may permit us to return to custom production methods—but this time in automated factories which will enable the customer to decide more exactly what he wants and then obtain almost immediate delivery. This may cause drastic changes in internal company affairs, including sales forecasting, production scheduling, warehousing, and so on.

As we move through the text, you should see that some of the major advances in business have come from creative and early recognition of new ways to do things. Additional breakthrough opportunities probably will arise as our technological base continues to change.

A marketing manager could help his firm see such opportunities by trying to understand the "why" of its present techniques, and what is keeping it from doing things more effectively. Then, as new developments come along, he will be sensitive to their possible application and be able to see how potential opportunities can be turned into profitable realities.

Further, he can make a contribution to his firm's effort by cultivating a sense of what technical developments would be acceptable to society. Given the growing concern about environmental pollution, the quality of life and working conditions, and so on, it is possible that some potentially attractive technological developments should be rejected because of their long-run implications. Perhaps what might be good for the firm and the economy's *economic* growth, might not fit with the cultural and social environment, and subsequently the political and legal environment. The marketing manager's closeness to the market could give him a better feel for what people are thinking and enable him to help the firm avoid blunders.[17]

Resources of the firm

■ A smart marketing manager recognizes that his firm has some resources, and hopefully some unique resources, which can be capitalized upon when developing his marketing strategies. As a result of its own history, experiences, and personnel, it should have strengths and weaknesses that distinguish it from other firms. A good strategy would seek a differential advantage, making extensive use of the firm's strong points, while avoiding direct competition with firms having similar strong points. Various resources to consider when developing a marketing strategy are discussed below.[18]

Financial strength

■ Some industries such as steel and public utilities require large amounts of capital to achieve "economies of scale." For them, the cost of production per unit decreases as the quantities produced increase. Therefore, smaller producers would be at a great disadvantage if they tried to compete in these lines. Some industries, however, do not have economies of scale and smaller, more flexible firms may be quite effective. In fact, large companies often have difficulties when they enter low-investment-type businesses. For example, a large chemical processor attempted to make and sell decorated shower curtains because it was producing the basic plastic sheets. It lost heavily on the experiment, however, because the smaller shower curtain manufacturers and distributors were much more flexible, changing their styles and price policies more rapidly. Here, financial strength was an asset in the basic plastic sheet business, but not where style and flexibility in adapting to customer needs was important.

Raw material reserves

■ Firms that own or have assured access to basic raw materials have a head start in businesses that require these resources. But companies, large or small, that are not in this position may find—especially in times of short supply—that they have difficulty even staying in business. Chemical and paper manufacturers, for example, usually attempt to control timber resources. And the metals and petroleum companies have controlled their own resources. Now that we see a growing scarcity of raw materials, it probably would be desirable for a firm to control or have assurances of supply before building a marketing strategy which depended upon raw materials.

Physical plant

■ Some lines of business require large physical plants which must be owned by the firm. If these are well located, this may be an asset. On the other hand, badly located or obsolete plants or wholesale or retail facilities may be real liabilities. The existing physical plant can have a considerable bearing on marketing strategy planning because one of the firm's objectives probably will be to use the existing plant as fully as possible. Any logical strategy will, therefore, attempt to make use of the existing facilities, or provide for their disposal so that the capital can be used more effectively elsewhere.

Patents

■ Patents are of primary concern to manufacturers. A patent owner has a 17-year "monopoly" to develop and use his new product, process, or material as he sees fit. If a firm has a patent on a basic process, potential competitors may be forced to use second-rate processes, and their efforts may be doomed to failure. Clearly, if a firm has such a patent it is a resource, while if its competitors have it, it may be a liability which cannot be overcome with other aspects of a marketing mix.

Public acceptance

■ If a firm has developed a loyal following of customers—a *customer franchise*—for its product or service, others may have difficulty invading this market. A strong customer franchise is a valuable asset that a marketing manager should use in developing his marketing strategy.

Skill of personnel

■ Some firms deliberately pay high wages in order to attract and retain skilled workers so they can offer high quality products or services. A skilled sales force is also an asset, whereas lack of good salesmen may restrict strategy planning. Even if skilled employees can produce a new product, the sales organization may not have the contacts or know-how to sell it. This is especially true when a firm moves from consumer goods to industrial products or vice versa.

Management attitudes

■ The attitude of top management toward growth is an important factor in company planning, especially as it affects the development and introduction of new products.

The president of a New England manufacturing company was enthusiastic about the prospects for a new product. But after evaluating the attitude of his company personnel, and especially his management people, he dropped his plans for the product. Why? He found that his employees had no ambition or interest in growth.

Objectives of the firm

■ It might have been best to treat the objectives of the firm first, perhaps even before marketing strategy was discussed, since the company's objectives shape the direction and operation of the entire business. But we have saved our discussion of objectives until this point because it is easier now to see how they can affect the development of marketing strategies.

Should set firm's course

■ A business organization should know where it is going or it is likely to fall into the trap expressed so well by the quotation: "Having lost sight of our objective, we redoubled our efforts."[19] In spite of their importance, objectives are seldom stated explicitly. In small businesses, they appear to be stated *after the fact!* And in some large businesses, there may be *several* implicit – but conflicting – objectives held by different executives. The relative importance of any of these objectives seems to depend upon the point of view of the man being interviewed.[20]

It would be convenient if a company could set one overriding objective, such as making a profit, and let that serve as a guide. Actually, however, setting objectives is much more complicated – which explains why it is done so poorly, or sometimes not at all.

Setting objectives that really guide the present and future development of the company is a soul-searching procedure that forces top management to look at the entire business, relate its present needs and resources to the external environment, and then plot the broad outlines of the company's future course.

■ Given the importance of objectives and the fact that they are often so poorly stated, we will discuss objective setting in the following paragraphs. This can be important to a marketing manager, because he may have to help set company objectives just so he can know what his marketing strategy planning is supposed to accomplish.

Taken together, the following three objectives provide a useful starting point for objective setting for a particular firm. These three objectives could be phrased and made more specific in many ways. But they should be sought together because, in the long run, a failure in even one of the three areas could lead to total failure of the enterprise.

1. Engage in some specific business activity that will perform a socially and economically useful function.
2. Develop an organization to perpetuate the enterprise and implement its strategies.
3. Achieve sufficient profitability to survive.[21]

Should be socially useful

The first objective suggests that the company should do something useful. This is more than a platitude. Businesses exist at the discretion of consumers, and if the activities of a business appear to be at variance with the consumer "good," that firm can be wiped out almost overnight by political or legal action or the customers' own negative response.

Should view business broadly as customer-satisfying activity

The first objective also implies that the firm should view its mission as satisfying customer needs, rather than focusing only on internal concerns such as using the company's resources, exploiting a patent, and so on. The firm should define its efforts broadly, as we did in Chapter 4, when we focused on the refrigera*tion* market rather than the refrigera*tor* market. This should lead the company to *need-satisfying goals* rather than product-oriented goals.

The importance of a broad view should be obvious if objectives are supposed to help a company plan for the future. Too narrow a view may lead the company into a product area in which the product itself, because of changing customer needs, will soon be obsolete.[22]

Should organize to innovate

In a macro-marketing sense, consumers have granted businesses the right to operate and to make a profit if they can. But they do not expect them simply to exploit the status quo. Businesses are supposed to be dynamic — agents of change, adjusting their offerings to customers' needs. Competition is supposed to encourage innovation and efficiency. Assuming that our society will continue this approach, a business firm should develop an organization that will ensure that these consumer-assigned tasks are effectively carried out and that the firm itself continues to prosper.

Should achieve some profit

It is sometimes assumed that profit is the only objective of business, and it certainly is true that in the long run a firm must make profits to survive. But simply stating that a firm seeks to make a profit is not enough. The time period involved must also be specified, since long-run profit maximization may require losing money during the first few years of a plan.

Further, seeking to maximize profit will not necessarily lead to good profits. Competition may be so fierce that poor results may be almost inevitable in an industry. It might be more desirable to set some target rate of profit return that would tend to guide the business into avenues having some possibility of such a return. In fact, some firms probably should seek even higher rates of return than they are now achieving and more than is available in their *present* activities.

Further complicating objective setting is the desirability of specifying the degree of risk that management is willing to assume for larger returns. Very large profits might be possible in the oil prospecting business, for example, but the probability of success in that field might be quite low. If the business is to take a long-run view, if it intends to survive and be a useful member of the business community, it probably should include the costs of risk and potential losses in its calculations of long-run returns.

Both hands must work toward the same goal

■ Whatever objectives are selected by top management, they should be compatible with each other, or frustrations and even failure may result. The three broad objectives suggested above would help a firm avoid the blunder of working at cross-purposes with its various plans. But as these three guidelines are made more specific, care must be exercised. For example, management might choose to specify a 10 percent return on investment each year as one objective, while at the same time specifying that the current plant and equipment be utilized as fully as possible. Competition might be such that it would be impossible to use the resources fully and achieve this return, but the company managers might try to follow the resource-use objective through the course of the year and discover the incompatibility only at the end of the year!

Top management myopia may straitjacket marketing

■ We are assuming that it is the marketing manager's job to work within the framework of objectives provided by the top executives. But some of these objectives may restrict marketing strategies, perhaps to the detriment of the entire business. This is why it is desirable for the marketing manager to help shape the company's objectives.

A few examples will help to illustrate how the marketing manager might have to choose undesirable strategies.

A quick return on investment is sometimes sought by top management. This might influence the marketing manager to select marketing strategies that would yield quick returns in the short run but kill his "customer franchise" in the long run.

Top management might decide on diversification. This might force the marketing manager to choose strategies that are poorly suited to the company's resources.

Some top managements want a large sales volume or a larger

market share, seemingly for its own sake. This can lead to good profits, but not necessarily. Ampex almost went out of business seeking growth for its own sake. And Ford Motor Company shifted its objectives toward *profitable* sales growth when it realized that the two do not necessarily go together.[23]

Marketing manager must set own objectives

■ The marketing manager may have no choice in determining the overall company objectives, but he can and should set his own objectives within the framework of these overall objectives. In subsequent chapters, we will discuss such objectives and the policies which are needed to implement them. Here, it will be useful to see a set of objectives which was developed by American Can Company. (See Figure 5–2.) Note that the three basic objectives are involved here, along with some specifics for the marketing area.

Conclusion

■ This chapter has been concerned with the forces which, while beyond the marketing manager's control, profoundly affect the strategies and time-related plans he will develop. Some uncontrollable variables can change faster than others. But all can change, requiring adjustments in his plans. Ideally, likely changes would be considered in his planning.

As we have seen, he must develop marketing mixes appropriate to the customs of the people in his target markets. He must be aware, for example, that promotion which is appropriate in Gary, Indiana, may be offensive to citizens of New Orleans, Louisiana, or Yokohama, Japan.

The marketing manager also must be aware of the legal restrictions on his actions, and sensitive to changing political climates. The growing interest in consumerism may force many changes.

The economic environment – the chances of business cycle fluctuations, or spiraling inflation – also will affect his choice of strategies, and the marketing man must try to anticipate, understand, and deal with such changes.

He must also examine the existing business structure itself: How well entrenched are his competitors? What action can he expect them to take? What is the nature of competition? Recall our discussion of this topic in Chapter 3.

Finally, he must bear in mind the resources and objectives of his firm, for his strategies should be planned to gain those objectives within the constraints imposed by the firm's resources.

Developing good strategies is obviously a very complicated procedure. The marketing manager must be well informed. He can benefit by increased knowledge in the social and natural sciences. Most important, he must know his own field thoroughly, for he will have to use the information he has drawn from all these sources in the formation of his own strategies. Marketing management is clearly an integrating and challenging discipline.

Figure 5–2
American Can Company, statement of marketing department objectives

Marketing Department Objectives
⋈ ⋈ ⋈

The broad objective of the Marketing Department is to direct all of the Company's capabilities to its markets so as to achieve and maintain the position of acknowledged leadership in all of its fields of operations. In selling the Company's products in optimum quantity to produce maximum profit, the Marketing Department will:

1. *Establish and maintain an aggressive, highly motivated, and well-trained organization oriented to our principal markets.*

2. *Through marketing research, and with the support of corporate planning and economic research, determine trends, industry needs, and customer preferences for optimum product and facility planning.*

3. *Establish each year specific volume goals for each major product line aimed at maintaining and increasing market share.*

4. *Based on product profitability, direct major emphasis and support programs and services toward markets and products with highest return.*

5. *Develop and sell complete packaging systems to strengthen our total influence on the market.*

6. *Maintain constructive and cooperative relationships with customers based on business dealings of the highest in-*

tegrity, delivery of high quality products, and dependable service.

7. *Direct and coordinate the Company's efforts in new product development, including exploitation of new opportunities for existing products, with emphasis on products with high profit potential and likelihood of company franchise.*

8. *Recognize the need and take positive action where indicated to obsolete present products and be ready with successor products.*

9. *Establish or recommend price policy and specific prices that will return maximum profit consistent with the Company's total responsibility as the leader in its field.*

10. *Organize marketing services to provide maximum assistance to marketing management, maximum support to field selling, at the lowest reasonable cost.*

AMERICAN
CAN COMPANY

questions and problems

1 For a new design of haircomb, or one of the items mentioned in Question 8 of Chapter 4, discuss the uncontrollable factors that the marketing manager will have to consider.

2 Discuss the relative importance of the uncontrollable variables, given the speed with which these variables move. If some must be neglected because of a shortage of executive time, which would you recommend for "neglect"?

3 Which way does the U.S. political and legal environment seem to be moving (with respect to business-related affairs)?

4 Why is it necessary to have so many laws regulating business? Why has Congress not just passed one set of laws to take care of business problems?

5 What and whom is the government attempting to protect in its effort to preserve and regulate competition?

6 For each of the *major* laws discussed in the text, indicate whether in the long run this law will promote or restrict competition (see Figure 5–1). As a consumer, without any financial interest in business, what is your reaction to each of these laws?

7 Discuss the probable impact on your hometown of a major technological breakthrough in air transportation which would permit foreign producers to ship into any U.S. market for about the same transportation cost that domestic producers must incur.

8 Specifically, how would various company objectives affect the development of a marketing mix for a new type of baby shoe? If this company were just being formed by a former shoemaker with limited financial resources, list the objectives he might have and then discuss how they will affect the development of his marketing strategy.

9 Discuss how a company's financial strength might have a bearing on the kinds of products it might produce. Will it have an impact on the other three Ps as well? If so, how? Use an example in your answer.

notes

[1] David C. McClelland, "Business Drive and National Achievement," *Harvard Business Review,* July–August 1962, pp. 99–112.

[2] "FDA To Order Cosmetic Contents On Labels, Warnings On Inadequately Tested Products," *Wall Street Journal,* October 14, 1973. See also *Wall Street Journal,* October 12, 1971, p. 36; and "Del Monte Living With New Labeling Rules," *Business Week,* February 3, 1973, pp. 42–45.

[3] "The U.S.'s Toughest Customer," *Time,* December 12, 1969, pp. 89–98.

[4] "Crash Suit Costs Ford $450,000," *Detroit Free Press,* December 14, 1972; see also "A&P Is Ordered to Pay Damages of $32.7 Million," *The Wall Street Journal,* July 26, 1974, p. 14.

[5] See *Wall Street Journal,* May 1, 1972, p. 22; "Ottawa Restricts U.S. Ads," *Business Week,* September 4, 1965, p. 36; and "Mexico Tightens Up on Foreign Investment," *Business Week,* April 28, 1973, pp. 94–97.

[6] The *Wall Street Journal,* July 27, 1973, p. 30.

[7] "Detroit Gets Nod in Japan," *Business Week,* August 31, 1969, p. 58.

[8] "U.S. Lifts Bar to Trade Offer for the Have-Nots," *Business Week,* May 30, 1970, p. 71.

[9] Louis W. Stern and John R. Grabner, Jr., *Competition in the Marketplace* (Glenview, Ill.: Scott, Foresman and Co., 1970), pp. 98–99.

[10] "Business Responds to Consumerism," *Business Week,* September 6, 1969, p. 95; see also H. C. Barksdale and W. R. Darden, "Consumer Attitudes Toward Marketing and Consumerism," *Journal of Marketing,* October 1972, pp. 28–35.

[11] See Upton Sinclair, *The Jungle* (Pasadena, Calif.: Upton Sinclair, 1920).

[12] *Journal of Marketing,* October 1970, p. 85; and *Business Week,* December 26, 1970, p. 21.

[13] W. Jensen, Jr., E. M. Mazze, and D. M. Stern, "The Consumer Product Safety Act: A Special Case in Consumerism," *Journal of Marketing,* October 1973, pp. 68–71; R. E. Wilkes and J. B. Wilcox, "Recent FTC Actions: Implications for the Advertising Strategist," *Journal of Marketing,* January 1974, pp. 55–61; and "Dictating Product Safety," *Business Week,* May 18, 1974, pp. 56–62.

[14] See: "Is John Sherman's Antitrust Obsolete?" *Business Week,* March 23, 1974, pp. 47–56.

[15] "Dividends from the Drop," *Time,* July 8, 1970, p. 66; "The Boom in Wood that Busted," *Business Week,* October 25, 1969, p. 138.

[16] "Britain's Devaluation Hurts Export-Based Economy of Asian Land," *Wall Street Journal,* December 4, 1967, p. 1; "The Floating Dollar Takes Its Toll," *Business Week,* June 13, 1970, p. 46; see also "Petroleum Price Rises Mean All Bets Are Off on Economies of West," *The Wall Street Journal,* January 9, 1974, p. 1 f; "A Recreational Vehicle Shakeout," *Business Week,* December 8, 1973, p. 92; and David W. Cravens, "Marketing Management in an Era of Shortages," *Business Horizons,* February 1974, pp. 79–85.

[17] George C. Sawyer, "Social Issues and Social Change: Impact on Strategic Decisions," *MSU Business Topics,* Summer 1973, pp. 15–20; and P. Kotler, "What Consumerism Means for Marketers," *Harvard Business Review,* May–June 1972, pp. 48–57.

[18] Charles H. Kline, "The Strategy of Product Policy," *Harvard Business Review,* July–August 1955, pp. 91–100.

[19] Charles H. Granger, "The Hierarchy of Objectives," *Harvard Business Review,* May–June 1964, p. 63.

[20] Robert F. Lanzillotti, "Pricing Objectives in Large Companies," *American Economic Review,* December 1958, pp. 921–40; and F. Parker Fowler, Jr., and E. W. Sandberg, *The Relation of Management Decision-Making to Small Business Growth* (Management Research Summary [Washington, D.C.: Small Business Administration, 1964]).

[21] These were adapted from Peter F. Drucker, "Business Objectives and Survival Needs: Notes on a Discipline of Business Enterprise," *Journal of Business,* April 1958, pp. 81–90.

[22] This point of view is discussed at much greater length in: Theodore Levitt, "Marketing Myopia," *Harvard Business Review,* July–August 1960, p. 45 ff.

[23] "A Painful Attempt to Aid Ampex," *Business Week,* February 12, 1972, p. 17; and "Ford Motor Company Adopts New Tactics to Boost Its 'Big Three' Standing," *The Wall Street Journal,* May 15, 1973, p. 1 f.

Part two

Selecting target markets

The consumer's freedom of choice

Understanding submarket
needs . . . why people buy . . .
intermediate customers . . .
world markets . . . forecasting
market opportunities

makes businesses choose their target markets carefully

6

Applying market gridding

■ In Chapter 4 we introduced the concept of market gridding and showed how important the relevant dimensions of a market are to marketing strategy planning. Target marketers usually segment markets as they search for their target markets. As we will see in this chapter, the market grid concept is a useful way of thinking about market segmentation.

The importance of market gridding helps explain why we are going to spend the next six chapters (Chapters 6–11) on the topic of selecting target markets. This chapter will discuss how one can go about market gridding. The next few chapters will discuss what we actually know about possible dimensions. Finally, in Chapter 11, we will turn to evaluating the potential in alternative markets. Market gridding is not just an academic exercise. Ultimately, we want to estimate the potential in alternative target markets (given the appropriate marketing mixes) and then select the most attractive strategies for implementation.

It is not the size of the market, but profitable sales that is important

■ Before beginning our discussion of market gridding, it is extremely important to recognize that target marketing and market gridding are trying to locate attractive opportunities, *not* just smaller markets. Some production-oriented businessmen seem to shy away from target marketing because they are worried about unduly restricting the size of their potential market. They aim at everybody in hopes of reaching at least enough customers to achieve a reasonable sales volume. In contrast, the target marketer focuses his efforts on seemingly smaller markets, but expects to be able to satisfy them more exactly and, therefore, achieve not only a much larger share of his smaller market but also a larger and more profitable sales level than the mass marketer.

Market gridding is an aggregating process

■ A target marketer starts out with the assumption that everyone is an individual and does have unique needs. He does not mechanically break down the whole market into sub-markets using one or a few "hopefully" relevant dimensions. Instead, he aggregates. He assumes that each individual has his own set of relevant dimensions and tries to aggregate together those persons who happen to have somewhat homogeneous sets of relevant dimensions.

Aggregating loses detail

■ Once he starts the *aggregation process*, he knows that he is losing some individual detail. This can be seen in Figure 6–1, where the many dots show the position of the people in a market with respect to two dimensions — status and dependability. Every individual has his own unique position in this picture of a market. In order to obtain three (an arbitrary number) relatively homogeneous groups that possess somewhat similar needs, the analyst might aggregate all of these people into three groups — A, B, and C. The A group might be called status-oriented, and the C group, dependability-oriented. The B group wants both (and its members may have to compromise with themselves if satisfying both needs at the same time turns out to be very expensive). Note that some people have not been included in the three groups, because they are "too far" from others in the groups. Presumably, each group represents a homogeneous set of people — a market segment — and the larger the group is made, the less homogeneous it becomes. At some point, it is necessary to draw a line and say "this is the boundary of this group."

One of the agonizing aspects of aggregating is that some potential customers just don't "fit" neatly into potentially profitable market segments. They could be forced arbitrarily into one of the groups, but this would be defeating the purpose. Alternately, additional segments could be created, but this might be too artificial. Some people's needs may be just too "unique," and it may not be possible to lump them together with others into homogeneous groups.

This is not a defect of market gridding. Market gridding is an aggregation process and there is a limit to how far the process can be carried and still be meaningful. The "unique" customers may have to be lumped into a grid box called "all others" until some marketer is willing and able to identify and cater to smaller market segments.

How far should the aggregating go?

■ There is not much point in treating each individual in a market area as a separate market segment if each one's needs and preferences are roughly similar to others in the market — i.e., if they are all

Figure 6–1
Every individual has his own unique position in the market —
those with similar positions can be aggregated into potential
target markets

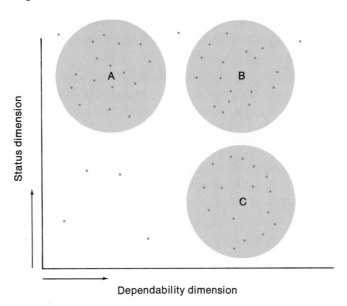

Dependability dimension

basically the same then there is no point in having more than one
group. Typically, however, there are some differences and market
gridding is helpful. But it is necessary to have a decision rule as to
how far to go.

Basically, one would want to continue to aggregate as long as an
appropriate marketing mix would be reasonably satisfying to all
those within the segment *and* the firm would be able to offer this
marketing mix at a profit. The interaction of customer needs with
what the firm can offer profitably should be noted. We do not pick
a target market first and then develop a marketing mix. We develop
whole strategies. As a practical matter, this means that cost considerations would probably encourage greater aggregation while
demand considerations would suggest less aggregation. Profit is
the balancing point — determining how unique a marketing mix the
firm can offer to some market.

Criteria for selecting market segments

■ Ideally, "good" market segments would meet the following
criteria:

1. The people within a particular market segment should be
    as homogeneous as possible with respect to their needs and
    preferences, and their likely responses to the marketing mix
    variables.
2. Buying behavior should vary from segment to segment —
    there is no point in segmenting on dimensions that have no
    relevance to buying behavior.

3. The dimensions should be useful for specifying particular marketing mix variables — there is no point in having a relevant dimension which does not have operational significance.

Criterion 3 is especially critical because it is possible to find dimensions which are useless because they cannot be made operationally significant. A personality trait such as moodiness, for example, might be found among the traits of particularly heavy buyers of a product, but what could one do with this knowledge? Personal salesmen would have to take a personality inventory of each prospective buyer — clearly an impossible task. Similarly, advertising media buyers or copywriters could not make much use of this information. So, although moodiness might be related in some way to previous purchases, it would not be a useful dimension for marketing purposes.

Criterion 3 may lead to the deliberate inclusion of readily available dimensions, such as demographics, to aid marketing mix planning. Dimensions such as age, income, location, and family size may be very useful, at least for place and promotion planning. In fact, it would be difficult to make some place and promotion decisions without information about such dimensions.

Number of potential dimensions is large

Dimensions are primary or secondary

■ There are many potential market grid dimensions. For now, we will divide them into two types: secondary and primary. Primary dimensions require the collection of new data (or management assumptions if they are unable or unwilling to collect data). Secondary dimensions, on the other hand, are concerned with demographic attributes for which data is readily available, usually from government sources.

Table 6–1 suggests some possible secondary dimensions. Table 6–2 lists some primary dimension possibilities, including needs, attitudes, and behavior patterns. These are *not* exhaustive lists. Potential dimensions will be discussed in more detail in Chapters 7–10. Now, however, it is important to note that if secondary dimensions *are* relevant in a particular case, then it will be easier to estimate market potential later. Secondary dimensions are basically *attributes* of potential customers and it is usually easier to link attributes to each other. Primary dimensions, on the other hand, usually require more judgment (or original research) to link them to secondary dimensions. But some linking probably will be necessary to obtain quantitative estimates of the size of possible target markets.

There may be both qualifying and determining dimensions

■ We have already stressed that consumers are multidimensional. Some dimensions may be more important than others, however,

Table 6-1
Potential secondary dimensions (basically demographic attributes of potential customers for which published data is usually available from Census or other government sources)

Geographic location	Demographic characteristics

City, county, SMSA, state, region, country
Urban versus rural versus suburban
	Age:
	   Household head, housewife, children
	Sex:
	   Household head, housewife, children
	Marital status
	Income
	Education
	Occupation
	Race
	Nationality
	Household:
	  Dwelling characteristics
	  Goods owned
	Business firms, size:
	  Dollars of sales and number of employees
	  Nature of business (SIC codes)

and it is useful to distinguish between qualifying and determining dimensions. A consumer would have to have enough money to be in the market, for example, but this might only qualify him as a prospect. It does not tell us which kind of product he is likely to purchase or which brand. Several such qualifying dimensions may have to exist and still we will not have determined what he will do. A prospective car owner, for example, would have to have enough income or credit to purchase a car but also would have to be of driving age, and have or be able to obtain a driver's license. This still does not determine that he will buy a car. He may simply rent one, or continue borrowing his parents' or friends' car, or hitchhike. He may not get around to actually buying a car until not having one is annoying—until, for example, his status with his buddies is falling because he doesn't have "wheels." This need may lead him to buy *some* car, but it is not determining with respect to a specific brand or a specific model within a particular brand.

How specific the determining dimensions have to get depends on whether one is concerned with a general product class or a specific brand. This is shown in Figure 6–2, where we start with both secondary and primary dimensions. Either or both types of dimensions may be qualifying and/or determining in a particular case. The more specific we want to be, the more particular the determining dimensions may have to be. In a particular case, the determining dimensions may seem minor, but they are important because they *are* the determining dimensions.

Table 6–2
Potential primary dimensions (needs, attitudes, and behavior patterns about which new data must be collected and/or management judgments made)

Possible needs		Attitudes toward	Behavior patterns
identification	nourish, aid, or protect the helpless	Marriage and family	Usage rate (nonuser
individuality	order	planning	to heavy)
conformity	recognition	Work versus leisure	Brand loyalty (none
pleasure	imitate or emulate	Mobility	to insistence)
social approval	reject, snub, or ignore	Saving versus spending	Store loyalty
entertainment	comply and accept punishment	Life style (swinger, . . .)	Willingness to shop
personal interest	achievement		Media use
affection	acquire possessions and property		Life style
variety	affiliation		Social class (lower
comfort	aggression		to upper)
economy	autonomy		
newness	obey and to avoid blame		
freedom	explore and to seek knowledge		
curiosity	collect and preserve things		
power	organize and build		
prestige	act differently from others		
success	defeat and retaliate		
creativeness	defend and justify one's actions		
health	serve a leader		
adventure	dominance		
welfare of loved ones	exhibition to attract attention		
privacy	give information, explain, interpret		
distinctiveness	avoid failure		
self-realization	preserve one's self-respect		
convenience	play		
attract the opposite sex	save things		
feel superior	seek aid, protection, or sympathy		

Determining dimensions may be very specialized

■ The behavior of a female schoolteacher buying gasoline illustrates this idea. The teacher always bought major brands of gasoline because she was afraid that cheap brands would ruin her car's engine. She bought several major brands at various times because she felt that all of them were quite similar. She never drove into a gas station unless it looked clean, and normally she patronized the stations nearest her home so that they would recognize her and be ready to give advice when she had mechanical problems.

From this description, it would appear that the qualifying factors here were experience, price, convenience, dealer's service, and prestige. Yet these factors did *not* determine her choice.

Her requirements were met by three major-brand service stations – Standard, Shell, and Mobil – located on different corners of the same intersection, one block from her house. Although the margin of choice seemed narrow, she stated that until recently she had been patronizing the Mobil station. After considerable questioning, she admitted she felt the Mobil station was larger than the

Figure 6–2
Finding the relevant dimensions

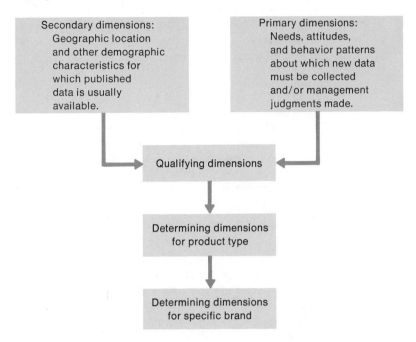

others and had extensive repair facilities. The added weight of the dealer's service facilities appeared to be the determining factor.

But this was still not an absolute determinant, it turned out. Two months earlier, she had acquired some Standard Oil stock—and this ownership factor had caused her to switch her purchases to the Standard dealer. So a minor factor proved to be the determining one, although the qualifying factors were vital to the narrowing of her choice.[1]

In the early stages of the market gridding process, it is not necessary to follow each potential customer in the detail we did for the gasoline buying example. We are attempting to aggregate markets and so we can ignore the peculiarities of individuals. But, note, we must do this with care or we will end up with relatively heterogeneous segments and be no better off than the mass marketer.

Qualifying dimensions are important, too

■ The qualifying dimensions are necessary to narrow down to the determining dimensions. For example, demographic dimensions can be very useful to a golf cart manufacturer who would probably be especially interested in older, more affluent golfers. However, these qualifying dimensions still don't explain *why* specific people buy specific products or brands, although they might explain *some* behavior and be useful in planning marketing mixes.

Once the determining dimensions have been identified, we can go back to the qualifying dimensions for additional insights which can aid mix planning and implementation. In other words, qualifying and determining dimensions work together to bring it all together. We saw this earlier, in Chapter 4, where we outlined three basic classes of dimensions: (1) geographical location and other demographic characteristics, (2) behavioral needs, and (3) urgency to get need satisfied, and desire and willingness to compare and shop. Here, we have called class one a secondary dimension and classes two and three primary dimensions, but later (Chapter 14 and on) we will make good use of the third class.

We will say more about the interrelation of dimensions in the following chapters. For now, it is important only to see that the multidimensional aspect of buying behavior—with some dimensions more important than others—helps the marketing strategy planner develop a more complete description of a market segment.

A seven-step approach to market gridding

■ Now that we have discussed the philosophy underlying market gridding, let's go on to a logical, "rough and ready" approach to gridding. This approach has been used successfully without expensive marketing research or computer analyses. More sophisticated approaches are discussed later.

Once one accepts the marketing concept and the market grid concept, then he begins to see markets in a new way. Just careful observation of what is going on may reveal opportunities and sometimes really significant breakthrough opportunities. Until this kind of intuitive market gridding becomes a part of one's way of thinking, however, it does help to have a logical approach.

The seven-step approach presented here is workable and has led to the development of successful strategies. It is especially useful for finding the qualifying and determining dimensions for *product types*. When it is necessary to move down to specific brands, especially when there are several competing brands in an existing market, then more sophisticated techniques may be necessary.

So that you can clearly grasp this approach to market gridding, we will list each step separately, explain its significance and provide a common example to illustrate and show how each step works. The example we have chosen concerns rental housing and, in particular, the apartment market.

1. *Select the product-market area that will be considered.*

After the firm has defined its objectives, it must determine, roughly, what business it wants to be in. If the company already has some committed resources and some knowledge of product-market areas, it is likely that attractive product-markets will be related to its present business. The grass is *not* always "greener on the other side of the fence."

Possible product-market areas should be defined in market terms (market needs)—not only in product terms (product characteristics). If the firm has some production or technology-related skills which may lead to some differential advantage, then using *some* product-related dimensions would be reasonable. But using *only* product terms would be unduly limiting.

Example: The firm might presently be building small, austere apartments for low-income families. A narrow view of market gridding – considering only products being produced now – might lead it to think *only* in terms of low-income housing for other low-income families. A bigger view, however – considering more product-market needs – might see these compact, unexciting apartments as only a small part of the total apartment or even housing market.

Ultimately, some balance has to be struck between defining the market too narrowly (same old product and same old market) and too broadly (the whole world and all its needs is our market). Here, the focus is on the whole apartment market because that is where the firm had had some experience and wanted to work.

2. *List all needs that all potential customers may have in this product-market area.*

This is just a "brainstorming" step. We want to write down as many needs as we can as quickly as possible. The list does not have to be exhaustive at this step. The idea here is to have enough input to stimulate creativity in the next several steps. Some need dimension which is just "thrown in" now may be *the* determining dimension for a market segment. If that need were not included at this stage, it is possible that the existence of that market segment would be neglected.

Possible need dimensions may be identified by reviewing a list of dimensions, but also by thinking analytically about the present offerings in this product-market area and why some people buy them. If the products are selling, presumably they are satisfying somebody's needs for something. They may not be doing it very well, but at least they are doing it better than competitive offerings. Therefore, a market gridder should critically appraise the need-satisfying characteristics of all of the competitive offerings in his product-market area.

Example: In the rental apartment market, it is fairly easy to list the following needs which might be relevant: need for basic shelter, parking, safety and security, distinctiveness, economy, play space, privacy, convenience (to something), enough living area, attractive interiors, and good supervision and maintenance to assure trouble-free and comfortable living.

3. *Assuming that some market segments will have different needs than others, select out of the above list the most relevant ones for yourself, then a friend, then several acquaintances from widely different demographic groups. Continue until at least three different segments emerge.*

This is obviously an intuitive and judgmental process, but, at the very least, one should have some thoughts about his own behavior. Then, if he is willing to accept the assumption that he is unique and that therefore everyone else is different, he must begin to identify some of the differences. Once one starts down this path, it is really quite remarkable how good one's judgment is about what motivates others, and how similar different peoples' views are on the same subject. They may differ over their preference about alternative offerings in the market, but their perceptions about who buys what and why are fairly stable.

Example: A college student living off campus would probably want his apartment to provide basic shelter, parking, economy, convenience to school or work, and enough room either in his own apartment or in common facilities to have parties. A newly married friend of his, on the other hand, might have quite different needs — perhaps for basic shelter and parking, but also privacy and perhaps good supervision so he would not have to put up with the rowdy party environment which might be attractive to his friend. An older acquaintance with a family would also be interested in shelter and parking, but they might be faced with a financial squeeze and, therefore, be interested in economy while getting enough room for the children to live and play.

4. *Review the lists of needs in each market segment, and remove any that are common as they apparently are not segmenting dimensions (although they may be very important to all segments).*

A potential dimension such as low price or a good value may be relevant for all potential customers and, therefore, not useful as a segmenting variable. In fact, it may be an important qualifying dimension, but it may also be a need that all competitive products will have to satisfy. Therefore, for market gridding purposes it may be qualifying, but not determining.

Example: With our apartment "hunters," the need for basic shelter, parking, and safety and security appear to be common needs. Therefore, in this step, we will remove them from the need list.

5. *Review the remaining needs, segment by segment, and tentatively name each segment.*

This step requires creativity and imagination. (Even the sophisticated techniques to be discussed below require judgment at this stage.) What is required here is a feel for the relative importance of the remaining dimensions. This will lead to tagging each market segment with meaningful people-related words.

Example: We can logically identify the following apartment segments: Swingers, sophisticates, newly married, family, job-centered, home-centered, and urban-centered. (See Figure 6–3.) Each of the segments has a different pattern of determining dimensions, as shown in Figure 6–4. Such a figure might be developed after this step but, more likely, it would develop out of step 6.

6. *Determine what is already known about the needs and behavior of each segment and add any new dimensions to each list. (This may lead to splitting and renaming some segments.)*

After tentatively naming some segments, as we did in step 5, a

Figure 6–3
Market grid for apartments (in Dallas, Texas).

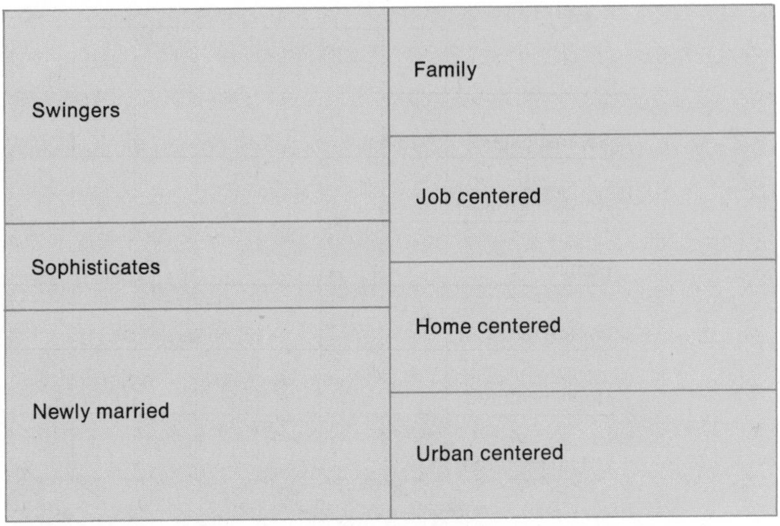

Swingers	Family
	Job centered
Sophisticates	
	Home centered
Newly married	
	Urban centered

Swingers—young, unmarried, active, fun-loving, party going.
Sophisticates—young, but older than swingers, more mature than swingers, more income and education than swingers, more desire for comfort and individuality.
Newly married—focuses on future home, not a swinging place. Apartment is a transitional place, not enough money to buy a house. Wife works, therefore economy not necessary.
Job centered—want to be near job, single adults, widows or divorcees, interested in economy.
Home centered—former homeowners but still want some aspects of suburban life.
Urban centered—former homeowners in suburbs—want to be close to attractions of city.
Source: *House & Home,* April 1965, pp. 94–99.

more serious consideration of the needs and behavior of each segment is necessary in order to deepen understanding about how and why some market segments behave the way they do. It may also help to explain why some competitive offerings are more successful than others. This can easily lead to a splitting and renaming of some segments.

Example: Some young married couples may still be swingers while others have begun to shift their focus toward buying a home and the apartment is only a transitional place. At the same time, some other newly marrieds may be more like the sophisticates and should be placed in that market segment.

Additional information on the needs and behavior of each of the segments in this example is given at the bottom of Figure 6–3. There, it can be seen that the newly married have quite different views than the sophisticates and probably should be treated as a separate segment. Note however, that if the newly marrieds happen to have enough income, they might end up in a sophisticates apartment development while waiting to move into a home of their own. The same apartment development might be able to cater to the sophisticates and some of the newly married at the same time, but the advertising and personal selling appeals might be quite differ-

Figure 6–4
Determining dimensions in the market for apartments
(in Dallas, Texas)

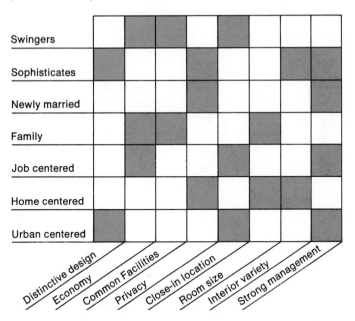

ent. The point here is that these differences might only be discovered in step 6 and, it would be at this stage that the newly married segment would be named.

7. *Link each segment to demographic characteristics, if possible, to help determine the size of each market segment.*

Eventually, we are looking for a profitable opportunity, so we must determine the size and market potential of alternative market segments. As already noted, there is a substantial amount of measurable data on demographic characteristics. Therefore, we should attempt some linkage to this data to facilitate estimating market potential. Without such hard data, the risks go up rapidly — some market grid boxes may be almost empty!

Example: It is possible to make a good linkage between the swingers and demographic data. Most of them are young, in their twenties, and the U.S. Census Bureau has very detailed information about age. Given age data and an estimate of what proportion are swingers, it is easy to estimate the actual number of unmarried "swingers" in various areas.

Grid dimensions suggest a good mix

■ Once we have followed all seven steps, it is then possible to consider what kind of marketing mix can be offered. Let's take a look:

We know that "swingers" are active, young, unmarried, fun-loving and party-going. The housing needs blocked out in Figure

6-4 indicate what the swingers want in an apartment (as an aside, it is interesting to note what they *do not want* – strong management. Most college students will probably understand why!)

It is now easier to develop an appropriate marketing mix. A very successful appeal to the swingers in the Dallas, Texas, area includes a complex of apartments with a swimming pool, a putting green, a night club that offers jazz and other entertainment, poolside parties, receptions for new tenants, and so on. And to maintain their image, management insists that tenants who get married move out shortly so that new swingers can be accommodated.

As a result, apartment occupancy rates were extremely high in such buildings.

At the same time, other builders were experiencing difficulties filling their apartments, mostly because the units offered were hardly more than "little boxes" with few uniquely appealing characteristics.[2]

More sophisticated clustering techniques may help in market gridding

■ The seven-step approach described above is logical, practical, and it works. But a marketing manager no longer is limited to such an intuitive, judgmental approach. Some new techniques are evolving to help. Roughly called "clustering" techniques, they seek to do mechanically some of what previously required much intuition and judgment.

The basic thrust of clustering techniques (which require a computer) is to try to find similar patterns within sets of customer-related data. This data could include anything which might possibly turn out to be relevant, including demographic characteristics, attitudes toward the product-market area or life in general, and previous purchasing behavior. The computer searches among all of the data for homogeneous groups of people. When such groups have been found, then the dimensions of the people in the groups must be analyzed by humans for insights as to why the computer clustered them together. If the results make some sense – if they have face validity – they may suggest new or at least better marketing strategies. For example, they may suggest where a firm should "position" itself in the market and who its direct competitors will be.[3]

A cluster analysis of the toothpaste market, for example, might show that some people buy toothpaste for its sensory satisfaction (the sensory segment), while others are concerned with the effect of clean teeth on their social image (the sociables). Others are worried about decay (the worriers), and some are strictly interested in the best value for their money (the economic men). Each of these market segments calls for a different marketing mix, although some of the four Ps may be similar, and a marketing manager would have to decide where he wanted to position his offering(s).[4]

Much experimental work is being done with these techniques,

and the results are encouraging. As more work of this kind is done, we may see similar kinds of clusters reoccurring in different product classes, for example (besides those mentioned above): The status seeker, the swinger, and the conservative.

It should be clear, however, that these techniques only aid the manager. Judgment is still required to develop an original list of possible dimensions and then to name the resulting clusters, if they make market sense.[5]

Clustering can work for services too

■ These clustering techniques have general applicability — for both goods and services, and consumer goods and industrial goods.

In a study of the commercial banking market for example, six distinctive groups were isolated, each having relevance for marketing strategy planning. These groups were called the: nonborrowers, value-seekers, nonsaving convenience seekers, loan seekers, one-stop bankers, and a representative group (which was not particularly distinguished on any dimensions). Subsequently, changes were made in the bank's strategy, focusing on each of the markets and treating them as the basis for separate strategies. Instead of the previous "we are friendly people" advertising campaign, the bank decided to focus on its various products and services in an attempt to appeal to the different markets. The nonborrowers segment was appealed to with messages about the bank's checking account, bank charge card, insurance, and investment counseling. For the convenience seekers, on the other hand, stress was placed on faster teller service, express drive-in windows, overnight drop boxes, and deposit-by-mail accounts. In an effort to reach the loan seekers, some promotional efforts stressed auto-loan checking accounts, mail-loan request forms, and a greater emphasis was placed on loan programs through automobile dealers.[6]

Gridding is a circular process

■ Selecting the right qualifying and determining dimensions for the firm's target market(s) is a dynamic circular process requiring continuous analysis *and* judgment. After potentially relevant dimensions are identified, the marketing manager must see if he can develop attractive and profitable mixes, within the uncontrollable constraints. In the process, he may discover new ways to segment the market. And he may find that some markets cannot be served profitably. He may return to looking at grid box dimensions, developing and evaluating potential mixes, refining the dimensions, and so on, many times. Finally, he will have to select the target market(s) and mix(es) which are "right" for his firm. This is not an easy job, and it is the subject of this whole text, not just this chapter.

Grid boxes define target markets

■ *Hereafter, whenever we speak of target markets, we will mean customers in one or more grid boxes.* Each box may require several dimensions, however, to fully describe the customers in it.

The market for a particular firm may consist of the customers in one or several of these boxes. At any one time, and for a specific product area, a particular customer probably would be in only one box. Markets are not static, however, so shifts must be anticipated, and marketing strategy planning must be adjusted accordingly.

In our increasingly affluent society, some customers may have different demands which might place them in two or more customer groupings simultaneously. Consider, for example, the large family with teen-agers. The family might need more than one car and desire quite different things in each car because of different uses. It is possible that these demands can only be satisfied by quite different products, perhaps from different producers, say, an Oldsmobile sedan, a VW sedan, and a Ford station wagon.

In general, each unique target market requires a unique marketing mix – which is why it is imperative to consider customer needs rather than product characteristics when planning marketing strategies. The latter is a hangover from the production-oriented era.

Conclusion

■ This chapter is an introduction to the extremely important task of market gridding. Chapters 7–11 will continue with this topic and the balance of this text will use market gridding in marketing strategy planning.

Although the discussion of market gridding in Chapter 4 might have led you to think of it as a process of breaking a market into sub-sets, actually market gridding is a process of aggregating essentially unique individuals into homogeneous customer groupings. The more similar customers needs and preferences are, the larger some market segments can be. From a firm's point of view, it might like to deal with large market segments because there may be some economies of scale in production and distribution, but the larger the market segments are made, the greater the likelihood of ignoring some unique customer dimensions. Some conditions for optimal market segmentation were presented, because the aggregation process really involves trade-offs between trying to satisfy each customer's needs uniquely and the costs of doing so.

A seven-step approach to market gridding was presented and illustrated. This approach relies heavily on judgment, but it is workable and useful. Where more precise gridding is economically possible or desirable, more sophisticated techniques can be used. The nature of these clustering techniques was discussed briefly.

A good marketing man should be an expert on markets and likely relevant dimensions. He should not rely only on stereotypes or guesses. Instead, he should become familiar with what we already know and evolving research. As a start, the student should take the study of the next several chapters seriously. Guessing about things we already know about is foolhardy and not becoming of a professional businessman.

questions and problems

1 Illustrate the concept that market gridding is an aggregating process by referring to the apparent admissions policies of your own college and a nearby college or university.

2 Evaluate how "good" the following market segments are with respect to the three criteria for selecting good market segments: *(a)* the seven markets in the market grid for apartments (see Figure 6–3), and *(b)* the British home decorating market (see Figure 4–8).

3 Review the list of possible primary and secondary dimensions in Tables 6–1 and 6–2 and select the ones which you feel should be combined to fully explain the market grid box which you are or will be in when you buy an automobile. Do not hesitate to list several dimensions, but when you have done so, then attempt to develop a shorthand name, like "swinger," to describe your market grid box. Then try to estimate what proportion of the total automobile market would be accounted for by your market segment. Next, explain if there are any product offerings which come close to meeting the needs of your market. If not, what sort of a marketing mix is needed? Do you feel it would be economically attractive for anyone to try to satisfy your market segment? Why or why not?

4 Identify the determining dimension or dimensions which explain why you bought the specific brand you did in your most recent purchase of a: *(a)* soft drink, *(b)* pen, *(c)* shirt or blouse, and *(d)* larger, more expensive item, such as a bicycle, camera, boat, and so on. Try to express the determining dimension(s) in terms of your own personal characteristics rather than the product's characteristics. Estimate what share of the market would probably be motivated by the same determining dimension(s).

5 Apply the seven-step approach to market gridding to the college-age market for off-campus recreation, which can include eating and drinking. Then, roughly evaluate whether the needs in your various market segments are being met in your area, or whether there is an obvious "breakthrough opportunity" waiting for someone.

notes

[1] William F. Brown, "The Determination of Factors Influencing Brand Choice," *Journal of Marketing*, April 1950, pp. 699–706.

[2] "Singles Swing for Landlords," *Business Week*, March 5, 1966, pp. 38–40; "Segmented Demand," *House & Home*, April, 1965, pp. 94–99; and "More Builders Prosper by Offering Tenants Organized Recreation," *The Wall Street Journal*, January 22, 1969, p. 1; but this market is becoming saturated, see: "Closing the Door on Singles Housing," *Business Week*, March 4, 1972, pp. 31–32; and "Where Day Care Helps to Sell Apartments," *Business Week*, September 30, 1972, pp. 60–61.

[3] "Positioning Ads—Why Is Schaefer Beer the One Beer to Have When Having More . . . ?" *The Wall Street Journal*, December 13, 1973, p. 1; "To Position Strategically, Find Right Priorities, Get Quantifiable Market Data," The AMA *Marketing News*, October 15, 1973; "Perceptual Mapping to Reposition Brands," *Journal of Advertising Research*, February 1971, pp. 39–42; and John H. Holmes, "Profitable Product Positioning," *MSU Business Topics*, Spring 1973, pp. 27–32.

[4] Russell I. Haley, "Benefit Segmentation: A Decision-Oriented Research Tool," *Journal of Marketing*, July 1968, pp. 30–35; and "Beyond Benefit Segmentation," *Journal of Advertising Research*, August 1971, pp. 3–8; "CP's Peak, Alive and Well, Expands Into Central U.S.," *Advertising Age*, June 10, 1974, p. 1; and Richard M. Johnson, "Market Segmentation: A Strategic Management Tool," *Journal of Marketing Research*, February 1971, pp. 13–18.

[5] The details of these techniques are beyond our scope, but for discussion see: William L. Wilkie, "The Product Stream and Market Segmentation: A Research Approach," American Marketing Association Combined Conference Proceedings, Spring and Fall 1971, Series No. 33, pp. 317–321; and R. E. Frank, W. F. Massy, and Y. Wind, *Market Segmentation* (Englewood Cliffs, N.J.: Prentice-Hall, 1972). (This book has an extensive bibliography.); see also Paul E. Green and Frank J. Carmone, *Multi-Dimensional Scaling and Related Techniques in Marketing Analysis* (Boston: Allyn and Bacon, Inc., 1970).

[6] S. Arbeit and A. G. Sawyer, "Benefit Segmentation in a Retail Banking Environment," presented at the American Marketing Association Fall Conference, Washington, D.C., August 1973.

7

Consumers: Characteristics of the United States market

■ The *Customer* is the focal point of all business and marketing activity. Customers in the aggregate are markets—people with the ability (buying power) and willingness to spend their money to satisfy their needs.

The market grid concept leads us to think of any market as many smaller, more homogeneous submarkets. Unique and profitable marketing strategies may be discovered by more fully understanding the needs of some submarkets. Ideally, we want to find those dimensions which really make a difference, in terms of the needs, preferences, and attitudes of the potential customers. And we also would like to know how many think this way and where they are. Then we would be better able to plan attractive marketing strategies for them.

Three important questions should be answered regarding any potential market:

1. What are its relevant dimensions?
2. How big is it?
3. Where is it?

The first question—about relevant dimensions—is basic. Judgment—perhaps aided by analysis of existing data and new findings from marketing research—is needed in picking the right dimensions. To help build your judgment regarding consumer buying behavior, this and the following three chapters will discuss what we know about consumers.

Forget the
Texas or
New York
stereotypes

■ The marketing manager should not fall into the trap of accepting common stereotypes about the size or potential of various markets, such as those illustrated in one artist's version of a New Yorker's and a Texan's view of the United States (Figure 7–1), which may be humorous but is of no real value.

When valid data is available, there is no excuse for decisions based on such misconceptions or regional propaganda. Try to see the data in the next few chapters in terms of selecting relevant dimensions and estimating the potential in market grid boxes. Also, check your own assumptions against this data. Marketing decisions often must be made in a hurry, under pressure. Then, if you feel you really do know the relevant market dimensions, you may decide without even looking at the available data. Now is a good time to get the "facts" straight.

Population

Present
population
and its
distribution

■ Table 7–1 shows the population by states for 1970. The first rank of California should sober the New Yorker and the Texan, and explain why some marketers are going after the West Coast market. On the other hand, the heavy concentration of population in New York and a few adjacent states—altogether twice as populous as the entire West Coast—does lend a certain validity to the New Yorker's view of the U.S. market. The population of Texas is large, but its partisans' views are based on area, not population, and now that Alaska has been admitted to the Union, Texas is no longer even the biggest state.

The map in Figure 7–2 emphasizes the concentration of population in various geographic regions. It shows the area of each state in proportion to its population. Notice the importance of the mid-western states and the southern states when viewed as a group. These regions, too, are often viewed as unique target markets by marketers anxious to avoid the extremely competitive East and West Coast markets. Note, too, the relative scarcity of people in the Plains and Mountain states, which explains why some mass marketers pay less attention to these areas. Yet these states can provide an opportunity for an alert marketer who is looking for less competitive market situations.

Where are
the people
today and
tomorrow?

■ Population figures for a single year fail to convey the dynamic aspects of markets. The U.S. population has been growing continuously since the founding of the country, more than doubling in the 60 years from 1910 to 1970. But—and this is important to marketers—the population did *not* double everywhere. Some states have seen very rapid growth, while others have grown only a little and at a slower rate.

California and the southwestern states, as well as Florida, have seen very rapid growth, while the New England and Plains states have grown more slowly. Some states even lost population from

Figure 7-1
A New Yorker's eye view of the United States

A Texan's eye view of the United States

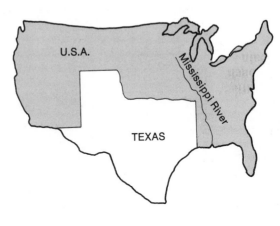

1960-70 – including West Virginia, Mississippi, North Dakota, South Dakota, and Wyoming.

These different rates of growth are especially important to marketing. For example, sudden growth in one area may create a demand for many new shopping centers, while existing facilities may be more than adequate in other areas. In fact, the introduction of new marketing facilities in slow-growing areas can create severe competitive problems for existing merchants, while in other areas demand may be growing so rapidly that even poorly planned and managed facilities can be profitable.

Population will keep growing

■ It seems certain that U.S. population will continue to grow, at least for another 50 years or more. The big questions are, "How much and how fast?" The birthrate is currently declining and may continue to drop. It fell below the "replacement level" in 1972, and if it drops further, "zero population growth" might be achieved eventually. This may be quite a few decades off, however, because there are so many young people in the population. Even a steady replacement level of fertility would not result in zero population growth for about 70 years. Therefore, we can expect continued population growth. In fact, the U.S. Census Bureau projects that actual births will continue to climb so that in 1980 we can expect over 4 million births – the same level that was reached in the peak baby-boom year of 1957.[1]

These projections might be changed, however, by new attitudes toward marriage, family size, and family planning. These trends should be watched carefully by marketers, because they obviously have an impact on future market sizes. For the present, however, it is clear that population will continue to grow and that most of this population expansion will center in already crowded metropolitan areas.

Table 7–1
Population by states and for Puerto Rico: 1960 and 1970

State or other area	Population (1,000) 1960	Population (1,000) 1970	Percent change 1960 1970	State or other area	Population (1,000) 1960	Population (1,000) 1970	Percent change 1960 1970
United States	179,323	203,212	13.3	East South Central	12,050	12,803	6.3
New England	10,509	11,842	12.7	Kentucky	3,038	3,219	5.9
Maine	969	992	2.4	Tennessee	3,567	3,924	10.0
New Hampshire	607	738	21.5	Alabama	3,267	3,444	5.4
Vermont	390	444	14.0	Mississippi	2,178	2,217	1.8
Massachusetts	5,149	5,689	10.5	West South Central	16,951	19,321	14.0
Rhode Island	859	947	10.1	Arkansas	1,786	1,923	7.7
Connecticut	2,535	3,032	19.6	Louisiana	3,257	3,641	11.8
Middle Atlantic	34,168	37,199	8.9	Oklahoma	2,328	2,559	9.9
New York	16,782	18,237	8.7	Texas	9,580	11,197	16.9
New Jersey	6,067	7,168	18.2	Mountain	6,855	8,282	20.8
Pennsylvania	11,319	11,794	4.2	Montana	675	694	2.9
East North Central	36,225	40,252	11.1	Idaho	667	713	6.8
Ohio	9,706	10,652	9.7	Wyoming	330	332	0.7
Indiana	4,662	5,194	11.4	Colorado	1,754	2,207	25.8
Illinois	10,081	11,114	10.2	New Mexico	951	1,016	6.8
Michigan	7,823	8,875	13.4	Arizona	1,302	1,771	36.0
Wisconsin	3,952	4,418	11.8	Utah	891	1,059	18.9
West North Central	15,394	16,319	6.0	Nevada	285	489	71.3
Minnesota	3,414	3,805	11.5	Pacific	21,198	26,523	25.1
Iowa	2,758	2,824	2.4	Washington	2,853	3,409	19.5
Missouri	4,320	4,677	8.3	Oregon	1,769	2,091	18.2
North Dakota	632	618	−2.3	California	15,717	19,953	27.0
South Dakota	681	666	−2.2	Alaska	226	300	32.8
Nebraska	1,411	1,483	5.1	Hawaii	633	769	21.5
Kansas	2,179	2,247	3.1	Puerto Rico	2,350	2,712	15.4
South Atlantic	25,972	30,671	18.1				
Delaware	446	548	22.8				
Maryland	3,101	3,922	26.5				
D.C.	764	757	−1.0				
Virginia	3,967	4,648	17.2				
West Virginia	1,860	1,744	−6.2				
North Carolina	4,556	5,082	11.5				
South Carolina	2,383	2,591	8.7				
Georgia	3,943	4,590	16.4				
Florida	4,952	6,789	37.1				

Source: *Statistical Abstract of the United States,* 1973, pp. 12–13.

Shift to urban and suburban areas

■ Migration from rural to urban areas has been continuous in the United States since 1800. In 1920, about half the population lived in rural areas, but by 1950 the number living on farms had dropped to 15 percent and in 1970 it was about 5 percent. Clearly, we have become an industrialized society, and it seems that farming will

Figure 7-2
Map showing each state's area in proportion to its 1970 population

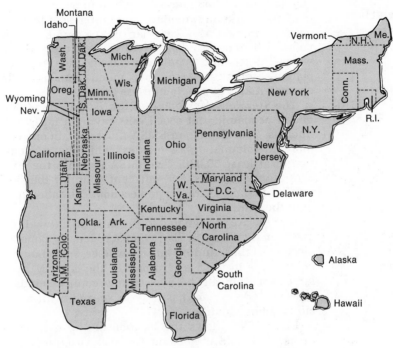

eventually be dominated by corporate agricultural enterprises. This subject is explored further in Chapter 9.

From city to suburbs to city again

■ Since World War II, there has been a continual race to the suburbs. In 1970, more people were living in the suburbs than in the central cities. As people moved to the suburbs, retail and service businesses followed. And as middle-income people have moved out of the cities, lower-income consumers, often with different racial and national backgrounds, have moved in, thereby changing the nature of target markets in the center of the city.

A partial reversal of this trend seems possible, however. Some families have become disenchanted with the suburban dream, which they found to be a nightmare of commuting, yard and housework, rising local taxes, and gossiping neighbors.

The movement back to the city is most evident among older and sometimes wealthier families. Their children are usually married or ready to leave home. They feel hemmed in by the rapid expansion of suburbia and especially by the large number of lower-income families moving in. These older families are showing increased interest in condominiums and high-rise apartments close to downtown shopping, recreational, and office facilities.

Developing a new concept of the urban area

■ These continuing shifts to and from urban and suburban areas mean that the usual practice of recording population by arbitrary city and county boundaries may lead to misleading descriptions of markets. Marketing men are more interested in the size of homogeneous marketing areas than in the number of people within political boundaries. To meet this need, the U.S. Census has developed a separate population classification, the Standard Metropolitan Statistical Area, and much data is collected on the characteristics of people in these areas.

The *Standard Metropolitan Statistical Area* (SMSA) is an integrated economic and social unit having a fairly large population nucleus. Specifically, an SMSA must contain one city of 50,000 or more inhabitants, or "twin cities" which have a combined population of at least 50,000. The SMSA includes the county of such a central city or cities and adjacent counties that are found to be metropolitan in character and economically and socially integrated with the central city.

SMSAs are designated differently in New England because many of the cities in that compact, densely populated region are closer together, and counties must be split. Some SMSAs, especially those in the western part of the country, are exceptionally large geographically because of huge county boundaries. Generally, however, SMSAs are basically urbanized, with a central city and surrounding suburbs.

Figure 7–3 shows the location of the nation's biggest urban areas: 263 SMSAs account for over two-thirds of the country's population. Notice that this map further emphasizes the concentration of population in specific places – here, in SMSAs.

Big targets are easier

■ Some national marketing organizations are concerned solely with these metropolitan areas because of the large concentrations of population within easy reach of their major distribution facilities. Table 7–2 shows the size of the top 15 SMSAs in 1972.

These larger target markets also offer greater sales potential in dollars and cents than population alone would indicate, in part because of generally higher wages in metropolitan areas and the concentration of higher-paying occupations.

The SMSAs should be considered as potential dimensions in market grid analysis. The farther customers are from major marketing centers, the more expensive they are to serve. Densely populated areas offer great opportunities – *if* the competition is not too strong!

The age of the continuous city

■ Despite the return of some families to the central cities, the trend to the suburbs seems likely to continue. An expanding population must go somewhere, and the suburbs can combine pleasant neighborhoods with easy transportation to higher-paying jobs in the city. Further, the continuing decentralization of industry may move jobs closer to the suburbs than to the central city. Not only people but industries have been fleeing the old cities.

Figure 7–3
Standard Metropolitan Statistical Areas

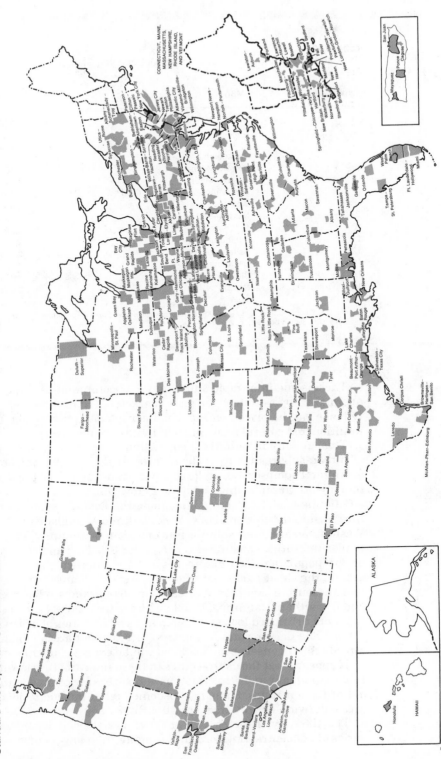

Table 7-2
Rank and population of top 15 Standard Metropolitan Statistical
Areas in 1972

Rank	SMSA	Population
1	New York, N.Y.–N.J.	9,943,800
2	Chicago, Ill.	7,084,700
3	Los Angeles–Long Beach, Calif.	6,999,600
4	Philadelphia, Pa.–N.J.	4,877,500
5	Detroit, Mich.	4,488,900
6	Boston, Mass.	3,417,000
7	San Francisco–Oakland, Calif.	3,131,800
8	Washington, D.C.–Md.–Va.	2,998,900
9	Nassau–Suffolk, N.Y.	2,597,300
10	St. Louis, Mo.–Ill.	2,399,800
11	Pittsburgh, Pa.	2,395,900
12	Dallas–Fort Worth, Tex.	2,383,800
13	Baltimore, Md.	2,125,000
14	Cleveland, Ohio	2,045,500
15	Newark, N.J.	2,082,000

Source: U.S. Department of Commerce, U.S. Bureau of the Census, *Current Population Reports*, Series
P-25, No. 506, September 1973, p. 23.

These sometimes rapid shifts into new communities can create overnight opportunities for alert marketers. Here, however, less reliance can be placed on the usual census data; it's too old. Both intuition and careful study of local trends are necessary.

This growth in suburban population may create a new kind of urban-suburban strip called *"interurbia"* or *"megalopolis."* J. Walter Thompson Co.–a large advertising agency that has done much work in projecting population growth in various areas–sees a 600-mile-long "city" stretching along the East Coast and joining the citizens of Boston, New York, Baltimore, Philadelphia, and Washington and their suburbs into one giant community. This particular interurbia constitutes 6 percent of U.S. land and 20 percent of the population (see Figure 7-4). Other interurbia areas occur around the Great Lakes and adjoining areas in Pennsylvania, Ohio, and Missouri; in southern Florida; in the San Francisco Bay region; and in southern California. People who see the whole world becoming more urbanized look at these areas as laboratories of urban evolution. The darker parts in Figure 7-4 represent areas which are already fairly densely populated and can be expected to grow more.

It appears that the central cities in these interurbia areas will be rebuilt gradually and attractively as slum areas are cleared with the aid of federal funds. Some may become higher-income residential areas, drawing heavily from the suburbs.

The U.S. city of the past 70 or 80 years has been depicted as a series of concentric rings or bands ranging from low-income slums

Figure 7-4
Projected growth of "interurbias"

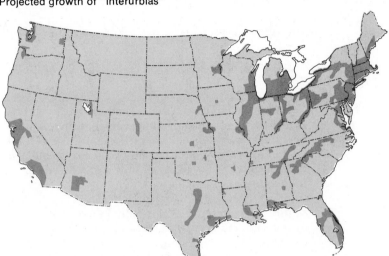

at the city center outward through progressively higher-income areas to the wealthy suburban areas at the outer fringe. The city of tomorrow will probably be more heterogeneous with many small neighborhoods – some wealthy, some middle income, and some poor – intermingled throughout the area from the central city to the suburbs. This pattern of urban redevelopment already can be seen in the Los Angeles, Chicago, and Philadelphia areas. This new urban population structure will make the use of the market grid concept even more important.

The mobile ones are an attractive market

■ It is important to remember that none of these population shifts is necessarily permanent. People move, stay awhile, and then move on again. In fact, approximately 20 percent of Americans move each year. It appears that mobile people represent an important economic market, because their moves are often caused by promotions and job transfers and they have money to spend. Moreover, it is clear that they must make many market-oriented decisions fairly quickly after their move. They must locate new sources of food, clothing, medical and dental services, and household goods. Alert marketers are well advised to try to locate these people and inform them of their market offering.[2]

Not only are Americans mobile with respect to their home base, but they are also willing to travel about and try new things. The development of better highways has encouraged more distant vacationing and ownership of second homes, vacation cabins, travel trailers, and boats. This, in turn, has led to the development of additional retail facilities, marinas, and recreational areas. Even the growth of suburban areas was facilitated by the willingness of the breadwinner to travel farther to work. And these suburban developments have encouraged the growth of outlying shopping centers. Given the energy crisis, we may not see as much growth of this kind. In fact, there may have to be a reversal. This could present new opportunities for alert marketers closer to population centers.

Income

■ So far we have been concerned primarily with geographic characteristics. It is obvious, however, that unless a person has money or the assurance of acquiring it, he cannot be regarded as a potential customer. The amount of money he can spend also will affect the type of goods he is likely to buy. For this reason, most marketing men study income data too.

Growth probably will continue

■ Income is derived from producing and selling goods or services in the marketplace. A widely available measure of the output and the growth of the economy is the gross national product, which represents the total market value of goods and services produced in a year. The GNP has increased at the rate of approximately 3 percent a year since 1880. This means that GNP doubles, on the average, every 20 years. If past trends continue, as is expected, the economy will probably continue to grow at about the same rate, that is, doubling every 20 years.

All the forecasts call for a continued growth of GNP. It is government policy to seek "full employment," which would tend to increase GNP as the population continues to grow. The current energy crisis, and rethinking about the desirability of growth may have a negative effect on future growth. But the interrelation of employment and growth cannot be neglected, because while it might be desirable to inhibit growth, perhaps to reduce pollution, this might also lead to unemployment and severe hardships. Politically, this may be very difficult to manage. It seems more likely that we will continue to see a growth in GNP, although different kinds of goods and services may be produced.

The income pyramid capsizes!

■ These aggregate GNP figures are more meaningful when expressed in terms of family income and its distribution. Family income has been moving up, but even more important to marketing men is that the *distribution of income* has been changing drastically and will probably continue to change. Figure 7–5 shows that as recently as 1930 most families were bunched together in the lower income levels, and the distribution looked something like a pyramid. The data in Figure 7–5 is in terms of 1965 dollars, which means the effects of price inflation over the years have been removed.

By 1965, we see that the pyramid had turned over! Projections into the future indicate that real income will not only continue to grow but that more families will find themselves above the middle of this income distribution. One forecaster expects that by 1980,

Figure 7-5
Redistribution of income—a revolution

Percent of families in income class, 1965 dollars

		1930	1965	1980
$10,000 & over		2	22	29
7,500-9,999		3	18	25
5,000-7,499		11	26	28
4,000-4,999		7	9	7
3,000-3,999		14	8	5
2,000-2,999		21	7	3
1,000-1,999		24	6	2
Under 1,000		18	4	

Source: Reprinted from the October 16, 1965 issue of *Business Week* by special permission. Copyrighted © 1965 by McGraw-Hill, Inc.

two out of every three families will have incomes of $10,000 a year or more. And, of course, some families will have substantially higher incomes.[3]

Is $10,000 bare subsistence?

■ The importance of the income distribution data in Figure 7-5 cannot be stressed too much. Bad marketing strategy errors have been made by overestimating the amount of income available in various target markets. It is all too easy for businessmen to fall into such errors because of the natural tendency we all have of associating with others in similar circumstances and then assuming that almost everyone lives the same way. This was brought home most forcefully to the author when a group of students confronted him with what they felt was an error in a textbook. They questioned the statement in the book that many people made less than $5,000 a year. No one, they felt, could possibly survive on such a low income. They felt that $10,000 or more a year was necessary for "bare subsistence." This was in 1955. Figure 7-5 shows that 10 years later— 1965—only 22 percent of the country's families made more than $10,000. Furthermore, 34 percent of the families were making less than $5,000 a year.[4]

The $10,000 income figure is a useful reference point, because a 'recent college graduate might earn almost this much (and a working couple together can easily go over this figure). This will seem like a lot in the initial flush of making money, but it is surprising how soon needs and expenses rise and adjust to available income. Before long it's difficult to see how anyone can live on less. Then, the fact that there *is* an income distribution and that some families must make do on much less should not be forgotten in marketing strategy planning.

Consumer spending patterns related to population and income

■ We have been using the term *family* income because consumer budget studies suggest that most consumers spend their incomes as part of a family or household unit. If the wife or children work, they usually pool their income with the husband or father when planning family expenditures. Thus, most of our discussion will be on how households or families spend their income.

Disposable income is spendable income

■ It should be remembered, however, that families do not get to spend all of their income. Taxes take a share and what is left is called *disposable income*. Out of its disposable income – together with gifts, pensions, cash savings, or other assets – the family makes its expenditures. Some families do not spend all of their disposable income, saving part of it. Therefore, we should distinguish between disposable income and actual expenditures when trying to estimate potential expenditures in market grid boxes.

Discretionary income is elusive

■ As we have already noted, peoples' incomes have been growing and probably will continue to grow. But not all of the growing income is uncommitted. Most households allocate a goodly portion of their income to "necessities" – food, rent or house payments, car and housefurnishings payments, insurance, and so on – which are defined in various ways by different researchers and consumers. A family's purchase of "luxuries" comes from what's left, or what is called *discretionary income*.

Discretionary income is a rather elusive concept, because the definition of necessities varies from family to family and over a period of time. But it is also an important concept, because if consumers do not feel they have *any* discretionary purchasing power, they may stop buying certain luxuries altogether. Also, discretionary income may jump substantially with a small growth in income. One study, for example, shows that a family with $8,000 gross income may have almost four times the discretionary income of a family with $6,500 gross income.[5] Again, much would depend on the attitudes of people in the target markets. A color television set might be purchased out of discretionary income by a lower-income family but be considered a necessity by a higher-income family.

People's needs for "necessities" also may continue to grow, outstripping their purchasing power. It was recently estimated that only "54 percent of American families can afford what is now perceived as a 'low moderate' life standard. And very few can afford the leisure-class life-styles popularized by the spread of education and promoted by mass media."[6]

Engel's laws show basic spending relationships

■ Before looking at hard expenditure data, some generalizations are possible about consumer spending patterns. These generalizations are commonly referred to as "Engel's laws" because they grew out of the work of a German statistician who published the first study of consumer spending patterns in 1857. Followers have rephrased these laws, until now they are stated in three parts:

1. As a family's income increases, the percentage spent on food will decrease.
2. As a family's income increases, the percentage spent on housing and household operations will be roughly constant (with the exception of fuel, light, and refrigeration, which will decrease).
3. As a family's income increases, the percentage spent on all other categories and the amount saved will increase (with the exception of medical care and personal care items, which are fairly constant).

Engel was primarily concerned with working-class families who spent *all* their income. This fits in with our emphasis on analyzing consumer *expenditures*. Note that it is implied in Engel's laws that as a family's income increases, *more money will be spent in total in all categories*. The decreases or increases occur as a percentage of the total.

Engel's laws are useful only for predicting the behavior of an individual family or groups of families moving from one income category to another. They should be used with care when it comes to predicting the spending pattern that develops in the whole economy when the gross national product changes. Engel's laws were not based upon such movements, but rather on a comparison of the budgets of individual families. They can still be useful to marketing men, however. An established retailer, for example, might use Engel's laws to forecast how the expenditure patterns of his present customers would change if a new industrial plant coming into the community were likely to increase their incomes.

Expenditure data provides harder numbers

■ Generalizations such as Engel's laws are valuable when precise data is not available, but fortunately we do have some detailed information on consumer expenditure patterns. The National Industrial Conference Board (NICB) has developed an extremely comprehensive breakdown of data gathered by the Bureau of Labor Statistics as part of its project to revise its Consumer Price Index.

To make this revision, approximately 12,000 nonfarm families were interviewed during 1961–62 concerning their purchases of approximately 700 individual products and services. All of this data has been analyzed and cross-classified with 11 different family characteristics, and presented in detailed tables.[7]

It must be understood that this data is somewhat dated now and incomes have since gone up. Nevertheless, the basic interrelationships probably still hold, and it is currently the most comprehensive and detailed data easily available. Some updating of the income distribution data from a source such as *Sales Management's* "Survey of Buying Power"[8] probably would be desirable if this data were to be used in a real business situation. But for our purposes we will discuss and illustrate the use of this basic information.

Table 7–3
Average annual family expenditures by family income

Item	Total	Family income (before taxes)					
		Under $3,000	$3,000– $5,000	$5,000– $7,500	$7,500– $10,000	$10,000– $15,000	$15,000 and over
Percent distribution of:							
All families	100%	22.4%	20.8%	26.2%	16.1%	10.7%	3.7%
Total expenditures	100	8.9	15.6	27.1	21.2	18.0	9.1
Average family size	3.2	2.1	3.0	3.5	3.7	3.9	3.8
Expenditures for current consumption:	$5,152	$2,043	$3,859	$5,315	$6,788	$8,679	$12,687
Food	1,259	600	1,015	1,318	1,624	1,970	2,550
Alcoholic beverages	81	21	55	81	117	152	242
Tobacco	93	42	84	105	123	126	134
Housing and household operations	1,236	620	968	1,263	1,552	1,889	3,002
Housefurnishings and equipment	269	83	185	284	376	476	690
Clothing and accessories	525	145	348	528	720	1,001	1,550
Transportation	781	176	560	848	1,093	1,450	1,891
Medical care	342	174	269	350	425	539	771
Personal care	148	61	118	156	194	241	312
Recreation and equipment	205	48	133	201	291	419	597
Reading and education	100	26	55	88	126	215	440
Other expenditures	113	47	69	93	147	201	508

Source: Adapted from Fabian Linden (ed.), *Expenditure Patterns of the American Family* (New York: National Industrial Conference Board, 1965), p. 18.

Why lower-income consumers may be ignored

■ Table 7–3 shows the average annual spending by households for major categories of expenditures, as developed in this study. These aggregate measures serve as bench marks, and as noted earlier, should keep you from making wild estimates based only on your own experience.

The data in Table 7–3 shows that those in the upper-income categories spend a large share of the total spent for goods and services. The families making over $7,500, for example, comprised only 30 percent of the population but accounted for almost half the expenditures. This may not be surprising information, but it does help to explain why some business organizations tend to ignore the lower-income consumers.

Estimating how potential customers spend their money

■ Data such as that in Table 7–3 can help a marketing manager understand how his potential target markets spend their money. For example, if he is seriously considering consumers in the $15,000-and-over income bracket, he can analyze how families in this category distributed their expenditures. Then he can consider how they would have to rearrange their spending to purchase his product. A swimming pool manufacturer could calculate that such families spend about $600 a year on recreation and equipment. If his pool costs approximately $600 a year, including depreciation and maintenance, it follows that for the average family in this income category, such a purchase would necessitate a substantial realignment in its life-style.

Clearly, the data will not give the pool maker the answer that he seeks, but it may supply some of the raw materials he needs to make a sound decision. If he feels that he needs more information, he can use various marketing research techniques. For example, he might want to make a budget study on consumers who already have swimming pools to see how they adjusted their spending patterns. He might also want to incorporate differences in spending habits due to other factors for which data is available in the NICB study, such as age of household head, stage in the family life cycle, and so on.

Expenditure patterns vary with other measurable factors

■ Income has a direct bearing upon spending patterns, but there are other factors that should not be neglected in any careful analysis of market grids.

Expenditures are affected by location of household

■ The NICB data show that the location of a consumer's household does have a distinct bearing on the household's spending habits. We will not present detailed tables here, but will summarize a few of the important differences. The more detailed NICB data that is available should be analyzed to answer specific questions.

Expenditures on transportation, housing, and food do seem to vary by geographic location. Consumers in central cities spend much less on transportation and much more on housing than those in outlying areas, probably because of higher land and construction costs and greater population density. A rural family spends a larger share on food, perhaps because there is less competition in rural areas for a grocery dollar. But incomes tend to be lower in rural areas, and Engel's laws may explain some of this.

Also, by geographical boundaries

■ Geographical boundaries also are relevant to expenditures. Total expenditures in the South are lower than in other regions because incomes there are lower. But the important differences are in the relative shares going for housing and household operations and transportation. Consumers in the northeastern part of the United States tend to spend more on housing and household operations (for utilities and higher land costs) while spending substantially less on transportation because of the greater availability of public transportation and the greater density of population.

Stage of life cycle affects spending

■ Two other population dimensions—age and number of children—seem to have a direct bearing on expenditure patterns. Put together, these dimensions are concerned with the life cycle of a family. Younger families without children behave differently than those with children. And as the children grow older, budgets must be changed. When the children leave, the "empty-nesters" may suddenly have ample discretionary income to satisfy needs which have long been neglected. Finally, they become "senior citizens" and again we see different expenditure patterns.

Young families accept new ideas

Younger people seem to be more receptive to new products, such as household products and house furnishings. Further, younger families – usually with no children – are still accumulating durable goods such as automobiles and house furnishings. They need less food. It is only as children begin to arrive and grow that the family emphasis shifts to soft goods and services such as education, medical, and personal care. This tends to occur when the household head reaches the 35–44 age bracket.

Reallocation for teen-agers

The teen-ager and young adult markets are important and may be key markets for decades. See Figure 7–6 and note the size and forecast of continued growth for the "under 25 years" market. Considerable attention has been directed to the babies born in the period from 1940–60, and it is fairly easy to project their numbers and when they will mature.

With respect to teen-agers, we know that they eat more, begin to wear more expensive clothes, and develop recreational and educational needs that are hard on the family budget. Their parents may be forced to reallocate their expenditures to cover these expenses, spending less on durable goods such as appliances, automobiles, household goods, and houses.

As these teen-agers grow into young adults, we can expect a sharp increase in marriages, and *perhaps* a continuing baby boom. These young adults, in turn, will buy durable goods until their children become older, and then they, too, will have to reallocate their budgets to provide for food, clothing, education and recreation.

Selling to the "empty nesters"

There is an important group in the 50–64 age category that is sometimes called the *"empty-nesters."* Their children are grown, and they are now able to spend their money in other ways. It is an elusive group, however, because some people marry later and are still raising a family as they move into this age group. It is empty-nesters who move back into the smaller, more luxurious apartments in central cities. They may also be more interested in travel, small sports cars, and other things that have not been realistic possibilities for them until now. Much depends on their income, of course.

Old folks are a new market

Finally, the *"senior citizen"* market is one that should not be neglected. The number of people over 65 is increasing rapidly because of modern medicine, improved sanitary conditions, and better nutrition. This group now constitutes 10 percent of the population.

Although older people generally have reduced incomes, they

Figure 7–6
Population growth projection by age groups

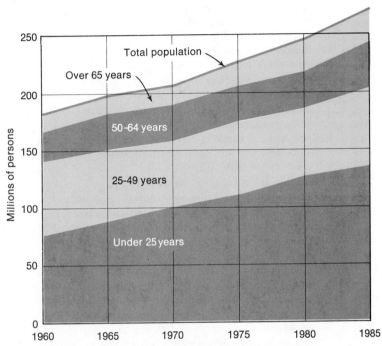

Source: Reprinted from the May 15, 1965 issue of *Business Week* by special permission.
Copyrighted © 1965 by McGraw-Hill, Inc.

represent a unique target market. Many firms, in fact, are already catering to the senior citizen market. Special food products and diet supplements have been developed, and there are even housing developments designed especially to appeal to older persons.[9]

Are savers spenders?

■ One factor logically related to consumers' ability and willingness to spend money is their asset position. It is reasonable to assume that if a consumer has a substantial bank account or a nest egg of savings bonds, he will be more willing to spend his current income and even go into debt. This concept has interested the Federal Reserve System, which has some control over credit policies, and it collects data on the subject.

This data shows that about 10 percent of the families have $10,000 or more in liquid assets while about 20 percent have none, and the average family would have less than $1,000. Companies planning to sell expensive products, homes for example, which would have to draw on savings should bear this data in mind.[10]

Nationality, race, and purchasing

■ America may be called the "melting pot," but there are still relatively distinct racial and nationality groups that require special consideration when the marketing man is dimensioning a market grid. This is obvious for some products, but there are other differences that may be ignored by the superficial observer.

It is in this area that stereotype thinking is the most common and where some original marketing research may be especially desirable. All blacks, for example, do not have big cars—in fact, black consumers spend less on automobile transportation than do whites with comparable incomes.[11] And those of Irish extraction do not eat just corn beef and cabbage or potatoes, just as those of Italian extraction buy food products other than pasta.

These possible dimensions must be studied and watched carefully, because they may be subtle and fast changing. Hair straighteners, for example, are no longer selling well to the black market.[12] But different kinds of cosmetics and hair preparation products do seem to be needed for the black market. At the same time, a young, middle-income, black working couples' market may be developing. This may be an "almost ignored" $25 billion a year market. These working couples have accepted the values of middle America but they have their own needs and ways of thinking—and importantly they live in different areas and read different media. It would certainly be wise to consider having separate dimensions for them.[13]

The median age of U.S. blacks and Chicanos is considerably lower than that of whites. This means that many more are in earlier stages of the life cycle and, therefore, are a better market for certain goods, especially durable goods.

Some minority groups seem to be striving for what they believe to be white middle-income standards in material goods and current products may be quite acceptable. Others have abandoned this goal in favor of identification with their own set of values. Clearly, separate strategies may be needed for nationality or racially defined markets. Perhaps, some of these strategies would only require changes in place and promotion, but nevertheless they would be separate strategies.

When the wife earns, the family spends

■ A relatively new phenomenon in spending patterns that deserves attention is the growing number of married women who hold jobs. In 1972, over 19 million wives were on the nation's payrolls—more than double the number when employment of wives was at a high level during World War II.

In families where the wife works, about 40 percent of all the family spending power is derived from her income. Half of all U.S. families in the $10,000-to-$15,000 income bracket have achieved this income because the wife is working.

A study by the U.S. Department of Agriculture showed that while a wife's employment outside the home seems to have little effect on the nutritive value of her family's food, working wives do *spend more* for food and do choose more expensive types of food.

Families with working wives also spend more on clothing, alcohol and tobacco, housefurnishings and equipment, and automobiles.

In short, when a wife works, it has a very distinct effect on the spending habits of the family. This fact must be considered when developing market grids.

Conclusion

■ In our study of the American consumer, we have moved from the general to the particular. We first studied population data, dispelling various misconceptions about how our more than 200 million people are spread over the United States. In so doing, it became apparent that the potential of a given market cannot be determined by numbers alone. Income, stage in life cycle, geographic location of people, and other factors are important, too.

We also noted the growth of interurbia, such as the megalopolis of the Atlantic Seaboard. These urban-suburban systems suggest the shape of future growth in this country. It is also apparent that one of the outstanding characteristics of the American is his mobility. For this reason, even relatively new data is not foolproof. The wealth of available data can only aid judgment, not replace it.

Engel's so-called "laws" are useful generalizations about consumption patterns. They help predict individual and family buying behavior. But the American consumer is different from Engel's workingman in a very important respect, namely, he is the most affluent in the world, and this affluence affects his purchasing behavior. Beyond the necessities of life, he is able to buy a wide variety of products. In fact, it could be argued that little that he buys is an absolute necessity.

The kind of data discussed in this chapter can be very useful for estimating the market potential within market grids, but, unfortunately, it has not been very helpful in explaining actual customer behavior—why people buy *specific* products and *specific* brands. And such detailed forecasts are obviously important to marketing managers. Fortunately, improved estimates can come from a fuller understanding of consumer behavior. This may require more sophisticated and different kinds of analysis. More will be said on this in Chapter 8, where we discuss the decision-making behavior of individual consumers and of household groups.

questions and problems

1 Some demographic characteristics are likely to be more important than others in determining market potential. For each of the following characteristics, identify two products for which this characteristic is *most* important: (a) size of geographic area, (b) population, (c) income, (d) stage of life cycle.

2 If a large new atomic research installation were being built in a formerly small and sleepy town, how could the local retailers use Engel's laws in planning for the influx of newcomers, first of construction crews and then scientists?

3 Name three specific examples (specific

products or brands—not just product categories) illustrating how demand will differ by geographic location *and* market location, that is, with respect to size and location inside or outside a metropolitan market.

4 Explain how the continuing mobility of consumers as well as the development of "interurbia" areas should affect marketing strategy planning in the future. Be sure to consider the impact on the four Ps.

5 Explain how the redistribution of income has affected marketing planning thus far and its likely impact in the future.

6 Explain why the concept of the Standard Metropolitan Statistical Areas was developed. Would it be the most useful breakdown for retailers?

7 With the growing homogeneity of the consumer market, does this mean that the market grid idea is less useful? Do you feel that all consumers of about equal income will probably spend their incomes similarly and demand similar products?

notes

[1] Replacement rate is defined as the number of births per woman at completion of the child-bearing years. "The Burgeoning Benefits of a Lower Birth Rate," *Business Week,* December 15, 1973, pp. 41–42; "The Surprising Decline in Birth Rate," *Business Week,* June 3, 1972, pp. 66–68; "Thinking Old," *Newsweek,* May 6, 1974, pp. 68–70; and J. D. Foust and A. D. Southwood, "The Population Fizzle," *Business Horizons,* February 1973, pp. 5–20.

[2] James E. Bell, Jr., "Mobiles—A Possible Segment for Retailer Cultivation," *Journal of Retailing,* Fall 1970, pp. 3–15; James E. Bell, Jr., "Mobiles—A Neglected Market Segment," *Journal of Marketing,* April 1969, pp. 37–44; James E. Bell, Jr., *Selection of New Suppliers by the Mobile Family* (Bureau of Business & Economic Research, Michigan State University, 1969), 101 pp.; Alan R. Andreasen, "Geographic Mobility and Market Segmentation," *Journal of Marketing Research,* November 1966, pp. 341–49.

[3] Martin Gainsbrugh, "The Consumer Market: The Coming Decade of Change," *4A Newsletter,* American Association of Advertising Agencies, April 29, 1970, p. 10; and "Who Has the Wealth in America," *Business Week,* August 5, 1972, pp. 54–56.

[4] For a fuller discussion of the growth of the mass market and the implication for marketing strategy planning, see Walter Gross, "Income Flow Diffusion and Marketing Strategies," *MSU Business Topics,* Autumn 1966, pp. 70–77.

[5] Thomas T. Semon, "Family Income and Spending Capacity," *Journal of Marketing,* April 1962, pp. 26–30.

[6] "Price of the Good Life Will Get Stiffer," *Business Week,* December 6, 1969, p. 197.

[7] Fabian Linden (ed.), *Expenditure Patterns of the American Family* (New York: National Industrial Conference Board, 1965).

[8] See Chapter 11.

[9] George W. Schiele, "How To Reach the Young Consumer," *Harvard Business Review,* March–April 1974,

pp. 77–86; "Retirees Live Better As Private Pensions, Social Security Rise," *The Wall Street Journal,* January 23, 1974, p. 1f; "New Life in Retirement Communities," *Business Week,* July 8, 1972, pp. 70–72; "The Power of the Aging in the Marketplace," *Business Week,* November 20, 1971, pp. 52–58; see also James U. McNeal, "The Child Consumer: A New Market," *Journal of Retailing,* Summer 1969, pp. 15–22; Paul Gilkison, "What Influences the Buying Decisions of Teen-agers?" *Journal of Retailing,* Fall 1965, p. 33; William H. Reynolds and James H. Myers, "Marketing and the American Family," *MSU Business Topics,* Spring 1966, pp. 57–66.

[10] See also, a basic study: Robert J. Lampman, *The Share of Top Wealth-Holders in National Wealth* (Princeton, N.J.: Princeton University Press, 1962).

[11] Marcus Alexis, "Some Negro-White Differences in Consumption," *American Journal of Economics and Sociology,* January 1962, pp. 11–28; K. K. Cox, J. E. Stafford, and J. B. Higginbotham, "Negro Retail Shopping and Credit Behavior," *Journal of Retailing,* Spring 1972, pp. 54–66; Gerald E. Hills, Donald H. Granbois, and James M. Patterson, "Black Consumer Perceptions of Food Store Attributes," *Journal of Marketing,* April 1973, pp. 47–57; Donald E. Sexton, Jr., "Black Buyer Behavior," *Journal of Marketing,* October 1972, pp. 36–39; and Thomas W. Whipple and Lester A. Neidell, "Black and White Perceptions of Competing Stores," *Journal of Retailing,* Winter 1971-2, pp. 5–20.

[12] "When Black Is Beautiful," *Business Week,* September 8, 1973, p. 51.

[13] *Marketing News,* American Marketing Association, September 15, 1973, p. 5.

[14] "Women Win More Credit," *Business Week,* January 12, 1974, pp. 76–78; and "More Moms on Payroll," *Business Week,* December 31, 1966, p. 59; *U.S. Department of Agriculture Food and Home Notes,* July 13, 1960; and Margaret S. Carroll, "The Working Wife and Her Family's Economic Position," *Monthly Labor Review,* April 1962, pp. 366–74.

8

Consumers: A behavioral science view

■ How can marketing management predict which of a given group of products will be purchased by consumers? In what quantities? Why does a consumer select a particular product?

Basic data on population, income, and consumer expenditure patterns in U.S. markets were presented in the last chapter. With such information, it is possible to predict basic trends in consumer expenditure patterns.

Unfortunately, when many firms sell similar products, this traditional demographic analysis is of relatively little value in predicting which *products* and *brands* will be purchased. Yet the question of whether its products and brands will be chosen, and to what extent, is extremely important to a firm.

The behavioral sciences help understand behavior

■ To find better answers, we need a better understanding of people. For this reason, many marketing analysts have turned to the behavioral sciences for insight and help. The approaches and thinking in psychology, sociology, and the other behavioral disciplines are the topic of this chapter.

Buying in a black box

■ A simplified way of summarizing the way various behavioral scientists understand consumer purchasing behavior is shown in Figure 8–1. Potential customers are subjected to various stimuli, including the marketing mixes of various competitors and an al-

Figure 8–1
Simplified buyer behavior model

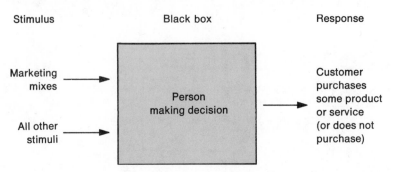

most infinite number of other potentially influencing factors. Somehow, an individual person internalizes some or all of these stimuli (he is the "black box" in Figure 8–1), and then he might purchase some product or service of interest to the researcher.

This is the classical *stimulus-response model* of buyer behavior and was the model we were implicitly using in the last chapter. There, we hoped to find some relationship between demographic characteristics (of customers in the black box), products (stimulus), and the customer's purchasing behavior (response). We did find some relationships, but now we want to go even deeper. This will require a better understanding of how the consumer decision-making process works.

There are many black boxes

■ Depending on a person's behavioral science training and the theories he subscribes to, we find many descriptions of how the black box works. These varying theories lead to different predictions about how consumers will react, so it helps considerably to have some feel for the various differences.

How the economist views the black box

■ The economist, for example, typically assumes that consumers are *economic men*, rationally evaluating alternatives in terms of cost and value received, in an effort to maximize their utility or satisfaction while spending their always scarce resources of time and money. Therefore, the economist collects and analyzes demographic data when trying to predict consumer behavior. It was a logical extension of the economic man theory which led us to look carefully at demographic characteristics in the last chapter. Certainly, there is validity to this model, since consumers must at least have income to be in the market. But other behavioral scientists suggest that the black box works in a more complicated way than postulated by the economic-man model.

The black box is multidimensional

■ In the balance of this chapter, we will briefly review behavioral science thinking, with a view to integrating it into one model to help the marketing manager find promising submarkets for which he will know what to offer, and when and where.

Figure 8–2
The individual decision maker (shown as a dot) is nestled in
an environment

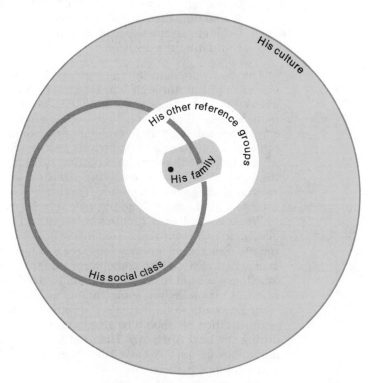

To help your perspective in the following discussion, Figure 8–2 is presented. Note that the individual consumer decision maker— shown by the dot in the center of the diagram—is surrounded by many other influencing factors. Presumably he has his own needs and motivations. These, in turn, may be influenced by his family, social class, other reference groups, and the culture in which he lives. No man is an island. Yet, ultimately, the individual makes decisions, so we must understand both how he solves his problems and how his environment affects him. Markets are made up of many individuals. We may think of them and appeal to them as a group, but in the final analysis, we must sell to them one by one.

Consumers are problem solvers

■ It is generally agreed by behavioral scientists that people are problem solvers; that individuals are motivated by drives or needs; that unsatisfied needs lead to tension and the desire to solve that problem. How the individual solves his problem depends on his own makeup and his environment. Nevertheless, given some needs, there does seem to be a basic problem-solving process.

The basic process consists of five steps:

1. Becoming aware of or interested in the problem.
2. Gathering information about possible solutions.
3. Evaluating alternative solutions, perhaps trying some out.
4. Deciding on the appropriate solution.
5. Evaluating the decision.[1]

Three levels of problem solving are useful

■ The basic problem-solving process indicates the steps a consumer might go through while trying to find a way to satisfy his needs, but it does not show how long he will take or how much thought he will give each step. Some individuals have had much experience solving certain problems and can move quickly through some of the steps or almost directly to a decision.

It is helpful, therefore, to recognize three levels of problem solving: *extensive problem solving, limited problem solving,* and *routinized response behavior.*[2] These problem-solving approaches might be used for any kind of product or service.

When a need or a product or service is completely new to a person, then he may turn to extensive problem solving. It may take time to understand a newly felt need and to perceive how it can be satisfied. A new college student, for example, may have feelings of loneliness, a need for companionship, a need for achievement, and so on. It may take him some time to get his bearings on how and what he wants to do. After some initial decision making and experimentation, he should be able to fulfill these needs more quickly during the next few years. His need for companionship, for example, might be quickly solved by meeting with friends in familiar surroundings. A daily trip to the local "hangout" might become a routine answer to these problems.

Problem solving is a learning process

■ The reason problem solving becomes simpler with time is that people learn from experience—both positive and negative things. As a person approaches the problem-solving process, he brings with him attitudes, shaped by previous experiences and social training. Each new problem-solving process may then contribute to or modify this attitude set.

Learning theorists have isolated a number of steps in the learning process. They see a *drive* as a strong stimulus that motivates the individual to some *response* in an effort to satisfy the drive. The specific response chosen depends on the *cues* existing in his environment and, of course, his previous attitudes.

Reinforcement of the process occurs when the response is followed by satisfaction, that is, a reduction in the drive tension. Reinforcement strengthens the relationship between the environmental cue and the response and may lead to a similar response the next time the drive occurs. Repeated reinforcement obviously would lead to the development of a habit, thereby making the decision process routine for the individual.

The learning process can be illustrated by a hungry person. The hunger drive could be satisfied by a McDonald's hamburger (response) if the person happened to be driving around and saw a McDonald's sign (cue) along the highway. If the experience were satisfactory, *reinforcement* would occur, and our friend might be quicker to satisfy this drive in the same way in the future. This also emphasizes the importance of developing good products which live up to the promises of the firm's advertising. Learning happens with negative experience also![3]

Adoption process is problem solving

■ Behavioral scientists especially interested in the process of accepting new ideas have identified the "adoption process," which explains how new ideas are learned and accepted. This process is similar to the problem-solving process, but makes clearer the role of learning and the potential contribution of promotion in a marketing mix.

The adoption process for individuals moves through some fairly definite stages, as follows:

1. Awareness – The potential customer comes to know about the product but lacks details. He may not even know how it works or what it will do.
2. Interest – *If* he becomes interested, he gathers general information and facts about the product.
3. Evaluation – He begins to make a mental trial, applying the product to his personal situation.
4. Trial – The customer may buy the product so that he can experiment with it in use. A product that is either too costly to try or cannot be obtained for trial may face severe difficulties in being adopted.
5. Decision – He decides on either adoption or rejection. A satisfactory evaluation and trial may lead to adoption of the product and regular use. According to psychological learning theory, reinforcement will lead to adoption.
6. Confirmation – The adopter continues to rethink his decision and searches for support for his decision – i.e., further reinforcement.

Selective processes facilitate problem solving

The searching that takes place during the awareness and interest stages may be facilitated by three selective processes. People seem to (1) seek out or read only some information sources (*selective exposure*), (2) screen out ideas, messages, and information not immediately relevant to solving their problems (*selective perception*), and (3) remember only what they want to remember (*selective retention*). This helps explain why some people are not at all affected by some advertising, even offensive advertising – they just don't "see it."

Riskiness may complicate decision making

The factor of risk also has a bearing. Trying a new candy bar does not involve much of a loss if it doesn't suit your taste. But trying a new car or clothing style involves a bigger risk, and a much more careful evaluation is called for.[4]

Dissonance may set in after the decision

After his decision has been made, a buyer may have second thoughts. He may have had to choose from among several attractive alternatives – weighing the pros and cons and finally making a decision. Subsequent doubts, however, may lead to "dissonance" – a form of tension arising out of uncertainty about the rightness of a decision. Dissonance may lead a buyer to search for additional information to confirm the wisdom of his decision and, thereby, reduce his tension. This points up the importance to the marketing manager of providing the information the consumer might seek at this stage. Without this confirmation, the adopter might buy something else next time and, further, would *not* give very positive comments to others.[5]

Several processes are related and relevant to strategy planning

■ The interrelation of the problem-solving process, the adoption process, and learning can be seen in Figure 8–3. It is important to see their interrelation and to note that they can be modified or accelerated by promotion. Also, note that the problem-solving behavior of a potential buyer would affect the design of distribution systems – if he is not willing to travel far to shop, then more facilities may be needed if you want his business. Similarly, his attitudes may help determine what price to charge. Clearly, a knowledge of how a target market handles these processes would facilitate marketing strategy planning.

The balance of this chapter will be concerned with some of the more important behavioral science structures and findings which affect the basic problem-solving process. Our starting point will be the individual – how he sees needs and products – and the impact others have on his decision making.

How a person sees his needs and products

Needs lead to wants and purchasing decisions

■ Everybody has certain *needs* and *wants*. Some needs are physiological, concerned with a person's physical body. Examples are needs for food, drink, sex, and shelter. Other needs are psychological or sociological or cultural – they are concerned with the individual's view of himself and his relationships to others. Wants are less basic; these are learned during the course of the individual's life.

When a need or a want is not satisfied, it leads to a *drive*. The food need, for instance, leads to a hunger drive. The drive state is one of tension in which the individual tries to find ways of satisfying his drive. Drives are, in effect, the reasons or motives underlying certain behavior patterns. Drive tensions lead to behavior that will satisfy the need or want and thereby reduce the drive tension.

Are needs learned?

■ Trying to separate learned from unlearned needs is not very useful and we will not try to do so here. But brief consideration of

Figure 8–3
Relation of problem-solving process, adoption process, and learning
(given a problem and drive tensions)

Problem-solving steps	Adoption process steps	Learning steps
1. Becoming aware of or interested in the problem.	Awareness and interest	
2. Gathering information about possible solutions.	Interest and evaluation	Cues ←– – – – – – – – – – ⌐
3. Evaluating alternative solutions, perhaps trying some out.	Evaluation, maybe trial	⏐ Reinforcement
4. Deciding on the appropriate solution.	Decision	↓ Response – – – – – – – – – →⌐
5. Evaluating the decision.	Confirmation	

the idea is desirable because some critics feel that marketing creates and warps many needs.

It might be argued that all *basic* needs are innate in humans. A small child develops strong desires for "things," certainly before advertisers have had a chance to influence him.

Even the need for status, which some marketing critics feel is related to the influence of advertising, is found among animals and in human societies where there is no such influence. Studies of birds show that there is a definite pecking order in flocks. In a study of jackdaws, for instance, it was found that the female, upon mating, acquires the status of her mate. In the human realm, African villagers raise domesticated cattle and goats purely as signs of wealth and social status. For food, they hunt wild animals.[6]

Liking hamburger is learned behavior
■ Some needs may be culturally (or socially) determined, however. When a human baby is born, his needs are simple. But as he grows, he learns various and complex behavior patterns to satisfy the drives stemming from these needs. As his needs become more sophisticated and specific, they can be described as wants. The need for food, for instance, may lead to many specific food wants, depending on the experience of the person. The resulting hunger drive may be satisfied only by the specific food desired. The people of Western nations like beef, and our children learn to like it. In

India, however, Hindus regard the cow as sacred and will not eat beef. Hindu children learn to eat and like other foods. Many foods, in other words, can satisfy the hunger drive—but in a particular culture, an individual might *want* a hamburger, and the hunger drive might not be fully satisfied until he has eaten one.

Are there hierarchies of motives?

■ Some schools of thought in psychology make distinctions between motives and drives. Others dismiss motives as far too simple an explanation of consumer behavior. Some feel that a person may have several motives for buying as he does, and they see that person attempting to develop a balance between the forces driving him.

Maslow saw a hierarchy

Still other psychologists portray motives in a hierarchy. Maslow, for example, proposed five levels of needs, in a diminishing order of "prepotency" for the individual:

1. Physiological needs (lowest, most prepotent level).
2. Safety needs.
3. Belongingness and love needs.
4. Esteem and status needs.
5. Self-actualization needs (highest, least prepotent level).

This concept sees consumers attempting to satisfy "lower" needs before "higher" needs, although they may be willing to satisfy the lower-level ones only partially before moving up to others. Food, for example, may have a high priority, but not all the consumer's expenditures will go for food. After an adequate supply of food has been assured, money may be allocated to satisfy progressively higher-level needs for housing, clothing, medical or beauty care, companionship, and education. But, clearly, one product might satisfy several needs at the same time in a modern society; food, for example, could be used to satisfy all five levels of need (assuming it is prepared in different ways and served in different settings).[7]

The many possible need dimensions presented in Chapter 6 (Table 6–2) would fit into this hierarchy. Some marketing organizations use checklists of needs which run to hundreds of motives. All of them, except the economic motives to be discussed below, would logically fit within this five-level framework and it is valuable to see the progression from basic physiological needs to higher-level needs.

Consumers may be more aware of some motives than others

■ Trying to determine the relevant need dimensions, either informally or through research, is complicated by the fact that consumers may not be willing to discuss, or even be aware of, the motives which drive them. At this point, it may be helpful to consider three *degrees of awareness* of motives on the part of consumers: *conscious, preconscious,* and *unconscious.*[8]

At the *conscious* level, the consumer is aware of his motivations and is willing to talk to others about them. At the *preconscious* level, however, he may be aware of the motives but would rather not discuss them with others; or perhaps he's not fully conscious why he behaves the way he does. A desire for status might be quite strong in an individual, but he might feel the need to rationalize a purchase in terms of its usefulness. Finally, at the *unconscious* level, a person is not even aware of what forces are driving him. A straightforward promotion appeal directed to such motives would not be effective.

Emotional motives drive many consumers

■ The motives discussed above are usually thought of as emotional, and they are important because we do make emotional decisions. Americans, perhaps because of their cultural heritage, are generally reluctant to admit this fact, preferring to rationalize their actions in terms of economic necessity or other practical factors they are willing to talk about at the conscious level. People in other countries, for example, the Latin nations, are much less concerned about economic or practical justifications.

Economic motives can be important too

■ In contrast to emotional motives, economic motives are primarily concerned with making the most effective use of the customer's limited resources. A product that is easier to use or which will last longer, at lower cost, clearly accomplishes this purpose. Eight categories are listed below:

1. Handiness.
2. Efficiency in operation or use.
3. Dependability in use.
4. Reliability of auxiliary service.
5. Durability.
6. Enhancement of earnings.
7. Enhancement of productivity of property.
8. Economy of purchase or use.

Here, more quantitative or specific appeals can be used – in contrast to the more subtle or descriptive appeals designed to reach emotional motives. Specific dollar savings, differences in weight, length of product life, and other such measurable factors can be emphasized.

Motives help market gridding, if they are relevant

■ A production-oriented businessman might feel that consumers should logically buy a particular product because it is the "best buy" economically. Based on economic considerations only, he could be right. But people have a wide range of different motives, and emotional motives may be stronger than economic ones in a particular case. This is implicit in the market grid concept, but it is important to note here that the same product may satisfy different motives and, therefore, become part of different mixes, aimed at different market grid boxes. And the relevant dimensions of these grid boxes may include both economic and emotional motives.

Imagination and creativity may be needed to see the interactions among economic and emotional motives and then to come up with an accurate description of each market grid box. This is a real challenge, but if done well it facilitates marketing mix planning and may even lead to a breakthrough opportunity.

Impact of others on personal buying behavior

■ So far we have been discussing insights which can be developed from psychology. Yet consumer behavior may be determined not only by a person's particular psyche and drives but also by his relations with others.

Social psychologists and sociologists see market behavior as a response to the attitudes and behavior of others. We will review this thinking in terms of the interaction of the individual with his family, social class, and reference groups.

Family considerations may overwhelm personal ones

■ Most decisions are made within a framework developed by experience within the family. An individual may go through much of the thinking discussed above when developing his own preferences for various products and services. But this analysis may be only one of the influences in the final decision. Social processes — such as power, domination, and affection — may be involved, too. This decision-making behavior is often the result of much social learning.

A boat for father or a TV for mother

The interaction of various social forces can be illustrated by a choice between two products — a television set and a boat with outboard motor.

The husband in a family might be particularly interested in the boat and motor for his camping and fishing trips. Weekend pleasure outings with the family would be only incidental. But in his arguments, he can present his preference in the desirable terms of *family wants and uses.* At the same time, his wife might prefer a new television set. It would enhance the beauty of her home and, secondarily, would be used as an entertainment medium for herself, her husband, and the children. She, too, could argue that this purchase is *for the family.*

The actual outcome in such a situation is unpredictable. It depends on the strength of the husband's and the wife's preferences; their individual degree of dominance of the family; who contributes the most money to the family's income; the need for affection; and the response of other family members.

Knowing how all these forces interact would be most helpful to the marketing manager. Unfortunately, each family behaves differently, and a marketing strategy usually has to deal with groups. Yet an individual retail salesman in direct contact with the family might sense how the family operates and be able to adjust his marketing mix, especially his sales presentation, accordingly.

Who is the real decision maker?

Although one person in the family often makes the purchase, in planning strategy it is important to find out who is the real decision maker.

Traditionally, the housewife has been considered the family

purchasing agent. She has normally been the one who had the time to shop and run the errands. As a result, most product promotion and advertising have been aimed at women. But the situation may be changing. As more women work, and as night shopping and Sunday shopping become more popular, the housewife may be playing a less dominant role as family buyer and decision maker. One study found that 80 percent of the wives check with their husbands on any purchase of $50 or more, and nearly half consult him on smaller purchases.

Men now have more time for, and interest in, shopping, and they may make decisions involving large purchases or buy products of special interest to them, such as beer, liquor, automobiles, tires, life insurance, air conditioners, electric shavers, shaving creams, and outboard motors.[9]

The nature of the decision makes a difference

Apparently the father is usually concerned with buying decisions that involve functional items. Of the two parents, he tends to be more concerned with matters external to the family. The mother is more likely to make those buying decisions that have expressive values, and she is more concerned with internal matters. These distinctions may apply even if the user of a purchased product is the other parent. For example, the wife may buy the husband's clothing accessories, while the husband might buy household appliances.

The husband and wife may work together where internal-functional or external-expressive matters are involved, because the husband-wife roles may overlap. Husbands and wives may share in home improvements, for example, because they involve both functional and internal matters.[10]

The question of spending by the family is not limited to mothers and fathers. As the life-cycle stages of the family change, the children begin to handle and spend more money.

In many cases, however, the person actually doing the shopping is merely acting as an agent for persons who may have specified which products should be bought. Small children may want specific kinds of cereals; the father may want a certain brand of cigarettes or golf balls.

Clearly, we still need greater understanding to see why different families come to widely different decisions when faced with a choice among many available products.

Social class affects buying of specifics

■ Up to now, we have been concerned with the individual and his relation to his family. Now let's consider how society looks at an individual and perhaps his family – in terms of social class.

The mere mention of class distinctions in the United States provokes a defensive reaction. We like to think of America as a land of equality. We have been brought up to revere the statement in the Declaration of Independence, "All men are created equal."

Our class system is far less pronounced than those in European and Asiatic nations where the system is tied to religion, blood kinship, or landed wealth. Nevertheless, sociological research bears out the contention that a class structure *does* exist in this country.

In discussing class structure, we will use the traditional technical terms, "upper," "middle," and "lower." But a word of warning is needed. The choice of these terms, even though in general use, is unfortunate, because they have a connotation of superior and inferior. In sociological and marketing usage, however, no value judgment is implied. In fact, it is not possible to state that a particular class is "better" or "happier" than any other.

Some people strive to enter a "higher" class because they find the values of that class more admirable; others are comfortable with the standards of their own group and prefer to remain where they are.

The marketing man's goal should be learning the characteristics and typical behavior patterns of each class so that he will be better able to develop unique marketing strategies involving class differences.

Characteristics of U.S. class system

The U.S. class system is an individual and a family system. While a child is a member of a family, his social status will probably depend on the status of his family. But grown children often "join" a different class than their parents. This is especially the case when they attain higher educational levels or take up different occupations from those of their parents.

The U.S. class system is related to several dimensions: income, occupation, and housing arrangements. The early work on social class in the United States was done by Lloyd Warner, a social psychologist, who developed a class system for cities in the 10,000–25,000 population range.

Later, the *Chicago Tribune,* under the guidance of Warner, developed a population breakdown for metropolitan Chicago, which is probably typical of a big industrial city. Many of the findings are interesting to marketing managers. Let us look at the *Chicago Tribune's* five-class breakdowns first and then consider some of the findings.

1. *Upper Class* (0.9 percent of population). This was defined as old families (upper-upper class) and the socially prominent new rich (lower-upper class). This group has been the traditional leader in the American community. Most large manufacturers, bankers, and top marketing executives belong to it. It represents, however, less than 1 percent of the population. Being so small, the two upper classes were merged into one in this study. In some of the *Chicago Tribune* studies, these two classes are broken out separately, and a six-class breakdown is used.

2. *Upper-Middle Class* (7.2 percent of population). These are the successful businessmen, professionals and top salesmen. The advertising professional usually is part of this class, reflecting the tastes and codes of the first two groups. Yet,

combined, groups 1 and 2 still represent only 8.1 percent of the population.

3. *Lower-Middle Class* (28.4 percent of population). These are the white-collar workers – small tradesmen, office workers, teachers, technicians, most salesmen. The American moral code and the emphasis on hard work has come from this class. This is the most conforming, churchgoing, morally serious segment of society. We speak of America as a middle-class society, but the middle-class value system stops here. Two thirds of our society is *not* middle-class.

4. *Upper-Lower Class* (44.0 percent of population). These are the factory production workers, the union labor groups, the skilled workers, the service workers, and the local politicians and union leaders who would lose their power if they moved out of this class.

5. *Lower-Lower Class* (19.5 percent of population). This group includes unskilled laborers, racial immigrants, and people in nonrespectable occupations.[11]

What do these classes mean?

The *Chicago Tribune* class studies suggest that an old economic maxim, "A rich man is simply a poor man with more money," may not hold true. While Engel's laws may still apply in general, it appears that a person belonging to the lower class, given the same income as a middle-class individual, handles himself and his money very differently. The various classes patronize different stores, would prefer different treatment from salesmen, buy different brands of products (even though their prices are approximately the same), and have different spending-saving attitudes. Some of these differences are summarized in Table 8–1.

The marketing implications of this and other studies are most interesting. Selection of media in advertising should be related to social class, for example. Customers in the lower classes would have little interest in *Fortune, Holiday, Vogue,* or *Ladies Home Journal,* while the middle and upper classes probably would have little desire to read *True Story.*

Class differences also have a bearing on product design, and the assortment carried by retailers. In a study[12] on lamps and furniture, for example, the lower-class half of the market selected completely different styles than did the top half. This lower group did not want the severely plain, functional styling of furniture preferred by the higher classes. Instead, they preferred overstuffed and ornate furnishings (sometimes called "borax" goods).

Once marketing men are aware of these differences, they can adjust their mixes. Understanding that lower classes are concerned about the present, for example, stores aiming at these classes frequently emphasize credit sales so that target consumers can satisfy their needs *now*. In such stores – such as credit jewelers and credit furniture stores – it is often difficult even to determine the total price of a product. Salesmen talk about the small down payment

Table 8–1
A comparison of attitudes and characteristics for two social classes

Middle class	Lower class
1. Pointed to the future.	1. Pointed to the present and past.
2. His viewpoint embraces a long expanse of time.	2. Lives and thinks in a short expanse of time.
3. More urban identification.	3. More rural identification.
4. Stresses rationality.	4. Nonrational essentially.
5. Has a well-structured sense of the universe.	5. Vague and unclear structuring.
6. Horizons vastly extended or not limited.	6. Horizons sharply defined and limited.
7. Greater sense of choice making.	7. Limited sense of choice making.
8. Self-confident, willing to take risks.	8. Very much concerned with security and insecurity.
9. Immaterial and abstract in his thinking (idea-minded).	9. Concrete and perceptive in his thinking (thing-minded).
10. Sees himself tied to national happenings.	10. World revolves around his family.

Source: P. Martineau, "The Pattern of Social Classes," in R. L. Clewett (ed.), *Marketing's Race in Scientific Management* (Chicago: American Marketing Association, 1957), pp. 246–47.

and easy monthly payments with little mention of the number of such payments.

The lower classes seem to be confused by variety and apparently have difficulty in making choices. As a result, such buyers look on furniture salesmen, for example, as friends and advisers. The middle-class buyers are much more self-confident in contrast. They know what they want and prefer a furniture salesman to be an impersonal guide.[13]

From this review, it is obvious that social class cannot be ignored when analyzing market grids and developing marketing strategy.[14] Fortunately, it appears that some fairly objective and readily available data can be used for determining social class and estimating market sizes.[15] In particular, U.S. Census measures of occupation, education, and expenditures on housing may be of service.

Reference groups have relevance too

■ A reference group is composed of people whom the individual looks to when forming his opinions, attitudes, and beliefs. A person normally has several reference groups for various subjects. Some he meets face-to-face, while others he may just aspire to emulate. In either case, he may take his values from "them" and make purchasing decisions based on what he feels they would accept. *Playboy* magazine, for instance, and the "in" people who presumably read it, might be a reference group for *Playboy* readers.

The importance of reference groups depends somewhat on the nature of the product and on whether anyone else will be able to

Figure 8–4
Reference-group influence

Brand type \ Product class	Weak	Strong
Weak	Canned peaches Laundry soap Refrigerator (brand) Radios	Air conditioners* Instant coffee* TV (black and white)
Strong	Clothing Furniture Magazines Refrigerator (type) Toilet soap	Cars* Cigarettes* Beer (premium versus regular)* Drugs*

* Classification by the extent to which reference groups influence their purchase based on actual experimental evidence. Other products listed are classified speculatively on the basis of generalizations derived from the sum of research in this area and confirmed by the judgment of seminar participants.
Source: Bureau of Applied Social Research, Columbia University.

"see" which product and which brand is being used. Figure 8–4 suggests the interrelations here. For example, an individual may smoke cigarettes because his reference group smokes, and the group's preference may even determine the brand he chooses. At the other extreme, most people in our society use laundry soap, and which brand is not readily determinable. In this case, reference group influence may be negligible.

Inner versus other directed man

The reference-group concept has grown in importance in recent years as more people live and work together in today's larger organizations. The "organization man" seems to be especially responsive to group pressures and puts "getting along" with the group above other values.

This group consciousness has been described by Riesman as a sign of the transition from the "inner-directed" man to the "other-directed" man. The inner-directed man has his own value system and directs his own activities, whereas the other-directed person is the one whose character is formed chiefly by those around him. Other-directed people—a large proportion of our society according to Riesman—are led by each other, and consequently there is a strong tendency to conform.[16]

Reaching the opinion leaders who are buyers

■ A trend toward other-directedness could have a profound effect on marketing through its effect on the way individuals and groups change their values and desires. Advertising, and promotion in general, might have to be more concerned with affecting opinion leaders.[17] We will say more about affecting the "web-of-word-of-mouth" from opinion leaders to others when we talk about promotion planning in Chapter 20.

In this drive for conformity, some people are more effective than others as "opinion leaders" or "communicators." It is important to note that these communicators are not restricted to the higher-income people or the better educated. Rather, they are spread throughout all levels of society in varying proportions. Communicators on one subject are not necessarily communicators on another.

Housewives with larger families may be consulted for advice on cooking, while young girls may be leaders in new clothing styles and cosmetics. And all of this may take place within the various social classes, with different opinion leaders in the various classes.[18]

Integrating the behavioral science approaches

■ We have been examining various approaches to explaining why individuals and families buy as they do. Hopefully, the decision processes within the consumer's "black box" are somewhat clearer. But we also have to acknowledge that the behavioral sciences have not answered all of the questions. It would be most desirable to have an integrating framework to relate the various influences on buying behavior and the theories about these influences. Unfortunately, we do *not* have such a framework. As of now, after the marketing manager has reviewed all of the behavioral data, he still has to rely on his own intuition and marketing research to help him estimate expected behavior in various market grid boxes.

Some integrating theories have been presented, however, and to try to tie all of this together we will discuss a recent effort which forces us to think beyond the typical stereotypes (or our own misconceptions) about consumer behavior. This model does not provide answers, but it presents a comprehensive view of what is happening in the black box.

Howard-Sheth model of buyer behavior

■ Figure 8–5 presents the Howard-Sheth theory of buyer behavior, with its many interactions. This is basically an elaboration of the stimulus (black box) response model introduced in the beginning of the chapter.

On the left side of the diagram, we see the input or stimulus variables. The *significative stimuli* include the *physical* aspects of the firm's and competitors' marketing mixes, including the quality and price of the products, service offered, and availability of the product or service. The *symbolic stimuli* include the image-making information about the significative stimuli, for example, the written or pictorial material available on packages or in advertising. Finally, the *social stimuli* include all information which a potential buyer would get from his family, reference groups and social class.

All of these stimuli then enter into the consumer's black box for processing. This is shown in Figure 8–5 as entering into the perceptual subsystem. How this information is processed, however, depends upon how much attention is given to these particular stimuli

Figure 8–5
A simplified description of the Howard-Sheth theory of buyer behavior

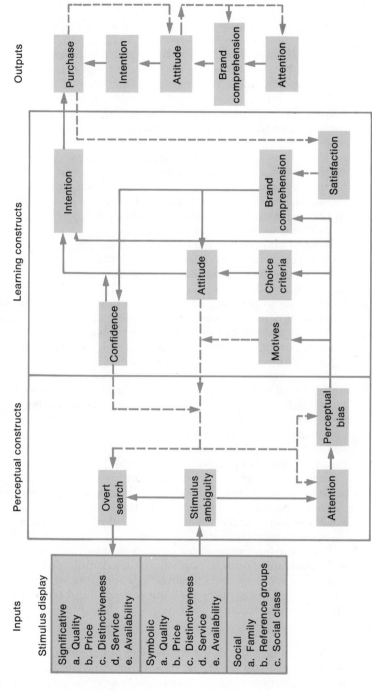

Source: John A. Howard and J. N. Sheth. *The Theory of Buyer Behavior.* (New York: John Wiley & Sons, Inc., 1969) p. 30.

by the consumer, how clear the stimuli are, and the perceptual bias which is used by the individual in translating them.

The information, if any, which passes through the perceptual subsystem would then be processed by the learning subsystem. Here the individual's motives, his methods of making choices, attitudes, brand comprehension, confidence about making decisions, and intentions with regard to purchasing, all interact with his satisfaction, if any, with previous experiences of the type being evaluated.

The output of all of this information processing might be a purchase, shown at the right-hand side of the diagram. And depending on the satisfaction with this purchase, the buyer's intentions, attitudes, brand comprehension, and attention may be modified and in turn affect subsequent decision making.

Can aid marketing strategy planning

Such a framework is useful for estimating what form of problem-solving target customers are likely to use.

Extensive problem solving may be necessary if the information in a number of the boxes is inadequate and the consumer must develop such information on his own in order to make his decision. Routine buying behavior, on the other hand, could result if the consumer were quite familiar with the incoming stimuli, perceived them accurately (at least in his mind), and had already learned that a particular product would be very satisfactory.

Such a framework is also useful for the marketing manager— helping him to focus on what he does and does not know about his target customers' decision making. He may be willing to assume some things, while others will require some marketing research.

The model also indicates where his marketing plans might have some impact. If there is perceptual bias, for example, a promotional effort could be developed to clarify the information entering the buyer's "black box." Or if there is confusion about choice criteria, personal selling efforts could help potential customers evaluate various offerings. Or if the product's physical characteristics are not what the buyer perceives them to be, promotional effort could be directed to correcting this situation.

Can aid understanding of new research findings

Finally, this framework gives the marketing manager a chance to handle new research findings in a meaningful way. Instead of just saying, "Well, that's very interesting" (and wondering how it all fits), he can organize and classify his thoughts within this framework.[19]

Intuition and judgment still needed for marketing planning

■ The present state of our knowledge about consumer behavior is such that we still must rely on intuition and judgment to develop useful descriptions of the "whys" of consumer behavior in various market grid boxes. Demographic characteristics help some. Behavioral theories provide insights too, and new multi-dimensional research approaches, called *psychographics*, which try to capture the whole of a person's or market's "life-style" may be helpful.[20]

But, finally, the marketing manager will have to mix in a dash of his own intuition and judgment to isolate homogeneous groups of potential customers. And, as we discussed in Chapters 4 and 6, if he is able to invert "shorthand" names which capture the essence of the determining characteristics of each of his potential target markets (e.g., swingers, cost-conscious-couples, and so on) he will have taken a giant step forward in marketing strategy planning.

Conclusion

■ In this chapter we have analyzed the individual consumer, the consumer operating in a group, and the way individuals and groups view products. We have stressed that consumers are problem solvers, but that individual consumers behave very differently, sometimes motivated by economic and sometimes by emotional considerations, and often by a combination of the two. To assume that everyone behaves the way we do – or even the way our friends or families do – may lead to grave marketing errors.

Consumer buying behavior is the expression of the consumer's efforts to satisfy his needs and wants. We discussed some motives that suggest why consumers buy, but saw that consumer behavior cannot be explained only by a list of motives.

We also saw that our society is characterized by social classes, which does help explain some consumer behavior. Fortunately, it is possible to develop some estimates of the size of social classes, using readily available data on education, occupation, and housing expenditures. The impact of reference groups was discussed too.

A framework was presented in this chapter to help the student interpret and integrate the present findings and any new data he might obtain from marketing research. As of now, the behavioral sciences can only offer insights and theories which the marketing manager must blend with his own intuition and judgment in developing his marketing strategies.

Marketing research may have to be used to answer specific questions. But if neither the money nor the time is available for research, then management will have to rely on the available description of present behavior and "guesstimates" about future behavior. You should study the popular magazines and the nation's leading newspapers carefully, for these publications often mirror the public's shifting preferences. You also should be familiar with the many studies concerning the changing consumer that are published regularly in the business and trade press. This material, added and related to the information in these last several chapters, will aid your own decision making.

Remember that the consumer, with all his likes and preferences, may be elusive – but not invisible. We have more data and understanding of consumer behavior than is generally used by businessmen.

questions and problems

1 What is the behavioral science concept which underlies the "black-box" model of consumer behavior? Does this concept have operational relevance to the marketing manager, i.e., if it is a valid concept, can he make use of it?

2 Illustrate the three levels of problem solving with an example from your own personal experience.

3 Cut out two recent advertisements: one full-page color ad from a magazine and one large display from a newspaper. Indicate which needs or motives are being appealed to in each case.

4 How do society's values have an impact on purchasing behavior? Give two specific examples.

5 How should the social class structure affect the planning of a new restaurant in a large city? How might the four Ps be adjusted?

6 What social class would you associate with each of the following phrases or items?
a. Sport cars.
b. *True Story, True Romances,* etc.
c. *New Yorker.*
d. *Playboy.*
e. Women watching "soap operas."
f. TV bowling shows.
g. Families that serve martinis, especially before dinner.
h. Families who dress formally for dinner regularly.
i. Families which are distrustful of banks (keep money in socks or mattress).
j. Owners of French poodles.
In each case, choose one class, if you can. If you are not able to choose one class, but rather feel that several classes are equally likely, then so indicate. In those cases where you feel that all classes would be equally interested or characterized by a particular item, choose all five classes.

7 Illustrate how the reference-group concept may apply in practice, by explaining how you personally are influenced by some reference group for some product. What are the implications of such behavior for marketing managers?

8 What new status symbols are replacing the piano and automobile? Do these products have any characteristics in common? If they do, what are some possible status symbols of the future?

9 On the basis of the data and analysis presented in Chapters 7 and 8, what kind of buying behavior would you expect to find for the following products: (1) canned peas, (2) toothpaste, (3) ball-point pens, (4) baseball gloves, (5) sport coats, (6) dishwashers, (7) encyclopedias, (8) automobiles, and (9) motorboats? Set up a grid for your answer with products along the left-hand margin as the row headings and the following factors as headings for the columns: (1) how do you think consumers would shop for these products, (2) how far would they go, (3) would they buy by brand, (4) would they wish to compare with other products, and (5) any other factors which they should consider. Insert short answers—words or phrases are satisfactory—in the various grid boxes. Be prepared to discuss how the answers you put in the grid boxes would affect each product's marketing mix.

notes

[1] Adapted from James H. Myers and William H. Reynolds, *Consumer Behavior and Marketing Management* (Boston: Houghton Mifflin Co., 1967), p. 49.

[2] John A. Howard and Jagdish N. Sheth, *The Theory of Buyer Behavior* (New York: John Wiley & Sons, Inc., 1969), pp. 46–48.

[3] Gerald Zaltman, *Marketing: Contributions from the Behavioral Sciences* (New York: Harcourt Brace & World, Inc., 1965), pp. 20–21; and Peter D. Bennett and Robert M. Mandell, "Prepurchase Information Seeking Behavior of New Car Purchasers—The Learning Hypothesis," *Journal of Marketing Research,* November 1969, pp. 430–33.

[4] James W. Taylor, "The Role of Risk in Consumer Behavior," *Journal of Marketing,* April 1974, pp. 54–60.

[5] For further discussion on perception and dissonance see Myers and Reynolds, *Consumer Behavior and Marketing Management;* J. R. B. Ritchie, "An Exploratory Analysis of the Nature and Extent of Individual Differences in Perception," *Journal of Marketing Research,* February 1974, pp. 41–49; and James F. Engel, David T. Kollat, and Roger D. Blackwell, *Consumer Behavior* (New York: Holt, Rinehart & Winston, Inc., 1968).

[6] Robert Ardrey, *African Genesis* (New York: Antheum Publishers, 1961), Chapter 4.

[7] A. H. Maslow, *Motivation and Personality* (New York: Harper & Bros., 1954); John McFall, "Priority Patterns and Consumer Behavior," *Journal of Marketing,* October 1969, pp. 50–55, for an extension of this concept to the order in which consumers buy appliances.

[8] G. H. Smith, *Motivation Research in Advertising and Marketing* (New York: McGraw Hill Book Co., 1954), pp. 19–21.

[9] *Male vs. Female Influence on Purchase of Selected Products, an Exploratory Depth Interview Study with Husbands and Wives* (New York: Fawcett Publications, Inc., 1958), p. 6; and "Liquor Store Survey Uncorks Potent Data: Two-Fifths of the Customers Are Women," *Business Week,* May 13, 1967, p. 187.

[10] W. H. Reynolds and James H. Myers, "Marketing and the American Family," *Business Topics,* Spring 1966, pp. 58–59; see also: R. Ferber and L. C. Lee, "Husband-Wife Influence in Family Purchasing Behavior," pp. 43–50, and H. Davis and B. P. Rigaux, "Perception of Marital Roles in Decision Processes," pp. 51–62, *Consumer Research,* June 1974.

[11] Adapted from Pierre Martineau, *Motivation in Advertising* (New York: McGraw-Hill Book Co., 1957), p. 164.

[12] Martineau, *Motivation in Advertising,* p. 168; See also, Richard P. Coleman, "The Significance of Social Stratification in Selling," in Martin L. Bell (ed.), *Marketing: A Maturing Discipline* (Chicago: American Marketing Association, 1961), pp. 171–84.

[13] *Advertising Age,* February 22, 1960, p. 63.

[14] For more discussion on this, see Joseph N. Fry and Frederick H. Siller, "A Comparison of Housewife Decision Making in Two Social Classes," *Journal of Marketing Research,* August 1970, pp. 333–37. See also James H. Myers and John F. Mount, "More on Social Class Versus Income as Correlates of Buying Behavior," *Journal of Marketing,* April 1973, pp. 71–73.

[15] James A. Carman, *The Application of Social Class in Market Segmentation* (Berkeley, Calif.: Institute of Business and Economic Research, University of California, 1965). See also, William H. Peters, "Relative Occupational Class Income: A Significant Variable in the Marketing of Automobiles," *Journal of Marketing,* April, 1970, pp. 74–78.

[16] David Riesman, N. Glaser, and R. Denney, *The Lonely Crowd* (Garden City, N.Y.: Doubleday & Co., Inc., 1950). For additional discussion on reference groups, see James H. Donnelly, Jr., "Social Character and Acceptance of New Products," *Journal of Marketing Research,* February 1970, pp. 111–116.

[17] Harold H. Kassarjian, "Social Character and Differential Preference for Mass Communication," *Journal of Marketing Research,* May 1965, pp. 146–53; and James H. Myers and Thomas S. Robertson, "Dimensions of Opinion Leadership," *Journal of Marketing Research,* February 1972, pp. 41–46.

[18] Carman, *The Application of Social Class,* pp. 21 and 61; Elihu Katz and Paul E. Lazarsfeld, *Personal Influences* (Glencoe, Ill.: Free Press, 1955); see also John O. Summers, "The Identity of Women's Clothing Fashion Opinion Leaders," *Journal of Marketing Research,* May 1970, pp. 178–86; and Charles W. King and John O. Summers, "Over-lap of Opinion Leadership Across Consumer Product Categories." *Journal of Marketing Research,* February 1970, pp. 43–50.

[19] For a fuller discussion of the Howard-Sheth model, see John U. Farley, John A. Howard, and L. Winston Ring, *Consumer Behavior—Theory and Application* (Rockleigh, N.J.: Allyn and Bacon, Inc., 1974); also John U. Farley and L. Winston Ring, "An Empirical Test of the Howard-Sheth Model of Buyer Behavior," *Journal of Marketing Research,* November 1970, pp. 427–438.

[20] Joseph T. Plummer, "The Concept and Application of Life Style Segmentation," *Journal of Marketing,* January 1974, pp. 33–37; Thomas P. Husted and Edgar A. Pessemier, "Industry's Use of Life Style Analysis: Segmenting Consumer Market with Activity and Attitude Measures," in *American Marketing Association Combined Conference Proceedings,* Spring & Fall 1971—Series No. 33; and William D. Wells (ed) *Life Style and Psychographics* (Chicago: American Marketing Assn., 1974).

Intermediate customers and their buying behavior

■ The term *customer* is interpreted by most of us to mean the individual final consumer (or family). Yet most ultimate consumers probably would be startled to find that the bulk of purchases are made, not by them, but by intermediate customers.

This chapter will be devoted to these intermediate customers — who and where they are, and what their buying habits are. There are misconceptions about the nature and size of these "other" markets. In fact, there are great marketing opportunities in serving intermediate customers, and it is quite probable that a college-level student will eventually work in this area.

We want to show that the market grid concept may have even greater application here because of the great diversity of demand and types of intermediate customers. While we will limit our discussion to the United States to keep it specific, many of the ideas are applicable to the world market.

Market gridding for intermediate customers

■ In our macro-marketing system, there are many kinds of intermediate customers between producers of basic raw materials and final consumers. The various types and their numerical importance are shown in Table 9–1. There are only about 12 million intermediate customers in the United States, compared to over 200 million final consumers. These customers do a wide variety of jobs and many different market grid dimensions would be needed to describe all of these different markets.

Table 9–1
Kind and number of intermediate customers in 1970

Agriculture, forestry, and fisheries	3,179,000
Service industries	2,964,000
Retailers	2,210,000
Contract construction	875,000
Wholesalers	470,000
Manufacturers	409,000
Governmental units	78,000
Others	1,751,000

Source: *Statistical Abstract of the United States*, 1970, pp. 405 and 468 and 1973, pp. 412 and 471.

We know much less about segmenting markets in these areas. However, there are some similarities in buying behavior, and we will focus on some of these in this chapter. As shown in Figure 9–1, a first step in gridding in this area is to determine the kind, size, and location of potential intermediate customers. Then, some of the variations caused by differences among buyers and the buying situation will provide other bases for segmentation.

Although manufacturers are not the most numerous intermediate customers, they will be the primary focus in this chapter because we know the most about their behavior. Besides, it appears that others behave similarly, especially with respect to the way they buy plant and equipment.

We will also discuss the way retailers and wholesalers buy the goods they plan to sell, because some new concepts are relevant here. And we will treat the farm market and the government market because they are so large and also they differ from the other markets in some important respects.

The important point to remember as we begin our discussion of intermediate customers is that we are interested in finding the relevant dimensions of these markets. Market gridding is not well developed in this area, but we do know that some firms have had great success with strategies based on the relevant dimensions. Competition is extremely rugged in some intermediate markets, and even "trivial" differences may be determining. Further, intermediate customers typically are approached directly by a salesman, so there is a greater opportunity to adjust the marketing mix for each individual customer. This makes studying the nature of the buyer and the individual buying situation even more important. In other words, in these markets it is possible that every individual customer should be thought of as the basis for an individual marketing strategy. The basic product offered, and perhaps the price, may be the same, but other services and promotion might be tailored to the needs of each individual customer.

Figure 9–1
Bases for gridding for intermediate customers

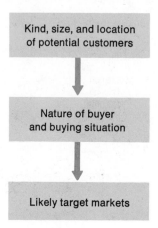

Manufacturers are important customers

There are not many big ones

■ One of the most striking facts about manufacturers is how few of them there are compared to final consumers. In the industrial market, there were about 306,000 factories in 1967 and the majority of these are quite small, as indicated in Table 9–2. The owners may also be the buyers in the small plants, and they will approach the buying process much more informally than in the relatively few large manufacturing plants which employ the majority of workers, and produce a substantial share of the value added by manufacturing. In 1967, plants with 250 or more employees numbered only 13,512–4.3 percent of the total, yet they employed 60 percent of the production employees and produced 65 percent of value added by manufacture. Clearly, these large plants represent an important market, and it may be desirable to segment potential customers on the basis of size.

Customers cluster in geographic areas

■ In addition to concentration by size, industrial markets are characterized by concentration in particular geographic areas—both regions and cities. The Middle West, Middle Atlantic states, and California are important industrial markets. Beyond this, the big metropolitan areas are also big industrial markets.

The buyers for some of these larger manufacturers are even further concentrated in home offices which often are located in the large metropolitan areas. One of the large building material manufacturers, for example, does the bulk of its buying for more than 50 plants from its Chicago office. In such a case, a salesman may be able to sell his products all over the country without leaving his home city. But, this makes it not only easier for the salesman, but also for his competitors, and he may have to compete in an ex-

Table 9–2
Size distribution of manufacturing establishments, 1967

Size in terms of number of employees	Number of establishments	Value added by manufacturing (millions dollars)	Total number of employees (1,000)	Percentage of firms	Percentage of value added	Percentage of employees
1–4	117,514	2,756	197	38.5	1.1	1.1
5–9	39,349	3,349	265	12.9	1.3	1.5
10–19	41,678	7,166	581	13.7	2.8	3.2
20–49	48,942	18,250	1,536	16.0	6.9	8.3
50–99	24,923	20,888	1,740	8.2	8.0	9.4
100–249	19,762	38,922	3,069	6.4	14.9	16.5
250–499	7,749	36,268	2,681	2.5	13.8	14.5
500–999	3,450	34,768	2,361	1.1	13.2	12.8
1000–2499	1,639	39,171	2,433	0.5	15.0	13.1
2500 or over	674	60,446	3,629	0.2	23.0	19.6

Source: *1967 Census of Manufactures.*

tremely competitive market. The importance of these big buyers has led some companies to set up "national account" sales forces which are specially trained to cater to their needs. A geographically-bound salesman can be at a real disadvantage against such competitors.

Concentration by industry

■ Not only do we see concentration by size of firm and geographical location, but also by industry. Manufacturers of advanced electronics systems are concentrated in the Boston and New York areas and on the West Coast, for example. The steel industry is heavily concentrated in the Pittsburgh, Birmingham (Alabama), and Chicago areas. Other industries have similar concentrations based on the availability of natural or human resources.

Much data is available on industrial markets by SIC code

■ It should be clear that in industrial markets, marketing managers can focus their attention on a relatively few clearly defined markets and be within reach of the majority of the business. Their efforts can be aided by the availability of very detailed information. The federal government regularly collects data on the number of establishments, their sales volumes, and number of employees of a large number of industry groups, broken down by county and SMSA. The data is reported for Standard Industrial Classification code industries (SIC codes). These codes greatly facilitate research by firms who can relate their own sales to their *customers'* type of activity. SIC code breakdowns start with such broad industry categories as food and kindred products (code 20), tobacco products (code 21), textile mill products (code 22), apparel (code 23), and so on.

Within each two-digit industry breakdown, much more detailed data may be available for three-digit and four-digit industries (that is, subindustries of the two- or three-digit industries). Within the apparel (23) industry, for example, the three-digit industry 232—men's, youths', and boys' furnishings, work clothing and allied garments—contains the following four-digit industries: shirts, collars, and night wear (2321), underwear (2322), neckwear (2323), separate trousers (2327), work clothing (2328), and NEC (not elsewhere classified) (2329).

Four-digit detail is not available for all industries in every geographic area, of course, because industries do tend to concentrate. But, the point is that a lot of good basic information is available. If companies aiming at industrial target markets can specify clearly who they are aiming at, readily available data organized by SIC codes may be extremely valuable. Besides the federal government, most trade associations and private organizations which gather data in the industrial area do so according to SIC code.[1]

It should be obvious that SIC code breakdowns may be an important dimension in market gridding for the industrial market. At the very least, SIC codes and geographic dimensions could serve as a starting point in gridding. Then, behavioral dimensions might have to be added as more is learned about each market segment.

Industrial buyers are problem solvers

■ Some people think of industrial buying as something entirely separate from consumer buying, but a deeper analysis of buying processes suggests that there may be more similarities than was once thought. In fact, it appears that the basic problem-solving framework which was introduced in Chapter 8 can be applied here. Similarly, the Howard-Sheth model may have general applicability.

Three kinds of buying processes are useful

■ In Chapter 8 we discussed three kinds of buying by consumers: extended, limited, and routine buying. In industrial markets, it is useful to adapt these concepts slightly and work with three similar buying processes; a *new-task buying* process, a *modified rebuy* process, or a *straight rebuy*.[2]

New-task buying

New-task buying would occur when a firm has a new need. In this case, it must develop a great deal of information, and perhaps even set up the criteria for selection. New-task buying can be quite important because it establishes product specifications, sources of supply, and an order routine which can be followed in the future if satisfactory results are obtained.

Modified rebuy buying

The *modified rebuy* is the in-between process where some additional analysis or rethinking of the buying situation is done, but not nearly as much effort is involved as in the new-task situation. Since buyers may want additional information, an alert marketer would provide it.

Straight rebuy buying

A *straight rebuy* is a routine purchase which may have been made many times before. Buyers probably would not bother looking for new information or even new sources of supply. The majority of a company's purchases might be this type, but they would occupy a relatively small amount of the buyer's time if he is well organized.

The fact that the identical product or service might be considered in any of the three ways cannot be overemphasized. It points up the importance of careful market grid analysis to determine how the firm's products are accepted, and by whom. A new-task buy will take much longer than a straight rebuy and provide considerably more chance for promotional impact by the seller. This can be seen in Figure 9–2, which shows the time and the many influences involved in the purchase of a special drill.

Industrial buyers are becoming specialists

■ The large size of some manufacturers has made the buying function extremely important. Many have developed buying specialists, known as purchasing agents. Some of these have banded together, forming the National Association of Purchasing Agents in an effort to improve the effectiveness and status of professional buyers. This is the knowledgeable modern-day buyer who confronts those who wish to sell to the industrial market.

The industrial buyer, or purchasing agent, usually is the man all salesmen must see first before contacting any other employee. The buyer holds an important position and may take a dim view of salesmen who attempt to bypass him. In large companies, he may even specialize by product area and be quite expert.

Some purchasing agents have expanded their job concept to include an analysis of whether the products requisitioned should be purchased at all, or if they are the most suitable for the job. This broader approach, called *value analysis,* requires that the purchasing agent become involved with areas outside his own department, including engineering and manufacturing.

Rather than being "sold," these buyers expect precise and accurate information that will help them buy wisely. They like information on new products and services and tips on potential price changes, strikes, and other changes in business conditions. Most industrial buyers are serious, well-educated men, and salesmen should treat them accordingly.

Basic purchasing motives are economic

■ Industrial buyers are usually less emotional in their buying habits than final consumers.

Specifically, buyers tend to look for certain product characteristics, including economy, both in original cost and in use, productivity, uniformity, purity, and ability to make the buyer's final product more suitable.

In addition to product characteristics, buyers consider the

Figure 9–2
Decision network diagram of the buying situations: Special drill

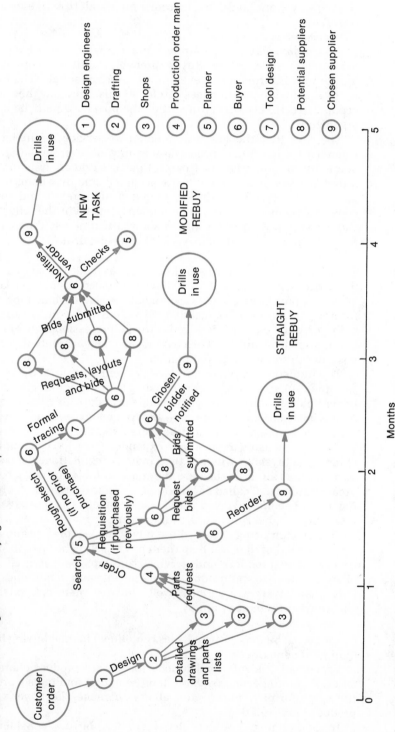

Source: Patrick J. Robinson and Charles W. Faris. *Industrial Buying and Creative Marketing* (Boston: Allyn & Bacon, Inc., 1967), p. 33. Reprinted by permission of the publisher.

reliability of the seller, his general cooperativeness, his ability to provide speedy maintenance and repair, past and present relationships (including previous favors), continuous supply under all conditions, and reliable fast delivery.

Emotional motives are relevant, too

■ Industrial purchasing does have some emotional overtones, however. Modern buyers are human, and they want to have friendly relationships with suppliers. Some buyers seem eager to emulate progressive competitors, or even to be the first to try new products. Such "innovators" might deserve special attention when new products or concepts are being introduced.

Buyers are also human with respect to protecting their own interests, and their own position in the company. Most buyers, like people everywhere, seek to survive and improve their chances for promotion, without taking too many risks.

"Looking good" may be an especially serious matter for some purchasing executives. They often have to buy a wide variety of things from many sources. Perhaps more than other executives, they have to make decisions involving many factors beyond their control. A new source may deliver low-quality materials, for example, and the buyer may be blamed. Or, poor service or late delivery may reflect on his ability. Any product or service or vendor, therefore, that assures the buyer that he will look good to higher-ups has a definite appeal. In fact, this one factor might make the difference between a successful and an unsuccessful marketing mix.

Supply sources must be dependable

The matter of dependability deserves further stress. There is nothing worse to a purchasing agent and a production executive than shutting down a production line because vendors have not delivered the goods. And product quality is important, too. The cost of a small item may have little to do with its importance. If it causes malfunctioning of a larger unit into which it is incorporated, it may cause a large loss completely out of proportion to its own value. To try to assure dependable quality, some vendors set up statistical quality control procedures to inspect all incoming lots. And other buyers deliberately give preference to producers who seek to make products that are slightly better than required specifications, thereby giving greater assurance of reliability and quality. This is *the* important selling point for some firms. In effect, this "makes" their marketing mix because it gives the buyer an extra margin of safety.

Clearly, a seller's marketing mix should satisfy both the buyer's company objectives as well as his own individual goals. Therefore, it helps to seek some overlapping area where both can be satisfied. See Figure 9–3 for a graphic model of this concept.

Multiple influences on buying

■ Much of the work of the typical purchasing agent consists of straight rebuys – routine placing of orders to fill requisitions flowing from various production, warehouse, and office departments. For

Figure 9-3
A model of individual industrial buyer behavior — showing overlapping goals (shaded area)

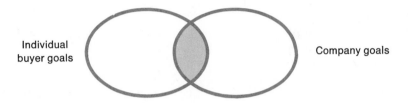

Individual buyer goals   Company goals

such requisitions, he may place the order without consultation with anyone.

In other cases, especially in new-task buying, the buyer may share the purchasing decision with several executives, perhaps even top management. Each of these buying influences may be interested in different aspects of the buying situation, and the salesman should study each case carefully. A salesman might have to talk to every one of the possible influencers, but he would take up different topics and stress different factors for each of them. This not only complicates the promotion job, but also lengthens it. Approval of a routine order may take anywhere from a week to several months. But on very important purchases — say, the purchase of a new computer system, a new plant, or major equipment — the selling period may stretch out to a year or more.

Basic methods and practices in industrial buying

■ Not only the nature of the buyer but also the nature of the buying situation may be grounds for segmenting markets. Some firms use different methods of evaluating products and vendors. And because of their methods of buying, there may be times when the market potential dries up completely or there is no way for a new supplier to break into a market. These topics are discussed below, and it is important to see that they could serve as potential dimensions in market gridding.

Basic approaches for evaluating and buying

■ Industrial buyers (really, buyers of all types, including final consumers) can use four basic approaches to evaluating and buying products: (1) inspection, (2) sampling, (3) description, and (4) negotiated contracts.

In modern economies, most products are purchased by description or negotiated contracts. By contrast, in less developed economies, most buying is done by inspection or sampling, regardless of the products. The reason is skepticism and uncertainty about quality, or lack of faith in the seller. An understanding of the differences in these methods is important.

Inspection

The inspection method is used for products that are not standardized and require examination. Here, each product is different, as in the case of some fruits and vegetables, and livestock. One-of-a-kind products, such as used buildings and cars, must also be inspected. These products are often sold in open markets or at auction, especially if there are several potential buyers. Potential buyers inspect the merchandise and either "haggle" with the seller or bid against competitors for the product.

Sampling

As products become more standardized, perhaps because of more careful grading and better quality control, buying by sample becomes feasible. The general price level may be set by demand and supply factors, but the actual price may be adjusted from this level depending on the quality of the specific sample. This kind of buying is used in the U.S. grain markets, for example, where the actual price is set based on a sample which has been withdrawn from a carload of grain and analyzed.

Description

Today, most manufactured items and many agricultural commodities can be subjected to more rigid quality control or grading. When quality almost can be guaranteed, buying by description — grade, brand, or specification — may be satisfactory, at least when there is mutual trust between buyers and sellers. In recent years, more wholesale and retail buyers have come to accept government grading standards for some fruits and vegetables. Now, much of this merchandise is packed in the fields and sold without any further inspection or sampling. This, of course, reduces the cost of buying and is used by buyers whenever practicable.

Negotiated contracts

The three methods discussed above are concerned with tangible products or products and services which can be described sufficiently well so that suppliers know what is wanted and can submit definite prices or bids. Usually a price is set for each shipment or order, or perhaps for a series of shipments against the same order. But a price is set for some fairly definite, agreed upon, product and marketing mix.

Sometimes, however, the buyer knows roughly what he wants but cannot describe it exactly. Perhaps he plans to change the specifications or total requirements as the job progresses, or maybe some of the details cannot be anticipated. This is found, for example, in research and development work and in the building of special-purpose machinery and large buildings. In such cases, the general project is described, and a basic price may be agreed upon, with provision for adjustments both upward and downward. Or a supplier may be willing to work under a contract that provides some type of incentive, such as full coverage of costs plus a fixed fee, or full costs plus some percentage profit based on costs. The whole contract may even be subject to renegotiation as the work proceeds.

Buyers may favor loyal, helpful suppliers

■ To be assured of dependable quality, a buyer may also develop loyalty to certain suppliers. This is especially important when buying nonstandardized products. When a friendly relationship is developed over the years, the supplier practically becomes a part of the buyer's organization.

Most buyers have a sense of fair play, and when a salesman proposes a new idea that saves the buyer's company money, he usually attempts to reward that salesman with orders. This encourages future suggestions. In contrast, buyers who use a bid system exclusively—either by choice or necessity, as in some government and institutional purchasing—may not be offered much beyond the basic products or services. They are interested primarily in price. Marketing managers who have developed better products and technical or other assistance programs may not solicit such business, at least with their better mix. That is, they may use buyer loyalty and buying methods as segmenting dimensions.

But buyers must spread their risk— seeking several sources

■ Even if a firm has developed the most ideal marketing mix possible, it probably will not get all of the business of its industrial customers. Purchasing agents usually seek several dependable sources of supply, to protect themselves from unpredictable events, such as strikes, fires, or floods in one of their suppliers' plants. But still, a good marketing mix is likely to win a larger share of the total business.

Some buy by computer

■ Some buyers have been able to delegate a considerable part of their routine order placing to computers. They develop decision rules that tell the computer how to order and leave the details of following through to the computer. Then they watch the general movement of economic conditions, and when conditions require, the buyers modify instructions to the computer. When nothing unusual happens, however, the computer system can continue to routinely rebuy as needs develop—printing out new purchase orders to the established suppliers.

It is extremely important, then, for a supplier to be one of those that the computer will consider. In such a situation, the critical thing is not whether a particular salesman will get a particular order, but whether he will be considered one of the major suppliers. Obviously, this is a much bigger "sale." It also is obvious that such a buyer might be more favorably impressed by an attractive marketing mix, perhaps for a whole line of products, rather than just a lower price for a particular order. It might be too costly and too much trouble to change his whole buying system just because somebody is offering a low price on a particular day. Obviously, such buying situations are different and can be the basis for meaningful market segmentation.

Inventory policy may determine purchases

■ Industrial firms generally try to maintain an adequate inventory —at least enough to ensure that production lines keep moving. There is no greater calamity in a factory than to have a production line close down.

Adequate inventory often is expressed in terms of number of days' supply—for example, 60- or 90-days' supply. But what constitutes 60- or 90-days' supply depends upon the level of demand for the company's products. If the demand rises sharply, say by 10 percent, then total purchases will expand by more than 10 percent to maintain customary inventory levels *and* meet the new needs. On the other hand, if sales decrease by 10 percent, actual needs *and* inventory requirements decrease, and total purchases may decrease drastically while the inventory is being "worked off." During such a contraction, a seller would probably have little success with efforts to stimulate sales by reducing price or offering more favorable credit terms. The buyer is just not in the market at that time.

Reciprocity helps sales, but . . .

■ Reciprocity implies that if "you buy from me, I'll buy from you." If a company's customers also can supply products which the firm purchases, then the sales departments of both buyer and seller may seek to "trade" sales for sales. Purchasing agents generally resist reciprocity, but often it is forced upon them by their sales departments.

Reciprocal buying and selling is commonplace in some industries, particularly in paints, chemicals, and petroleum. Usually both prices and product qualities are competitive, and it becomes difficult to ignore the pressures of the sales departments involved. One chemical company brought purchasing under marketing to handle this problem.

When prices and quality are competitive, an outside supplier seldom can break such a reciprocal relationship. He can only hope to become an alternate source of supply and wait for his competitors to let quality slip or prices rise.

The U.S. Justice Department also frowns upon reciprocity. It has launched a program to block reciprocal buying on the grounds that it is an attempt to monopolize, restricting the normal operation of the free market. This may force those firms that place heavy reliance on reciprocal dealing to reevaluate their marketing strategies.[3]

Buying practices vary by product

■ These general buying methods and practices apply in the purchase of many industrial products. Specific habits and practices, however, vary according to the type of product, which is a subject covered in Chapter 15.

Retailers and wholesalers are problem solvers, too

■ Retailing and wholesaling involve so many different kinds of operations that it is difficult to find generalizations that cover the behavior of both the small firms and the highly specialized buyers in large firms. Still, there are some common characteristics, and then other characteristics which might be useful for segmenting these markets.

They must buy for their customers

■ Most retail and wholesale buyers see themselves as purchasing agents for their target customers, remembering the old maxim: "Goods well bought are half sold." Typically, they do *not* see themselves as sales agents for manufacturers. They buy what they think they can sell, and in the case of wholesalers, they buy what they think their retailers can sell. They do not try to make value judgments about the desirability or "worth" of what they are selling, but rather focus more on the needs and preferences of *their* target customers. Recognizing the close relationship of buying and selling, in some smaller firms the buyers are also responsible for sales and the sales force. This permits immediate feedback from the sales people to affect buying.

They must buy too many items

■ Most retailers carry a large number of items—drug stores up to 12,000 items, hardware stores from 3,000 to 25,000, and grocery stores up to 8,000 items—and they just do not have the time to pay much attention to individual items. Often retail buyers are annoyed by the number of wholesalers' and manufacturers' representatives who call on them. These retailers feel that their sales of each item are so small that they cannot afford to spend much time choosing each product.

Wholesalers, too, handle so many items that they cannot give continual attention to each one of them. A grocery wholesaler may stock up to 20,000 items; a drug wholesaler, up to 125,000; and a dry-goods wholesaler up to 250,000 items.

Understandably, most retailers and wholesalers buy the bulk of their products on a routine, automatic reorder basis—straight rebuys—once the initial decision to stock products has been made. Clearly, a seller to these markets must recognize the sheer magnitude of the buyer's job and have something to say when he comes calling. His marketing mix might even be more successful if he sold full lines and emphasized display and shelf arrangement or sales aids rather than focusing on product features.

In larger firms, on the other hand, we see buyers spending more time on individual items. Buyers may begin to specialize in certain goods; some large chains buy such large lots that they can assign buyers to find additional and lower cost sources of supply.[4]

They must watch inventories and computer output

■ The large number of items bought and stocked by wholesalers and retailers makes it imperative that inventories be watched carefully. Most modern retailers and wholesalers attempt to carry adequate but *not* excessive inventories. Instead, they seek to maintain a selling stock and some reserve stock, and then depend on a continual flow through the channel. Smaller firms use hand inventory control methods, but increasingly we find even small firms moving to automatic inventory control procedures. And large ones use quite sophisticated computer-controlled inventory control systems. Large retail discounters have even moved to unit control systems in order to quickly pinpoint sales of every product on their shelves. As one discounter put it, "we are not satisfied to know what we are selling in a thousand-foot area—we want to know quickly what we are selling on each table."[5] Similarly, drug wholesalers maintain perpetual inventory on their important items. One drug wholesaler maintains a perpetual inventory record on 800 items that are extremely important to his operation. And a plumbing-heating wholesaler maintains an automated perpetual inventory on 13,000 items. The system so speeds pricing and other activities, thereby cutting his other costs, that this inventory control system operates "for free."[6] For this reason, more and more wholesalers and retailers are adopting such systems. This is especially relevant to marketing managers selling to them because buyers with this kind of information know their needs better and become more precise and demanding about dependability of delivery. They also are more knowledgeable about how goods move and where promotional assistance might be desirable.

Some are not always "open to buy"

■ Just as manufacturers may sometimes be attempting to reduce their inventory and, therefore, are "not in the market," retailers and wholesalers may stop buying for similar reasons. No amount of special promotion or price concessions will cause them to buy in these situations.

In retailing, another dimension may become relevant. A buyer may be controlled by a fairly strict budget. This is a miniature profit-and-loss statement for each department or merchandise line. In an effort to make a profit in his area, the buyer attempts to forecast sales, merchandise costs, and expenses. The figure for "cost of merchandise" is the amount the buyer has to spend over the budget period. If he has not yet spent it all, he is "open to buy." This buyer, therefore, does have considerable latitude to exercise his judgment, *if he is open to buy.*

Owners or professional buyers may buy

■ The buyers in small stores or for many wholesalers are the owners or managers, since there is a very close relationship between buying and selling. In larger operations, buyers may specialize in certain lines, but they still may supervise the sales people who sell what they buy. These buyers, therefore, are in close contact with their customers, *and* with their sales people, who are sensitive to the effectiveness of the buyer's efforts—especially when they are on commission. A buyer may even buy some items to satisfy the preferences of his sales people, therefore they should not be neglected in the promotion effort. The multiple buying influence may be determining.

As sales volumes rise, a buyer may specialize in buying only and have no responsibility for sales. Sears is an extreme case, to be sure, but it has a buying department of more than 3,000, supported by a staff department exceeding 1,400. These are professional buyers who may know more about prices and quality and trends in the market than their suppliers. Obviously, these are big potential customers and should be approached differently than the typical small retailer.[7]

Resident
buyers may
help a firm's
buyers

■ Many retailers and wholesalers work with independent buying agents, called *resident buyers,* in the central markets of New York, Chicago, Los Angeles, and San Francisco. They cover new styles and fashions on the spot, and buy fill-in items as their customers run out of stock during the year. Some resident buying organizations buy everything except furniture, shoes, and food for their stores. Some resident buyers have hundreds of employees and buy more than $1-billion worth of goods a year.

Resident buying organizations fill a need to reach the many small manufacturers who cannot afford large selling organizations. Resident buyers' usually are paid an annual fee based on their purchases.

Committee
buying
happens too

■ In some large organizations, especially in grocery and variety lines, the major decisions – to add or drop lines or change buying policies – may be delegated to a committee. The seller still will contact the buyer, but the buyer does not have final responsibility. In some organizations, the buyer prepares forms summarizing proposals for new products. The seller completes these forms but may not get to present his story in person to the buying committee.

This rational, almost cold-blooded, approach reduces the impact of the persuasive salesmen, but it has become necessary because of the flood of new products. Consider the problem facing grocery chains. In an average week, 150 to 250 new items are presented for consideration to the buying offices of the larger food chains. If all were accepted, 10,000 new items would be added during a single year, more than their present stock! Obviously, buyers must be hardheaded and impersonal. About 90 percent of the new items presented to food stores are rejected.

Wholesalers' and manufacturers' marketing managers must develop good marketing mixes when buying becomes so sophisticated and competitive. This approach is likely to become more common as computers improve sales and inventory analysis. Clearly, how possible target markets buy should affect market gridding and marketing strategy planning.

The farm market

■ Agriculture is fundamental to almost all economies. In some countries, agriculture absorbs almost all of the work force, but in the United States the percentage of the population engaged in agriculture has been declining steadily to about 6 percent of the population.

The farmers are the most numerous intermediate customers, but just as the percentage of the population engaged in agriculture is declining, so is the number of farms. In the 30-year period from 1940 to 1970, more than 3 million farm units disappeared, the total dropping from more than 6 million to less than 3 million farms. The remaining farms have absorbed some of this acreage, and from

1940 to 1970, the average farm increased in size from fewer than 200 acres to almost 400 acres.

Just as in manufacturing, however, there are still many small units while the large ones produce most of the output. About half the farmers produce almost 90 percent of the total farm output. Many of the small farmers are not much more than subsistence farmers and they are not an especially attractive market. Quite simply, many farmers do not have the money to buy much.

The owners of large farms are another matter. They tend to run their farms as a business, rather than a way of life and, consequently, are susceptible to presentations stressing savings and increases in productivity. Further, they are more knowledgeable and receptive to change—and, they may have the assets to act on their decisions.

Some studies of farmer purchasing behavior, however, indicate that for some products, buying motivations are not much different from those for consumer goods.

Many farmers seem unwilling to shop around for the lowest price, preferring the convenience of patronizing the nearest farm implement or feed dealer. Some emulation is found, especially in the purchase of farm machinery. This is understandable when you consider that a farmer's home and place of business are the same. Some manufacturers take pride in office facilities and factories, and the same sort of motive may affect farmer purchasing behavior. Among owners of smaller farms, a new tractor may offer just as much status as a new car would to an urban resident. Moreover, the farmer's roles as a businessman and a final consumer sometimes overlap. For example, a station wagon might be used for carrying feed and the family's groceries. Thus the motives that drive both final consumers and businessmen may become intertwined.

Tailoring products to customers' specialization
■ Another important factor is that farmers are tending to specialize in one or a few products—such as wheat alone, or wheat plus oats and corn, or fruit and nuts, or poultry. These farmers are interested in only specific kinds of products.

A cotton farmer, for example, may have little interest in hen houses or antibiotics. Or a wheat farmer in the northern plains where hard wheat is grown would have different needs from those of a farmer further south where soft wheat is preferred.

Market grids for such different customers should be developed in great detail. Fortunately, much data is available from the U.S. Department of Agriculture.

Marketing mixes may have to be tailored for each individual farmer—and in some cases this is happening. Fertilizer producers have now moved far beyond selling an all-purpose bag of fertilizer. Now they are able to blend the exact type needed for each farm and load it directly onto fertilizer spreaders which do the job more economically than manual methods. Some producers, in fact, are working directly with farmers, providing a complete service—including fertilizing, weeding, and debugging—all tailored to each individual farmer's needs.[8]

Agriculture is becoming agri-business

■ Another increasingly important factor is the tendency for farmers to engage in contract farming. Here, the farmer obtains his supplies and perhaps working capital from local dealers or manufacturers who agree to purchase his output, sometimes at guaranteed prices. This limits his buying freedom, since he becomes, in effect, an employee. Such arrangements are becoming more frequent, especially in raising chickens and turkeys and in growing fresh vegetables for commercial canning. These arrangements give stability to the agricultural structure but also limit the markets for sellers. It is all part of the move toward bigger and more businesslike agricultural enterprises – what has been called "agri-business."

Where such contractual arrangements (or actual ownership) are common, marketing managers will have to adjust their marketing mixes. They may have to sell directly to large manufacturers or dealers who are handling the arrangements rather than to the farmer himself.

In summary, the modern farmer is becoming more knowledgeable and more businesslike and seems willing to accept help and new ideas – but only when he feels sure they will help him improve production.

The government market

Size and diversity

■ Government is the largest customer in the United States. Approximately 33 percent of the gross national product is spent by various governmental units. These units buy almost every kind of commodity. They not only run schools, police departments, and military organizations but also supermarkets, public utilities, research laboratories, offices, hospitals, and liquor stores. And government expenditures for all these operations are growing constantly. They cannot be ignored by an aggressive marketing manager.

Bid buying is common

■ Many government customers buy by description, using a *mandatory bidding procedure* which is open to public review. Often the government buyer is forced to accept the lowest bid. His biggest job, after deciding generally what he wants, is to correctly describe his need so that the description is unambiguous and complete. Otherwise, he may find sellers bidding on a product he does not want. By law, he might have to accept the low bid for an unwanted product.

Drawing specifications carefully is not an easy task, and buyers usually appreciate the help of knowledgeable salesmen. Legally, the buyer cannot draw the specifications so that only one supplier will be able to meet them (although this has been done!), but if all the relevant specifications are included, then the bidding must be on the items desired. The customer can then obtain the product he wants. And the knowledgeable salesman may get the business, even though his bid is not the lowest, because the lower bids do not meet the minimum specifications.

Not all of the items that governments buy, however, create specification difficulties. Many branded items or items for which there are widely accepted standards are routinely purchased through the conventional bidding procedures. School supplies, construction materials, and gasoline, for example, would fall into this category.

Negotiated contracts are common too

■ For items that are not branded or easily described, or for products requiring research and development, or in cases in which there would be no effective competition, contracts may be negotiated directly. Depending on the government involved, the contract may be subject to audit and renegotiation, especially if the contractor makes a larger profit than was expected.

Negotiation often is necessary when there are many qualitative and intangible factors. Unfortunately, this is exactly where favoritism and "influence" can slip in. Such influence is not unknown, especially in city and state governments. Nevertheless, negotiation is an important buying method in government sales, and there is a definite need for a marketing mix that emphasizes more than just price.

Approximately 90 percent of the items purchased by the U.S. Defense Supply Agency are acquired through negotiation. This has led the USDSA to seek new ways of evaluating the total cost of buying. Elaborate value analysis and cost accounting studies are being employed to determine what items *should* cost to produce, and use over their life. In other words, regular experimenting takes place with new approaches to buying that may replace the traditional low-bid practice.[9]

Learning what government wants

■ Since most government contracts are advertised, the prospective supplier focuses on the government agency he wants to cater to and learns the bidding procedures of that particular agency or department. The marketing man can make a big contribution at this point, because there are so many different bidding procedures and possibilities.

The marketing man should be an expert on potential government target markets, using the assistance available from government directories. For example, the U.S. government offers a purchasing and sales directory that explains its procedures;[10] and various state and local governments also offer assistance. There are trade magazines and trade associations providing information on how to reach schools, hospitals, highway departments, park departments, and so on. These are unique target markets and must be treated as such when developing marketing strategies.

Conclusion

■ In this chapter we have considered the number, size, and buying habits and practices of various intermediate customers with a view to identifying logical bases for market gridding. Kind of customer is a logical basis, as well as the customer's size and location. Further, the nature of the buyer and the buying situation may be relevant dimensions. In fact, we saw that the basic problem-solving models of buyer behavior introduced in Chapter 8 are applicable here, with modifications.

The primary focus was on the nature of buying in the industrial market because we know more about how those buyers behave and we assume buying in other markets is similar. We did discuss some specific differences in buying by retailers and wholesalers, especially with respect to the buying of goods which they resell. We also discussed some of the characteristics of the farm market and the government market. In the farm market, we emphasized the rapid changes taking place there, and the trend toward fewer, larger, more productive farms with better informed and more progressive farmers. Finally, we saw that the government market is an extremely large, complex market which obviously requires much market gridding. But fortunately, there are many sources, including government manuals, which explain how to sell to the many government markets. Here, a good marketing man would simply have to do his homework – to obtain the relevant market dimensions as well as what is wanted when and what pricing procedures are required.

This review of intermediate customer buying habits and practices has tried to suggest possible gridding dimensions. A clear understanding of these buyers' needs and preferences will facilitate marketing strategy planning. And since there are fewer intermediate customers than final consumers, it may even be possible for some marketing managers (and their salesmen) to develop a unique strategy for each potential customer.

This chapter has suggested some general principles which would be useful in strategy planning, but the nature of the products being offered may require some adjustments in the plans. The nature of specific industrial products is discussed in Chapter 15. And the nature of specific consumer goods which might be sold by retailers and wholesalers is discussed in Chapter 14. These variations by product may provide additional segmenting dimensions to enable the marketing manager to more finely tune his marketing strategies.

questions and answers

1 Discuss the importance of applying the market grid concept when analyzing intermediate customer markets. Be sure to consider how easy it is to isolate homogeneous market segments.

2 Explain how SIC codes might be helpful in evaluating and understanding industrial markets.

3 Compare and contrast the problem-solving approaches used by final consumers and industrial buyers.

4 Describe the situations which would lead to the use of the three different buying processes for a particular product, such as computer tapes.

5 Compare and contrast the buying motives of final consumers and industrial buyers.

6 Distinguish among the four methods of evaluating and buying (inspection, sampling, etc.) and indicate which would probably be most suitable for furniture, baseball gloves, coal, and pencils, assuming that some intermediate customer is the buyer.

7 Discuss the advantages and disadvantages of reciprocity from the industrial buyer's point of view. Are the advantages and disadvantages merely reversed from the seller's point of view?

8 Is it always advisable to buy the highest-quality product?

9 How does the kind of industrial good affect manufacturers' buying habits and practices? Consider lumber for furniture, a lathe, nails for a box factory, and a sweeping compound.

10 Considering the nature of retail buying, outline the basic ingredients of promotion to re-tail buyers. Does it make any difference what kinds of products are involved? Are any other factors relevant?

11 Discuss the impact of the decline in number of commercial farmers on the marketing mixes of manufacturers and middlemen supplying this market. Also consider the impact on rural trading communities which have been meeting the needs of farmers.

12 The government market is obviously an extremely large one, yet it is often slighted or even ignored by many firms. "Red tape" is certainly one reason, but there are others. Discuss the situation and be sure to include the market grid concept in your analysis.

13 Based on your understanding of buying by (1) manufacturers, (2) farmers, and (3) governments, outline the basic ingredients of promotion to each type of customer. Use two products as examples for each type. Is the promotion job the same for each pair?

notes

[1] For more detail, see *Industry Profiles — 1958–1966* and *Facts for Marketers,* U.S. Department of Commerce, Business and Defense Services Administration.

[2] Patrick J. Robinson and Charles W. Faris, *Industrial Buying and Creative Marketing* (Boston: Allyn & Bacon, Inc., 1967), chap. 2; see also: Frederick E. Webster, Jr., and Yoram Wind, "A General Model for Understanding Organizational Buying Behavior," *Journal of Marketing,* April 1972, pp. 12–19; Urban B. Ozanne and Gilbert A. Churchill, Jr., "Five Dimensions of the Industrial Adoption Process," *Journal of Marketing Research,* August 1971, pp. 322–328; and Donald R. Lehmann and John O'Shaughnessy, "Difference in Attribute Importance for Different Industrial Products," *Journal of Marketing,* April 1974 pp. 36–42.

[3] "Federal Suit Charges GE With Reciprocity on Purchasing; Vigorous Defense Is Vowed," *The Wall Street Journal,* May 19, 1972, p. 2; see also Reed Moyer, "Reciprocity: Retrospect and Prospect," *Journal of Marketing,* October 1970, pp. 37–54.

[4] For a detailed discussion of supermarket chain buying, see: J. F. Grashof. *Information Management for Supermarket Chain Product Mix Decisions* (Ph.D. thesis, Michigan State University, 1968.)

[5] "What's the Sales Potential of Those Products Taking Up Space on a Store's Valuable Shelves," *Systems Management,* January 1962, pp. 35 ff.

[6] "Aaron Company's Total Inventory Control of 13,000 Items," *Supply House Times,* February 1959, pp. 48–70.

[7] "Why Sears Stays the No. 1 Retailer," *Business Week,* January 20, 1968, pp. 65–73.

[8] "Monsanto Moves Into Farmers' Back Yard," *Business Week,* February 6, 1965, pp. 60–62; see also "Agricorporations Run Into Growing Criticism as Their Role Expands," *The Wall Street Journal,* May 2, 1972, p. 1 f.

[9] "A Radical Shift in Setting Profits," *Business Week,* May 13, 1972, pp. 102–04; "Picking the Winners with a New System," *Business Week,* May 13, 1967, pp. 62–67; and " 'Should-Cost' Is the New Weapon to Test," *Business Week,* May 30, 1970, pp. 48–49.

[10] *U.S. Government Purchasing and Sales Directory.*

10

International markets

■ Most Americans know that the United States is a wealthy country. They also know that our government has been spending billions of dollars annually on foreign aid programs to help the "less developed countries" of the world. It is only natural, therefore, that many Americans think of foreign countries as poor, with little market potential. While this may be true in some areas, such thinking ignores the fact that there are many opportunities in international markets. Some foreign consumers already have high standards of living, and markets in many countries are growing, some very rapidly. Further, some U.S. firms are deeply involved in international markets, earning more there than in the United States.

Market gridding may be even more complex in international markets, because of their greater heterogeneity. Foreign markets must be treated as separate target markets. Lumping all foreign people together as "foreigners," or assuming that they are just like U.S. customers is almost a guarantee of failure. There has been even more stereotype thinking with regard to international markets than domestic markets, and this chapter seeks to sweep away some of these misconceptions and to suggest some possible dimensions for market gridding.

Importance of international markets to the United States and U.S. firms

As a nation grows, its trade grows

■ All countries trade to some extent, since we live in an interdependent world. But it may surprise Americans to know that the United States is the largest exporter and importer of goods in the world. Our share of the world's foreign trade is approximately 13 percent. Even the United Kingdom and Japan, which have built their growth on exports and imports are below the United States.

Most of the largest traders are highly industrialized nations. Trade seems to expand as a country grows and industrializes.

But while the United States is the biggest trading nation in the world, foreign trade does not dominate our economy. On a per capita basis, it is less important to us than it is to many other nations. This is because of the larger size of our gross national product. Our foreign trade makes up a relatively small part of our GNP—less than 10 percent—but the smaller part is, nevertheless, greater in total dollars than in other major trading countries.

There are profitable opportunities in world markets

■ Attractive opportunities in foreign countries have led many companies into worldwide operations. The marketing concept is less well understood in some foreign markets and, consequently, there are great opportunities for those who know how to work with it and want to apply it abroad.

Some companies simply move from strictly domestic operations to exporting and licensing of foreign producers. Such operations are often treated as separate little departments, with resultant neglect. Increasingly, though, some companies are aggressively pursuing foreign market prospects, and often find foreign operations more profitable than domestic operations. As a result, they are paying more attention to worldwide markets. Domestic and foreign operations may even be integrated under one executive. Deere & Company, a farm machinery manufacturer, and Procter and Gamble, for example, have taken this step. Companies such as Eastman Kodak, Warner-Lambert, Pfizer, Anaconda, Goodyear, Ford, IBM, IT&T, Corn Products, 3M, National Cash Register, H. J. Heinz, Gillette, and others get over 30 percent of their total sales or profits abroad. And Coca-Cola recently moved past the halfway point—more than half of its profits come from international operations, and they foresee the day when as much as 75 percent of their earnings may come from abroad.[1]

Multinational marketing makes sense to some firms

■ As firms move more deeply into international markets, some ultimately reach the point where the firm sees itself as a worldwide enterprise. The chief executive of Abbott Laboratories, a pharmaceutical company with plants in 22 countries, said: "We are no longer just a U.S. company with interests abroad. Abbott is a world enterprise, and many major, fundamental decisions must be made on a global basis."[2]

A Texas Instruments executive had a similar view: "When we consider new opportunities, and one is abroad and the other domestic, we can't afford to look upon the alternative here as an inherently superior business opportunity simply because it is in the U.S. We view an overseas market just as we do our market in, say, Arizona, as one more market in the world."

A General Motors executive sees this trend as: ". . . the emergence of the modern industrial corporation as an institution that is transcending national boundaries."

These multinational companies are expanding worldwide, in part for profit, but also because of the force of competition and the problems of acting solely as exporters. At one time, foreign sales were handled by exporting domestic production, but exporting was a stepchild which was encouraged only when domestic business was poor.

Increasingly, multinational companies are finding it economically sensible to actually set up factories and distribution facilities in other countries, not just export to them. Capital and technical know-how and parts may be exported, but basic production often is handled in the country involved. Already, sales of U.S. subsidiaries located abroad are roughly six times U.S. exports. Clearly, this is a different kind of sales growth. And it seems likely that this kind of growth will continue. At the same time, foreign multinational companies are growing, too, and beginning to not only export but set up operations around the world, including in the United States. Japan's Sony has set up a TV assembly plant in San Diego and a TV tube plant is going up nearby. Volvo is planning an auto assembly plant in Virginia. And several European multinational companies are just buying controlling or complete interest in U.S. firms. Nestlé's recently purchased Stouffer Foods from Litton Industries, for example. Others, like Nestlé, Shell, and Lever Brothers, are already well-accepted "foreign" brands, not only in the United States but around the world.[3]

Multinational companies transcend national boundaries

■ One reason for the movement of some multinational firms into the United States is that labor costs in their own countries (including Japan) have been rising. Considering the total cost including transportation costs, it may be more economical to produce products for the U.S. market here.[4]

From an international perspective, multinational firms must be seen as organizations which transcend national boundaries. They see world market opportunities and position their production and distribution facilities without regard to national boundaries. This has annoyed some nationalistic businessmen, and politicians. But some of these multinational operations may be difficult to stop, because they are no longer just importing. They live locally, employ local residents, build plants, and may even be jointly owned with local businessmen and politicians. These are powerful organizations which have learned to cope with nationalistic feelings and the typical national barriers and quotas – treating them simply as uncontrollable variables.

Some of the multinational firms see continued growth as the only route for their survival. They see increasing competition among multinational firms and expect that only the most well-managed will survive in the long run. The general manager of a French electrical equipment manufacturing group predicts that by 1980 there will be only seven or eight major electrical equipment groups in the world, and said "we plan to be one of them." To get there, the firm has been expanding and buying control in a variety of electrical equipment firms, including one in Canada and two in the United States.[5]

We may not have "one world" politically as yet, but business is rapidly moving in that direction. We may have to develop new kinds of corporations and laws to govern multinational operations, because the limitations of national boundaries on business and politics will make less and less sense in the future.[6]

International marketing requires more market gridding

■ Success in international markets requires even more attention to market gridding. At the same time, this becomes more difficult as there are more potential dimensions. Further, as one contemplates moving from one country to another, he must recognize that the political, legal, and cultural variables which he could treat as "uncontrollable" in the domestic market now become "controllable" by choosing which countries or regions the firm will work in (until the entry decision is made, and then they too are uncontrollable). There may be substantial differences in language, customs, beliefs, religion, and race, and even income distribution patterns as one moves from one country to another. What makes it even worse is that there is much less good data as one moves into international markets, i.e., while the number of variables increase, the quantity and quality of the data declines. It may even be nonexistent. This is one reason why some multinational firms insist that local operations be handled by natives—they at least have a "feel" for their markets.

There are more dimensions —but there is a way

■ Segmenting international markets may involve more dimensions, but a reasonable approach seems to involve a several step process, focusing first on country or regional characteristics which might be similar for the product-market area the firm is considering. Then, depending upon whether the firm is aiming at final consumers or intermediate customers, it would consider other potential dimensions. (See Figure 10–1.) For final consumers, one would evaluate specific customer or product-market characteristics, as we discussed in Chapters 7 and 8. For intermediate customers, one would consider the kind and size and location of potential customer types, and then drop down to focusing on the nature of the buyer and the buying situation, as we discussed in Chapter 9.

With the spreading impact of multinational companies, analysis of the likely behavior of intermediate customers probably will be easier, in that they will tend to behave like well-managed firms anywhere. Increasingly, they are specialists at management and technology transfer, and their behavior is much more economic and predictable than final consumers.

Figure 10–1
Bases for gridding in international markets

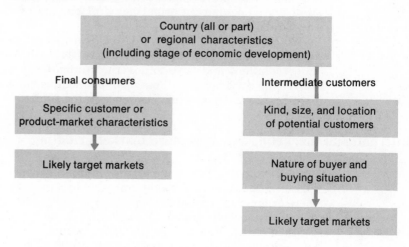

For this reason, most of the discussion in this chapter will emphasize likely *final consumer* differences, as well as regional groupings and stages of economic development which can provide additional insights for market gridding. Ultimately, even more judgment is required in international markets – this is no place for production-oriented businessmen and their sometimes pathetically naïve stereotypes about "foreigners."

New economic groups are moving beyond national barriers to adopt cooperative arrangements

■ While national boundaries are a common and logical dimension for gridding, we do see nations banding together in cooperative groups to speed their development and to facilitate trade. They have dared to abandon old ideas and nationalistic prejudices in favor of cooperative efforts to reduce tariffs and other restrictive arrangements which are commonly applied at national boundaries. Tariffs – taxes on incoming goods – vary depending upon whether the country is attempting to raise revenue or restrict trade. Restrictive tariffs often block all movement, but even revenue-producing tariffs lead to red tape and discourage free movement of goods. Quotas act similarly to restrictive tariffs in that they set specific quantities of goods which can move in or out. In other words, there might be great market opportunities within a country, but import quotas might bar outsiders from entering.

In the following paragraphs we will consider some economic arrangements which have moved beyond nationalistic boundaries and are currently relevant to market gridding.[7]

GATT works on tariff reduction

■ Until 1948, most countries in the world made bilateral arrangements on trade. In 1948, most of the nations of the free world accepted the idea of multilateral negotiations, when they signed the General Agreement on Tariffs and Trade (GATT). They agreed to meet every two years and negotiate for reductions in tariffs. This organization is still going strong, and through six major negotiation conferences has been very effective in lowering tariffs and encouraging greater trade.

This multilateral bargaining is especially important because most major trading nations use the "most-favored-nation" clause, which says that a significant tariff reduction offered to one nation immediately will be offered to all participating nations.

OEEC and OECD work on all economic problems

■ Also in 1948, 17 European nations signed the Convention for European Economic Cooperation, forming the Organization for European Economic Cooperation (OEEC). This group of nations agreed to work toward a common solution of their economic problems while retaining full national sovereignty.

In 1960, OEEC evolved into OECD (Organization for Economic Cooperation and Development). This organization now includes not only 18 European countries as full members, but also Japan, Canada, and the United States. This is a consultant agency only, however, and has no binding power over its members.

Coal and Steel Community surrendered some national sovereignty

■ The first supranational economic institution developed in 1952 when Belgium, France, Germany, Italy, Luxembourg, and The Netherlands signed the Coal and Steel Community Pact. In this agreement, some national sovereignty was surrendered to the higher body for the purpose of establishing a free market for iron ore, steel scrap, coal, and steel.

The goal of the Coal and Steel Community was development of a regional, rather than national, pattern for the production and distribution of these products. Since none of these countries was self-sufficient in steel production, the agreement made considerable sense. It showed that economic integration, even without political integration, was possible when it was logical and desired by the countries involved.

European Economic Community works toward full economic union

■ As a result of the smooth functioning of the Coal and Steel Community, these same six nations met in Rome in 1957 to sign a treaty establishing a European Economic Community (EEC) and a European Atomic Energy Community. They were, in effect, applying the concept behind the Coal and Steel Community to their entire economic life. These six nations formed the nucleus of the European Common Market.

By the middle 1960s, it was obvious that this large free-trade market was breaking down old nationalistic and restrictionist attitudes, expanding employment and investment, reducing prices, and generally helping to raise the standard of living in these communities. So impressive are the advances made by the Common

Market nations that a number of other nations are applying for or thinking about membership in the Common Market. Denmark, Ireland, and the United Kingdom joined in 1973. Over 20 other nations in Western Europe and Africa are associate members. And others have concluded free-trade agreements with the EEC, covering the removal of all customs duties on industrial products.

Other groups are following the EEC

■ Organizations akin to the European Common Market have formed in Africa, the Middle East, and Latin America. The Latin American Free Trade Association (LAFTA) was formed in 1960 and included Argentina, Brazil, Chile, Mexico, Paraguay, Peru, Uruguay, and later, Colombia and Ecuador. The second group, also formed in 1960, is known as the Central American Common Market (CACM) and consists of El Salvador, Guatemala, Honduras, Nicaragua, and later, Costa Rica.

These groups have not had the same success as the EEC, because of a few border and civil wars and revolutions, and strong nationalistic protectionist tendencies.[8]

In spite of some setbacks in the development of common markets elsewhere, the success of the European Common Market bodes well for the concept. It probably will encourage other cooperative arrangements as well, and long-range marketing plans should include the possibility of such developments.

Stages of economic development help define markets

■ International markets are so varied that it is impossible to generalize easily. Some markets are much more advanced and/or growing more rapidly than others. And some countries (or parts of a country) or regions are at different stages of economic development, which means that their demands and even their marketing systems will vary.

To get some perspective on the many possible differences in potential markets, we will discuss six stages of economic development. These stages must be qualified, however, because they greatly oversimplify the real world for a number of reasons. First, different parts of the same country may be at different stages of development, so it is not possible to identify a single country or region with only one stage. Second, the growing influence of multinational companies, and eager governments in some less developed countries, has led to the skipping of one or two stages due to the infusion of outside or government capital. For example, the building of uneconomic steel mills in order to boost a nation's "pride" or the coming of one or a few multinational corporations might lead to a substantial jump in stages. These "stage-jumping" developments do not invalidate the six stage process which provides a foundation for understanding what is happening in less dynamic situations. Rather, they merely show why more rapid movements have taken place in some situations.

**Stage 1 —
agricultural
self-
supporting**

■ In this phase, most people exist as subsistence farmers. There may be a simple marketing system — perhaps occasional weekly markets — but most of the people are not even in a money economy. Some parts of Africa and territories such as New Guinea are in this stage. In a practical marketing sense, these people do not represent a market, since they have no money to purchase goods.

**Stage 2 —
preindustrial
or commer-
cial**

■ Some countries in Sub-Sahara Africa and the Middle East are in this second stage. During this phase of economic development, we see more market-oriented activity. Raw materials such as oil, tin, and copper are extracted and exported. Agricultural and forest crops such as sugar, rubber, and timber are grown and harvested for the market and exported. Often this is done with the aid of foreign technical skills and capital. A commercial economy may develop along with, but unrelated to, the subsistence economy. These activities may require the beginnings of a transportation system to link the extracting or growing areas to shipping points. A money economy functions at this stage.

In this phase, there are demands for imports of industrial machinery and equipment, and huge construction projects may require many specialized supplies. Buying for these needs may be handled by purchasing agents and engineers in industrial countries. There is also the need for imports, including luxury goods, to meet the requirements and living standards of technical and supervisory personnel; these may be handled by company stores rather than local retailers.

The relatively few large landowners and those who benefit by this commercial activity may develop expensive tastes. The few natives employed by these larger firms and the small businessmen who serve them may develop into a small, middle-income class. But the majority of the population is still in the first stage, for practical purposes not in the market. This total market may be so small that local importers can easily handle the demand, with little incentive for local manufacturers to attempt to supply it.

**Stage 3 —
primary
manufactur-
ing**

■ In the third stage, there is some processing of metal ores or the agricultural products that formerly were shipped out of the country in raw form. Sugar and rubber, for example, are both produced and processed in Indonesia, and the same is true for sisal in Tanzania and oil on the Persian Gulf. And multinational companies may set up factories to take advantage of low-cost labor, exporting most of the output but, nevertheless, stimulating local development. More local labor becomes involved at this stage, and a domestic market develops. Even small businesses are starting to handle some of the processing or to service larger firms.

Even though the local market expands in this third stage, a large segment of the population is still at the subsistence level and almost entirely outside the money economy. There may still be a large foreign population of professionals and technicians essential to the developing agricultural-industrial complex. The demands of this group and of the growing number of wealthy natives are still quite different from the needs of the lower class and the growing middle class. A domestic market among the local citizenry begins to develop, but local manufacturers still may have difficulty finding enough demand to justify operation.

Stage 4 — nondurable and semidurable consumer goods manufacturing

■ At this stage, small local manufacturing begins, especially in those lines requiring low capital investment relative to output. Often these industries are an outgrowth of small firms that developed to supply the primary manufacturers dominating the last phase. For example, plants making sulfuric acid and explosives for extracting mineral resources might expand into soap manufacturing. And recently, multinational firms have accelerated development of countries at this stage with infusions of capital where the opportunities were right.

Paint, drug, food and beverage, and textile industries develop in this phase. The textile industry is usually one of the first to develop. Clothing is a necessity, and the articles imported for the upper-income and foreign markets are too expensive for the majority of potential customers now entering the money economy. This early emphasis on the textile industry in developing nations is one reason the world textile market is so vigorously competitive.

Some of the small manufacturers become established members of the middle or even upper-income class, and help to expand the demand for imported goods. But as this market grows, local entrepreneurs begin to see sufficient volume to operate profitably. The heavy dependence on imports for nondurable and semidurable goods then declines, though consumer durables and capital goods are still imported.

Stage 5 — capital goods and consumer durable goods manufacturing

■ In this phase, the production of capital goods and consumer durable goods begins. These classes of goods include automobiles, refrigerators, and machinery for local industries. Such manufacturing in turn creates other demands — raw materials for the local factories, and food and fibers for clothing for the rural population entering the industrial labor force.

Full-fledged industrialization has begun. But the economy is still heavily dependent upon exports of raw materials, either wholly unprocessed or slightly processed.

It still may be necessary to import specialized heavy machinery and equipment to build the capital facilities needed at this stage. Imports of consumer durable goods may still compete with local products. The foreign community and the status-conscious wealthy may prefer imports, and this demand can continue to provide an attractive market.

Stage 6 — exporting of manufactured products

■ Countries that have not progressed beyond the fifth phase are primarily engaged in exporting raw materials and in importing manufactured goods and equipment to build their industrial base. In the sixth stage, export of manufactured goods becomes dominant. The country may specialize in certain types of manufactured goods, such as iron and steel, watches, cameras, electronic equipment, and processed food. Large countries (Germany or Japan are examples) may have many specialities.

Opportunities for importing and exporting at this stage are great, since the countries have grown more affluent and have needs (and the purchasing power) for a great variety of products. In fact, countries in this stage often carry on a great deal of trade with each other, each trading those goods in which they have production advantages. In this phase, almost all consumers are in the money economy, and there may be a large middle-income class. The United States and most of the Western European countries are at this last stage today.[9]

It is important to recognize, here, that it is not necessary to label a whole country or geographic region as being in one stage. Certainly, different parts of the United States have developed differently and might properly be placed in different stages. It may help to understand the full implications of the stages if you try to identify geographic areas within the United States which are in each of these stages. Then, by careful thinking about the kind of public and private facilities found in these areas, one can get a deeper understanding about the likely character of international markets at the same time.

How these stages can be useful

■ A good starting point for evaluating present and future market potentials in a country (or part of a country) is to estimate its present stage of economic development and whether and how fast it is moving to another stage. Actually, the speed of movement, if any, and the possibility that stages may be skipped, may be the most critical factors in whether market opportunities are there or are likely to open. But just identifying the present stage can be very useful in achieving perspective, to help one decide what to look at and whether there are likely prospects for what the firm can offer.

Suggest marketing possibilities
■ Manufacturers of automobiles, expensive cameras, or other consumer durable goods, for example, should not plan to set up a mass distribution system in an area that is in the preindustrial (stage 2) or even primary manufacturing (stage 3) phase. The market would be too limited.

Among the foreign population and the wealthy landowners, nevertheless, there may be a small but very attractive market for luxury models, and a simple distribution system with one or a few distributors may be quite adequate. The market for U.S. "necessities," however—items such as canned foods or drug products—may not yet be large. Large-scale selling of these consumer items requires a large base of cash or credit customers, and as yet too few are part of the money economy.

On the other hand, an area in the nondurable-goods manufacturing phase has more potential, especially for durable-goods producers. Incomes and the number of potential customers are growing, yet there is no domestic competition.

Opportunities might still be good for durable-goods imports in the fifth stage, while domestic producers are attempting to get started. But more likely, the local government would raise some restrictions to aid local industry. Then the foreign producer might have to start licensing local producers or building a local plant.

Pursuing that enticing inverted pyramid

■ Areas or countries in the final stage often represent the biggest and most profitable markets. While there is obviously greater competition, there are many more customers with higher incomes. We have already seen how income distribution shifted in the United States from a pyramid to a more equal distribution, with a large middle-income market. This kind of development can be expected during the latter stages.

As incomes rise, we begin to see expenditure patterns somewhat similar to our own. This can be seen developing in Western Europe, and it should not be surprising, since the original work on Engel's laws was done in Europe. The "middle-income" market is growing fast in increasingly affluent Japan, too.

Other market dimensions are necessary, too

■ A consideration of country or regional differences, including stages of economic development in these areas, can be useful as a first step in segmenting international markets. After some potentially attractive areas have been identified (or, more likely, unattractive ones eliminated) then it is necessary to consider more specific customer or product-market characteristics, as discussed earlier in the chapter.

While several chapters have been devoted to potential dimensions in the U.S. market, it is clearly impossible to cover all of the possible dimensions in all world markets. On the other hand, some of the concepts discussed there certainly apply elsewhere. So here, we will simply sketch some of the dimensions of international markets and present some examples to emphasize that relying on stereotypes and half-truths about "foreigners" will not do in the increasingly competitive international markets.[10]

The number of people in our world is staggering

■ Although you may be overwhelmed by the crowds of people you have to compete with in our urban areas, the over 200 million population of the United States is less than 5 percent of the world's population of over 4 billion.

Sheer numbers are important

Instead of a tedious breakdown of population statistics, let's look at a map showing area in proportion to population. Figure 10–2 reduces the United States to relative insignificance because of our small population in relation to land area. The same is true of Latin America and Africa. In contrast, Western Europe is considerably larger and Far Eastern countries are even bigger.

Figure 10–2
Map of the world showing area in proportion to population

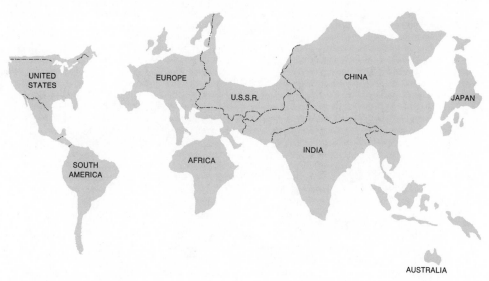

Source: Drawn by Joe F. McCarthy.

But people are not spread out evenly

There is a worldwide movement off the farm and into industrialized and urbanized areas. Shifts in population, combined with already dense populations, have led to extreme crowding in some parts of the world.

Figure 10–3 shows a map of the world emphasizing density of population. The darkest shading indicates areas with more than 250 persons per square mile.

The developing interurbias in the United States show up clearly as densely populated areas. Similar areas are found in Western Europe, along the Nile River valley in Egypt, and in many parts of Asia. In contrast, many parts of the world, like our western plains and mountain states, are sparsely populated.

Your own knowledge of the United States should help you avoid misreading a population density map. There are cities throughout the world, just as in the sparsely populated western United States, that are important markets even though surrounding areas have few people. These cities can be extremely important as markets if they serve as trading centers for a large region. Still, for locating large numbers of people, population density maps are invaluable.

Population densities are likely to increase in the foreseeable future. Birthrates in most parts of the world are high (higher in Africa, Latin America, Asia, and Oceania than in the United States), and death rates are declining as modern medicine is more widely accepted. Generally, population growth is anticipated in most countries, but the big questions are, How rapidly?, and Will output increase faster than population? This has great relevance for

200

Figure 10-3
Map of the world emphasizing density of population

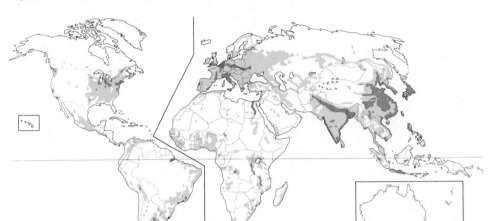

Adapted from *Atlas of Economic Development* by Norton Ginsburg by permission of the University of Chicago Press. © 1961 by The University of Chicago.

marketing men because it determines how rapidly some econo-mies evolve to higher stages of development and the kinds of goods that consumers have the income to buy.

You must sell where the income is

■ Profitable markets require income as well as people. The best available measure of income in most countries is gross national product. Unfortunately, this may understate consumer well-being in many countries because the methods commonly used for calcu-lating GNP may not be directly comparable for widely different cultures and economies. For instance, do-it-yourself activities, household services, and the growing of produce or meat by family members for their own consumption are not normally calculated as part of GNP. Since the activities of self-sufficient family units are not included, GNP can greatly underestimate economic well-being in less developed countries.

Gross national product, nevertheless, is useful and sometimes the only available measure of market potential in many countries. Table 10-1 shows the population and GNP of major regions of the world, except the U.S.S.R. and mainland China. It is quite clear that the more developed industrial regions have the lion's share of the world's GNP. This is why so much trade takes place between these countries, and why many companies see them as the more im-portant markets.

Income per capita can be more revealing

■ Since individuals and families rather than whole countries are buyers, GNP per capita may be a more relevant statistic. This is a commonly available figure—but it can be misleading regarding market potential. When GNP per capita is used for comparison, we

Table 10–1
Population and gross national product of major geographical regions
of the world (as of 1970)

Region	Population (millions)	Percent	GNP ($ millions)	Percent
North America	230	8.6	1,059	32.9
Latin America	291	10.8	142	4.4
Europe*	466	17.4	1,440	44.7
Near East	79	2.9	36	1.1
Africa	354	13.2	58	1.8
South and East Asia†	1,245	46.3	447	13.9
Oceania	20	.8	38	1.2
	2,685	100.0	3,220	100.0

* Except U.S.S.R.
† Except China.

Source: *Statistical Abstract of U.S. 1973*, p. 813 and *U.N. Statistical Yearbook 1972*, p. 8.

assume that the wealth of each country is distributed evenly among all consumers. However, this rarely is the case, as we noted earlier. In an underdeveloped economy, 75 percent of the population may be supported by agriculture but receive 25 percent or less of the income.[11] And there may be unequal distribution along class or racial lines. In South Africa, for example, the average family income in 1970 for whites was $5,830, for Asians $2,352, for mulattos $1,411, and for blacks $538.[12]

To provide some bench marks, the GNP per capita for a variety of countries is presented in Table 10–2. The range is wide, from $65 (U.S.) per capita per year in Ethiopia to $4,300 in the United States.

A business, and a human opportunity

These data indicate that a large share of the world's population lives in extreme poverty. Many of these countries are in the early stages of economic development, with large parts of their population engaged in agriculture and living only barely within the money economy.

These people, however, have needs, and many who have been exposed to Western ways are now anxious to better themselves. But they may not be able to raise their living standards without outside help. This presents a challenge and an opportunity to the industrialized nations and their business firms.

Some companies, including American firms, are attempting to do something constructive for the people of less developed countries. Corporations such as Pillsbury, Corn Products, Monsanto, and Coca-Cola have developed nutritious foods that can be sold cheaply, but profitably, in poorer countries. One firm sells a milk-based drink with 10 grams of protein in the Middle East and the Caribbean area. Such a beverage can make an important contribu-

Table 10–2
Gross national product per capita for major regions of world
and selected countries (in 1970 U.S. dollars) and population (in
millions in 1970)

	GNP/capita for countries	GNP/capita for regions	Population (1,000)
North America		$4,670	230,000
United States	$4,300		207,000
Canada	3,200		21,600
Latin America		510	291,000
Argentina	980		23,000
Brazil	380		93,000
Haiti	90		4,200
Mexico	630		48,000
Europe		1,950	466,000
United Kingdom	2,000		55,000
France	2,600		50,000
West Germany	2,700		60,000
Italy	1,600		54,000
Sweden	3,700		8,000
Portugal	600		8,500
Near East		366	79,000
Israel	1,600		3,000
Turkey	350		35,500
Africa		202	354,000
Algeria	300		14,000
Egypt	200		34,000
Ethiopia	65		25,000
Ghana	265		8,500
Kenya	130		11,000
Nigeria	85		55,000
South Africa	700		21,500
Rwanda	55		3,700
South and East Asia		240	1,245,000
India	90		550,000
Pakistan	130		128,000
Japan	1,660		103,000
Vietnam	170		40,000
Indonesia	90		118,000
Oceania		2,504	19,800
Australia	2,700		12,700
New Zealand	2,000		2,800

Source: *Statistical Abstract of U.S. 1973*, p. 813 and *U.N. Statistical Yearbook 1972*, pp. 8, 67–79
and 621–23.

tion to some persons' diets, as poor residents in less developed lands typically obtain only 8–12 grams of protein per day in their normal diet.[13]

Reading, writing, and marketing problems

■ The ability of a country's people to read and write has a direct bearing on the development of the economy and on business firms' marketing strategy planning. Certainly, the degree of literacy affects the communication of information – which in a marketing context means promotion.

An extensive analysis of literacy data in 136 countries showed that only 56 percent of the world's population is literate.[14] But this number must be interpreted with care. Most of this information is based on census materials that were compiled by asking the question, "Can you read and write?" A simple yes, as a second-grader might answer, would not pinpoint a person's literacy level.

Generally, there is a band of countries with low literacy rates extending from Latin America through Africa and the Near East to eastern Asia. At the other extreme, higher rates of literacy are found in Australia, Canada, United States, Western Europe, the Soviet bloc of Europe, Japan, and some Latin American countries.

Low literacy sometimes causes difficulties with product labels and with instructions for which we normally use words. In highly illiterate Africa, some manufacturers have found that placing a baby's picture on food packages is unwise, since illiterate natives believe that the product is just that – a ground-up baby! Singer Sewing Machine Co., met this lack of literacy with an instruction book which used no words.[15]

Even in Latin America, which has generally higher literacy rates than Africa or Asia, a substantial proportion of the population cannot read and write. Promotional programs have to use symbols, colors, and other nonverbal means of communication if they wish to reach the masses.

Careful market gridding is vital

■ The opportunities in international marketing are exciting ones, but their diversity presents a real challenge to marketing management. Obviously, the market grid concept should find special application when a firm is considering these markets.

The gridding concept is especially important since there often are subtleties that we would not pick up unless we were aggressively seeking out all the possibilities. Our neighbor, Canada, affords an excellent example.

Canadians are different

■ Some Americans think of Canadians only as our northern neighbors and as being pretty much like themselves. Actually, however, they have as much (or more) diversity as we have in the United States. The province of Quebec, for example, which has 30 percent of Canada's population, is a unique market. Quebec is predominantly French in heritage and language. Some French-Canadians feel they have suffered at the hands of the English-speaking majority of Canada. This attitude finds its expression in the marketplace, where French-Canadians support local producers, buying their goods in preference to those of firms from other parts of Canada or Great Britain or the United States.

What are you drinking?

■ Tastes do differ across national boundaries. French Burgundy wine intended for Belgian export must have a higher sugar content than the Burgundy intended for consumption in France. Burgundy shipped to Sweden must have still another sugar concentration to be sold successfully there.

Milk-drinking habits also differ substantially. Scandinavians consider milk a daily staple, while Latins feel that milk is only for children. A former French premier was able to get his picture on the front page of every Paris newspaper simply by drinking a glass of milk in public.

Who wears the makeup in France?

■ The great diversity in international markets almost demands marketing research to learn the habits and preferences of the many market grid boxes. Prejudices and stereotypes will not do.

The need for marketing research to avoid common stereotypes can be dramatized by the following results from a large-scale survey of European Common Market adults:

> The average Frenchman uses almost twice as many cosmetics and beauty aids as his wife.
>
> The Germans and the French eat more spaghetti than the Italians.
>
> French and Italian housewives are not as interested in cooking as their counterparts in Luxembourg and Belgium.[16]

Conclusion

■ The international market is large and keeps growing in population and income. New economic groupings such as the European Common Market are being developed in the hope of expanding output and income even more. Many American companies are becoming aware of the enormous opportunities open to alert and aggressive businessmen.

The great variations in stages of economic development, income, population, literacy, and other factors, however, mean that foreign markets must be treated as many separate target markets—and each studied carefully. Lumping foreign nations together under the common and vague heading of "foreigners" or, at the other extreme, assuming that they are just like U.S. customers, is almost a guarantee of failure. So is treating them like common movie stereotypes. It is clear that marketing management, marketing research, and the market grid concept all can play a significant role in international marketing.

Much of what we will discover about American marketing in subsequent chapters will also apply in the world market. Actually, not too many adjustments are necessary to sell to the world market —*except* to realize that the all-important customer may behave differently from what we would expect or hope.

The major stumbling block to success in international markets is an unwillingness to learn about and adjust to different peoples and cultures. To those who are willing to make these adjustments, the returns can be great.

questions and problems

1 Discuss the long-run prospects for (a) multi-national marketing by U.S. firms producing in the United States only, and (b) multinational firms which are willing to operate anywhere.

2 Discuss the prospects for a Latin American entrepreneur who is considering building a factory to produce machines which would manufacture cans for the food industry. His country happens to be in stage 4 — the non-durable and semidurable consumer goods manufacturing phase. The country's population is approximately 20 million and there is some possibility of establishing sales contacts in a few nearby countries.

3 Discuss the value of gross national product per capita as a measure of market potential. Refer to specific data in your answer.

4 Discuss the possibility of a multinational marketer using essentially the same promotion campaign in the United States and in many international markets.

5 Evaluate the growth of "common markets" in relation to the phases of economic development of the members. Is this basically a movement among the developed countries which are seeking to "catch up"?

6 Discuss the kinds of products which you feel may become popular in Europe in the near future. Does the material on U.S. consumption behavior discussed in the last chapter have any relevance here?

7 Discuss the probable importance of the market grid concept within the European Common Market.

notes

[1] "How Coke Runs a Foreign Empire," *Business Week,* August 25, 1973, pp. 40–43.

[2] "Multi-national Companies," *Business Week,* April 20, 1963, pp. 62–86; "Multi-national Firms Now Dominate Much of World's Production," *The Wall Street Journal,* April 18, 1973, p. 1 f; "ITT Europe Rings Up Profits; A Low Profile Keeps Troubles Minor," *The Wall Street Journal,* January 9, 1974, p. 1 f.

[3] "The New Competition From Foreign-Based Multi-Nationals," *Business Week,* July 7, 1973, pp. 56–58.

[4] "Foreign Ventures Fetch More Profit for U.S. Firms Based in the United States," *The Wall Street Journal,* November 1, 1973, p. 1.

[5] "The New Competition From Foreign-Based Multi-Nationals," *Business Week,* July 7, 1973, p. 56.

[6] Franklin R. Root, "Public Policy Expectations of Multi-national Managers," *MSU Business Topics,* Autumn 1973, pp. 5–12; "Domesticating the Multinationals," *Business Week,* May 26, 1973, p. 15; "Multinationals:

The Public Gives Them Low Marks," *Business Week,* June 9, 1973, pp. 42–44; and "The Unions Move Against Multinationals," *Business Week,* July 24, 1971, pp. 48–52.

[7] This discussion is based upon George Donat and Lawrence Dowd, "Formation of the European Economic Community," in L. P. Dowd, *The European Economic Community* (Michigan Business Reports, No. 36 [Ann Arbor: Bureau of Business Research, University of Michigan, 1961]).

[8] "11 Latin American Countries Make Trading Progress in Small Steps," *Marketing News,* May 15, 1974, p. 7; and Harry A. Lipson and Douglas F. Lamont, "Marketing Policy Decisions Facing International Marketers in the Less-Developed Countries," *Journal of Marketing,* October 1969, pp. 24–31.

[9] This discussion is based on William Copulsky's, "Forecasting Sales in Underdeveloped Countries," *Journal of Marketing,* July 1959, pp. 36–37. Another set of stages is interesting although less marketing-oriented. See: W. W.

Rostow, *The Stages of Economic Growth—A Non-Communist Manifesto* (New York: Cambridge University Press, 1960).

[10] The *Statistical Abstract* and the U.S. Department of Commerce Bureau of International Commerce would be a good place to start locating current data. In its publication, *International Commerce*, the Department of Commerce issues a semiannual checklist of material it feels will be helpful to businessmen interested in the world market. The *Statistical Year Book* of the Statistical Office of the United Nations is also a good source of basic data.

[11] Donald G. Halper, "The Environment for Marketing in Peru," *Journal of Marketing*, July 1966, pp. 42–46.

[12] (Lansing, Mich.) *State Journal*, February 10, 1970, p. D-7.

[13] *Wall Street Journal*, August 8, 1968, p. 1.

[14] Norton Ginsberg, *Atlas of Economic Development* (Chicago: University of Chicago Press, 1961).

[15] Edward Marcus, "Selling the Tropical African Market," *Journal of Marketing*, July 1961, p. 30.

[16] Robert L. Brown, "The Common Market: What Its New Consumer Is Like," *Printers' Ink*, May 31, 1963, pp. 23–25.

11

Forecasting target market potential and sales

■ Estimates of market potential and likely sales volumes are vital for effective marketing management. But a manager cannot develop a sales forecast until he has some tentative plans. In other words, forecasting and marketing strategy planning are interdependent. Sales are not just "out there for the taking." Market opportunities may be out there, but whether a particular firm converts these opportunities into sales depends upon which marketing strategy is selected. A strategy, therefore, should be incorporated into the sales forecasting process.

Most of this chapter is concerned with approaches for estimating *market potential* or "opportunities." The term "opportunities" will be used sometimes to emphasize that market potential is concerned with what a whole market segment might buy, while *sales potential* is concerned with how much the firm can hope to sell to that segment. We must first estimate the market potential before we can estimate what share a particular firm may be able to realize.

Our primary focus will be on forecasting for a reasonable planning period, such as a year, rather than long-run "blue-sky" estimates, or weekly or monthly forecasts to guide current operations. These forecasts require different techniques and are beyond our scope.

Two basic approaches to forecasting

■ Many techniques are used in forecasting potential and sales, but they can be grouped under two basic approaches: (1) extending past behavior; and (2) anticipating future behavior. The large number of techniques may seem confusing at first, but in fact this variety proves to be an advantage. Forecasts are so important that management often prefers to develop forecasts in two or three different ways, and then reconcile the differences before preparing a final forecast.

Extending past behavior — trend extension

■ When we forecast for existing products, we usually have some historical data to go on. The basic approach is to project past sales experience into the future. See Figure 11-1.

Ideally, when extending past sales behavior, one should determine *why* sales fluctuate. This is a difficult and time-consuming aspect of sales forecasting. Usually we can gather a lot of data about the product or market or about the economic environment. But unless the *why* of past sales fluctuations is known, it is difficult to predict in what direction and to what degree sales will move. Graphing of the data, and statistical techniques, including correlation and regression analysis, can be useful here. These techniques are beyond our scope; they are discussed in beginning statistics courses.

Once we know why sales fluctuate, it generally is quite easy to develop a specific forecast. Sales may be moving directly up as population or income grows, for example, and we can simply obtain or develop an estimate of how population and income are expected to grow and make the appropriate calculations. Or, sometimes trend lines can be used to project the past data into the future.

The big limitation of the trend-extension method is that it assumes conditions in the past will continue unchanged into the future. In fact, the future is not always like the past, and, unfortunately, trend-extension techniques usually will be wrong whenever there are important fluctuations. For this reason, although they may extend past behavior for one estimate, most forecasters seek another method to help them anticipate sharp economic changes.

Anticipating future behavior

■ When we try to anticipate what will happen in the future, rather than just extending the past, we have to use other methods and add a bit more judgment. Some of these methods, to be discussed later, include: juries of executive opinion, salesmen's estimates, surveys, panels, and market tests.

Three levels of forecast are useful

■ We are interested in forecasting the potential in specific market grid boxes. To reach this goal, it helps to make several kinds of forecasts.

Some economic conditions affect the entire economy. Other factors may influence only one industry, and some may affect only a specific company or a particular product's sales potential. For this reason, a common approach to sales forecasting is to:

1. Develop a *national economic forecast* and use this to. . . .

Figure 11–1
Straight-line trend projection — extends past sales into the future

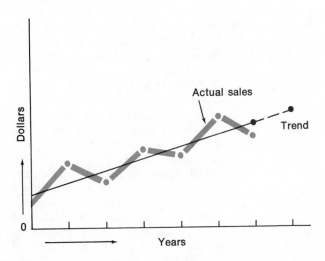

2. Develop an *industry sales forecast,* which in turn is used to. . . .
3. Develop *specific company and product forecasts.*

Developing national economy forecasts

■ Gross national product (GNP) is widely used as an estimate of the economic health of the economy. GNP is an estimate of the market value of goods and services produced in a year and is roughly equal to the national income.

An estimate for GNP is a good starting point for developing industry and company sales forecasts, since sales curves usually rise when GNP goes up, and vice versa. A variety of trend extension methods and macro-economic models are used to forecast GNP and its various macro components. The models use data on actual consumer, business, and government expenditures, and surveys on their expectations. Some analysts merely add together the forecasts secured from various sources. Others use these data to develop mathematical equations for forecasting purposes.

Developing national economy forecasts is a specialty in itself. Fortunately, aggregate forecasts are available in business and government publications, so individual businessmen can simply accept one source's forecast, or combine several together into their own estimate.

Developing industry sales forecasts

■ Once the future course of the entire economy has been estimated, the next step is to make a forecast for industry sales; i.e., sales in the firm's general product-market area. Since the two are often closely related, simply extending this past relationship may be effective. Automobile sales, for example, reflect the level of national income, since auto sales normally go up as national income rises. But it would be most unusual for such a relationship to be direct; i.e., a 1 percent increase in some national aggregate seldom leads to a 1 percent increase in industry sales. Therefore, some statistical analysis has to be done to determine the degree of relationship between the two (or more) variables.

Someone else may forecast

Just as a marketing manager does not have to do all of the work in developing national economy estimates, he may not have to do industry estimates either. Some (for broad categories such as steel, cement, plywood, and housing) industry estimates are published regularly by government agencies, banks, trade associations, and business publications. Private firms also do forecasting for others at reasonable prices.

While a marketing manager doesn't have to gather and analyze all this data himself, he should know what is going on. Then he can use the forecast properly at the next step—forecasting his own company and product sales—where less outside help is available. However, the more targeted a marketing manager's planning has become, the less likely it is that readily available industry data will be appropriate. In fact, he may have created his own little "industry" and thus must move directly to forecasting for his company and for specific products.

Developing company and product forecasts

■ Now the marketing manager must forecast magnitudes which are of interest only to people in his own firm. He may use some of the techniques applied by macro-level forecasters, but here he must focus on specific market grid boxes. This is the subject of the rest of this chapter.

Forecasting sales for new products is a tougher assignment than forecasting for established products, and also calls for slightly different techniques. Therefore, we'll discuss these two forecasting jobs separately.

Forecasting sales for established products

Sales analysis shows what is going on

■ A detailed breakdown of a company's sales records can be very illuminating, especially the first time it is done. At the very least, the marketing manager ought to know what the market grid in his general area looks like, and what his company has done, to give him a solid basis for forecasting in the future. Then, a simple extension of past behavior would permit the marketing manager to make one forecast at least.

Too often, men who have moved into management positions are not aware of specific changes that have taken place in the field since they were out there. This is especially true of managers who have assistants to handle details. Yet the broad marketing decisions for which they are responsible are made on the basis of their knowledge of the business, however outdated or incomplete it may be.

Some managers resist sales analysis, or any analysis for that matter, because they do not fully appreciate how valuable it can be to them. One top executive in a large consumer products firm made no attempt to analyze his company's sales, even by geographical area. When asked why, he replied: "Why should we? We're making money!"

But today's profit is no guarantee that you'll make money tomorrow. In fact, ignoring market analysis can lead not only to poor sales forecasting but to poor decisions in general. One manufacturer did extensive national advertising on the premise that the firm was, in fact, selling all over the country. A simple sales analysis, however, revealed that the vast majority of his customers were within a 250-mile radius of the factory. In other words, the firm did not know who and where its customers were and was wasting most of the money it spent on national advertising.

But marketing manager must ask for it

Detailed sales analysis is only a possibility, however, unless management makes definite arrangements for gathering the data. Valuable sales information is regularly buried in sales invoice files after the usual accounting functions are completed. Manual analysis of such records is so lengthy and burdensome that it is seldom undertaken.

Today, with electronic data processing equipment, effective sales analysis can be done easily and at comparatively small cost — if marketing management makes up its mind to do it. In fact, the information desired can be obtained as a by-product of basic billing and accounts receivable procedures. The manager simply must be sure that identifying information on dimensions important to him, such as territory, salesman, and so forth, are recorded in machine-processable form. Then, sales analysis and simple trend projections can easily be run.

What to ask for varies

There is no one best way to analyze sales data. One or several information breakdowns may be appropriate, depending on the nature of the company, product, and which market grid dimensions are relevant. Typical breakdowns which are often useful include:

1. Geographical region — state, county, city, salesmen's territory.
2. Product, package size, grade, or color.
3. Customer size.
4. Customer type or class of trade.
5. Price or discount class.
6. Method of sale — mail, telephone, or direct salesman.
7. Financial arrangement — cash or charge.
8. Size of order.
9. Commission class.

While this information might be readily available on invoices, and useful for some types of analyses, relevant market grid dimensions might not be included. As we saw in Chapters 4 and 6, the relevant market grid dimensions are not always readily measurable. It is also likely that they will not be available on the firm's invoices. Nevertheless, simply extending the past data, even without the relevant dimensions, can give one sales forecast which can be compared with those obtained by other techniques.

Single factor method looks ahead

■ Naïve extension of past sales yields one forecast but it usually is desirable to relate future sales to something more than the passage of time and the continuation of past trends. The single factor method attempts to remedy this situation.

With the single factor method, one tries to find a relation between the company's sales and some other data which is readily available, perhaps forecasted by others. This approach may yield more accurate forecasts than would be possible with simple extension of the firm's own sales data.

The following example for a bread manufacturer shows how forecasts can be made for many geographical market grid boxes using available data. This general approach can be useful for any firm, be it a manufacturer, wholesaler, or retailer.

Analysis of past sales relationships may show that a particular bread manufacturer regularly achieved one half of 1 percent (0.005) of the total retail food sales in his target markets. Estimates of retail sales for the coming period in these areas, then, could be used by the firm to forecast its bread sales (by multiplying 0.005 times the expected retail food sales in each market).

Retail sales estimates can be based on past sales figures from sources such as *Sales Management* magazine. Figure 11-2 shows the kind of geographically detailed data available each year in a summer issue of *Sales Management*.[1] Similar data is available for industrial markets.

This data is carefully updated year after year and has correlated with surprising accuracy with the U.S. censuses upon which it is based. Evanston, Illinois, for example, accounts for 0.0382 of the U.S. population, but has a much larger share, .0520, of buying power. The food sales dollar figure—$37,585—is an estimate of last year's food sales in this city. Thus, by extending past trends, our bread manufacturer can estimate future food sales. Then, by finding his firm's usual share—0.5 percent—he would have his own sales estimate. Or if he planned an especially aggressive promotion campaign, he might increase his estimates by multiplying forecasted food sales by 0.0055 rather than 0.005, to provide for an expected sales increase of 10 percent.

Multiple factor method uses more data

■ Consumer behavior is definitely multidimensional. If a firm has data on each of its relevant dimensions and some idea of the relation of these dimensions to buying behavior, then it may be able to multiply all of this data together to obtain an estimate of sales potential.

A West Coast manufacturer of sets of novelty beer mugs, for

Figure 11-2
Sample page from *Sales Management*, "Annual Survey of Buying Power," retail sales estimates—Illinois

Illinois (Cont.)
SM ESTIMATES SS

COUNTIES / CITIES	Met. Area Code	POPULATION 12/31/73 Total (thousands)	% of U.S.	House-holds (thousands)	Net Dollars ($000)	EBI 1973 Median Hsld.	% Hslds. By EBI Group (A) $0–2.999 (B) $3,000–4.999 (C) $5,000–7.999 (D) $8,000–9.999 (E) $10,000–14.999 (F) $15,000 and Over						Total Retail Sales ($000)	% of U.S.	Food ($000)	General Mdse. ($000)	Furn. House. Appl. ($000)	Auto-motive ($000)	Drug ($000)	Buying Power Index
							A	B	C	D	E	F								
Cook	.56	5,539.3	2.6264	1,890.5	28,306,511	11,557	8.5	6.1	13.7	12.9	28.3	30.5	14,119,659	2.7468	2,805,124	2,256,240	731,137	2,279,364	555,528	2.9563
Arlington Heights		73.2	.0347	21.4	458,698	15,754	3.4	2.0	5.0	7.8	29.5	52.3	191,715	.0373	44,190	15,728	15,412	60,904	13,366	.0442
Berwyn		51.0	.0242	20.7	285,835	11,521	8.8	6.4	11.8	13.9	29.7	29.4	159,174	.0310	32,761	21,221	9,880	31,699	9,935	.0304
▲Chicago		3,291.9	1.5608	1,185.3	15,112,916	9,959	11.3	8.0	17.2	13.8	25.6	24.1	7,858,729	1.5288	1,405,110	1,425,904	424,448	1,073,417	298,172	1.6288
Chicago Heights		42.5	.0202	13.2	185,751	11,460	7.3	5.2	14.0	14.4	31.2	27.9	169,685	.0330	32,579	22,598	13,152	44,969	6,620	.0245
Cicero		65.4	.0310	25.6	337,678	11,227	7.7	5.6	14.2	15.1	30.7	26.7	127,504	.0248	30,492	9,665	3,868	23,114	4,683	.0328
Des Plaines		56.2	.0266	17.6	337,393	14,247	3.0	2.4	6.5	10.2	32.8	45.1	266,836	.0519	66,270	15,983	4,351	95,517	12,531	.0400
Evanston		80.5	.0382	29.3	557,568	13,143	9.5	5.6	11.5	9.8	21.5	42.1	217,907	.0424	37,585	25,410	15,514	75,748	6,563	.0520
Oak Lawn		63.8	.0303	18.4	337,343	13,989	3.0	2.0	6.3	11.5	34.1	43.1	242,232	.0471	55,887	39,413	6,127	70,769	8,455	.0393
Oak Park		62.1	.0294	23.9	425,270	12,791	10.2	5.3	10.9	10.2	24.1	39.3	177,734	.0346	30,737	16,284	8,290	69,992	5,923	.0404
Park Ridge		45.1	.0214	14.6	335,011	16,791	5.8	2.6	6.3	7.7	22.5	55.1	107,498	.0209	19,719	5,171	6,080	44,579	5,877	.0296
Skokie		71.1	.0337	22.9	523,405	16,482	2.7	2.1	5.9	7.7	27.1	54.5	381,967	.0743	53,076	79,102	24,183	72,959	9,996	.0587
Crawford		21.9	.0104	8.4	85,482	8,601	19.6	11.6	15.4	11.5	24.6	17.3	42,144	.0082	10,053	2,887	2,140	10,118	1,782	.0094
Cumberland		10.3	.0049	3.7	41,643	8,465	17.0	10.7	19.3	12.7	18.6	21.7	19,698	.0038	3,190	3,750	1,177	2,305	1,614	.0045
De Kalb		72.4	.0343	21.2	290,598	10,645	11.8	7.0	14.7	13.1	26.8	26.6	172,904	.0336	32,397	14,597	9,132	38,446	5,097	.0334
De Witt		16.3	.0077	6.0	65,053	8,934	15.3	11.0	17.1	14.1	22.8	19.7	48,150	.0094	10,385	2,466	2,644	10,911	550	.0081
Douglas		19.1	.0091	6.6	68,864	8,557	16.4	11.0	18.6	14.4	23.1	16.5	46,235	.0090	8,093	1,690	2,792	11,631	1,035	.0084
▲Du Page	.56	519.6	.2464	152.4	2,976,737	14,192	4.0	2.9	7.3	10.4	30.3	45.1	1,727,475	.3361	360,274	291,594	49,912	341,796	66,839	.3191
Elmhurst		52.3	.0248	15.9	331,930	15,468	4.3	2.8	6.3	8.1	27.1	51.4	173,393	.0337	30,239	22,886	2,863	63,791	5,321	.0339
Edgar		21.5	.0102	7.9	78,769	7,693	18.7	13.1	20.3	13.6	18.5	15.8	48,710	.0095	11,526	3,313	1,392	11,310	1,787	.0093
Edwards		7.0	.0033	2.7	25,969	7,193	22.8	12.9	19.9	11.3	17.1	16.0	10,353	.0020	2,253	215	419	3,024	106	.0027

Buying Power index (BPI) is a weighted average of each market's strength. Each market's share of U.S. population is multiplied (weighted) by 2, its income by 5, and its retail sales share by 3. The resulting sum is divided by 10 (the total weighting) to give the BPI.
▲ SMSA.

Boldface type indicates county data.

Source: *Sales Management*, July 8, 1974, p. D-34. © 1974, Sales Management Survey of Buying Power; further reproduction is forbidden.

example, might be interested in the potential for his products in the New York City area. If his target market consisted of young, low-income families without children, and he expected that about 10 percent of these people could be expected to buy his $5 sets within a one-year period, then he could multiply the appropriate numbers together as shown below and determine that 7,344 buying families will spend $5 each for a total sales potential of $36,720.

Families in New York City	2,000,000
× Percent earning under $5,000	43.2
	864,000
× Percent under 25 years	20.0
	172,800
× Percent without children	42.5
Number of families	73,440
× Share of market (percent)	10.0
	7,344
× Price of product (in dollars)	5
Total sales potential	$36,720

Direct use by a retailer

This kind of analysis is applicable not only to large manufacturers, but to retail store managers as well. To illustrate we will use the NICB average annual family expenditure data like that introduced in Chapter 7. Here we will look at the problem of a soft goods retailer who is thinking about adding refrigerators and similar large appliances. The NICB study does have data on refrigerator purchases, and 700 other products and services.

The store manager knows that he is now serving a lower-income target market and wants to get an idea of the relative magnitude of their current refrigerator purchases. His credit records give him a good measure of the number and income of his regular customers. He finds that about half are in the under-$3,000-a-year family income bracket, while the other half are in the $3,000-to-$5,000 bracket.

One of the tables in the NICB study shows that while the average expenditure for refrigerators was $14.56, the lowest income category spent only $6.17 for refrigerators, and the $3,000-to-$5,000 income group spent only $12.90.[2]

As would be expected, the higher-income group spent more, probably reflecting both more frequent purchases and purchases of larger units. Data did show, nevertheless, that the lower-income consumers were buying refrigerators. By multiplying the average purchase per family times the number of families in each of the income groups, the department store manager developed an estimate of the total purchases in his target market. By making similar calculations for the other major appliances he was considering, he could estimate the total spending for such commodities.[3]

After the department store manager has developed an estimate of the expenditures of his target customers, he would then have to estimate the likelihood of his getting a share of this business. He would also have to evaluate the possibility of attracting other people, including those like his present customers, if he added appliances to his line. And before the final decision was made, the manager would have to consider competition. At the start, however, the expenditure data would add hard facts to the analysis.

Manipulating available data

Sometimes several factors have to be manipulated in some logical way, perhaps dividing one by another, or using regression analysis to determine appropriate coefficients. Figure 11–3 shows how one analyst estimated the market for fiber boxes for a particular county. In this case, widely available data by SIC code was used and it is extremely important for the student to recognize that such data is available and used. In this case, the value of box shipments by SIC code category were collected by a trade association. This data in turn was divided by employment statistics tabulated by SIC code and available from the U.S. Census Bureau to obtain the typical consumption per employee in each SIC industry group. This average consumption figure was then multiplied by the actual employment in the subject county to obtain a market potential estimate for each group. Then, the sum of all of these estimates became the total market potential in that county. A firm thinking of going into that market would have had to estimate what share it felt it could get with its own marketing mix.

Note that this approach can also aid management's control job. If the firm were already in this industry, it could compare its actual sales (by SIC code) with the potential and see how it is doing. If its typical market share is 10 percent of the market and it is obtaining only 2–5 percent of the market in various SIC sub-markets, then some marketing mix changes may be in order.

Time series and leading series may help estimate a fluctuating future

■ Not all past economic or sales behavior can be neatly extended with a straight line or some manipulation. Much economic activity is characterized by ups and downs. To cope with such variation, statisticians have developed time-series analysis techniques. A detailed discussion of these techniques is beyond the scope of this book, but it should be noted that there are techniques to handle daily, weekly, monthly, seasonal, and annual variations.[4]

The dream of all forecasters is to find an accurate leading series. This is a time series which, for some reason, changes in the same direction *but ahead of* the series to be forecasted. No single series has yet been found that leads GNP or other important quantities. Lacking such a series, forecasters develop indices – statistical compilations of several series – in an effort to find some index that will lead the series they are attempting to forecast. Some indices of this type are published by the Census Bureau of the U.S. Department of Commerce in a booklet, *Business Cycle Developments*.[5] And business magazines, such as *Business Week*, publish their own series.

Input-output analysis helps some forecasters

■ Another sophisticated forecasting technique which we cannot treat fully here is input-output analysis. Simply extending past data may be extremely risky if a seemingly remote development in one part of the economy may have a direct impact on another part, and

Figure 11–3
Estimated market for corrugated and solid fibre box by industry groups, Phoenix, Arizona
Standard Metropolitan Statistical Area, 1962

SIC major group code	Using industry	Value of box shipments by end use ($ 000)[1] 1	Employment by industry groups[3] 2	Consumption per employee by industry groups (1 ÷ 2) (dollars) 3	Maricopa County Employment by industry groups[3] 4	Estimated share of th market (3 ⨯ ($ 000) 5
20	Food & Kindred Products	586,164	1,578,305	371	4,973	1,845
21	Tobacco	17,432	74,557	233	–	–
22	Textile Mill Products	91,520	874,677	104	–	–
23	Apparel	34,865	1,252,443	27	1,974	53
24	Lumber & Products (except furniture)	19,611	526,622	37	690	26
25	Furniture & Fixtures	89,341	364,166	245	616	151
26	Paper & Allied Products	211,368	587,882	359	190	68
27	Printing; Publishing, & Allied Industries	32,686	904,208	36	2,876	104
28	Chemicals & Allied Products	128,564	772,169	166	488	81
29	Petroleum Refining & related Industries	28,328	161,367	175	–	–
30	Rubber & Misc. Plastic Products	67,551	387,997	174	190	33
31	Leather & Leather Prod.	8,716	352,919	24	–	–
32	Stone, Clay & Glass Prod.	226,621	548,058	413	1,612	666
33	Primary Metal Industries	19,611	1,168,110	16	2,889	46
34	Fabricated Metal Products	130,743	1,062,096	123	2,422	298
35	Machinery; except Electrical	58,834	1,445,558	40	5,568	223
36	Electrical Machinery, Equipment & Supplies	119,848	1,405,382	391	6,502	553
37	Transportation Equipment	82,804	1,541,618	53	5,005	265
38	Professional, Scientific Instruments, etc.	13,074	341,796	38	–	–
39	Misc. Manufacturing Industries	200,473	369,071	543	376	204
90	Government	10,895	–	–	–	–
	Total	2,179,049[2]	–	–	–	4,616

[1] Based on data reported in *Fibre Box Industry Statistics 1963*, Fibre Box Association.
[2] U.S. Bureau of the Census, *1962 Annual Survey of Manufacturers: General Statistics for Industry Groups and Industries* (M62(AS)-1 Revised) Table 1—General Statistics for Industry Groups and Industries: 1962, 1961, and 1958, p. 10.
[3] U.S. Bureau of the Census, *County Business Patterns, First Quarter 1962*, Parts 1 and 9.

in particular the part of interest to the marketing managers' firm.[6]

For example, a manufacturer of sulfuric acid, used in manufacturing paper pulp, can predict future industry sales of his product more accurately with an input-output analysis involving interactions such as the following: An additional $1 billion appropriated for federal aid to education would lead to a predictable increase in the number of textbooks used, which in turn would increase paper consumption and paper pulp manufacturing, which uses his firm's sulfuric acid. But if the manufacturer based his forecast only on past sales in the paper pulp business, his forecast might be seriously in error.

Some forecasting methods call for more judgment and some "opinions"

Jury of executive opinion

■ The methods discussed above make use of "hard" data, projecting past experience into the future on the assumption that the future will be somewhat like the past. But in dynamic markets, adding judgment to hard data is increasingly important. Further, competitors' and the firm's own marketing mixes affect both potential and current sales.

One of the oldest and simplest methods of forecasting—the "jury" approach—is an attempt to work in the opinions of several executives, perhaps from marketing, production, finance, purchasing, and top management. The idea here is to utilize as much seasoned management judgment as possible in combination with analysis of past data.

The main advantage of the jury approach is that it can be done quickly and easily. On the other hand, the results may not be spectacular, because they represent the consensus of a number of viewpoints. In addition, the jury method is most suitable for aggregate estimates, but what operating managers ultimately need is a more precise breakdown by products, time intervals, and specific geographic markets.

Salesmen's estimates

■ This approach is similar to the jury approach, except that the opinions sought are those of sales personnel. This approach can be much more reliable where competition is dynamic.

The sales force is more likely than home office analysts to be familiar with customer reactions, to know what competitors are doing, and is, therefore, more able to anticipate changes. Salesmen's estimates are especially useful in industrial markets with a limited number of customers who are well known to the salesmen. But this approach is useful in any type of market. A good retail clerk has a feel for his market, and his observations should not be ignored.

Two qualifications concerning the use of salesmen's estimates, however, should be kept in mind.

First, salesmen normally are not familiar with anticipated changes in the national economic climate, nor even with proposed changes in the company's marketing mix. As a result, their estimates must often be adjusted by the home office in light of national and industry forecasts and other factors.

Second, sales force estimates must be used with care if there is high turnover in sales personnel and if the estimates are used for other purposes. If subsequent performance and compensation are based on estimates, for example, then the estimates may be low. Alternately, if the promotion money budgeted to each territory is based on sales prospects, then the estimates may be high. In these cases, it is only human for salesmen to tailor their forecasts to their own advantage.

Keeping these qualifications in mind, sales force estimates can provide another basis for comparison before final forecasts are developed.

Surveys, panels, and market tests

■ Instead of relying heavily upon salesmen to estimate customers' intentions, it may be desirable to use some marketing research techniques (to be discussed more fully in Chapter 28). Special surveys of final buyers, retailers, and wholesalers can be illuminating, showing what is happening in different market segments. Some firms use panels of stores or final consumers to keep track of buying behavior and to determine when simply extending past behavior has become inadequate.

Survey techniques are sometimes combined with market tests when the company wants to estimate the reaction of customers to possible changes in the marketing mix. In one such market test, a product increased its share of the market by 10 percent when its price was dropped 1 cent below competition. Yet this extra business was quickly lost when the price increased 1 cent above competition.[7]

Such market experiments enable the marketing manager to make realistic estimates of future sales when one or more of the four Ps are changed.

Forecasting sales for new products

■ Forecasting sales for new products is the most difficult task of all—and the most risky. If the product is really new, there is no relevant historical data that can be projected. It is also unrealistic to expect potential customers or even salesmen to have valid opinions about things with which they are unacquainted.

The situation is not hopeless, however. The substitute method, need analysis, and market tests can be useful here.

Substitute method

■ Since few products are entirely new, careful analysis of the sales of products which the new one may displace can provide, at the least, an upper limit on potential sales. With imagination and research, a company can list most possible uses and determine the potential in the present markets. Once the potential upper limits of the markets have been ascertained, these figures can be scaled down by market realities, including likely customer preferences at various price levels.

Figure 11–4
Size of market possibilities

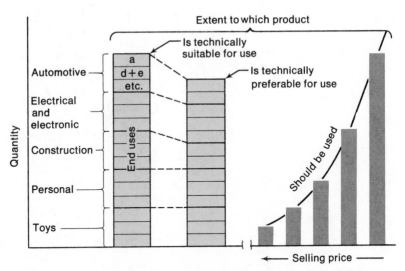

Source: G. T. Borchert, "Design of the Marketing Program for a New Product," in Robert L. Clewett (ed.), *Marketing's Role in Scientific Management* (Chicago: American Marketing Association, 1957), p. 64.

This procedure can be illustrated by the forecasting done by Du Pont for a plastic resin product.

The chemical company began by estimating the size of the various end-use markets—shown as the left series of boxes in Figure 11–4. These were markets where the resin product was technically suitable for use, including automotive, electrical, electronic, construction, personal, and toy products. The sum of the potential in all of these boxes indicated the upper limit on demand. Then a harder look at the suitability of the product in comparison with those currently being used indicated that one of the planned automotive and construction applications should be dropped.

The markets where the new product was technically preferable for use are shown in Figure 11–4, in the second bar from the left. These first two market-possibility bars, however, ignore potential selling prices which are realities in any market. So the potential demand at various selling prices was considered. The five right-hand bars in Figure 11–4 show the various quantities of the product that technically should be used at various price levels. The extreme right-hand bar indicates that if prices were low enough, all of the potential users would use the product.

Many potentials but one forecast

The data in Figure 11–4 are shown in a different way and with more detail in Figure 11–5.

Here the relation of the market grid concept, demand curves, and marketing strategy planning becomes clearer. At a high selling

Figure 11–5
Framework of market possibilities

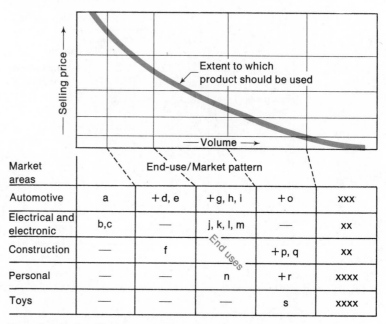

Market areas		End-use/Market pattern			
Automotive	a	+d, e	+g, h, i	+o	xxx
Electrical and electronic	b,c	—	j, k, l, m	—	xx
Construction	—	f		+p, q	xx
Personal	—	—	n	+r	xxxx
Toys	—	—	—	s	xxxx

Source: G. T. Borchert, "Design of the Marketing Program for a New Product," in Robert L. Clewett (ed.), *Marketing's Role in Scientific Management* (Chicago: American Marketing Association, 1967), p. 66.

price, interest would be shown by one of the potential automotive markets and by electrical and electronic users (markets a, b, and c). If the price were dropped slightly, additional automotive users (d and e) and a construction industry user (f) would add to the potential market. In other words, potential target markets are being specified as part of the sales forecasting procedure.

This approach, however, merely indicates market potentials. Determining a specific sales forecast requires a decision to go after particular target markets with the necessary marketing mixes. Many marketing strategy decisions — one for each potential target market — must be made. When all of these decisions are made and combined with judgments about the probability of achieving certain market shares, the sales forecast develops as a by-product.

Need analysis in possible market grid boxes

■ If the product is so new that no present product-market can be used as a guide, then the marketing manager may have to use a survey to determine who might be interested in the product and why. And the seven-step approach to market gridding introduced in Chapter 6 could be applied. Even an informal survey may be illuminating. This kind of forecasting may seem crude in comparison with the techniques described previously, but it is no less important. Careful analysis of this type may produce clear alternatives. It may show that the highest attainable sales volume for a product either is too small to warrant further research and development, or the outlook may prove to be so attractive that, despite the crude estimate, enthusiasm seems justified.

Calculations killed this slide rule

The following simple example illustrates this approach.

A firm developed a 5-inch plastic slide rule that would help the housewife determine which was the "best buy" among several products and packages at a supermarket. After discussion with a few friends, the company's executives were sure that some housewives would be interested. But how many? And which ones? Men probably should have been considered, too, because they do some shopping, but the executives limited their initial investigation to housewives.

A small-scale survey of women was discouraging, with only 5 percent of the housewives questioned showing any interest. The survey was not large enough to determine all characteristics on a housewife market grid, but it appeared that only the more highly educated, younger housewives were the ones who might be interested—and only if the retail price of the slide rule were under 70 cents.

The company then talked to retailers to see how they reacted to the product. Informal investigation with some retailers indicated a lack of enthusiasm, though some were willing to give it a try.

It looked as if the achievable potential would be quite low. Specific figures confirmed this. The 5 percent of the housewives who *might* be interested, multiplied by approximately 50 million American families, suggested an upper limit of 2.5 million units. When potential retail availability was considered, this potential upper limit was reduced to 100,000 units *or less*. In view of the fact that a premium price could not be obtained (the rule itself would cost about 25 cents to make), and that repeat sales were highly unlikely, the project was dropped.

Market tests — what will the S-curve look like?

■ Sometimes the only way to estimate the market potential of a new product is to actually try it in the market. Several test markets can be used, and assuming they are fairly representative (a very large assumption!), the results can be projected to a larger area.

Forecasting from market test results, however, can be misleading, since the very novelty of the product seems to attract some customers. This means that analysis of the sales pattern in the market test must consider what is called the "S-curve" effect. This refers to the phenomenon of sales shooting up just after the product is introduced and then declining quickly, leveling off, and then *perhaps* rising as a market of repeat customers develops.

Haste makes mistakes . . . or success

The major problem is estimating where the market will level off, not the initial peak. This may require continuing market research over several months or even a year or two, depending upon the product and the eventual repeat customer rate.

Some companies have been misled by the initial sales boom. Others have been misled by the early results *plus* their eagerness to market their product ahead of competition. Hurried testing (or none at all) may lead to costly mistakes — and the failure rate is very high on new products. But more extensive market testing may prove a luxury in our highly competitive markets, especially if more venturesome competitors are monitoring the test and then beat the innovator to national distribution. This has happened often enough to discourage some firms from testing new products.

Accuracy of forecasts

■ The accuracy of forecasts may vary considerably, depending upon the number of components in the magnitude being forecast. The more general the value being forecast, the more accurate the forecast is likely to be. This is because small errors in various components of the estimate tend to offset each other and make the aggregate estimate more accurate.

Annual forecasts of national aggregates, such as GNP, may be accurate within 5 percent. Industry sales forecasts, which tend to be more specific, are usually accurate within 10 percent, depending upon the inherent variability of the industry.

When estimates are made for individual products, there is even less chance of offsetting errors, except where errors from one salesman or territory offset those in another. Where style and innovation are important factors in an industry, forecast errors of 10 to 20 percent for *established products* are not uncommon. The accuracy of specific *new-product* forecasts is even lower. Many new products fail completely, while others are overwhelmingly successful.

One forecaster of new consumer and industrial products claimed he had an excellent overall forecasting average for a particular year. He was off by only 2 percent on the average. His inaccuracy on specific product forecasts, however, was frightening. Many products did not sell at all — he missed by 100 percent, in other words — and others exceeded his expectations by 200 to 300 percent.[8]

Conclusion

■ This chapter has discussed several approaches to forecasting market opportunities. The most common approach is to extend past behavior into the future. Where market conditions are fairly stable, reasonably good results can be obtained with this method. Techniques here include straightforward extension of past sales data, the single factor method, the multiple factor method, time series analysis, and input-output models. Unfortunately, projecting the past into the future is weak whenever sharp market changes are likely to occur — and it is precisely at those times that good forecasts are most needed. To compensate for this possible weakness, the manager must use his own experience and judgment. He also may be able to bring in the judgment of others in the firm using the jury of executive opinion method and salesmen's estimates, and he may also be able to use surveys, panels, and market tests.

Forecasting potential for new products is even more difficult than for established products. There is no past data to extend. The substitute method can be useful, however, as well as need analysis and market tests. In the end, of course, considerable judgment is required.

We saw that the accuracy of forecasts depends on how general a forecast is being made – with the most inaccuracy when specific forecasts for products, and especially new products, are made.

Even though forecasts are subject to error, they still must be made. Without some estimate of potential sales, it is not possible to evaluate alternative strategies. Further, such forecasts require consideration of the likely attractiveness of the planned marketing mixes. In other words, forecasting and marketing strategy planning are interrelated. This should be kept in mind as we move on into planning marketing mixes in Chapters 12–26. Marketing mixes are designed to satisfy potential customers, and if good mixes are planned and implemented, then sales (and profits) result as forecasted.

questions and problems

1 Explain the difference between a forecast of market opportunities and a sales forecast.

2 Suggest a plausible explanation for sales fluctuations for (a) bicycles, (b) baby food, (c) motor boats, (d) baseball gloves, (e) wheat, (f) woodworking tools, and (g) latex for rubber-based paint.

3 Discuss the relative accuracy of the various forecasting techniques. Explain why some are more accurate than others.

4 Explain the difference between the single factor method and the multiple factor method and how one would decide which method to use.

5 Given the following annual sales data for a company which is not planning any spectacular marketing strategy changes, forecast sales for the coming year (7) and explain your method and reasoning.

A		B	
Year	Sales (in 000's)	Year	Sales (in 000's)
1	200	1	160
2	230	2	155
3	210	3	165
4	220	4	160
5	200	5	170
6	220	6	165

6 Discuss the relative market potential of Cicero and Evanston, Illinois, for: (a) prepared cereals, (b) automobiles, and (c) furniture.

7 Discuss how a General Motors market analyst might use the substitute method if the company were considering the potential for an electric car which might be suitable for salesmen, commuters, housewives, farmers, and perhaps other groups. The analyst is trying to consider the potential in terms of possible price levels— $1,000, $1,500, $2,000, $3,000, and $4,000 — and driving ranges—10 miles, 20 miles, 50 miles, 100 miles, and 200 miles—which would typically be desired or needed before recharging. He is assuming that gasoline-powered vehicles would become illegal for use within the major urban cities. Further, it is expected that while personal gasoline-driven cars still would be used in rural and suburban areas, they would not be permitted within some suburban areas, especially around the major metropolitan areas.

notes

[1] Look for the "Survey of Buying Power" issue. Similar current data are published by others. Standard Rate and Data Service, for example, provides less detailed monthly data of this type. *The Editor and Publisher Market Guide*, and *Industrial Marketing* magazine also publish annual data supplements.

[2] Fabian Linden (ed.), *Expenditure Patterns of the American Family* (New York: National Industrial Conference Board, 1965), pp. 70–75.

[3] The NICB study provides a variety of data, including information on the following appliances: refrigerators, home freezers, dishwashers, gas stoves, electric stoves, floor waxers, garbage disposal units, vacuum cleaners, washing machines, dryers, air conditioners, dehumidifiers, sewing machines, and ironers.

[4] See most basic statistics textbooks under time-series analysis; and U.S. Bureau of the Census, *Estimating Trading Day Variation in Monthly Economic Time Series* (Technical Paper No. 12 [Washington, D.C.: U.S. Government Printing Office, 1965]).

[5] *Business Cycle Developments* also includes about 70 other indicators and about 350 series of various economic magnitudes. One or a combination of several of these might be more useful in a particular case than the aggregate measures, such as GNP, that are being discussed. This may require considerable analysis, but the general approach discussed above would be used. Some forecasters are also experimenting with combinations of

series, called diffusion indices, which they hope will better describe the fluctuations in the economy. See *Diffusion Indices* (Technical Paper No. 13 [New York: National Industrial Conference Board, Inc., 1963]). NICB's diffusion indices are published weekly and monthly in its own publications.

[6] For more discussion on this topic see: E. D. Ranard, "Use of Input/Output Concepts in Sales Forecasting," *Journal of Marketing Research*, February 1972, pp. 53–58.

[7] R. J. Weber, "The Relationship of Advertising to Pricing Policy," *Pricing and Prosperity* (Marketing for Executives Series No. 1 [Chicago: American Marketing Association, 1956]), pp. 16–17. For more discussion on forecasting techniques see: "A Manager's Primer on Forecasting," *Harvard Business Review*, May–June 1973, pp. 6ff, and "How To Choose the Right Forecasting Technique," *Harvard Business Review*, July–August 1971, pp. 45–74.

[8] Checking accuracy of forecasts is a difficult subject. See: "A Loss of Faith in Pollsters," *Business Week*, June 1, 1974, p. 25; Rex V. Brown, "Just How Credible Are Your Market Estimates?" *Journal of Marketing*, July 1969, pp. 46–52; Robert J. Piersol, "Accuracy of Estimating Markets for Industrial Products by Size of Consuming Industry," *Journal of Marketing Research*, May 1968, pp. 147–54.

Part three

Developing marketing mixes

A good marketing mix requires creative blending of all four Ps —

total product planning
and consumer buying
habits . . . industrial
goods buyers . . . channels
of distribution . . . retailing
and wholesaling . . . who
will haul and store . . . promotion
to satisfy target market needs . . .
pricing policies
depend on objectives

a good product in the right place,

carefully promoted at the right price

Once a Campbel
always a Campbe

nce you start a couple of kids on Campbell's Chicken Noo
stopping them. They keep coming back for more of the se
th two chicken stocks for extra flavor, juicy bites of tender
icken and lots of enriched golden egg noodles. When it
mes to Campbell's Chicken Noodle Soup, Campbell
kids know you can't get too much of a good thing.
Sit right down and get your Campbell's worth.

12

Product planning

■ Beginning in this chapter and continuing through the next several chapters, we will look at the demanding job of developing products and product lines to satisfy the ever changing desires of customers. This involves developing the right Product, which then can be put in the right Place, and sold with the right Promotion and Price.

Developing the right product is not an easy task. Not only are customer needs and preferences changing but competition also continually makes current products obsolete. In some lines of business, new-product development is so rapid that 50 percent or more of the products made by a given firm were not even in the planning stages 5 to 10 years earlier.

In Chapters 12–15, we will consider the role of products in marketing strategy planning. This may have first-job relevance to you, because many companies have organized their production and marketing activities along product lines. Some multiple-product producers, for example, maintain separate sales forces for each of the company's product lines, and wholesalers and retailers frequently have salesmen and buyers who specialize along product lines.

What is a product?

Customers buy satisfaction, not input

■ First, we must decide what we mean by a "product."

If we sell a washing machine, are we selling a certain number of nuts and bolts, some sheet metal, an electric motor, and a plastic agitator?

If we sell the detergent to be used in this washing machine, are we selling several chemical raw materials?

If we sell a delivery service, are we selling so much wear and tear on a delivery truck and so much operator fatigue?

The answer to all of these questions is *no*. Instead, what we are really *selling is the capacity to provide the satisfaction, use, or perhaps the profit desired by the customer.*

All the housewife asks is that her washing machine do a good job of washing and continues to run. She does not care how it was made. Furthermore, she wants to clean with her detergent, not analyze it. And when she orders something, she doesn't really care how much out of the way the driver had to go or where he has been. She just wants *her* package.

When producers and middlemen buy products, they are interested in the profit they will get from their purchase, through use and resale, not how the products were made.

The concept of product as potential customer satisfactions or benefits cannot be overstressed. Many business executives, trained in the production side of business, get wrapped up in the number of nuts and bolts, the tightness of the nuts, the fertilizer application per acre, and other technical problems. Middlemen, too, are often concerned with technical details. But while these are important to *them*, they have little bearing on most customers' conceptions of the product. What is important to customers is how *they* perceive what is being offered—and these two views may be far apart.

Total product is more than just a physical thing

■ The *total product* is more than just a physical product with its related functional and aesthetic features. It includes accessories, installation, instruction on use, the package, perhaps a brand name which fulfills some psychological needs, and the assurance that service facilities will be available to meet the customer's needs after the purchase.

When the product is a service

■ The *total product* may not include a physical product at all! The product of a barber or hair stylist is the design, trimming or styling of your hair. A medical doctor may simply look at you, neither taking anything away or giving you anything tangible. Nevertheless, each satisfies needs, and therefore provides a product in the sense we will use "product" in this book.

Satisfaction comes from the *total* product

■ This broader view of the product concept must be understood thoroughly, because it is too easy to slip into a physical product orientation. In fact, marketing has traditionally focused on physical goods almost to the exclusion of services. Actually, however, services represent a very important and growing share of total GNP. We certainly cannot ignore services, and at the same time we do not want to treat them as greatly different from physical goods. Customer needs are satisfied not only by tangible products but also by services, or some combination of them. Indeed, one author has suggested that there are very few pure (physical) products or pure services. Most goods are a combination of both.[1] If the objective of the firm is to satisfy customer needs, it must see that service is part of the product and must be provided as part of the marketing mix. An automobile without access to repair service, for example, is not a very useful product.

Some market-oriented firms are designing more quality into their products and then offering longer and stronger guarantees or warranties. Some companies, such as Proctor-Silex Corp. and Sears Roebuck and Co., have gone even further by extending a one-year *replacement* — not just repair — guarantee on some of their appliances. And still other businesses, Whirlpool, for example, have developed appliance service systems including "hot lines" so the customer can air his complaints right away.

We will not make a distinction between goods and services but will call them all products. Where the intangibility of a service as contrasted to the physical nature of a product is of special significance, we may take special notice of the distinction. For the most part, however, we will focus on the similarities — based on customer-buying habits and preferences.

Within this broader concept of a product, we can also consider the offering of a wholesaler or retailer as a total product. This will enable us to generalize about marketing strategy planning for any kind of a firm.

The need for total product planning

■ We have been emphasizing a single physical product and the related services that make up a single total product. But customer needs cannot always be satisfied by a single product. Long ago, when economies were much simpler, most products were commodities — more or less homogeneous products that were in general demand. The idea of planning products to satisfy specific customers' demands was not very prevalent.

Today's more aggressive competitors strive to satisfy specific markets. Modern production processes permit a growing number of choices. Manufacturers and wholesalers may have to offer a complex total product to their customers. Likewise, retailers may have to offer a wide assortment in their total product. This may include the total assortment of goods they offer as well as related services. Good parking facilities, gift wrapping, charge accounts, and delivery services probably should be considered as part of the retailer's product. Clearly, total product planning is necessary.

In our discussion, we will focus mostly on a single total product for convenience of exposition. But it should not be forgotten that several products and/or services might have to be combined to develop the most effective marketing strategy.

Products have life cycles

■ Since products, like consumers, have life cycles, it is even more essential that a company do total product planning. Competitors are continually developing and copying ideas and products, making existing products obsolete more quickly than ever. We will discuss the product life-cycle concept in detail here because it is extremely important and underlies ideas to be found later in the text.

The life of a product can be divided into four major stages: product introduction, market growth, market maturity, and sales decline. A product's marketing mix must change during these stages, because: (1) customers' attitudes and needs may change through the course of the product's life cycle; (2) entirely different target markets may be appealed to at different stages in the life cycle; and (3) the nature of competition moves toward pure competition or oligopoly.

In addition, the sales history of the product varies in each of its four stages, and more importantly, the profit picture changes. It is significant that the two do not necessarily move together. Profits may decline while sales rise. Their general relationships can be seen in Figure 12–1.

Product introduction — investing in the future

■ In the introduction stage, a company needs promotion to *pioneer* the acceptance of the product, since it is not sought out by customers. Potential target customers must be told about the existence, advantages, and uses of the new product.

Even though a firm has successfully carved out a new market for itself, the product may not be an immediate success. This introductory stage usually is characterized by losses, with much money spent for promotion and product and place development. Funds, in effect, are being invested with the expectation of future profits.

Market growth — many competing products and better profits

■ In the market growth stage, the innovator usually begins to make substantial profits. Competitors start coming into the market, and each tries to develop the best product design. There is much product variety. Some competitors copy the most successful products. Monopolistic competition with downsloping demand curves is characteristic of both the product introduction and market growth stages.

During this stage, the sales of the industry are rising fairly rapidly as more and more customers enter the market. This second stage may last from several days to several years, depending on whether the product is hula hoops, credit card service, or color television sets. This is the time of peak profitability — *and also the beginning of the decline of profits.*

Market maturity — competition up, profits down

■ By the market maturity stage, many competitors have entered the market, unless oligopoly conditions prevail. In either case, competition becomes more aggressive, with declining profits. Industry profits decline throughout the market maturity stage because promotion costs climb, and some competitors begin to cut prices to attract business. Even in oligopoly situations, there is a long-term downward pressure on prices. Prices actually may be cut even as total industry volume is rising.

Figure 12–1
Life cycle of a typical product

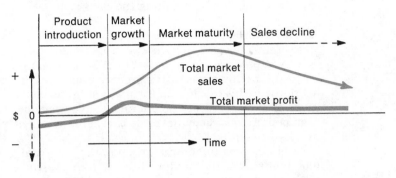

Promotion becomes important during the market maturity stage. Products differ only slightly (if at all), because most of the companies have discovered the most effective appeals to the market. There is a tendency to copy competing features. And in the industrial goods sector, buyers tend to encourage the development of oligopoly conditions when they buy by specifications and want to have several sources of supply.

In monopolistic competition situations we see increasing competitiveness on product, price, and promotion. The basic product similarities cause firms to resort to emotional appeals as the only remaining way to add value to the product. Although each firm may still have its own demand curve, the curves are becoming increasingly elastic as the various products become almost homogeneous in the minds of many potential consumers.

In the United States, the markets for most automobiles, boats, many household appliances, most groceries, television sets, and tobacco products are in the market maturity stage.[2] This period may continue many years until a basically new product idea comes along to completely change the market. Gasoline-powered automobiles, for example, replaced horse-drawn carriages, and eventually may be replaced by some other method of transportation, such as electric autos and high-speed mass transit.

Sales decline — a period of replacement ■ In the fourth and final stage of the life cycle, new products replace the old. Price competition from dying products may become more vigorous, but products with strong customer franchises may make profits almost till the end. These firms will have downsloping demand curves because they have successfully differentiated their products.

As the new products go through the introductory stage, the old ones may retain some sales by appealing to the most loyal target customers, perhaps older people or those who found unique satisfactions.

Our earlier discussion of consumer behavior showed that some customers accept new ideas more readily than others. The former would "discover" the new product; more conservative buyers might switch later, smoothing the sales decline.

Product life cycles are getting shorter

■ The total length of the cycle may vary from 90 days, as in the case of hula hoops, to possibly 90 years for automobiles. In general, however, product life cycles seem to be shortening.

In the highly competitive grocery products industry, they may be down to 12–18 months for really new concepts. Simple variations of such a grocery product may have even shorter life cycles. Competitors may copy flavor or packaging changes in a matter of weeks or months.

And large manufacturers, even in the industrial goods area, are not immune to the product life cycle. A top Du Pont executive said: "Lead time is gone . . . there's no company so outstanding technically today that it can expect a long lead time in a new discovery."[3] Du Pont had nylon to itself for 15 years, but in just 2 years a major competitor, Celanese Corp., came out with something very competitive to Delrin, another synthetic fiber discovery that Du Pont considered potentially as important as nylon. Similarly, six months after U.S. Steel came out with a new commercial "thin tin" plate, competitors were out with even better products.

Even copying of products is not uncommon, and this speeds up the cycle. Westinghouse found a company copying its new hair dryer *and* instruction book almost exactly.[4] And patents may not be much protection. The product's life may be over before a case would get through the courts.

The early bird makes the profits

■ What the accelerating speed of the product life cycle means is that the modern firm must be developing new products continually and must seek to have a marketing mix (and not just a product) that will make the most of the early stages of the life cycle when profits are highest.

Length of cycle influences strategy planning

■ The probable length of the cycle must figure in strategy planning to assure that realistic plans are made for the latter stages. A company does not have to sit by in frustration and watch its products go through a complete product life cycle. It has options. It can either significantly improve the product and let it start off on a new cycle, or withdraw it before it completes the cycle. These two alternatives are illustrated in Figure 12–2.[5]

Market areas are related to product life cycles

The market should be defined

■ To fully understand the *why* of a product life cycle, we should carefully define the market area we are considering. The way we define a market is quite relevant to the way we see product life cycles and who we have as competitors. If a market is defined very generally, then there may be many competitors and the market may

Figure 12–2
A. Significantly improved product starts a new cycle, but maybe with short introductory stage. B. Profit-oriented firm dropping out of market during market maturity stage.

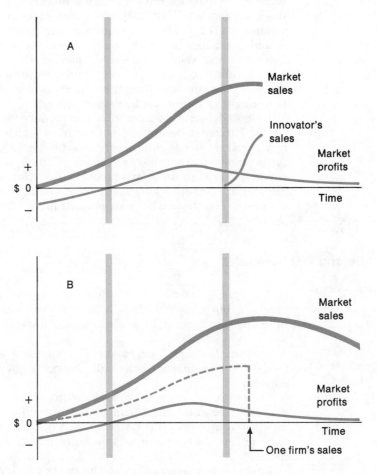

appear to be in market maturity. On the other hand, if we focus on a narrow area and a particular way of satisfying specific needs, then we might see much shorter product life cycles as improved products come along to replace the old. For example, there may be an ongoing general market demand for copies of letters, term papers, and book pages. If we add the annual sales of all the copying machines which have come on the market during the last few decades and treat them as the sales of one product, it probably would appear to be in the market growth stage. If we think of individual kinds of machines applying different technical principles, however, we see relatively short life cycles as new generations of machines come along.[6] In this case, earlier machines have already gone through the sales decline stage and have disappeared from the market.

Each market has its own product life cycle

■ In some cases it might be useful to consider more than one market area. Our earlier discussion of the relevant market dimensions in market gridding would be helpful here. If a businessman produces or sells exercise machines, he can focus on the "exercise machine market," but it really makes more sense to sell to the "fitness market." Then he competes not only with other exercise machine makers but with health clubs, and suppliers of jogging suits, athletic shoes, and other sporting goods as well. In this case, he has two product markets and life cycles to work with—the exercise machine and the fitness markets. The growth patterns in both might or might *not* be closely related.[7]

It should be emphasized that the product life-cycle concept is useful but must be applied with care to realize full benefit. Ongoing market needs might be stable (as for food) or growing (as for copying), and particular product efforts to satisfy these needs would go through their own product life cycles. Depending on the number of competitors (as in the fitness market) and the fickleness of consumers, these particular product life cycles can be relatively short.

Style and fashion cycles

■ The concept of the product life cycle applies generally to most products, but a special kind—a fashion cycle—can be seen clearly in markets where style or fashion are important to consumers.

The short happy life of fads

■ The words "style" or "fashion" commonly are used synonymously by consumers. Technically, however, they should be differentiated.

Style is a "characteristic or distinctive mode or method of expression, presentation, or conception in the field of art."[8] Various residential architectural styles such as colonial, Cape Cod, ranch, and modern have come to popularity during certain periods of history.

Fashion, however, refers to the *currently* accepted or popular style in a given field. A particular style of house such as a ranch house or A-frame may be in fashion for a time and then lose its popularity. Or a certain color and style of women's dresses, such as mini style, may be in fashion one year, then outdated the next. It is still a style but no longer a fashion.

A *fad* is a particular fashion that seems fashionable only to certain groups who are enthusiastic about it but so fickle that it is short-lived as a fashion. Some teen-agers' music tastes can be called fads. And chlorophyll, which deodorizes cigarettes, socks, and soap and makes toothpastes, mouthwashes, and even vitamins smell good, has been labeled a fad.

Fashion cycles have stages, too

■ Consumer acceptance of fashions usually goes through a cycle closely related to consumer buying motives. A fashion cycle is commonly composed of three stages: the *distinctiveness, emula-*

tion, and *economic emulation* stages, which roughly parallel the product life-cycle stages.

In the *distinctiveness* stage, some consumers seeking new styles are especially interested in, and willing to pay for, products that are different from those possessed by the majority. They have products custom-made or patronize manufacturers or distributors who offer goods in small quantities.

If a particular style catches on with a number of style leaders, then other consumers, because of their desire to emulate, may copy them. *Emulation* may come easier as manufacturers begin to make larger quantities of the products that seem to be catching on. This stage can be likened to the early market growth stage of the product life cycle.

Then, if it seems assured that a fashion is going to be popular with a large segment of the population, the product moves into a third stage, economic emulation. Manufacturers mass-produce large quantities of the product at low cost, and we move quickly through the market growth stage and maybe through the market maturity stage into sales decline.

Perhaps in the second stage, and certainly in the third stage, the style that began as the private fling of the few becomes less attractive to these original style leaders. They already are trying other styles – which eventually may become fashions and run through another cycle.[9]

How a particular fashion gets started is not well understood. Most present fashions are adaptations or resurrections of previously popular styles. Designers and entrepreneurs continually seek styles that will suit those consumers who want distinctiveness. The results may be exaggerations of earlier styles or perhaps new adaptations of styles from Japan, India, or Egypt.

Predicting what will sell is not easy. Fortunes can be lost in the fashion business by guessing wrong about consumer behavior. Ambrose Bierce once wrote, "Fashion is a despot whom the wise ridicule – and obey." And Thoreau commented, "Every generation laughs at the old fashions but follows religiously the new."

Despite the chancy nature of any fashion-oriented enterprise, businessmen keep trying to find new fashions.[10] It is mostly "trial and error," but there are a few generalizations which are relevant to marketing.

1. Fashions cannot be forced, but many styles can be presented, and when one becomes fashionable, its cycle may be accelerated by aggressive promotion.
2. A higher standard of living and greater mobility encourage a greater interest in fashions.
3. The speed of communication affects the rate of change or acceptance of fashions.
4. Speed in change of fashions increases the cost of producing and marketing products. There are losses due to trial and error in finding acceptable styles, then producing them on a limited basis because of uncertainty about the length of the

cycle. These increased costs are not always charged directly to the consumer, since some firms lose their investment and go out of business. But in the aggregate, fashion changes cost consumers money.

Designing new products

Find out what the customer wants

■ All people who handle, sell, or use a product must be considered when developing a new product. The market grid concept is relevant here again. The needs and preferences of the customers in a market segment should determine the product design for that target market. However, a company must not only consider final customers, but intermediate customers as well. Retailers or wholesalers might need a wider product line than a manufacturer is currently providing. Coca-Cola added several new products to its line – Fanta, Sprite, Tab, Fresca, and even orange juice – to satisfy bottler and consumer demands.[11]

Safety should be considered in design too

■ The marketing concept would certainly lead to the design of safety into products, if potential customers want it. And, as already noted, the consumerism movement is focusing greater attention on this subject. The Consumer Product Safety Act of 1972 demands more awareness of safety in product design and production. The Consumer Product Safety Commission can order costly repairs or returns of "unsafe" products, and can back up its orders with fines and jail sentences. This act brings added importance to the Product area and reemphasizes the need for production-oriented businessmen to become more market-oriented.

Large court settlements for defective designs and tough enforcement of the Product Safety Act have increased business' interest in safety. But consumers' newfound interest in safety is worth noting also. Early efforts (in the late 1940s and early 1950s) to "sell" seat belts to American motorists were not successful. The Ford Motor Company backed off from its efforts to sell safety when it found that consumers were not too concerned about needs which they personally did not feel. Now, a change in the social environment has caused much more interest in the matter by both politicians and businessmen.[12]

The final choice and design of the product should be compatible with a company's overall objectives and provide for effective use of resources. The company might choose to modify present products to satisfy a new market's needs (or the changing needs of present markets). Or, the product might not be changed, but perhaps it still should be treated as a "new" product if it is part of a new mix aimed at old or new markets.

What is a new product – lemons!?

■ In this text, we will consider a product as new if it is *new in any way* for the company concerned. To be considered new, there need not even be a physical change in the product, package, or brand – if different target markets are sought. Lemons illustrate the point.

Figure 12–3
Good design: Does your product have it?

		Yes	No
1.	Does the product's present design reflect quality?	——	——
2.	Is the present design economical to manufacture?	——	——
3.	Is the design well accepted by wholesalers, retailers, salesmen and customers?	——	——
4.	Is the design in tune with current design trends?	——	——
5.	Does the design have a comparatively long life?	——	——
6.	Are the details of the product well designed?	——	——
7.	Does the design contribute to the product's usefulness, safety, and convenience?	——	——
8.	Are the materials used practical for product's end use?	——	——
9.	Is the color right for use and environment?	——	——
10.	Is the size right for best use?	——	——
11.	Is the weight right for best use?	——	——
12.	Does the design stand up well with competition?	——	——

In the marketing of lemons by one organization, no physical changes were made, but extensive promotion and consumer education created many "new" products. The same old lemons were promoted successfully for lemonade, mixed drinks, diet supplements, cold remedies, lemon cream pies, a salad condiment, dressing for fish, and many other culinary uses. For each of these markets, the product had to go through the early stages of the product life cycle.[13]

A product can be called new for only a limited time. Six months is the maximum time that a product should be called new, according to the Federal Trade Commission. To be called new, says the FTC, a product must be entirely new or changed in "a functionally significant or substantial respect."[14] While six months may seem a very short time for production-oriented businessmen, it may be reasonable in the light of our earlier discussion of the length of product life cycles.

Keeping score on product design

■ An analysis of potential customers' needs and preferences, as well as the needs of potential channel members is obviously vital in product design. Nevertheless, some management judgment will still have to be used. Consumers have been notoriously unreliable in predicting what they will like.

Since some judgment and risk will probably always be involved, the checklist in Figure 12–3 may help management to narrow the areas in which judgment is necessary.[15] This checklist is useful because it usually is safer to make 12 separate small judgments than one large "yes" or "no" judgment.

On this checklist, a score of "yes" on 11 or 12 questions would indicate a good design; 9 or 10 points, a fair design (with "no" answers indicating weak spots to be corrected); and below 9 points, a poor design, probably indicating that profits will be reduced through lost sales and possibly through high manufacturing costs. This list is suitable for all manufactured products except high-fashion women's apparel – which is a world of its own. Adaptations must be made for services.

New-product development: A total company effort

Some organization helps

■ A new-product development department or committee helps assure that new ideas for products are carefully evaluated and good ones profitably marketed. Delays may lead to late test marketing or market introduction and give competition a head start in the product life cycle. A delay of even six months may make the difference between a product's success or failure in a competitive market.

A well-organized development procedure might even enable a firm to copy others' attractive innovations quickly and profitably. This possibility should not be overlooked. No one company can hope to be first always, with the best.[16]

Top-level support vital

■ New-product development must have the enthusiastic support of top management. New products tend to disrupt the old routines that managers of established products may try in subtle but effective ways to maintain. So someone should be responsible for this effort. The organizational arrangement may not be too important, as long as new-product development has top-level support.[17]

Complicated integrated effort needed

■ Developing new products should be a total company effort, as Figure 12–4 shows. Here, we see that the whole process is sequential, involving personnel in management, research, production, promotion, packaging, and branding. The process moves from an early exploration of ideas and concepts (see Figure 12–4) to development of the product and product-related concepts. Technical development of the product itself is not the first step in new-product development. Concept appraisal comes first. Many "odd-ball" items can be produced, but who wants them?

After the product and related concepts have been developed, the total concept – really, the total marketing mix – is developed and matched against the company's resources to see whether the product looks profitable.

If the answer is yes, then management must make another decision: Does it want to test-market (say in one or two markets) before a full-scale market introduction? This is not a trivial decision, because although test marketing may test out ideas, it also may tip the company's hand to competition. After seeing the speed of product life cycles, we can better understand why some managements are reluctant to test-market.

Figure 12–4
New-product market development sequence

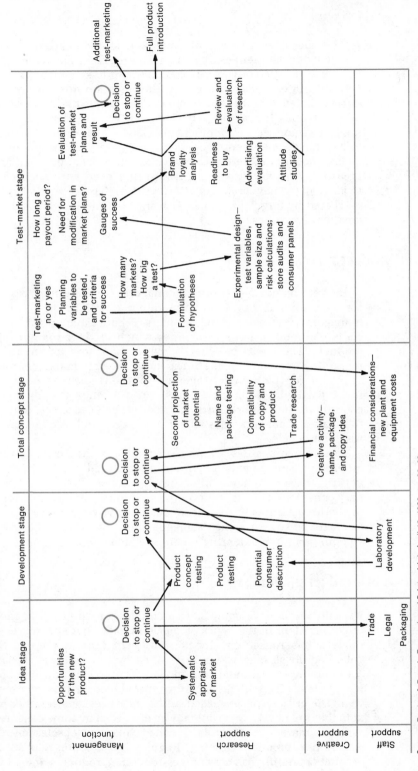

Source: Benton & Bowels Research and *Printers' Ink*, April 13, 1962, pp. 22–23.

■ The role of marketing management and top management in product development is shown in Figure 12–4. Management has the power to push or veto development, but to keep it going it must commit more funds. As a result, the rejection rate for new ideas during this new-product development process is high. One study of 80 companies found that only 1 out of 40 new ideas survive the kind of organized development process we have just discussed.[18]

As the development process moves along, the sequential decisions become more difficult because the costs and risks are increasing. And executives are aware that even with such careful studies, many new products *do* fail. About 50 percent of all of those marketed by large companies fail, and the rate is even higher for smaller companies.[19]

Need for product managers

■ Product managers (or brand managers) are sometimes responsible for the job of new-product planning as well as the continuing management of established products. Product managers are especially common in large companies which produce many kinds of products. There may be several product managers serving under a marketing manager. Sometimes these product managers are responsible for the profitable operation of the whole marketing effort for a particular product. In this capacity, they usually have to coordinate their efforts with those of other executives, including the sales manager, advertising manager, and production and research people.

In some companies the product manager has much power. In other situations he may be primarily concerned with planning and getting the promotional effort implemented. Product managers vary considerably in their activities and there is much controversy in the literature as to the proper role of a product manager. What is clear, however, is that someone must be responsible for developing and implementing product-related plans.[20]

Evaluation of product planning

■ Deliberately developing new products, sometimes only slightly updating them in the hopes of replacing older but still serviceable models, has roused the ire of some critics of marketing. Such "planned obsolescence," as it is called by its critics, is especially common in the automobile, appliance, and clothing industries, where new styles or fashions are introduced at least once each year. The critics are concerned, among other reasons, because products that are not yet worn out may be discarded by some consumers.

Some marketers see this so-called "planned obsolescence" as simply new-product planning. Regular introduction of such new products certainly has advantages for some producers and middlemen, since new models may help them out of the market maturity stage of a product life cycle and back into the more profitable market growth stage. The effectiveness of this approach may depend on which part of the market grid is the target. Volkswagen customers seem satisfied with little change from year to year, while many others are attracted by yearly model changes.

Much of the continued innovation that is manifested in new-model introductions seems to have been forced upon producers by the demands of some market segments and competitive pressures. Continued novelty seems to satisfy some consumer needs. Marketing research sometimes shows that customers truly prefer a face-lifted model to the old model simply because it is new, perhaps for prestige reasons. Recall our discussion of the early stage of the fashion cycle. Catering to such needs can even be seen as target marketing. Without this continued newness, these innovation-minded segments of the market would not be truly satisfied.[21]

It can be argued further that planned obsolescence not only satisfies many customers but also encourages research and investment, helping to maintain high levels of employment.

"Old" products, moreover, are not always wasted. There is a large secondhand market in those markets where innovation and product changes are more rapid. In fact, a strong secondhand market seems to encourage change, making it less costly and economically more feasible for more customers. In the automobile market, for example, there is a ready secondhand market. A car may be sold several times before it is finally junked. The furniture market, on the other hand, has no organized secondhand market, and furniture is not replaced nearly as rapidly, to the sorrow of many housewives.

"Obsoles-cence" seems to be what the customer wants

■ Further support for aggressive and continuing product development comes from an unexpected source.

The early Soviet practice of producing only homogeneous products was not successful. And so, responding to consumer wishes, Soviet production agencies have been expanding product variety. The Soviet radio-TV industry offers 30 to 40 different brands of radios and phonographs and about 20 types of television sets.

In fact, Soviet interest in product variety has even spread to laundry soap and detergents, important areas of new-product development in the United States. Witnessing this development, one American specialist on Soviet economic affairs feels that many American critics of marketing may have underestimated the advantages of our present economic system and ought to reevaluate their thinking.[22]

Clearly, what the critics call "planned obsolescence" and the marketing practitioners call "product planning," may have a number of desirable characteristics. In any case, these practices seem to be responses to some customer demands in a competitive marketplace. A question still remains as to whether we should satisfy them. Should we? More will be said on this in Chapter 30.

Conclusion

■ This chapter has explored the concept of a *product* very broadly. The product may not even involve a physical product at all. It may be a service, or some combination of a physical product and a service. A product is the firm's offering which satisfies the needs of its target customers. In this sense, a retailer or wholesaler's offering can be thought of as a product, as can physicians' services, automobiles, appliances, wheat, or coal. By *product* we will mean the *total product*, which *may* include a physical product but also could involve a package, brand, installation, repair services, and so on—whatever it takes to meet the target customers' and channel members' needs.

Product planning is an increasingly vital activity in a modern economy because it is no longer very profitable to sell just "commodities." And product planning must be continuous to meet the dynamic and innovating competition which is causing product life cycles to shorten.

The product life-cycle concept is especially important to marketing strategy planning because it shows that different marketing mixes, and even strategies, are needed as a product moves through its cycle. This is an important point because profits change during the cycle, with most of the profits going to the innovators or fast copiers.

We pointed out that a new product is not limited to physical newness. We will call a product "new" if it is new in any way—to any target market.

New products are so important to the survival of firms in our competitive economy that some organized method for developing them is needed. A general approach was discussed, but it is obvious that it must be a total company effort to be successful.

The failure rate of new products is high, but it is considerably lower for larger and better-managed firms that have recognized product planning as a vital function in the business process. Some firms have appointed product managers to manage individual product lines and new-product committees to assure that the process is carried out successfully. It is clear that modern product planning can help improve marketing strategy planning in a competitive world where more and more products are being demanded and offered.

questions and problems

1 Define, in your own words, what a product is.

2 Explain how the addition of guarantees, service, and credit can improve a "total product." Cite a specific case where this has been done and explain how customers viewed this new "total product."

3 What "products" are being offered by an exclusive men's shop? By a nightclub? By a soda fountain? By a supermarket?

4 Cite two examples of products which you feel are currently in each of the product life-cycle stages.

5 Explain how different conclusions might be reached with respect to the correct product life-cycle stage(s) in the automobile market, especially if the market grid concept is used.

6 Discuss the life cycle of a product in terms of its probable impact on a manufacturer's marketing mix. Illustrate, using battery-operated toothbrushes.

7 Distinguish among a fad, style, and fashion. How should a retailer adapt to them? Some people maintain that fads or fashions can be created by businessmen. Can you give an example of any business firm that has *consistently* created successful fads or fashions? *Consistently* is important, because anyone can be lucky a few times; the successes are publicized but the failures are not.

8 Discuss how the checklist "Good design: Does your product have it?" (Figure 12–3) could be used to evaluate: (*a*) a can opener, (*b*) a baby stroller, (*c*) men's hats (fedoras), (*d*) a coffeemaker.

9 Explain the importance of an organized new-product development process and illustrate how it might be used for: (*a*) an improved phonograph, (*b*) new frozen-food items, (*c*) a new children's toy.

10 Discuss the social value of planned obsolescence policies, especially when they encourage people to discard products which are not "all worn out." Is this an economic waste? How worn out is "all worn out"? Must a shirt have holes in it? How big?

notes

[1] John M. Rathmell, "What Is Meant by Services?" *Journal of Marketing*, October 1966, pp. 32–36; and "Services Grow While the Quality Shrinks," *Business Week*, October 30, 1971, pp. 50–57.

[2] "Decline in Color-TV Sales Brings Worry that More Makers May Fall by Wayside," *The Wall Street Journal*, April 2, 1974, p. 36; "Sales of Major Appliances, TV Sets Gain: But Profits Fail to Keep Up, Gap May Widen," *The Wall Street Journal*, August 21, 1972, p. 22; "Gillette Company Struggles As Its Rivals Slice at Fat Profit Margin," *The Wall Street Journal*, February 2, 1972, p. 1f.

[3] "The Short Happy Life," *Time*, March 29, 1963, p. 83.

[4] *Time*, March 29, 1963, p. 83.

[5] See also T. Levitt, "Exploit the Product Life Cycle," *Harvard Business Review*, November–December 1965, pp. 81–94.

[6] "Xerox Unveils First of 'New Generation' of Copying Machines," *Wall Street Journal*, May 20, 1970, p. 11.

[7] "Getting Fat by Making Others Slim," *Business Week*, March 22, 1969, pp. 140–44.

[8] P. H. Nystrom, *Economics of Fashion* (New York: Ronald Press Co., 1958), p. 3.

[9] M. T. Copeland, *Principles of Merchandising* (New York: A. W. Shaw Co., 1942), p. 167; and Claude R. Martin, Jr., "What Consumers of Fashion Want to Know," *Journal of Retailing*, Winter 1971–72, pp. 65–71.

[10] Alfred H. Daniels, "Fashion Merchandising," *Harvard Business Review*, May 1951, pp. 51–60. See also, Chester R. Wasson, "How Predictable Are Fashion and Other Product Life Cycles?" *Journal of Marketing*, July 1968, pp. 36–43.

[11] "Coke Tries New Ways to Refresh," *Business Week*, August 24, 1963, pp. 100–110.

[12] "Dictating Product Safety," *Business Week*, May 18, 1974, pp. 56–62; L. A. Bennigson and A. I. Bennigson, "Product Liability: Manufacturers Beware!" *Harvard Business Review*, May–June 1974, pp. 122–32; Walter Jensen, Jr., Edward M. Mazze, and Duke N. Stern, "The Consumer Product Safety Act: A Special Case in Consumerism," *Journal of Marketing*, October 1973, pp. 68–71; and L. J. Loudenback and J. W. Goebel, "Mar-keting in the Age of Strict Liability," *Journal of Marketing*, January 1974, pp. 62–66.

[13] See Chester R. Wasson, "What Is 'New' about New Products?" *Journal of Marketing*, July 1960, pp. 52–56.

[14] *Business Week*, April 22, 1967, p. 120.

[15] Victor Petertil, "Is Your Product Designed to Sell?" *Management Methods*, July 1958, p. 48; and "Putting Products Through an Audit Wringer," *Business Week*, February 2, 1974, pp. 60–61.

[16] See T. Levitt, "Innovative Imitation," *Harvard Business Review*, September–October 1966, pp. 63–70.

[17] Philip R. McDonald and Joseph O. Eastlack, Jr., "Top Management Involvement with New Products," *Business Horizons*, December 1971, pp. 23–31; William A. Bours, III, "Imagination Wears Many Hats," *Journal of Marketing*, October 1966, pp. 59–61; John H. Murphy, "New Products Need Special Management," *Journal of Marketing*, October 1962, pp. 46–49; E. J. McCarthy, "Organization for New Product Development?" *Journal of Business of the University of Chicago*, April 1959, pp. 128–32.

[18] Paul Stillson and E. Leonard Arnof, "Product Search and Evaluation," *Journal of Marketing*, July 1957, pp. 33; and "How Ideas Are Made into Products at 3M," *Business Week*, September 15, 1973, pp. 224–27.

[19] *Management of the New Product* (Chicago: Booz-Allen & Hamilton, 1960), p. 14; and "New Product Success Ratio," *The Nielsen Researcher*, No. 5–1971.

[20] "The Brand Manager: No Longer King," *Business Week*, June 9, 1973, pp. 58–66; Stephens Dietz, "Get More Out of Your Brand Management," *Harvard Business Review*, July–August 1973, pp. 127–36; Gary R. Gemmill and David L. Wilemon, "The Product Manager As an Influence Agent," *Journal of Marketing*, January 1972, pp. 26–30.

[21] See, for example, H. M. Case, "Designed Decay," *Harvard Business Review*, January–February 1966, pp. 126–31.

[22] Marshall I. Goldman, "A New Perspective on Product Differentiation and Advertising: The Soviet View," *Business Review*, Boston University, Spring 1962, pp. 3–12.

Packaging and branding

■ A total product is much more than a physical product. But if a physical product is involved, it probably will need some packaging. Physical products *and* services probably should be branded to make sure that they are clearly identifiable. Moreover, brands, including corporate and store names, can carry much meaning for customers and potential customers.

In the same sense, there is much more to packaging and branding than just buying a cardboard box and sticking on the company's name. In some cases, the packaging and branding decisions may be more important than physical product decisions. They may enable a firm to differentiate its homogeneous physical product or service and avoid pure competition.

In this chapter we will emphasize the decisions of manufacturers or the middlemen who must make packaging and branding decisions.

Growing importance of packaging

■ Sometimes a distinction is made between packing and packaging —the former being concerned with protection and the latter with promotion. We will *not* make this distinction because the difference is seldom clear-cut. Modern packaging tries to do both jobs.

Amount spent large and rising

■ The importance of packaging is partially illustrated by its cost. About $14 billion was spent on packaging *materials* alone in 1965. This total was estimated at $21 billion in 1972 and is expected to continue rising in coming years.[1] For perspective, this is roughly equal to the total amount spent on advertising. And the actual cost of packaging might be twice as high, if all of the costs of handling, storing, and moving containers were included. These rising outlays for packaging are due in part to a shift from an earlier almost sole emphasis on protection to the current interest in protection *and* the promotional potential of the package – both in terms of greater convenience and the messages it can carry.

Higher corporate status for packaging

■ The purchasing agent used to be in charge of packaging in many companies when protection was the major function of the package. But now, some companies are establishing corporate packaging staffs. And in some the product manager or a specialist in packaging has taken over the job.[2]

General Foods Corp. appointed a manager of packaging development and procurement services when it reached the conclusion that packaging is an important tool of management. This manager coordinates packaging activities with the various product managers. The National Biscuit Co. has a vice president of packaging acting as chairman of the packaging committee.[3]

This newfound status for packaging occurred in part because of the growing competitiveness in many markets. This status also reflects the costliness of packaging errors and the difficulty of correcting them. A poor package could have long-term effects, killing the product for customers who try it and creating ill will among middlemen. In other words, packaging can have great strategic importance.

Strategic importance of packaging

■ Marketing strategy planning tries to match target market needs and preferences to the marketing mix offered – and packaging is definitely a part of the mix. In some cases, it may be a vital part.

May improve or create a "new" product

■ A new package can become the major factor in a new marketing strategy by significantly improving the total product. A better box, wrapper, can, or bottle may even enable a relatively small, unknown firm to compete successfully with the established competitors. Carter Products Co., not previously in the men's toiletries field, introduced its first men's product, Rise shaving cream, in aerosol cans and was able to compete effectively. The normal tube and carton might not have been so successful.[4]

A package change often creates a "new" product by giving either the regular customers or new target markets the existing product in a new form or quantity that is more satisfactory. Packaging frozen vegetables in 1-pound packages instead of 10-ounce packages served larger families better. The small package held too little for them, while two packages held too much. Some producers are carving large turkeys into quarters to stimulate year-round sales. One such experiment expanded sales 200 percent.[5]

Multiple packs can be the basis of a new marketing strategy, too. Consumer surveys showed that some customers were buying several units at a time of products such as soft drinks, beer, and frozen orange juice. This suggested an overlooked market grid box. Manufacturers tried multiple packaging of units in 4-, 6-, and 8-packs, and have gained wide acceptance.

May lower total distribution costs

■ Better protective packaging is especially important to intermediate customers, such as manufacturers and wholesalers, who may have to absorb the cost of goods damaged in transit. Sometimes the cost of such damage can be charged to the transportation agencies, but there still are costs for settling such claims – and getting them settled is a nuisance. Moreover, goods damaged in shipment may delay production and cause lost sales.

Packaging is vital to retailers. They benefit from both the protective and promotional aspects of packaging. Packaging which provides better protection, supermarket operators claim, can reduce store costs by lessening breakage, shrinkage, and spoilage, preventing discoloration, and stopping pilferage. Packages that are easier to handle can cut costs by speeding price marking, improving handling and display, and saving space. And packaging can increase sales by such promotionally oriented moves as offering smaller or larger sizes, more multi-packs, better pictures of the product itself, illustrations of the product in use, and more effective use of color.

Food retailers attach such importance to packaging that they have formed supermarket industry committees to criticize manufacturers' packages and to encourage improved packaging. Retailers also make their feelings known individually. In South Bend, Indiana, for example, some supermarket operators refused to carry one manufacturer's gelatin products because he would not supply the products in larger cartons. The storekeepers maintained that the firm's small cartons, designed to serve small retailers, were a nuisance and cost too much to handle.

May be "better" than advertising

Packaged goods are regularly seen in retail stores and may actually be seen by many more potential customers than the company's advertising. An effective package sometimes gives a firm more promotional impact than it could possibly afford with conventional advertising efforts.

Promotionally oriented packaging also may reduce the total distribution costs. An attractive package may speed turnover so that total costs will decline as a percentage of sales. While more will be said on this in subsequent chapters, rapid turnover is one of the important ingredients in the success of self-service retailing. Without packages that sell themselves, self-service retailing would not be possible.

Or . . . may raise total costs

■ In other cases, total distribution costs may rise because of packaging – and yet *everyone may be satisfied* because the packaging improves the total product. Packaging expenses as a percentage of the manufacturer's selling price vary widely ranging from 1 to 70 percent.

Consider sugar as an example. In 100-pound bags, the cost of packaging sugar is only 1 percent of the selling price; in 2- to 5-pound cartons, 25–30 percent; and for individual serving envelopes, 50 percent. Yet most housewives do not care to haul a 100-pound bag home, and are quite willing to pay the added costs for more convenient packages. Restaurants use one-serving envelopes of sugar, finding that they reduce the cost of filling and washing sugar bowls and that customers prefer the more sanitary little packages. In both cases, packaging adds value to the total product — or more accurately, it creates new products and new marketing strategies.

What makes a good package design?

The right packaging, enough packaging

■ Experience shows that *a specific package must be developed for each specific product*. The package must safely transport its contents, serve in a specific climate (especially if the product is to be exported), and last for a specific time. To provide such packaging, the manufacturer must know his product, his customers, and how the product will be delivered to them. *Under*packaging costs money for damage claims or poor sales, but *over*packaging also costs money because dollars are spent but no gains are realized. Glassware, for example, needs to be protected from even relatively light blows that might smash it. Heavy-duty machinery seldom needs protection from blows but may need protection from corrosion caused by moisture.

Packaging suppliers can offer suggestions

■ Packaging suppliers have recognized the importance of packaging and their salesmen and staffs are usually highly trained to help a firm do a better job. Typically they will insist on knowing something about the needs and preferences of the potential customers and the middlemen who are likely to be handling the packages. With this kind of information, then, they will make recommendations about how to blend the package into the total marketing strategy.

Consumers versus packaging

■ Despite all the time and money now spent on packaging, there is still much room for improvement. In one survey, 85 percent of the housewives interviewed told of having been hurt when opening a package. Women were especially vocal about having to use knives to open containers of frozen strawberries. Complaints were general about bottles that break, metal containers with sharp edges, re-closable baby-food jars that are practically unopenable, sardine tins without windup keys, sugar bags that are almost impossible to open, and flour bags that invariably spill.[6] The result is unsatisfied target markets.

Some consumers complain about partially filled packages. Others are confused by the many and varied sizes. Critics of business allege that some package designs are misleading, perhaps deliberately so. They feel that the great variety of package designs makes it difficult for consumers to make value comparisons readily.

■ The concern of some consumers finally led to the passage of the *Federal Fair Packaging and Labeling Act* of 1966. This law basically requires that consumer goods be clearly labeled in understandable terms, in order to give the customer more information. The law also calls upon government agencies and industry to try to reduce the number of package sizes. The Food and Drug Administration is made responsible for foods, nonprescription drugs, and cosmetics. The Federal Trade Commission is responsible for nonfood items. And the Commerce Department is expected to seek voluntary agreements by industry groups with respect to package proliferation.

Some progress has been made, such as the reduction by industry groups of the number of toothpaste sizes from 57 to 5, and paper-towel packages from 33 to 8. But major problem areas still exist in the analgesics (aspirin and other pain-killers) and toiletry goods, such as hair spray, deodorants, mouthwashes, and aftershave lotions. The toilet goods people, for example, have not shown much interest because they feel consumers are more concerned with how the products feel or smell or look than with price comparisons.

Food products must now carry more informative labeling with respect to their nutrients and weight and volume. But there is some question as to whether many consumers understand and know what to do with this information or whether this is the relevant information they are seeking. At the same time, it is difficult to provide the kind of information some are seeking, for example regarding taste, color, and texture.[7] Clearly the intentions are good but there are difficulties implementing laws which must rely upon easily measurable, but perhaps less relevant, standards such as weight and volume.

■ Weight and volume are not completely irrelevant, however. There is continuing interest in *unit-pricing* which would facilitate comparison shopping using weight and volume standards. Unit-pricing involves placing some indication of the cost per ounce or some other standard measure on *or* near the product. Some large supermarket chains have voluntarily adopted unit-pricing and it is claimed that many consumers do appreciate this service.[8]

Branding — why it developed

■ Brands are so numerous and commonplace that we are inclined to take their significance for granted. In the grocery products area alone, there are approximately 38,000 brands, even though the average supermarket can stock only about 6,500.[9] The following section discusses the importance of branding for individual firms and for the economy as a whole.

From our review of Western economic history, it will be recalled that production for the marketplace began early in recorded history, lapsed after the fall of Rome and during the Middle Ages, and expanded again as the feudal villages began to trade with each other. During this revival, craft guilds (similar to labor unions) and merchant guilds formed to control the quantity and quality of production. One requirement was that each producer mark his goods so that output could be restricted when necessary. This also meant that inferior quality, which might reflect unfavorably on other guild products and discourage future trade, could be traced back to the offending producer. Early trademarks also were a protection to the buyer, who could now determine the source of the product.

Not restriction but identification

■ More recently, brands have been used primarily for identification rather than restriction of output.

The earliest and most aggressive brand promoters in America were the patent medicine manufacturers. They were joined by the food manufacturers, who grew in size after the Civil War. Some of the brands started in the 1860s and 1870s, and still going strong, are Dr. Lyon's Tooth Powder, Borden's Condensed Milk, Quaker Oats, Vaseline, Pillsbury's Best Flour, and Ivory Soap.[10]

Today, a good brand usually assures high or at least consistent quality and encourages repeat purchasing. This works where there is some trust of sellers by buyers. This is generally true in the United States, but much less so elsewhere.

Customers are willing to buy by brand rather than by inspection when there is some assurance of quality. In many countries, however, the consumer doesn't feel he has any such assurance. In India, inspecting the product is common because there is a complete lack of confidence in packaged goods and brands. This distrust has a solid foundation. In 1957, it was estimated that in Delhi, 25 percent of all food was adulterated. Sawdust, husks, colored earth, and ground seeds accounted for 10–50 percent of the weight of many products. As a result, some Indian customers avoid buying packaged or prepared foods.[11]

Soviets adopted brands

■ The importance of brands in a nation's economy can be seen clearly in the Soviet experience. The U.S.S.R. evolved toward an enthusiastic use of branding—after instances of economic disaster forced it upon them.

Several Russian factories were manufacturing supposedly identical 17-inch TV sets, but actually one of the plants was shipping "lemons." When customers became aware of this, they stopped buying *all* 17-inch sets, because they could not identify the bad ones. This obviously caused considerable inventory problems for the central planners. It also caused some public discontent with the Soviet system. Shortly thereafter, factory numbers on products were required to help the planners identify the production source.

Subsequently, consumers discovered the factory numbers, and plants that were producing poorer quality products began to have difficulties meeting their economic plans. Soviet consumers rather than planners forced the plants to pay more attention to quality. Interestingly, before long there were more than 25 state-sponsored advertising agencies to tell people about the "quality" of various factories. Now, advertising courses are even offered in Russian universities![12]

The important thing to note here is that the "brands" were created by the customers rather than the planners. The factory identification numbers had been added originally to help the planners—but the consumers quickly adapted them to their own use.

Why branding is advantageous to customers

Makes shopping feasible

■ Well-recognized brands make shopping feasible in a modern economy. Think of the consumer's dilemma in a grocery store, for example, if she had to consider seriously the advantages and disadvantages of each of 6,500 items every time she went shopping.

Assures regular satisfaction

■ Many customers are willing to buy new things, but having gambled and won, they like to buy a "sure thing" thereafter. The customer may even be willing to pay a premium for brands with which she has had favorable experience.

Dependable guides to quality

■ There is considerable evidence that if the housewife used well-known brands rather than high prices as an indication of good quality, she might be further ahead. One study of grocery products found that the known brands usually had fairly consistent quality, but there was little assurance that a high price meant high quality.[13]

Branded drug products may also be better than unbranded ones which meet the same minimum specifications. This is an important political and social matter, because some branded drug products are prescribed by doctors and are priced substantially above unbranded ones in the same generic class. Business critics have been very vocal here. Industry representatives argue that there are differences, and some tests suggest that this is the case. In other cases, there is not even agreement over which test should be used, or if it is possible to measure effectiveness.[14]

Brands may satisfy status need

■ Lower-class housewives may buy well-recognized manufacturers' brands, not for status, but for assurance of quality within their more narrowly perceived range of choices.[15] Other customers, however, seem to be less concerned with the physical characteristics of the product and more concerned with the symbolic value. They seem to derive psychic satisfaction from the use of well-known branded articles, perhaps because they feel some of the status or prestige of the product may rub off on them. You may recall that both the physical and symbolic aspects of products were incorporated into the Howard-Sheth model.

Why branding is advantageous to branders

Encourages repeat buying
■ Brands obviously would not be used so aggressively by companies if target customers did not respond to them. Many of the advantages of brand promotion to the branders are a function of the advantages to customers. A good brand speeds up shopping for the customer, and so it reduces the marketer's selling time and effort. When a customer finds it convenient to repeat purchases by brand, promotion costs are reduced and sales volume is increased. A marketing manager who consistently attempts to provide a good buy and maintain quality can be assured of his reward by using brands.

May develop customer franchise
■ Another important advantage of successful branding is that the brander may be able to carve out a market for himself among loyal customers. Whether the brander is a manufacturer, wholesaler, or retailer, this brand loyalty protects him from competition, because the brander, in effect, is given a customer franchise by the customers he is reaching. In other words, he achieves a monopolistic competition situation or even a little monopoly, and this gives him greater control in planning his marketing mix.

May help segment markets
■ A brander also can use various brands to segment markets and meet the needs of various intermediate customers. Instead of just selling "motor oil," for example, the marketing manager could offer three grades (and brands) to cater to final consumers' varying demands for oil quality. Or, if he were selling this oil to various competing wholesalers and retailers who did not want to compete directly with each other, he might offer them identical or almost identical products under different brand names. Such practices help explain why there are so many brands on the market.

Branding may return more than it costs
■ By offering customers what amounts to a "guarantee" of quality, branders may be able to obtain a price that is higher than the cost of giving this guarantee. This is important because maintaining quality and providing a guarantee do, in fact, cost something. One study showed that customers were willing to spend approximately 13 percent more for well-known food brands.[16]

A good brand may build corporate image
■ Good brands can enhance the company's name, simplifying the introduction of additional products. Or the company may use its own name as a brand for many of its products. This is of special importance in the industrial goods area, where branding of individual products is more difficult. Here, it is really the company's total personality which it would like to project, positively.

The idea of improving the company's corporate image, as well as its brands, has been growing. When customers think a company is big and successful, they often have a better impression of it and its products. The U.S. Steel Corp., with its many large subsidiaries, found that industrial customers who were aware of the relationship of U.S. Steel to its subsidiaries viewed the subsidiaries more favorably. This was important in their choice of supplier, especially when competing products were basically similar. For this reason, in 1958, U.S. Steel redesigned its trademark and began to identify all the subsidiaries with it.[17]

Growing acceptance of the idea that a good customer image is important has led some companies to change their corporate name so that the name either is more descriptive of the firm's activity or is more inclusive of a variety of activities. Cities Service, for instance, took the name Citgo, and spent a lot of money popularizing the new name and the new symbol because the old name seemed inappropriate. And U.S. Rubber, with its various foreign subsidiaries, adopted the Uniroyal name and trademark because it felt that the new name was a more accurate designation.[18]

Conditions favorable to branding

■ Most marketing managers accept branding as desirable and are primarily concerned with assuring the success of the brand name of the product(s) they are marketing.

The following conditions would be favorable to successful branding:

1. The demand for the general product class or in the selected target market(s) should be large enough to support a profitable marketing plan.
2. The demand should be sufficiently strong so that the market price will offer a large enough margin over additional promotion cost to make the effort worthwhile.
3. It is best when there are economies of mass production. If the branding were really successful, the cost of production would decline with additional volume, thereby increasing profits.
4. The product quality being offered should be the best for the price in the market being served, and the quality should be easily maintained.
5. The product should be easily identifiable by a brand or trademark. This is easier said than done. Many products do not lend themselves easily to conspicuous marking. Few consumers would like to have a furniture manufacturer's label sewn conspicuously on their sofa or lounge chair. But if the label or mark is inconspicuous, then much of the brand prestige value is lost.

Some producers are ingenious in placing labels. Walnut and orange growers stamp their brand names directly on their products; some coal producers color their coal; and large meat-packers place metal foil brand labels inside self-service meat packages.

6. Consistent and widespread availability is necessary. When a customer starts using a brand, she should be able to continue finding it in her stores.

7. Brand promotion will be more successful if the brander can be assured of favorable positioning of his products in the stores. For some manufacturers, this is just a hope or a goal for their salesmen. But when wholesalers and retailers brand their own products, this is something they can control.

Achieving brand familiarity is not easy

■ It is clear that recognition and respect for a brand must be earned by means of a good product and persistent promotion. There are many brands which, for practical purposes, are valueless because they have no meaning to target customers.

There are four levels of familiarity

■ Four degrees of brand familiarity are useful for strategic planning: (1) nonrecognition, (2) recognition, (3) preference, and (4) insistence. The adoption process and the types of problem solving discussed in Chapter 8 are directly relevant here.

The degree of brand familiarity achieved by the brander (*and* his competitors) obviously affects the planning for the balance of the marketing mix, and especially influences decisions on where the product should be made available and what promotion is needed.

Nonrecognition of brand

Some products are seen as essentially homogeneous. Their brands are not recognized by final consumers at all. And they may never be, although middlemen may use the brand names for identification and inventory control and this may mislead production-oriented manufacturers. Examples here are: school supplies, novelties, inexpensive dinnerware, and similar goods found in variety stores and mass merchandising outlets.

Brand recognition

"Brand recognition" means that customers remember having seen or heard of the brand. This can be a significant achievement if there are many nondescript brands on the market. Potential customers could have either positive or negative feelings about a brand, of course, but here we will emphasize the positive aspects only.

Brand preference

Rather than just gaining brand recognition, some branders would prefer to reach the stage called "brand preference" in which target customers will choose the brand out of habit or past experience. At this stage, the firm may have achieved a favorable position in a monopolistic competition situation.

Brand insistence

"Brand insistence," a logical extension of brand preference, is the stage at which customers insist upon a product and would be willing to search extensively to find it. This stage is the goal of most target marketing activities. Here, the firm has developed a strong customer franchise and may enjoy a very inelastic demand curve.

Knowing how well you're known may take research ■ While the degree of brand familiarity achieved will have an important bearing on the development of a marketing mix, marketing research may be necessary to determine exactly what the firm has achieved and in which target markets. In many situations, company executives feel their products have achieved or will achieve a higher degree of brand familiarity than is really the case, and the firms develop their marketing mixes accordingly. This self-delusion can only lead to overburdening the other ingredients in the marketing mixes. Studies show that some brands do not reach even the brand recognition stage. One study, for example, revealed that two out of every five housewives could not even name the brand of furniture they owned.[19]

Choosing a brand name

■ Brand name selection is still an art, but management judgment may have to enter because the matter is important. It is difficult to pinpoint what constitutes a good brand name, because some of the successful brand names seem to defy even the obvious rules. Many of these names, however, got started when there was relatively little market competition.

A good brand name can make a difference, helping to communicate something important about the company or its product. Just using the company's name or a family member's name is no longer adequate in our highly competitive markets. A good brand name should be:

Short, simple, and easy to spell and read.
Easy to recognize and remember.
Pleasing when read and easy to pronounce.
Not disagreeable sounding.
Pronounceable in only one way.
Always timely (does not get out of date).
Adaptable to packaging or labeling requirements.
Available for use (not in use by another firm).
Pronounceable in all languages (for goods to be exported).
Not offensive, obscene, or negative.
A selling suggestion.
Adaptable to any advertising medium (especially billboards and TV).

What is a brand?

■ We have used the terms *branding, brand names*, and *trademarks* interchangeably so far, but it is important to distinguish among them because of the legal implications each term has.

Branding refers to the use of a name, a term, a symbol, or design (or a combination of these), to identify goods or services of one seller or a group of sellers and to distinguish them from those of competitors. This is a broad term that includes the use of brand names, trademarks, and practically all other means of product identification.

Brand name has a narrower meaning. It is a word, letter, or a group of words or letters that can be spoken.

Trademark, however, is essentially a legal term and includes only those words, symbols, or marks that the law designates as trademarks.

The word *Buick* can be used to illustrate these distinctions. The Buick car is *branded* under the *brand name* "Buick," whether it is used orally or printed in any manner. When "Buick" is printed in a certain kind of script, however, it becomes a *trademark*. A trademark need not be attached to the product. It need not even be a word. A symbol can be used.

These distinctions may seem technical, but they are very important to business firms that spend much money to protect their brands.

Protecting brand names and trademarks

■ Common law assures the rights of the true originators and users of trademarks and brand names, stating that the ownership of brand names and trademarks is established by continued usage without abandonment. Clearly, by now Morton Salt, Coca-Cola, and Bon Ami are unmistakably identified with particular products.

The exact procedure for protecting trademarks and what could be protected were not clear, however, until the passage of the federal *Lanham Act* in 1946. This act specifies what types of marks (including brand names) can be protected by law, and it makes provision for registration records to facilitate their protection. It applies to goods shipped in interstate or foreign commerce.[20]

No federal tests or policing

■ The Lanham Act does not make registration compulsory. Even getting onto the registration records does not establish ownership of a mark. It is still necessary to show that the firm was the first to use the particular trademark and that the trademarked product actually has been offered for sale on a continuing basis. Further, registration does not imply that the federal government endorses the product or that the product has passed any federal tests of quality. Neither does registration mean that the government will police the owner's rights to a mark. He himself still must bring suit against any infringers.

A principal reason for registering under the Lanham Act is to protect a trademark to be used in foreign commerce. Some countries require that a trademark be registered in its home country before it can be protected in that country.

A legally valid trademark can be a real asset to a company. Every effort should be made to develop a trademark that will not become a common descriptive term for that kind of product. A unique product group may come to be known by its leading brand name rather than its common descriptive name. When this occurs, the brand name or trademark becomes public property, and the owner loses all his rights to it. This happened with the names *cellophane, aspirin, shredded wheat,* and *kerosene,* and there was concern that *Scotch Tape* and *Frigidaire* might become public property.

What kind of brand to use?

The old established family name

■ Branders who manufacture or handle more than one item must decide whether they are going to use the same brand name for all of their items – called a family brand – or individual brands for each item.

The use of the same brand for many products is sensible if all are essentially the same in nature and quality. The goodwill attached to one or two products may reflect on the others. This reduces the promotional overhead, tends to build a customer franchise for the family brand, and paves the way for the introduction of new products.

Examples of family brands are the Heinz "57" food products, A&P brands (Ann Page, Sultana, and Iona, each in different price classes), Sears, Roebuck's Kenmore appliances, and the Pittsburgh Plate Glass line of paints and other home products.

Individual brands: outside and inside competition

■ Individual brands frequently are used by a manufacturer when his products are of varying quality or type. If the products are distinctly different, such as meat products and glue, individual brands are preferable. Or the quality and higher price of one of the company's well-known names may be protected while another brand (perhaps identifying a lower priced line) is used as a *fighting brand* to meet competition. Use of individual brands is preferred, too, if there is any risk of the failure of one product damaging the reputation of others.

Sometimes firms use individual brands to stimulate competition *within* the organization. Each brand is the responsibility of a different group; management feels that internal competition keeps everyone alert. The theory is that if anyone is going to take business away from them it ought to be their own brand. This kind of competition is found among General Motors' brands, where Chevrolet, Pontiac, Oldsmobile, Buick, and even Cadillac compete with each other in some markets.

Who should do the branding?

■ Frequently wholesalers and retailers decide to use their own brands in preference to manufacturers' brands, commonly called "national brands" because of their promotion across the nation or in large regions. Such manufacturers' or national brands include Kellogg's, Stokely, RCA-Whirlpool, International Harvester, Sheetrock, and IBM.

The term *national* is not always an accurate designation, however, since many wholesalers' and retailers' brands have achieved national distribution and are advertised nationally, while some manufacturers' products have only regional distribution. Kroger, A&P, Sears Roebuck, and Montgomery Ward brands, for example, are all advertised and distributed more widely than many so-called national brands.

For this reason, instead of the term *"national brands,"* we will use *manufacturers' brands* to refer to this type—as contrasted to wholesalers' and retailers' brands. These latter brands frequently are called *"private brands."* But to reduce confusion, we will call the wholesalers' and retailers' brands *dealer brands.*

So far we have been focusing on the value of branding in general, but branding has some special advantages and disadvantages for dealers. This is especially relevant with respect to whether they should use manufacturer's brands or develop their own dealer brands. These advantages and disadvantages are discussed below.

■ The major advantage of selling a popular manufacturer's brand is that the product already is presold to some target customers. Furthermore, it may bring in new customers. It can encourage higher turnover with a reduced selling cost, and some of the prestige of the manufacturer's brand may rub off on the dealers. And in case the manufacturer doesn't maintain his quality, *he* receives the blame, not the dealer, and the customer can be shifted to another manufacturer's brand or a dealer brand. The dealer does not lose *his* customer.

Since manufacturers' brands usually are readily available at the wholesalers' or manufacturers' warehouses, the dealer needs to carry less inventory. Another major advantage for some retailers is that the retailer can advertise special prices on items which are carried in other stores and thereby call attention to his store as a source of bargains.

■ The major disadvantage of manufacturers' brands is that manufacturers normally offer a lower gross margin than the dealer might be able to earn with his own brands. This, however, may be offset by higher turnover.

Another disadvantage is that the manufacturer still maintains control of his brand and may withdraw it from the dealer at any time. Wholesalers are especially vulnerable in this respect. If customers become loyal to a manufacturer's brand and the dealer does not or cannot carry the product, then the customers may go elsewhere. Here, loyalty may be tied to the brand rather than to the dealer.

Advantages of dealer brands — loyal salesmen, the best shelves

■ In some respects, the advantages of dealer brands are the converse of the disadvantages of manufacturers' brands. The dealer may be able to buy products at lower prices and so be able to obtain higher gross margins even with lower retail prices. He can have greater price flexibility with his own brands because price comparisons are not as easy as with manufacturer's brands and also because there is no manufacturer to dictate pricing policy.

Another advantage of dealer brands is that dealers easily can change from one supplier to another if any one firm can't offer the quality and price needed. By using their own brands, dealers may be able to protect themselves from the arbitrary action of manufacturers.

Dealer brands protect wholesalers from the defection of their salesmen — and the salesmen's customer following — to other wholesaling firms. Why? Dealer brands give the wholesaler, rather than his salesmen, a claim to customer loyalty.

Since the dealer's own brand ties customers to him, he may be able to estimate demand and buy more effectively. His salesmen can also control the point of sale and may be able to give their products special shelf position or displays.

Disadvantages of dealer brands — taking the blame, buying big quantities

■ The dealer must stimulate his own demand, and this may be costly, especially if turnover is typically slow in his lines. He must take the blame for inferior quality. He may have difficulty getting consistently good quality at low prices, especially during times of short supply such as wartime or inflationary periods. And the dealer must purchase in fairly large quantities from suppliers, assuming the risk and cost of carrying inventory.

Dealer brands have a chance if . . .

■ Branding by dealers begins to move them into the traditional role of a manufacturer. They must assume all of the marketing responsibilities of a manufacturer and plan their marketing strategy accordingly. Therefore, the decision to go into dealer branding should not be made lightly. The chances of a dealer brand being successful are helped if a number of conditions exist:

1. If there are several manufacturers' brands, none should be strongly entrenched in the market.
2. A dependable quality and quantity of ingredients or raw materials for the dealer brand should be available at a reasonable price to ensure a good margin in case the brand meets with acceptance.
3. It helps if manufacturers' brands are overpriced, so the dealer brand can be priced under them, yet with a larger-than-normal gross margin, to cover higher promotional costs.
4. Although the dealer's brand must be promoted, the promo-

tion should not be so expensive as to use up the extra gross margin.

5. There should be an adequate, well-established market; dealers may find it expensive to pioneer the introduction of new products.

6. Product quality should be easily and economically determined by inspection or use—customers will be more willing to experiment if a dealer's brand does not present too much of a risk.

7. If the dealer brand is lower priced, depressed business conditions may help its sale—customers are more price conscious then.

Dealer brands in the food and drug lines usually are offered at slightly lower prices than manufacturers' brands. Dealer brands, however, are not always priced lower. Sometimes dealers, having analyzed their target market, choose to offer a prestige-laden, higher quality product and then price it even higher than major manufacturers' brands.

The battle of the brands—who's winning?

■ Manufacturers and dealers have been vying with each other in what has been called the "battle of the brands." No criticism of branding is implied in the term battle. It is simply a question of whose brands are to be more popular and who is to be in control.

Some research findings suggest, for food products at least, that manufacturers' brands may be losing ground. In 1951, manufacturers' brands seemed to be preferred by a ratio of 2 or 3 to 1. Even higher prices were accepted. This strong preference has continued to decline, and in 1970 one survey showed that 45 percent of the consumers had shifted to dealer brands. And younger households may be leading here.[21]

One of the reasons for this shift is that some of the manufacturers' brands have come to symbolize elegance and are regarded as a luxury, while the dealer-branded chain store products are seen as necessities.[22] Then, too, the chains' dealer-branded products *are* more likely to be in stock. One consumer's statement may be revealing in this connection: "When something is highly advertised, I find it short in the supermarkets."[23]

The growth of dealer branding has also been pushed by the established chain stores using their brands as a competitive weapon against discount houses. But this, in turn, sometimes leads manufacturers to bring out lower-priced lines of their own.[24] Goodyear, for example, brought out a third-line nylon tire to compete with dealer-branded tires being sold at lower prices. Department stores, supermarkets, service stations, clothiers, appliance dealers, and drugstores are all going more deeply into dealer branding.

The battle of the brands certainly is far from over, but the former dominance of manufacturers' brands may have ended. Some retailers are becoming so large that dealer brands frequently sell in large volume and are nationally advertised. Some wholesalers have developed extremely strong brands and have ties to regional chains with literally hundreds of stores.

Manufac-turers may become only manufac-turers

■ In the future, retailer-controlled brands may seek broader distribution among other retailers and perhaps wholesalers too. It seems logical that as retailers begin to advertise nationally but have only a limited number of sales outlets, they may find it profitable to permit others to carry their brands. This might be a serious challenge to manufacturers' brands.

If this trend continues, manufacturers could become just that — only the manufacturing arms of dealers. Retailers and wholesalers might come to dominate marketing. Certainly, the latter are closer to final consumers and may have greater control of the final sale situation.[25]

Conclusion

■ Packaging and branding can create a new total product. Variations in packaging can make a product salable in various target markets. Branding can be used by the marketer in creating and building a customer franchise for a given product.

A specific package must be developed for each product. Both underpackaging and overpackaging can be expensive. Although the final customer remains the ultimate factor, the packager also must remember the needs of wholesalers and retailers. A small retailer might prefer the smaller package units that a supermarket operator would resist. Both promotional and protective packaging can cut total distribution costs.

To customers, the main significance of brands is an assurance of quality. This confidence leads to repeat purchasing. For marketers, such "routine" buying means reduced promotion costs and increased sales.

Should brands be stressed? The decision depends on whether the costs of brand promotion and honoring the brand guarantee can be covered and made profitable by a higher price or more rapid turnover, or both. The cost of branding may reduce other costs by relieving pressure on the other three Ps.

In recent years, the strength of manufacturers' brands has declined and dealer brands have become more important. The dealer-labeled products may win in the battle of the brands, perhaps because dealers are closer to customers and may choose to promote their own brands more aggressively.

Branding gives a marketing manager considerable latitude. He can add brands and use individual or family brands. Ultimately, however, customers express their approval or disapproval of the total product (including the brand). The degree of brand familiarity obtained is a measure of management's ability to carve out a separate market, and has considerable impact on Place, Price, and Promotion decisions.

questions and problems

1 Explain the increasing interest in packaging, not only for consumer goods but industrial goods. Is this likely to continue?

2 Suggest an example where packaging costs probably: (a) lower total distribution costs, and (b) raise total distribution costs.

3 Is there any difference between a brand name and a trademark? If so, why is this difference important?

4 Is a well-known brand valuable only to the owner of the brand?

5 Would it be profitable for a firm to expend large sums of money to establish a brand for any type product in any market situation? Why, or why not? If the answer is no, suggest examples.

6 Evaluate the suitability of the following brand names: (a) Star (sausage), (b) Pleasing (books), (c) Rugged (shoes), (d) Shiny (shoe polish), (e) Lord Jim (ties).

7 Explain family brands. Sears, Roebuck and A&P use family brands but they have several different family brands. If the idea is a good one, why don't they have just one brand?

8 What is the "battle of the brands"? Who do you think will win and why?

9 What does the degree of brand familiarity imply about previous promotion efforts and the future promotional task? Also, how does the degree of brand preference affect the Place and Price variables?

10 If you have been operating a small supermarket with emphasis on manufacturers' brands and have barely been breaking even, how should you evaluate the proposal of a large wholesaler who offers a full line of dealer-branded groceries at substantially lower prices? Specify any assumptions necessary to obtain a definite answer.

notes

[1] *Modern Packaging Encyclopedia and Planning Guide,* 1972–73 Issue.

[2] "Brand Manager Spans the Packaging Gap," *The* (AMA) *Marketing News,* January 1, 1973, p. 3; and David J. Luck, "Interfaces of a Product Manager," *Journal of Marketing,* October 1969, pp. 32–36.

[3] "The New Power of Packaging: Management Takes Control," *Printers' Ink,* June 11, 1965, pp. 13–18.

[4] "New Packaging Concepts Sell, Resell, and Satisfy Customers," *Printers' Ink,* November 21, 1958, pp. 21–27.

[5] "Packaging Brings a Sleeper to Life." *Printers' Ink,* March 22, 1963, pp. 48–49.

[6] "The Perfect Package: It's Not Here Yet," *Business Week,* August 12, 1961, pp. 106–8; See also William N. Gunn, "Packagers and the Environmental Challenge," *Harvard Business Review,* July–August 1972, pp. 103–11; "Oregon: A Test Case for Returnable Containers," *Business Week,* July 28, 1973, pp. 76–77; and Carl D. McDaniel, Jr., "The Social Costs of Disposable Packaging," *Business Horizons,* February 1971, pp. 46–48.

[7] W. A. French and L. O. Schroeder, "Package Information Legislation: Trends and Viewpoints," *MSU Business Topics,* Summer 1972, pp. 39–43; and M. L. Dean, J. F. Engel, and W. W. Talarzyk, "The Influence of Package Copy Claims on Consumer Product Evaluations," *Journal of Marketing,* April 1972, pp. 34–39.

[8] H. R. Isakson and A. R. Maurizi, "The Consumer Economics of Unit Pricing," *Journal of Marketing Research,* August 1973, pp. 277–85; K. B. Monroe and P. J. LaPlaca, "What Are the Benefits of Unit Pricing?" *Journal of Marketing,* July 1972, pp. 16–22; and M. J. Houston, "The Effect of Unit Pricing on Choices of Brand and Size in Economic Shopping," *Journal of Marketing,* July 1972, pp. 51–63.

[9] *The Nielsen Researcher,* No. 1 (1967), p. 11.

[10] Frank Presbrey, *The History and Development of Advertising* (New York: Doubleday & Co., Inc., 1929).

[11] Ralph Westfall and Harper W. Boyd, Jr., "Marketing in India," *Journal of Marketing,* October 1960, p. 17.

[12] T. Levitt, "Branding on Trial," *Harvard Business Review,* March–April 1966, pp. 28–32.

[13] Robert H. Cole, "The Battle of Brands in Canned Goods," in S. H. Rewoldt (ed.), *Frontiers in Marketing Thought* (Bloomington, Ind.: Bureau of Business Research, Indiana University, 1955), pp. 153–59.

[14] "Just How Good?" *Time*, July 7, 1967, pp. 66–67; and "FDA Has Doubts on Generic Names," *Business Week*, January 13, 1968, p. 36.

[15] James A. Carman, *The Application of Social Class in Market Segmentation* (Berkeley: Institute of Business and Economic Research, University of California, 1965), p. 28.

[16] J. O. Peckham, *Planning Your Marketing Operations for 1959 . . . and the Years Ahead* (Chicago: A. C. Nielsen Co., 1958), p. 15; and "How A Small Packer Does Better than the Giants," *Business Week*, November 22, 1958, pp. 140–52.

[17] "What's Behind the New Look That U.S. Steel Is Sporting," *Business Week*, March 29, 1958, pp. 88–93.

[18] "One Name to Girdle the Globe," *Business Week*, August 1, 1964, pp. 74–75; John E. Mertes, "The Genesis of the Corporate Image," *MSU Business Topics*, Winter 1971, pp. 35–46; William J. E. Crissy, "Image: What Is It?" *MSU Business Topics*, Winter 1971, pp. 77–80; see also "Exxon Victorious," *Time*, March 5, 1973, p. 63.

[19] *Business Week*, February 20, 1960, p. 71; see also: Frank M. Bass and William L. Wilkie, "A Comparative Analysis of Attitudinal Predictions of Brand Preference," *Journal of Marketing Research*, August 1973, pp. 262–69; F. B. Kraft, D. H. Granbois, and J. O. Summers, "Brand Evaluation and Brand Choice: A Longitudinal Study," *Journal of Marketing Research*, August 1973, pp. 235–41; Dik W. Twedt, "How Does Brand Awareness-Attitude Affect Marketing Strategy?" *Journal of Marketing*, October 1967, pp. 64–66; and "Women Flunk Identity Test," *Business Week*, April 6, 1965, pp. 50–52.

[20] Thomas F. Schutte, "The Semantics of Branding," *Journal of Marketing*, vol. 33, no. 2 (April 1969), pp. 5–11; Philip C. Burger and Barbara Schott, "Can Private Brand Buyers Be Identified?" *Journal of Marketing Research*, May 1972, pp. 219–22; and Barbara D. Coe, "Private Versus National Brand Preference Among Lower and Middle-Income Consumers," *Journal of Retailing*, Fall 1971, pp. 61–78.

[21] *Marketing Communications*, August 1970, p. 13; "Is the Private Label Battle Heating Up?" *Grey Matter*, vol. 44 (July 1973) no. 7.

[22] E. Dichter, "Brand Loyalty and Motivation Research," *Food Business*, January and February 1956.

[23] "Private Brands Score Well," *Printers' Ink*, May 12, 1967, p. 3.

[24] "A Wider Track for Tire Sales," *Business Week*, March 20, 1965, pp. 55–58.

[25] "Private Label Products Gain Increased Space on Many Retailers' Shelves," *The Wall Street Journal*, February 11, 1971, p. 1; "A&P's Own Brand of Consumerism," *Business Week*, April 11, 1970, p. 32; Victor J. Cook and T. F. Schutte, *Brand Policy Determination* (Boston: Allyn & Bacon, Inc., 1967).

14

Consumer goods

■ Product classifications can be extremely valuable in planning marketing strategies. In fact, we will use these classifications to help integrate the material in the balance of the text. The consumer goods categories introduced in this chapter and the industrial goods categories introduced in Chapter 15 should be studied carefully — they are not just academic trivia. They can greatly accelerate your development as a marketing strategy planner because they are logical and their implications follow logically. Your firsthand observations applied to this analytical framework will speed the development of your "marketing sense."

Depends on who will use the product

■ *Consumer goods* are those goods and services destined for the ultimate consumer. These contrast with *industrial goods*, which are those goods and services destined for use in producing other goods or services. All goods fit into one or the other of these two categories.

There are two major problems in discussing consumer goods. One is that it is impossible to discuss the marketing process for thousands of goods. The other is that some products usually considered consumer goods also may be industrial goods, since they are destined for use by intermediate customers. Examples include typewriters, typing paper, rugs, decorators' services, lighting fixtures, brooms, and plumbing services.

The type of customer who will finally use the good determines whether it should be classified as consumer or industrial. Although the same product may be involved, the two types of customers may need entirely different marketing mixes.

Need for a classification system

Simplifies the
process of
relating
products to
marketing
mixes

■ Within the consumer goods area, the same or similar products, may require entirely different marketing mixes even though they are appealing to the same "type" of customer. Fresh meat, canned salmon, and lettuce are all foods, yet all are marketed differently. Hosiery and women's party dresses are clothing items, but the marketing mixes for each are quite dissimilar. Hosiery is available in many different types of outlets and has a much simpler fitting problem. Hosiery has been successfully branded, but relatively few women's dress brands are widely known.

There are many other examples of apparently similar products with dissimilar marketing problems. How people view the product has considerable bearing on how the four Ps are combined in a marketing mix. To avoid treating every product as unique, we must try to develop sensible, if tentative, generalizations about how products are related to marketing mixes. If we can classify products this way, it can be highly useful as a starting point for developing marketing mixes for new products and evaluating present mixes.

A number of classification systems are conceivable. One type might be based on the kind of outlet through which the products are marketed. Another could be based on a division of all products into either of two categories: durable versus nondurable, perishable versus nonperishable, or necessities versus luxuries. A third could be classification by the degree of demand elasticity. Each has its deficiencies.

A useful classification system

■ A particularly workable and useful product classification system would be one based on *the way people buy products*. Since the purpose of the marketing process is to satisfy customer needs, basing product classification on customer behavior makes the most sense and follows logically from the market grid concept.

The problem-solving approach discussed in Chapter 8 has relevance here. Some consumers regularly engage in extended problem solving to satisfy certain needs. They will spend a lot of time searching for the right product to satisfy those needs. At the other extreme, other consumers have found routine ways of fulfilling the same needs and therefore do not shop extensively. These problem-solving processes help us understand the goods classification system introduced here and applied throughout subsequent chapters.

In our goods classification system, which is based on customer buying behavior, goods can be separated into four categories: (1) convenience goods, (2) shopping goods, (3) specialty goods, and (4) unsought goods.

Convenience goods are those that customers want to buy immediately with minimum shopping effort, i.e., where the busy customer feels she stands to gain little from making price and quality comparisons. In other words, she wants to use routinized buying behavior.

Shopping goods are those goods for which customers do shop, comparing the price and quality of various brands by visiting several stores, studying performance evaluations, and reading advertisements. Here we might see either limited or extended problem-solving behavior.

Specialty goods are those that customers insist upon having, and are willing to search for until they find them. Here the consumer already has done extended problem solving and decided on a particular product as a solution. If the product's availability is unknown, she is willing to search for it. If only one place has it, as with some services, then she will only buy there.

Unsought goods are those items that potential customers don't want yet, or don't know they can buy, or aren't looking for. Here, the need has not yet arisen, or the consumer has not recognized that she has a problem, or that it can be solved with a particular good.

Helps define one set of possible grid dimensions

■ In Chapter 4 we introduced three basic classes of potential market grid dimensions and indicated that, ideally, we would be able to describe all potential market grid boxes in terms of all three types — generally, (1) demographic characteristics, (2) behavioral needs, and (3) urgency to get need satisfied, and desire and willingness to compare and shop.

If we had all of this information, it would be "relatively easy" to develop an "ideal" marketing mix. In fact, however, it should be increasingly obvious that we do not always know as much as we would like to know about our potential customers. It is usually impossible to define each potential target market precisely using all three classes of grid dimensions mentioned above. This is where product classifications can help.

A marketing planner may be able to make reasonably good judgments about the third dimension class — how urgent his potential customers are to get the needs satisfied and how willing they are to compare and shop. These judgments may help him specify the appropriate goods classifications which we are discussing. And these classes will have immediate relevance to marketing planning.

It should be understood that product classifications are not grid dimensions. They are shorthand descriptions which can be used to summarize grid dimensions. However, in the interests of convenience and simplicity, we will use the product classifications as grid dimensions. And they can be very useful in summarizing how *some* target customers view the product.

Focusing on goods classifications is a practical approach. And goods classes will provide a thread through the balance of this text. Research does support this approach, having found that these product classifications are relevant to marketing mix planning.[1]

Figure 14–1
How the motel market looks to some motel owners

More than one product classification might be needed in a market

■ There is no simple, automatic classification for a particular good. While this may be bothersome, it means that there is no need to memorize a long list of products according to classifications. However, since different target markets sometimes react differently to similar goods or services, two or more product classifications, combined with two or more marketing strategies might be needed to satisfy all potential customers in a general market area.

A tale of
three motels

■ Motels are a good example of a service that is viewed as three different kinds of goods. Some motorists – tired ones – are satisfied with the first motel they come to (a convenience good); other travelers shop for the best facilities at the best price (a shopping good); still others study their road guides and drive or phone ahead until they find a vacancy in a recommended motel (a specialty good).

Perhaps the same motel could satisfy all potential customers, but it would take some doing to produce a marketing mix attractive to everyone. Those looking for convenience would want easy access; the shopping tourists would want attractive appearance and comfort relative to price; specialty-goods travelers would require a listing in their touring guides.

The market grid for motels in one geographical area might appear as shown in Figure 14–1, with a very large convenience-goods market. This might suggest that motel owners should try harder to get convenient locations even if it means skimping on facilities that would appeal to the shopping-goods travelers.

In other areas, the market grid might look more like Figure 14–2, which shows large shopping-goods and specialty-goods markets – which may be the best view of the motel market today. The newer motels not only are conveniently located but also have more luxurious layouts and offer charge card and free reservation services

Figure 14–2
Another view of the motel market

to your next stop. Some are low-price oriented, while others are not.[2]

These motel examples show that if each marketing manager analyzed his own potential target markets in terms of these goods classifications, it would force him to clarify his thinking about consumers' behavior and marketing mixes. Certainly he would like to know more about his potential customers than is summarized in the product classifications. But this could be a "quick and dirty" beginning which could also be vital to his subsequent planning.

In the more thorough discussion of product classes that follows, you will notice that goods classifications can be subdivided even further according to other relevant dimensions. Generally, we are looking for homogeneous market segments so we can design marketing mixes to satisfy each market grid box more exactly.

Convenience goods

■ Convenience goods—those goods the customer wants but isn't willing to spend much time shopping for—include such items as cigarettes, soap, drugs, newspapers, magazines, chewing gum, candy, and most grocery products.

These products are bought frequently and readily, require little service or selling, are not very expensive, and may even be bought by habit. The classic cigarette slogan, "I'd walk a mile for a Camel," tried to imply that Camels were not a convenience good, but it is doubtful that many consumers think of their own cigarette brand in this light.

At the same time, you should also be careful about too readily classifying goods as convenience goods. Consider the attitudes of your target customers as they are influenced by income, wealth, and other factors. A 10-cent novelty might be a convenience good for most adults, but it might be a shopping good for a child with a 20-cent weekly allowance.

Convenience goods can be further classified into three subtypes, again primarily on the basis of how customers think about products and buy them, *not* the characteristics of the products themselves. These subclassifications are (1) staples, (2) impulse goods, and (3) emergency goods.

Staples — purchased and used regularly

■ The staple food and drug items used regularly in every household are usually bought frequently, and routinely, without much thought beyond the initial decision to buy. Here, branding becomes important because brand recognition helps the customer reduce shopping effort.

Staple items are offered for sale in such convenient places as food stores, drugstores, and hardware stores, as well as vending machines, because customers don't want to search far for them. Some customers, in fact, value convenience so highly that they prefer to have such goods as milk, bread, newspapers, and orange juice delivered directly to their homes. This may cost slightly more, but some customers are willing to pay for the convenience.

Shopping for staples might not even be planned. Since many housewives do their meal planning while passing shelves in the supermarket, modern supermarkets have been laid out to facilitate this behavior. Complementary goods such as strawberries and shortcake mix (biscuit mix) or sponge cake are sometimes placed next to each other. This encourages even more spontaneous buying.

Such purchasing of convenience goods does not mean that it is completely haphazard. One study did show that the purchase of about 50 percent of all grocery items might be classed as unplanned, but nearly 86 percent of these purchases were products and brands that had been bought before.[3]

Unplanned purchasing of this kind is sometimes called "impulse buying," but this may be a misuse of the term. Rather, it would seem that some customers — especially experienced shoppers and those buying large quantities — are shifting their routine meal planning from the home to the store; this may be a very sensible way for them to buy. This kind of buying should be analyzed carefully because it is *not* impulsive and some underlying patterns may exist, including buying by preferred brand. Further, the products may be used regularly as part of the consumer's consumption system, leading to even more routinized buying behavior.

Impulse goods — purchased immediately on sight

■ Impulse goods are bought as unplanned purchases, but not in the same sense as are unplanned purchases of staples. Customers typically are not out shopping for impulse goods. True impulse goods are items that the customer decides to purchase on sight, probably has bought the same way many times before, and wants immediately.

If a housewife passes a street corner vendor, for example, and gets a sudden urge for ice cream and purchases an ice-cream bar, it would be considered an impulse good. The important distinction is that if the same housewife were to buy a box of ice-cream bars in the supermarket with the intention of using them for a family dessert, the bars would be regarded as staples because she was *looking* for desserts.

There is an important distinction between buying something to satisfy a *strongly felt current need* and buying to satisfy *ongoing needs*, perhaps for *subsequent use*. If the customer does not purchase an impulse good immediately, that need may disappear and no purchase will be made. But if the customer needs some desserts, she will eventually buy them.

This distinction is important because it affects Place and the whole marketing mix. Place is extremely important for impulse goods, because if the buyer doesn't happen across them at the "right" time, the potential sale may be lost forever. As a result, special methods have developed for selling impulse goods. Impulse-good specialists, such as ice-cream vendors, specialize in putting these goods where they'll be bought. Department stores often place impulse goods on the first floor near main doors; supermarkets and drugstores put them near the checkout counter. Impulse goods sometimes achieve a strong brand preference—as in the case of Coca-Cola and some brands of candy bars.

Emergency goods— purchased only when urgently needed

■ Emergency goods are purchased only when the need is urgent. The customer wants these products immediately; price and perhaps even quality are of small concern. The demand for such goods may be extremely inelastic.

Examples are ambulance services, umbrellas or raincoats during a rainstorm, and tire chains during a snowstorm.

Some retailers deliberately handle emergency goods to meet such needs. They know that many potential customers will face certain kinds of emergencies, and they set up their operations to help these customers solve their problems as easily as possible. Small gasoline stations in rural areas and big service stations on turnpikes carry tires to meet emergency needs. The buyer probably could get a tire at a lower price back home, but with a damaged tire on his car, he will pay what he has to.

Some small, neighborhood grocery stores meet the "fill-in" needs of customers who make only one major buying excursion to the supermarket each week and need something else between trips. Usually these small stores charge higher prices for this service, but customers find it worthwhile because they take a different view of the products they buy there. One study found that almost 80 percent of the housewives used such a "fill-in" store.[4]

Place is an important part of the marketing mix for emergency goods. Clearly, the marketing mix for emergency goods will be different from the one for staples, at least regarding where goods are placed.

Everything is becoming a convenience

■ Convenience goods traditionally have been regarded as small, frequently purchased items. We accept this view, except that emergency goods are not purchased as often. But as consumers grow increasingly affluent, they seem to enjoy the luxury of treating more goods as convenience goods, and even as impulse goods.

In addition to foods, some consumers seem to be buying toys, jewelry, cosmetics, some women's clothing, books, and phonograph records on impulse. The author has seen a $300 freezer bought without any comparison shopping—an isolated example, perhaps, but one that may become more common in the future.

You should watch the growing tendency to buy goods quickly, with little shopping, because this kind of buying may drastically alter marketing distribution patterns in the future. There seems to be a trend among neighborhood drugstores, variety stores, and grocery stores to carry increasingly high-priced goods that apparently are bought as convenience goods.

Shopping goods

■ Shopping goods are those products that a customer feels are worth the time and effort to examine carefully and compare with competing products. Extended problem solving is involved here.

Shopping goods can be divided into two classifications, depending on what customers are seeking: (1) homogeneous and (2) heterogeneous shopping goods.

Homogeneous shopping goods—the price must be right

■ Homogeneous shopping goods are products that the customer sees as standardized and wants the lowest price.

Our earlier discussion of homogeneous products—those that consumers view as essentially similar—begins to bear fruit here. You will recall that when consumers view the various brands of a product as basically the same, each competitor has an almost perfectly elastic demand curve. Since a slight price cut on such products could substantially increase sales volume, we might expect vigorous price competition.

This, in fact, is the condition in many markets. Some consumers feel that certain sizes and types of refrigerators, television sets, washing machines, and even automobiles are essentially similar, and are primarily concerned about shopping for the best price.

Each manufacturer seeks to emphasize his differences, and every retailer tries to promote his "better service." But if the customers do not believe these differences are real, your Ford dealer who "wants to make you happy . . . keep you happy . . . " may not get the chance unless the price is right. This is particularly true in large urban areas where there are many firms selling the same physical product and similar services.

In a study of automobile purchasing behavior, about 56 percent of those interviewed wanted the "best price or deal," and about half of those interviewed did shop at more than one dealership.[5] And three out of four supermarket shoppers are reported to shop for advertised specials every week.[6]

Some consumers, interested only in price, try to simplify their search by attempting to obtain comparative prices by telephone.

But some retailers refuse to give prices by telephone, feeling that they are selling more than the physical product—and want to be able to tell the customer face-to-face about their services.

This buyer emphasis on price helps explain the rise of certain types of discount houses.

Low-price items seen this way, too

Even some inexpensive items like butter, coffee, and other food items may be considered homogeneous shopping goods by some people. Some customers carefully read food store advertising for the lowest prices on these items, and then go from store to store getting the items—doing what is known as "cherry picking" in the grocery trade. Still, these customers may fill other needs while on their rounds, and this could enable the store to make profitable sales to offset the bargains they offer.

Heterogene-
ous shopping
goods—the
product must
be right

■ Heterogeneous shopping goods are products that the customer sees as nonstandardized and wants to inspect for quality and suitability. Examples are furniture, draperies, dishes, and clothing. Style is important, and price is secondary.

Even if an item costs only $5 or $10, consumers sometimes will seek it in three or four stores to be sure they have done a good job of shopping.

Price is not totally ignored in this kind of buying. But for non-standardized merchandise, there are fewer bases for price comparison. Once the customer has found the right product, he may not be too worried about price, provided it is reasonable. That is, the demand for the product may be quite inelastic. The more close substitutes there are, the more elastic becomes the demand. But it does not approach the extreme elasticity found with homogeneous shopping goods.

Branding may be less important for heterogeneous goods. The more a consumer wants to make his own comparisons of price and quality, the less he relies on trade names and labels. However, as with other types of products, if the customer is unsure about several apparently similar items, he may choose the brand he recognizes or which he thinks carries status.

Often the buyer of heterogeneous shopping goods not only wants but expects some kind of help in buying, the kind and degree depending on the demographic status or other relevant dimensions of the purchaser.

If the purchase is costly, the buyer may want expensive service, such as alterations of clothing or installation of appliances. For most customers, a sport shirt picked up on the run, as a convenience good, need not fit so precisely as a good suit—a heterogeneous shopping good.

Specialty goods

■ Specialty goods are those consumer goods that a significant group of buyers want and will make a special effort to buy. The buyer knows he wants the product. Shopping for a specialty good doesn't mean comparing but merely finding it. If such goods are readily available, their purchase may look like routine staple buying. Therefore, it is not the *extent* of searching, but rather the customer's *willingness to search* that is the determining factor. Although some customers might be willing to look hard to locate it, the following conditions in the competitive market structure might make extensive searching unnecessary:

1. If many retailers want to obtain a share of this specialty-goods market.
2. If the manufacturer, uncertain of his success in creating a specialty good, tries to obtain distribution in more outlets than really are needed to satisfy the specialty-goods market.
3. If the product is basically a staple convenience good and the major effort is directed at that target market.

Specialty goods usually are not product categories but specific branded products that have passed the brand preference stage and achieved brand insistence.

There are some instances in which a unique new product, even though not branded, also might be a specialty good. This could be true of a new drug or fertilizer, available only by generic name. Generally, however, a specific brand is involved.

Accept no substitutes! ■ Contrary to a common view, specialty goods need not be relatively expensive, durable items that are purchased infrequently. Any branded item that develops a strong customer franchise may achieve specialty-goods status. Consumers have been observed asking for a drug product by its brand name and, when offered a substitute (even though chemically identical), actually leaving the store in anger.

As might be expected, the demand for specialty goods will be relatively inelastic, at least within reasonable price ranges, since target customers are willing to insist upon the product.

Unsought goods

■ Unsought goods are those that potential customers do not yet want or know they can buy and, therefore, do not search for at all. In fact they probably would not buy these goods even if they came upon them unless additional promotion were used to show them the value of the goods or services. Needs (problems) these goods might solve are not yet recognized.

There seem to be two types of unsought goods: *new* unsought and *regularly* unsought.

New unsought goods ■ The *new* unsought goods are products offering *really new* concepts with which potential customers are not yet familiar. The concepts are such, however, that informative promotion can help convince consumers to accept or even seek out the product, thereby ending its unsought status.

Not all new products are new unsought goods. There may be lots of good substitutes available already. Just another new brand of shoe polish, for instance, would not be an unsought good. Dow-Corning's Shoe-Saver, a silicone waterproofing product for shoes, was another matter, however. Dow-Corning fought an uphill battle to gain acceptance for Shoe-Saver. It was not a polish, and cost more than polishes. The marketing manager's job, here, was to end its unsought status by informing potential target markets that a new kind of product was available for shoe protection. Subsequently, Shoe-Saver was accepted by retailers and consumers as another convenience good.

Regularly unsought goods

■ *Regularly* unsought goods are products such as life insurance, encyclopedias, and gravestones that may remain unsought but definitely not unbought forever. These products may represent some of the biggest expenditures a family ever makes, but few people would even drive around the block to find them. There may be a need, but the potential customers are not motivated to satisfy it. Goods such as encyclopedias and life insurance must be promoted continually to achieve any sales. And there probably is little hope that they will move out of the unsought category for most consumers. For this type of challenge, greater stress is needed on Promotion, and it is likely that aggressive promotion will have to continue.

By imaginatively searching for unsatisfied customer needs, however, it may be possible to locate some target market that would find the unsought good so attractive that customers might go after it, or at least buy with enthusiasm. Demand might even be fairly inelastic.

A producer of grave markers, for example, recently abandoned the not very productive approach of relying on a location close to cemeteries in the hope that customers would simply come in. Instead, he began using aggressive sales techniques.

He had considerable success with a TV advertising appeal, finding a good market particularly among guilt-ridden sons and daughters who long ago had buried their parents without a gravestone. Now, after years of uneasiness about the poorly marked grave(s) and with a newfound affluence, the heirs were willing to seek out the gravestone seller and discuss price and quality.[7]

One product may be seen as several goods

■ We have been focusing on one good at a time, but let's also understand that the *same product* might be viewed as *different goods* by *different target markets* at the *same time*.

The marketing manager might find that his general market consists of several clusters of people each of whom has similar attitudes toward his product, as shown in Figure 14–3. This diagram

Figure 14–3
How potential customers might view some product*

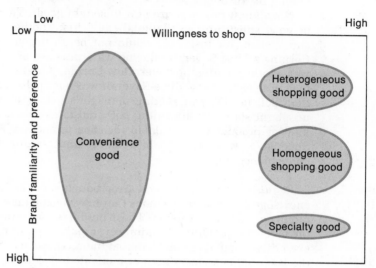

* The number of people holding each view is indicated roughly by the size of the cluster. This figure was suggested by Professor Y. Furuhashi of the University of Notre Dame.

clusters people in terms of their willingness to shop, and brand familiarity or preference – and is a simple way of summarizing our discussion of goods.

Each of these clusters might require a different marketing strategy. Or closer analysis of each might suggest the possibility for several profitable strategies, depending on how homogeneous the clusters are. Generally, we are looking for homogeneous market segments so we can design marketing mixes to satisfy each market grid box more exactly.

Clustering by goods classifications and then subdividing these clusters where necessary can be very revealing. Further, it is a commonsense approach which enables anyone with some market judgment to organize his thinking without extensive preliminary marketing research.

Need for consumer research to properly classify goods

■ Although the marketing manager can use his market judgment to classify a good, he probably could do a more reliable job by using marketing research. A formal research effort can uncover consumer attitudes and needs related to the product class and the company's particular product. Such an analysis might not only show the relevant dimensions for determining the appropriate goods class or classes but also the other two types of grid dimensions: demographic characteristics, and behavioral needs.

Clearly, consumers are multidimensional and there are many

boxes on a market grid. So the more we know about these potential customers, the better job we can do in marketing mix planning. But sometimes, consumer behavior is so mystifying that conclusions about goods classes may be the only ones that a marketing manager is willing to make with some feeling of certainty. In these cases, it is likely that the goods classes will have an important bearing on his planning and the mix that he actually chooses to implement.

Even rough judgments will suggest strategy implications

■ The product classifications we have introduced may seem somewhat arbitrary, but they are workable. In developing marketing strategies, even rough judgments about how substantial groups of customers view products are helpful. Since we will use these goods classifications throughout the rest of this book, you should have a real understanding of them.

A new view may suggest breakthrough opportunities
■ Looking at products the way customers do may create significant breakthrough opportunities for a firm. Too often production-oriented people in the factory or product-oriented people in the wholesale or retail firm see things very differently from their customers. As a result, they develop marketing mixes which are logical to them but not really satisfying to customers.

A simple illustration will help show that a "new view" may appear obvious *after* some one has had it, and that it also may be the key to getting ahead rapidly in business. A top executive of General Electric, Mr. Fred J. Borch, started out as an auditor in the lamp division in Cleveland. He moved quickly up through the marketing side of the business, however, after he developed a plan to sell light bulbs in grocery stores. At the time, the hardware store was virtually the only outlet for lamp bulbs because it was assumed that light bulbs were shopped for by men. Mr. Borch, however, regarded the light bulb as something that *housewives* would buy almost as an "impulse good," but these women were more likely to be found in grocery stores than in hardware stores.

Within our goods framework, he recognized that different segments of the market grid would buy light bulbs in different ways in different places and he built his marketing mixes accordingly. Light bulbs are now widely distributed because somebody had a new view and helped move his company in a new direction.[8] These are the breakthrough opportunities which progressive firms seek. Hopefully, this goods framework will help stimulate your thinking and insight.

For best results in planning actual marketing strategies, we should probably use marketing research to determine the goods classifications in various market grid boxes. In the following examples, however, we will use an intuitive approach to classifying products in order to clearly demonstrate what these goods classifications mean and their potential impact on strategy planning.

Prescription drugs . . . specialties and bargains

■ How should the drugs listed on a doctor's prescription be classified? The patient is seeking a specific product and will probably pay whatever price is charged. This has all the earmarks of a specialty good, yet the consumer has little or no choice of product, brand, or price.

In some markets, pharmacists will fill the prescription with similar products but at different prices. While it might be worthwhile for the patient to shop around, comparing prices is somewhat impractical and could be embarrassing to some customers because at each store they would have to ask the pharmacist to decipher the prescription and then quote his price. Besides, the customer buying a prescription usually wants his order filled as quickly and as conveniently as possible. Most consumers, therefore, probably think of prescriptions as convenience goods, either staples or emergency goods.

For an alert pharmacist, there is an opportunity in this situation. He could promote his establishment so effectively that consumers would have greater confidence in his products and his ability to fill prescriptions. If successful, he might turn his service into a specialty good. Other pharmacies have thought of their products as homogeneous shopping goods, emphasizing lower prices in their efforts to attract customers.

Saltine crackers — a "new" product?

■ How are saltine crackers classified? Major commercial baking firms produce a number of well-advertised saltine cracker brands. Does this mean that these individual brands of soda crackers are specialty goods or close to it?

Researchers found that most consumers thought of a saltine as just a saltine—they saw little difference among brands and were not interested in investigating other crackers. This implied a staple convenience good, and attempts by the bakers to distinguish their crackers through promotion met with considerable indifference.

Additional research on saltines found, however, that consumers *did want* their crackers fresh and crisp. This led one firm to develop a new inner-seal package, enabling consumers to open only part of the package at a time, preserving the freshness and crispness of the other unopened crackers. This package modification, creating a "new" product, allowed the baker using it to differentiate his product, obtaining some brand recognition and even brand preference for the product, even though it remained a convenience good.

Ski resorts must have snow

■ Ski resorts probably fit into the heterogeneous shopping-goods category. Skiers watch the snow reports carefully and go to the lodges where the snow is good. Their preference for a ski instructor and chalet accommodations may be qualifying factors but seldom overcome the one determining factor—snow.

In an effort to eliminate snow as a variable, some ski resorts have been installing snow-making machines. This puts an end to shopping for snow and has made it possible for some resorts to differentiate their service and to become specialty goods in the minds of some customers.

**A mutual
fund at
Sears,
Roebuck**

■ How is a mutual fund classified, especially when it is sold by Sears, Roebuck? Sears has been selling various kinds of life insurance for years, both in its 1,500 stores and door-to-door. But now the company has moved into selling shares in the "Allstate Enterprises Stock Fund." Automobile insurance probably should be seen as a staple, especially in states where auto insurance is mandatory. But how do you classify shares of common stock?

Do Sears customers actively shop for such things? The feeling in the mutual fund industry is that they emphatically do not. But Sears has found that its large sales force, particularly the life insurance salesmen, can sell the fund shares to customers who pass by their sales booth and become curious. The strategy, as seen by a stockbroker, is that "Allstate is prospecting for people who wouldn't seek out an investment firm because they wouldn't know how they would be treated."[9]

In this case, for these customers, it would seem that the unsought-goods classification would be most appropriate. But the Sears name and reputation among its regular customers gives it an inside track and facilitates the introduction and sale of these unsought goods. Lesser-known mutual fund sales organizations, on the other hand, often have to go after customers with more aggressive promotion efforts because many potential customers not only are not looking for mutual funds, but are completely unfamiliar with the concept or the seller.

**Butter and
other
agricultural
products**

■ Butter is probably a homogeneous shopping good for many people. Why some consumers have focused so much attention on this product is not clear, but their practice of shopping for the lowest butter prices has made the retail butter market extremely competitive.

To escape from this extreme competition, Land-O'-Lakes Creameries, Inc., a producers' cooperative, branded its butter as "quality butter" and sought to promote Land-O'-Lakes butter to a specialty-goods status. Land-O'-Lakes has had some success in its efforts, as have the Idaho potato growers and the Sunkist orange growers in similar programs.

Brand preference and even insistence is so strong for products in *some* segments of the market that producers can command a slightly higher price, in addition to a substantial share of the market. Among some customers, these cooperatives may have achieved the specialty-goods status. Yet they continue to distribute these products as convenience goods because most customers probably see them this way.

Conclusion

■ A consumer product classification system based on consumers' buying habits and behavior has been introduced in this chapter. These classifications are workable and convenient. They will simplify our study of marketing and the development of marketing mixes because the attitudes of target customers *almost* determine the marketing mix which should be designed to serve them.

The four major categories of goods—convenience, shopping, specialty, and unsought—provide a framework for subsequent analysis. They also relate to the concept of elasticity of demand. If customers do not give much thought to price when purchasing a product, as in the case of convenience goods, or if consumers have extremely strong brand insistence, as for specialty goods, then the demand for these products will be relatively inelastic. On the other hand, if consumers have a strong interest in comparing the products, as they do with shopping goods, then demand may be more elastic.

You should become familiar with these classifications and their subclassifications and begin to observe how marketing institutions handle specific products. Your firsthand observations applied to this analytical framework will speed the development of your "marketing sense."

The way customers in various market grid boxes view the same product may help explain how seemingly poor or irrational marketing mixes can become successful. Much of the diversity and complexity of the marketplace can be explained in terms of different product classifications.

questions and problems

1 What kinds of goods are the following: (a) fountain pens, (b) men's shirts, (c) cosmetics? Explain your reasoning and draw a market grid in each case to help illustrate your thinking.

2 Some goods seem to be treated perpetually as "unsought goods" by their producers. Give an example and explain why.

3 Illustrate what is meant by the statement: "Convenience goods and shopping goods are at either ends of a continuum of customer shopping effort."

4 How would the marketing mix for a staple convenience good differ from the one for a homogeneous shopping good? How would the mix for a specialty good differ from the mix for a heterogeneous shopping good? Use examples.

5 Which of the Ps would receive greatest emphasis in the marketing mix for a new unsought good? Explain why, using an example.

6 Would the marketing mix for all convenience goods be essentially the same? Discuss, using an example for each type of convenience good.

7 In what types of stores would you expect to find: (a) convenience goods, (b) shopping goods, (c) specialty goods, and (d) unsought goods?

8 Draw market grid boxes showing your view of the relative sizes of the markets for the products discussed in the last few pages of the chapter, i.e., specifically (a) prescription drugs, (b) saltine crackers, (c) ski resort services, (d) a mutual fund, and (e) butter. (Hint: Apply the seven-step approach from Chapter 6.)

notes

[1] J. B. Mason and M. L. Mayer "Emperial Observations of Consumer Behavior as Related to Goods Classification and Retail Strategy," *Journal of Retailing,* Fall 1972, pp. 17–31; Arno K. Kleinenhagen, "Shopping, Speciality, or Convenience Goods?" *Journal of Retailing,* Winter 1966–67, pp. 32–39 ff; Louis P. Bucklin, "Testing Propensities to Shop," *Journal of Marketing,* January 1966, pp. 22–27; William P. Dommermuth, "The Shopping Matrix and Marketing Strategy," *Journal of Marketing Research,* May 1965, pp. 128–32; Richard H. Holton, "The Distinction Between Convenience Goods, Shopping Goods, and Specialty Goods," *Journal of Marketing,* July 1958, pp. 53–56; Perry Bliss, "Supply Considerations and Shopper Convenience," *Journal of Marketing,* July 1966, pp. 43–45; S. Kaish, "Cognitive Dissonance and the Classification of Consumer Goods," and W. P. Dommermuth and E. W. Cundiff, "Shopping Goods, Shopping Centers, and Selling Strategies," *Journal of Marketing,* October 1967, pp. 28–36; Edward M. Tauber, "Why Do People Shop?" *Journal of Marketing,* October 1972, pp. 46–49; and Fred D. Reynolds and William R. Darden, "Intermarket Patronage: A Psychographic Study of Consumer Outshoppers," *Journal of Marketing,* October 1972, pp. 50–54.

[2] "A No-Frills Chain for Holiday Inns," *Business Week,* April 16, 1972, p. 87; "Economy Motels Lure Travelers with Prices as Low as $6 a Room," *The Wall Street Journal,* December 26, 1972, p. 1 f; "Royal Inns Tries to Learn Innkeeping," *Business Week,* August 7, 1973, p. 28; "A Rougher Road for Motel Chains," *Business Week,* March 30, 1974, pp. 94–96; "A Motel Room at Bargain Rates," *Business Week,* August 22, 1970, p. 20, and "Riches from Royal Treatment," *Time,* November 16, 1970, p. 87.

[3] David T. Kollat and Ronald P. Willett, "Customer Impulse Purchasing Behavior," *Journal of Marketing Research,* February 1967, pp. 21–31. See also: David T. Kollat and Ronald P. Willett, "Is Impulse Purchasing Really a Useful Concept for Marketing Decisions?" *Journal of Marketing,* January 1969, pp. 79–83.

[4] M. Alexis, L. Simon, and K. Smith, "Some Determinants of Food Buying Behavior," in M. Alexis, R. Hancock, and R. J. Holloway, *Empirical Foundations of Marketing: Research Findings in the Behavioral and Applied Sciences* (Skokie, Ill.: Rand McNally & Co., 1969).

[5] L. P. Feldman, "Prediction of the Spatial Pattern of Shopping Behavior," *Journal of Retailing,* Spring 1967, pp. 25–30 ff.

[6] "If You Don't Give the Lady What She Wants, She'll Go Elsewhere," *Marketing News,* January 1, 1968, p. 11.

[7] See also: "Nashville's Choice: Six Feet Under or Twenty Stories Up," *The Wall Street Journal,* June 12, 1973, p. 1 f.

[8] "A New Team Rewires GE for the Future," *Business Week,* March 30, 1968, pp. 99–109.

[9] "Something New in Stock for Sears Shoppers," *Business Week,* April 25, 1970, pp. 120–22.

Industrial
goods

■ While a consumer goods classification system is useful for developing effective marketing mixes, an industrial goods classification is even more valuable since, over the years, industrial firms have developed a rational system of buying that is related to these goods classes. They are based on how buyers regard products and how they are to be used.

Before looking at the various product *differences*, however, we will note some important product *similarities* that have a direct impact on marketing strategy planning for industrial goods.

General characteristics of industrial goods[1]

One demand derived from another ,

■ The outstanding characteristic of the industrial goods market is derived demand—i.e., the demand for industrial goods is derived from the demand for final consumer goods. There would be little need for fertilizer if there were no demand for food products.

Derived demand is clearly illustrated in the steel industry. Almost all forms of steel, such as beams, plate, and rods, are sold to manufacturers for the production of other products. About one fifth of all steel products goes to the automotive industry, which is highly dependent on final consumer demand. If a car manufacturer hopes to sell 50,000 cars of a particular model each month, then he will order enough steel to produce those automobiles. No amount of price cutting or other adjustments in the marketing mixes by the steelmakers will increase the total amount of steel demanded by this auto producer, because he is limited by expected final consumer sales.

As long as business is good and markets are growing, the derived nature of this demand does not seem very important. But it assumes great importance when final consumer preferences are shifting rapidly or in times of recession, when even the most efficient and aggressive companies lose sales because their customers cannot get business.

At such times, even a seemingly good marketing mix aimed at intermediate customers may not be very effective unless it has some impact on final consumer demand. Industrial goods producers sometimes advertise directly to consumers, in an effort to stimulate demands. Cement and earthmoving equipment manufacturers, for example, have promoted road building to final consumers in an effort to build demand for *their* products.

Price increases might not reduce quantity purchased

■ The fact that demand for most industrial goods is derived means that industry demand will be fairly inelastic. To satisfy final consumer needs, producers need a certain quantity of each of the components of their products, almost regardless of price. Since each of the components costs only a fraction of the total cost of their product, the price behavior of any one item may have relatively little to do with the quantity of that item purchased. The cost of the spice in a box of cake mix, for example, might represent only one half of 1 percent of the cake manufacturer's total cost. Even if the price of this spice were doubled and passed directly along to consumers, it would have relatively little impact on the cake producer's price or the quantity demanded by final consumers. Therefore the price increase might not reduce the quantity of spice purchased.

But suppliers may face almost pure competition

■ *Although the industry demand may be inelastic, the demand facing individual sellers may be extremely elastic.* This will be true if competitive products are essentially homogeneous, and there are many sellers – that is, if the market approaches pure competition.

In the case of the spice ingredients, if the spices available from all suppliers are basically similar and one spice supplier increases his price while his competitors do not, buyers probably will shift their purchases to the competition. Thus *there may be nearly pure competition among the suppliers of a product even though there is an inelastic industry demand.*

Buyers will help make the market as competitive as they can. Most industrial buyers would prefer to have several sources of supply in order to ensure production in their own plants. Therefore they seek out several sources of supply. Further, their job is to buy as economically as possible and we can expect that they will be quick to spread the word that competitors are offering lower prices. The fact that many industrial goods are bought by specifications further increases competition. Each seller, in effect, must bid on an essentially homogeneous product. Sometimes these specifications are established by large buyers. Other times the specifications are commonly accepted ones for those commodities. In either case, the tendency is to move the market toward pure competition or oligopoly for these essentially homogeneous products.

Backward chain reactions can cause booms

■ Demand at the industrial goods level may fluctuate much more than demand at the final consumer level. This is true because demand for industrial goods, which may be several steps removed from the final consumer demand, reflects in part the expectations and buying practices of various middlemen and other producers. Intermediate customers attempt to: (1) anticipate price changes, (2) reduce costs by quantity buying, (3) anticipate demand, which may not materialize, and (4) place rush orders when their sales forecasts prove inadequate.

If intermediate customers believe prices are going to drop further, they may postpone all purchases. If they feel that prices are at their lowest point, they may buy in substantial quantities, anticipating future needs. Or firms may buy in large quantities to obtain quantity discounts and then work off the inventory as needed. On slow-moving items, this may mean that a firm will buy three to six months' inventory at one time to obtain a lower price.

Sales swings at the manufacturer level may be even more extreme when other intermediate customers try to anticipate growing demand. Home air-conditioners, for example, are sold to final consumers primarily when hot weather arrives. Orders for air-conditioner compressors, however, may be heavy before the summer selling season as retailers and wholesalers attempt to build their stocks. Compressor producers may have to accelerate production, perhaps even going on overtime. If really hot weather never comes, though, the retailers, wholesalers, and air-conditioner manufacturers may become overstocked, and the orders for compressors will stop completely. Yet, if there is a prolonged heat wave, it may deplete retailers' stocks—and a chain reaction will start backward to component manufacturers.

If this sort of chain develops in an industry that is less seasonal than air-conditioners, there may be pressures to expand the producer's plant capacity. Rush orders may develop for new plant and machinery, causing sudden boom conditions for these manufacturers.

These extreme but typical fluctuations have an impact on the nature of competition and the development of marketing mixes. Drastic changes in both price and promotion may be needed to handle these shifting conditions.

Paying taxes affects spending for equipment

■ How the cost of a particular purchase is handled on a firm's profit and loss statement may have a significant effect on the buyer. If, in computing profits, the cost of a large machine could be charged to the current year's expenses, the company executives might be more willing to buy it. Even though the cost of the equipment reduced current profits, it also would reduce tax liability and increase the company's assets. Typically, however, such purchases *cannot* be charged off in one year!

There are two general methods of charging costs: as capital and as expense items. Both are determined primarily by U.S. Internal Revenue Service regulations.

Capital items

Most large machinery and other durable, relatively long-lived items are treated as capital items. They are often called "capital goods." Internal Revenue regulations and accepted accounting procedure require that only a portion of the original cost be charged off or depreciated each year for a total depreciation period of 2 to 50 years, depending on the item. The depreciation rate usually is specified by the Internal Revenue Service.

In recent years the federal government has liberalized and then tightened depreciation rules to stimulate the economy and then later to cool an inflationary boom. These efforts have been effective, and it is clear that businessmen do look at capital investments differently from the way they view expense items. The purchase of capital items is likely to lead to "new-task" purchasing because of its importance to the company, in the short run and the long run.

Businessmen generally are slow to buy capital items. The purchase of a capital item is, in effect, a long-term claim against future revenues. Yet management cannot predict exactly what the future holds. Since an error in judgment can have an influence for many years, company executives understandably are hesitant to make quick decisions. There seems to be little agreement on the best approach to capital expenditure decisions,[2] however, and emotional considerations may become important.

Expense items

In contrast to capital items, expense items are charged off as they are used – usually in the year of purchase. The potential value is more easily forecast and can be compared with the cost. Since the company is not putting a lien against its future when it buys expense items, it tends to be less concerned about these costs, especially if business is good. The multiple buying influence is likely to decline here, and straight rebuys may become more likely. If a firm's sales decline, however, some expense purchases may be cut back sharply or eliminated temporarily. There may also be a reversion to the modified rebuy process, as buyers are expected to reevaluate their sources of supply and the prices being offered to them.

Industrial goods classifications

■ Industrial goods buyers do relatively little shopping, compared to consumer goods buyers. The accepted practice is for the seller to come to the buyer. This means that a product classification system based primarily on shopping behavior is not appropriate.

The classification system we will use here is determined by how buyers regard products and how the products are to be used. Relatively expensive and/or long-lived products are treated differently from relatively inexpensive items. And products that become a part of a firm's own product are seen differently from those which only facilitate production. Finally, the size of a particular purchase can be relevant; an air compressor may not be very important to a buyer for General Motors, but it might be a very important purchase for a small garage owner.

The categories of industrial goods are: (1) installations, (2) accessory equipment, (3) raw materials, (4) component parts and materials, (5) supplies, and (6) services.

While the consumer goods classification is tentative and perhaps arbitrary, the industrial goods classification is keyed directly to the way industrial purchasing departments and accounting control systems operate day to day. Buyers, for example, often specialize by product categories. And categories similar to our industrial goods classifications are used for buying, maintenance, costing of orders, and control purposes.

The authority of certain plant executives to requisition and buy is limited frequently to one or more categories, either directly or by a dollar limit. Accessory expenditures, for example, might be limited to $10,000 an item to allow the department foreman some latitude in his requisitioning and, at the same time, to control expenditures. Under other control systems, perhaps the only items a plant foreman could buy without higher approval would be supplies, but it is remarkable what kinds of small machines and other accessories can be called supplies in this situation.

Our industrial goods classification system generally does make sense and is used extensively in the industrial goods market.

Installations, major capital items

■ Installations are large and expensive items that do not become a part of the final product but are expended, depleted, or worn out during years of use. All installations are *capital items.*

There are two major classifications of installations: *buildings and land rights,* and *major equipment.*

Buildings and land rights include assets such as factories, farms, stores, office buildings, mining deposits, and timber rights. Major equipment includes large items of machinery and production facilities such as diesel engines, tractors, papermaking machines, printing presses, and kilns.

Major equipment can be subdivided into two types: (1) custom-made and (2) standard.

Custom-made equipment is built to specification for a particular company. *Standard* installations are regular production items such as tractors, general-purpose diesel engines, lathes, and printing presses.

For our purposes in this text, *buildings* and *custom-made equipment* are treated alike, since both require special negotiations for each individual product. *Standard major equipment*, being more homogeneous, can be treated more routinely. All installations, however, are important enough to require high-level and even top-management consideration. New-task buying or modified rebuy buying will be involved here.

Size of market small at any time

■ Installations are long-lived goods, and the number of potential buyers at any particular time usually is small. For some custom-made machines, there may be only a half-dozen potential customers at any one time, compared to a thousand or more potential buyers for standard machines of similar type and capacity.

Potential customers generally are in the same or a related industry, permitting industry specialization by sales executives. Their plants are likely to be geographically concentrated. The automobile industry, for example, is heavily concentrated in and around Michigan, the tire industry in Ohio, copper mining in the western states, and the aircraft industry – from a global view – in the United States.

Multiple buying influence important

■ The importance of these items leads to considerable multiple buying influence. Negotiations can stretch over months or even years and often involve the top executives of the company, especially for buildings or custom-made products. This may complicate promotion, since these executives may be concerned with quite different problems than purchasing agents and may not use the same evaluation procedures. The top executive may be less concerned, for example, with the product's suitability for current needs than with its flexibility and possible usefulness in a new venture he is considering. The seller may need different sales approaches to cope with each of the possible influences.

Buying motives essentially economic

■ Buying motives are essentially economic, and concerned with the projected performance of the installation over its expected life. After comparing expected performance to present costs and calculating interest, the expected return on capital can be calculated. Yet emotional motives, such as a desire for industry leadership and status, also may be involved.

Industry demand may be very inelastic, but sellers see elastic demand curves

■ The demand for a particular installation may be completely inelastic up to a certain price, especially if the firm badly needs expanded capacity. The potential return on the new investment may be so attractive that any reasonable price might be acceptable.

While the buyers' demand can be very inelastic, however, the situation for sellers may be different. There may be many suppliers, such as building contractors, and so buyers of installations may be able to request bids and buy in a highly competitive market.

Installation industry, a "boom-or-bust" business

■ The installation industry has been described as a "boom-or-bust" business. During the upswing of a business cycle, businessmen want to expand production capacity rapidly and are willing to pay almost any reasonable price to do it. Competition is less vigorous, and profits are higher for the installation sellers. But during a downswing, buyers will have little or no need for new installations, and sales can fall off precipitously.

Installation manufacturers can even suffer a bust because consumer demand, although high, is no longer rising. At such times, the producers who previously needed additional installations to meet *rising* consumer demand are no longer in the market — except for replacements.

Installations may have to be leased or rented

■ Since installations are relatively expensive, the producer often will lease or rent the product rather than sell it outright. Examples are buildings and land rights and some specialized equipment, including electronic data processing machines.

Such lease or rental arrangements are attractive to some target markets because they shift the expenditure from a capital item to an expense item.[3]

Specialized services needed as part of the product

■ Since the expected return on an installation is based on efficient operation, the supplier may have to make service provisions to assure this efficiency. The sales contract may stipulate regular visits by servicemen; a serviceman may even be permanently attached to the company. Computer manufacturers sometimes station service personnel with the machines. The cost is included in the price or rent.

The more homogeneous the installation, the more likely it is that the seller will try to differentiate his product by offering specialized services such as aid in installing his machine in the buyer's plant, training employees in its use, supplying repair service, and taking trade-ins on long-lived installations that a potential buyer already may have on hand.

Accessory equipment — important but short-lived

■ Accessory equipment, like installations, does not become a part of the buyer's final product. These products usually are less expensive and shorter-lived than installations and generally can be depreciated more quickly, but are still *capital items*.

Accessory equipment is very similar to the smaller standard installations and includes tools and equipment that facilitate production or office activities. Examples include portable drills, sanding machines, electric lift trucks, typewriters, filing cases, accounting machines, wheelbarrows, hand trucks, and small lathes. Here, the modified rebuy process may be more typical, although sellers certainly will try to move their brands to straight rebuys. This might happen if a product is part of a "system," say, of office equipment or a production line, and the buyer wants to modify or expand his present facilities.

More target markets requiring different marketing mixes

■ Accessories are even more standardized than installations and are usually needed by more target markets. A large, special-purpose belt sanding machine, for example, might be produced as a custom-made installation for woodworking firms, but small sanding machines would be considered accessory equipment for general use in a variety of shops and factories. Since there is a larger number of target markets and less geographical concentration, different marketing mixes would be required for accessory equipment than for installations.

Multiple buying influences less important

■ Since these products cost less and last a shorter time than installation equipment, the multiple buying influence is less important. Operating personnel and purchasing agents rather than top-level executives may do the buying. Purchasing agents have more say in buying accessories as these become more standardized and are bought by brand or at least by widely recognized standards.

The nearer accessory items come to being expense items, charged off in one year, the less the consideration given to these purchases by higher-level management. Some small accessories are treated as expense items, even if the Internal Revenue Service might prefer otherwise.

Might prefer to lease or rent

■ Leasing or renting accessories is attractive to some target markets because the costs can be treated as expenses. A manufacturer of electric lift trucks, for instance, was able to expand its sales by selling the basic truck outright but charging for the expensive battery system by the amount it was used. This expanded sales because, as one of the company executives said: "Nobody worries about costs which are buried as an operating expense."[4]

Buyers may have many substitutes — and sellers elastic demand curves

■ As accessory items become smaller and more standardized, the more likely it is that there will be competitive substitutes. Then, although buyers may have inelastic demands, they still are able to purchase in fairly competitive markets. And competition will be accentuated because when purchasing agents are buying less important items, they will be more willing to experiment with alternate suppliers.

Special services may be attractive

■ Ordinarily, engineering services or special advice is less important for accessory equipment because of its simpler operation. Yet some companies have managed to add attractive services to their accessories, as in the case of the office equipment firms that offer advice on office layouts and office systems.

Raw materials—farm products and natural products

■ Raw materials are products that have been processed only as much as needed for safe, convenient, economical transport and handling. *Unlike installations and accessories, raw materials become part of a physical product.*

Raw materials are *expense items* and may be purchased routinely—as straight rebuys—by purchasing agents. But top executives may take part in buying when certain raw materials represent a large part of the firm's costs, as with wheat in the flour milling business. Moreover, to assure sources of supply, top executives may help negotiate the annual contracts for some important raw materials.

It is useful to break raw materials into two broad categories: (1) farm products and (2) natural products. *Farm products* include crops, livestock, and other commodities such as cotton, wheat, strawberries, sugar cane, cattle, hogs, poultry, eggs, and milk. *Natural products* include animal, vegetable, and mineral products as they occur naturally, including, for example, fish and game, lumber and maple syrup, and copper, zinc, iron ore, oil and coal.

Some raw materials, such as fruits and vegetables, poultry, eggs, and milk, can be used directly by final consumers. In this text, we will treat raw materials sold directly to consumers or through middlemen *for sale to consumers* as consumer goods, not industrial goods.

As we will see later, the buying attitudes and practices of the various middlemen handling raw materials will be quite different from those handling consumer goods.

Farm products

Involve grading, storage and/or transportation

■ The need for grading is one of the important factors distinguishing these products from other industrial goods. Nature produces what it will, and someone must sort and grade the wheat, corn, tobacco, cotton, and other similar products to satisfy various market segments. Some of the top grades of fruits and vegetables may find their way into the premium-quality consumer goods market, while the lower grades will be treated as industrial goods and be used in juices, sauces, and frozen pies.

Most farm products are produced seasonally, yet the demand for them is fairly constant throughout the year. As a result, storage and transportation are major activities in their marketing process.

As noted, buyers of industrial goods normally do not seek out suppliers. This is a complicating factor in marketing farm products, because the many small farm producers usually are widely scattered, sometimes far from potential buyers, and selling direct to final users would be difficult for them. Place and Promotion consequently are important factors in marketing mixes for these products.

Large buyers may want contract production

■ Most buyers of farm products have specific uses in mind and generally prefer that products be sorted and graded. But since large buyers may have difficulty getting the quantities of the grades and types they want, contract production has developed. Here, the buyer deliberately seeks out potential sources of supply and makes contracts that assure the supplier a market for his goods. This has several effects. It tends to make the supplier a part of the buyer's operation and removes one more producer from the competitive market. This may be desirable from the suppliers' point of view, because it isolates him from a purely competitive market.

Each seller's demand curve is elastic

■ Most farm products have an inelastic *market* demand, even though the many small producers are in nearly pure competition. The market demand becomes more elastic when there are many substitutes (such as beef for pork or corn for wheat). But within the usual price ranges, the demand for agricultural products is generally inelastic, and so it helps agricultural producers to control output and prices, perhaps through U.S. Department of Agriculture programs.

Most attempts to control prices in the farm products market are frustrated by slow adjustment of supply and the difficulty of organizing the many producers. Once a crop is planted, the potential supply is more or less fixed (subject to weather, pests, and so on), and it is too late to change crop size that year. For some animal products, the planning cycle may be two or three years, and this further accentuates the problem of adjustment in supply.

At the end of a growing season, the quantity of available farm products is fixed. If this supply is large, the market price can be extremely low; if it is small, the price may be high. This can be seen in Figure 15–1 where vertical lines are used to show that in the short run, farmers would supply the same quantity regardless of the price.

This relatively long planning period has led to some peculiar cycles in production and prices. The poultry farmers in the Delaware, Maryland, and Virginia area traditionally went through boom-and-bust periods on an annual basis. High poultry prices one year attracted many growers the following year, who then overproduced, driving prices down below cost. This caused many small producers to leave the market, creating an inadequate supply and again raising price to a high level. Recently, however, the entry of a few large producers with better planning and control over supply has reduced this seesawing of supply and prices.

Natural products

■ In contrast to the farm products market, with its many producers, natural products are produced by fewer and larger companies. There are some exceptions, of course, such as the coal and lumber industries, but generally oligopoly conditions are common.

Figure 15-1
Effect of changes in supply on price in agricultural markets

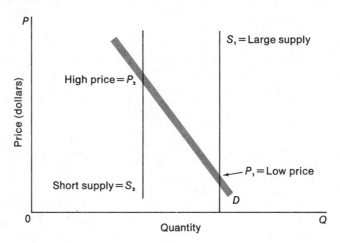

Typically, the total supply of natural products is limited and cannot be expanded readily. But the supply harvested or mined in any one year *is* adjustable.

Most of the products are bulky and pose transportation problems. But storage is less important, since fewer are perishable and some can be produced year-round. Major exceptions are fish and game, which have runs or seasons and resemble farm animal products more than forest or mineral products in their marketing patterns.

Vertical integration or contract buying

■ As with farm products, buyers of natural products usually need specific grades and dependable supply sources to assure continued production in their own plants. Large buyers, therefore, often seek to buy, or at least control, their sources of supply. This is easier than with farm products because fewer and larger production facilities are involved.

One way to control supply sources is *vertical integration* — ownership of the natural product producer by the user. Examples are synthetic fiber and paper manufacturers who control timber resources, oil refiners who control crude oil sources, and tire manufacturers who control rubber plantations. Probably the best known are the steel producers who control not only iron ore and coal deposits but also the ships and trains to carry ore and coal.

When a great deal of integration has taken place in a given industry, there may be an erratic or spotty open market. This is because buyers and sellers will come into the market only when their own captive sources are producing too much or too little or the wrong quality.

In these markets, sellers who do not integrate with users normally find that their customers buy in large quantities and are interested in assuring themselves dependable sources of supply.

This usually is done through contracts or "understandings," perhaps negotiated by top-level executives and referring to standard grades or specifications for products.

■ The industry demand for natural products is derived and basically inelastic. The large producers understand and are quite responsive to market demands and are inclined to limit supply to maintain stable prices. In the coal and lumber industries, however, where there are many producers, there is close to pure competition.

Component parts and materials—the sum is no better than . . .

■ Like raw materials, *component parts and materials become a part of a finished product.* Both are treated as *expense items.* Component parts, however, undergo more processing than is required for raw materials and may require different marketing mixes. All three buying processes may be seen here.

Component parts include those items that are (*a*) finished and ready for assembly or (*b*) nearly finished, requiring only minor additional processing (such as grinding or polishing) before being assembled into the final product.

In the parts category are automobile batteries, small motors, tires, and forgings or castings, all of which are incorporated directly into a finished product. It also includes other items, such as automobile jacks, that are sold with the product but not physically attached to it or incorporated into it.

Component materials are items such as wire, paper, textiles, or cement. They have already been processed but must be processed further before becoming part of the final product.

■ Some component parts are custom-made and much negotiation may be necessary between the engineering staffs of both buyer and seller to arrive at the proper specifications. If the price of the item is very high or if it is an extremely important component of the final product, top-level executives may become involved, as with raw materials. New-task buying is found here to help set the specifications and sources.

Other component parts and materials are more likely to be processed to commonly accepted standards or specifications and produced in quantity. For such items, engineering or production people in the buying firm may specify quality. The purchasing agent will do the actual buying and he will want several dependable sources of supply. Modified rebuys and straight rebuys are seen here.

■ As with other types of industrial goods, the motives involved in buying components are basically economic and concern price, availability, quality, and suitability. Assurances of availability and prompt delivery are most important. A purchasing agent must do everything in his power to avoid a plant shutdown caused by unavailability of materials. Moreover, an assured source of supply will enable the buyer to reduce his inventory, reducing both his inventory investment and the risk of damage to, and obsolescence of, goods in stock.

Since components are incorporated into the firm's own product, quality is extremely important, too. The buyer's own name and whole marketing mix are at stake. Quality may be less important for component parts, however, if they are well branded—such as a tire or spark plug—and the blame for a defective product can fall upon the component supplier. Generally, however, a progressive buyer would attempt to buy from component sources that would help assure a satisfactory product to the final customers.

Market may be very competitive

■ Although the industry and individual buyers' demand may be fairly inelastic for components, there usually are many possible suppliers, enabling buyers to purchase in a fairly competitive market. In fact, the market for many component parts and materials is extremely competitive. There are several reasons for this competition.

1. Most component buyers want to have several sources of supply, and encourage new suppliers.
2. There usually are many small producers—small tool-and-die shops, machine shops, and foundries—with general-purpose machinery that can produce a great variety of component parts.
3. There often are many suppliers of component materials willing to produce to widely accepted specifications or standards.

Design services may help

■ Design services may be important for some components, and this enables an alert seller to achieve an inelastic demand curve. Or if the seller has obtained some design patents or in some way developed a particularly unique (heterogeneous) product, he may achieve an extremely inelastic demand curve.

Replacement markets may develop

■ Since component parts are incorporated into a finished product, a replacement market often develops. This market can be both large and very profitable, as in the case of automotive tires and batteries.

This replacement market may involve new target markets. The part originally may have been considered a component part when it was sold in the *OEM (original equipment market)*, but as a replacement the same product might become a consumer good. The target markets are different, and probably different marketing mixes will be necessary.

Some component parts suppliers may be eager to have their parts used in the OEM market because the "after" market composed of final consumers is attractive.

The Mallory Battery Co. worked hard to get its small batteries installed as original components in cameras, watches, hearing aids, and dictating equipment because marketing research had told them that half of all final consumer battery buyers don't know what kind of battery powers their equipment. They simply walk into a store and say, "Gimme one just like this."

Mallory coordinated its efforts in both markets – the components and final consumer markets – and achieved a 50 percent increase in profits.[5]

Supplies – everybody wants them but how much?

■ Firms consume supplies currently, just as they do raw materials and component parts and materials. Supplies are, therefore, *expense items*. But unlike raw materials and components, *supplies do not become a part of a physical product* and may be treated less seriously by buyers. Although they are necessary, most supplies are not as vital as the products in the first four classifications – and when a firm economizes, orders for supplies may be the first to go.

Supplies can be divided into three categories: (1) maintenance, (2) repair, and (3) operating supplies, giving them their common designation, *MRO items*.

Maintenance items include such things as paint, nails, light bulbs, sweeping compounds, brooms, and window-cleaning equipment. *Repair items* are nuts and bolts or parts needed to repair existing equipment. *Operating supplies* include lubricating oils and greases, grinding compounds, coal, typing paper, ink, pencils, and paper clips.

Most supply items are used by industry in general and are similar to the kinds of items purchased by final consumers in hardware stores. Some supplies are more important than others, as noted below.

Important operating supplies

■ Some operating supplies needed regularly and in large amounts receive special treatment from buyers. Some companies buy coal and fuel oil in carload or tank-car quantities. Usually there are several sources for such homogeneous products, and large volumes may be purchased in highly competitive markets. Or contracts may be negotiated, perhaps by high-level executives. Such contracts have several advantages. Subsequent purchase requisitions may be drawn routinely against them – as straight rebuys. They sometimes assure lower prices, and they eliminate the buyer's concern about a dependable source for these important operating supplies.

When several dependable sources are available and orders are large, reciprocity may become important. If quality and price are roughly the same, it becomes more difficult to refuse the sales department's request for reciprocity relationships. Purchasing departments usually resist such overtures, but this is one place where the sales department's arguments are strong.

Maintenance and small operating supplies

■ These items are similar to consumer's convenience goods and are so numerous that a purchasing agent cannot possibly be an expert in buying all of them. There usually is little multiple buying influence. They may not even justify modified rebuying.

Each requisition for maintenance and small operating supplies may be for a relatively few items. The purchase requisitions can amount to only $1 to $2. Although the cost of handling a purchase order may be from $5 to $10, the item will be ordered, because it is needed, but as simply as possible.

Branding may become important for such products. It makes product identification and buying of such "nuisance" items easier.

Industry demand for supplies is fairly inelastic, and sellers may see pretty inelastic demand curves, too. Since only small amounts of money are involved and shopping around for bargains would hardly be worth the time, a purchasing agent might find several dependable sources of supply and patronize them for the bulk of such items.

A new company offering only one supply item might have trouble entering such a market. The job of buying these many small items is difficult enough, and buyers usually don't have time to review the small advantages of some new product or supplier. The purchasing agent wouldn't be as interested in price for such items – the breadth of assortment and dependability of the source are of utmost importance in buying supply items. Yet a characteristic of a dependable source of supply is that it offers good values, and a skilled purchasing agent continually shops for good value. The threat of losing a substantial amount of business from one buyer tends to keep the various suppliers' prices in line.

Repair items

■ The original supplier of installation or accessory equipment may be the only source of supply for repairs and parts. The cost of repairs relative to the cost of disrupted production may be so small that buyers are willing to pay the price charged – whatever it is.

Demand for repair items is quite inelastic. But if the demand for such items is large and steady – say, for truck mufflers or power transmission belts – there may be many suppliers. The market then may become quite competitive even though each buyer's demand is relatively inelastic.

Services – you pay for what you get

■ Services supplied by specialists frequently are valuable in supporting the operations of a firm.[6] Engineering or management consulting services can improve the plant layout or the organization of the company. Design services can supply designs for the physical plant, products, and graphic materials. Outside maintenance services can handle window-cleaning, painting, or general housekeeping services. Other organizations can supply in-plant lunches and piped-in music to improve employee morale and production.

All these services are considered *expense items.* The cost of buying them outside the firm is compared with the cost of having company personnel provide them. For special skills needed only irregularly, an outsider can be the best source. Specialists are proliferating in our increasingly complex economy.

The demand for special services is often inelastic if the supplier has a unique product. And the supply may be fairly inelastic, too. The suppliers may consider themselves professionals and charge accordingly. For example, engineers, architects, and medical doctors have commonly accepted fee schedules, and the competition among them is not based on price but on quality of service.[7]

Industrial goods classes and buying behavior are related

■ The previous focus on kinds of goods may not seem very exciting, but it is important because the nature of goods has an effect on how the buyers will accept and buy them. And this obviously has a direct bearing on the planning of marketing mixes.

Buyers often specialize by product categories

■ Don't forget that an individual buyer may behave differently toward different kinds of goods. Or, in a larger company, there may be specialists buying the various goods. This can both simplify and complicate the selling process. Buying specialists may be easier to deal with — at least they are more expert and, therefore, require less education about technical points. On the other hand, if there are many buying specialists in a company, then a salesman cannot casually conclude that he is calling on the entire company just because he calls on one person.

Each buyer of each type of good should be treated as an entirely separate customer (as though he were in a different firm). He may behave and think quite differently when he is buying different products. He may not feel any obligation to give a salesman any special consideration just because he happens to sell another buyer in the company. In fact, this might even be a handicap, in that the two buyers might have quite different philosophies about purchasing. Being able to get along with one might not be viewed as an asset by the other!

The organization of buyers in a large purchasing department may help illustrate these ideas. Figure 15–2 shows the layout of a centralized purchasing department for a large manufacturer, with plants throughout the country. Seventeen men work under a vice president of purchasing. Some of these buyers (shown by rectangles in the figure) report to group supervisors (shown in offices along the left edge of the figure), who also do some buying and report directly to the vice president. As you can see, each of the buyers specializes in certain types of *goods* classes that have been discussed in this chapter.

Figure 15–2
Layout of the purchasing department of a large manufacturer

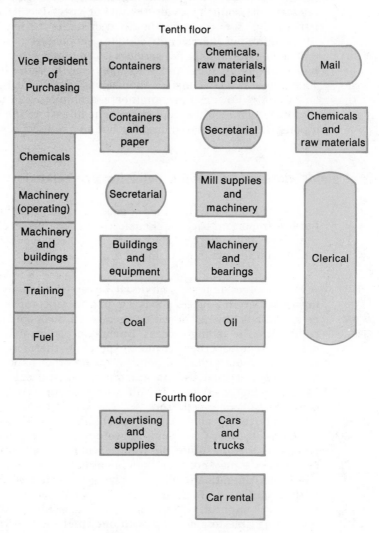

Tenth floor

Vice President of Purchasing	Containers	Chemicals, raw materials, and paint	Mail
Chemicals	Containers and paper	Secretarial	Chemicals and raw materials
Machinery (operating)	Secretarial	Mill supplies and machinery	
Machinery and buildings	Buildings and equipment	Machinery and bearings	Clerical
Training			
Fuel	Coal	Oil	

Fourth floor

| Advertising and supplies | Cars and trucks |
| | Car rental |

**Requisition-
ing and
ordering in
practice**

■ The basic ordering process used by this firm is as follows. Whenever a department or plant wants to buy anything, it fills out a requisition which, after approval by some operating supervisor, is forwarded to the centralized purchasing department for placement with the "best" vendor. The requisitions flow in large numbers to the mail desk and then are sorted to the various buyers by a clerical supervisor in the clerical pool. The nature of the product facilitates this sorting to buyers. The requisitions have already been approved, and now the buyer is responsible for placing a purchase order and obtaining delivery by the date requested on the requisition.

Ordering may be routine after requisitioning

The requisitions are converted to purchase orders as quickly as possible. Straight rebuys are usually made the day the requisition is received, while new task and modified rebuys take longer. If time is important, the buyer may place the order by telephone, and then a confirming purchase order is typed in the clerical pool and sent out. More routine straight rebuys would consist of the buyer (1) deciding which of his several vendors would get this order, (2) filling in the vendor's name and other details on the face of the requisition, and (3) forwarding it to the clerical pool for typing into a purchase order and mailing.

It pays to know the buyer

Notice the importance of being one of the regular sources of supply. The buyers do not even call potential sources for straight rebuys. Vendors' salesmen regularly call on these buyers, typically *not* to sell a particular item but to cement relations, or to become a source, and/or to point out new developments which might cause the buyer to reevaluate his present "straight rebuy" procedure and give more favorable attention to the salesman's company.

The fact that buyers do specialize by product, and that a considerable amount of buying is of the "straight rebuy" type, points up the vital importance of treating each buyer as a separate target market and understanding how and why he works the way he does. It also shows us the importance of being on the buyer's list of potential vendors. The salesman cannot always be there exactly when the requisitions come in, and the buyer may not consult all potential sources before placing his orders.

It also makes sense to recognize the potential advantage to a salesman of the buyer having a favorable image of him. Unless a definite percentage share of the business is to be allocated to each of several sources, it is likely that a favored source might achieve a slightly larger share than he would otherwise get. Moving from a 20 percent to a 30 percent share may not seem like much from the buyer's point of view, but for the salesman it represents a 50 percent increase in his sales!

The salesman who fully understands and satisfies the needs and preferences of his customers clearly can get significantly better results. And the goods classes are a great help in summarizing how and why individual buyers behave as they do, so that a satisfying marketing mix can be developed for them.

Conclusion

■ The industrial goods classification system developed in this chapter is considerably easier to use than the one for consumers' goods because it starts with products and the way they are used. Customer buying behavior and product-market competition are related to the product classifications.

You should have a thorough understanding of the various kinds of products and their distinguishing characteristics, since this has a significant bearing on where and how these products are distributed, promoted, and priced.

A vital characteristic of industrial goods is that demand is derived from demand for consumer goods. Further, *industry demand for industrial goods tends to be inelastic, but because of competition among suppliers, the demand facing any one industrial goods seller may be quite elastic.* Derived demand and industrial buying practices also may lead to violent and hard-to-forecast fluctuations in sales. Capital-goods producers, in particular, experience boom-and-bust cycles, because of changes in final consumer buying patterns.

In contrast to consumer buying, which may be emotionally motivated, industrial purchasing of all categories of goods is more concerned with economic factors. Multiple buying influence may be important too. Some industrial goods even warrant top-level decisions.

While consumer goods classifications are somewhat arbitrary, those for industrial goods are not. Industrial goods buyers usually know what they want and need and often specialize according to these product classifications.

The following chapters will begin to use these product classifications to bring order out of a complex marketing structure. Before reading these chapters, you will profit by a serious consideration of what kinds of marketing institutions might develop to distribute specific products and the functions which they would provide. This will enable you to better appreciate why certain marketing specialists have developed and why they use certain marketing practices.

questions and problems

1 Cite two examples of industrial goods which require a substantial amount of service in order to make them useful "products."

2 Would you expect to find any wholesalers selling the various types of industrial goods? Are retail stores required (or something like retail stores)?

3 What kinds of goods are the following?
a. Nails and screws.
b. Paint.
c. Dust-collecting and ventilating systems.
d. An electric lift truck.
Explain your reasoning.

4 What impact does the fact that demand for industrial goods is derived and fairly inelastic have upon the development of industrial goods marketing mixes? Use examples.

5 How do farm product raw materials differ from other raw materials or other industrial goods? Do the differences have any impact on their marketing mixes? If so, what, specifically?

6 How would an Internal Revenue Service relaxation of depreciation regulations affect the marketing mixes of industrial goods? Would it affect all of them equally?

7 Discuss how much latitude an industrial buyer has in selecting the specific brand and the specific source of supply for that product, once a product has been requisitioned by some production department? Consider this question with specific reference to pencils, paint for the offices, plastic materials for the production line, a new factory, and a large printing press. How should the buyer's attitude affect the seller's marketing mix?

8 For the kinds of goods described in this chapter, complete the following table (use one or a few *well-chosen* words).

Goods	1	2	3
Installations			
Buildings and			
land rights			
Major equipment			
Standard			
Custom-made			
Accessory equipment			
Raw materials			
Farm products			
Natural products			
Components			
Parts			
Materials			
Supplies			
Operating supplies			
Maintenance and			
small operating			
supplies			
Services			

1—Kind of distribution facility(ies) needed and functions they will provide.
2—Caliber of salesmen required.
3—Kind of advertising required.

notes

[1] Many of the ideas presented in this chapter are based on R. S. Alexander, "Goods for the Market: Industrial Goods," in C. F. Phillips (ed.), *Marketing by Manufacturers* (Homewood, Ill.: Richard D. Irwin, Inc., 1950), pp. 34–60.

[2] Donald F. Istvan, *Capital-Expenditure Decisions: How They Are Made in Large Corporations* (Indiana Business Report No. 33 [Bloomington: Indiana University, 1961]), p. 97; James D. Edwards, "Investment Decision Making in a Competitive Society," *MSU Business Topics*, Autumn 1970, pp. 53–60; see also "Banquet Days for Capital Goods Producers," *Business Week*, June 22, 1974, pp. 72–77.

[3] "Can Leasing Make Ownership Obsolete?" *Business Week*, March 8, 1969, pp. 50–54.

[4] "Switching the Charge on Batteries," *Business Week*, March 13, 1965, pp. 132–34.

[5] "Will Tiny Cells Power Big Sales," *Business Week*, January 14, 1967, pp. 60–64.

[6] For a discussion of the marketing problems associated with technical services, see James G. Hauk, *Technical Service in the American Economy: A Problem in Marketing Management* (Michigan Business Studies, vol. 31, no. 1 [Ann Arbor: University of Michigan, 1962]). For further discussion of the opportunities and problems of marketing services, see E. B. Turner, "Marketing Professional Services," *Journal of Marketing*, October 1969, pp. 56–61; "Here's a Company That's Cleaning Up," *Business Week*, October 26, 1968, pp. 176–80; "A Builder 'Packages Everything,'" *Business Week*, November 2, 1968, pp. 146–48.

[7] Warren J. Wittreich, "How to Buy/Sell Professional Services," *Harvard Business Review*, March–April 1966, pp. 127–38.

16

Development of channel systems

■ Your product may be the best in the world, but it will be of little use to the customer if it is not *where* he wants it *when* he wants it. In the next four chapters, we will take a look at all of the activities and institutions needed to provide "place."

Place decisions are concerned with the location of marketing facilities and the selection and use of marketing specialists including transportation and storage agencies, wholesalers, and retailers—really with developing channel systems.

For simplicity, we will use the term "Place" to refer to the many factors that go into providing the time, place, and possession utilities needed to satisfy target customers, just as we use Product to mean the "total product" offered.

Place decisions hard to change

■ The marketing manager's decisions on Place may be the most important ones he makes because they have long-range implications and are harder to change than Product, Price, and Promotion decisions. It is difficult to move retail and wholesale facilities once leases have been signed and customer movement patterns have been established. Cordial working arrangements with middlemen can take several years and a good deal of money to develop. Place decisions are likely to be the *one-time strategic decisions* whose importance we discussed in Chapter 2.

Specialists and channel systems develop to adjust discrepancies of quantity and assortment

■ A goal of any producer is to ensure that his product reaches the final customer. However, the assortment and quantity of goods wanted by a customer has little direct relation to the assortment and quantity of goods normally produced. Specialists may be needed to adjust these discrepancies.

Discrepancy of quantity

■ It is economically sensible for a firm to specialize and offer those products (or services) that it can produce most efficiently, given its resources and objectives. This specialization causes manufacturers to produce large quantities of a few items. For example, most manufacturers of golf balls produce in large quantities such as 200,000 to 500,000 in a given time period. The average golfer, however, is interested only in a few balls at a time. For a golf ball manufacturer to deal directly with thousands of golfers would be a Herculean task. Each individual order would have to be mailed to the customer's home (unless he lived right around the corner). And then there would be a question of credit.

The solution to this problem would be a local specialist – a retailer – who could fill the various needs of individual consumers for a product and ease the manufacturer's headaches. We now have one link in our channel system chain.

But there still might be a great discrepancy between the quantity the manufacturer produced and the quantity each retailer wanted. The solution to this problem would be wholesalers. They could serve perhaps 100 retailers each – another link in our channel system chain.

If we limit our discussion to the golf ball example alone, however, we only partially explain the development of specialists. Why doesn't the producer simply open his own wholesale branches and retail outlets to adjust for these discrepancies in quantity? Typically, he cannot afford to do this. To understand why requires a consideration of discrepancy of assortment.

Discrepancy of assortment

■ The typical consumer usually doesn't want a large quantity of particular items but rather an assortment of products. The typical golfer, for example, needs more than golf balls. He wants a full line of golf supplies including golf shoes, gloves, clubs, and so forth. Probably, he would prefer not to shop around for each item.

It is the job of specialists – wholesalers and retailers – to assemble assortments for their target customers. If retailers offer a wide assortment to their customers, then the aggregate quantity that they buy of a variety of items may represent an attractive and economical transaction for wholesalers. Along with orders for golf balls, for example, they might also place orders for golf shoes, gloves, and so on for delivery at the same time. The wholesalers, in turn, while assembling attractive size orders for their manufacturers, are also able to run a profitable operation because of the large sales volumes they achieve representing not one, but many manufacturers.

In actual practice, bringing goods to customers is not quite so simple as in the golf example. Specializing only in golfing products may not achieve all of the economies which are possible in a channel of distribution. Sporting goods retailers may carry even wider assortments of goods to accommodate their customer's desires. And they may acquire the various products in their assortment from a variety of wholesalers who specialize by product line. And some of these wholesalers may be supplied by other wholesalers. These complications will be discussed later. The thing to remember is that discrepancies in quantity and assortment may cause distribution problems for manufacturers and explain why specialists develop.

How channel specialists deal with and adjust to discrepancies

■ To overcome discrepancies of quantity and assortment, it may be necessary to use *regrouping activities:* accumulation, allocating, sorting-out, and assorting. When one or more of these activities is required, a marketing specialist might develop to deal with and fill this need.

Adjusting quantity discrepancies

■ The job of adjusting quantity discrepancies may require development of two quite different types of specialists, because two kinds of regrouping processes may be needed: accumulation and allocation.

The accumulation process

As we mentioned earlier, most producers specialize in certain products and produce in quantity. But some products are not even produced in sufficient quantity to be handled economically further along in the channel. This is particularly true of agricultural commodities. As a result, specialists develop to *increase* the quantity discrepancy. Collecting substantial supplies of such products is called the *accumulation process.* This process is commonly practiced to obtain the lowest possible transportation rate by accumulating and shipping goods in truckload or carload lots. The goods must then move through several specialists before reaching final consumers.

The allocation process

Once economical quantities have been accumulated and moved closer to potential customers, then breaking bulk — *the allocation process* — begins. Sometimes this starts at the manufacturer's level, as in our golf example. In any case, the homogeneous supply is broken into smaller quantities during the allocation process since the next level or group of customers has less need for such quantities. This process may involve many marketing specialists. Depending upon the product, wholesalers may sell smaller quantities to other wholesalers or directly to retailers. The retailers continue the allocation process as they break bulk for their customers.

Adjusting assortment discrepancies

■ The job of adjusting assortment discrepancies may also require development of two different types of specialists, because two kinds of regrouping processes may be needed: sorting out and assorting.

The sorting-out process

Because of the inherent variability of some production processes — all products are not created equal — channel members may be needed to adjust these inevitable discrepancies. They do this through the *sorting-out process*. A manufacturer has quality control operations that handle this function. And growers or wholesalers grade agricultural products such as apples, oranges, or wheat as a way of sorting out.

Sorting-out may create assortments that are not desired by the producers or middlemen. They may be of lower quality or may not fit into the company's product line at all and must be distributed to entirely different target markets. Minor defects in clothing, tires, and sporting goods, for example, may require the marketing manager to offer them, perhaps at little profit, as "seconds" in regular or even special outlets.

The assorting process

Other assortments are created deliberately to develop a product line. This approach, called the *assorting process*, means putting together a line of heterogeneous products to give a target market what it wants. This usually is done by those closer to the final consumer or user; that is, retailers or wholesalers who are attempting to supply a wide assortment of products for the convenience of their customers.

An electrical goods wholesaler may take on a line of lawnmowers or garden products for the convenience of his hardware retailer-customers. Even manufacturers participate in the assorting process when they attempt to develop a more complete product line to satisfy their present customers.

Watching for changes

■ Sometimes, however, these discrepancies are adjusted badly, especially when there have been rapid shifts in buying habits and preferences. Some producers and marketing specialists do not adjust to these changes and continue to offer the same marketing mixes. When this happens, marketing opportunities may open up for new firms, or, breakthrough opportunities may occur if a marketing specialist can see a "better way." This might include eliminating some specialists. Specialists should develop to adjust discrepancies *if they must be adjusted*. But there is no point in having intermediaries just because "that's the way it has always been done."

Good classifications suggest "ideal" Place objectives

■ The needs and preferences of potential target markets should obviously be considered when developing Place. Presumably, the people in a particular target market would have similar attitudes and, therefore, could be satisfied with a similar Place arrangement. Their attitudes about urgency to have needs satisfied and willingness to shop have already been summarized in the goods classifications. Now we should be able to use these goods classifications to suggest how Place should be handled.

The relationship between goods classes and ideal Place objectives is shown in Figure 16–1 for both consumer and industrial

Figure 16–1
Place objectives

Consumer goods

1. *Convenience goods*
   a. *Staples*—need maximum exposure—need widespread distribution at low cost.
   b. *Impulse goods*—need maximum exposure—need widespread distribution but with assurance of preferred display or counter position.
   c. *Emergency goods*—need widespread distribution near probable point of use.

2. *Shopping goods*
   a. *Homogeneous*—need enough exposure to facilitate price comparison.
   b. *Heterogeneous*—need adequate representation in major shopping districts or large shopping centers near other, similar shopping goods.

3. *Specialty goods*—can have limited availability, but in general should be treated as a convenience or shopping good (in whichever category product would normally be included), to reach persons not yet sold on its specialty-goods status.

4. *Unsought goods*—need attention directed to product and aggressive promotion in outlets—or must be available in places where similar products would be sought.

Industrial goods

1. *Installations*
   a. *Buildings (used) and land rights*—need widespread and/or knowledgeable contacts, depending upon specialized nature of product.
   b. *Buildings (new)*—need technical and experienced personal contact, probably at top-management level (multiple buying influence).
   c. *Major equipment*
      1. *Custom-made*—need technical (design) contacts by person able to visualize and design applications, and present to high-level and technical management.
      2. *Standard*—need experienced (not necessarily highly technical) contacts by person able to visualize applications and present to high-level and technical management.

2. *Accessory Equipment*—needs fairly widespread and numerous contacts by experienced and sometimes technically trained personnel.

3. *Raw Materials*
   a. *Farm products*—need contacts with many small farmer producers and fairly widespread contact with users.
   b. *Natural products*—need fairly widespread contacts with users.

4. *Component Parts and Materials*—need technical contacts to determine specifications required—widespread contacts usually not necessary.

5. *Supplies*
   a. *Maintenance*—need very widespread distribution for prompt delivery.
   b. *Repairs*—need widespread distribution for some, and prompt service from factory for others (depends on customers' preferences).
   c. *Operating supplies*—need fair to widespread distribution for prompt delivery.

6. *Services*—most need very widespread availability.

goods classifications. These Place objectives should be studied carefully, since they set the framework for solving the whole Place problem.

Just as there are no automatic classifications of products, we cannot automatically determine the one best Place arrangement. If there are two or three market grid boxes holding different views of the product, then different Place arrangements may be required as well. Place selection depends on what customers would like best, as well as what the various channel members can provide profitably. But different place arrangements often lead to inter-channel competition.

Channel systems can be complex

■ The complexity and inter-channel competition that can develop in actual markets is illustrated in Figure 16–2, involving both consumer and industrial goods. This figure shows the many channels used by manufacturers of household, cartridge, and auto fuses. It should be noted that household fuses go through grocery, drug, variety, and hardware wholesalers, all of which supply goods to retailers who are accustomed to different gross margins. Among such channels, there is a great deal of opportunity for competition, including price competition because of the different margins. If this leads to open price warfare, especially on well-known and branded merchandise, considerable ill will can result all along the channel.

The management of competing channels is a continuing and difficult problem for marketing managers. It may be made even more difficult if one of the managers in a channel system segments the market grid more finely than some of his present channel members. This may lead him to joining or developing additional channel systems to reach some target markets more effectively. Some appliance manufacturers, for example, try to sell through discounters, department stores, and small appliance stores at the same time because they feel that these different store types cater to different customer segments. Not all retailers see the market grid split up so neatly however, and resist the encouragement of more competition in the market.

Dual distribution may develop

■ When a manufacturer uses several competing channels he may be accused of *dual distribution*. This approach is resented by some established middlemen because they do not particularly appreciate competition anyway, and especially competition set up by their own suppliers. Dual distribution is often used, however, because the present channel members may have become inadequate or there is a desire to reach additional target markets which can only be reached through middlemen who also serve some of the firm's existing customers. These are unpleasant realities to some middlemen but realities, nevertheless, in a competitive marketplace.

Figure 16–2
Sales of fuses are made through many kinds of wholesalers

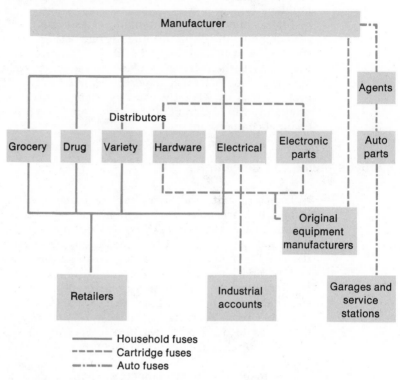

Source: Edwin H. Lewis, "Distributing Electrical Products in a Dynamic Economy," *Electrical Wholesaling*, June 1958, p. 111.

Sometimes there is no choice

■ This example seems to suggest that there are plenty of middlemen around to form almost any kind of a channel of distribution. This is not always the case. Sometimes there is only one key middleman serving a market, and he may have a virtual monopoly. To reach the markets he serves, small producers may have no choice but to use him.

Sometimes there are just no middlemen at all, and a producer has to go directly to target customers. One large U.S. apparel maker described this kind of situation as follows: "There is a production super-highway and a retailing super-highway, but a cowpath in between." This manufacturer found it necessary to set up his own retail chain, building a channel directly from producer to the retail level.

Channel system may shift and share functions

■ Ultimately the channel system must deliver the goods and services desired by target customers. Regardless of whether the marketing manager uses long or short channels, the channels must provide all the functions of marketing. Some buying and selling are required. Transporting, storing, grading or sorting, financing, risk-taking, and market information functions are necessary in all channels. These functions can be shifted and shared, but not eliminated. Note that the customer can participate in this shifting and sharing also. And how costly the whole process is depends on how well the functions are combined *and* how much work has to be done.

If a manufacturer has been extremely successful in differentiating his mix in the minds of customers, there may not be much for other channel members to contribute, and the manufacturer might not have to offer channel members very attractive returns for their efforts. Auto and appliance manufacturers, for instance, offer dealers a lower margin on fast-selling, lower-priced models than on less popular, top-of-the-line models.

Even if a producer takes goods directly to the user, the channel functions are not eliminated. The direct-to-user route may reduce the number of times the functions are performed—but it does not eliminate them, and it may *or may not* reduce the cost.

Channel captain needed to guide channel planning

■ Until now, we have considered the individual marketing manager as the integrating force in marketing planning. But now we see that there may be several firms and managers in a single distribution channel. If we follow the systems concept, we see that each *channel* should act as a unit, directed by someone we can call a "channel captain." The question is, which marketing manager should be the captain?

The concept of a single channel captain is useful, but we must recognize that some channels may not have an acknowledged captain, since the various firms are not acting as a system. The reason may be lack of leadership or lack of understanding that members of the system are interrelated. Many businessmen, more concerned with those firms immediately above and below them, seem almost unaware that they are part of a channel.[1]

But, like it or not, firms are interrelated, even if poorly, by their policies. It would seem to make a lot more economic sense to make a whole channel work efficiently by trying to reconcile the areas of potential conflict before they become big problems.

Manufacturer or middleman?

■ In the United States, manufacturers frequently take the initiative in channel relations. Middlemen wait to see what the manufacturer intends to do and what he wants done. After the manufacturer sets his pricing, promotion, and place policies, middlemen decide whether their roles will be profitable and whether they want to participate in the manufacturer's plans. Middlemen may not play an active role in building the channel, but they must be considered by manufacturers in their planning, if only because they (middlemen) have the power to say no.

There are large or strategically located middlemen who do take the initiative, especially in foreign markets where there are fewer large manufacturers. Such middlemen may determine the types of products their customers want and then seek out manufacturers – perhaps small ones – who can provide products at reasonable prices.

Such middlemen may develop their own dealer brands. Or they may handle manufacturers' brands, but on their own terms. These strong middlemen can even become, in effect, manufacturers. They specify the whole marketing mix for a product and merely delegate production to a factory.

Large middlemen are closer to the final user or consumer and are in an ideal position to assume the channel captain role. It is even possible that middlemen, especially retailers, may dominate the marketing structure of the future.

Our captain, the producer

We cannot overemphasize the importance of a whole channel system seeing itself in competition with other systems. Without this self-conception by members of the channel, one firm might adopt policies that clearly would be unfavorable to another member of his own system. In the short run, a stronger firm might succeed in forcing its policies by sheer weight of market power. Yet in the long run this might lead to the failure, not only of a weaker channel member but of the whole team.

A good example of how *not* to act as channel captain is the manufacturer who loads his retailers with excessive inventory. He may make money in the short run, but he will not be welcomed back by the overloaded firms.

Clearly, the person or firm that helps direct an integrated system of action is the leader. We will consider him our channel captain. His identity may change from time to time – depending on the success of product development or promotional programs, financial reserves, and management personalities – but this does not change the concept or its impact on marketing.

For convenience, we will assume in the following discussion that the channel captain is a producer. Remember, though, that a middleman may play this role too.[2]

Product-market commitment can guide channel strategy planning

■ It helps to think of the members of a cohesive channel system as having a *product-market commitment,* with all members focusing on the same target market at the end of the channel, and sharing the various functions in appropriate ways.

The job of the channel captain is to arrange for the performance of the necessary functions in the optimum way. This might be done as shown in Figure 16–3 in a manufacturer-dominated channel system. Here, the manufacturer has selected the target market and developed the product, set the price structure, done some mass promotion and promotion in the channels, and developed the place

Figure 16–3
How channel strategy might be handled in a manufacturer-dominated system

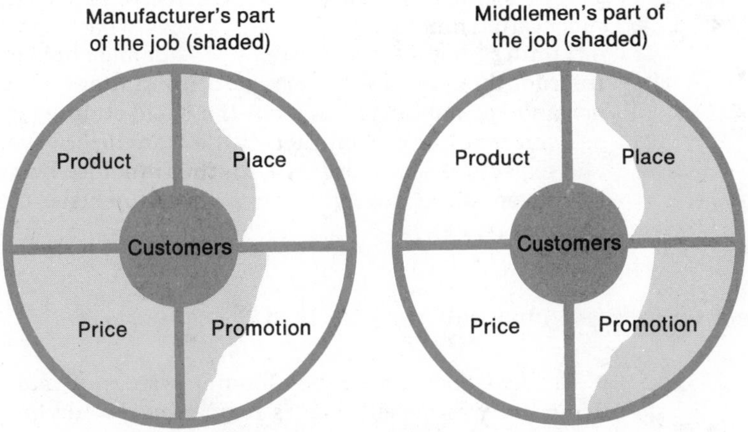

Source: D. J. Bowersox and E. J. McCarthy, "Strategic Development of Planned Vertical Marketing Systems," in Louis Bucklin (ed.), *Vertical Marketing Systems* (Glenview, Ill.: Scott, Foresman & Co., 1970.)

setup. Middlemen are then expected to finish the promotion job in their respective places.

In a middleman-dominated channel system, we would see quite different diagrams. In the extreme, in a channel similar to that dominated by Sears, Roebuck, the middleman circle would be almost completely shaded for some products, and manufacturers would be almost solely concerned with manufacturing the product and perhaps designing it to meet the specifications set by Sears.

New and better ways of organizing channel systems might evolve out of this way of thinking. By rearranging who does what functions, unnecessary and costly duplication may be avoided and information and physical goods flows smoothed and speeded.

A good channel system can help everyone

■ A channel system where the various members have accepted a common product-market commitment can function very well, even though not everyone in the channel system is strongly market-oriented. As long as someone, say, the channel captain, is market-conscious, it should be possible for him to win the confidence and support of production-oriented firms and make the whole channel work effectively. He can convince his channel partners that he knows what he is doing and that a commitment to mutual cooperation is well worth their while.

Small production-oriented producers in Japan or Hong Kong, for example, may become part of an effective channel reaching the U.S. market if there is a middleman who correctly diagnoses market needs and relays them clearly to his producers. The producers may not even know where their products are going, but the system still can be competitive with other systems.

Franchising
—following
a channel
strategy

■ Franchising organizations are also illustrations of channel systems in which the members have made the same product-market commitment. In the fast food franchising industry, for example, a successful franchiser who really knows what he is doing will have a training program for prospective franchise holders and carefully instruct them in how to carry out this strategy effectively. The importance of not deviating from the basic strategy may be stressed, or even required by contract. If the franchiser knows his business and expects to share profits with the franchise holder, then he will feel even more strongly about the franchisee carrying out the channel strategy.[3]

Direct or indirect channels may be best

■ In ideal terms, a whole channel system of marketing-oriented firms, fully aware of what is happening, would be preferable to a marketing-oriented producer working through stodgy middlemen. This, unfortunately, is the position many progressive manufacturers find themselves in, and it is why some have chosen to take over more and more of the distribution job themselves.[4] Remember the best channel system is the one that satisfies customers' wants *and* meets the needs of the various channel members.

Direct
channel
systems
may be
desirable,
sometimes

■ Many producers would prefer to handle the whole distribution job themselves. Perhaps they have a desire to control large organizations, or perhaps it is simply a case of, "If you want a job done right, do it yourself." In any event, there are genuine advantages in selling directly to the final user or consumer.

When the producer is close to his target customers, marketing research is easier. He is more sensitive to changes in customer attitudes and preferences and is in a better position to promptly adjust his marketing mix. If aggressive selling effort or special technical service are needed, he can be sure that his sales force receives the necessary training and motivation.

Some products typically have short channels of distribution, and a direct-to-user channel is not uncommon. It is not always necessary to use middlemen.

Integration may shorten channels

Some channels normally contain several firms, but we also find integrated firms developing full-channel systems. Integration usually refers to the acquisition of other firms. With corporate ownership ranged all along the channel, we can say that the firm is going direct, but actually it may be handling manufacturing, wholesaling, *and* retailing.

HORIZONTAL INTEGRATION At first, it might seem that *horizontal integration* — the acquisition of firms at the same level of activity — would have little to do with channels of distribution, which are usually depicted as vertical. But discrepancies of quantity and assortment must be considered, too, and it is for these reasons that horizontal integration can make sense.

To have the sales volume to integrate vertically, a firm might have to integrate horizontally or expand its horizontal operations by internal expansion. Woolworth's, Kresge's, A&P, National Tea Co., Safeway Stores, Kroger, Florsheim Shoes, Genesco, and J. C. Penney have expanded or integrated horizontally at the retail level. General Motors Corp. and U.S. Steel Corp. are integrated horizontally at the producer level.

VERTICAL INTEGRATION In *vertical integration,* control is expanded to two or more successive stages of production or distribution. A retailer might go into wholesaling and perhaps even manufacturing. Some companies are integrated both horizontally and vertically. A&P, Kroger, Genesco, Florsheim Shoes, and J. C. Penney are wholesalers or manufacturers as well as retailers. A&P, for example, has fish-canning plants. Genesco and Florsheim make their own shoes, and J. C. Penney controls textile plants. Firestone Tire and Rubber Co. has rubber plantations in Liberia, tire plants in Akron, Ohio, and Firestone label wholesale and retail outlets all over the United States.

There are many advantages to vertical integration, such as stability of operations, assurance of materials and supplies, better control of distribution, better quality control of products, an opportunity for larger research facilities, greater buying power, and reduction in executive overhead expense.

The economies of vertical integration may benefit the consumer, too, through lower prices and better products. Vertical integration brings smooth, routine operation of the traditional marketing functions and can cut costs. The business transactions that once required negotiations between separate firms now are routine requisitions, acknowledgements, and internal accounting transactions.

In conclusion, we can see that vertical integration is a method for assuring exclusive arrangements in a channel. Provided that the discrepancy of quantity and assortment is not too great at each level in a channel—that is, the firms fit together well—vertical integration may be extremely efficient and profitable.[5]

Indirect channel systems may be necessary

■ Although a producer might prefer to handle the whole distribution job himself, this is just not economically feasible for many kinds of goods. He may have to use middlemen whether he likes it or not. There are various types of indirect channel systems, and the survival of a firm may depend on what type it joins or develops.

Traditional channel systems

In a traditional channel system, the various channel members make little or no effort to cooperate with each other. They buy and sell from each other and that is that. In some highly independent channels, buyers may even prefer to wait until sellers desperately need to sell, hoping to force the price down. This leads to erratic production, inventory, and employment patterns that can only increase total costs.[6] Traditional channel members may have their independence, but they may pay for it too. As we will see below, such channels are declining in importance—with good reason. But they are still typical in some industries.

Administered channel systems

The inherent advantages of an integrated system have been understood by some progressive businessmen. But instead of integrating corporately, they have tried to develop formal and informal relationships with others in the channel system. Some have achieved the advantages of corporate integration while retaining some of the flexibility of the traditional system.

Norge Division of Borg-Warner Corp., for example, developed an arrangement with its independent distributors to provide them automatically and continually with a six weeks' inventory of appliances, based on current inventory and sales, plus projected sales. Every week, Norge makes a thorough item-by-item analysis of 125,000–130,000 major appliance units valued at around $18 million. These units are located in many warehouses operated by 87 distributors throughout the country. Each week, all of this data is analyzed by the president and his managers of distribution, sales, and marketing research (as well as his manufacturing heads), and plans for production and sales activities for the following week and weeks are established.

Similar systems have been developed and coordinated by middlemen in the grocery, hardware, and drug industries. In fact, a retailer in these lines almost has to be a member of such a system to survive.

Channel systems— new wave in the marketplace

■ In addition to their other virtues, smoothly operating channel systems also appear to be competitively superior.

In the consumer goods field, corporate chains that are at least partially vertically integrated account for about 26 percent of total retail sales; firms aligned with various administered systems account for an additional 37½ percent. This gives vertical systems in the consumer goods area a healthy majority of retail sales. Importantly, it appears that such systems will continue to increase their share in the future. The inevitable conclusion is that vertical marketing systems are becoming the principal competitive units in the U.S. distribution system.[7]

The best channel system should achieve ideal market exposure

■ The best Place system does not happen automatically. Someone must plan the system and the Place objectives introduced earlier suggest the kind of system that should be developed. But then, someone must make specific decisions about how much market exposure will be needed in each geographic area. Although it might seem that all marketing managers would want their products to have maximum exposure to potential customers, this is not the case. Some goods classes require much less market exposure than others.

Generally, the ideal market exposure should meet target customers' needs and preferences—but not exceed them. Excessive exposure would merely increase the number and kinds of outlets, the work involved, and probably the total marketing cost.

<table>
<tr><td>

Three
degrees of
market
exposure
may be ideal

</td><td>

■ We will discuss three degrees of market exposure: *intensive distribution, selective distribution,* and *exclusive distribution.* As we move from intensive to exclusive distribution, we give up exposure in return for some other advantage—including, but not limited to, cost reduction.

Intensive distribution is the sale of a product through any responsible and suitable wholesaler or retailer who will stock and/or sell the product. *Selective distribution,* as the name implies, refers to the choice or selection of only those middlemen who will do a good job with the product. *Exclusive distribution* is the choice of only one middleman in a particular geographic area.

In practice, this means that cigarettes are handled, through *intensive distribution,* by at least a million U.S. outlets, while Rolls Royces or expensive chinaware products are handled through *exclusive distribution,* by only a limited number of middlemen across the country.

A more detailed explanation of each of the three degrees of market exposure will clarify the differences.

</td></tr>
<tr><td>

Intensive
distribution
—sell it
where they
buy it

</td><td>

■ Intensive distribution is commonly needed for convenience goods and for industrial supplies—such as pencils, paper clips, and typing paper—used by all plants or offices. Customers want such goods nearby.

Manufacturers of "new" unsought goods that must compete with convenience goods want to achieve intensive distribution. They may not be able to get this degree of exposure, because customers aren't demanding their products and the channel consequently isn't willing to carry them; nevertheless, these manufacturers have an intensive distribution policy.

The seller's intent is important here. Intensive distribution refers to the *desire* to sell through *all* responsible and suitable outlets. What this means depends on customer habits and preferences. If target customers normally buy a certain product at a certain type of outlet, then, ideally, we would specify this type of outlet in our Place policies. If customers prefer to buy hardware items only at hardware stores, we would solicit all hardware stores to achieve intensive distribution. If, however, as it seems today, many customers will buy certain hardware items at any convenient outlet, including drugstores and food stores, an intensive distribution policy logically requires use of these outlets—using more than one channel to reach one target market.

</td></tr>
<tr><td>

Selective
distribution
—sell it
where it
sells best

</td><td>

■ Selective distribution covers the broad band of market exposure between intensive and exclusive distribution. It may be suitable for all categories of products. Only the better middlemen, chosen on some predetermined basis, are used here. The usual purpose in going to selective distribution is to gain some of the advantages of exclusive distribution while still achieving fairly widespread market coverage.

A selective policy might be used to avoid selling to wholesalers

</td></tr>
</table>

or retailers who (1) have a poor credit rating, (2) have a reputation for making too many returns or requesting too much service, (3) place orders that are too small to justify making calls or providing service, or (4) are not in a position, for any other reason, to do a satisfactory marketing job.

Selective distribution is growing in popularity over intensive distribution as firms decide it no longer is necessary to obtain 100 percent coverage of the market in order to justify or support national advertising. Often, the majority of sales come from a relatively few customers, while a large number are clearly unprofitable to serve.

Selective distribution may produce greater profits for all channel members because of the closer cooperation among them. Here, the systems concept is relevant. Transactions become more routine, requiring less negotiation in the buying and selling process. Wholesalers and retailers may be more willing to give aggressive promotion to products if they know they are going to obtain the majority of sales produced through their own efforts. They may carry more stock, wider lines, do more promotion, and provide more service, all of which contribute to increased sales.

Selective distribution makes sense for shopping and specialty goods, and for those industrial goods that require special effort from channel members. If the channel captain selects only "good" members for his team, this reduces interchannel competition and gives each of the members a greater opportunity to profit if they do a good job.

When selective distribution is used by manufacturers, fewer sales contacts have to be made, and fewer wholesalers may be needed. In fact, as in the garment industry, a manufacturer may be able to contact retailers directly if selective distribution is suitable at the retail level.

In the early part of the life cycle of a new unsought good, a manufacturer's marketing manager may have to use selective distribution to encourage enough distributors to handle his product. He wants to get his product out of the unsought category as soon as possible, but he can't as long as it lacks distribution. Well-known middlemen may have the power to get a product introduced – but sometimes on their own terms, which often includes limiting the number of competing wholesalers and retailers.

Exclusive distribution sometimes makes sense

■ Exclusive distribution is merely an extreme case of selective distribution – one (only) middleman is selected in each geographic area. Besides the various advantages of selective distribution, exclusive distribution is sometimes used by manufacturers as a device to help control prices and the services offered in a channel. For years, Magnavox Corporation maintained its list prices and service standards by selling through 3,000 exclusive franchised dealers. These dealers were willing to go along with Magnavox' exclusive distribution system (which did provide good service) because they had the assurance that prices would not be cut by nearby dealers.

Unlike selective distribution, exclusive distribution arrangements usually entail a verbal or written agreement stating that channel members will buy all or most of a given kind of product or product line from a particular firm. In return, these middlemen are granted the exclusive rights to that product in their territory. Many dealers are so anxious to get a manufacturer's exclusive franchise that they will do practically anything to satisfy the manufacturer's demands. In effect, the dealer becomes a part of the manufacturer's organization. Obviously, there may be economic advantages for both the producer and the dealer, but especially for the dealer. As a result, retailers of shopping goods and specialty goods often seek to obtain exclusive distribution rights in their territories.

But is limiting market exposure legal?

■ Marketing managers must operate within the law, and any consideration of Place must raise the question of the legality of limiting market exposure.

Exclusive distribution, per se, is not illegal. But current interpretation of the various antimonopoly laws gives the impression that almost any exclusive-dealing arrangement could be interpreted as an injury to some competitor somewhere. For example, horizontal arrangements among competing retailers, wholesalers, and/or manufacturers to limit sales by customer or territory are illegal, as shown by recent decisions of the Supreme Court in the Sealy mattress case and the General Motors case. Similarly, the Supreme Court decision in the Schwinn case discourages vertical relationships that would limit territories.[8] And a recent case involving a large retailer who allegedly blocked sales of certain manufacturers' lines to nearby competitors may tend to limit the power of some large retailers.[9] The matter of conspiracy and its impact on competition is important in all these cases.

In general, it would seem that companies should be cautious about entering into any exclusive-dealing arrangements. Apparently the law would allow some exclusive arrangements in order to permit the introduction of a new product or to enable a new company to enter a market, but these arrangements probably should be restricted to less than three years.[10] The same cautions probably apply to selective distribution; here, however, less formal and binding arrangements are typical and the possible impact on competition more remote.

Pushing or pulling through the channel system

■ A producer has a special challenge with respect to channel systems: How to win channel cooperation to ensure that his product reaches the end of the channel. Middlemen, and especially retailers, don't have this problem, since they already control that end of the channel.

The two basic methods of achieving channel cooperation are *pushing* and *pulling.*

Pushing policy—get a hand from the boys in the channel

■ Pushing a product through the channels means using normal promotional effort—personal salesmen and advertising—to help sell the whole marketing mix to possible channel members. This method is common, since these sales transactions are usually between rational, presumably profit-oriented businessmen. The approach emphasizes the importance of building a channel and securing the wholehearted cooperation of prospective channel members in a total system of action. The channel captain, in effect, tries to develop a team that will work well together to get the product to the user.

Pulling policy—make them reach for it out there

■ By contrast, a manufacturer pulls a product through the channels when he tries to develop channel support by making consumers want his product. This entails highly aggressive promotion to final consumers or users, perhaps using coupons or samples, and temporary bypassing of middlemen. If the promotion works, the middlemen are forced to carry the product to satisfy their customers.

This method, familiar in the soap industry, may be necessary if many products are competing already in all of the desired outlets, and the channel members are reluctant to handle a new product. They may be told about the promotion beforehand so that they can anticipate demands if the promotion is successful.

Regardless of how channel cooperation is won, potential channel members must be convinced that the channel captain knows what he is trying to accomplish and why. The marketing manager's salesmen must be able to tell prospective channel members what is expected of them and how much competition they may get from other channels. And it may be a good idea to spell out how the firm and channel will react to probable competitive marketing mixes. In other words, Place policies must be integrated with the rest of the marketing mix if implementation is to be effective.

Conclusion

■ This chapter has discussed the role of Place in an economic system. Place decisions are especially vital because while they may be the one-time strategic decisions that make for unique strategies, the Place decisions may also be difficult to change.

Marketing specialists and channel systems develop to adjust discrepancies of quantity and assortment. These adjustment processes are basic in any economic system, and adjusting them provides opportunities for innovative businessmen.

"Ideal" Place objectives were outlined, based on the goods classifications. These objectives suggest the kind of distribution system and the degree of market exposure which might be "ideal." These ideal objectives can be achieved with either direct or indirect channels of distribution.

Various types of channel systems were discussed (direct, integrated, traditional indirect, and administered) and it was stressed that each channel system may have to compete with other channels. Therefore, a marketing manager of a particular firm should not only consider his own firm's needs and goals but also the needs of others in his channel system. A marketing manager or channel captain could even conceive of a channelwide strategy which would center around a product-market commitment to which all of the members of the channel system would contribute.

In the final analysis, it is channel systems which compete with each other. The "battle of the brands," for example, can be seen in a broader context as only a skirmish in the battle between various channel systems. Finally, it should be emphasized that producers are not necessarily channel captains. Often, middlemen control or even dominate channels of distribution. The degree of this control must be considered by producers when they decide whether they should try to push or pull their product through a channel system.

questions and problems

1 Explain "discrepancies of quantity and assortment" using the clothing business as an example. How does the application of the concept of discrepancies change when coal for sale to the steel industry is considered rather than clothing? What impact does this have on the number and kinds of marketing specialists required?

2 Explain the four steps in the regrouping process with an example drawn from the building supply industry (nails, paint, flooring, plumbing fixtures, etc.) Would you expect many specialists to develop in this industry or would the manufacturers handle the job themselves? What kind of marketing channels would you expect to find in this industry and what functions would be provided by various channel members?

3 In view of the Place objectives suggested for convenience goods, what kinds of specialized marketing institutions would the manufacturer hope to find when he went into the market to implement the objectives? What kinds for shopping goods? For unsought goods? For industrial goods? (In your answer, don't be concerned with whether there are any such institutions, just indicate ideally what you would like to find.)

4 Discuss the Place objectives and distribution arrangements which might be ap-

propriate for the following products (indicate any special assumptions required to obtain a definite answer):
a. A postal scale for products weighing up to two pounds.
b. Children's toys: (1) electric train sets costing $20 or more, (2) balloons.
c. Pneumatic nut tighteners for factory production lines.
d. Caustic soda used in making paper.

5 If a manufacturer has five different markets to reach, how many channels is he likely to use? If only one, why? If more than one, what sort of problems will this raise?

6 Find an example of horizontal integration within the confines of your city. Do there appear to be any particular advantages from this horizontal integration? If so, what are they? If there are no such advantages, how do you explain the integration?

7 Explain how a "channel captain" could help independent firms compete with integrated ones.

8 Discuss the possibility of retailer-organized integrated channels (either formally integrated or administered) dominating consumer goods marketing.

9 Relate the nature of the product to the degree of market exposure desired.

10 Why would middlemen seek to be exclusive distributors for a product? Why would producers seek exclusive distributors? Would middlemen be equally anxious to obtain exclusive distribution for any type of product? Why or why not? Explain with reference to the following products: cornflakes, razor blades, golf clubs, golf balls, steak knives, hi-fi equipment, and industrial woodworking machinery.

11 Explain the present legal status of exclusive distribution. Describe a situation where exclusive distribution is almost assured to be legal. Describe the nature and size of competitors and the industry, as well as the nature of the exclusive-dealing arrangement. Would the exclusive dealing arrangement so described be of any value to the producer or distributor?

12 Discuss the promotion a grocery products manufacturer would need in order to develop appropriate channels and move goods through these channels. Would the nature of this job change at all for a dress manufacturer? How about for a small producer of installations?

13 Discuss the advantages and disadvantages of either a pushing or pulling policy for a very small manufacturer who is just getting into the candy business with a line of inexpensive candy bars. Which policy would probably be most appropriate for him? State any assumptions you need in order to obtain a definite answer.

notes

[1] Phillip McVey, "Are Channels of Distribution What the Textbooks Say?" *Journal of Marketing,* January, 1960, pp. 61–65; but awareness of channel thinking may help spot opportunities. See: Bruce Mallen, "Functional Spin-Off: A Key to Anticipating Change in Distribution Structure," *Journal of Marketing,* July 1973, pp. 18–25.

[2] For further discussion on the idea of channel control, see: Shelby D. Hunt and John R. Nevin, "Power in a Channel of Distribution: Sources and Consequences," *Journal of Marketing Research,* May 1974, pp. 186–193; Adel I. El-Ansary and Robert A. Robicheaux, "A Theory of Channel Control: Revisited," *Journal of Marketing,* January 1974, pp. 2–7; Louis W. Stern, Brian Sternthal, and C. Samuel Craig, "Managing Conflict in Distribution Channels: A Laboratory Study," *Journal of Marketing Research,* May 1973, pp. 169–79; Louis P. Bucklin, "A Theory of Channel Control," *Journal of Marketing,* January 1973, pp. 39–47; and Bert Rosenbloom, "Conflict and Channel Efficiency: Some Conceptual Models for the Decision Maker," *Journal of Marketing,* July 1973, pp. 26–30.

[3] Shelby D. Hunt, "The Socioeconomic Consequences of the Franchise System of Distribution," *Journal of Marketing,* July 1972, pp. 32–38; P. Ronald Stephenson and Robert G. House, "A Perspective on Franchising," *Business Horizons,* August 1971, pp. 35–42; and Bruce J. Walker and Michael J. Etzel, "The Internationalization of U.S. Franchise Systems: Progress and Procedures," *Journal of Marketing,* April 1973, pp. 38–46.

[4] For further discussion on this point, see E. J. McCarthy, "Are Effective Marketing Institutions Necessary and Sufficient Conditions for Economic Development?" in S. A. Greyser (ed.), *Toward Scientific Marketing* (Chicago: American Marketing Association, 1964), pp. 393–404.

[5] This discussion is based on the advantages and disadvantages discussed in Nugent Wedding (ed.), *Vertical Integration in Marketing* (Bulletin 74 [Urbana: Bureau of Economic and Business Research, University of Illinois, 1952]), pp. 11–12, 30.

[6] For more discussion on this interaction, see Jay Forrester, "Industrial Dynamics—A Major Break-Through for Decision-Makers," *Harvard Business Review,* July–August 1958, pp. 37–66.

[7] Bert C. McCammon, Jr., "The Emergence and Growth of Contractually Integrated Channels in the American Economy," a paper presented at the Fall Conference of the American Marketing Association, Washington, D.C., September 2, 1965.

[8] "Ever Tighter Limits on Franchising Power," *Business Week,* May 25, 1974, p. 62; S. Powell Bridges, "The Schwinn Case: A Landmark Decision," *Business Horizons,* August 1968, pp. 77–85; "Are Supermarkets for Autos Next?" *Business Week,* May 7, 1966, p. 33; "Is the Franchise System Legal?" *Business Week,* April 3, 1965, pp. 66–68.

[9] "Antitrust Verdict Rocks the Stores," *Business Week,* July 26, 1969, p. 29.

[10] *Business Week,* July 2, 1966, p. 30.

17

Retailing

■ Marketing managers of consumer goods at all channel levels must understand retailing since it involves the sale of goods to the *ultimate* consumer. If the retailing effort is not effective, the goods may not be sold, and *all* members of the channel will suffer.

Retailing is not concerned with industrial goods nor the sale of consumer goods to retailers or wholesalers. *Retailing consists primarily of buying a satisfying assortment of goods for some market segments, making these goods available at a reasonable price, and often convincing the target customers that the goods will satisfy them.* The term *merchandising* is often used to cover all these activities.

Since Place decisions at the retail level may determine the success or failure of a particular product or service, we will consider, in this chapter, the nature and development of retail facilities and likely trends. We will *not* cover the promotional and pricing aspects of retailing here. These problems are similar for all firms and are discussed in the Promotion and Price chapters.

Why consumers select particular stores — patronage motives

■ We have talked about buying behavior in terms of why individuals or families make decisions about *products*. But why do they select particular stores? We will take up this topic now, following essentially the same line of discussion as in Chapter 8. In fact, it is possible to consider a retailer's store as his "product," meaning that much of what we said in earlier chapters would apply directly.

Economic motives — the importance of price

■ The motives listed below are similar to the economic motives for products and help explain why consumers buy at one store rather than another.

1. Convenience.
2. Variety or selection.
3. Quality of goods — freshness, purity, craftsmanship, and so on.
4. Courtesy of sales personnel.
5. Integrity — reputation for fairness in dealings.
6. Services offered — delivery, credit, returned-goods privileges.
7. Value offered.

Customers patronize stores that offer the conveniences and services they want, at the lowest prices consistent with all the service they want. Some consumers want a great deal of service and are willing to pay for it. The conventional thinking in retailing, however, tends to emphasize economic motives, especially the value offered or, more narrowly, low prices.

Emotional motives — the importance of social class

■ There may also be important emotional reasons for patronizing particular stores. Some people visit a store because they may meet their friends there. Others feel certain stores are distinctive and wear the labels of these institutions with pride. As a result, others may patronize these same stores to emulate the leaders. By contrast, they might not patronize another store because they would be embarrassed to carry home packages bearing the insignia of an obviously "inferior" store.

Social class seems to be especially important in consumers' selection of stores. In one study, it was found that the lower-class woman thinks that if she goes into a higher-class store, the clerks and the other customers in the store may "punish" her in various subtle ways. "The clerks treat you like a crumb," one woman said.[1]

Different stores do seem to attract different classes of customers and ignorance about the relevant dimensions, including the social class dimensions, could obviously lead to serious errors in marketing strategy. There is no one "right" answer as to whom a store should appeal. In fact, not all stores have, or want, a distinct image. Some try to avoid creating a class image because they want to appeal to a wide audience. Macy's in New York, for example, tries to create a fairly universal appeal. John Wanamaker, in Philadelphia, thinks of itself as a family store with a friendly atmosphere; as a result, it (like Macy's) has departments that carry some very expensive merchandise and others that handle goods for the mass market. Carson Pirie Scott & Co., in Chicago, caters to the large middle majority. Its objective is to have a friendly family store that will satisfy the broad market, some of which might feel uncomfortable in a high-fashion outlet.

By contrast, Robert Hall Clothes, Inc., a national clothing chain, aims at the lower-class market. It tries to attract the average family who wants good clothing, not *high* fashion, and it emphasizes lower prices.

Goods classes tied to store types

■ Building on our earlier discussion of consumer behavior and the goods classifications, we can classify three types of stores: convenience stores, shopping stores, and specialty stores. There is no point in discussing unsought stores. They have no image at all and cannot last long unless they do acquire an image in the eyes of some market segments.

These labels do not limit any store to one type of merchandise, for example, a convenience store might stock specialty goods. Rather, the classification refers to the customers' image of the store.

If a store is centrally located or "in the neighborhood," it may be perceived as a *convenience store*—i.e., a convenient place to shop. These convenience stores may draw many customers, even for shopping goods, simply because they are so accessible.

Certain other stores seem to be favored by consumers shopping for such items as clothes, furniture, and household appliances. These stores carry all types of merchandise, but their attraction is the width and depth of their assortments. Such stores are classified as *shopping stores*.

Finally, a customer may develop an extremely strong allegiance to a particular store. Whatever his reasons—service, selection, or store reputation—the customer consistently will buy convenience, shopping, and specialty goods at this store. It would be classified as a *specialty store*.

Store type affects retailer and channel strategies

■ A retailer's planning must allow for customers' attitudes toward both the products and the store—that is, the planners must view product and patronage motives together. Classifying stores by type of goods, as shown in Figure 17–1, is a good way to understand this complete view.

A retailer can better understand his potential market and competition by estimating the relative size of each of the market grid boxes, shown in Figure 17–1, and then identifying which retailers are satisfying which boxes. He may find that he and his competitors are all charging head on for certain kinds of customers, and completely missing a substantial number of others.

When the retailer sees more clearly what he is doing, he may continue his present marketing strategy more vigorously or he may alter it. The manager of a shopping store, for instance, might decide to widen his assortment.

A decision on store type should be part of a retailer's overall strategy; it affects a retailer's whole marketing mix. Type-of-store classification also is important to the strategies of manufacturers and wholesalers. If, for example, the majority of a manufacturer's target customers patronize convenience stores, widespread distribution may be necessary.

Store type could be used as another dimension on a multidimensional market grid to provide greater understanding of the needs, preferences, and behavior of customers. A dealer-branded product might be no better than a manufacturer's brand, but if the dealer's

Figure 17-1
How customers view store-product combinations*

Store type / Product type	Convenience	Shopping	Specialty
Convenience	Will buy any brand at most accessible store.	Shop around to find better service and/or lower prices.	Prefer store. Brand may be important.
Shopping	Want some selection but will settle for assortment at most accessible store.	Want to compare both products and store mixes.	Prefer store but insist on adequate assortment.
Specialty	Prefer particular product but like place convenience too.	Prefer particular product but still seeking best total product and mix.	Prefer both store and product.

* For more discussion of these ideas, see Louis Bucklin, "Retail Strategy and the Classification of Consumer Goods," *Journal of Marketing*, January 1963, pp. 50–55.

store is a specialty store for such products for some target customers, then the product may sell well despite its lack of superiority. An example involves Sears, Roebuck's washing machines, which are similar to competing manufacturers' brands. Some target customers seem to view Sears as a specialty store, and Sears' share of the home-laundry business regularly has been over 25 percent.

To determine store type requires detailed evaluations of individual retailers. Since implementation efforts are beyond our scope, we will de-emphasize store types in this chapter and continue to stress the goods classifications introduced earlier. But remember that a store's entire offering of goods and services can be described as its Product. Thus many of the concepts discussed below with respect to products would be directly applicable to retail store planning and management.

Number and size of actual facilities available

■ Since retailers sell to final consumers, they usually are located nearer to people than to production facilities. Retailers also are much more numerous than manufacturers because customers are widely dispersed and have greatly varied wants and needs. In 1967, there were almost 1.8 million retailers compared to about 310,000 wholesalers and 310,000 manufacturers.

Table 17-1
Retail trade, 1967 – United States, sales by size of establishment

Sales size of establishments	Establishments			Sales volume		
	Number (000)	Percent	Cumulative percent	Sales ($000,000)	Percent	Cumulative percent
Total, all establishments	1,763			$310,214		
Establishments operated entire year, total	1,671	100.0		299,430	100.0	
With annual sales of:						
$1,000,000 or more	50	3.0	3.0	132,876	44.4	44.4
$500,000–999,999	55	3.3	6.3	38,464	12.9	57.3
$300–499,999	74	4.4	10.7	28,110	9.4	66.7
$100,000–299,999	359	21.5	32.2	60,290	20.1	86.8
$50,000–99,999	323	19.3	51.5	22,888	7.6	94.4
$30,000–49,999	227	13.6	65.1	8,769	2.9	97.3
$29,999 or less	583	34.9	100.0	8,033	2.7	100.0

Source: *U.S. Census of Business, 1967,* Vol. I

Retailing: many small businesses

■ The large number of retailers might suggest that retailing is a field of small businesses. To an extent, this is true. In 1967, the date of the last Census for which completed data is available, 34.9 percent of the nation's retailers accounted for only 2.7 percent of total retail sales, grossing less than $30,000 each annually.

Yet in the aggregate, retailing is big business. Retail sales in 1967 totaled $310 billion, making retailing a key element in the U.S. economy. The larger retail stores – those selling more than $1 million in goods or services annually, such as supermarkets – do most of this business. Only 3.0 percent of the retail stores fell in this bracket, yet they accounted for more than 44 percent of all retail sales. Table 17-1 gives details on the number of retailers and the sales volume by various sales classes.

The many small retailers, however, cannot be ignored, especially because they frequently cause the marketing manager difficult problems. Their large number and relatively small sales volume make it expensive to work with them, and they often require additional marketing mixes. Yet these stores reach many consumers and often are invaluable channel members for some products and target markets.

Evaluation of conventional retailing facilities

■ Marketing managers, faced with selecting retailer channel members, have a wide variety from which to choose. Similarly, those interested in retailing have many choices because there are many kinds of retailing institutions – each fulfilling some function.

In the following section we will discuss why and how present retailing facilities have evolved and why there are so many stores — especially so many small stores.

Actually, there is continuous change occurring in the retailing area and a solid understanding of the "why" of various kinds of retailing facilities will help you plan better marketing strategies now, and in the future.

Door-to-door retailers

■ Door-to-door selling in the United States is an old but still effective method inherited from the Yankee peddler. Today, it is a relatively insignificant form of retailing, accounting for less than 1 percent of retail sales. But it does have an important advantage — it offers marketing managers an opportunity to control their whole channel of distribution. It may be especially useful during the introductory stage of the product life cycle, for sales of unsought goods, or during a recession when goods need a special push.

This is an expensive method of selling. Markups range from 30 to 50 percent and often are higher. To be sure, overhead costs are lower because the door-to-door retailer has no store, but travel is costly and the number of personal contacts possible in a day is limited.

Success can be achieved with this method, however, if it meets the needs of certain segments of the market grid. Vacuum cleaners may be an unsought good for some housewives, for example, and therefore no store type will reach them. If a demonstration is needed to show how a vacuum cleaner will meet the housewife's needs, then door-to-door selling may be indicated. Electrolux has sold vacuum cleaners door-to-door since its introduction from Sweden decades ago. And it still claims the top position in the vacuum cleaner business selling all of its cleaners at list price! The same kind of success has been seen by the Avon ladies who sell cosmetics directly to housewives.[2] And Fuller Brush, Tupperware, and most encyclopedia companies use this approach successfully.

Trading posts — general stores

■ Historically, trading posts or general stores sold anything the local consumers would buy in sufficient volume to justify carrying it. Before the Civil War, they were the main type of retail outlet in this country.

The main advantage of the general store is its convenient location for some target customers. It sometimes serves, too, as a social center and a collecting point for agricultural produce.

Such stores are still found at rural crossroads and in some small towns, carrying mainly food and other convenience goods, but there are so few now that the U.S. Bureau of Census no longer reports them as a separate category.

Single-line, limited-line stores

■ Single-line stores became common after the Civil War, when the continuing expansion in the volume and variety of consumer goods began to make it impossible for the general store to offer depth and breadth in all its traditional lines. Some stores began specializing in certain lines such as dry goods, apparel, furniture, or groceries. Some stores not only specialize in a single line, such as food, but in a limited line within the category—in the food classification: meat, staples, fresh produce, or bakery goods. The modern convenience food store is a limited-line store in that it limits its assortment to meet particular needs.

. Most retail stores are single- and limited-line stores—specializing in groceries, or hardware, or gasoline, or clothing, or sporting goods—and this probably will continue to be true as long as customer demands are numerous and varied. The main advantage of a single-line, and especially a limited-line, store is that it can satisfy some target markets better, perhaps achieving a specialty-store status, by adjusting its marketing mix—including store hours, credit, and product assortment—to suit certain customers. Several stores, catering to various parts of the market grid, can satisfy the whole market.

Such stores face a major disadvantage in having to stock some items in depth that are slow-moving but must be carried to satisfy each store's target market. Further, many of these stores have the disadvantage of being small, with high expenses relative to sales. It is stores of this type which have traditionally applied the retailing philosophy of "buying low and selling high." They are the "conventional" retailers who have been, and probably will continue to be, squeezed by newer forms of retailing.

There are some extremely large single-line and limited-line stores—supermarkets and furniture stores, for example—especially in larger cities. But a manufacturer's or a wholesaler's marketing manager must remember that there are many more small stores in *both* large cities and small towns and adjust his strategies accordingly.

Specialty shops

■ The specialty shop is a type of limited-line store found in downtown areas, fashionable shopping districts, and large shopping centers. It usually is small, has a distinct personality, and aims at a carefully defined market segment by offering a unique product assortment, knowledgeable salesmen, and better service. Boutiques are examples of specialty shops that project an image of excitement as they invite customers to "be uniquely you."

Usually the specialty-shop designation is reserved for stores dealing in special types of shopping goods, such as high-quality sporting goods, men's exclusive ties, high-fashion dresses, clothes in special sizes, and women's shoes.[3]

Using the term "specialty" should not cause us to confuse specialty *shops*, specialty *stores*, and specialty *goods*. A successful specialty shop might achieve the specialty-store status, discussed earlier in the chapter, among a small group of target customers, but the owner probably would be more satisfied to be well known among a larger group for the distinctiveness of its line and the special services offered. Similarly, a specialty shop might carry specialty goods, but only if they fit into its narrow line and they could benefit by the additional service and display the specialty shop offers.

The specialty shop's major advantage is that it caters to certain types of customers whom the management and salespeople come to know well. This familiarity simplifies buying, and the resulting quicker turnover cuts the costs due to obsolescence and style changes.

Specialty shops probably will continue to be a part of the retailing scene as long as customers continue to have such varied tastes and the money to satisfy them.

Department stores

■ Department stores handle a *wide* variety of goods, such as women's ready-to-wear and accessories, men's and boys' wear, piece goods, housewares, and housefurnishings.

The distinguishing characteristic of department stores is that they are organized into separate departments like limited-line stores and specialty shops – for purposes of promotion, service, and control. They normally are large stores.

Some specialty shops, grown large and departmentalized, appear to be department stores, and we will treat them as such. As a rule, however, specialty shops do not carry complete lines. They frequently omit housewares, housefurnishings, and furniture, and prefer instead to emphasize depth of line and distinctiveness in the lines they do choose to carry. Neiman-Marcus in Dallas, for example, is departmentalized, but insists it is a specialty shop.[4]

Department stores generally try to cater to customers seeking shopping goods. Originally they were located in downtown districts close to other department stores and convenient to many potential customers. Historically, this close grouping developed to facilitate shopping at the junctions of major railroad and streetcar routes, the principal forms of urban public transportation in the 19th century, when the major U.S. department stores began.

Since World War II, many downtown department stores have opened suburban branches in shopping centers to serve the middle- and higher-income groups who moved to the suburbs. The big J. L. Hudson store in Detroit was a leader in the movement toward building shopping centers around a large branch department store.

Some downtown department stores now are making efforts to renew the appeal of their traditional downtown locations by (1) carrying wide lines in the major shopping-goods items for which they have long been famous; (2) attracting the trade of conventioneers and tourists; and (3) appealing to low-income groups remaining in the residential neighborhoods near the downtown area. New urban trends, including downtown apartment units and urban redevelopment, may provide new markets for the big downtown stores.[5]

Department stores are often looked to as the retailing leaders in a community. Leaders, first, because they seem to be so generous in giving the customer services he can't get elsewhere – credit, merchandise return, delivery, fashion shows, and Christmas displays. And leaders also because of their size. In 1967, the annual sales volume of U.S. department stores averaged more than $5 million, compared to about $175,000 for the average retail store. The biggest — Macy's, Field's, and Hudson's — each top $100 million in sales annually. Although department stores account for about one third of 1 percent (5,792) of the total number of retail stores, they accounted for over 10 percent of total retail sales in 1967.

Certain department stores have a strong grip on their market. Some market grid segments can be reached *only* through particular department stores. These stores have achieved a strong specialty-store status, and their buyers can make it tough on suppliers. In other words, instead of playing the role of channel captain because of their strength, they simply demand all of the concessions they can get. These might include restricting suppliers from selling preferred lines to their competitors.[6]

Mail-order retailing

■ Mail-order retailing should not be ignored by marketing managers. It may be useful for reaching widely scattered markets with products that otherwise might be unsought. Some mail-order houses aim at narrow target markets, selling only electronic components, phonograph records, or health foods. Others, such as the big mail-order houses, offer both convenience goods and shopping goods. These houses have continued to grow with the U.S. economy, numbering almost 6,000 establishments in 1967. Yet they have never achieved more than 1.3 percent of total U.S. sales, and in 1967, they were down to about 1 percent.

Some of the early mail-order houses, including Sears, Roebuck and Montgomery Ward, were started after the Civil War, as railroads and postal service expanded. They were so successful with their low prices and wide variety that some conventional retailers sought legislation to restrict their operations.

Today, mail-order selling isn't what it used to be. The emphasis is no longer solely on low-price selling by mail. There is an increasing emphasis on high-fashion women's and girls' wear, and luxury items. And some companies offer catalog stores, telephone service, convenient pickup depots, and delivery, to make it easier to buy out of their catalogs. The big mail-order houses started this practice, but now department stores and limited-line stores are seeing the profit possibility and selling by mail, too. Not only can they obtain additional business this way, but costs may be lower because they can use warehouse-type buildings and limited sales help. They may even be able to offer wider selections at lower prices than conventional retailers. Sears' mail-order and catalog operation typically undersells its own retail stores by about 10 percent.

Vending machines

■ Although vending machines are the newest revolution in marketing methods, and their growth has been spectacular, automatic vending still represents less than 2 percent of total U.S. retail sales. But in certain lines, the vending machine is an important factor — 16 percent of all cigarettes sold in the United States, 20 percent of the candy bars, and 25 percent of the bottled soft drinks are sold through machines.[7]

The largest part of the vending-machine business (about 40 percent) is in cigarettes, and the next largest share is from hot and cold beverages (36 percent). For some target markets, clearly, the marketing manager cannot ignore this retailing method.

The major stumbling block in vending is high cost of operation. The machines are relatively expensive for the volume they sell, and they require much stocking time and repair labor. Mass marketers of similar, nonvended products can operate profitably on a margin of about 20 percent; the vending industry seems to require about 41 percent, and so usually must charge higher prices.[8] If costs come down and consumers' income and desire for convenience rises, perhaps we will see more growth in this method of retailing.

Planned shopping centers

■ The planned shopping centers that have grown rapidly in the last 15 years can be viewed as both a new development and a variation of old marketing institutions. Shopping centers' forerunners were the early villages and country fairs, and department stores composed of many individual shops leased to merchants who operated them as limited-line and specialty shops within one large building.[9] The new shopping centers also are similar to the old shopping districts in larger cities, except shopping centers are planned as a unit, perhaps around a mall.

Usually there are substantial parking facilities, and some are pleasantly landscaped. Although the centers are composed of independent merchants, they sometimes act together for promotional purposes.

Shopping centers have been classified into three basic categories based on the type of tenant and the size of the market they must serve to be profitable: (1) the neighborhood center, (2) the community center, and (3) the regional center.

Neighborhood shopping centers

These centers, similar to the many "strips" of convenience stores found in most cities, usually include a supermarket, drug store, hardware store, beauty shop and barbershop, laundry, dry cleaners, gas stations, and others, such as a bakery or appliance shop. They normally serve 7,500 to 40,000 people living within 6 to 10 minutes' driving distance.

Community shopping centers

These larger operations usually include a variety store or a small department store in addition to the stores found in the neighborhood center. There is more emphasis here on shopping goods (apparel and home furnishings), but the bulk of sales are of convenience goods. These centers must serve 40,000–150,000 people within a radius of 3 to 4 miles.

Regional centers

These are much larger units. They include one or two large department stores and as many as 100 smaller stores. Most of these emphasize shopping goods; in fact, the stores that emphasize convenience goods often are at the edge of the center, where they will not interfere with customers primarily interested in shopping.

Regional centers must serve 150,000 or more persons within a radius of 5 or 6 miles. They closely resemble downtown shopping districts of larger cities and usually are found near suburban areas.

One aspect of shopping center development, important to manufacturer and wholesaler marketing managers, is that the financial requirements of shopping center developers often have barred small independent stores from the centers in favor of national chain stores. This sometimes has blocked manufacturers' brands from these important centers, since some chains tend to emphasize their own dealer brands.[10]

Evolution of new, mass merchandising institutions

Mass merchandisers see things differently from conventional retailers

■ So far we have been describing retail institutions primarily in terms of the number of lines carried and their physical facilities. This is the traditional or conventional way of thinking about retailing. But there are some important retail institutions that cannot be adequately described this way. Supermarkets and discount houses, for instance, can be shoved into our previous classifications. But by so doing, we would miss their essence, just as some conventional retailers did when these stores first developed.

Mass merchandisers reject the conventional retailer's notion of a fixed demand for a territory and also the "buy-low-and-sell-high" philosophy. The mass merchandiser's approach is to offer lower prices to achieve faster turnover and substantial sales volumes by appealing to larger markets. Some mass merchandising institutions were started by nonretailers who were willing to depart from the conventional wisdom of existing retailers. Their success is history now.

Some conventional retailers have adopted mass merchandising methods and prospered. Other retailers missed the boat and are out of business today. And others have ignored these methods and continue to operate, perhaps because they satisfy different segments of the market grid. To understand more fully what mass merchandising really is, we will discuss its evolution from the development of supermarkets and discounters to the mass merchandisers.

Supermarkets started move to mass merchandising

■ A supermarket is essentially a large store specializing in groceries. As late as 1930, most food stores were relatively small single- or limited-line operations. In the early depression years, some innovators felt that price appeals could move merchandise in volume. Their early experiments in vacant warehouses proved an immediate success. Conventional retailers, both independents and chains, quickly copied the innovators – emphasizing lower prices and self-service.[11]

According to the Super Market Institute, $1 million is considered the minimum annual sales volume for a store to be classified as a supermarket. In 1972, there were 28,010 supermarkets, about 14 percent of all grocery stores, and they handled about 67 percent of total grocery sales. Today supermarkets are beginning to reach the saturation level, yet new ones still do well when they are wisely located. Supermarkets are growing in popularity all over the world, with several thousand in Europe alone.[12]

Supermarkets sell convenience goods, but in quantity. Their target customers don't want to shop for groceries every day as was common in pre-supermarket times. To facilitate volume shopping, supermarkets generally offer free parking facilities.

Present-day supermarkets are planned for maximum efficiency; some carefully analyze the sales and profit of each item, and allocate space accordingly. This approach helps sell more merchandise in less time, reduces the investment in inventory, makes stocking easier, and reduces the cost of handling goods. Such efficiency is essential. Grocery competition is keen, and net profits after taxes in grocery supermarkets usually run a thin 1 percent of sales, or *less*.

Discount selling preceded mass merchandisers

■ Discount selling has become quite popular since World War II, but price cutting or discounting goes back to the earliest days of marketing. Bargaining has always been the way to get a better price. And clergymen, teachers, members of labor unions, and members of various social groups have long received discounts in certain stores.[13]

Some discounting has been done through brokers and in "open showrooms" where furniture and similar bulky items ostensibly are shown only to wholesalers or retailers but actually are shown to anyone. Others used "wholesale" catalogs which *were used* by small retailers but the "wholesaler" was also willing to sell to final consumers, perhaps at "wholesale" prices. Usually these operations were not well publicized and accounted for a small portion of retail sales. Recently, however, they have expanded their activities markedly. Using catalogs and more complete showrooms with large backup inventories, the average discount cataloger can deliver 95 percent of his items on the showroom floor. Price is the important variable here and important savings can be shown in the jewelry, gifts, luggage, and small appliance areas where they have tended to focus their efforts.[14]

Discount selling did not bother the conventional retailers because the operations were not well publicized and they accounted for only a small portion of retail sales. If the discount sellers had been as aggressive as the current catalog retailers, it might have been another story. But instead, discount houses developed.

Discount houses upset some conventional retailers

■ Right after World War II, some retailers moved aggressively beyond discount selling into operating discount houses. They were much more open about their operations than those retailers who were simply offering discounts to selected customers or to those who happened to hear about their catalog operation. These retailers sold hard goods such as appliances, cameras and jewelry, and furniture at substantial price cuts. To get the lower prices, the discount house customer would have to go to the discounter's low-rent facilities, pay cash, and take care of service and repair problems himself, because the lower prices didn't cover such extras (although manufacturers' guarantees were available on some items). The emphasis in these discount houses was on price cutting to obtain fast turnover.

Word-of-mouth advertising made the discount houses well known, and eventually some advertised through local media. Such steps were taken very cautiously, however. Sales and profits were growing, and the discounters did not wish to antagonize their manufacturer-brand suppliers or conventional competitors for fear that they might – as in fact they eventually did – put pressure on their sources to cut off the discounter's supplies.

In the early 1950s, with war shortages finally ended, goods became more plentiful, and a buyers' market developed. Discount houses became more attractive to suppliers, and the discounters themselves became more aggressive. Earlier they had emphasized products that had been bought cheaply but often with little regard to assortments. Now they were able to offer full assortments.[15]

At this stage, many discounters sought respectability, moving to better locations and offering more services and guarantees. They began to act more like regular retailers, but kept their prices lower than conventional outlets to keep turnover high.

Discount houses are a new approach to retailing. In the face of discount house competition, some conventional retailers have resorted to price cutting on highly competitive items. But these purely defensive tactics are just that – price cutting – while discounters make a standard practice of selling all of their goods with small markups.

More than price cutting is involved, however. Careful buying with the firm's target markets in mind is essential, to assure high turnover. A major discounter's first venture into apparel sales flopped, for instance, because its buyers were appliance experts and knew little about fashions. The discount approach worked only after they hired experienced buyers from department stores.

Mass merchandisers are more than discounters

■ Unlike the early discount houses – which emphasized manufacturer-branded hard goods, such as appliances and TV sets, where it was easier to show that discounts were being given – the mass merchandisers tend to emphasize soft goods and, more recently, groceries. These "discount" stores are a force to reckon with. They are selling more food (among other things) per store than the chain supermarkets!

The mass merchandisers are simply large, departmentalized stores that are larger than the supermarkets and follow the discount house's philosophy of emphasizing lower margins to win faster turnover. They offer a wider range of goods than some supermarkets and discount houses, stress lower prices and self-service and, inevitably, are bigger.

In 1972, there were over 4,000 such outlets. By definition their minimum floor space is 10,000 square feet, but the average mass merchandiser has over 60,000 square feet — three to four times the size of the average supermarket.[16]

Mass merchandisers typically are fully committed to a self-service operation, with checkout counters in the front of the store and little or no sales help on the floor. This is in contrast to more conventional retailers, such as Sears and Penney's, who still offer some service and have sales stations and cash registers throughout the store. The more conventional retailer may attempt to replenish sizes and stocks in lines it carries, whereas some mass merchandisers make little effort in this regard. They want to move merchandise — quickly, they hope — and are less concerned with continuity of lines and assortment.

The mass merchandisers are usually operated as chains. Some were started by relative newcomers to retailing. Two important competitors, however, are Kresge with its K Marts and F. W. Woolworth with its Woolco stores. The K Marts are 100,000-square-foot, full-line department stores that sell top-quality manufacturers' and dealer brands at moderate prices. Kresge also has a slightly lower-price operation — the Jupiter Stores.

The mass merchandisers may have already reached saturation levels in many markets. The profits are declining and some have gone bankrupt. The number expanded so rapidly in some areas that they were no longer taking customers from conventional retailers but from each other. Well-managed ones which are able to adjust to local needs seem to be surviving and thriving and there will probably be a continued expansion by such firms, with fallout by others.[17]

The success of mass merchandisers clearly indicates that at least some customers in the market grid were not fully satisfied with the conventional retailers' strategies. Mass merchandisers already have made a substantial dent in the market, accounting for about 5 percent of total grocery sales, 17 percent of health and beauty aid sales, and a larger but more difficult to estimate share of some general merchandise lines. Clearly, there is a demand for this type of operation, and it is likely that the mass merchandisers will continue to use their present methods, because they see these methods as "conventional" for their type of operation.

Even larger stores may be seen in the future. The French already have over 200 *hyper markets* with up to 200,000 square feet. And a 240,000-square-foot monster is being tried in Montreal. If this works, the developers are planning to move south into the United States.[18]

Super-stores may be coming

■ Some supermarkets have moved into nonfood items, and some mass merchandisers have taken on groceries. When a store attempts to carry not only foods but also all of the other goods and services which the consumer purchases routinely, then it has accepted a new concept — the *super-store concept*. Such a store may look like a mass merchandiser, but it is different in concept in that it is attempting to meet *all* of the customer's *routine needs*, at a low price. This will cause it to move not only into foods, but also personal care products, alcoholic beverages, tobacco products, some apparel products, low-priced housewares and hardware items, leisure-time products including magazines, books, etc., some lawn and garden products, gasoline, stationery and sewing supply products, and household services such as laundry, dry cleaning, shoe repair, check cashing, and bill paying.

The super-store concept is much bigger than the supermarket or mass merchandising concept. Some firms have already moved in this direction and it is estimated that if the trend continues, the food-oriented supermarkets may suffer badly. Many are not large enough to move into the super-store category and it is estimated that over the next decade super-stores could render obsolete 50 percent of the existing supermarkets.[19]

Will scrambled merchandising continue?

Who's selling what to whom?

■ Current retailing might be called "scrambled merchandising." Variety stores (the old 5-and-10-cent stores) are almost indistinguishable nowadays from department stores and some discount houses. Mass merchandisers are selling groceries. Some discount houses are becoming department stores and want to be called "promotional department stores." Supermarkets are selling anything they can move in volume.

The Wheel of Retailing, the ladder of success

■ What is behind this scrambled merchandising? According to the "Wheel of Retailing" hypothesis, new types of retailers enter the market as low-status, low-margin, low-price operators. If successful, they evolve into more elaborate establishments and offer more services, with resulting higher operating costs and higher prices. They are then vulnerable to new low-status, low-margin, low-price outlets—and the wheel turns again.

Early department stores began this way, then became higher priced and built basement departments to serve the more price-conscious customers. The 5-and-10-cent store and the mail-order house were developed on a price basis, as were the food chains, economy apparel chains, drug chains, and the automotive accessory chains which developed during the 1920s. The supermarket, in turn, was started with low prices and little service.

Some innovators start high on the ladder

■ The wheel theory, however, does not explain all major retailing developments. Vending machines entered retailing as high-cost, high-margin operations. The branch trend of the department stores and the development of shopping centers have not been low-price oriented. On the contrary, they sometimes have even been high-price operations. Nor have all innovations been immediate successes. Some of the first department stores failed, while vending-machine history is filled with failures.

The probable cause of these crosscurrents has been summarized very well by Hollander:

> . . . retailers are constantly probing the empty sectors of competitive strategy with many failures until someone uses exactly the right technique at the right time. In at least some cases, the merchant prince's skill may have been in judging opportunities rather than in originating techniques.[20]

The market grid concept may help explain scrambled retailing

■ A clearer view of the present retailing scene can be achieved by building on the market grid concept. Figure 17–2 is a simplified view of the market which suggests that three consumer-oriented dimensions affect the types of retail facilities customers choose. These dimensions are: (1) width of assortment desired; (2) depth of assortment desired, and (3) a price/service combination. Within this three-dimensional market grid it is possible to position most of the retail facilities now operating.

Figure 17–2, for example, suggests the *why* of vending machines. Some people – in the front upper left-hand corner – have a pressing need for a specific item and are not interested in the width of assortment, the depth of assortment, *or* the price.

On the other hand, some people have very specific needs in mind and would like to be able to select from a very deep assortment and a range of price alternatives as well. Various kinds of specialty shops have been developed to fill these needs. This market can be seen in the lower left front corner of Figure 17–2.

At another extreme, if a customer wanted to shop for a broad assortment of items with reasonable depth, he might choose a large department store or a mass merchandiser, depending upon his price/service preferences.

Drawing a three-dimensional grid is relatively easy, but it does not guarantee that all parts of the grid have equal quantities of market needs to be satisfied. In fact, it is quite possible that certain grid boxes would be almost empty. This emphasizes the importance to retailers of focusing on market needs *before* developing their offerings.

Product life-cycle concept helps too

■ The market grid concept helps explain why a variety of marketing institutions can develop, but we need to apply the product life-cycle concept to retail institutions to understand fully the evolutionary process. The merchant prince may exploit new opportunities for a while, but if his judgment is correct, he can count on fairly prompt imitation and a squeeze on his innovator's profits.

Some conventional retailers are far along in their cycle, some have already declined, while current innovators are still in the market growth stage. The retailers who are bewildered by the scrambling that is going on around them don't see this evolutionary process and don't understand that some of their more successful competitors are focusing on the needs in different market segments rather than just selling products. These product-oriented retailers

Figure 17–2
A three-dimensional view of the market for retail facilities and probable position of some
present offerings

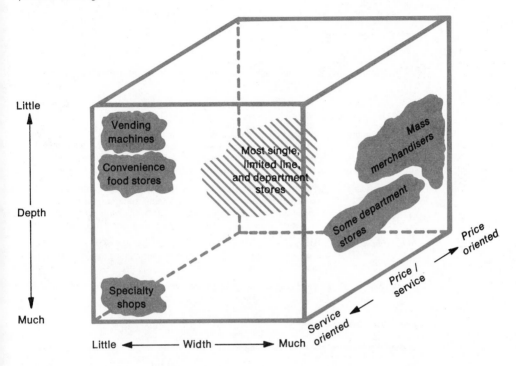

can get away with focusing primarily on their internal problems
during the early stages of the life cycle of a particular kind of
retail institution. But as each market gets saturated with that particular kind of institution, market maturity sets in and profits are
squeezed. Then they too may blindly scramble for more profitable
opportunities.

It is not surprising to find that some modern success stories in
retailing are among firms which aim at needs along the edges of the
market grid shown in Figure 17–2. The convenience food store
chains, for example, don't just sell food, but deliberately sell a
particular assortment-service combination to meet a special need.
The same can be said for certain specialty-shop and boutique chains
as well as some of the mass merchandisers and department store
chains.[21]

**Will retailers
keep
scrambling
for profits?**

■ Scrambled merchandising may continue into the future. There
are still many inflexibilities and rigidities in our marketing system,
including the inflexibility of the traditional retailers' pricing
policies. Pricing will be discussed in detail later, but it should be
noted here that many retailers have traditionally used fixed percentage markups for *all* items, regardless of the rate of turnover.

Table 17–2
Gross margins in selected retail trades for recent years

Gross margin ranges	Retail trades
50 percent or more	Custom tailors, monuments, florists and nurseries, bakery shops, furs.
40 to 50 percent	Garages, jewelry, restaurants, eating places, furniture, and undertaking.
35 to 40 percent	Musical instruments, housefurnishings, dairy and poultry products, gifts, novelties, souvenirs, books, furniture, drinking places, taverns, bars, office equipment and supplies, floor coverings, shoes (family stores), electric and gas household appliances.
30 to 35 percent	Paint, wallpaper, glass, confectionery, drugs, women's accessory and specialty stores, men's clothing, stationery, men's furnishings, women's ready-to-wear, limited-price variety, automobile accessories and parts, family clothing, coal and other fuel.
20 to 30 percent	Hardware, sporting goods, dry goods, general merchandise, lumber, cigar stores and stands, filling stations, meats, hardware and farm implements.
Below 20 percent	Alcoholic beverage package stores, farm implements, motor vehicles, groceries and meats, groceries.

Source: Dun & Bradstreet.

The fast-moving items contributed nicely to profit, while the slow-moving items tended to reduce profits. If a firm were looking for opportunities, it would sell these fast-moving, high-profit items. And it is exactly these items that are crossing traditional lines and appearing in unexpected places.

Table 17–2 shows the ranges of gross margins conventional retailers have found necessary, to assure staying in business and making *some* profit. *Some* is emphasized because typically the net profit—the difference between a seemingly big gross margin and apparently necessary expenses—is only 1 or a few percent.

Mass merchandisers and discounters like to operate on gross margins and markups of 15 to 30 percent but, as shown in this table, conventional retailers usually require much higher percentages. This table should give you a better idea of the *why* of scrambled merchandising and suggest possible directions it will take. This table shows, for example, why scramblers want to sell bakery goods, jewelry, appliances, refreshments, and gifts. Try to analyze why some of the conventional retailers have such high gross margins and why other types of retailers can operate more economically.

Retailer size and channel system thinking

■ As already noted, mass production is not the only source of economies related to larger size. A few specific comments on how the advantages and disadvantages of larger size apply to retailing will help show why some retailers have grown and why channel system thinking is vital.

Small size may be hard to overcome

■ The small independent retailer may satisfy his own psychic needs by being his own boss, and he can be very helpful to some target customers because of his flexibility. But his shop may only *seem* profitable because some of the costs of doing business are ignored. He may not be allowing for depreciation or for family members clerking or keeping books without pay. Sometimes he can keep the doors open only because he operates the store and has a full-time job elsewhere. As we noted already, about 580,000 small retailers gross less than $30,000 of sales annually, which, after expenses, leaves hardly enough to support one person.

Even the average retail store is too small to gain economies of size. Annual sales for the average store of only $175,000 is not very impressive, especially considering that net profits as a percentage of sales range from 1 to 5 percent. We gain some perspective on size when we realize that a grocery supermarket sells more than $1 million worth of goods per year!

But although larger stores may be able to buy in quantity at lower prices, take advantage of mass advertising, and hire specialists, larger size alone does not guarantee more efficient operation. A large department store may be made up of many small-scale specialty shops and limited-line stores that require special management skills. Leasing of some departments – optical goods, hats, restaurants – may be necessary if specialized skill is required to operate them. Moreover, the departments in a department store might not be any larger than independent limited-line stores, and so there may be little or no possibility for volume buying.

Being in a chain may help

■ The disadvantages of small size, even among large department stores, has led to chain operations to achieve the benefits of large-scale operations.

Chains grew slowly until after World War I, then spurted ahead during the 1920s. The first Census of Distribution in 1929, designed in part to determine the importance of chains, found that more than 7,000 chain organizations controlled about 21 percent of all retail sales and a much larger share in certain lines. This discovery caused a number of states to pass antichain store legislation. The Robinson-Patman Act of 1936 was intended, in part, to stop certain chain store practices, especially demanding and getting lower prices because of their size.

This legislative reaction may have inhibited some managements. Chains did continue to grow, but at a less dramatic rate. In 1948,

23 percent, and in 1969 about 29 percent, of the country's retail sales were made by chain stores.

Chains have done even better in certain lines. Variety store chains have 80 percent of sales in that field. Department store chains are an important factor across the nation in selling general merchandise. Such chains as Sears, Montgomery Ward, and J. C. Penney are in this category.

Independents form chains too

■ One of the reasons chain store sales have been climbing recently is that chain management is paying more attention to achieving the economies of scale in distribution, either corporately or through administered systems. We already have mentioned corporate chains, but here we must note the development of cooperative and voluntary chains.

Retailer-owned *cooperative chains* are formed by independent retailers in their efforts to compete with chains. They band together to set up their own wholesaling organization, and cooperation in such groups has enabled many "independents" to meet chain competition effectively. Sales of cooperative chains have been rising.

Wholesaler-sponsored *voluntary chains,* operating similarly to cooperative chains except that they are sponsored by wholesalers, also have been most helpful to the "independent" retailers. Some are linked together by contracts specifying common operating procedures and the use of common storefront design, store name, and joint promotional efforts. Examples include IGA and Super Valu in groceries, Ace in hardware, and Western Auto in auto supplies.

Franchising is similar

■ *Franchise operations* – such as McDonald's Carry-Out Restaurants and Colonel Sander's fried chicken shops – are similar to voluntary chains. Someone has developed a good marketing strategy, and the members of the group carry it out. The voluntary chains have tended to work with existing retailers, whereas franchisers like to work with newcomers whom they train and get started. Sometimes they will locate the site, as well as supervise building and the initial promotion and opening.[22]

Cooperatives are something else

■ Cooperative and voluntary chains should not be confused with *consumer cooperatives,* which are groups of *consumers* who have banded together into voluntary buying associations and normally operate on a nonprofit basis with voluntary or poorly paid management. These consumer cooperatives have never been sizable in the United States, their high point being 1 percent of retail sales in 1954.

Such cooperatives have been more successful in Europe where most retailers apparently have been high priced and inefficient. Most U.S. markets, on the other hand, have been so competitive that the cooperative patronage dividends, basic to co-op customer loyalty, have not been attractive enough to keep the customers coming to the typically out-of-the-way store for the (sometimes) unknown or co-op dealer brands.

The fate of consumer cooperatives is further evidence that size or goodwill alone do not make an efficient channel system. Economies of scale may be possible, but it takes some hardheaded business decisions to link the members of a channel system efficiently. As always, the final test is customer approval. Some large horizontal and vertical linked systems seem to be getting this approval.

What does the future look like?

■ The changes in retailing in the last 30 years have been extremely rapid. No end to this pace seems to be in sight. Scrambled merchandising may become more scrambled. Some analysts are forecasting larger stores while others are predicting smaller ones.

The new
age of
servoselling

■ Any effort to forecast trends in such a situation is extremely risky, but the market grid approach can be helpful. Those who suggest bigger and bigger supermarkets and discount houses may be primarily concerned with the mass market. Those who look for more small stores and specialty shops may be anticipating more small but increasingly affluent target markets which are able to afford higher prices for different products.

To serve these smaller but affluent markets, small, convenience-type grocery stores may continue to spread, and sales by vending machines — even with their higher operating costs and prices — may grow steadily. Certainly, some customers are getting tired of the large supermarkets that take so much of their time. Logically, convenience goods should be offered at the customer's, rather than the retailer's convenience, as has been the case. Some retailers still fight night and weekend hours, for example, when it is most convenient for many families to shop.

Telephone shopping is another possibility. The catalog houses and department stores already find phone business attractive. Telephone supermarkets, now a reality, sell only by phone and deliver all orders. Linking the phone to closed-circuit TV would enable the customer to see the goods at home while hearing well-prepared sales presentations. Then the customer could place an order through a small computer system or through a telephone system and have the billing and delivery arranged automatically. Simpsons-Sears, Ltd., in Toronto, is experimenting with just such a system. Customers with Touchtone telephones are placing their own orders straight into an IBM 360–65 computer. Along with taking the order, the computer automatically checks the customer's credit and the company's inventory levels. If there is any problem, a human operator will call the customer. Otherwise this selling process is completely automated.[23]

We now have far greater electronic capabilities than we are using. There seems to be no reason why the customer couldn't shop from his home instead of traipsing up and down the aisles of larger and larger shopping facilities. Such automated retailing – perhaps the equipment involved would warrant the name "servoselling" – could take over a large share of the convenience good and homogeneous shopping good business. The super-stores may be a first step in this direction. The next step may be to eliminate any need for actually going to such a store.

Retailers becoming manufacturers and vice versa

■ We also may see more horizontally and vertically administered channel systems. This would have a major impact on present manufacturers who already see retailers developing their own brands and using manufacturers primarily as production arms.

The large manufacturers themselves may go into retailing in the future for self-protection. General Electric and Westinghouse are experimenting along this line. But they would not be the first, since Rexall Corp., Sherwin-Williams, B. F. Goodrich, Van Heusen, and others already control or own retail outlets.[24]

The function of retailing clearly will continue to be needed, but the role of individual retailers, and even the concept of a retail store, may have to undergo considerable change. There will always be customers' needs and they will probably want to satisfy these needs with combinations of goods and services. But retail stores are not necessarily the best way of accomplishing this in all cases.

Renting may eliminate buying

■ Just as builders of tract homes shifted some home appliance sales from retailers, the builders of new cities may sell completely furnished homes and eliminate the need for retail home furnishing stores. And catering to the mobile young, apartment builders may rent furnished apartments or offer assortments of furniture for rent from a selection owned by the management. This may fit the needs more precisely of a mobile population less interested in the possession of goods. But it will also have a direct impact on present retailers. Many may just not be needed at all!

Retailers must face the challenge

■ One thing is certain – change in retailing is inevitable. For years, traditional retailers' profits have declined. Even some of the newer discounters and shopping centers have had disappointing records. Department stores and food and drug chains have experienced profit declines. The old variety stores have fared even worse. Some are shifting into mass merchandising operations, and that picture is less attractive now.

A few firms, among them Sears, J. C. Penney, and Kresge have avoided this general profit squeeze. But generally, declining profits have helped cause the sometimes desperate moves into scrambled merchandising. Where it will all end is not yet clear, but it is safe to say that the imaginative marketing manager will find opportunities as well as problems in this unsettled situation.

Conclusion

■ Modern retailing is scrambled, and we will probably see even more changes in the future. In such a dynamic environment, a producer's marketing manager must choose among the available retail facilities very carefully. Or a retailer's marketing manager must plan his offering with his target customers' needs in mind, while at the same time assuring that he is part of an effective channel system.

We described a wide variety of retail facilities, and saw that each has its advantages and disadvantages. We also saw that modern retailers have abandoned conventional practices. The old "buy low and sell high" philosophy is no longer an effective guide. Faster turnover with lower margins seems to be the more common philosophy as retailers move from discounting into mass merchandising. But even this is no guarantee of success as retailers' product life cycles move on.

Scrambled merchandising will probably continue as the many competitors seek ways of developing differential advantage. But retailing is not completely chaotic. The market grid concept helps to understand what has been going on and what is likely to go on. And some generalizations about the development of retailing institutions are possible. These can be summarized as follows:

1. Certain types of retailing facilities are extremely stable. It is likely that in every city in the country there are stores with ancient Roman counterparts, such as limited-line food and clothing stores.

2. Although the development of new retailers has frequently been viewed with alarm by conventional retailers, these newcomers have tended (a) to become a stable part of the retailing system, and (b) now account for only a relatively small percentage of retail sales. This has been true for the department store chains, mail-order houses, and most recently, discount houses.

3. Changes in retail institutions appear to be evolutionary, not revolutionary, and usually reflect changes at the consumer level. Even changes caused by uncontrollable variables – the laws passed in the political environment, for instance – may be traced to the consumer. When very rapid changes do occur, it is usually because orthodox retailers have not recognized, or made adjustment to, changes in consumer behavior. Unmet demands open the door to innovators, and then conventional retailers may have to make swift and dramatic modifications to catch up. Such a situation very well may be in the making now.

questions and problems

1 Identify a specialty store selling convenience goods in your city. Explain why you feel it is that kind of a store and why an awareness of this status would be important to a manufacturer. Does it give the retailer any particular advantage? If so, with whom?

2 What sort of a "Product" are specialty shops offering? What are the prospects for organizing a chain of specialty shops?

3 A department store consists of many departments. Is this horizontal integration? Are all of the advantages of horizontal integration achieved in a department store operation?

4 Many department stores have a bargain basement. Does the basement represent just another department, like the hat department or the luggage department for example, or is some whole new concept involved?

5 Distinguish among discount houses, discount selling, and mass merchandising. Forecast the future of low-price selling in food, clothing, and appliances.

6 In view of the wide range of gross margins (and expenses) in various lines of trade, sug-gest what the supermarket or scrambled merchandising outlet of the future may be like. Use care here. Are products with high gross margins necessarily highly profitable?

7 List five products which seem suitable for automatic vending and yet are not normally sold in this manner. Generally, what characteristics are required?

8 Apply the "Wheel of Retailing" hypothesis to your local community. What changes seem likely? Does it seem likely that established retailers will see the need for change or will entirely new firms have to develop?

9 Discuss the kinds of markets served by the three types of shopping centers. Are they directly competitive? Do they contain the same kinds of stores? Is the long-run outlook for all of them similar?

10 Explain the growth and decline of various types of retailers and shopping centers in your own community, using the market grid and product life-cycle concepts and treating the retailers' total offering as a "Product."

notes

[1] Martineau, "The Pattern of Social Classes," in R. L. Clewett (ed.) *Marketing's Role in Scientific Management* (Chicago: American Marketing Association, 1957) p. 234.

[2] See also: "Apparel Salesmen Take Samples to the Party," *Business Week*, July 15, 1967, pp. 148–52.

[3] See, for instance, a description of the operation of a sporting goods retailer of this type (Abercrombie & Fitch), "Caterer to the Outdoor Man," *Business Week*, December 16, 1961, pp. 84–89; see also "Abercrombie's Hunts for a Comeback," *Business Week*, October 21, 1972, p. 21.

[4] "The Merchant Prince of Dallas," *Business Week*, October 21, 1967, pp. 115–18 f; and "The Showdown at Post Oak," *Business Week*, February 28, 1970, pp. 124–25.

[5] Louis H. Grossman, "Merchandising Strategies of a Department Store Facing Change," *MSU Business Topics*, Winter 1970, pp. 31–42; "Suburban Malls Go Downtown," *Business Week*, November 10, 1973, pp. 90–94.

[6] "Anti-Trust Verdict Rocks the Stores," *Business Week*, July 26, 1969, p. 29.

[7] "Vendors Pull Out All Stops," *Business Week*, August 15, 1970, pp. 52–54; "Vending in 1964, and Vending in 1961," National Automatic Merchandising Association, Chicago, Ill.; and Malcolm L. Morris, "Growth Parameters for Automatic Vending," *Journal of Retailing*, Fall 1968, pp. 31–45.

[8] Douglas J. Dalrymple, "Will Automatic Vending Topple Retail Precedence?" *Journal of Retailing*, Spring 1963, pp. 27–31.

[9] Paul E. Smith, "Prescription for a Successful Shopping Center," *Business Topics*, Autumn 1966, p. 17; see also "Suburban Malls Are Trying Harder," *Business Week*, March 9, 1974, p. 53; "He Builds Shopping Centers Around the World," *Business Week*, December 1, 1973, pp. 47–50; "Suburban Malls Go Downtown," *Business Week*, November 10, 1973, pp. 90–94.

[10] "The FTC Zeroes In on Shopping Centers," *Business Week*, February 19, 1972, p. 22; and "Shopping Centers and New York State's Retail Economy," *New York State Commerce Review*, September 1958, p. 2.

[11] David Appel, "The Supermarket: Early Development of an Institutional Innovation," *Journal of Retailing*, Spring 1972, pp. 39–53.

[12] *Progressive Grocer*, April 1973, p. 97 and April 1970, p. 53.

[13] Discount selling and discount houses have been discussed extensively in the literature. See a special-interest

bibliography compiled by S. C. Hollander, *Discount Selling, Retail Price-cutting, and Resale Price Controls* (Chicago: American Marketing Association, 1956).

[14] "Discount Catalogs: A New Way To Sell," *Business Week*, April 29, 1972, pp. 72–74; and "Catalog Discounting Is A Small Man's Game," *Business Week*, October 13, 1973, pp. 70–76.

[15] For a description of a discount house that has gone through these stages—Polk Brothers in Chicago—see "Chicago's Red Hot Merchandiser," *Fortune*, September, 1955, pp. 130–54.

[16] Mass Merchandisers: A Pause in Growth? *Nielsen Researcher* No. 4 (1973).

[17] "Hard Times Hit the Discount Stores," *Business Week*, February 10, 1973, pp. 87–90.

[18] "Carrefour: A Superdiscounter Eyes the U.S.," *Business Week*, December 15, 1973, p. 78–80; *Business Week*, February 24, 1973, p. 48, and *Grey Matter*, vol. 44, no. 11, November 1973.

[19] Walter J. Salmon, Robert D. Buzzell, and Stanton G. Cort, "Today the Shopping Center, Tomorrow the Superstore," *Harvard Business Review*, January–February 1974, pp. 89–98; "Super-stores May Suit Customers to a T—a T-Shirt or a T-Bone," *The Wall Street Journal*, March 13, 1973, 1f; and *The Super-Store—Strategic Implications For the Seventies*, the Marketing Science Institute, Cambridge, Mass., 1972.

[20] Stanley C. Hollander, "Retailing: Cause or Effect?" in William F. Decker, *Emerging Concepts in Marketing*, American Marketing Association, December, 1962, pp. 220–30.

[21] For more discussion on gridding of retail markets, see "Fast-Food Franchisers Invade the City," *Business Week*, April 22, 1974, pp. 92–93; "Korvettes Tries for a Little Chic," *Business Week*, May 12, 1973, pp. 124–26; Philip D. Cooper, "Will Success Produce Problems for the Convenience Store?" *MSU Business Topics*, Winter 1972, pp. 39–43; "Levitz: The Hot Name in 'Instant' Furniture," *Business Week*, December 4, 1971, pp. 90–93; David L. Appel, "Market Segmentation—A Response to Retail Innovation," *Journal of Marketing*, April 1970, pp. 64–67; Steven R. Flaster, "A Consumer Approach to the Specialty Store," *Journal of Retailing*, Spring 1969, pp. 21–31; A. Coskun Samli, "Segmentation and Carving a Niche in the Market Place," *Journal of Retailing*, Summer 1968, pp. 35–49.

[22] E. H. Lewis and R. Hancock, *The Franchise System of Distribution* (Minneapolis: University of Minnesota Press, 1963). See also, the special issue on franchising in the *Journal of Retailing*, Winter 1968–69.

[23] *Business Week*, October 27, 1973, p. 60.

[24] "Westinghouse Tries Its Hand at Appliance Retailing in Deal with West Coast Chain," *Business Week*, August 5, 1967, p. 57.

Wholesaling

■ Wholesaling is extremely important in the marketing process. Wholesalers are a vital link in many channel systems. To understand their role better, you should look at wholesalers primarily as members of channels rather than separate entities.

In this chapter we will discuss how wholesalers have evolved, how they fit into various channels, why they are used, or, more specifically, what functions they perform.

What is a wholesaler?

■ This question is hard to answer precisely, but one way to get at the definition is to find out why a given firm wants to be considered a wholesaler rather than a retailer. There are several reasons why he might seek this classification.

How to tell a wholesaler from a retailer

■ *First*, in some channels, manufacturers permit only wholesalers to buy directly from them. The wholesalers, in turn, are expected to sell only to retailers. Exactly which firms will be permitted to buy from the manufacturer depends on how the manufacturer defines what a wholesaler is.

Second, and related to the first point, is the amount of discount granted. If retailers in a certain line normally expect a 30 percent discount off the suggested retail list price, then the wholesalers supplying them may be given a 45 percent discount off retail list. They, in turn, are expected to pass on a 30 percent discount to their retailers. In practice, this can be much more complicated.

Some manufacturers set up a scale of wholesale discounts depending on the size of the wholesaler and the services he offers. Called "trade discounts," these are discussed further in the Pricing chapters. Correctly determining which firms are entitled to what trade discounts is especially important to manufacturers because of the provisions of the Robinson-Patman Act, prohibiting price discrimination and discriminatory discounts.

Third, some cities and states have retail sales taxes or taxes on inventories or gross receipts that apply only to retailers. These levies require record keeping and occasionally out-of-pocket costs when the retailer fails to collect the tax from the consumer. It is natural, therefore, that some firms should try to avoid classification as a retailer.

Fourth, fair-trade laws usually are binding only on retail sales to consumers. Some discount houses have sold below the fair-trade price to consumers who were buying as "wholesalers." Being a member of a buying group – such as a labor union, church group, or local business concern – was sufficient rationalization for the purpose. Interestingly, some discount houses, although operating as wholesalers to avoid the manufacturer's ire, have not wished to risk prosecution by state taxing units and have charged a retail sales tax on these "wholesale" sales.

Any of these four points explains why a firm might wish to be labeled a wholesaler rather than a retailer. The *fifth* point operates in reverse. Some retailers, but not wholesalers, are exempt from federal minimum-wage legislation, including the requirement that overtime be paid for more than 40 hours' labor a week.[1] •

A wholesaler – by any other name – is still a middleman

■ Despite the apparent difficulty in writing a single, hard definition of wholesaling, the *main* source of confusion is not simply semantic, but rather the wide variation in how wholesale firms operate – the functions performed, the cost of operations, and the operating policies followed.

Many wholesalers perform more functions than we traditionally associate with the term. Some wholesalers engage in all four of the regrouping steps, and some of their sorting-out and accumulation activities may even seem like manufacturing. As a result, we find some firms calling themselves manufacturer and jobber, or manufacturer and dealer. In addition, some use general terms such as merchant, dealer, distributor, or jobber because their actual operations are flexible, and they do not wish to be narrowly classified.

To avoid a prolonged technical and semantic discussion, we will use the U.S. Bureau of Census definition, the essence of which is:

Wholesaling is concerned with the activities of those persons or establishments which sell to retailers and other merchants, and/ or to industrial, institutional, and commercial users, but who do not sell in significant amounts to ultimate consumers.

It should be noted that producers who take over wholesaling functions are not considered wholesalers. However, if separate establishments, such as branch warehouses, are set up, those facilities are counted as wholesalers by the U.S. Bureau of Census.

Wholesaling is a middleman activity. When a manufacturer goes direct, he still must assume the marketing functions that an independent wholesaler might provide. This is important from a channel standpoint. Wholesaling functions usually must be performed by some channel member, whether a wholesaler or the manufacturer himself.

Possible wholesaling functions

■ Wholesalers may perform certain functions for both their own customers and their suppliers — in short, for those above and below them in a channel. These wholesaling tasks really are elaborations of the basic marketing functions — buying, selling, grading, storing, transporting, financing, risk-taking, and gathering market information. These wholesaling functions are basic to the subsequent discussion and should be studied carefully now. But *keep in mind that these functions are provided by some, but not all, wholesalers.*

What a
wholesaler
might do for
his customers

■ 1. *Anticipate needs.* As a purchasing agent for his customers, the wholesaler forecasts his customers' demands and buys accordingly.

2. *Regroup goods.* The wholesaler provides at least one and sometimes all four of the regrouping steps in an effort to provide the assortment wanted by his customers at the lowest possible cost.

3. *Carry stocks.* The wholesaler carries inventory, relieving his customers of the necessity to carry a full inventory.

4. *Deliver goods.* The wholesaler frequently has transportation facilities and can provide prompt delivery service at low cost. Speed may be essential to keep factory production lines rolling or to satisfy a retailer's customers.

5. *Grant credit.* The wholesaler has traditionally extended credit to many of his customers, sometimes for several months. This financing function may be especially important to small customers and is sometimes the reason why they buy through wholesalers rather than directly from the manufacturer. Generally, the smaller the customer, the more financially dependent he is on wholesalers.

6. *Provide information and advisory service.* The wholesaler and his salesmen may be specialists in the products in which they deal. They are in a position to provide price and technical information as well as suggestions on how to install and sell products.

7. *Provide part of buying function.* Many customers appreciate the wholesaler having salesmen call on them. This relieves customers of the responsibility of looking for supply sources — that is, it simplifies *their* buying function. They have only to evaluate the worth of the various products offered.

8. *Own and transfer title to goods.* Ownership of inventory per-

mits a wholesaler and his customer to complete a sale without benefit of other intermediaries (such as a manufacturer or broker), thus facilitating the whole transaction.

What a wholesaler might do for his producer-suppliers

■ 1. *Provide part of producer's selling function.* The wholesaler sometimes seeks out supply sources, decreasing the number of salesmen the producer needs. The wholesaler also may participate in the producer's advertising and sales promotion programs.

2. *Store inventory.* The classic wholesaling function of storing reduces a manufacturer's need for carrying large stocks, reducing his warehousing expenses.

3. *Help finance by owning stocks.* Some producers, especially small ones, need financial assistance. When the wholesaler carries inventory, this reduces the producer's need for working capital.

4. *Reduce credit risk.* A producer's customers—retailers and other producers—may be numerous, and some may be poor credit risks. It is expensive for a small producer, especially one far distant, to evaluate all of these potential credit risks when selling only one or a few products. The wholesaler who sells these customers many products is in a better position to evaluate their credit status. And if the wholesaler is a source of supply of many products, the customer may be more likely to pay him than to pay a manufacturer from whom he may not reorder.

5. *Provide market information.* The wholesaler is closer to the consumer and is in a better position to evaluate customer reactions. As an informed buyer and seller, he may reduce the producer's needs for market research.

Kinds and costs of available wholesale facilities

■ Table 18–1 lists the types, number, sales volume, and operating expenses of wholesalers operating in 1967, the latest date for which complete Census data is available. The differences in operating expenses suggest that each of these types performs or does not perform certain wholesaling functions. But which ones and why?

Why, for example, do manufacturers use merchant wholesalers costing 13.8 percent of sales when manufacturers' branches with stock cost only 11.3 percent?

Why use either when brokers cost only 3.2 percent?

Is the use of wholesalers with higher operating expenses the reason why marketing costs are high—if, in fact, they are?

Historical background will help answer these questions.

Each wholesaler found his niche

■ In this text, we are emphasizing the evolutionary character of change in our economy. This concept applies fully to wholesaling. America has transformed itself from colonial territory, dependent on the mother country for its finished goods in exchange for its

Table 18–1

Wholesale trade, 1967, United States, by type of operation

Type of operation	Establish-ments (number)	Sales (000,000)	Operating expenses (including payroll) percent of sales
United States, total	311,464	$459,476	
Merchant wholesalers' total	212,993	206,055	13.8%
Wholesale merchants' distributors	204,783	181,776	14.8
Importers	5,171	10,354	10.3
Exporters	2,272	9,508	4.1
Terminal grain elevators	767	4,418	4.5
Manufacturers' sales offices, sales branches, total:	30,679	157,097	7.2
Manufacturers' sales branches (with stock)	16,709	67,175	11.3
Manufacturers' sales offices (without stock)	13,970	89,922	4.1
Petroleum bulk plants, terminals, LP gas facilities, total	30,229	24,822	0.3
Merchandise agents, brokers, total	26,462	61,347	4.0
Auction companies	1,594	4,792	2.9
Merchandise brokers	4,373	14,030	3.2
Commission merchants	5,425	14,068	3.4
Import agents	270	1,791	2.2
Export agents	548	3,372	1.9
Manufacturers' agents	12,106	15,257	6.4
Selling agents	1,891	6,890	4.2
Purchasing agents and resident buyers	11,101	10,156	8.6
Assemblers of farm products, total	255	1,147	3.6

Source: *1967 Census of Business.*

raw materials, into a prime industrial nation. As output grew, so did the need for middlemen to handle it.

To serve the retail general stores of earlier times, early wholesalers carried a wide line of merchandise. They were called "general merchandise" wholesalers because their merchandise was so varied. We already have seen that the general store developed into a single- or limited-line store as towns grew and more goods became available. To serve these stores, "single-line" wholesalers evolved; those specializing in very narrow lines were called "specialty" wholesalers. Single-line wholesalers were well established in the eastern grocery and dry goods fields by the early 1800s. This same evolution took place a little later in the markets farther west.

Since wholesaling developed to distribute the greater production of the factories to an expanding population, wholesalers served not only retailers and final consumers but also manufacturers. Many manufacturers were so small that it was hard for them to contact the growing number of wholesalers or other manufacturer customers, and special wholesalers—called agents and brokers—developed to make these contacts. In general, specialized needs arose, and specialized wholesaling institutions developed to meet them.

Learn the pure to understand the real

■ One of a wholesaler's principal assets is his customer list. He attempts to offer a unique service to certain customers and may be the only one who does this particular job. The manufacturer who wishes to reach the market segment served by this wholesaler *may have to use him.* Who each possible wholesaler serves should be one of the first questions asked by a channel planner.

The next important question would be what functions does a particular wholesaler provide. Wholesalers typically specialize by product line—a fact which should be of considerable interest to product-oriented manufacturers! But they do provide different functions.

To get a clear understanding of wholesaling, we will identify and analyze as pure types several specific kinds of wholesalers. In practice, it may be difficult to find examples of these pure types because some wholesalers are hybrids. Further, the names commonly used in a particular trade may be misleading. Some so-called "brokers" actually behave as limited-function merchant wholesalers, and some so-called "manufacturers' agents" operate as full-service wholesalers. This casual use of terminology makes it all the more important for you to thoroughly understand the pure types before trying to understand the hybrids and the names they go under in the business world. Similarly, a manufacturer's or retailer's marketing manager should understand these differences *and* clearly specify *his* place objectives before trying to select suitable wholesalers.

In the following pages, we will discuss the major types of wholesalers which have been identified by the U.S. Bureau of Census to guide its data collection. There are difficulties with any definitional scheme, but this one is workable; and, importantly, detailed data is available by kind of business, by product line, and by geographic territory. Among other things, such detailed data can be valuable in strategic planning—especially in determining if there are potential channel members in a target market and the sales volumes achieved by the present middlemen. Also, because specific wholesalers might place different emphasis on various marketing functions, it is useful to look at each geographic territory as a separate channel-building problem. And this might lead to quite different channels of distribution in different geographic areas.

In international markets, we find the same kinds of wholesalers as we have in the United States, although good data may be lacking. In addition, different names may be used, and this again emphasizes the importance of understanding the pure types.

Merchant wholesalers are the most numerous

■ Merchant wholesalers are the most numerous of all wholesalers. In 1967, they constituted about 68 percent of wholesaling establishments – but handled only 45 percent of wholesale sales.

Their major distinguishing characteristic is that they take title; they assume the ownership of the goods they handle. They also provide some, or all, of the wholesaling functions. The two basic types of merchant wholesalers are: (1) service, sometimes called full-service, wholesalers, and (2) limited-function or limited-service wholesalers. Their labels are suggestive of their difference.

Service wholesalers provide all the functions

■ Service wholesalers normally provide all of the functions discussed previously. Within this basic group are three main subtypes: (1) *general merchandise*, (2) *single line*, and (3) *specialty*.

General merchandise service wholesalers

General merchandise service wholesalers handle a broad variety of nonperishable staple items such as hardware, electrical supplies, plumbling supplies, furniture, drugs, cosmetics, and automobile equipment. With this broad line of convenience and shopping goods, they serve general stores, hardware stores, drugstores, electric appliance shops, and small department stores. In the industrial goods field, the mill supply house (or distributor) operates in a similar way. Somewhat like a hardware store, the industrial supply house carries a broad variety of accessories and supplies.

Single-line or general-line wholesalers

This type of wholesaler differs from general merchandise wholesalers or mill supply distributors in restricting himself to a narrower line – and sometimes to a specific line – such as dry goods, groceries, wearing apparel, paint, hardware, or certain types of industrial tools or supplies. In consumer goods, he services the single and limited-line stores. In industrial goods, he covers a wider geographical area and offers more specialized service.

Specialty wholesalers

This type of wholesaler stocks only a narrow range of products. A *consumer goods* specialty wholesaler might carry only health foods or Oriental foods, rather than a full line of groceries. Or the specialty house might carry only automotive items, selling exclusively to mass merchandisers. One wholesaler, for example, is willing to arrange and stock his mass merchandisers' shelves, an important service to these retailers because their customers' behavior seems to vary according to geography. Final consumers in northern Indiana, for instance, respond to different shelf arrangements and products from those in southern Indiana.

The specialty wholesaler's task is to learn these differences, and adjust stocks and displays accordingly. In this effort, he goes further than most merchant wholesalers – providing some of his customers' selling functions, since displays do most of the selling in mass merchandising outlets.

For industrial goods, a specialty wholesaler might limit himself

Table 18–2
Functions provided by limited-function merchant wholesalers

Limited-function or limited-service merchant wholesalers

	Cash-and-carry	Drop-shipper (desk jobber)	Wagon or truck	Mail-order	Coopera-tives	Rack jobbers
Functions for customer:						
Anticipates needs	X		X	X	X	X
"Regroups" goods (one or more of four steps)	X		X	X	X	X
Carries stocks	X		X	X	X	X
Delivers goods			X		X	X
Grants credit		X	Maybe	Maybe	Maybe	Consignment (in some cases)
Provides information and advisory services		X	Some	Some	X	
Provides buying function		X	X	X	Some	X
Owns and transfers title to goods	X	X	X	X	X	X
Functions for producers:						
Provides producer's selling function	X	X	X	X	X	X
Stores inventory	X		X	X	X	X
Helps finance by owning stocks	X		X	X	X	X
Reduces credit risk	X	X	X	X	X	X
Provides market information	X	X	Some	X	X	Some

to fields requiring technical knowledge or service, perhaps electronics or plastics.

The Cadillac Plastic and Chemical Co., in Detroit, became a specialty wholesaler serving the needs of plastics makers and users alike because neither the large plastics manufacturers nor the merchant wholesalers with wide lines were in a position to give individual advice to the many users (who often have little knowledge of which product would be best for them). Cadillac now carries 10,000 items and sells to 25,000 customers, ranging in size from the very small firms to General Motors.

Limited-function wholesalers —certain functions

■ The limited-function wholesaler, as the name implies, usually provides only certain wholesaling functions. Table 18–2 outlines the services typically provided by the various limited-function merchant wholesalers. It shows what services are, and are not provided by each general type.

In the following paragraphs, the main distinguishing characteristics of each of the limited-function wholesalers will be discussed. Wholesalers operating solely or principally as limited-function wholesalers are not numerous; in fact, they are not itemized separately in the 1967 Census of Business. Limited-function wholesalers are, nevertheless, important in some trades.

Cash-and-carry wholesaler

Many small retailers, especially small grocers and garages, are too small to be served profitably by a service wholesaler. Discovering this fact, wholesalers establish a minimum charge or, in some cases, merely refuse to handle certain customers' business. Or, they may establish cash-and-carry subsidiaries to give the small retailer the products he needs in exchange for cash on the counter. This works like a retail store, but for small retailers; it can operate at lower cost because the retailer provides many of the wholesaling functions himself. And using cash-and-carry outlets may enable the small retailer to stay in business.

Drop-shipper (or desk jobber)

A drop-shipper obtains orders from wholesalers, retailers, or industrial users, then passes these orders on to producers, telling them to ship directly to these customers. He takes title and technically owns the goods, but he does not physically handle, stock, or deliver them. This lowers his operating costs.

Drop-shippers most commonly deal in products that are so bulky that additional handling would be expensive and possibly damaging. Or the quantities may be so large that there is little need for regrouping, as with rail carload shipments of coal, lumber, oil, or chemical products.

The drop-shipper's major function is selling, but he does have to locate supplies, arrange for transportation, finance customer purchases, and assume some of the risks that go with taking title to goods.

Wagon or truck wholesaler

This wholesaler is always on the go, selling his stock from a wagon or truck. Handling perishable commodities in general demand, such as tobacco, candy, potato chips, and salad dressings, the truck jobber may provide almost the same functions as a full-service wholesaler. His major contribution is delivery of perishable lines that regular wholesalers prefer not to carry because of the special problems involved.

Truck wholesalers sometimes supply small service stations and back-alley garages with local delivery of the many small items they often forget to pick up from the service wholesaler. Truck wholesaler operating cost ratios are relatively high because they do a lot for the little they sell.

Mail-order wholesaler

We discussed catalog selling in the chapter on retailing. Wholesale mail-order houses operate in much the same way. In fact, many wholesale mail-order houses also will sell to *final* consumers who may, in some way, have access to their wholesale catalogs. To bona

fide retailers, however, wholesalers give special discounts for ordering larger quantities. Otherwise, all the advantages and disadvantages of mail-order selling apply here. These houses operate in
the hardware, jewelry, sporting goods, and general merchandise
lines, often catering to small outlying stores.

Producers' cooperative

Producers' cooperatives are also limited-function wholesalers,
although they frequently attempt to give the same service as
service wholesalers. Here, the "profits" go to the cooperative's
customer-members – in the form of patronage dividends.

The successful producers' cooperatives have emphasized the
sorting-out process – to improve the quality of farm products offered to the market. They have also branded these improved products and then promoted the brands. These farmers' cooperatives
sometimes have had success in restricting output and increasing
price by taking advantage of the normally inelastic demand for
agricultural commodities.

Examples of such organizations are the California Fruit Growers
Exchange (citrus fruits), Sunmaid Raisin Growers Association, The
California Almond Exchange, and Land O'Lakes Creameries, Inc.

Aside from demand stimulation and supply restriction activities,
the cooperatives operate basically as service wholesalers.

Rack jobber – sells nonfoods in food stores

The rack jobber is a relatively new type of wholesaler, catering
mainly to food stores and especially to supermarkets. He specializes
in products, such as housewares, hardware items, and health and
beauty aids, that frequently are displayed on wire racks he provides.

Many grocers don't want to bother with reordering and maintaining displays of nonfood items, since it involves small quantities
of so many different kinds of goods. Regular wholesalers who were
handling such items were not too interested in this business either,
because opening up this new channel might jeopardize relations
with their present customers. While many wholesalers specialize by
product line, the rack jobber must handle a scrambled assortment
because this is what consumers want.

The rack jobber is practically a service wholesaler, except that
he usually is paid cash for the amount of stock sold or delivered.
This is a relatively expensive operation, with operating costs of
about 18 percent of sales. Although the large volume of nonfood
sales from these racks has prompted some large chains to experiment with handling such items themselves, it appears now that
rack jobbers can provide this service as effectively as (or more effectively than) the supermarket chains.

Manufacturers' sales branches provide wholesaling functions

■ The drive toward economic integration that began in the late
1880s had its effect in wholesaling, too. Many manufacturers set
up their own sales branches whenever the sales volume or the

nature of their products warranted it. By 1967, less than 10 percent of wholesale establishments were manufacturers' sales branches, but they handled 34 percent of the total wholesale sales.

One reason for this disproportion is that these branches are usually placed in the most fertile market territories. This helps explain why their operating costs often are lower. But cost comparisons between alternate channels can be misleading, since cost allocation methods may differ. Sometimes the cost of selling is not charged to the branch but to the manufacturer's sales expenses. If all expenses were allocated similarly, it is likely that manufacturers' sales branches would prove more costly than they appear to be.

The U.S. Bureau of Census collects extensive data showing the number, kind, location, and operating expenses of manufacturers' sales branches. Such data can help manufacturers determine competitors' distribution systems and probable costs. If many competitors are going direct, it may mean that there are no good specialists available — or at least none who can provide the functions desired.

Petroleum bulk plants, terminals, and LP gas facilities

■ Another major census bureau wholesale classification (see Table 18–1) covers petroleum distribution. These specialized wholesalers work closely with the major oil companies. We will not treat them in detail here, since their major contribution to the marketing process is providing storage and handling facilities that are not generally applicable to other marketing management problems.

Agents and brokers are strong on selling

They do not take title

■ All merchant wholesalers at least take title to the goods, even when they do not actually handle them. These are the middlemen that most people picture when thinking of wholesalers. Yet there is another important group of middlemen — the merchandise agents and brokers — who do *not* take title. Their main service is to facilitate the buying and selling functions. They normally provide even fewer functions than the limited-function merchant wholesalers. In certain trades, however, their contribution is extremely valuable, and they may operate at relatively low cost, say 2 to 6 percent of selling price.

Agents and brokers, like merchant wholesalers, generally specialize by customer type and by product or product lines, and so it is extremely important to determine exactly what each agent or broker does.

In the following paragraphs, only the most important points about each type of agent or broker will be stressed. For details on the functions provided by each, see Table 18–3, which continues the scheme used for merchant wholesalers, based on functions per-

Table 18–3
Functions of agents and brokers

Functions	Auction companies	Brokers	Commission merchants	Manufacturers' agents	Selling agents
Functions for customers:					
Anticipates needs		Some		Sometimes	
"Regroups" goods (one or more of four stages)	X		X	Some	
Carries stocks	Sometimes		X	Sometimes	
Delivers goods			X	Sometimes	
Grants credit	Some		Sometimes		X
Provides information and advisory services		X	X	X	X
Provides buying function	X	Some	X	X	X
Owns and transfers title to goods	Transfers only		Transfers only		
For producer:					
Provides selling function	X	Some	X	X	X
Stores inventory	X		X	Sometimes	
Helps finance by owning stocks					
Reduces credit risk	Some				X
Provides market information		X	X	X	X

formed. It is obvious from the large number of vacant spaces in Table 18–3 that agents and brokers provide fewer functions than merchant wholesalers.

Auction companies — display the goods

■ Auction companies provide a place where buyers and sellers can come together and complete a transaction. Auction companies are not numerous (see Table 18–1), but they are extremely important in certain lines such as fruit, livestock, fur, tobacco, and used-car markets. For these products, demand and supply conditions change rapidly, and the product must be seen to be evaluated. Buyers and sellers, therefore, are brought together by the auction company, and demand and supply interact to determine the price while the goods are being inspected.

Facilities can be plain, keeping overhead costs low. Frequently, auction sheds are close to transportation facilities so that the commodities can be reshipped quickly. The auction company charges a set fee or commission for the use of its facilities and services.

Brokers — provide information

■ The broker's principal function is to bring buyers and sellers together but, unlike the auction company, his facilities are not crucial. He may not even have a separate office but may operate out of his home, perhaps with the aid of an answering service. His "product" is information about what buyers need and what supplies are available. He aids in buyer-seller negotiation and if the transaction is completed, earns a commission from whichever party engaged him.

Usually, some kind of broker will develop whenever and wherever market information is inadequate. Brokers are especially useful for selling seasonal products. For example, they could represent a small food canner during the canning season, then go on to other activities. Some have expanded their operations, still calling themselves "food brokers," but operating more like manufacturers' agents. They are discussed later.

Brokers also are active in used machinery, real estate, and even ships. These products are dissimilar, but the marketing functions needed are not. In each case, buyers come into the market infrequently, and someone with extensive knowledge of available products is needed to help both buyers and sellers complete the transaction quickly and inexpensively.

Commission merchants— handle and sell the goods

■ Commission merchants are common in agricultural markets. When a producer does not use a local auction to sell his output, he may ship it to a big-city central market. There he needs someone to handle the goods as well as to sell them for him, since it is obviously not practical to accompany every shipment.

Commission merchants have grown up to meet this need. They are especially common in markets for livestock and grain, both commodities that buyers want to inspect and if they so choose, buy immediately. Commission merchants, although they do not take title, are generally permitted to sell goods at the market price or the best price obtainable above some stipulated minimum. They usually are numerous in central markets, each competing with the others and trying to get the highest price for his producer-sellers. Since prices in these markets usually are a matter of public record, the producer-seller has a check on the performance of his commission merchant. Usually costs are low because commission merchants handle large volumes of goods and buyers usually come to their central market location.

A commission merchant is similar to a broker, except that he actually handles goods, completes transactions, and remits the selling price (less his commission) to the seller.

Commission merchants sometimes are used in other trades, too, such as textiles, where many small producers wish to reach buyers in a central market without having to maintain their own sales forces.

Manufacturers' agents— freewheeling salesmen

■ A manufacturers' agent works for several manufacturers almost as if he were each company's own salesman. He may cover one city or several states. If the sales potential of an area is low, he may be used in lieu of a company's own salesmen. Or a small firm may have to use agents everywhere because sales volume is inadequate to support a sales force.

Manufacturers' agents can be useful in any field where many small manufacturers need representation. They are used frequently in the sale of machinery and equipment, dry goods, electrical goods, automotive products, clothing and apparel accessories, furniture, and some food products.

Manufacturers' agents usually know their own territory quite well and handle the noncompeting lines of several manufacturers. They work on commission and often can operate profitably in situations where a producer's sales force cannot. This is mainly because they have well-established contacts, detailed knowledge of an industry, and a wide line of goods obtained by representing several companies. This wide product line enables them to spread fixed selling costs over many products.

As with a manufacturer's salesman, the agent's main job is to call on wholesalers or industrial customers or both. Orders picked up are sent to the producer, or the customer sends them directly to the producer, but in either case the agent is credited with the sale. Agents seldom have any voice in setting prices or determining the producer's policies.

As a service to customers, manufacturers' agents sometimes stock goods and make deliveries, but the majority concentrate on sales calls. The producer delivers the merchandise and bills the customers.

The distinguishing characteristic of manufacturers' agents is a rather freewheeling, independent, and aggressive approach to selling — especially in the sale of new products.

When practicing their specialty of developing markets for new products, manufacturers' agents charge a healthy 10 to 15 percent commission. By contrast, their commission for large-volume established goods may be quite low — perhaps only 2 percent. The higher rates often come to be the agent's major disadvantage, from the manufacturer's point of view. The original commission rate may have seemed small when the product was new and sales volume was low, but once the product is selling well and large commissions are going to the agent, the agreed rate may seem high. At about this time, the firm often begins using its own salesmen, and the manufacturers' agent must look for other new products to develop.

Food brokers — fill a gap ■ Food brokers, operating like manufacturers' agents, have become extremely important in grocery distribution. More than half the processed goods handled by grocery stores is sold by these brokers.

Food brokers call on grocery wholesalers and large retailers for their manufacturer clients. Some aggressive food brokers have become quite involved with their client's marketing strategy planning — more than the typical manufacturers' agent. They may even work closely with the producer's advertising agency.[2] They are consulted for these roles because they are so intimately familiar with their territory.

For the usual commission of 5 percent of sales, these firms may take over the entire selling function for a manufacturer. Some even suggest what prices and advertising allowances should be offered to particular retailers. For a small manufacturer, they can perform a vital service; for large firms with many small divisions they can be equally helpful.

Each food broker organization specializes in a given territory. Most manufacturers can achieve national distribution with between 70 and 100 food brokers.

The food broker fills a gap in the sales efforts of many manufacturers. The brokers generally have an effective sales force because they pay their salesmen well and keep them in the field. In contrast, manufacturers often use their sales territories as training grounds, and promote their good salesmen to larger territories or home offices as soon as (and sometimes before) they have really become effective in their sales areas.

Selling agents — almost marketing managers

■ The selling agent operates somewhat like the manufacturers' agent, only he may handle competing lines. He usually takes over the whole *marketing* job nationally — not just the *sales* contacts in one area. He handles the entire output of one or more producers and has almost complete control of pricing, selling, and advertising. In effect, he becomes each producer's marketing manager.

Financial trouble is one of the main reasons a producer calls in a selling agent. The selling agent may provide working capital, but in turn he may take over the affairs of the business.

These agents have been especially common in highly competitive fields such as textiles and coal, and they also have been used for marketing lumber, certain food products, clothing items, and some metal products. In all these industries, marketing is much more important than production for the survival of firms. The selling agent provides the necessary financial assistance and marketing know-how.

International marketing is not so different

■ We find agents in international trade, too. Most operate much like those just described. *Export* or *import agents* are basically manufacturers' agents. *Export* or *import commission houses* and *export* or *import brokers* are really brokers. A *combination export manager* serves as a blend of a manufacturers' agent and a selling agent, handling the entire export function for a number of manufacturers of allied but noncompetitive lines.

As with domestic agents, it is necessary to determine exactly what functions each institution provides before deciding to use it in a channel system. Agents are more common in international trade because of the critical problem of financing in that field. Many markets include only a few well-financed merchant wholesalers. The best many manufacturers can do is obtain local representation through agents and then arrange for financing directly, often through banks with specialized services in international trade.

Assemblers of farm products help farmers *and* others in channel

■ Assemblers are specialists in agricultural products. As already indicated, there are many small producers in the agricultural market. Output must be accumulated and sorted to ship it to market in the most economical quantities. Once accumulation and sorting are completed, the wholesalers already described may handle these commodities.

The specialists who do the sorting and accumulation are assemblers. They also usually handle transportation, storage, grading, and financing, taking the risks these functions involve. The assembler's costs may be relatively modest, but for perishable items such as fresh fruits and vegetables, operating expenses may exceed 25 percent of their sales. Such high handling costs help explain why farmers receive only 10 to 25 percent of the retail price for some agricultural commodities.

Other specialized middlemen fill unique roles

Factors— like a credit department

■ Factors are important specialists in financing. In effect, they are wholesalers of credit. They buy their clients' accounts receivables. Usually they specialize in certain lines of trade and are willing to extend credit for longer periods than commercial banks. Sometimes factors provide management advice or assistance and almost become selling agents. In fact, some are former selling agents who have concentrated on financing rather than selling. Like selling agents, factors are especially common in the highly competitive textile industry.

In buying accounts receivables, factors provide their clients with working capital. The factor's lending charge varies from 6 to 18 percent, depending on interest rates and whether he has any recourse to the seller for collection in case of nonpayment. He may charge extra for his advice in customer selection and collection, and these additional charges may be 1 to 3 percent of the invoice face value. In effect, the factor may assume the function of a credit department, relieving his client of this expense.

Usually factors have many clients in a given line, such as textiles, and so are able to spread their risks over many customers. By specializing in a certain line, they get to know most of the buyers in the trade and are better able to evaluate the credit risks. One result is that while a buyer, for example, might be willing to delay payment to a single seller, he might not run a similar risk when he owes money to a factor. The factor might seriously hurt his credit rating or even cut off all future credit.

Field ware-housemen — cash for goods on hand

■ Another specialist in financing is the field warehousing organization. If a firm has accounts receivable, it can use a factor or even borrow at a bank. But if it has financial problems and its goods are not yet sold, then borrowing may be more difficult. One solution to this problem is to move the goods to a public warehouse and obtain a warehouse receipt, which can then be used as collateral for borrowing at a bank. But moving goods can be expensive.

In field warehousing, the selling company's own warehouse is used, but a portion is formally segregated by the field warehouseman. The seller retains title to his goods, but control of them passes to the field warehouseman. He in turn issues a warehouse receipt, as collateral in borrowing. These field warehousing organizations usually know capital sources and may be able to arrange loans at lower cost than obtainable locally.

Using this method, large stocks may be maintained at various distribution points in anticipation of future needs. Or economical production runs can be made and then stored at the factory against future needs.

Sales finance companies — do floor planning

■ Sales finance companies normally deal only in consumer credit, but a number have become interested in financing inventories for middlemen, especially auto and appliance dealers. This type of financing is called "floor planning." Many auto dealers, for example, do not own outright any of the cars on their display floors. They may have only a 10 percent interest in each of them, the other 90 percent belonging to a sales finance company. The auto dealer has physical possession, but the finance company owns the cars, and the proceeds from sales may go directly to it.

In effect, these companies are providing part of the dealer's financing function. But because the goods are usually well branded, and therefore easily resold, there is relatively little risk. The charge to the dealer for these services may be as low as 10 percent a year, depending on the finance company's cost of borrowing money in the capital markets.

Geographical concentration of wholesalers

Different wholesalers are found in different places

■ Some wholesalers such as petroleum distributors and assemblers, are located close to producers, but the bulk of wholesaling is done in or near large cities. Almost half of all wholesale sales in 1967 were made in the 15 largest Standard Metropolitan Statistical Areas.

This heavy concentration of wholesale sales in large cities is caused, in part, by the concentration of manufacturers' sales offices and branches in these attractive markets. It also is caused by the tendency of agents and brokers to locate in these large cities near the many large wholesalers and industrial buyers. Some large manufacturers buy for many plants through one purchasing department located in the general offices in these cities. And large general merchandise wholesalers often are located in these transportation and commerce hubs.

The prominent role played by the New York City area should be especially noted—13 percent of all wholesale sales. This results partly from the concentration of much of the U.S. wholesale clothing and jewelry industries in this one market. But it also points up the important role played by large commercial cities. This is true not only in the United States but in world markets. Wholesalers tend to concentrate together—near where there are transporting, storing, and financing facilities as well as a large population.

Comeback and future of the wholesaler

■ In the 1800s, the wholesaler held a dominant position in marketing. The many small producers and small retailers needed his services. As producers became larger, some bypassed the wholesaler by setting up their own sales organizations or by selling directly to industrial customers. When retailers also began to grow larger—and especially during the 1920s, when chain stores began to spread rapidly—many predicted a dire future for the wholesaler. Chain stores normally assume the wholesaling functions, and it was thought that the days of the independent wholesaler were numbered.

Not fat and lazy, but enduring

■ Some analysts and critics felt that the decline of the wholesaler might be desirable from the social point of view, for many wholesalers had apparently grown "fat and lazy," contributing little more than breaking bulk. Their salesmen often were only order takers; the selling function was neglected; high-caliber management was not attracted to the wholesaling industry, and it became a domain of vested interests which many persons felt should be eliminated.

Our review here, however, has shown that wholesaling functions *are* necessary, and wholesalers have not been eliminated. True, their sales volume declined from 1929 to 1939, but wholesalers have since made a comeback. By 1954, they had regained the same relative importance they had in 1929, and they have continued to hold their own since then.[3]

Producing profits, not chasing orders

■ Wholesalers have held their own, in part, because of new management and new techniques. To be sure, there are still many operating in the old ways, and wholesaling has had nothing comparable to the rapid changes in retailing. Yet progressive wholesale firms have become more concerned with their customers and with channel systems. Some are offering more services to their independent customers, and others are developing voluntary chains, as noted in Chapter 16, that bind them more closely to their customers. Some of this ordering is done routinely by mail or telephone, or directly by telephone to computer.

Today's *progressive* wholesaler is no longer a passive order taker.

As part of the new look in wholesaling, not only have many salesmen been eliminated, but in place of the old order takers, wholesalers are now using order slips similar to those used between a chain warehouse and chain retail stores.

Some modern wholesalers no longer require all customers to pay for services simply because certain customers use them. This traditional practice had the effect of encouraging limited-function wholesalers and direct channels. Now, some wholesalers are making a basic service available at a minimum cost, then charging additional fees for any special services required. In the grocery field, for instance, the basic servicing of a store might cost the store 3 to 4 percent of wholesale sales. Then promotional assistance and other extra aids are offered at extra cost.

Modern wholesalers also are becoming more selective in picking customers, as cost analysis shows them that many of their smaller customers are clearly unprofitable. With these less desirable customers gone, the wholesaler can give even more attention to preferred customers. In this way, he is helping to promote healthy retailers who are able to compete in any market.

Some wholesalers have renamed their salesmen "store advisers" or "supervisors" to reflect their new roles. These representatives provide many management advisory services, including location analysis; store design and modernization; legal assistance on new leases or adjustments in old leases; store-opening services; sales training and merchandising assistance, and advertising help. Such salesmen, really acting as management consultants, must be more competent than the mere order takers of other days.

Progress — or fail

■ Training a modern wholesaler's salesmen is not an easy task, and it is sometimes beyond the capacity of management in small wholesale firms. In some fields, such as the plumbing industry, wholesaler trade associations have taken the problem in hand. They organize training schools designed to show wholesaler salesmen how they, in turn, can help retailers manage their businesses and promote sales. These schools may give instruction in bookkeeping, figuring a markup, collecting accounts receivable, advertising, and sales planning — all in an effort to train salesmen to improve retailers' effectiveness as channel members.[4]

Some wholesalers are now using electronic data processing systems to control inventory, and in the next chapter, we will see what some wholesalers are doing to modernize their warehouses and physical handling facilities.

Some wholesalers are offering central bookkeeping facilities for their retailers, realizing that their own survival is linked to their customers' survival. In this sense, some wholesalers are becoming more channel system minded, no longer trying to overload retailers' shelves but now trying to clear the merchandise *off* the retailers' shelves.[5] They follow the adage, "Nothing is really sold until it is sold at retail."

Perhaps
goodbye
to some

■ Despite these changes, however, not all wholesalers today are progressive. Many still follow outmoded practices; some of the smaller, less efficient ones may have difficulty in the future. While the average operating expense ratio is 13.8 percent for merchant wholesalers, some small wholesalers have expense ratios of 20 to 30 percent.

Low cost, however, is not the only criterion for success. The higher operating expenses for some smaller wholesalers may be a reflection of the special services they offer to some segments on a market grid. Truck distributors are usually small and have high operating costs, yet some customers are willing to pay the higher cost of this service. Some of the apparently expensive, older, full-service wholesalers probably will continue operating because they offer the services and contacts needed by some small manufacturers. And, of course, some goods and some markets traditionally have slow turnover; wholesalers may be the best choice here even though they have high operating expenses.

Even making these allowances, though, it is clear that the smaller wholesalers and the larger, less progressive ones face future difficulty unless each has carved out a specific market for itself. Profit margins are not large in wholesaling, typically ranging from less than 1 percent to 2 percent. And they have been declining in recent years as the competitive squeeze has become tighter.

In short, the institution of wholesaling certainly will survive, but weaker, less aggressive wholesale firms may not.

Conclusion

■ Wholesalers can provide functions for those both above and below them in a channel of distribution. These services are closely related to the basic marketing functions. There are many types of wholesalers. Some provide all the wholesaling functions while others specialize in only a few. Eliminating wholesalers would not eliminate the need for the functions they provide, and we cannot assume that direct channels will be more efficient.

Merchant wholesalers are the most numerous and account for a sizable share, although not the majority, of wholesale sales. Their distinguishing characteristic is that they take title and often physical possession of goods. Agents and brokers, on the other hand, act more like salesmen for sellers or representatives for buyers, and usually they do not take title or possession.

Despite various predictions of the demise of wholesalers, they continue to exist, and the more progressive ones have adapted to a changing economic environment. No such revolutions as we saw in retailing have yet taken place in the wholesaling area and none seem likely. But it is probable that some smaller and less progressive wholesalers will fail.

questions and problems

1 Discuss the evolution of wholesaling in relation to the evolution of retailing.

2 What risks do merchant wholesalers assume by taking title to goods? Is the size of this risk about constant for all merchant wholesalers?

3 Why would a manufacturer set up his own sales branches if established wholesalers were already available?

4 What is an agent middleman's marketing mix? Why don't manufacturers use their own salesmen instead of agent middlemen?

5 Discuss the future growth and nature of wholesaling if low-margin retailing and scrambled merchandising become more important. How will wholesalers have to adjust their mixes if retail establishments become larger and the retail managers more professional? Might the wholesalers be eliminated? If not, what wholesaling functions would be most important? Are there any particular lines of trade where wholesalers may have increasing difficulty?

6 Which types of wholesalers would be most appropriate for the following products? If more than one type of wholesaler could be used, provide the specifications for the situation in each case. For example, if size or financial strength of a company has a bearing, then so indicate. If several wholesalers could be used in this same channel, explain this also.

a. Fresh tomatoes.

b. Paper-stapling machines.

c. Auto mechanics' tools.

d. Canned tomatoes.

e. Men's shoes.

f. An industrial accessory machine.

g. Ball-point pens.

h. Shoelaces.

7 Would a drop-shipper be most suitable for the following products: coal, lumber, iron ore, sand and gravel, steel, furniture, or tractors? Why, or why not? What channels might be used for each of these products if drop-shippers were not used?

8 Explain how factors differ from commercial banks and why factors developed.

9 Explain how field warehousing could help a marketing manager.

10 Which types of wholesalers are likely to become more important in the next 25 years? Why?

notes

[1] For a detailed discussion of the definition of wholesaling and the operation and management of a wholesale business, see T. N. Beckman, N. H. Engle, and R. D. Buzzell, *Wholesaling,* 3rd ed. (New York: Ronald Press Co., 1959).

[2] "Food Brokers: A Comprehensive Study of Their Growing Role in Marketing," in *Grocery Manufacture* (magazine), December 1969, This and others available from the National Food Brokers Association, 1916 M Street, N.W., Washington, D.C. 20036.

[3] Paul D. Converse, "Twenty-Five Years in Wholesaling: A Revolution in Food Wholesaling," *Journal of Marketing,* July 1957, pp. 40–41; and Richard S. Lopata, "Faster Pace in Wholesaling," *Harvard Business Review,* July–August 1969, pp. 130–43.

[4] *Dealer Development Institute* (Chicago: Central Supply Association.

Physical distribution

■ Physical distribution is the handling and moving of physical goods within individual firms and through channel systems. Nearly half the cost of marketing is spent on physical distribution.

It is very important to the firm and the macro-marketing system, since goods that remain in the factory or on the farm really have no "use" at all. And Possession utility is not possible until Time and Place utility have been provided. This usually requires the transporting and storing functions that are part of physical distribution.

Knowing who will haul and store is essential

■ As any marketing manager develops the Place part of his strategies, he should consider how transporting and storing functions can and should be divided within the channel. Who will store and transport the goods, and who will pay for these services? Merely deciding to use certain types of wholesalers or retailers does not automatically or completely answer these questions. A wholesaler may use his own trucks to haul goods from a producer to his warehouse and from there to retailers, but only because the manufacturer gives him a transportation allowance. Another wholesaler may want the goods delivered to him.

When developing a marketing strategy, the marketing manager must determine precisely how these functions are to be shared, since this will affect the other three Ps, and especially Pricing.

The truth is, however, that there is no ideal sharing arrangement. Physical distribution can be varied endlessly in a marketing mix and in a channel system.

In this chapter, we will discuss different physical distribution possibilities and also some important new developments including the distribution center, the total cost approach, and the physical distribution manager.

The transporting function

From backpacks to cargo planes

■ Before the advent of powered vehicles, transporting activities were slow and limited. The movement of goods was reduced to what a man could carry on his back or haul in a wagon. People lived where the goods were, on self-sufficient farms, and traded their surpluses in nearby markets.

Early societies developed along seacoasts or rivers partly because transportation of goods by water was easier than by land. Yet, most commercial river transportation was still one way – downstream.

And then the introduction of the steamboat in the early 1800s and the first practical steam locomotive in 1829 blasted the barriers that had confined transportation and a whole new era opened up.

In the United States, rail transport made it possible to ship midwestern farm products to the eastern industrial area, lowering food prices considerably. Later, motor trucks and highways brought even small towns and remote farms closer to the markets.

Today, the marketing manager generally has several carriers in one or more modes competing for his transportation business. There are five basic modes of freight movement: railroads, trucks, waterways, pipelines, and airplanes.

Table 19–1 shows the annual volume of intercity freight moved in the United States by each mode. Ton-miles carried is the most common method of measuring the importance of various methods of transportation. A ton-mile represents the movement of a ton of goods one mile. If, for example, 10 tons of sand were carried 10 miles, the total movement would be 100 ton-miles.

Using this measure makes it obvious that railways are the backbone of the U.S. transportation system. Following in consecutive importance are trucks, oil pipelines, and barges. Relatively speaking, airplanes do not yet move a significant volume of freight.

The numbers in the table do not tell the whole story, however, since they do not identify the amount of goods shipped. Information on this subject is sketchy, but it is likely that at least 75 percent of all freight moves by trucks, at least part of the way, from producer to user. Railroads may carry goods for long distances, but trucks haul the bulk of the short-haul movement. The trucking industry slogan, "If you have it, it came by truck," is certainly accurate for consumer goods, although many industrial goods are still delivered by railroads or other transportation modes.

The point to remember is that without transportation, there could be no mass distribution with its regrouping activities or any urban life as we know it today. We understand this most clearly during a major rail or truck strike.

Table 19–1
The intercity freight movement in the United States

| | Ton-miles carried in 1971 | |
	Billions	Percent of total
Railways	$ 746	38.6
Motor Vehicles	430	22.3
Inland Waterways	307	15.9
Pipelines	444	23.0
Airways	3	.2
Total	1,930	100.0

Source: *Statistical Abstract of the United States, 1973,* p. 538.

Transporting can be costly

Can you afford to get to the target?

■ The cost of shipping an average product by rail is about 5 percent of wholesale cost.[1] For many bulky or low-value products, however, the percentage of cost is much higher. Transporting sand and gravel, for example, costs about 55 percent of its value; bituminous coal, 42 percent; cabbage, 38 percent; watermelons, 38 percent; and iron ore, 20 percent. At the other extreme are lighter or more valuable commodities, such as copper ore and copper concentrates and business and office machines, at less than 1 percent of wholesale cost; cigarettes, and butter, less than 2 percent.[2]

Transportation costs may limit the target markets that a producer's or middleman's marketing manager can consider. Shipping costs increase delivered cost, and this is what really interests the customer. High costs for goods in outlying areas, caused by higher transportation costs, encourage local production. The high costs of shipping sand and gravel dictate that these materials be sold in the limited geographical areas near the pits where they are extracted.

If a product is unique in some way, however, customers who really want it will have to bear the transportation costs. A unique clay product selling for only $12.50 a ton in Georgia costs an additional $12 a ton to ship to an Ohio paint factory. A unique paint ingredient, pyrophyllite, costs only $20 a ton in the Carolinas but another $21 a ton to transport to a California paint plant.

Common carriers versus contract carriers

■ The transportation rates we have been referring to are those charged by *common carriers*, such as the railroads and major truck lines. These carriers, given a franchise by a government regulatory body, must accept merchandise from any shipper and maintain regular service. They usually must obtain permission to discontinue service or change their rates.

In contrast to common carriers are *contract carriers,* who are less strictly regulated and do not maintain regular schedules. They make up a more freewheeling group. They can work for anyone for an agreed sum and for any length of time. Like agents and brokers, they appear wherever needed.

Development of the transportation rate structure

■ In our discussion of transportation rates, we will concentrate on *rail common carrier rates,* since they set a competitive standard. Most other transportation rate structures have similar characteristics.

The development of the railroad rate structure was guided by governmental regulatory commissions. The underlying rationale of the rate structure was that the railways could carry the heavy and bulky items—such as sand and gravel—at a relatively low charge per ton; carry the more valuable, less bulky items at higher rates per ton; and then balance the low charges against the high charges to show a profit. As we will see, however, this has not worked out as planned. The railroads have been carrying the heavy bulky items at low rates, but trucks and airlines have been taking the high-rate business.

There are three basic types of rates: (1) class, (2) commodity, and (3) exception. These three kinds of rates are quoted for carloads (*CL,* 60,000–100,000 pounds), truckloads (*TL,* 15,000 pounds or more), less than carloads (*LCL*), and less than truckloads (*LTL*).

Rates on less than full carloads or truckloads vary but are often twice as high as those on full loads. These rate differentials are one reason for the development of wholesalers, who buy in larger quantities than most users need, to get the advantage of full-load rates and then sell in the smaller quantities the users *do* need.

Bear in mind that there is nothing final about the present rate structure; since it is man-made, it could be changed. If it were changed, it might lead to a vastly different, and perhaps more efficient or more equitable, transportation system. In some other countries, for instance, these rate differentials are much smaller or nonexistent. As a consequence, goods are shipped in much smaller quantities, freight cars are smaller, and wholesalers and retailers handle smaller quantities.

Class rates—higher rates for smaller volume

The railroads handle so many different products that they have had to develop a freight classification system covering more than 10,000 different articles or groups of articles. Each class is assigned rates based on the cost and value of the service, the size of the shipment, and the distance shipped.

Most of the goods shipped under class rates are general manufactured products that are shipped in volumes too small to justify much negotiation by shippers. Between 2 and 4 percent of the volume shipped by rail comes under these rates, and these are the rates which were supposed to offset the low rates on bulky, low-value items.

Commodity rates—lower rates for big bulk

In many instances, there is no provision within the 10,000 class-rate classifications for the specific characteristics of certain commodities, especially bulky or low-value items. Commodity rates are set for transporting specific commodities, usually between specific points or over specific routes. These rates frequently develop out of negotiation between shippers and railroads.

There are special commodity rates for most bulky items, such as wheat, iron ore, coal, lumber, or any products shipped regularly in substantial volume. Some of the negotiated commodity rates are called "blanket rates," because the same rate applies over a large geographical area regardless of the distance between specific points within that area. Fresh fruits and vegetables, for example, can be shipped from the West Coast to almost any place on the East Coast for the same rate. Approximately 90 percent of the rail carload traffic moves under commodity rates.

Exception rates—special rates for special conditions

If a certain producer needs lower rates so that he can compete in other markets, or if competition from other methods of transportation is especially strong, the carriers sometimes are forced to reconsider their costs and set special rates.

Railways have granted "exception rates" on many items to meet truck competition in certain territories. But less than 10 percent of carload traffic moves under these rates.[3]

Correct rate not easy to determine

■ The large number of rate classes, and the many exceptions, make traffic management a difficult job. A freight agent frequently charges a higher rate when a lower rate should apply. Some companies find it profitable to audit all freight bills before payment. There are even private firms specializing in this kind of work, earning a share of the savings.

It is not that carriers are deliberately overcharging, but rather that the agents who determine the appropriate rates must choose from a vast number of possible routes, rates, and rate combinations. Determining the best routing for the lowest rate gets more complex each year, since more than 150,000 rate changes are made annually.[4] And the basic rate books do not show cross-references to all of these new rates. Because of this complexity, and possibility of error, some channel members prefer to have prices quoted on a delivered basis.

Marketing manager may affect rates

■ The previous discussion has been concerned primarily with how to operate within the existing rate structure. Yet, as noted, the rate structure is not *permanently fixed*. Carriers can and do initiate changes, and if no one objects, the new rates usually go into effect. Rate changes can be made relatively quickly (1 to 30 days) and easily, as indicated by those 150,000 changes made each year.

Capitalize
on carrier
competition

■ Most rates are based originally on supply considerations; that is, the cost of providing necessary services – loading, product liability, regular scheduled service even though it is not used, special equipment such as refrigerated cars, and so on. But supply factors are not the final determinants of transport rates. Rather, they determine the rate the carrier *would like to charge.* The rates actually charged are determined by competition among the various carriers and alternate methods of transportation. It is by capitalizing on these factors that an aggressive marketing manager can influence the cost of the transporting function.

Carriers are usually interested in stimulating business in their areas. If the marketing manager can show that he could expand his business if lower rates were granted into certain territories, the carriers may be willing to grant these lower rates. In fact, considerable adjustment has taken place so that now distance traveled and total transportation costs are often not very closely related. New England railroads, for example, long have charged the same rates from New England as from New York on shipments going west, thereby enabling their New England customers to compete on equal terms with respect to transportation costs. Similarly, southern railroads reduced their rates on finished cotton goods so southern mills could sell in northern territories in competition with New England mills.[5] Note the behavior here of competing channel systems, with the railroads as part of the channel.

The creative marketing manager, by bargaining for rate changes, can help his channel system members with the transportation function. In fact, some manufacturers and middlemen maintain *traffic departments* staffed by ten or more employees to deal with carriers. These departments can be of great aid not only to their own firm but also to their suppliers and customers.

Which transportation alternative is best

■ The best transportation alternative should not only be as low in cost as possible, but also provide the level of service (e.g., speed and dependability) which is required. Obviously, the transporting function should fit into the whole marketing strategy, and in order to do this well, the marketing manager should fully understand the advantages and disadvantages of the various transportation modes, but it is important to see from the beginning that lowest transportation cost is not the only criterion in selecting the best method.

Railroads –
workhorse
of the
nation

■ The railroad, the workhorse of U.S. transportation, has been important mainly for carrying heavy and bulky freight such as coal, sand, and steel. By handling large quantities of such commodities, according to standardized methods and in a variety of standardized car types, the railroads are able to transport at relatively low cost. But railroads have had profit difficulties in recent years, in part because trucking firms have set their rates low enough to compete for the more profitable, less bulky items that the railroads were counting on to offset the low rates on the bulky commodities.

Competition has forced railroads to innovate

■ The railroads have taken various steps to bring their profits up. Computerization and automation of rail facilities has helped. Catering more specifically to the needs of some target customers has helped, too. By introducing an efficient triple-deck carrier for automobiles, the rails were able to win back from trucks a substantial share of the new-car transport. And now, a specially designed railcar can carry 30 small automobiles–twice as many as the triple-deck carriers–by stacking them vertically rather than horizontally. And the design of special refrigerator cars, tank cars, hopper cars, and cars especially suited for loading and unloading livestock has helped attract and hold business.[6]

Rails now offer more special services

■ To be more competitive, the railroads also have offered a variety of special services and shipping alternatives. Some of these are discussed below.

Piggyback service

Operating with the apparent philosophy, "If you can't beat them, haul them," railroads have offered more flexible service by loading truck trailers onto specially designed flatcars and hauling them "piggyback." The trailers are picked up at the producer's location, loaded onto rail flatcars, hauled as close to the customer as rail lines run, then picked up by a truck tractor and delivered to the buyer's door. Such service provides all the flexibility of trucking, and on some routes it costs even less. A loaded truck trailer can be shipped piggyback from the Midwest to the West Coast for approximately half the cost of sending it over the highways.

Fast freight

Many of the goods shipped by rail are not particularly perishable or in urgent demand, and as a result, much railroad freight moves more slowly than truck shipments. But when speed is needed, a train can really move.

Some railroads have instituted a "fast freight" service for perishable or high-value items. Such trains, highballing at 60 m.p.h. and stopping only to change crews and load water and ice, can be competitive in speed with trucks, provided shippers and receivers are located near rail lines.

Pool cars

Railroads are most efficient at handling full carloads of goods. Less-than-carload (LCL) shipments take a considerable amount of handling and rehandling. They usually move slowly, and at a higher price per 100 pounds than carload shipments.

To counter the shortcomings of low speed and high cost and still encourage the business of small shippers, some railroads encourage groups of shippers to cooperate and pool their shipments as a full car. This service enables one producer to ship to several buyers in a single area at greater speed and under the lower carload rates. If the buyers of these goods are not located in the same area, the goods may be shipped in a pool car at the carload rate to the first buyer and then broken up for further shipment at LCL rates.

Sometimes local retailers buying from a single area, such as New York City, consolidate their shipments in single cars. Local truckers deliver the goods when they arrive. When various commodities are shipped in the same car, it is called a *mixed car* rather than a *pool car,* and the highest rate for any of the commodities applies to the whole shipment.

Diversion in transit

Some railroads allow redirection of carloads already in transit. A carload of California oranges could be shipped toward Chicago or simply eastward toward no specific destination, and as market demand and supply conditions changed, the shipper could change or specify the destination. The railroad would then reroute the car for a small fee.

This service lets a marketing manager get his goods rolling but still stay flexible in his final target market selection.

Transit privilege

Some agricultural or industrial raw materials must be shipped from their original source to a processing plant and then to users. To facilitate this regrouping and processing, some railroads permit shippers to ship commodities, stop along the way for processing, and then reship them toward the final destination at the "through" rate—as long as the same general direction is maintained. This privilege is especially important in the flour milling industry, where the procedure is called "milling in transit."

Transloading privilege

A more recent innovation, the transloading privilege, speeds delivery of portions of an original carload shipment to two or more destinations. When goods are to be shipped in a car cross-country to customers at several destinations, the railroad does not pull the car from city to city, unloading it bit by bit, here and there. Instead, it moves a full carload of goods to the single point that is closest to the various customers, then reloads parts of the shipment into other cars for the remaining distance.

Since the transloading privilege makes LCL size deliveries feasible, customers can maintain smaller inventory, shifting the storage function back to the manufacturer or wholesaler. Like other privileges, transloading gives channel members more latitude in planning marketing strategies and sharing channel functions.

Trucks are flexible, fast, dependable, and indispensable

■ The flexibility of trucks makes them especially suitable for moving small lots of goods short distances. They can travel on almost any road, can serve broad areas without unloading and reloading, and give extremely fast service. Trucks also cause less breakage and rough handling than rails, an important factor because it may permit a reduction in packaging cost.

For short distances and for higher valued commodities, trucks may charge rates that are the same as (or lower than) railroad rates, yet provide much faster service. The way truckers compete with railroads for these high-charge items is somewhat like the way retailers compete in "scrambled merchandising." Going after such business is logical for the truckers because it is these smaller high-charge items that trucks are best equipped to handle.

Trucking has opened many new markets and permitted a considerable amount of decentralization by bringing fast, dependable transport to outlying urban areas, smaller towns, and rural areas. Whatever the truth may be about charges that trucks congest traffic and damage highways, it *is* a fact that trucks are indispensable to our present economic and marketing system.

Waterways are slow and seasonal, but inexpensive

■ Barges on the internal waterways are used chiefly for bulky, nonperishable products such as iron ore, grain, steel, petroleum products, cement, gravel, sand, coal, and coke. Water transportation is the lowest-cost method, but it is also the slowest and most seasonal. When winter ice closes freshwater harbors, alternate transportation must be used. Some shippers, such as those dealing in iron ore, ship their total annual supply during the summer months and store it near their production facilities for winter use. Here, low-cost transportation combined with storage reduces *total cost*.

The availability of ocean transport to the vast industrial and agricultural regions of the inland United States was made possible in 1959 by the completion of the St. Lawrence Waterway System. This 2,342-mile-long waterway opened the Great Lakes to 80 percent of all ocean vessels. Only the very largest ships are excluded.

A recent advance in coastal and transoceanic shipping is the redesign of ships to handle large standard-size containers or *containerized freight,* and truck trailers. Now ships combined with trucks can offer a *fishyback* service similar to rail piggyback handling of truck trailers. Door-to-door service is now being offered between the U.S. and European cities.[7]

Pipelines are used primarily by the petroleum industry

■ In the United States, pipelines are used primarily by the petroleum industry to move petroleum liquids and natural gas. Extensive lines in the Southwest bring oil from the fields to refineries. From there, the more flexible railroads, trucks, and ships usually transport refined products to customers.

Airways are fast and expensive

■ The most expensive means of cargo transportation yet developed is airfreight – but it also is fast! Airfreight rates normally are at least twice as high as trucking rates, but the greater speed may more than justify the added cost. Trucks took the cream of the railroads' traffic. Now airways are taking the cream of the cream. They also are creating new transportation business by carrying across continents and oceans perishable commodities that simply could not be moved before. Tropical flowers from Hawaii, for example, now are jet-flown to points all over the United States. And

California's strawberries are flown to the Midwest and East all through the winter. French bread comes into Detroit daily from Paris and Brazilian manufacturers sell goods throughout South America by air.

The bulk of airfreight so far has been fashions, perishable commodities, and high-value industrial parts for the electronics and metal-working industries.

But airplanes may cut total cost of distribution

■ An important advantage of air transport is that the cost of packing, unpackaging, and preparing the goods for sale may be reduced or eliminated when goods are shipped by air. One Los Angeles manufacturer of electronic products who makes all his deliveries beyond 150 miles by airfreight, merely wraps the complex 600-pound machines in heavy wrapping paper. His increased transportation costs are more than offset by the reduction in packaging costs, and he is now competing for business nationally. The speedy service at lower costs has improved the company's marketing mix *and* market position.

Although the *transportation cost* of air shipments may be higher, the *total cost of distribution* for a firm using airfreight may be lower.

Airfreight may enable a firm to reduce its inventory costs by eliminating outlying warehouses. And finally, valuable by-products of air transport's speed are the reduction of spoilage, pilferage, and damage. With less time from shipper to customer, goods are exposed to fewer hazards.

Freight forwarders are transportation wholesalers

■ Many marketing managers use freight forwarders to make optimum use of available transportation facilities, especially for the many small shipments that may have to move by varied transportation services.

Freight forwarders do not own their own transportation facilities, except perhaps for pickup and delivery trucks. Rather, they wholesale air, ship, railroad, and truck space. Accumulating small shipments from many shippers, they reship in larger quantities to obtain lower transportation rates. Their profits mainly come out of the difference in freight rates between small- and large-quantity shipments, though they sometimes make special service charges.

They help exporters

■ Freight forwarders can be especially helpful to the marketing manager who ships many small shipments to foreign markets. They handle an estimated 75 percent of the general cargo shipped from U.S. ports to foreign countries. More than 90 percent of all exporters, including companies with large shipping departments, use their services; a decisive reason is that the forwarders are located right at the exporting point and can more easily process all the complicated paper work necessary in overseas shipments.[8]

Should you do it yourself?

■ To cut transportation costs, some marketing managers provide their own transportation facilities rather than buy from specialists. Trucking has made it easier for a businessman to use do-it-yourself transport. Some large manufacturers own thousands of cars and trucks, and there are iron ore, gypsum rock, and petroleum producers who have their own ships.

It depends on discrepancies of quantity and shipment consistency

■ The concept of discrepancy of quantity is an important factor to be considered here. If there is a great difference between the quantity a firm normally ships and the quantity that carriers find most economical, the firm may have to ship via common carrier or freight forwarder. But if a company normally ships in the same quantities that common carriers find economical, it may save money by using its own trucks and avoiding the cost that common carriers must charge for maintaining a regular schedule or contract carriers must charge against future uncertainties.

If a marketing manager is fairly certain of his future plans, do-it-yourself transportation may be good business. One wholesale wine distributor in New Orleans found that he was paying considerably more to ship wine by rail from California than if he rented a tank truck and hired his own driver for the California run. Because this was a regular and frequent shipment, he bought a truck and operated it himself at a large saving.

The storing function

Store it and smooth out sales, increase profits and consumer satisfaction

■ Storing is the marketing function of holding physical goods between the time of production and the time of final use. It provides time utility.

Storing is necessary because production does not always match consumption. Some products, such as agricultural commodities, are produced seasonally though they are in demand year-round. If crops could not be stored when they matured or ripened, all the crop would be thrown onto the market at one time, and prices might drop sharply. The consumer might benefit temporarily from this surplus, but later in the year, when supplies were scarce and prices high, he would suffer. Storage, therefore, permits price stabilization throughout the consuming period, although prices usually do rise slightly over time to cover storage costs.

The practice of storing and therefore withholding products from the market to get better prices is the basic principle behind the U.S. Department of Agriculture's parity program and the occasional stockpiling of commodities such as rubber, coffee, and cocoa beans in other countries. Our federal government has stockpiled metals not only for defense but also to maintain prices. Storing, we can see, may be intimately related to Price as well as to Place.

Planning to use storage, some buyers purchase in large enough quantities to get quantity discounts. Goods also are sometimes stored as a hedge against future price rises, strikes, shipping interruptions, and other disruptions.

Finally, storing goods enables manufacturers and middlemen to keep stocks at convenient locations, ready to meet customers' needs. In fact, storing is one of the major activities of some middlemen.

Storing varies the channel system

■ Most channel members provide the storing function for varying lengths of time. Even final consumers store some things for their future needs. Since storing can be provided anywhere along the channel, the storage function offers several ways to vary a firm's marketing mix and its channel system by: (1) adjusting the time goods are held, (2) sharing the storage costs, and (3) delegating the job to a specialized storage facility. This latter variation would mean adding another member to the distribution channel.

Which channel members store the product and for how long affects the behavior of all channel members. If a manufacturer of groceries, for example, were to maintain a large local stock, wholesalers probably would maintain smaller inventories, since they would be assured of dependable local supplies.

Specialized storage facilities can be very helpful

Private warehouses

■ Private warehouses are those that are owned by individual companies for their own use. Most manufacturers, wholesalers, and retailers have some kind of storage facilities, either in their main buildings or in a warehouse district. Management of a manufacturer's finished-goods warehouse often is the responsibility of a sales manager, especially at sales branches located away from the factory. In retailing, storage is so closely tied to selling that the buyers may control this function.

Private warehouses are used when a large volume of goods must be stored regularly. Owning warehouse space, however, can be expensive, since it is a fixed cost and may limit flexibility in the company's operations. If sales should fall and warehouse stocks decline, the extra space may be hard or impossible to lease, and costs may remain constant while revenue declines.

Public warehouses fill special needs

■ The company that does not need permanent warehouse space may find public warehouses useful. The customer pays only for the space he uses and may, if he wishes, purchase a variety of additional services. Public warehouses are useful to manufacturers who must maintain stocks in many locations, including foreign countries.

Some public warehouses provide all the services that could be obtained in the company's own branch warehouse or from most wholesalers. These warehouses will receive goods in carload quantities, unload and store them, and later reship them in any size lots ordered by the company or its customers. They will inspect goods, package them, and even invoice customers. They will participate in the financing function by issuing warehouse receipts that can be used as collateral when borrowing from banks. Some public warehouses will provide desk space and telephone service for a company's salesmen. And the public warehouse is responsible for the risk of damage or the loss of the product in the warehouse.

Public warehouses are located in all major metropolitan areas and many smaller cities. Rural areas also have public warehouses for locally produced agricultural commodities.

General merchandise and bonded warehouses

General merchandise warehouses store almost every kind of manufactured goods. A special form of warehouse is the *bonded* warehouse used for storing imported goods or other goods, such as liquors or cigarettes, on which a tax must be paid before the goods are released for sale. If a long storage period is needed, say to age liquor, then these warehouses may lower costs by delaying payment of taxes or duties until the goods are removed. Private bonded warehouses also can provide this latter feature.

Commodity and cold-storage warehouses

Commodity warehouses and *cold-storage* warehouses are designed specifically for storing perishable or easily spoiled products such as apples, butter, and furs. Grain is stored in huge elevators.

Modernized warehousing facilities have emerged

■ The cost of physical handling is a major storage cost. The goods must be handled once when put into storage and again when removed to be sold. Particularly in older, multistoried warehouses, located in congested districts, these operations take many man-hours of high-cost labor. Difficult parking, crowded storage areas, and slow freight elevators all delay the process, increasing the cost of distribution.

Today, modern, one-story structures are replacing the old multistoried buildings. These new single-level designs eliminate the need for elevators and permit use of power-operated lift trucks, battery-operated motor scooters, roller-skating order pickers, electric hoists for heavy items, and hydraulic ramps to facilitate loading and unloading. Some grocery warehouses even have radio-controlled tractors that order pickers drive by remote control. Most of these new warehouses use lift trucks and pallets (wooden "trays" which carry many cases) for vertical storage and better use of cube space.

One Los Angeles drug wholesaler, through careful planning and use of electronic controls, has now almost eliminated physical handling for most of his repeat business—covering 1,800 items. The system of controls and conveyor belts now assembles, in a few seconds, the kind of order that an experienced stock clerk formerly spent 20 minutes putting together.[9]

The distribution center — a different kind of warehouse

Is storing really needed?

■ Storage is justifiable only if it helps achieve time utility. Storage is *not* necessary just because there is some discrepancy of quantity or assortment between one channel level and another. If there is a discrepancy *and* time must be used, then it can make economic sense to regroup and store at the same time. But if time is not needed, then no storage should be provided. This leads us to a whole new idea — the distribution center.

Don't store it, distribute it

■ A distribution center is a special kind of warehouse designed, *not* to stock goods, but to *speed* the flow of goods and eliminate unnecessary storage. It is a breaking-bulk operation. Turnover is increased, and the cost of carrying inventory is reduced. Such cost may run as high as 25 percent a year of the value of the average inventory.

The concept underlying the distribution center is the same one that led to the development of discount houses and mass merchandisers: *Reducing costs and increasing turnover will lead to bigger profits.*

There are many variations of the distribution center. The following example of its application in the Pillsbury Company shows it within an integrated operation. Some public warehouses try to offer similar services for smaller manufacturers, too. Eventually, it may be possible for a manufacturer to use only 10 or 15 such public warehouse centers and still service the country efficiently and at lower cost than with his present methods.

Pillsbury's distribution system was overwhelmed by expanding product lines and sales

■ The Pillsbury Co., a large manufacturer of baking mixes and flour, used to move its products in carload lots directly from factory to wholesaler or large retailer. Plants were as near to customers as possible, and each plant, initially, was equipped to produce the whole Pillsbury line. As lines were expanded, however, it became apparent that no plant could produce all the various products. When customers began to ask for mixed carload shipments and faster delivery, Pillsbury found itself adding warehouse space and hauling goods from plant to plant. By 1955, Pillsbury had set up 100 branch warehouses, controlled by 33 sales offices. Each sales office had its own accounting, credit, and other processing operations.

Later, one Pillsbury official was to say of this old system: "Turnover was slow, warehousing costs were high, and there was no effective control over inventories." It was then taking the company one week *just to process an order.*[10]

The distribution center brings it all together

■ Now, Pillsbury uses distribution centers which enable it to guarantee its customers "third morning delivery" anywhere in the United States. Each manufacturing plant specializes in a few product lines and ships in carload lots directly to the distribution centers, virtually eliminating warehousing at the factories. The field sales organization no longer handles physical distribution or inventory. Sales is its only activity, and it has been able to expand its branches from 33 to 52. The distribution centers are controlled by four regional data processing centers. Sales orders are routed to one of the data processing centers, which immediately determines where and when the goods are to be shipped for that "third morning delivery." Centralized accounting speeds invoices to customers, resulting in quicker payment. And because each distribution center always has adequate supplies, it is possible to route and ship orders directly from that point, by the most economical means.

Before these changes at Pillsbury, neither the production nor the sales departments had precise responsibility for what happened to goods between manufacture and sale. Now, the entire physical distribution effort is treated as one system, under a director of distribution who is equal in rank to the heads of manufacturing and sales.

Pillsbury salesmen have something extra to sell—better and faster service. Costs have been reduced and profits increased. Over a four-year period, the new system is credited with boosting the company's ratio of pre-tax income to sales from 2.9 percent to 4.9 percent.[11]

Physical distribution concept focuses on whole distribution system

■ We have been looking at the transporting and storing functions as separate activities, partly because this simplifies discussion but also because it is the traditional approach. In recent years, however, attention has turned to the *whole* physical distribution function, not just warehousing and transportation. This sometimes affects production, too, since these activities *are* interdependent. We just saw this in the Pillsbury case.

Physical
distribution,
a new idea
whose time
may come

■ According to the physical distribution (PD) concept, a relatively new business theory, all physical handling activities of a business and a channel system should be thought of as part of one system. It may be hard to see this as a startling development, but until just a few years ago, even the most progressive companies treated these various functions as separate and quite unrelated activities. Most firms still do.

In some firms, the production department is responsible for warehousing and shipping, and it builds inventories that are related to its production activities rather than market needs. In other companies, inventory may be a separate activity. If those in charge of inventory put little faith in sales forecasts, they may simply adjust stocks according to their own expectations.

This naïve focusing on individual functional activities may actually increase a firm's and channel's total distribution costs. Therefore, those who accept the PD concept usually study the total cost of alternative physical distribution systems—applying the "Total Cost Approach."

Evaluate PD systems with total cost approach

Searching for the lowest total cost

■ The total cost approach to evaluating PD systems simply requires that *all* of the costs of each alternative PD system be identified and totaled before a choice is made. This means that all costs, including some which are sometimes ignored, should be considered. Inventory carrying costs, for example, are often ignored because these costs may be buried in "overhead costs," yet they may represent 10 to 35 percent of the value of average inventory.

The tools of cost accounting and economics are used with this approach. Sometimes, total cost analyses reveal that unconventional physical distribution methods will yield services as good as or better than conventional means, and at lower cost. The following simple example illustrates the approach.

Evaluating rail/warehouse versus airfreight

■ Table 19–2 shows the result of a comparative cost analysis of two alternatives: airfreight with no warehouse versus rail freight with warehouse. The comparison was based on the distribution of 1,000 tons of a particular commodity during a definite period of time.

Comparing the final totals showed that using airfreight would be less expensive than the rail-warehouse combination, even though airfreight itself was considerably more costly than rail.

In any total cost analysis of this kind, all practical alternatives should be evaluated and compared. Sometimes alternatives are so numerous or complicated that advanced mathematical and statistical techniques, and perhaps a computer, are needed for their analysis.[12] For evaluating many alternatives, some companies have found it desirable to use a new approach: simulation with a computer. In simulation, the characteristics and costs of the many alternatives are described as carefully as possible, and then the computer tests the alternatives, using a trial-and-error technique. For many applications, however, the straightforward total cost analysis discussed previously is practicable and will show whether there is need for a more sophisticated analytical approach.

Physical distribution planning as part of a company's strategy planning

Physical distribution not just cost-oriented

■ Although cost reduction was the main focus of early physical distribution efforts, more attention is being directed now toward integrating physical distribution planning into the company's strategy planning. Perhaps by increasing physical distribution costs somewhat, service levels can be increased so that, in effect, a new marketing mix has been created.

Decide what level of service to offer

■ Figure 19–1 shows the typical relation between physical distribution costs and customer service level. When one chooses to minimize total costs he is also settling for a lower customer service level. Here, by increasing the number of distribution points the firm

Table 19-2
Comparative costs of airfreight versus rail and warehouse

		Total cost	Cost per ton
Rail and Warehouse			
(2)	Interest on inventory, 30-day cycle, 360-day interest year at 6% on $1,500,000 of inventory	$ 90,000.00	$ 90.00
(2)	Taxes on inventory	40,000.00	40.00
(2)	Warehouse cost	55,200.00	55.20
(1)	Transport expense (rail carload)	58,000.00	58.00
	Cost via rail and warehouse	$243,200.00	$243.20
Airfreight			
(2)	Interest on investment in inventory, 10-day cycle, 360-day interest year at 6% on $500,000 inventory	$ 30,000.00	$ 30.00
(1)	Airfreight	120,000.00	120.00
(1)	Local delivery	10,000.00	10.00
	Cost via airfreight	$160,000.00	$160.00

Note: Total sales = 1,000,000 units or 1,000 tons
(2) indicates fixed and variable expense; (1) indicates variable expense only.
Source: Reprinted with permission of the publisher from p. 76 of *Physical Distribution Management* by E. W. Smykay, D. J. Bowersox, and F. H. Mossman. Copyright 1961 by the Macmillan Co.

would be able to serve more customers within some time period, such as four days. Transportation costs would be reduced but warehousing and inventory costs would be increased and, therefore, total cost would be increased as more distribution points were added. The higher service levels, however, might greatly improve the company's strategy and the increased sales might much more than offset the increased costs. Clearly, the marketing manager has a strategic decision with respect to what level of service he wants to offer. Simply minimizing cost is obviously not the right answer.

Significantly increasing service levels may be extremely profitable in highly competitive situations where the firm has relatively little to differentiate its marketing mix — for example, in pure competition or oligopoly. Here, simply increasing the service level — perhaps through faster delivery or wider stocks — may enable the firm to make significant headway in the market without altering prices or promotion. In fact, improved service levels can put a marketing mix across, and competitors may not fully realize what has happened. As already discussed, buyers and especially industrial buyers usually must have several sources of supply, but each buyer has some option as to how much he buys from whom. A higher service level might lead a buyer to forget about splitting orders equally among three vendors in order to reward a supplier

382

Figure 19–1
Higher customer service levels are obtained at a cost

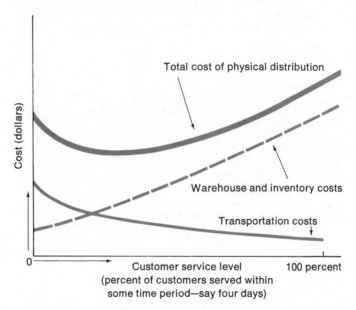

who is offering a higher service level. He has to buy from someone, so adjusting shares does not affect him. But see what happens if the supplier with the better marketing mix were given one half of the business rather than his customary one third. While not affecting the buyer (except that he gets better service), the seller would see a 50 percent increase in sales![13]

Need for physical distribution manager

■ Basic company reorganization may be necessary for full acceptance and exploitation of the physical distribution concept. It is even less accepted than the marketing concept. Just adding an executive called a "distribution manager" or a "manager of physical distribution," or simply giving the traffic manager or warehouse manager a new title will not in itself do the job. This would only be paying lip service to the concept, when what is really needed is the merging of production, warehousing, shipping, and sales into one integrated system. Such far-reaching changes may be a long time coming. Not only will departments which are typically production-oriented resist such moves, but many sales and marketing executives still have not recognized their responsibility for physical distribution. One survey found that in 43 percent of the firms the top marketing executive did not assume any responsibility for physical distribution, and in 35 percent of the firms he did not participate in discussions concerning this important phase of marketing.[14]

A real physical distribution manager would have a big job. He would be concerned not only with physical product flows but also the location of place facilities through which the flows would move. In some companies, it might be a good idea to have a separate distribution manager, coequal with the marketing manager, with centralized control of all physical distribution activities. There is much ferment and controversy in this area, because a "total system" is involved. But it is clear that major changes will be required in many companies if the marketing concept *and* the physical distribution concept are wholeheartedly adopted.

Future physical distribution problems and opportunities

■ The marketing system of the future, responding to new living patterns and technology, may change drastically in some urban areas. Urban redevelopment programs may cause even more significant shifts of population than we have seen so far. With mounting population pressure and the energy crisis, radical new regulations might be introduced, such as the exclusion of private automobiles from city streets, either by ordinance or by prohibitively high taxation.

Getting ready for an age of planning and people

■ New approaches must be found to mass transportation and urban living. Already, the federal government is subsidizing urban mass transportation systems. There are some limited attempts at developing new residential and commercial building arrangements. France and Sweden have experimented with communities combining residential, working, and recreation facilities in the same center.

Adjustments in transportation rate structures may lead to drastic changes in physical movement patterns and where and what goods are produced and sold. The railroads have seen more and more of their most profitable business go to competitors; but if this situation were to be adjusted on a grand scale, the changes might have a profound impact on the whole economy.

Suppose, for example, that the low rail rates charged on bulk commodities such as lumber were raised sharply. A lumber company in the Northwest might suffer. Contractors might shift to other types of building materials. Such a rate increase might even force the whole construction industry to revamp its methods and materials.

Similarly, higher fuel costs and pollution controls may increase the cost of truck and air movements and make the rails more appealing. And lower speed limits on trucks may make the railroads look even better. But such shifts will also affect where people live and work, and what they produce and consume. In other words, it will have an impact on our whole macro-marketing system.

Transportation is not one problem but many problems. Any major changes in the existing rate structure will affect manufacturers, wholesalers, retailers, and consumers. So far these adjustments have been made on a piecemeal basis, but a national transportation policy may be coming. The recent formation of a separate U.S. Department of Transportation could bring solutions to some of the problems, but change comes slowly and is resisted by vested interests and the sheer magnitude of the problem. The number of people, cars, trucks, and airplanes continues to grow, and no one wants to be restricted.

As always, the marketing manager who has been able to carve out a target market today will have to stay alert if he wishes to keep it tomorrow.

Conclusion

■ This chapter has dealt with providing Time and Place utility. We have discussed the various modes of transportation and their advantages and disadvantages. The railroad rate structure, particularly, seems in need of a drastic overhauling, and this might have a marked impact on our present marketing system.

Storage, the second aspect of physical distribution, was considered, together with the types of warehousing now available. Examples were given of modern techniques which can cut storage and physical handling costs.

Although we discussed transportation and storage separately, it was emphasized that both are related. The distribution center, a new approach in this area, is an attempt to integrate these two activities for the purpose of speeding turnover and lowering handling and storage costs. The physical distribution concept is concerned with integrating all the physical handling, storing, and transporting activities into a smoothly working system.

Although cost is an important factor in evaluating physical distribution alternatives, service must also be considered—along with its strategic implications. Management often wants to improve service and may select a higher cost alternative to improve its marketing mix. Or the total cost approach might reveal that it is possible *both* to reduce costs and to improve service, perhaps by eliminating warehouses and using airfreight to speed delivery.

New organizational structures including the addition of a physical distribution manager may be needed within the firm to achieve the potential benefits of integrating physical distribution activities. In addition, new thinking may be indicated if these activities are to be shared within a channel system. Here, the channel captain may have to take the lead. It should also go without saying that the specialized transporting and storing institutions could also contribute to this effort, by adopting the marketing concept themselves and showing how they can contribute to the better operation of channel systems.

questions and problems

1 Discuss the relative advantages and disadvantages of railroads, trucks, and airlines as transporting methods.

2 Describe how your college town would be changed if there were no incoming or outgoing transportation except by foot, horseback, or horse-drawn covered wagon.

3 Distinguish between common carriers and contract carriers. What role do the contract carriers play in our economic system? How would our economy be different if there were no common carriers?

4 Distinguish among the following types of railroad rates: class, commodity, and exception rates. If all three rates might apply in a particular situation, which one would probably be the lowest?

5 Explain which transportation method would probably be most suitable for shipment of goods to a large Chicago department store:
a. A 10,000-lb. shipment of dishes from Japan.
b. 15 lbs. of screwdrivers from New York.
c. Three couches from High Point, N.C.
d. 500 high-fashion dresses from the garment district in New York City.
e. 300 lbs. of Maine lobsters.
f. 60,000 lbs. of various appliances from Evansville, Indiana.

How would your answers change if this department store were the only one in a large factory town in Ohio?

6 Indicate the nearest location where you would expect to find substantial storage facilities. What kinds of products would be stored there and why are they stored there instead of some other place?

7 Indicate when a producer or middleman would find it desirable to use a public warehouse rather than a private warehouse. Illustrate, using a specific product or situation.

8 Discuss the distribution center concept. Is this likely to eliminate the storing function of conventional wholesalers? Is it applicable to all products? If not, cite several examples.

9 Clearly differentiate between a warehouse and a distribution center. Explain how a specific product would be handled differently by these marketing institutions.

10 Explain the total cost approach and why it may be necessary to have a physical distribution manager to implement the concept.

11 How would a distribution manager differ from a transportation manager? Would he really be any different than a marketing manager?

notes

[1] D. Philip Locklin, *Economics of Transportation*, 4th ed. (Homewood, Ill.: Richard D. Irwin, Inc., 1954), p. 35.

[2] D. Philip Locklin, *Economics of Transportation*, 7th ed. (Homewood, Ill.: Richard D. Irwin, Inc., 1972, p. 57.

[3] F. M. Cushman, *Transportation for Management* (New York: Prentice-Hall, Inc., 1953), pp. 173–74.

[4] C. A. Taff, *Traffic Management*, 3d ed. (Homewood, Ill.: Richard D. Irwin, Inc., 1964), p. 248.

[5] Locklin, *Economics of Transportation*, 6th ed. p. 54.

[6] "Railcars Haul Vegas Vertically," *Detroit Free Press*, August 6, 1970, p. 8–D; "High-Mountain Railroad with Profits to Match," *Business Week*, June 10, 1967, pp. 174–80.

[7] "Cooling the Rate War on the North Atlantic," *Business Week*, April 29, 1972, pp. 48–52.

[8] Paul V. Horn and Henry Gomez, *International Trade Principles and Practices*, 4th ed. (Englewood Cliffs, N.J.: Prentice-Hall, Inc., 1959), p. 521.

[9] "Automation Gets It Wholesale," *Business Week*, March 15, 1958, pp. 157–60.

[10] "New-fangled Routes Deliver the Goods–Faster and Cheaper," *Business Week*, November 4, 1959, pp. 108–10.

[11] Ibid.

[12] See Donald J. Bowersox, *Logistical Management* (New York: Macmillan Publishing Co., Inc., 1974); James L. Heskett, N. A. Glaskowsky, Jr., and R. M. Ivie, *Business Logistics* (New York: The Ronald Press Co., 1973).

[13] For more discussion on this point see Donald J. Bowersox, Edward W. Smykay, and Bernard J. La Londe, *Physical Distribution Management*, ref. ed. (New York: The Macmillan Company, 1968), pp. 314–21.

[14] Robert E. Weigand, *Business Topics*, Summer 1962, pp. 70–71.

[15] For more discussion on problems and opportunities, see: James L. Heskett, "Sweeping Changes in Distribution," *Harvard Business Review*, March–April 1973, pp. 123–32; Robert F. Jeffries, Jr., "Distribution Management–Failures and Solutions," *Business Horizons*, April 1974, pp. 55–66; "The Railroad Paradox: A Profitless Boom," *Business Week*, September 8, 1973, pp. 54–63.

20

Promotion— introduction

■ Promotion, one of the four major variables with which the marketing manager works, is communicating information between seller and buyer with a view to changing attitudes and behavior. The marketing manager's job is to tell target customers that the right product is available at the right place at the right price.

How he communicates depends upon what blend of the following promotional methods he chooses:

Personal Selling involves direct face-to-face relationships between sellers and potential customers.

Mass Selling is designed to communicate with large numbers of customers at the same time. Advertising is the main form of mass selling, but it also involves publicity.

Sales Promotion refers to specific activities that complement personal and mass selling such as point-of-purchase displays, booklets, leaflets, and direct mailings.

What the marketing manager communicates is basically determined when the target customers' needs and preferences are known.

Clearly, promotion is only a part of strategy planning, but it is an important part because it is what gets your customer's attention, tells him what you have to sell, and, hopefully, convinces him that you have the product he is looking for.

In this chapter, we will discuss basic promotion objectives, methods of implementing these objectives, and ways in which these methods can be blended for effective promotion. The next two chapters will be devoted to personal selling and mass selling, the two basic approaches to promotion.

Basic promotion objectives

Behavior change is the main goal

■ A good marketing man is not interested in just "communicating." He wants to communicate information in order to obtain action. He knows that if he has a better offering for some target market, informed customers are more likely to buy. Ultimately, he is interested in (1) reinforcing present attitudes if they lead to the kind of behavior he is interested in or (2) actually changing the attitudes and behavior of his target market. In some cases, this is a tall order. The Howard-Sheth model introduced in Chapter 8 showed the many influences on behavior – more than just positive attitudes. Here it is extremely important to recognize that actually changing behavior is a difficult job – but, nevertheless, the overriding objective of the promotion area.[1]

Informing, persuading, reminding are promotion objectives

■ If a firm's promotion is to be effective, agreeing on and defining promotion objectives is critical because the right promotion blend depends on what is to be accomplished.

While changing behavior is an overriding objective not only of promotion, but really of the whole marketing strategy, three broad promotion objectives are useful. These objectives are to *inform, persuade,* and *remind* target customers about the company and its marketing mix. All are concerned with providing more information.

A more specific set of promotion objectives that state *exactly who* we would want to inform, persuade, or remind and *why* is even more useful, but this is unique to each company strategy and too detailed to discuss here. Instead, we will confine ourselves to the three general promotion objectives, and how we might reach them.

The informing, persuading, and reminding objectives provide direction. Generally, we know that potential customers must have some knowledge about a product offering if they are to buy at all. Therefore, informing may be a critical initial objective. A persuading objective would indicate that the firm would attempt to evoke a favorable set of attitudes in order to affect behavior – comparative information could be supplied here. A reminding objective would lead the firm to reinforce previously satisfactory behavior by keeping cues in front of the customer.

In summary, promotion is concerned with communicating information. The learning process discussed in Chapter 8, is certainly relevant here, because we can do a better promotion job if we know how people accept and act on new information.

May need a blend from shout to soft sell

■ The firm with a distinctly new product may not have to do anything but *inform* consumers about its offering and show them how it works better than all the existing products. Newness and uniqueness in a product can simplify the promotion process and may even get free publicity for the seller. But when others offer similar products, as is usually the case, the firm must not only inform customers that a product is available, but also persuade them to buy its product. This is really two different jobs, and it is becoming more difficult and expensive as markets expand and more and more competitive products come into the market. To solve this problem, the firm may place greater reliance on advertising, which may be more economical for telling a large number of potential customers about the firm's total product.

But even after customers have been attracted and sold once, they are still subject to competitive influences which force the firm to continue persuading and reminding. In our highly competitive world, a firm must usually use several promotion methods, all at the same time, to inform, persuade, and remind.

May need a different blend for each market grid box

■ Each unique market grid box may need a separate marketing mix, and each may require a different promotion blend. This is mentioned here because some specialists in promotion have missed this point, and think mainly in mass marketing rather than target marketing terms. Aiming at the "mass market" may be needed in some situations, but unfortunately, promotion aimed at everyone can end up hitting no one. In the promotion area, we should be especially cautious about slipping into a "shotgun" approach when what is really needed is a "rifle" approach, with more careful aiming.

Promotion requires effective communication

■ Promotion obviously must get the attention of the target audience or it is wasted effort. What is obvious, however, is not always easily accomplished. Much promotion does not really communicate. Recent behavioral science studies indicate that the communication process may be more complicated than we imagine.

The same message may be interpreted differently

■ Researchers have demonstrated that the audience evaluates not only the message but also the source of the message in terms of trustworthiness and credibility. These studies have also shown that some persons are more easily persuaded than others. Persuasibility seems to be related to feelings of inadequacy and social inhibitions. While women seem to be more open to persuasion than men, persuasibility does not seem to be related to the level of general intelligence.[2]

Different audiences may perceive the same message in different ways and interpret the same words differently. Such differences are often obvious, and to be expected, in international marketing where there are translation problems. General Motors' "Body by Fisher" came out as "Corpse by Fisher" in Flemish.

Semantic problems in the *same* language may not be so obvious, and yet they must be recognized and solved to avoid giving offense. For instance, a large food company recently discovered that potential female customers didn't like being called "consumers" because they thought the word was too impersonal. They preferred "customers" or "homemakers," and married women, specifically, preferred the term "housewife."[3] These might seem like small

Figure 20-1
The communication process

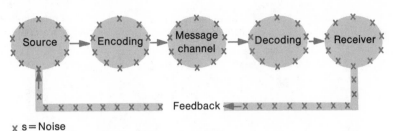

x s = Noise

differences, but it is just such subtleties that can make the target audience tune out a message, wasting the whole promotion effort.

The communication process—needs feedback

■ The communication process can be seen more clearly with the aid of a diagram (Figure 20-1). The relation to the stimulus-response model discussed in Chapter 8 should be noted here. But the critical importance of some feedback to direct the process should also be understood.

The *source* shown here is attempting to deliver a *message* to a *receiver,* perhaps a potential customer. The source can deliver his message in many ways. The personal salesman does it with his voice and actions, while advertising must do it with mass media, such as magazines, newspapers, handbills, posters, radio, and TV.

A major advantage of personal selling is that the source—the seller—may receive immediate feedback from the receivers. He can judge how his message is being received and adjust the balance of his message accordingly. This gives a real edge to the personal salesman. Mass sellers must rely on marketing research or aggregate sales results to measure what the salesman can see and feel.

The *noise* shown in Figure 20-1 refers to many factors which reduce the effectiveness of the communication process. Perhaps the source cannot agree on what should be said and how, and compromises with a general message. Or the receiver, a housewife, for example, may be distracted by children when the message comes out of her radio. Or other advertisers or salesmen may be saying essentially the same thing, and the receiver may become confused or ignore everyone. And the feedback process (including the salesman's interpretations and research results) may be filled with "noise."

Encoding and decoding depend on common frames of reference and fields of experience

■ The fundamental difficulty in the communication process occurs during encoding and decoding. The source must decide what it wants to say and then try to translate it into terms that will be decoded with the same meaning by the target audience. This can be very tricky because the meanings attached to various words and symbols may differ depending on the frames of reference and experience of the two groups. This can be seen in Figure 20-2. If there is no overlap, communication may be bad or impossible.

Figure 20–2
Another view of the communication process

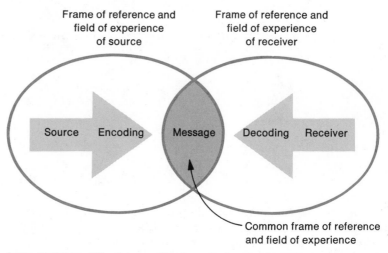

Source: Adapted from Wilbur Schramm, "How Communications Work," in Wilbur Schramm, *The Process and Effects of Mass Communication* (Urbana, Ill.: University of Illinois Press, 1960), p. 6.

The average car driver, for example, might think of the Ford Mustang as a sports car; if he constitutes the target audience, then his version of sports car terminology should be used in the message. Auto engineers and sports car buffs, however, do not consider the Mustang a true sports car, and when specifying, writing, or approving copy, they might encode the message in regular "small-car" terms, while their average-driver audience wants to hear about ease of handling, acceleration, and racing symbols such as wide tires. Errors could be minimized by knowing the relevant market grid dimensions, in terms of the needs and preferences of potential customers. This data should be available for strategy planning anyway, and here it would be especially useful.

Whether the message should emphasize only the positive features (one-sided arguments) or perhaps both positive and negative features (two-sided arguments) depends on the attitudes of the target market. Sometimes accenting the positive is desirable, since it's less confusing. But if the potential customers already know something of the pros and cons, it may be desirable to use a two-sided approach. Research on this and other topics with respect to putting together a message are beyond our scope, but it is important to realize that such matters may affect the effectiveness of communication.[4]

Message channel is important too

■ Further complicating the communications process is the receiver's awareness that the message is not only coming from a sender but that it is coming via some media. Consciously or subconsciously, the receiver may ascribe more virtue to a product if its message comes in a well-respected newspaper or magazine, just as the president of a company might seem more impressive than a junior salesman.

Effective communication leads to adoption

Adoption means behavior change

■ Effective communication means that a behavior change has taken place, or a previous behavior change has been successfully reinforced. The adoption process discussed in Chapter 8 is relevant to the problem of effective communication. There, we discussed consumer buying behavior as a problem-solving process in which buyers go through several steps on the way to adopting (or rejecting) an idea or product. Learning takes place during this process, and if the experience with a certain product is satisfying, then habits may form and subsequent problem-solving may become routine. In terms of the basic promotion objectives introduced in this chapter, informing and persuading might be needed to affect the potential customer's knowledge level and attitudes, and subsequently bring about the adoption. Then, subsequent promotion could simply remind the customer about the favorable experience, helping to confirm the adoption decision.

The AIDA framework can guide promotion planning

■ In our earlier discussion of the adoption process, we isolated six stages in this process: awareness, interest, evaluation, trial, decision, and confirmation. These stages in the adoption process dovetail very neatly with an action-oriented framework — called AIDA — which we will use in this and the following chapters to guide our discussion.

The AIDA framework consists of four fundamental and interrelated promotion tasks which have been recognized for many years: (1) to get *attention,* (2) to hold *interest,* (3) to arouse *desire,* and (4) to obtain *action.*[5] (As a memory aid, note that the initial letters of each key word spell out the four-letter word, AIDA, the well-known opera.)

The relationship of the stages of the adoption process to the AIDA promotion tasks can readily be seen:

Obtaining *attention* is obviously necessary if the potential customer is to become *aware* of the company's offering. Holding *interest* gives the communication a chance to really build the prospect's *interest.* Arousing *desire* favorably affects the *evaluation* process. And obtaining *action* includes encouraging *trial* and subsequent *adoption.* Continuing promotion is needed to *confirm* the adoption and assure continuing *action.*

These interrelations can be seen better in Figure 20–3. This action-oriented AIDA framework will guide our subsequent discussion. But it should be noted that this framework does not solve our problems. Most marketing managers deal not only with individuals going through the adoption process but with whole markets. Different promotional blends may be needed for different parts of

Figure 20-3
Relation of adoption process to AIDA tasks

Adoption process	AIDA tasks
Awareness	A (Attention)
Interest	I (Interest)
Evaluation	
Trial	D (Desire)
Decision	A (Action)
Confirmation	

the market. Some prospects may already have become aware of the product and developed considerable interest, while others have never heard of it. Still others might have adopted the product but want confirmation.

Good communication varies promotional blends along adoption curve

■ The communication and adoption processes discussed above concern individuals. This focus on individuals is important in order to understand the process. But it also helps to see markets in the aggregate and to understand that different customers within a market may behave differently—with some taking the lead in accepting products and, in turn, influencing others.

Adoption curve focuses on market segments, not individuals

■ Research on how *markets* accept new ideas has led to the development of the adoption-curve concept. The adoption curve shows how and when different groups accept ideas, and points up the need for varying the promotional effort as time passes. It also emphasizes the interrelations among groups, showing that some groups act as leaders in accepting a new idea. The adoption-curve concept is similar to the product life-cycle concept—both are concerned with the rate of acceptance of innovations.

Promotion for innovators leaves laggards behind

■ The adoption curve for a typical successful product or idea is shown in Figure 20-4. Some of the important characteristics of each of these potential customer groups are discussed below.

Innovators—3 to 5 percent of the market

The innovators are the first to adopt. They tend to be young and, at the same time, high in social and economic status. They are cosmopolites, with many contacts outside their own social group and community. Coupled with this is mobility and apparent creativeness.

Figure 20–4
The adoption curve

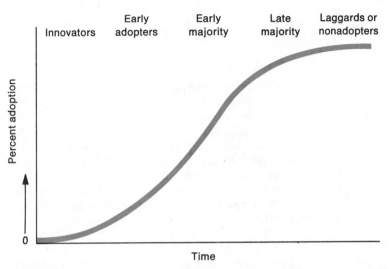

Business firms in the innovator class usually are large and rather specialized.

For promotion purposes, an important characteristic of innovators is that they tend to rely on impersonal and scientific information sources or other innovators rather than personal salesmen. They often read articles in technical publications or informative advertisements in "respectable" sources to get information.

Early adopters—10 to 15 percent of the market

This group is likely to be relatively high in social status, probably being opinion leaders. They may be younger, more mobile, and more creative than later adopters. But their social relationships are confined to their local group.

Business firms in this category also tend to be specialized.

This group tends to have the greatest contact, of all the groups, with salesmen. Mass media are important information sources, too.

Early majority—about 34 percent of the market

This group consists of those with above average social status. They usually will not consider an innovation until many early adopters have tried it. A long period may elapse between trial and adoption.

Average-sized business firms with less specialization would fit in this category.

The early majority have considerable contact with mass media and salesmen *and* early adopters.

Late majority—34 percent of the market

People in this group tend to be below average in social status and income. They are less likely to follow opinion leaders and early adopters. In fact, some social pressure from their own group may

Figure 20–5
The two-step flow of communication

| Message | Mass media | Opinion leaders | Word-of-mouth | Target groups |

be required before they try the product, but then adoption may follow quickly.

Business firms in this group tend to be smaller-sized firms with little specialization.

The late majority make little use of mass media and of salesmen. They tend to be oriented more to other late adopters than to outside sources of information.

Laggards or nonadopters—5 to 16 percent of the market

This group has the lowest social status and income, and tends to be tradition-bound.

The smallest businesses with the least specialization are often in this category.

The main source of information for laggards is other laggards, which certainly bodes ill for marketers who want to reach the whole market quickly or use one promotional method. In fact, it may not pay to bother with this group.[6]

Opinion leaders spread the word by mouth

■ Adoption-curve research reinforces our earlier discussion in Chapter 8 on opinion leaders and the *web of word of mouth*. It shows the crucial importance of the early adopters (not necessarily the innovators) because they influence the early majority—and help spread the word to many others. The *two-step flow of communications* concept is helpful to see this process.[7] Some firms deliberately use mass media to reach the opinion leaders and then count on word of mouth to reach their target groups, as shown in Figure 20–5.

Marketing men recognize the prime importance of these interpersonal conversations and recommendations by opinion leaders. If early groups reject the product, it may never get off the ground. But if the early groups accept the product, then what the opinion leaders in each social group say about it may be critical. The web of word of mouth may do the real selling job long before the customer ever walks into the retail store. This points up the importance of trying to reach the opinion leaders (communicators) in various social groups. And because all the communicators are hard to identify—recall from Chapter 8 that different kinds of people may be communicators for different products—mass media can play an important role in getting the message to them.

Less is known about the adoption process in industrial goods markets. It seems likely that the same general process is at work, but one study suggests that there is little word-of-mouth communication in these markets. This points up the importance of both personal selling and mass selling in communicating with industrial buyers *and* the multiple buying influencers.[8]

Successful promotion may be an economical blend

■ Once promotion objectives for a product have been established, a marketing manager may decide to use a blend of promotion methods, since certain jobs can be done more economically one way than another. This can be illustrated most clearly in the industrial goods market.

While personal selling dominates most industrial goods promotion budgets, mass selling is necessary, too. A blend usually is desirable. A personal salesman nearly always has to complete the sale, but it is seldom practical for him to carry the entire promotion load. In 1972 the average cost of a manufacturer's salesman's call was estimated at almost $60, and this figure is rising.[9] This relatively high cost comes from the fact that a salesman has only limited time, and much of what he does is expended on nonselling activities—traveling, paper work, sales meetings, and strictly service calls. Only 42 percent of his time is available for face-to-face selling.

The job of reaching all the buying influences is made more costly and difficult by the continuing turnover of buyers and influencers. An industrial salesman may be responsible for several hundred customers and prospects, with about four buying influencers per company. Clearly, he does not have enough time to get the company's whole message across to every potential customer. The problem is depicted in the classic McGraw-Hill advertisement shown in Figure 20–6. As the ad suggests, too much has been invested in a salesman to use his time and skill to answer questions that could be better handled through mass selling. Mass selling can do the general spadework; the salesman should concentrate on answering specific questions and clinching the sale. These mass selling "sales calls" can be made at a fraction of the cost of a personal call. One McGraw-Hill study found a mass selling "call" costing $0.0094 per call; a personal call, $22.[10]

Factors affecting selection of a promotion blend

■ Most business firms develop a promotion blend of some kind, because the various methods complement each other. But what blend is right in a particular situation?

Wholesalers invariably rely on personal selling, perhaps with good reason. Some retailers do, too, although other retailers may advertise aggressively.

At the same time, a food products manufacturer may develop a promotion blend composed of 10 parts advertising to 1 part personal selling, although some of this advertising money may be allocated to help his channel system retailers advertise. A lawn seed producer might emphasize advertising 4 to 1, while a paint manufacturer might reverse the ratio. Is there some logical pattern underlying these differences?

Figure 20–6

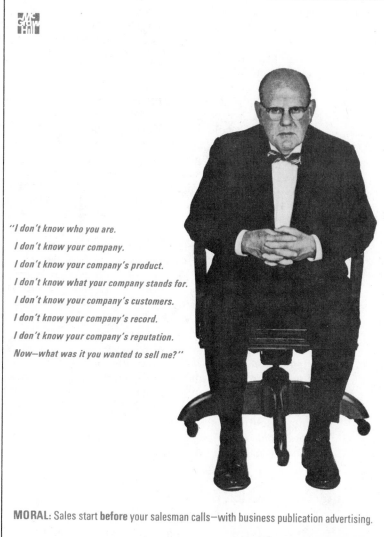

"I don't know who you are.

I don't know your company.

I don't know your company's product.

I don't know what your company stands for.

I don't know your company's customers.

I don't know your company's record.

I don't know your company's reputation.

Now—what was it you wanted to sell me?"

MORAL: Sales start **before** your salesman calls—with business publication advertising.

McGRAW-HILL MAGAZINES
BUSINESS•PROFESSIONAL•TECHNICAL

Each promotion blend is designed to accomplish the firm's over-all objectives. But the particular blend selected depends on a number of factors, including (1) the promotion budget available, (2) stage of product in its life cycle, (3) nature of the market situation, (4) target of the promotion, and (5) nature of the product.

Figure 20–6 (continued)

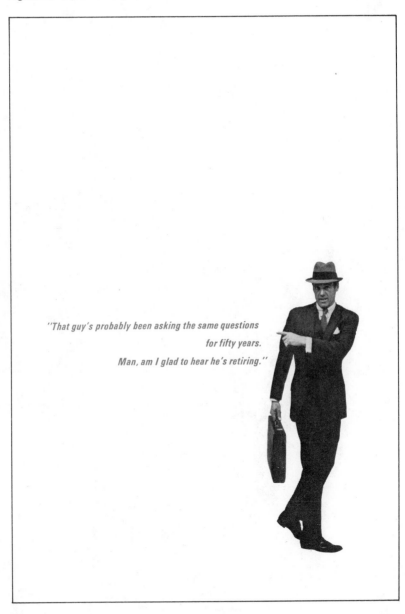

"That guy's probably been asking the same questions for fifty years. Man, am I glad to hear he's retiring."

Promotion budget affects promotion efficiency

■ There are some economies of size in Promotion. Network radio or television may reach more people more economically than local media. Local radio, TV, and newspapers may be more economical than neighborhood media or direct personal contact. But the minimum charge for some alternatives may force smaller firms, or those

Figure 20–6 (continued)

with small promotion budgets, to use the less economical alternative, in terms of cost per contact. For example, a small retailer
might like to use local television, but all he can reasonably afford
are handbills and perhaps ads in neighborhood newspapers, together with church and school bulletins. Some smaller manufacturers, out of necessity rather than choice, use personal selling as

Figure 20–6 (concluded)

"I don't know who you are.
I don't know your company.
I don't know your company's product.
I don't know what your company stands for.
I don't know your company's customers.
I don't know your company's record.
I don't know your company's reputation.
Now—what was it you wanted to sell me?"

MORAL: Sales start **before** your salesman calls—with business publication advertising.

McGRAW-HILL MAGAZINES
BUSINESS•PROFESSIONAL•TECHNICAL

their major promotion method. A personal salesman can be hired for $10,000 to $15,000 a year plus expenses. Sponsorship of a single hour of network television can cost from $50,000 to $100,000. The TV show might bring the firm's message to more people for less per person, but its total one-lump cost might be too high for a small firm.

A small budget, however, need not limit a firm to personal selling. Sales promotion, public relations, and direct mail are attractive possibilities. A small tire manufacturer who wanted to tell potential dealers about his product and was not in a position to compete with the big tiremakers' promotion programs decided instead to use direct mail. His carefully targeted campaign was extremely successful, yielding $196 in new business for every dollar invested.[11] A direct-mail expenditure of $1,861 brought in 101 new dealers and more than $360,000 of new business.

Stage of product in its life cycle

■ A new product seldom becomes a spectacular success overnight. The adoption curve discussed earlier in the chapter helps explain why. Usually the product must go through the several stages described in Chapter 12—introduction, market growth, market maturity, and sales decline. During these stages, promotion blends may be changed to achieve changing promotion objectives, including reaching different groups at varying stages of their adoption process.

Introduction stage—"this new idea is good"

During the introduction stage, the basic objective is to inform. If the product contains an entirely new idea, that idea must be sold—and not just the company's version of it. The promotion must pioneer acceptance of the product idea—not just the company's own brand. The purpose of this emphasis is to stimulate *primary demand,* a job which may be long and costly. There may be few potential "innovators" during the introductory stage. Personal selling can be very useful, especially for industrial products. But salesmen also are needed to select good channel members and then persuade them to carry the new product.

Since there are few competitors at this stage, mass selling can concentrate on the basic informing job. Initial advertisements might be designed to draw inquiries.

Market growth stage—"our brand is best"

In the market growth stage, competitors begin entering the market, and promotional emphasis must begin to shift from stimulating primary demand to stimulating *selective* demand for the company's own brand. The main job is to persuade customers to buy and stay with the company's own product, although informing is still important.

Now that more potential customers are trying and adopting the product, mass selling may become more economical. But personal salesmen must still work in the channels, expanding distribution.

Market maturity stage—"our brand is better, really"

In the market maturity stage, additional competitors have entered the market. Promotion must become increasingly persuasive rather than informative.

At this stage, mass selling may dominate the promotion blends of consumer products manufacturers. Industrial products might require more aggressive personal selling, perhaps complemented by more advertising. The total dollars allocated to the promotion blend may rise as the competitive frenzy rises.

Firms which have achieved a strong customer franchise are able to use reminder-type advertising, the type that seeks only to remind the customer of the product name and may be considerably less expensive than more persuasive efforts.

Sales decline stage – let's find those who still want our product

During the sales decline stage, the total amount spent on promotion may decrease as firms attempt to cut costs and remain profitable. Since the product may still be acceptable to some people, more targeted promotion is needed to reach these remaining customers. Firms with a strong customer franchise may use reminder-type promotion.

Nature of market situation requires different promotion

■ Closely related to the product life cycle is the nature of competition in the target market.

Firms in monopolistic competition may favor mass selling because they have differentiated their mix somewhat and apparently have something to talk about. Mass selling can be more economical, especially if they are trying to reach broad audiences.

As the market tends toward pure competition, or oligopoly, it is difficult to generalize about what will happen. Competitors in some markets aggressively seek to outpromote each other, using mass or personal selling or both. The only way for a competitor to stay in such a market is to match rivals' promotional efforts – unless, of course, his whole marketing mix can be improved in some other way. We see such competitive advertising in our daily newspapers all the time.

In markets that are drifting toward pure competition, some companies may resort to price cutting. This *may* increase their number of units sold, temporarily, but it may also reduce the revenue and the amount available for promotion *per unit*. And then competitive retaliation may reduce the temporary sales gains and drag price levels down faster. In such a situation, the cash revenues flowing into the business may decline, and all promotion will have to be cut back.

Once a firm is in pure competition, there would appear to be little reason to promote the product. But someone has to get the business, and using persuasive personal salesmen can be the way to get it. For the customer's part, he must buy needed products someplace, and often prefers to buy from friendly salesmen who call regularly.

This condition also exists in oligopoly situations. Only here, there may be enough sales revenue to support promotional efforts such as entertaining and business gift giving.

Target of promotion helps set the blend

■ Promotion can be directed to four different groups: final consumers, industrial customers, retailers, and wholesalers. The right promotion blend for each group can be slightly different.

Promotion to final consumers

The vast number of potential customers practically forces consumer goods manufacturers and retailers to use mass selling in their promotion blends. Effective mass selling may even establish brand preference to such an extent that little personal selling may be needed. Self-service and discount operations attest to this.

Mass communication may even be the way to supply information to those consumers who seek it. We noted earlier that there are innovators and early adopters, and communicators within social groups, to whom others look for guidance and suggestions. Mass selling may be necessary to reach these communicators because they are widely dispersed and it is not possible to identify or approach each one individually.

The predominance of mass selling in promoting to final consumers should not suggest that personal selling cannot be effective. Some retailers, in particular specialty shops, rely heavily on knowledgeable salesmen. And some door-to-door sales organizations have been very effective. But aggressive personal selling to final consumers usually is found only in relatively expensive channel systems (though a less costly system might not succeed at all).

Promotion to industrial customers

Industrial customers are much less numerous than final consumers, and there is more justification for a promotion blend emphasizing personal selling to such customers. Industrial customers may have specific questions or might need adjustments in the total product. A manufacturer's or wholesaler's personal salesman can be more flexible in adjusting his company's appeals to suit each customer. He is also able to call back later and provide the confirmation and additional information that often are necessary in bigger industrial sales. Personal selling becomes more practical as the size of each purchase increases, and larger unit purchases are more typical in the industrial goods field.

Although personal selling dominates industrial goods promotion blends, mass selling *is* used for some jobs, as we mentioned earlier, for economic reasons.

Promotion to retailers

As with industrial buyers, the relatively small number of retailers makes it feasible for manufacturers and wholesalers to emphasize personal selling. Sales promotion activities and some mass selling in trade magazines and newspapers are valuable, but the bulk of the promotion effort is by personal salesmen – who can answer retailers' questions about what promotion will be directed toward the final consumer, the retailers' own part in selling the product, and important details concerning price, markups, and promotional assistance and allowances.

In other words, promotion to retailers is primarily informative. But since the manufacturer's or wholesaler's salesman cannot *guarantee* the retailer a profit, promotion to retailers must also be persuasive. The salesman must convince the retailer that demand for the product exists and that making a profit will be easy.

Another reason personal selling is so important in dealing with retailers is that marketing mixes may have to be adjusted drastically from one geographical territory to another to meet competitive situations. The mixes in highly competitive urban areas, for example, may emphasize price more than those in outlying areas. Personal salesmen can judge these conditions. We already have seen the development of a specialist – the food broker – to assist producers' salesmen in the extremely competitive grocery industry.

Personal selling is also important in a promotion blend aimed at retailers because part of the selling job is to establish and maintain good channel relationships. The retailer must be shown that the manufacturer or wholesaler has his interest at heart. A channel is a human system and depends on the mutual trust and understanding of channel members which can be built only by personal relations.

Promotion to wholesalers

Promotion to wholesalers is very similar to promotion to retailers except that wholesalers are less numerous and perhaps even more conscious of demand and cost. They respond to economic arguments. They may be very interested in the promotion which the producer intends to direct at retailers and final consumers. But it is clear that personal salesmen are needed to cement the relationship between producer and wholesaler.

Nature of product makes a big difference

■ The target customers' view of the product is the common theme tying together all of the variables that must be combined into a marketing mix. Their view of the product affects the promotion blend too. The goods classes introduced in Chapters 14 and 15 had a direct bearing on the Place objectives introduced in Chapter 16. And these goods classes have a bearing on the development of promotion blends, too. These interactions are left as exercises for the student until all of these interactions are brought together in Chapter 26. Here, however, we should consider the impact of some general product characteristics on promotion blends.

Technical nature of product

An extremely technical industrial product may require a heavier emphasis on personal selling, preferably by technically trained salesmen. This is the only sure way to make the product understood and obtain feedback on how industry can use it. The technical salesman can meet with engineers, plant people, purchasing agents, and top executives, and can adjust the sales message to the needs and wants of these various influencers within the target market.

Mass selling, on the other hand, is feasible for many consumer goods because there is no technical story to be told. Or, if there are some technical factors – for example, with cars or appliances – they can be offered where there is demonstrated customer interest in them, perhaps in booklets at the dealer's showroom.

Degree of brand familiarity

If the product has already won a strong brand preference, perhaps after years of satisfactory service in the market, there may be no need for aggressive personal selling. Reminder-type advertising is usually adequate. Indeed, Hershey Chocolate long prided itself on not having to do any advertising! Recently, however, it did begin some advertising and sales promotion to counter increasing competition in the United States. But in Canada, where it is not well established, Hershey has advertised aggressively.[12]

If a manufacturer has not differentiated its product, and does not plan to invest in building a brand name—perhaps because its product is not different—then much heavier emphasis on personal selling is sensible. The major goals, then, should be building good channel relations and getting distribution in as many outlets as possible. Rather than spending—perhaps fruitlessly—to build a brand name, the firm could invest in Place development.

How typical promotion budgets are blended

■ There is no right promotion blend for all situations. Each must be developed as part of a marketing mix. But to round out our discussion of promotion blends, we can make some generalizations about how manufacturers have allocated their promotion budgets. They do vary considerably, depending on their situation and the various factors discussed above. Retailers' blends, similarly, may vary widely for similar reasons. Wholesalers' blends, on the other hand, use personal selling almost exclusively.

Figure 20-7 shows how manufacturers have tended to allocate their promotion budgets. It shows the ratios of advertising expenditures to personal selling which might be expected in various situations. It is common to find the ratios of advertising to personal selling varying from 10 to 1 to 1 to 10. Note, here we are referring to ratios, not actual expenditures. A 1 to 1 ratio would merely mean that the expenditures for advertising and personal selling were roughly equal.

The figure indicates that manufacturers of well-branded consumer goods (such as autos, breakfast cereals, and proprietary drugs), and especially those which are seeking to build brand preference, will tend to have heavier ratios in favor of advertising. And the ratio might be even higher in favor of advertising if the firm had already established its channel relationships.

At the other extreme, smaller companies with new consumer goods would tend to use more personal selling. This would be even more true if the consumer goods were relatively undifferentiated. The same thing applies for most industrial goods—because of buyers' preferences to have several sources of supply, personal selling is quite important in order to assure that the firm continues to satisfy and remain on the supplier list.

A balanced blend of personal selling and advertising might be expected where a firm sells both consumer and industrial goods. Now we are considering a blend for the whole company, not an individual product. The heavier emphasis on advertising which might be expected with consumer goods might be offset by a heavier emphasis on personal selling for industrial goods.[13]

The relatively heavier emphasis on personal selling which might be inferred from the figure is correct. As we will see in the next two

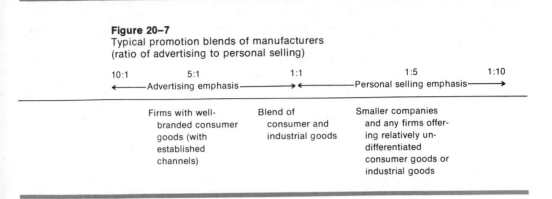

Figure 20–7
Typical promotion blends of manufacturers
(ratio of advertising to personal selling)

10:1	5:1	1:1	1:5	1:10
←——————Advertising emphasis——————→		←——————Personal selling emphasis——————→		

	Firms with well-branded consumer goods (with established channels)	Blend of consumer and industrial goods	Smaller companies and any firms offering relatively un-differentiated consumer goods or industrial goods

chapters, for the economy as a whole, far more is spent on personal selling than on advertising. The many advertisements one sees so commonly in magazines and newspapers and on television are impressive and costly. But they should not blind us to the fact that most retail transactions are completed by sales personnel and that behind the scenes there is much personal selling that goes on in the channels. In the aggregate, personal selling is several times more expensive than advertising.

Someone must plan and manage promotion blend

Good blending takes judgment

■ The selection of a promotion blend is a strategic-level decision which should jibe with the rest of the marketing strategy. The whole should be greater than the sum of the parts. Once the basic outlines of the promotion blend are set, then more detailed plans for the parts of the blend must be developed and implemented, perhaps by specialists such as the sales and advertising managers.

Deciding on the appropriate promotion blend is obviously difficult, dependent as it is on fitting together with the rest of a marketing strategy. Conceptually, this can be seen as a problem of balancing the alternative use of scarce resources among the various elements of a marketing mix. This still requires considerable judgment and experience and is why we show it as a job for the marketing manager.

Sales manager manages salesmen

■ Personal selling usually is the responsibility of a sales manager. Since most sales managers have been personal salesmen, they usually place great confidence in the power of personal contact.

The sales manager may be responsible for implementing Place policies, especially building good distribution channels, and in smaller companies, he often acts as the marketing manager.

Advertising manager works with ads and admen

■ An advertising manager, on the other hand, is concerned with mass selling effort via television, newspapers, magazines, billboards, and other media. His job is choosing the appropriate media for each purpose and developing the ads. He may implement this effort in an advertising department within his firm, especially if he is in retailing, or through an independent outside advertising agency.

Sales promotion manager, a jack of all promotion

■ The sales promotion manager often fills the gaps between the sales and advertising managers, enhancing their effectiveness. Nearly everything the sales promotion department does could be done by either the sales or advertising departments. But sales promotion activities are so varied that specialists tend to develop.

In some companies, the sales promotion manager works for the sales manager; in others, he is moving toward independent status with responsibility only to the marketing manager.

Marketing manager, talks to all, blends all

■ Because of differences in outlook and experience, the advertising, sales, and sales promotion managers may have difficulty working with each other as partners or equals, especially when each feels that his approach is the most important. In some companies, they are hardly on speaking terms. It remains the marketing manager's job to weigh the pros and cons of the various approaches and come up with an effective promotion blend, fitting the various departments and personalities into it and coordinating their efforts.

All of these jobs might have to be carried by one man in a smaller company, perhaps with the title of sales manager. In this case, *he* is responsible for developing an effective promotion blend.

Conclusion

■ Promotion is a vital factor in any marketing mix. Most consumers and intermediate customers can choose from among many products. To be successful, a manufacturer must not only offer a good product at a reasonable price but also must tell potential customers about his product and where it can be purchased. The producer must tell wholesalers and retailers in the channel about his product and his marketing mix. These middlemen, in turn, must use promotion to reach their customers.

The nature of the promotion job should fit logically into the strategy which is being developed to satisfy the needs and preferences of some target market. *What* should be communicated to them should be stated explicitly as part of the strategy planning.

The overriding promotion objective is changing behavior, but basic promotion objectives include informing, persuading, and reminding.

Various promotion methods can be used to reach these objectives and how the promotion methods are combined and used to achieve effective communication can be guided by some behavioral science findings. In particular, we know more now about the communications process, how individuals adopt new ideas, and how groups react.

An action-oriented framework called AIDA will help guide strategic planning of promotion blends, but finally the marketing manager is responsible for blending the alternative promotion methods into one promotion effort for each marketing mix. Special considerations which may affect the promotion blend are the size of the promotion budget, stage of product in its life cycle, the particular target customers who must be reached, the nature of the market situation, and the nature of the product.

In this chapter, we have considered some basic ideas. In the next two chapters we will treat personal and mass selling in greater depth.

questions and problems

1 Relate the three basic promotion objectives to the four tasks (AIDA) of the promotion job, using a specific example.

2 Discuss the communication process in relation to a manufacturer's promotion of an accessory good, say a portable air hammer used for breaking up concrete pavement.

3 Explain how an understanding of the way individuals adopt new ideas or products (the adoption process) would be helpful in developing a promotion blend. In particular, explain how it might be desirable to change a promotion blend during the course of the adoption process. To make this more concrete, discuss it in relation to the acceptance of a new sport-coat style.

4 Discuss how our understanding of the adoption curve should be applied to planning the promotion blend(s) for a new, small (personal) electric car.

5 Discuss the nature of the promotion job in relation to the life cycle of a product. Illustrate, using household dishwashing machines.

6 Promotion has been the target of considerable criticism. What specific types of promotion are probably the object of this criticism?

7 Might promotion be successful in expanding the general demand for: (a) oranges, (b) automobiles, (c) tennis rackets, (d) cashmere sweaters, (e) iron ore, (f) steel, (g) cement? Explain why or why not in each case.

8 Indicate the promotion blend which might be most appropriate for manufacturers of the following established products (assume average- to large-sized firms in each case) and support your answer:
a. Candy bars.
b. Men's T shirts.
c. Castings for automobile engines.
d. Car batteries.
e. Industrial fire insurance.
f. Inexpensive plastic raincoats.
g. A camera which has achieved a specialty-goods status.

9 Discuss the potential conflict among the various promotion managers.

notes

[1] Philip Zimbardo and Ebbe B. Ebbesen, *Influencing Attitudes and Changing Behavior* (Reading, Mass.: Addison-Wesley Publishing Co., 1969), pp. 85–93.)

[2] Abe Shuchman and Michael Perry, "Self-Confidence and Persuasibility in Marketing: A Reappraisal," *Journal of Marketing Research*, May 1969, pp. 146–55; Carl I. Hovland and Irving L. Janis (eds.), *Personality and Persuasibility* (New Haven, Conn.: Yale University Press, 1959), pp. 229–40.

[3] *Management Review*, June 1961, pp. 4 ff.

[4] For more discussion of basic studies in the communications area, see David K. Berlo, *The Process of Communication* (New York: Holt, Rinehart & Winston, Inc., 1960).

[5] M. S. Heidingsfield and A. B. Blankenship, *Marketing* (New York: Barnes & Noble, Inc., 1957), p. 149.

[6] For further discussion, see Gerald Zaltman, *Marketing: Contributions from the Behavioral Sciences,* (New York: Harcourt, Brace & World, Inc., 1965), pp. 45–56 and 23–37; Everett M. Rogers, *The Diffusion of Innovations* (New York: Free Press, 1962); Kenneth Uhl, Roman Andrus, and Lance Poulsen, "How Are Laggards Different? An Empirical Inquiry," *Journal of Marketing Research,* February 1970, pp. 51–54; see also C. W. King and J. O. Summers, "Overlap of Opinion Leadership Across Consumer Product Categories," *Journal of Marketing Research,* February 1970, pp. 43–50; Joseph R. Mancuso, "Why Not Create Opinion Leaders for New Product Introductions?" *Journal of Marketing,* July 1969, pp. 20–25; and Thomas S. Robertson, "The Process of Innovation and the Diffusion of Innovation," *Journal of Marketing,* January 1967, pp. 14–19.

[7] Elihu Katz, "The Two-Step Flow of Communication," *Public Opinion Quarterly,* Spring 1957, pp. 61–78.

[8] Frederick E. Webster, Jr., "Informal Communication in Industrial Markets," *Journal of Marketing Research,* May 1970, pp. 186–90; Leon G. Schiffman, and Vincent Gaccione, "Opinion Leaders in Institutional Markets," *Journal of Marketing,* April 1974, pp. 49–53; John A. Czepiel, "Word-of-Mouth Processes in the Diffusion of a Major Technological Innovation," *Journal of Marketing Research,* May 1974, pp. 172–80; and John A. Martilla, "Word-of-Mouth Communication in the Industrial Adoption Process," *Journal of Marketing Research,* May 1971, pp. 173–78.

[9] *Business Week,* July 27, 1974, p. 76.

[10] *The Mathematics of Selling* (New York: McGraw-Hill Publishing Company, Inc.).

[11] "Direct Mail Puts Jack with Giants," *Printers' Ink,* November 10, 1961, pp. 49–50.

[12] "Hershey's Sweet Tooth Starts Aching," *Business Week,* February 7, 1970, pp. 98–104; and "Big Chocolate Maker, Beset by Profit Slide, Gets More Aggressive," *Wall Street Journal,* February 18, 1970, pp. 1 f.

[13] Edwin H. Lewis, "Sales Promotion Decisions," *Business News Notes* (Minneapolis: School of Business Administration, University of Minnesota, November 1954).

21

Personal selling

■ Promotion is communication with potential customers, and a personal presentation is often the best way to do the communicating. While face-to-face with the prospect, a salesman can get more attention than an advertisement or a display. He can adjust the presentation as he goes along, stay in tune with prospect feedback, and if (and when) the prospect indicates that "this might be a good idea," the salesman is there to close the sale and take the order.

In this chapter, we will discuss the nature of the personal selling job and the sales management decisions that are needed to make it an effective part of a promotion blend and a marketing mix.

Importance and role of personal selling

■ We already have seen that personal selling is important in some promotion blends and vital in others. Some of its supporters feel that personal selling is the dynamic element which keeps our economy going.

Without question, our economy does need and use many salesmen. U.S. Census Bureau statistics show that almost 10 percent of the total U.S. labor force is in sales work. Keeping in mind that the Bureau is inclined to place many persons who are primarily personal salesmen into other classifications, it is likely that *at least* 10 percent of the nation's labor force, or over 7 million people, are engaged in personal selling. Contrast this with less than half a million people working in advertising. Any activity that engages so many people and is so important to the economy deserves study.

Death of a salesman?

■ Personal selling is vital to the survival of most businesses, but the role of the personal salesman has come in for considerable criticism. The aggressive and sometimes sharp practices of some salesmen, especially door-to-door peddlers, and the hucksters involved in county or street fairs, have soured some prospective personal salesmen. And the grinning glad-hander by the name of Willie Loman in the play *Death of a Salesman* established a pathetic stereotype for salesmen in some peoples' minds. There also has been criticism about the personal salesman's effectiveness, especially at the retail level. Many people have had experience with incompetent retail clerks who couldn't care less about the customer and her needs.

The poor image of personal selling in some peoples' minds, coupled with the ineffectiveness of many sales personnel, led some prophets to predict that personal selling would decline in importance. And this has happened to some extent in retailing, resulting in an increase in self-service.

Rebirth of the salesman

■ The personal salesman is far from dead. His role is simply being redefined and upgraded, as different types of sales tasks are required. And modern sales and marketing management have gone far toward redefining what needs to be done and then selecting, training, and motivating salesmen to perform effectively—while also providing them with personal satisfaction. In some cases, sales work is taking on the characteristics of a profession. Many high-caliber salesmen believe in the importance and value of personal selling, and often subscribe to codes of ethics.

It's more than "get rid of the product"

■ In discussing some of the fundamentals of selling, from the standpoint of marketing management, we will assume that the rest of the marketing mix the salesman is to sell is reasonably good. But in fairness to salesmen and salesmanship, this is not always the case, and a salesman should not be expected to compensate completely for his firm's failings. Production-oriented businessmen often feel that it is the salesman's job to "get rid of the product," whether it is good or not. But if the salesman can see that he doesn't have much to sell, it is easy to understand why his morale might slip and the whole promotion job suffer.

Helping to buy is good selling

■ Increasingly, good salesmen don't try to *sell* the customer, rather they try to *help him buy* by presenting both the advantages and disadvantages of their products and showing how they will satisfy his needs. They find that this helpfulness results in satisfied customers and long-term relationships. This new approach recognizes the growing sophistication of buyers, especially industrial buyers.

The old-line salesman with the funny story and the engaging grin is being replaced by the salesman who has something concrete to contribute. The smiling "bag of wind" with the big expense account is headed toward extinction.

Salesman represents the whole company

■ Increasingly, the salesman is recognized as a representative of the whole company, responsible for explaining its total effort to target customers, rather than just moving products. As evidence of this change in thinking, some companies now give their salesmen such titles as field manager, market specialist, sales representative, or sales engineer.

The salesman is both transmitter and receiver

■ A salesman is expected to do much more than just bring in new business, though this certainly is an important part of his job. But in terms of the communication process discussed earlier, he must both get action – the adoption of the product – and then continue to work with customers to help them confirm their decision and continue buying. This may take the form of regular follow-up calls to be sure the customer is satisfied with his last purchase.

At the same time, the salesman may gather feedback data to enable the company to do a better job in its subsequent planning. Recall that a feedback function is an integral part of both the communications process *and* the basic management process of planning, executing, and controlling.

The modern salesman, in other words, not only communicates the company's story to customers but also feeds back customer reaction to the company. He is a vital link both in the communication and marketing processes.

Salesman can be strategy planner, too

■ Some salesmen are expected to be the marketing managers in their geographic territories. In fact, some may become marketing managers by default because their own manager or top management has not provided clear strategic guidelines. In this case, he must fill the void – that is, develop his own marketing mix or even his own strategy. He may be given a geographic territory, but exactly who his customers are may be vague. He may have to start from scratch in his strategy planning, the only restrictions being the general product line which he is expected to sell and probably a price structure. He may have his own choice as to whom he aims at, which particular products in the whole line he will push aggressively, which middlemen he will solicit or work hard with, how he will allocate any promotion money that he controls and his own time, of course, and how he will adjust prices to the extent that he has latitude there.

A salesman who can put together attractive strategies and then implement them well can rise very rapidly. If a strategy will work in his territory, then it may work elsewhere and it is very likely that he will become responsible for larger and larger territories. The opportunity is there for those who are prepared.

And even the starting job may offer great opportunities. Some beginning salesmen, especially those working for manufacturers or wholesalers, are responsible for larger sales volumes than are achieved by average or even large-sized retail stores. This is a responsibility which must be taken seriously and should be planned for. Further, the sales job is often used as an entry level position –

to take a person's measure. And success in this job can lead to rapid promotion to higher level sales and marketing jobs and, of course, more money and security.

Basic sales tasks may be split

■ One of the difficulties of discussing selling is that every sales job is different. While the engineer or accountant can look forward to fairly specific duties, the salesman's job is constantly changing.

Selling is divided into three parts

■ There are three basic sales tasks which a salesman might have to perform. These tasks are: (1) *order getting,* (2) *order taking,* and (3) *supporting.* For convenience we will designate salesmen by these terms, referring to their primary task, although one salesman might have to do all three tasks in some situations.

As the names imply, order getters and order takers are specifically interested in obtaining orders for their company. In contrast, supporting salesmen are not directly interested in orders. Their function is to help the order-oriented salesmen.

While it is true that specific individuals with certain abilities, interests, and training may be best suited for specific jobs, note that there is a place in personal selling for nearly everyone.

Order getters develop new business

■ Order getting is concerned with developing new business. *Order getting, sometimes called "creative selling," means seeking out potential buyers aggressively with a well-organized sales presentation designed to sell a product, service, or idea.*

Order getters may sell complete lines or only a single line, in which case they may be called *specialty salesmen.* They may be interested in selling the advantages of buying from one company rather than from another, or shifting the share of purchases from others to the salesman's company, or finding completely new customers and even entirely new markets.

An order getter must have complete confidence in his abilities, his company, and his product, since his attitude shows through to customers. He must also know what he is talking about—not be just a contact man.

Order-getting salesmen work for manufacturers, wholesalers, and retailers. They normally are well paid—many earning more than $25,000 per year.

Manufacturers' order-getting salesmen

Manufacturers of all kinds of goods, but especially industrial goods, have a great need for order getters. They are needed to locate new prospects, open new accounts, visualize new opportunities, and help establish and build channel relationships.

High-caliber order getters are essential in sales of installations and accessory equipment, where substantial sums are involved and top-level management participates in the buying decision.

Top-level customers are more interested in ways to save or make more money than in technical details, and a good order getter caters to this interest. He sells concepts and ideas rather than physical products. The products are merely the means of achieving the ends desired by the customer.

In selling other industrial goods—such as raw materials, components, supplies, and services—skilled order getters also are necessary. Yet in these fields they may be required only for initial contacts. Since many competitors offer nearly the same product in this area, the salesman's crucial selling job here is getting his company's name "on the list." Persuasion of the highest order and sometimes deliberate social cultivation of top-executive prospects may be necessary.

Industrial goods order getters may be required to help solve the customers' problems which continually arise in the course of production. To supply themselves with technically competent order-getting salesmen, firms often give special technical training to business-trained college graduates. Such salesmen then can deal intelligently with their specialist customers. In fact, they may be more technically competent in their narrow specialty than anyone they are likely to encounter and so may be able to provide a unique service.

"WORMS," SAID THE SALESMAN The crucial need for technical training and an interest in service and problem solving can be seen in an incident in the career of a young salesman who was selling Ralston-Purina hog feed, (a component material) to hog raisers. This salesman had worked at Ralston Purina Co.'s huge (26,000 animals) experimental farm, which that firm uses as a training school for its salesmen. After training at this school, a salesman knows about the care and feeding of animals because he has fed and weighed many animals and recorded their gains in weight.

> One day he called on a hog raiser—one of the biggest buyers of hog feed in that part of the state. The farmer was not interested in Purina products. While our young salesman was talking with him, one of his hogs lay down and died in the mud right in front of them. "Worms," said the salesman. "No such thing!" said the farmer. *"I've had my hogs tested for worms and they don't have any."* "Give me a sharp knife and let's see," suggested the new graduate. So he performed an autopsy on that porker and revealed that it was full of worms.
>
> His next step was an offer of *service.* He said, "Now let's de-worm the rest of your hogs before you lose any more of them. I'll hang around and help you do it." He spent the best part of three days helping with this rather unpleasant chore, then made bold to suggest that the farmer would be wise to put a solid floor on his pens so that the hogs could live under cleaner conditions. By this time, the hog raiser was somewhat humbled and genuinely grateful; so he promised to make this improvement. Then, without being asked, he came across with the startling proposition: "Young fellow, you know hogs. You know things that I had never learned. I'd like your advice on how I should feed my hogs."
>
> Of course, he became one of the biggest buyers of Purina hog feed and, through his influence, almost an assistant salesman to our young friend.[1]

HE MUST KNOW OTHER MEN'S BUSINESS Business training also is important to enable the manufacturer's salesman to visualize the needs and potentials of particular prospects and to discuss prices and long-run business conditions with purchasing agents.

Wholesalers' order-getting salesmen—hand it to the customer, almost

We have seen already that progressive wholesalers are developing into counselors and store advisers rather than just order takers. In some situations, routine orders are simply handled by mail or telephone, with wholesalers' salesmen functioning as "partners" of retailers in the job of moving merchandise from the wholesale warehouse through the retail store to consumers.

The emphasis here is on *through*. Modern wholesalers attempt to cooperate with retailers rather than merely stocking them. The idea here is that nothing is really sold until the final consumer or user buys it.

These salesmen truly are in the order-getting class. Many have found it much more profitable to do an extremely good job with few accounts rather than wearing themselves out with large numbers of retailers, but selling little to each of them. These order getters practically become a part of the retailer's staff, helping to check stock, write orders, conduct demonstrations, and plan advertising, special promotions, and other retailing activities.

Agent middlemen often are order getters, particularly the more aggressive manufacturers' agents and brokers. They face the same tasks as manufacturers' order getters.

Retail order-getting salesmen—visionaries at the storm window

Order getters are necessary for unsought goods and desirable for some shopping goods.

UNSOUGHT GOODS NEED ORDER GETTERS Convincing customers of the merits of products they have not seriously considered takes a high degree of personal salesmanship. Encyclopedia salesmen, for example, must convince prospects that $300 or $400 is a small price for a lifetime of literacy and happiness.

Order getters may have to visualize how a particular product will satisfy existing needs now being filled by something else. Early salesmen for aluminum storm windows and other aluminum and plastic home improvements faced the difficult task of convincing skeptical prospects that these materials were not only durable but would save money and require less maintenance in the long run. Similar problems were faced by early refrigerator salesmen in the 1920s and air-conditioning salesmen in the 1930s, but encyclopedia salesmen will probably face them from now until doomsday.

Without order-getting salesmen, many of the products we now accept as part of our standard of living—such as refrigerators and window air conditioners—might have died in the introductory stage. Most people reject or wait for others to accept new ideas. It is the visionary order getter who helps bring products out of the introductory stage into the market growth and market maturity stages. It is the order getter who sells enough customers to get the web-of-word-of-mouth going. Without sales and profits in the early stages, the product may fail and never be offered again.

THEY HELP SELL SHOPPING GOODS Order-getting salesmen are desirable for selling *heterogeneous* shopping goods. Consumers shop for many of these items on the basis of price *and* quality, and they welcome useful information. Automobiles, furniture and furnishings, cameras and photographic supplies, and fashion items can be sold effectively by an aggressive, helpful order-getting salesman. Friendly advice, based on thorough knowledge of the product and its alternatives, may help consumers and bring profits to the salesman and retailers through the trade it attracts.

Many specialty shops and limited-line stores have developed a following because of the assistance offered by the stores' salesmen. Some retail salesmen notify their regular customers when they have special offerings. They frequently will advise a customer *not* to buy a particular product because it will not fit his needs, even though they do not have a suitable substitute. The store may lose an immediate sale, but this type of assistance in buying is profitable to retailers seeking loyal customers and repeat business.

Order takers — keep the business coming

■ Order takers complete the bulk of all sales transactions. After the customer acquires an interest in the products of a specific firm — either by an order-getting salesman, a supporting salesman, or through advertising or sales promotion — an order taker may be necessary to answer any final questions and complete the sale.

Order taking, which is defined as the routine completion of sales made regularly to the same or similar customers, accounts for much personal selling.

Sometimes sales managers or customers will use the term "order taker" in a snide way when referring to unaggressive salesmen, but such usage is often inaccurate and highly colored with prejudice. A salesman may perform so poorly that criticism of him is justified. But it is a mistake to downgrade the *function* of order taking. Order taking is extremely important whether handled by human hands or machines.

The order-taking function *can* sometimes be reduced to taking money mechanically and delivering the product, as by vending machine. Computers may take over many routine buying and selling transactions in the channel and in the industrial goods area; companies can now buy supplies in this way. But there are many aspects of order taking that demand the human touch.

Manufacturers' order takers — responsible for training and explaining

After order getters open up industrial, wholesale, or retail accounts, a day-in and day-out follow-up is necessary. Someone has to explain details, make adjustments, handle complaints, and keep customers informed on new developments. In selling certain products to manufacturers, it may be necessary to train the company's employees to use machines or products. In sales to dealers, it may be necessary to train the wholesalers' or retailers' salesmen. These activities are part of the order taker's job.

Usually these salesmen have a regular route with many calls, which they may make at fixed times. To handle these calls well, they must have considerable physical energy, persistence, enthusiasm, and a friendly personality that wears well over time.

Many times the order taker must set up displays, or place the company's sales promotion materials. He must continually explain the company's marketing mix to his customers. As it changes, he has to negotiate new prices, allowances, guarantees, credit terms, cooperative advertising, and other aspects of the mix.

Sometimes jobs that are basically order-taking tasks are used to train potential order getters and managers, since they may offer order-getting possibilities. This can be seen in the following description of his job by a young Colgate salesman, who moved rapidly into the ranks of sales management:

> Over many months, I worked carefully with Gromer's Super Market. It was an aggressive young store. After a few calls, I felt I had built up a warm friendship with the store personnel. They came to trust me and, more frequently than not, after I straightened shelves, checked out-of-stocks and did the usual dusting and rearranging, I gave them an order blank already filled in.
>
> It got to be a joke with big, husky Paul Gromer, the owner, and his hard-working manager-brother. They kept asking, "Well, what did we buy today?" and they signed the order book without checking.
>
> Naturally, I worked at the order like it was my own business, making certain that they were never stuck with dead stock or over-orders. They were making continual progress, though nothing sensational.
>
> Finally, Colgate came out with a good deal. I knew it was right for Gromer's and I thought the store ought to double its weekly order to 400 cases. I talked to Paul Gromer about it and, without any reason that I'm able to think of today, I said, "Paul, this is a hot deal and I think you're ready for a carload order."
>
> He looked at me for just a moment. I braced myself for an argument. Then he said, "Sure, why not? You've always been right before. Just ship it."
>
> It was the biggest order of soap Gromer's had ever taken—and the store soon became a regular carload buyer.[2]

Wholesalers' order takers—not getting orders, but keeping them

While manufacturers' order-taking salesmen handle relatively few items and sometimes even a single item, wholesalers' order takers may handle 125,000 items or more. Here, they obviously cannot be much more than order takers in the narrow sense of the word. In fact, the use of the term often applies specifically to wholesalers' salesmen.

Most order takers just sell out of their catalog. They have so many items that they cannot possibly give aggressive sales effort to very many of them, except perhaps newer or more profitable items. But once a new product has been featured, it is unlikely that the order taker will give it much attention for some time, if ever. He just has too many items to single any out for special attention. The order taker's strength is his wide assortment rather than detailed knowledge of individual products. Even if shown that he could expand sales of particular items substantially, he probably would not do it.

The wholesale order taker's main function is to keep in close contact with his customers, perhaps once a week, and fill any needs that have developed. Sometimes the salesman gets very close to industrial customers or retailers. Some retailers permit him to take inventory and write up his own order. Obviously, this position of trust cannot be abused. After writing up the order, this salesman normally checks to be sure his company fills the order promptly and accurately. He also handles any adjustments or complaints and generally acts as a liaison between his company and his customers.

Such salesmen are usually of the low-pressure type, friendly and easygoing. Usually these jobs are not as high paying as the order-getting variety but are attractive to many because they are not as physically taxing. Relatively little traveling is required, and there is little or no pressure to develop new accounts.

Retail order takers—often they are poor clerks

Order taking may be almost mechanical at the retail level, for example, at the supermarket checkout counter. For most convenience goods and for specialty goods which have already been thoroughly presold, not much needs to be done except fill the customers' order, wrap it, and make change. As a result, retail clerks often are expected to concentrate on setting up and arranging stock—and sometimes they seem to be annoyed by having to complete sales. Many are downright rude. This is most unfortunate because order taking *is* a vital function. They may be poor order takers, however, because they are not paid very well—often at the minimum wage. But they may be paid little because they do little. In any case, order taking at the retail level appears to be declining in quality and it is likely that there will be far fewer such jobs in the future as manufacturers and wholesalers make adjustments in promotion to offset poor sales personnel at the retail level. As we have already seen, more and more merchants are turning to self-service selling.

Supporting salesmen— inform and promote in the channel

■ There are two types of salesmen who *support and assist the order-oriented salesmen, but do not themselves try to secure orders.* These two types are *missionary salesmen and technical specialists.* Their activities, naturally, are directed toward obtaining sales, at least in the long run. For the short run, however, they are ambassadors of goodwill who provide specialized services. Almost all supporting salesmen work for manufacturers or are middlemen specialists who do this supporting work for manufacturers.

Missionary salesmen

A missionary salesman is employed by a manufacturer to work with his middlemen and their customers. His usual purpose is to develop goodwill and stimulate demand, help the middleman train his salesmen to do so, and often take orders for delivery by such middlemen.

Sometimes missionary salesmen are called *merchandising salesmen* or *detailers.*[3] They may be absolutely vital if a manufacturer uses the typical merchant wholesaler to obtain widespread distribution and yet knows that the retailers will need promotional assistance. These salesmen may be able to give an occasional shot in the arm to the company's regular wholesalers and retailers. Or, they may work regularly with these middlemen, setting up displays, arranging promotions, and, in general, supplying what his company's sales promotion specialists have developed. An imaginative missionary salesman may set up displays which double or triple the sales of his company's products. Naturally, this does not go unnoticed and missionary sales jobs are often a route to order-oriented jobs. In fact, this position is often used as a training ground for new salesmen.

Technical specialists

These men are usually scientists or engineers who have relatively little interest in sales. Instead, they have technical competence, plus the ability to explain the advantages of the company's product. Since they normally talk to the customer's technical people, there is little need for a high order of salesmanship. Prior to the specialist's visit, an order getter probably has stimulated interest. Then, the technical specialist can provide the details.

Frequently, it is the order getter's job to get past the purchasing agent or other company executives who serve as a screen for the company's engineering or technical personnel. The order getter locates a problem and suggests that his technical people can solve it. Then it is up to the technical specialist. The order getter probably will consummate the sale, but only after the customer's technical people give at least tentative approval. Some of these technical specialists eventually become fine order-getting salesmen, but the majority are more interested in establishing the technical excellence of their product than working closely with people to persuade them to buy it.

Most selling takes the right blend of all three —job descriptions are needed

■ We have isolated and described three sales tasks—order getting, order taking, and supporting. You should understand, however, that a particular salesman might be given at least two of these tasks and perhaps all three. Ten percent of a particular salesman's job may be order getting, 80 percent order taking, and the additional 10 percent supporting. Another salesman may have the same title but a far different blend of sales tasks.

The type of man required for a given sales position and the level of compensation will depend largely on which sales tasks are required and in what combination. This is why job descriptions for salesmen's positions are so important.

A careful job description should be written for each sales job as part of the marketing strategy planning effort. This, in turn, can guide implementation.

A good job description should show, in detail, what activities the salesman is expected to do. It might list 10 to 20 specific tasks which he is to accomplish as well as the routine prospecting and sales report writing. Each company must write its own job specifications—but when they are written, they should provide clear guidelines as to the kind of salesmen who should be selected and how they should be compensated and motivated. These matters are discussed later in the chapter.

Three kinds of sales presentations may be useful

■ We can deepen our understanding of the nature of the different kinds of selling jobs by considering three possible approaches to sales presentations. The approach that is selected and the type of salesman that is hired to implement this approach may be a strategic matter. The marketing manager can choose among three basically different sales presentation theories in his planning: the *stimulus-response* theory, the *selling formula* theory, and the *need-satisfaction* theory. Each of these approaches has its place, and is discussed below.

Stimulus-response theory

■ The basic stimulus-response model discussed in Chapter 8 applies here. Presumably, a customer faced with a particular stimulus will give the desired response – say, a yes answer to the salesman's request for an order. In applying this theory, however, the salesman usually does not have a very good idea about what goes on in the consumer's mind, and so he tries various appeals, one after another, hoping to get the desired response. This is shown in Figure 21–1. Basically, the salesman does most of the talking, see the shaded area in Figure 21–1, only occasionally letting the customer talk when he attempts to close. If one closing attempt does not work, he goes on with another standard presentation until he makes another try at closing. This procedure could go on for some time, until either the salesman runs out of material or the customer buys or decides to leave.

This theory can be effective and practical when the prospective sale is low in value and the time which can be economically devoted to selling is short. This would be true for many convenience goods in food stores, drugstores, and department stores. The presentation might be as simple as: "That's very nice, can I wrap it up?" or "That looks nice on you, would you like to take one?" or "Would you like to try it on?" or "Would you like a carton instead of a package?" or "Shall I fill'er up?" Each can be effective for some customers and, thus, all the situation demands.

This theory treats all potential target markets the same. It may work for some and not for others, and the salesman probably will not know why. Moreover, he doesn't really improve his performance as a result of experience, because he is just mechanically trying standardized presentations. This approach may be suitable for simple order-taking situations but is no longer considered good selling for more complicated selling situations.

Selling formula theory

■ This theory also builds on the stimulus-response model, but it assumes that we know something about the customer and his needs and preferences and can, therefore, take him through some logical steps to the final close.

This approach is illustrated in Figure 21–2, where we see that the salesman does most of the talking at the beginning of the presentation, because he knows what he wants to say to implement the strat-

Figure 21–1
Stimulus-response theory as applied to sales presentations

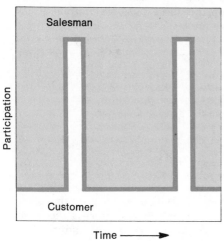

Source: Harold C. Cash and W. J. E. Crissy, "Ways of Looking at Selling," *Psychology of Selling*, 1957.

Figure 21–2
Selling formula theory as applied to sales presentations

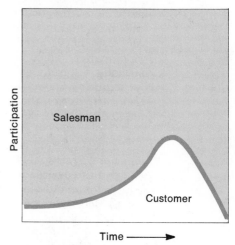

Source: Harold C. Cash and W. J. E. Crissy, "Ways of Looking at Selling," *Psychology of Selling*, 1957.

egy. As the sales presentation moves along, he brings the customer into the discussion to help clarify exactly what needs this customer has. Then he comes back to dominate the conversation in an effort to show how his product satisfies these needs and to close the sale.

This approach may be useful for both order-getting and order-taking situations where potential customers are quite similar in terms of their needs and preferences and relatively untrained salesmen (perhaps because of high turnover) must be used. It can be likened to using mass selling—where one general presentation must be tailored to a large audience—only here the presentation is being made face-to-face.

Need-satisfaction theory

■ With this approach, the salesman leads the customer into doing most of the talking at the beginning, in order to help the salesman pinpoint the customer's needs (see Figure 21–3). After the salesman feels that he understands the customer's needs more fully, he begins to participate more in the sales presentation, trying to help the customer understand his needs. Once they both agree on needs, the salesman attempts to show how his product will fulfill these needs and to close the sale.

The need-satisfaction theory can be useful if there are different needs held by various customers within the same target market. The salesman's job is to determine which of these various needs this particular person has and to help him to understand what his needs are.

It should be obvious that the need-satisfaction theory is applicable in most higher-level sales jobs. This type of selling provides

Figure 21–3
Need-satisfaction theory as applied to
sales presentations

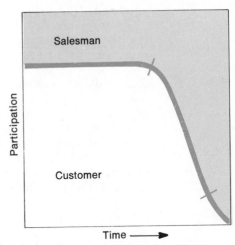

Source: Harold C. Cash and W. J. E. Crissy, "Ways of
Looking at Selling," *Psychology of Selling,* 1957.

great satisfaction for some salesmen, causing them to move toward
a professional status. Some become so deeply involved with satisfying their customers' needs that they see themselves as representatives of their *customers* in dealings with their own firms.

Using AIDA   ■ Each presentation (except for some simple stimulus-response
to plan   types), would tend to follow the AIDA sequence and "how-to-do-it"
sales   might even be specified as part of the marketing strategy. The time
presentations spent with each of the steps might vary depending upon the situation and the selling theory being applied, but it is still necessary to
begin a presentation by getting the prospect's *attention* and, hopefully, moving him to *action* through a close. The ways in which
these steps might unfold are discussed in the following paragraphs.

Attention
There is no sure way to get a prospect's attention. Much depends
on the salesman's instincts and his originality, as well as his knowledge of his customers. If a salesman calls on the same customers
frequently, he will want to use a new approach each time. If each
call is on a new prospect, a few successful attention-getters will
suffice.

At the first stage of his meeting with a customer, the salesman's
main purpose is to distract the potential customer from his current
thoughts and begin a conversation. He might do this by just introducing himself or saying, "Hello, can I help you?" as a retail clerk
might. Or a statement about the plans of the prospect's competitors
might get attention.

Whatever method is used, the attention-getter should be casual, not elaborate, so that the salesman can move quickly, naturally, and logically into the next step – creating interest. Otherwise, attention may be followed by a letdown.

Interest

Creating interest takes more time. The best way is to probe for the prospect's basic needs or problems, especially those which the salesman might be able to solve. A furniture store salesman should not make a prepared speech about rugs every time a customer comes in – some might want lamps, sofas, and so on. Getting the customer to talk begins a dialogue and gives the salesman the all-important feedback which guides his subsequent effort. Theoretically, he should select prospects from among the target customers of the marketing strategy or strategies he is implementing. Therefore, he should know roughly what they want and have a marketing mix that has been designed specifically for them. His job is to show how and why it fits their needs, in order to close the sale.

If the salesman has correctly selected his prospect, he may be able to use some visual aids specifically designed to hold interest and avoid having the presentation cut short. A slide or movie projector might communicate what the salesman's company sells or does. Or to appeal to his senses, the potential customer might be given a product or model to handle, or in the case of food, a sample to taste.

Desire

Arousing desire requires an even more persuasive effort. At this stage, the salesman definitely has to determine exactly what his prospect's problems and attitudes are. This enables the salesman to show how his product fits the need, counter any objections, and prepare for closing the sale. This feedback is vital to his sales presentation and is an important advantage of personal selling.

Knowing the prospect's specific needs, the salesman can explain *specifically* how the product could be used in the customer's factory or how it would be purchased by the buyer's customers.

One goal at this stage is to encourage the prospect to make a mental trial of the product to see how it could fit in with his needs. For example, the salesman might show a grocer statistics and testimonials on the success of the product in other stores.

Action

Finally, the salesman will try to summarize the important points he has made, tailor his arguments to the customer's needs and attitudes, and try to close the sale; i.e., affect the prospect's behavior. It is interesting to note that one of the most frequent reasons for the loss of a sale is that the salesman never *asks* for the order. Perhaps this is because he does not want to be refused. He's afraid that a direct request for the order is all too easily answered with a no.

There are ways, however, to avoid this awful word. The experienced salesman knows how to avoid a direct confrontation with human inertia and reluctance to make a decision. Without asking for a direct yes or no, he may begin to write up the order or ask which of various delivery dates would be preferable. He may inquire about the quantity the customer would like to try in a new display. This may lead the customer into taking action without consciously having to make a direct decision – a difficult step for some people.

Sales management must be planned, too

■ Marketing strategy planning must include some consideration for how the personal selling job will be carried out – in particular, how the jobs of selecting and compensating salesmen will be handled. Otherwise, planning may be unrealistic. We cannot cover the details of sales management, but we will discuss briefly these two sales management tasks.[4]

Selecting
salesmen
takes
judgment,
plus

■ It is extremely important to obtain *good, competent* salesmen. But since these descriptive terms mean different things to different companies, a careful job description should be used as a basis for the selection process.

The selection of salesmen in most companies is a hit-or-miss affair, normally attempted without any job description or serious thought about exactly what kind of man is needed. Friends and relations or people who are available may be used because many people feel that the only qualifications for sales jobs are friendliness and a presentable appearance. This approach has contributed to poor sales and high personnel turnover for many companies.

Progressive companies have attempted to use more scientific procedures in hiring, including multiple interviews with various executives, and psychological tests. Unfortunately, these techniques cannot guarantee success – but experiments have shown that using some kind of selection method brings in better personnel than using no selection aids at all.

The market grid concept and the company's own strategies may have to be given greater recognition in the selection of salesmen. Behavioral science research seems to indicate that the effectiveness of salesmen depends upon the kinds and personalities of the company's customers. Insurance salesmen, for example, seem to be more successful when dealing with individuals similar to them in age, height, income, religious affiliation, education, politics, and even smoking habits.[5]

Logically, this would mean that the sales manager should know as much as possible about his various target markets before selecting salesmen. He may need to hire a wide variety of men to meet different kinds of customers. Insurance companies, for example, probably make a mistake when they hire only college graduate athletes from middle-class backgrounds to sell for them. The former athlete may be very good for some potential customers but totally inappropriate for others.

■ While it is true that public recognition, sales contests, and simple personal recognition for a job well done may be highly effective in stimulating greater sales effort, most companies also use monetary spurs to sales personnel. Our primary emphasis here, too, will be upon monetary stimulation.

Two basic decisions must be made in developing a compensation plan: (1) determine the level of compensation and (2) establish the method of payment.

Level of compensation

The job description makes possible a careful appraisal of the salesman's role in the total marketing mix. This description shows whether any special skills or responsibilities are required that suggest higher pay levels.

To make sure that it can afford a given type of salesman with a certain set of responsibilities, the company should estimate, at the time this description is being written, how valuable such a salesman will be. A good order getter might be worth over $50,000 a year to one corporation, but only $5,000 to another company, simply because the firm does not have enough to sell. In the latter case, the company probably will have to redraft its job specifications or completely reshape its promotion plans, since the going compensation level for such salesmen is far higher than $5,000 a year.

To attract and retain men, most companies must at least meet the going market wage for salesmen of a particular caliber. Order getters are paid more than order takers. Some retail store clerks, basically low-level order takers, may not even be paid the federal minimum wage.

If there are particularly difficult aspects to a job, such as extensive traveling, aggressive pioneering, or contacts with less pleasant kinds of customers, the compensation may have to be increased. The salesmen's compensation level should correspond at least roughly with the pay scale of the rest of the firm, normally running higher than the compensation of the office or production force, but seldom exceeding that of the executives who supervise them.

Method of payment

Once the general level of compensation has been determined, then method of payment must be set. There are three basic methods of payment: (1) *straight salary*, (2) *straight commission*, or (3) *a combination plan.*

Straight salary normally supplies the maximum security for the salesman and straight commission, the maximum incentive. Because these two represent extremes, and most companies want to offer their salesmen some balance between incentive and security, the most popular method of payment is a combination plan which includes some salary and some commission. Bonuses and other goal-directed incentives are becoming more popular, too. Pensions, insurance, and other fringe benefits may be included, too, but salary and/or commission methods are basic to most combination plans.[6]

A sales manager's control over a salesman tends to vary directly with the proportion of the compensation which is in the form of salary. The straight-salary plan permits the maximum amount of supervision, while the man on commission tends to be his own boss. If the sales manager wishes the salesman to spend substantial time on supporting sales activities, repair work, or delivery services, then a straight-salary plan may be better. But a sales manager will have to give more supervision if he uses a straight-salary plan or one with a large salary element in it. If such supervision will be difficult, then the compensation plan should probably include some commission, or even a straight commission which provides built-in direction. That is, the commission rates should be set so that the salesman knows clearly what is wanted.

A straight-commission plan will probably provide the greatest incentive to increase sales. But a company may also use less direct incentives, such as a modest sharing of company profits. The incentive should be large only if there is a direct relationship between the salesman's effort and results. If the relationship is less direct, as when a number of people are involved in the sale—engineers, top management, or supporting salesmen—then each one's contribution to the final result is less clear and greater emphasis on salary may be appropriate. Strong incentives are normally offered order-getting salesmen, especially when a company wants to expand sales rapidly. Strong incentives may be used, also, when the company's objectives are shifting or varied. In this way, the salesman's activities and efforts can be directed and shifted as needed.

The marketing manager should probably seek to avoid excessively complex compensation plans or plans that change frequently. Complicated plans are hard for salesmen to understand, and costly for the accounting department to administer. Further, considerable dissatisfaction may result if salesmen cannot see a direct relationship between their effort and their income.

Simplicity is probably best achieved with straight commission. But in practice, it is usually better to sacrifice some simplicity in order to obtain some control over salesmen, while still providing flexibility and incentive.[7]

Sales management must coordinate with marketing management

■ There are, unfortunately, no easy answers to the compensation problem; it is up to the sales manager, in cooperation with the marketing manager, to develop a good compensation plan. The sales manager's efforts must coordinate with the whole marketing plan because he can accomplish his goals only if adequate funds are allocated to this task.

As already noted, it is the marketing manager's job to balance the promotion blend. The expected cost and performance of the sales force is only one of the many variables he must consider in making the final decision. To make these judgments, the marketing manager must know what a sales force should consist of, what its goals should be, and what it should cost.

Once the sales manager's basic plan and budget have been accepted, his job becomes one of implementing the plan, including directing and controlling the sales force. This would include determining and assigning sales territories, and the evaluation of performance.

More is said on this in Chapter 29, but it should be noted that the sales manager has more to do than fly about the country, sipping martinis, and entertaining customers. A sales manager is deeply involved with the basic management tasks of planning and control, as well as the ongoing execution of the personal selling effort.

Conclusion

■ In this chapter, we have discussed the importance and nature of personal selling. Selling is much more than just "getting rid of the product." In fact, a salesman who is not provided with strategic guidelines may have to become his own strategic planner.

Three *basic* kinds of sales tasks were isolated: (1) order getting, (2) order taking, and (3) supporting. Most sales jobs are a combination of at least two of these three tasks, and the nature of the job and the level and method of compensation depend, in large part, on the blend of these tasks. A job specification should be developed for each sales job. This, in turn, provides the guidelines for selecting and compensating the salesman.

Three kinds of sales presentations were identified. Each has its place but the need-satisfaction approach seems most applicable for higher-level sales jobs. It is in these kinds of jobs that personal selling is achieving a new, almost professional status, because of the competence and degree of personal responsibility required of the salesman. The day of the grinning glad-hander is passing in favor of the specialist who is creative, industrious, persuasive, knowledgeable, highly trained and, therefore, able to help the buyer. This type of salesman always has been, and probably always will be, in short supply. And the demand for high-caliber salesmen is continually growing.

questions and problems

1 What kind of salesman is required to sell the following products? If there are several selling jobs in the channel for each product, then indicate the kinds of salesmen required (specify any assumptions necessary to give definite answers):
a. Soya bean oil
b. Costume jewelry
c. Nuts and bolts
d. Handkerchiefs
e. Mattresses
f. Corn
g. Cigarettes

2 Distinguish among the jobs of manufacturers', wholesalers', and retailers' order-getting salesmen. If one order getter is needed, must all the salesmen in a channel be order getters? Illustrate.

3 Discuss the role of the manufacturers' agent in the marketing manager's promotion plans. What kind of salesman is he?

4 Discuss the future of the specialty shop if manufacturers place greater emphasis on mass selling because of the inadequacy of retail order taking.

5 Cite three actual local examples of the three kinds of sales presentations discussed in the chapter. Explain for each situation whether a different type of presentation would have been better.

6 Describe a need-satisfaction theory sales presentation which you have experienced recently and explain how it might have been improved by fuller use of the AIDA framework.

7 Explain how a straight commission system might provide flexibility in the sale of a line of women's clothing products which continually varied in profitability.

8 Explain how a compensation system could be developed to provide incentives for older salesman and yet make some provision for trainees who have not yet learned their job.

9 Describe the operation of our economy if personal salesmen were outlawed. Could the economy work? If so, how; if not, what is the minimum personal selling effort necessary? Could this minimum personal selling effort be controlled effectively by law?

notes

1 F. A. Russell and F. H. Beach, *Textbook of Salesmanship*, 6th ed. (New York: McGraw-Hill Book Co., 1951), pp. 113–14.

2 Michael F. Lennon, "Don't Limit Customer's Horizon," *Printers' Ink*, June 30, 1961, p. 43.

3 "Making Sure the Goods Get on the Shelves," *Business Week*, July 22, 1972, pp. 46–47.

4 For further treatment see W. J. Stanton and R. H. Buskirk, *Management of the Sales Force*, 4th ed. (Homewood, Ill.: Richard D. Irwin, Inc., 1973). See also A. F. Doody and W. G. Nickels, "Structuring Organizations for Strategic Selling," *MSU Business Topics*, Autumn 1972, pp. 27–34; Davis Fogg and Josef W. Rokus, "A Quantitative Method for Structuring a Profitable Sales Force," *Journal of Marketing*, July 1973, pp. 8–17; and Leonard M. Lodish, "'Vaguely Right' Approach to Sales Force Allocations," *Harvard Business Review*, January-February 1974, pp. 119–124.

5 Franklin B. Evans, "Selling Is a Dyadic Relationship —A New Approach," *American Behavioral Scientist*, May 1963, p. 79; see also James Holbert and Noel Capon, "Interpersonal Communication in Marketing," *Journal of Marketing Research*, February 1972, pp. 27–32.

6 For further discussion, see *The Conference Board, Incentives for Salesmen* (Experiences in Marketing Management, No. 14 [New York: National Industrial Conference Board, 1967]); and Richard C. Smyth, "Financial Incentives for Salesmen," *Harvard Business Review*, January-February, 1968 pp. 109–17; and H. O. Pruden, W. H. Cunningham, and W. D. English, "Nonfinancial Incentives for Salesmen," *Journal of Marketing*, October 1972, pp. 55–59.

7 For more discussion, see F. E. Webster, Jr., "Rationalizing Salesmen's Compensation Plans," *Journal of Marketing*, January 1966, pp. 55–58; and R. L. Day and P. D. Bennett, "Should Salesmen's Compensation Be Geared to Profits?" *Journal of Marketing*, October 1962, pp. 6–9.

Mass
selling

■ Mass selling facilitates mass distribution. Although a marketing manager might prefer to use personal selling exclusively, it can be expensive on a per-contact and a per-sale basis. Mass selling is a way around this roadblock. It is not as pinpointed as personal selling, but it does permit communication to large numbers of potential customers at the same time. Today, most promotion blends contain both personal and mass selling.

Primary emphasis in this chapter will be on the use of advertising as a mass selling tool. The need for advertising objectives, reaching target customers (via media), and communicating with target customers (with messages) will receive extensive treatment. The management and control of advertising also will be discussed.

Importance of advertising

$37 billion in ads by 1980　■ We saw in Chapter 20 that advertising can get results in a promotion blend. Good advertising results are obtained at a cost, of course. Expenditures in the United States for advertising have been growing continuously since World War II, and more growth is expected. In 1946, they were slightly more than $3 billion; by 1972, they topped $23 billion—and it is predicted that by 1980 the total annual advertising expenditure will be $37 billion.[1]

It's all done by less than half a million　■ While total advertising expenditures are large, the advertising industry itself employs relatively few people. The major expense is for media time and space. And in the United States, the largest share of this – 30 percent – goes for newspaper space. Television takes about 18 percent of the total and direct mail, about 14 percent.[2]

Fewer than 500,000 people work directly in the U.S. advertising industry. This would include all people who help create or sell advertising for advertising media, such as radio and television stations, newspapers, and magazines, as well as those in advertising agencies and those working for retailers, wholesalers, and manufacturers who handle their own advertising. The sometimes glamorous and often maligned 4,800 U.S. advertising agencies, however, employ only about 200,000 persons. Among these, not many are large, most employing fewer than ten persons and they are highly concentrated in New York and Chicago.[3]

Advertisers aren't really spending that much

■ U.S. corporations invest an average of only about $1\frac{1}{2}$ percent of their sales dollar in advertising. This is relatively small compared to the aggregate cost of marketing – perhaps 50 percent of the consumer's dollar – and the 20 to 50 percent gross margins with which we have been dealing at various channel levels.

Note that the total amount spent on a *particular* product may be greater because several firms in a channel may advertise for the same product. In the aggregate, total advertising expenditures account for a little over 2 percent of gross national product and about $3\frac{1}{4}$ percent of personal consumption expenditures.

Some spend more than others

■ Some industries spend a considerably larger percentage of sales for advertising than the average of $1\frac{1}{2}$ percent. One study showed that soap and related products manufacturers spent 14.2 percent, drug manufacturers 11.05 percent, and tobacco manufacturers 6.06 percent. At the other extreme, coal mining companies spent only 0.09 percent, construction companies 0.10 percent, men's and boys' clothing 0.11 percent, and wholesalers and retailers in the aggregate 1.05 percent.[4]

Clearly, advertising is an important factor in certain markets, especially the consumer goods markets. Nevertheless, we must keep in mind that in the aggregate it costs much less than personal selling.

Advertising objectives tied to marketing strategy

You get what you ask for

■ Every advertisement and every advertising campaign should seek clearly defined objectives. These should flow from the overall strategy and the job which has been assigned to advertising. It is not enough to say simply "promote the product." Some firms give their advertising agencies such a vague objective, but if they do they should not be surprised if the agency pursues its own objectives. The agency may develop somewhat reasonable objectives, but then begin to plan campaigns that will win awards within the advertising industry.

Progressive advertisers realize that without clearly defined objectives, preparing an advertising campaign is guesswork. They are beginning to describe their target audiences more precisely and to define specific objectives which advertising is supposed to accomplish. They will even set specific objectives for a particular advertisement.

If you want half the market, say so!

■ Advertising objectives can be extremely specific, probably much more specific than personal selling objectives. One of the advantages of personal selling is that the salesman can shift his presentation to meet customers' needs. Each advertisement, however, is a specific communication that must be effective, not just for one customer, but for thousands or millions of target customers.

A specific advertisement or advertising campaign might work toward objectives such as the following:

1. Aid in the introduction of new products to specific target markets.
2. Help obtain desirable dealer outlets.
3. Prepare the way for salesmen by presenting the company's name and the merits of its products.
4. Provide contact with the target customers even when the salesman is not available.
5. Obtain immediate buying action.
6. Help a buyer confirm his purchasing decision.

Even these objectives, however, may not be specific enough. If the advertiser really wants specific results then he should state what he wants. A general objective: "To assist in the expansion of market share," could be rephrased more specifically; "To increase traffic in our cooperating retailer outlets by 25 percent during the next three months."

Such a specific objective obviously has an impact on implementation plans. Advertising that might be right for building a good image among opinion leaders might be entirely wrong for getting customers into the retailers' stores. Here we might use contests or tie-in sales. And the media used would be pinpointed to help particular dealers, perhaps including local newspapers and billboards rather than national consumer magazines.[5]

Objectives determine kinds of advertising needed

■ The advertising objectives selected will largely determine which of two basic types of advertising to use—*product* or *institutional*.

Product advertising, as the name implies, is concerned with *selling a product.* It may be aimed at final users or channel members.

Institutional advertising, on the other hand, does not involve a product but rather a company or even an industry. It is intended

primarily to *develop goodwill toward the company or industry.*
The long-run goal is to improve sales and relations with the various
publics with whom the company deals. This includes not only consumers but current and prospective channel members or component suppliers, shareholders, and so on.

Product advertising — meet us, like us, remember us

■ Product advertising falls into three categories: pioneering, competitive, and reminder advertising.

Pioneering advertising — builds primary demand

Pioneering advertising is aimed at developing primary demand — i.e., for a product category rather than a specific brand. It is
needed in the early stages of the adoption process to inform potential customers about a new product or concept.

Pioneering advertising is used in the introductory stage of the
product life cycle and can be used with several advertising objectives (numbers 1, 2, and 3, for example). Its basic job is to inform,
not persuade.

Pioneering advertising doesn't have to mention the brand or specific company at all. The California olive industry promoted olives
as olives, not certain brands. This was so successful that after only
five years of promotion, the industry's surpluses had become shortages, and it diverted promotional funds to horticultural research to
increase production.

Competitive advertising — emphasizes selective demand

Competitive advertising stimulates selective demand by selling
a specific brand rather than a general product category. A firm can
be forced into competitive advertising as the product life cycle
moves along, to hold its own against competitors' products and promotion. The United Fruit Company gave up a two-decade pioneering effort to promote bananas in favor of advertising its own "Chiquita" brand. It launched a nationwide advertising campaign with
the theme, "We've put a seal on our peel." The reason for the
change was simple. While United Fruit was single-handedly promoting bananas, it slowly lost market share to competitors. The
competitive advertising program was launched to avoid further
inroads.[6]

Competitive advertising may be either direct or indirect.

The *direct type* is aimed at immediate buying action. The *indirect type* is intended to point out product virtues so that when the
customer is ready to buy, he will buy *that* product.

Much airline advertising is of the competitive variety. The various airlines are bidding for patronage, either immediately — in
which case the ads are of the direct-action type with prices, time-
tables, and phone numbers to call for reservations — or eventually,
in which case the ads are of the indirect-action type, suggesting
that you mention their name when talking to your travel agent.

Reminder advertising — reinforces earlier promotion

Reminder advertising may be useful when the product has
achieved a favored status, probably in the market maturity or sales

decline stage. The advertiser mainly wants to keep his product's name before the public and will use soft-sell ads that merely mention the name as a reminder. Much traditional Coca-Cola advertising has been of this variety.

Institutional advertising
— remember our name in St. Louis, Seattle, Charleston . . .

■ Institutional advertising focuses only on the name and prestige of a company or industry. It may seek to inform, persuade, or remind. A well-known Texas retailer, Neiman-Marcus, uses institutional ads that have reminder aspects. It does not expect the majority of its ads to pay for themselves immediately, but rather to maintain its image.

A persuading kind of promotion is sometimes used by large companies with several divisions. General Motors Corp., for example, does considerable institutional advertising of the GM name, emphasizing the quality and research behind *all* GM products. These are often keyed to GM's "Mark of Excellence."

Some large companies, such as General Motors and Du Pont, use institutional ads to emphasize the value of large corporations. Their ultimate goal is developing a favorable political and legal environment in which to work.

Sometimes an advertising campaign may have both product and institutional aspects because the federal government has taken an increasingly dim view of institutional advertising. The Internal Revenue Service has limited tax deductions on institutional advertising. And defense contractors are specifically barred from including advertising expenditures as a cost of doing business with the government.[7]

Cooperative advertising may buy more

Vertical cooperation in channels

■ The discussion above might suggest that only producers do product or institutional advertising. This is not true, of course, but producers can affect the advertising done by others. Sometimes a manufacturer knows what promotion job or advertising job he wants done but finds that it can be done more effectively or more economically by someone farther along in the channel. In this case, he may offer *advertising allowances* to buy the promotion he feels is needed by the channel system. In other cases, he advances only part of the money, and the middlemen are expected to add the balance — this is called *cooperative advertising*.

Cooperative advertising helps the manufacturer get more promotion for his advertising dollar because media rate structures usually are set up to give local advertisers lower rates than national firms. In addition, the retailer is more likely to follow through where he is paying a share of the cost.

Cooperative ad allowances are subject to abuse, however, because allowances can be given to retailers with little expectation that they will be used for ad purposes. This may become a disguised price concession and result in price discrimination. The Federal Trade Commission has recently become more interested in this problem, and some manufactures have pulled back from cooperative advertising. To avoid this, intelligent producers insist on advertising tearsheets and other proof of use.

Horizontal cooperation may be good, too

■ Some retailers, particularly those in shopping centers, may get together in joint promotional efforts. Similarly, the manufacturers of complimentary products, such as housefurnishings, may find it desirable to join forces. Generally, the objective is the same as in vertical cooperation—to get more for the promotion dollar.

Choosing the "best" medium

■ For effective promotion, specific target customers must be reached. Unfortunately, not all potential customers read all newspapers, magazines, or other printed media, or listen to all radio and television programs. So not all media are equally effective.

There is no simple answer to the question, "What is the best medium?" Effectiveness depends on how well it fits with the rest of a particular marketing strategy. To be more specific here, however, it depends on (1) your promotion objectives, (2) what target markets you are attempting to reach and (3) the funds available for advertising.

Specify promotion objectives

■ Before a firm can choose the best medium, it must first decide on promotion objectives. For example, if the objective is to inform, telling a long story with precise detail, and if pictures are desired, then the print media, including magazines and newspapers may be better.

If timeliness is not too critical, then weekly or monthly magazines may be practical. But if demonstrations are needed, then TV may become desirable.

If your objective is to provide technical information to a particular group, then you might have to choose specialized journals. Remember, you pay for the audience the media delivers, which may (or may not) be your target audience. The use of men's magazines such as *Esquire* and *True* to reach doctors would be highly inefficient. Medical journals and direct mail are the most effective advertising media for telling doctors about new drugs.

Specify target markets and match with media

■ To guarantee good media selection, the advertiser first must *clearly* specify his target markets—a step necessary for all our marketing strategy planning. Then, media can be chosen that are heard, read, or seen by these target customers (including, perhaps, all the purchase influencers).

Matching target customers and media is the major stumbling block to effective media selection, because it is not always certain who sees or hears what. To be sure, most of the major media have used marketing research to develop profiles of the people who buy their publications or live in their broadcasting area. Some have broken down their "audience" by sex, age, income, education, occupation, place of residence (such as farm or nonfarm), ownership of various appliances or automobiles, and ownership of homes or other articles of particular relevance.

But they cannot be as definite about who actually reads each page or sees or hears each show. And, they seldom tailor their marketing research to gather information on the market grid dimensions which *each* advertiser may deem important. Generally, media research focuses on demographic characteristics. But what if the really important dimensions are concerned with behavioral needs or attitudes which are difficult to measure or unique to a particular product or market?

The difficulty of evaluating alternative media has led some media analysts to focus excessively on objective measures such as cost in relation to audience size or circulation. But preoccupation with minimizing cost may lead to ignoring the relevant dimensions and slipping into "mass marketing." The media buyer may become mesmerized by the relatively low cost of "mass media" when, in fact, a more specialized medium might be a much better buy. Its audience might have more interest in the product, or more money to spend, or more willingness to buy.

Specialized media help zero in on target markets

■ Media are now directing more attention to reaching smaller, more defined target markets. National media may offer regional editions. *Time* magazine, for example, offers not only several regional and metropolitan editions, but also special editions for college students, educators, doctors, and businessmen.

Many magazines serve only special-interest groups, such as fishermen, radio and television enthusiasts, homemakers, religious groups, and professional groups. In fact, the most profitable magazines seem to be the ones which are aiming at clearly defined markets, while the mass magazines are experiencing difficulties. *Life* and *Look* went out of business, while magazines such as *Playboy, Car Craft, Skiing, Bride's Magazine,* and *Southern Living* have been doing well.

There are trade magazines in countless fields, such as chemical engineering, electrical wholesaling, farming, and the defense market. *Standard Rate and Data* provides a guide to the thousands of magazines now available. For those especially interested in the industrial market, *Industrial Marketing* magazine publishes the *Media Market Planning Guide.*

Radio suffered at first from the inroads of television. But now, like a number of magazines and newspapers, it has become a more specialized medium. Some stations cater to particular nationality, racial, and religious groups, such as Puerto Ricans, blacks, and Catholics, while others emphasize Western, popular, or classical music.

Perhaps the most specific medium is *direct-mail advertising.* The purpose of this medium is to go directly to the reader via his

Table 22–1
Examples of available mailing lists

Quantity of names	Name of list
425	Small Business Advisors
40,000	Social Register of Canada
5,000	Society of American Bacteriologists
500	South Carolina Engineering Society
2,000	South Dakota State Pharmaceutical Association
250	Southern California Academy of Science
12,000	Texas Manufacturing Executives
720	Trailer Coach Association
1,200	United Community Funds of America
50,000	University of Utah Alumni
19,000	Veterinarians

mailbox. The method is to send a specific message to a carefully selected list of names. There are organizations that specialize in providing mailing lists, ranging in number from hundreds to millions of names. The diversity of these lists is shown in Table 22–1 and indicates the importance of knowing specifically the firm's target market or markets.[8]

"Must buys" may use up available funds

■ Selecting which media to use is still pretty much an art. The media buyer may start with a budgeted sum and attempt to buy the best blend he can to reach the target audience. There may be some media that are obvious "must" buys, such as *the* local newspaper for a retailer in a small or medium-sized town. Such "must" buys may even exhaust the available funds. If not, then the media buyer must begin to think in terms of the relative advantages and disadvantages of the possible alternatives and recognize that he must make tradeoffs. Typically, media that have several advantages – for example, television which permits visual and audio presentations along with movement – are more expensive. So he might want to select a media blend which included some "expensive" media as well as some less expensive ones which may permit him to reach additional customers or reinforce the presentation from a different angle.

Ideally, the first media choice would reach a substantial part of the target audience. Then, each successive choice (if he could afford any more) would reach fewer who had not already been covered. Figure 22–1 illustrates the concept for four equally costly magazines. Here, the first choice reaches 60 percent of the target audience. The second choice adds only 20 percent who were not reached before. The third choice adds 10 percent and the fourth 5 percent. Five percent cannot be reached with only these four magazines.

436

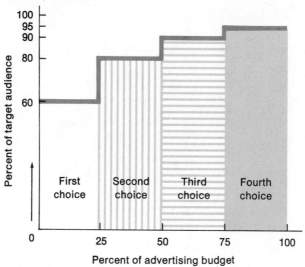

Figure 22–1
Increase in audience coverage as additional magazines
ads are purchased

Percent of target audience

First choice
Second choice
Third choice
Fourth choice

Percent of advertising budget

Planning the "best" message

**Some
messages
communicate
poorly**

■ Once the objectives of the advertising campaign determine
generally what is to be communicated, the key problem is how to
develop messages—both copy and illustrations—to communicate it.

Advertising must use general appeals, which is one source of
difficulty. It must communicate with large numbers of target
customers who have various and changing attitudes. The overall
promotion objective, of course, will be to affect the target customer's behavior; but because advertising uses more general
appeals, it sometimes has to be satisfied with merely affecting
attitudes.

**Communica-
tion process
theory is
relevant here**

■ Our understanding of the communication process helps guide
message planning, but adapting specific messages to the many
potential target customers is not easy. As we saw in Chapter 20,
common frames of reference and experience are desirable for good
communication. This is not a trivial matter in advertising, because
advertising professionals are often far removed from their target
audiences. Much advertising emanates from agencies in New York
City, and one advertising manager has deplored advertising "conditioned by our New York sophistication." His experience has
taught him that "New York's price of being New York is loss of
perspective; New York is not America."[9]

Some advertisers realize the complexity of the communication process and use marketing research to help them as much as possible. At the very least, such research may give clues about perceived needs and the words or ideas that potential customers use in the company's product area.

Other advertisers rely almost exclusively on their own "creative genius." This is at the root of many poor campaigns. Some are brilliant and others are miserable failures—and they don't know why.

There are relatively few tried-and-true rules in message construction. Everything we see and every new way we see it changes us in some way. An idea that may have worked a year ago can fail today. A highly successful advertising campaign that sold much beer in the New York area flopped in Los Angeles. And one industrial advertiser received more inquiries as it reduced the size of its ads.[10]

Behavioral science research does provide some help however. The concepts of motives, learning, and perception discussed in Chapter 8 are certainly relevant here. We know, for example, that consumers have a fantastic ability for selectively "tuning out" messages or ideas which are not of current interest. Just think of how much of the daily newspaper you actually "see" as you page through it. We do not see everything the advertisers want us to see or learn all they would like us to learn.

Let AIDA help guide message planning

■ Basically, the overall marketing strategy should determine *what* should be said in the message. Then management judgment, perhaps aided by marketing research, can be helpful in determining how this content can be encoded in order to have it decoded as intended.

As a guide to message planning, we can make additional use of the AIDA concept: getting Attention, holding Interest, arousing Desire, and obtaining Action. This approach is general, but these four steps can be a framework within which we can discuss the important problem areas.

Attention

Getting attention is the first job of an advertisement. If this is not done, it doesn't matter how many people can or do see it. Many readers leaf through magazines and newspapers without paying attention to any of the advertisements. Many listeners or viewers run errands or get snacks during commercials on radio and television.

The devices for catching the customer's attention are numerous. A large headline, newsy or shocking statements, pictures of pretty girls, babies, cartoon characters—or anything that is "different" or eyecatching—may do the trick. But . . . the attention-getting device must not distract from the next step—holding interest.

Interest

Holding interest is another matter. A pretty girl may get attention, but once you've seen her, then what? A man will pause to appreciate her, women will evaluate her. But if there is no relation between the girl and the product, observers of both sexes will move on.

More is known about holding interest than getting attention. The tone and language of the advertisement must be compatible with the field of experience and attitudes of target customers and their reference groups. A food advertisement featuring persons in riding costumes, for example, might be noted but passed over by many potential customers who do not ride to the hounds.

In addition to speaking the target customer's language, the advertising layouts should look right to the customer. Print illustrations and copy should be arranged so that the eye is encouraged to move smoothly through the ad, perhaps from the upper left-hand corner to the signature or brand name at the lower right-hand corner. Advertisements having this natural flowing characteristic are said to encourage *gaze motion*.[11]

Desire

Arousing desire to own or use a particular product is one of the most difficult jobs of an advertisement. It requires that the advertiser be successful in communicating with the customer. To communicate effectively, the advertiser should understand how his target customers think, behave, and make decisions.

To be successful, an advertisement must convince the customer that the product can meet his needs. *Pioneering* advertising may be useful to develop primary demand and show how the whole product class would satisfy latent wants. Later, in the market growth and market maturity stages, *competitive* advertising can show how a particular brand satisfies particular wants.

An advertisement may also have the function, especially during the market growth and market maturity stages, of supplying words that the customer can use for rationalizing his desire to buy. Although products may satisfy certain emotional wants, in our society many consumers find it necessary to justify their purchases on an economic or even moral basis. Desire may develop around emotional motives, but economic motives must also be reinforced.

Action

Getting action is the final requirement, and not an easy one. We now know, from communications research, that the potential customer should be encouraged to try the product before he adopts it. The prospective customer must be led beyond considering how the product might fit into his life to actually trying it or letting the company's salesman come in and show him how it works.

Strongly felt customer needs might be pinpointed in the ads to communicate more effectively. Careful research on the attitudes and wants in the target market may help uncover such strongly felt unsatisfied needs.

Appealing to these needs can get more action and also provide the kind of information the buyer seeks to confirm his decision. Post-purchase dissonance may set in and obtaining confirmation may be one of the important roles of advertising. Some customers seem to read more advertising *after* the purchase than before.

What is communicated to them may be very important if satisfied customers are to start or keep the web-of-word-of-mouth going. The ad may reassure them about the correctness of their decision and also supply the words they use to tell others about the product.

Advertising manager directs mass selling

■ Most companies have an advertising manager identified either by title or function. His job is to develop the company's mass selling effort.

Many advertising managers, especially those working for retailers, have their own advertising departments that plan the specific advertising campaigns and carry out the details. Others delegate much of the advertising task to specialists – the advertising agencies.

Advertising agencies often do the work

Evolution of agencies

■ Advertising agencies are specialists in handling the mass selling details we have been discussing. Agencies play a useful role because they are independent of the advertiser and have an outside viewpoint. They bring broad experience to bear on the individual client's problems because they work for many other clients.

In addition, agencies become specialists in the various phases of technical preparation and placement of advertising, and often can perform these functions more economically than a company's own department. Agency discounts in the media rate structure also help cover some or all of the costs of their services *for national advertisers* (a term used to distinguish this class of advertisers from *local* advertisers who pay lower rates).

Historically, advertising agencies started as space salesmen (brokers) working for a commission *from the media.* The amount of the commission paid to space salesmen has varied, but until recently it was about 15 percent of the price paid by national advertisers.

In the early days, space salesmen earned their income by selling empty time or space. As competition grew, these salesmen helped their customers fill this time or space by writing the advertisements. In time, the advertisers became even more demanding, and the original space or time salesmen have moved closer to customers than to media. Nevertheless, the commission system has continued. It is ironic to note that many media now find it necessary to hire salesmen to call on the advertising agencies, who ostensibly are selling space for them.

As they moved closer to the space buyers, advertising agencies took on more and more functions. Agencies sometimes handle overall marketing strategy planning as well as marketing research, product and package development, and the development of sales promotion aids. Some agencies make good marketing partners and almost assume the role of the firm's marketing department.

One of the ad agency's virtues is that the advertiser is free at any time to cancel the arrangement. This provides extreme flexibility for the advertiser. Some companies even use their advertising agency as a scapegoat. Whenever anything goes wrong, it's the advertising agency's fault, and the advertiser shops around for a new one. But a more fundamental advantage of the agency is that it is normally able to use specialists more effectively and continuously than individual advertisers. For this reason, it may be able to do a better job at less cost.

Agency compensation: Is it fair?

■ The major users of advertising agencies are manufacturers or national distributors, because of the media rate structure in the industry. Normally, media have two prices: one for national advertisers and another, lower one for local advertisers, such as retailers. The agencies earn their discount, usually 15 percent, of the media's price, only when time or space is purchased at the higher national rate. National distributors or manufacturers have a real incentive to use advertising agencies because the 15 percent discount is allowed to any authorized agency they choose, but it is not available to them. Retailers, who are entitled to the lower local rates, seldom use agencies.

There is a growing resistance to the present method of agency compensation. The chief complaints are that the agencies receive the flat 15 percent commission, regardless of work performed, and also that the commission system makes it hard for the agencies to be completely objective about low-cost media or promotional campaigns that use little advertising space or time.

Not all agencies are satisfied with the present arrangement, either. Some would like to charge additional fees as they see rising costs and advertisers demanding more services.

The commission system is most favored by those accounts, such as producers of industrial goods, that require extensive service but buy relatively little advertising. These are the firms the agencies would like to, and sometimes do, charge additional fees.

The commission system is generally opposed by very large consumer goods advertisers who do much of their own research and planning, and require only basic services from their agencies. Some of these accounts can be very profitable for agencies, and naturally their agencies would prefer the fixed-commission system.

Fifteen percent no longer mandatory

The Federal Trade Commission worked for many years to change the method of advertising agency compensation. Finally, in 1956, the American Association of Advertising Agencies signed a consent decree with the Justice Department, indicating that by joint action they would no longer require the maintenance of the 15 percent commission system. This opened the way to discounts and fee increases.

Agency arrangements are changing

■ The advertising agency business has seen considerable ferment and profit squeezes in recent years. Some agencies have given up the full-service approach (for 15 percent) and become more specialized, for example, in media buying or creative functions. Other agencies have gone out of business and others have been purchased by advertisers. Many of the changes probably can be traced to the work of less efficient agencies who, under the umbrella of the 15 percent commission, were able to obtain business primarily through social contacts rather than business ability.

Internal conflict causes changes

Some of the changes in the advertising business are due to internal struggles between the creative and the business types, with the latter winning many of the battles because the very survival of the agencies is involved. Some of the creative types might properly be labeled as "production-oriented."[12]

At the root of this tension is the fact that the advertiser's product manager or brand manager may be personally responsible for the success of a particular product and feels, therefore, that he has some right to direct and even veto the work of the creative people. This has resulted in confrontations in which the agency often loses, because the advertiser is paying the bills. One agency woman turned client said she had lost patience with the "ego-dominated creative type who is blindly in love with his own efforts." She feels the yardstick of successful advertising is whether advertising communicates what it's supposed to communicate to its target audience.[13] It is advertisers such as this woman who pay the bills and who have been partly responsible for the changes which are occurring in the agency business.

FTC interested in agencies — and deceptive advertising

■ Advertising agencies face a challenge from another direction. The growing indignation over deceptive advertising, a reaction encouraged by the consumerism movement, has affected agencies. According to a recent Federal Trade Commission opinion, agencies should share equal responsibility with the client for advertising which is false, misleading, or unfair. This is of special interest to agencies and advertisers because of the possibility of large financial penalties, and/or the need to spend money on corrective ads. The FTC is serious and some advertisers, and especially those aiming at children, may have to develop new ways of communicating. And more and better substantiation will be needed to avoid charges of misleading or unfair advertising.[14]

Measuring advertising effectiveness is not easy

Success depends on the total marketing mix

■ It would be convenient if we could measure the results of advertising by a simple analysis of sales. Unfortunately, this is not possible, although the advertising literature is filled with success stories that "prove" advertising has increased sales. The total marketing mix, not just promotion generally or advertising specifically, is responsible for the sales result. The one exception to this rule, as it concerns advertising, is direct-mail advertising. If it doesn't produce immediate results, it is considered a failure.

Research and testing can improve the odds

■ Ideally, management should pretest advertising before it is run rather than relying solely on the judgment of creative people or advertising "experts," who too frequently judge solely on the basis of originality or cleverness of the copy and illustrations. Management people may be no better, if as good, at divining how good an ad will be.

Some progressive advertisers now demand laboratory or market tests to evaluate the effectiveness of ads. In addition, before ads are run, opinion and attitude research is sometimes used. Researchers try to evaluate consumers' reactions to particular advertisements or parts of advertisements, sometimes using laboratory-type devices which measure skin moisture or eye reaction.

Hindsight may lead us to foresight

■ After the advertisements have been run, researchers may attempt to measure how much is recalled about specific products or advertisements. Inquiries from customers may be used as a measure of the effectiveness of particular ads.

The response to radio or television commercials or magazine readership can be estimated using various survey techniques to check the size and composition of audiences (the Hooper, Crosely, Nielsen, and Starch reports are produced routinely) with implicit assumptions that larger audiences lead directly to greater purchases.

These specific measurements are relevant only when the advertiser knows what he is trying to accomplish. When detailed advertising objectives are set, research can provide feedback on the effectiveness of the advertising.

While such advertising research techniques are far from foolproof, they are probably far superior to reliance on pure judgment by advertising "experts."

Until more effective advertising research tools are developed, moreover, the present method of carefully defining specific advertising objectives, choosing media and messages to accomplish these objectives, testing plans, and then evaluating results of actual advertisements, would seem most productive.

Conclusion

■ Theoretically, it may seem relatively simple to develop a mass selling campaign. Simply pick the media and develop a message. Yet, this is no simple process. Effectiveness depends upon using the "best" medium and the "best" message considering: (1) promotion objectives, (2) the target markets, and (3) the funds available for advertising.

The specific advertising objectives will determine what type of advertising to use – product or institutional. If product advertising is needed, then the particular type must be decided – pioneering, competitive (direct or indirect action), or reminder. And cooperative advertising may be helpful.

There are many complications involved in mass selling and specialists – advertising agencies – have evolved to handle some of these tasks. But specific objectives must be set for them, or their advertising may have little direction and be almost impossible to evaluate.

Ultimately, effective advertising should affect sales. But the whole marketing mix affects sales, and the results of advertising cannot be measured by sales changes alone. Advertising is only a part of promotion, and promotion is only a part of the total marketing mix that the marketing manager must develop to satisfy target customers.

questions and problems

1 Discuss the relation of advertising objectives to marketing strategy planning and the kinds of advertising actually needed. Illustrate.

2 Present three examples where advertising to middlemen might be necessary. What would be the objective(s) of such moves?

3 What does it mean to say that "money is invested in advertising"? Is all advertising an investment? Illustrate.

4 Find advertisements to final consumers which illustrate the following types of advertising: (a) institutional, (b) pioneering, (c) competitive, (d) reminder. What objective(s) does each of these ads have? List the emotional and economic motives utilized in each of these advertisements.

5 Describe the type of media which might be most suitable for promoting: (a) tomato soup, (b) greeting cards, (c) an industrial component material, (d) playground equipment. Specify any assumptions necessary to obtain a definite answer.

6 Discuss the use of testimonials in advertising. Which of the four AIDA steps might testimonials accomplish? Would they be suitable for all types of products? If not, for which types would they be most suitable?

7 Find an advertisement which seeks to accomplish all four AIDA steps and explain how you feel this advertisement is accomplishing each of these steps.

8 Discuss the future of independent advertising agencies now that the 15 percent commission system is not required.

9 Does mass selling cost too much? How can this be measured?

10 How would retailing promotion be affected if all local advertising via mass media such as radio, television, and newspapers were prohibited? Would there be any impact on total sales? If so, would it probably affect all goods and stores equally?

notes

[1] *Advertising Age*, November 21, 1973, p. 6.

[2] Ibid, p. 7.

[3] Exact data on this industry is elusive. But see "Showing Ad Agencies How to Grow," *Business Week*, June 1,

1974, p. 50–56; and "How Many People Work in Advertising?" *Printers' Ink*, December 6, 1957, p. 88.

[4] *Advertising Age*, September 18, 1967, pp. 77–78.

[5] For further discussion on this, see Russell H. Colley,

Defining Advertising Goals for Measured Advertising Results (New York: Association of National Advertisers, Inc., 1961), Part 2, and *Setting Advertising Objectives* (Studies in Business Policy, No. 118 [New York: National Industrial Conference Board, 1966]); and S. H. Britt, "Are So-Called Successful Advertising Campaigns Really Successful?" *Journal of Advertising Research,* June 1969, pp. 3–9.

[6] "Chiquita, United Fruit's 'Banana Girl,' to Narrow Her Field of Sales," *Business Week,* May 25, 1963, p. 108; and "At War with Chiquita Banana," *Business Week,* June 16, 1973, pp. 54–55.

[7] "Will Defense-Contractor Ads Run into New Snags in Washington?" *Printers' Ink,* January 4, 1963, p. 7; and Nugent Wedding, "Advertising Mass Communication, and Tax Deduction," *Journal of Marketing,* April 1960, pp. 17–22.

[8] "Mailing-List Brokers Sell More Than Names to Their Many Clients," *The Wall Street Journal,* February 19, 1974, p. 1 f.

[9] *Advertising Age,* May 27, 1963, p. 90.

[10] "More Than Ads Sell Rheingold," *Business Week,* September 21, 1957, p. 70; "How to Advertise *Not* by The Book," *Printers' Ink,* September 6, 1963, pp. 47–48.

[11] See Otto Kleppner, *Advertising Procedure,* 5th ed. (New York: Prentice-Hall, Inc., 1966).

[12] "The days of fun and games are over," *Business Week,* November 10, 1973, p. 84.

[13] Helen Van Slyke, Vice President, Advertising, Helena Rubenstein, Inc., New York, in a speech to the meeting of the American Association of Advertising Agencies, April 25, 1970.

[14] Robert E. Wilkes and James B. Wilcox, "Recent FTC Actions: Implications for the Advertising Strategist," *Journal of Marketing,* January 1974, pp. 55–61; "FTC's Chief May Supply Some People with a Strong Attack on TV Ads for Kids," *The Wall Street Journal,* June 3, 1974, p. 24; *Guidelines on Advertising Substantiation,* a Report of the Sub-council on Advertising and Promotion of the National Business Council for Consumer Affairs, September 1972; "4A's Suggest Guidelines for Comparative Advertising," *The 4A Newsletter,* May 20, 1974; and "The Industry Gets a Controversial Watchdog," *Business Week,* May 12, 1973, pp. 130–133.

23

Pricing objectives and policies

■ Price is one of the four major variables that the marketing manager controls. His Price decisions affect both the firm's sales and profits.

Uniqueness of the product, creative promotion, or simple availability may be more important than Price in some cases. But Price can never be ignored when developing a marketing mix. And, in some cases, it may be critical.

Guided by the company's objectives, a marketing manager must develop a set of pricing objectives and then policies. He must spell out what price situations the firm will face and how it will handle them. These policies should state: (1) how flexible his prices will be, (2) at what level they will be set, (3) how pricing will be handled during the course of a product life cycle, (4) how transportation costs will be handled and (5) to whom and when discounts and allowances will be given. These topics are the subject of this chapter.

Pricing objectives should guide pricing

■ Pricing objectives should flow from, and fit in with, company-level objectives. Ideally, they should be *explicitly stated*, because they have a direct effect on pricing policies and the price determination methods which are employed.

The various types of pricing objectives we will discuss are diagrammed in Figure 23–1.

Profit-oriented objectives

Target
returns
provide
specific
guidelines

■ Seeking a target return is a common objective. The target may be a certain percentage return on sales, or on investment. Or very small family-run firms may seek a fixed dollar amount of profit to cover living expenses.

Common long-run targets seek somewhere between 10 and 20 percent return on investment after taxes. The actual size may depend partly on industry or market practice and partly on competition. Some companies seem to set a relatively moderate objective to discourage potential competitors. Others, expecting relatively little competition, may set extremely high targets for the short run.

A target return objective has some administrative advantages in a large company. It simplifies measuring and controlling the performance of the many divisions and departments, all of which are using capital. Some companies will eliminate divisions or drop products not yielding a certain predetermined rate of return on investment. Naturally, then, managers use target return pricing, trying to hit this desired figure. This is not an easy matter. Too large a return may invite government action. Too small a return may put the division out of business.

Long-run targets are used by companies that have carved out markets for themselves or that are, at least, leaders in their fields, such as Alcoa, Du Pont, General Motors, International Harvester, and U.S. Steel.

For such companies, a long-run target return objective makes considerable sense. These companies might be considered public utilities. They are well aware that the public and the government are keeping an eye on them. They frequently play the role of price leaders and wage setters, and the public seems to expect them to follow a policy that is popularly referred to as being "in the public interest."

Profit maxi-
mization
has its
supporters

■ Objectives seeking to maximize profits might be stated as a desire to achieve profit growth and rapid return on investment or, more bluntly, "all the traffic will bear."

Profit maximization objectives seem to be found more frequently among smaller firms, especially small merchants and manufacturers who are out of the public limelight or who have successfully carved out their own market.[1]

The public, and many businessmen, have come to associate a profit maximization objective with high prices and monopolies. Many people feel that anyone attempting to maximize profits is operating contrary to the public interest.

Economic theory, however, does not support this reaction. Profit maximization does not necessarily lead to high prices. True, if competition cannot offer effective substitutes, then demand and supply *may* bring extremely high prices. But this happens *if, and only if,* demand is highly inelastic. If demand is highly elastic, it might be in a monopolist's interest to charge relatively low prices so that sales will be expanded.

Figure 23–1
Possible pricing objectives

Profit maximization can have desirable results for both business and consumers. Profit can be viewed as a return for efficiency. If the customer is served poorly, there might be no profit at all. If he is served more adequately, profit may be larger. Competitors will see the company's high profits and want to emulate it. In this way, competition — even the monopolistic competition variety — will eventually reduce profits (and probably prices, too). We saw this process at work in Chapter 12 in the rise and fall of profits during the life cycle of a product. Contrary to common belief, a profit maximization objective may be desirable from a social viewpoint.

Some just seek satisfactory profits

■ Some management theorists maintain that *satisfactory* profits is the level of profit sought by some businessmen today. To be sure, they work for profits, but they aren't nearly as aggressive as they might be if they were seeking maximum profits. They do want to convince stockholders of their competence and assure the firm's survival, but as long as profits are *satisfactory* for these purposes, they will have achieved their ends.[2]

Sales-oriented objectives

Does sales growth mean big profit?

■ Some business executives, especially in larger companies, seem more concerned about growth in sales than in profits. The popularity of this objective is probably due to the tendency to equate growth with profitability. This naïve belief is dying, however, since major corporations have faced a continuing profit squeeze over the last 20 years while sales have grown. More recently, greater attention has been aimed at profits as well as sales.[3]

Another explanation for the popularity of growth-oriented objectives is that the manager's salary may be more closely related to sales than to profits.[4] As noted in Chapter 21, compensation systems should be used to get desired results. Here, it seems that compensation systems may have had a bearing on the selection of objectives rather than vice versa.

Getting your market share

■ Just *maintaining* market share—the percentage of the market you are "entitled" to because of your size and reputation—seems to be extremely important to some managers. This may be in part because market share is easier to measure than whether profits are being maximized. It is fairly easy to determine by surveys whether a company has maintained its percentage of a market. Consequently, as long as some profit is returned, the managers may prefer emphasizing market share instead, especially if job promotions are based on market share performance!

Note, however, that some large companies do not want more than a certain percentage of the market. Why?

Some companies don't want to arouse government officials. Some observers feel that General Motors is not as aggressive as it could be in certain markets because it doesn't want to get substantially more than 50 percent of the market. One GM executive, commenting on his corporation's share of the market, stated: "Yes, it's a little better. Our market penetration in March was under 53 percent. In February, you remember, we took more than 57 percent."[5]

Aggressive and especially smaller companies often emphasize an objective of *increasing* their market share or even dominating a market. In some businesses, economies of scale can be gained by larger operations, and a firm may work both to increase market share and maximize profits. In other cases, however, firms blindly follow the market expansion goal, and this leads to pricing goods practically at cost in order to get more of the market. These growth preferences sometimes lead to profitless prosperity, where slight miscalculations may lead to bankruptcy.

Status quo objectives

More time for golf or nonprice competition

■ These can be described as *don't-rock-the-boat* objectives. The purpose of these objectives is stated variously as "meeting competition," or "avoiding competition," or "stabilizing prices."

Often a status quo objective is held by a conservative management that wishes to minimize the risk of loss, preferring instead a comfortable way of life and some assurance of profit. Maintaining stable prices may forestall competition and eliminate the need for hard decisions, and managers may have more time for golf.

On the other hand, status quo pricing objectives can be part of an extremely aggressive marketing strategy. The *pricing* objective may seem conservative, but the intention could be to avoid price competition in favor of aggressive action on one or more of the other Ps. This is called *nonprice competition.* A firm in oligopoly might logically follow this course, for example.

Most prices are administered — to reach the firm's objective

■ Specific pricing policies are vital for any firm. Otherwise, the marketing manager has to reexamine his strategy every time a customer asks for a price. This not only would be a drain on executive time, but customer goodwill easily could be lost if quoted prices did not appear to follow a logical pattern.

Specific price policies should lead to consciously set prices aimed at reaching the firm's objectives. In other words, rather than let daily market forces determine their prices, most firms (including *all* of those in monopolistic competition) set their own prices, sometimes holding them steady for long periods of time. For this reason, most prices are called *administered prices.*

Some firms handle pricing rather mechanically and unimaginatively — simply "meeting competition" or, worse, marking up their costs with little consideration for demand. Actually, however, they do have many factors to consider and many options. They *should* administer their prices, and carefully, because, finally, it is the price which customers have to decide to pay before a whole marketing mix is a success. In the balance of this chapter, we will discuss the policies a marketing manager must set to do an effective job of administering Price.

Government administers price too
■ Before going on to firm-level pricing, it is important to note that the government sometimes controls prices too. Usually, this is done in an attempt to control inflation or otherwise make the macro-marketing system work better. But the fact is that the many facets of our pricing system do not always work together well and some government officials are asked to move in. This makes it even more important to know how and why businesses should and do price. It also points up that price is a complex variable which may need administering, certainly by individual businessmen. Simple market forces may set the framework, but there are many decisions which must be made by individual businessmen (or government planners if they try to control prices).

Price flexibility policies

■ One of the first decisions any marketing manager has to make is to choose between one price and flexible prices.

One-price policy

■ A one-price policy means offering the *same price to all customers* who purchase goods under essentially the same conditions and in the same quantities. A majority of U.S. producers adopt a one-price policy, mainly for administrative convenience and to maintain goodwill among customers. Most food stores, department stores, and even the modern discount houses and mass merchandisers use a one-price policy, too.

A one-price policy may make pricing easier for the seller, but the marketing manager must be careful to avoid rigid adherence to a one-price policy. Such a policy could amount to broadcasting a price which his competitors could undercut—especially if his prices were somewhat high. One reason for the growth of discount houses is that conventional retailers applied traditional margins and rigidly stuck to them.

Flexible-price policy

■ Under a flexible-price policy, the same products and quantities are offered to *different customers at different prices*, depending on their bargaining ability, family relationship, or other factors.[6]

Flexible pricing was most common when businesses were small, products were not standardized, and bargaining was traditional. These conditions still exist in most foreign countries.

Flexible pricing does have advantages, however, and is often used in the channels, in direct sales of industrial goods, and at retail for more expensive items and homogeneous shopping goods. It allows a salesman to make adjustments for competitive conditions rather than having to turn down an order. An aggressive salesman might first emphasize the quality of his product rather than its price. He may charge a higher price to those customers who will pay it and cut the price for those who won't.

The use of flexible prices can cause legal difficulties as we will see later in the chapter. A flexible pricing policy has other disadvantages, too. The customer who finds that others have obtained lower prices for what he feels is the same marketing mix is not going to be happy. The time needed for bargaining may increase, and the cost of selling may rise as buyers become aware that this could be profitable to them. Finally, some salesmen may let the practice of offering price cuts become a habit. This could eliminate price as a competitive tool and lead, instead, to a new and lower price level.

Price-level policies

■ When a marketing manager administers his prices—as most do—he must consciously make another policy decision: Will his prices be set below the market, at the same level as competition, or above the market? If the firm is in pure competition, of course, no policy is really necessary; to offer goods above or below the market price would be foolish. We will be concerned, therefore, with those less than purely competitive situations in which the marketing manager does have a choice. Further, we will assume that the firm is seeking at least some profits. Other objectives might lead one to think about price level policies in quite a different way. A very sales-oriented marketing manager, for example, might try to set "below the market" prices with the hope of drastically expanding sales.

Is it below, at, or above the market?

■ Some firms seem to emphasize below-the-market prices in their marketing mixes. Retail discounters and mass merchandisers offer goods below the prices charged by conventional retailers. And some manufacturers, such as Volkswagen with its "beetle," consistently sell products which appear to be offered below the market. At the other extreme, manufacturers such as Zenith Radio Corporation have proudly claimed that their prices start well above those of competing models and that one of the reasons for their outstanding success in recent years is that while other companies cut prices and skimped on quality, Zenith consistently maintained high quality.

The question is: Do these various strategies contain prices which are above or below the market or are they simply different prices in different markets? Perhaps *some* target customers *do* perceive important differences in the physical product, or in convenience of location, or in the whole marketing mix. Then what we are really talking about are different marketing strategies, not different price levels. Seemingly lower prices are merely lower prices in different marketing strategies. The retail discounters, for example, may have lower prices than conventional retailers, but they may not be direct competitors. The economic shoppers may be comparing prices between discounters—a fact which some discounters are beginning to discover to their dismay.

Obviously, the market grid concept is relevant here. If some market grid box was not previously satisfied and a more attractive marketing mix is offered to it with a higher price, then that price probably should not be thought of as above the market, but rather a new price which is part of a new marketing mix. Similarly, a "lower" price may not automatically cause the firm to be "below the market." It may be the price that is needed to make a good mix and compete with similar "low price" mixes—i.e., it is "at the market" against these mixes.[7]

Meeting competition may be best in oligopoly

■ In highly competitive markets, and especially in oligopoly situations, pricing "at the market" may be the only sensible policy. To raise prices might lead to a substantial loss in sales unless competitors follow the price rise. And cutting the price would probably lead to competitors price cutting also, downward along an inelastic industry demand curve. As we saw in Chapter 3, this can only lead to a decrease in total revenue for the industry and probably for each of the firms. Therefore, a meeting competition policy may make sense for each firm and price stability may develop without any *conscious parallel action.*

Pricing over the product life cycle

■ When the original price level for a new product is established, the product life-cycle concept must be considered, because it will affect how fast the product moves through the cycle. A high price, for example, may lead to attractive profits but also competition and a faster cycle. With this in mind, should its initial price be a *skimming* or a *penetration* price?

Skimming pricing — feeling out demand at a good price

■ A skimming policy is aimed at getting the "cream" of the market (the top of the demand curve) at a high price before catering to the more price-sensitive segments of the market. Skimming frequently is practiced to maximize profits on new products — particularly in the product introductory stage when demand is fairly inelastic, at least in the upper price ranges.

Skimming is useful for feeling out demand — for getting a better understanding of the shape of the demand curve. It is easier to start with a high price that customers can refuse and then reduce it, than to start with a low price and then try to raise it.

A skimming policy can lead to a slow reduction of the price in a step-down or "cascading" process. The step-down technique, however, is part of a dynamic process. As the prices are lowered, new target markets are sought. New place and promotion policies may be needed, too. In short, a skimming pricing policy may involve changing prices through a succession of marketing strategies during the course of the product life cycle.

Penetration pricing — get the business even at a loss

■ A penetration policy is the opposite of a skimming policy. The intention is to try to sell the whole market at one price; that is, a low price on the firm's demand curve where the quantity demanded is larger. This policy might be indicated where there is no "elite" market — that is, where the whole demand curve is fairly elastic, even in the early stages of the product life cycle.

A penetration policy will be even more attractive if, as volume expands, substantial economies of scale reduce costs, or if the firm seriously expects strong competition *very soon* after introduction. A *low* penetration price may be called a "stay-out" price, since it is intended to discourage large competitors from entering the market.

Introductory price dealing — okay, get in there and fight!

■ Outright price cuts do attract customers. Retailers or producers offering new products, therefore, often use *temporary* price cuts to speed their entry into a market. These temporary price cuts should be distinguished from low-penetration prices, however, because the intention is to raise prices as soon as the introductory offer is over.

Established competitors often choose not to meet this introductory price dealing, as long as the introductory period is not too long or too successful. But realizing that customers may shift their loyalties if they try competitors' products, some aggressive competitors do meet such introductory price cuts.

Once price dealing gets started in a market, it may continue for some time, so an introductory dealing policy must be chosen with care.[8]

Legality of price flexibility and price level policies

■ From our general discussion of legislation in Chapter 5, you might have gotten the impression that companies have little latitude in pricing or may even need government approval for their prices. Generally speaking, this is *not* the case. As long as businessmen don't conspire with their competitors or discriminate against some of their customers, they can charge what they want, even "outrageously high" prices (unless emergency price controls have been imposed).

There *are* restrictions on pricing, however, and these are discussed in the following paragraphs. But here it should be noted that difficulties with pricing, and perhaps violation of price legislation, usually occur only when competing marketing mixes are quite similar. When the success of an entire marketing strategy depends upon price, there is pressure (and temptation) to conspire or discriminate. This is not a trivial matter, because as noted in Chapter 5, some business executives have gone to jail for violating business legislation!

The first step to understanding pricing legislation is to appreciate the thinking of legislators and the courts. Ideally, they attempt to design and administer laws which will help the economy perform more effectively in the consumers' interest. In practice, this does not always work out as neatly as planned. But generally their intentions are good, and if we take this view, we may get a better idea of the "why" of legislation. And this helps us to anticipate and evaluate future rulings. We will stress U.S. legislation here so that we can be specific, but other countries have similar legislative constraints on pricing.[9]

Unfair trade practice acts control some minimum prices

■ The "unfair trade practice acts" which have been passed in more than half the states are designed to put a floor under prices, especially at the wholesale and retail levels. Deliberate selling below cost in these states is illegal. Wholesalers and retailers are normally required to take a certain minimum percentage markup over their merchandise-plus-transportation costs. The most common markup figures are 6 percent at retail and 2 percent at wholesale.

If a specific wholesaler or retailer can show that his operating costs are lower than the minimum required figure, he may be permitted to offer lower prices. But he must prove conclusively that he does have lower costs and in the typical case this is almost impossible.

Even the most vigorous discounters know enough about their costs to seek larger markups than these minimums. The practical effect of these laws is to protect certain limited-line food retailers, such as dairy stores, from the kind of "ruinous" competition that full-line stores might offer if they chose to sell milk as a leader, offering it below cost for a lengthy period.

Antitrust legislation permits some price fixing— with "fair trade"

■ Price fixing is generally prohibited under the Sherman Act and more specifically under the Federal Trade Commission Act. There are special cases, however, in which collusion and price fixing are specifically permitted by law.

Fair-trade (or *resale price maintenance*) laws permit price fixing by manufacturers or wholesalers *who choose to do so.* These state laws, for example, will permit a manufacturer to sue retailers for not adhering to the 79-cent retail price set by the maker for a tube of toothpaste.

Too much competition for small retailers

These price-fixing laws were a product of the depression of the 1930s when drastic price cutting was used to try to stimulate sales. California retailers led the way in getting legislation which would permit manufacturers or wholesalers to set retail prices for trade-marked goods—the ones commonly discounted—by signing price-fixing agreements with their retailer customers. With the passage of a *nonsigner's clause,* all retailers in the state were bound if one retailer signed a price-fixing contract.

Wholesalers and retailers in other states, seeing the success of the California law, lobbied for such legislation, and eventually 45 states passed them.

Fair trade is basically a state-by-state matter

All of this legislation was alike in being limited to *intra*state trade. The question remained whether price-fixing agreements in *inter*state commerce were legal. In 1937, the *Miller-Tydings Act* was passed by the U.S. Congress, allowing branders in interstate commerce to make such agreements in states which had fair-trade laws, without violating federal antitrust legislation. This was an *enabling act,* since it permitted such agreements only in states that had such laws.

The Miller-Tydings Act, however, did not specifically contain a nonsigner's clause. In 1951, price cutting broke out around the country when the U.S. Supreme Court ruled that the Miller-Tydings Act applied only to signers. But the following year, 1952, Congress passed the *McGuire Act,* which said, in effect, that Congress had intended the nonsigners' clause to be in the Miller-Tydings Act. With this ambiguity cleared up, fair trade became effective again in those states having such laws. But fair traders have not had free sailing, since some states have repealed their laws. Less than half still have such legislation, but fair-trade supporters continue to offer fair-trade bills in state legislatures.

Fair trade can be a useful managerial tool but it is declining

Fair trade has been used effectively for well-differentiated products with relatively inelastic demands and with manufacturing costs that represent a small percentage of the price. Drug and cosmetics products are the best examples.

While fair trade has only been used for 5 to 10 percent of retail goods, it is strongly supported by conventional retailers such as those selling drugs and cosmetics and small appliances. These retailers want to protect themselves from discounters and, at times, have put heavy pressure on their manufacturer and wholesaler suppliers to fair trade their goods. Some manufacturers have given into this pressure because these retailers represented the best channel to their customers. Also, these retailers sometimes provide a needed promotional push, while discounters frequently provide a place for the product, and emphasize price while ignoring promotion. In other words, they might use only three of the four Ps, skimming the "cream" by dealing only with customers who were presold or easily sold, and ignoring the balance of the market.

With the growth of discounters and mass merchandisers, the dominance of these conventional retailers has eroded and fair trade is less commonly used. Another factor contributing to the decline of fair trade is that the legislation is normally permissive rather than mandatory. A manufacturer does not have to use fair trading, but if he chooses to do so, then the burden of policing is on him. Sometimes it is difficult to secure prompt injunctions against discounters. And then extensive court cases may be involved. And the relatively small penalties awarded to the producer, together with the ill will generated among channel members may overbalance the benefits of fair-trade pricing.

Finally, fair trade may be declining because some manufacturers did not feel that it was justified from a consumer viewpoint. Its main purpose is to stabilize or increase the price level. This is certainly not in tune with current thinking about running a more efficient macro-marketing system.

Antitrust legislation prohibits price discrimination unless . . .

■ Price level and price flexibility policies can lead to price discrimination. And, as discussed in Chapter 5 the *Robinson-Patman Act* of 1936 specifically makes unlawful, in interstate commerce, any price discrimination between different purchasers of "commodities of like grade and quality" which may *tend to injure competition.* This law does permit some price differentials, but they must be based on cost differences or the need to "meet competition." Both buyers and sellers are liable to prosecution if they knowingly enter into discriminatory agreements. This is a serious matter and price discrimination suits are common.

What does "like grade and quality" mean?

The Robinson-Patman Act permits a marketing manager to charge different prices for similar products if they are not of like grade and quality. But the crux of the matter is, how similar can they be? The FTC position is that if the physical characteristics of a product are similar, then they are of like grade and quality. The FTC's view was upheld in a 1966 U.S. Supreme Court ruling against the Borden Company. The Court held that a well-known label *alone* does not make a product different from the one with an unknown label. The issue was rather clear-cut in the *Borden* case because the company acknowledged that the physical characteristics of the canned milk it sold at different prices under different labels was essentially the same.

The FTC's "victory" in the *Borden* case was not complete, however. Although the U.S. Supreme Court agreed with the FTC in the *Borden* case with respect to like grade and quality, it sent the case back to the U.S. Court of Appeals to determine whether the price difference actually injured competition, which is also required by the law. In 1967, this court found no evidence of injury and further noted that there could be no injury unless Borden's price differential exceeded the "recognized consumer appeal of the Borden label." How "consumer appeal" is to be measured was not spelled out and may lead to additional litigation.[10] Eventually, what the consumer thinks about the product may be the determining factor. For now, however, it would appear safer for producers who want to sell several brands or dealer brands at lower prices than their main brand to offer actual physical differences, and differences that are genuinely useful, not merely decorative or trivial. Another possibility for differentiation that has won some support in the courts is packaging differences.[11]

Can cost analysis justify price differentials?

The Robinson-Patman Act supposedly allows price differentials if there are cost differences. Justifying cost differentials is a difficult task, however, since costs usually must be allocated to several products, and perhaps arbitrarily. It is easy, then, to raise objections to whatever allocation method is used. Such objections frequently are raised, in part, because there can be differences of opinion about how to allocate costs, but perhaps more basically because the FTC has been especially concerned about the impact of price differences on competition, and small competitors in particular. The FTC has even sought to control the size of quantity discounts on the grounds that big discounts, although justified on a cost basis, may be unfair to small competitors.[12]

Can you legally meet price cuts?

Meeting competition is permitted as a defense in price-discrimination situations under the Robinson-Patman Act, although the FTC normally has taken a rather dim view of this argument.

In a significant 5–4 decision in 1956, the U.S. Supreme Court said that "meeting competition" in "good faith" is a permissible defense if it can be shown that the price discrimination occurred as a *defensive* rather than an offensive action. The dissenting justices saw the implications and suggested that this ruling "crippled the enforcement of the act." They added that if price cutting should begin generally, the majority decision could permit a great deal of price cutting—*perhaps to the detriment of less efficient outlets.*[13]

A major objective of antitrust legislation is to protect competition, not competitors, and "meeting competition" in "good faith" still seems to be acceptable, even if it is large firms which meet the lower prices of small firms.

Are functional discounts discriminatory?

Can functional discounts be considered price discrimination? Legislation is not completely clear on this issue, but court decisions appear to have settled the matter with emphasis on functions provided.[14] At the root of the situation is the distinction between wholesalers and retailers, since wholesalers are entitled to certain discounts from producers to provide wholesaling functions.

Generally, the courts have felt that the identification of a firm as a wholesaler or a retailer depends, not on the quantity he buys or handles, but on the nature of the service he provides. A producer could legally refuse to give a wholesale discount to a large retail grocery chain, although the chain might handle a much larger volume than small wholesalers. The justification is that functional discounts are imperative for the small wholesaler if he is to cover his costs and still sell to retailers at prices low enough to permit the retailers to be competitive.

A chain probably would not have to pay the same price offered a small retailer, however. A special functional discount could be set up for chain stores. As long as a functional discount seems to reflect the nature of the job required in the channel, the courts probably would consider it legal.

Brokerage allowances may be illegal

Brokerage allowances can be troublesome. Brokers normally are allowed a trade discount for their services. But sometimes large organizations, such as grocery chains, act as their own brokers and request the broker's trade discount in the form of a brokerage allowance. Under the Robinson-Patman Act, such brokerage allowances for buyers or buyers' representatives are illegal. In highly competitive fields, however, the marketing manager may feel he has to grant such an allowance, perhaps calling it an advertising allowance but without any expectation of obtaining additional promotion. In effect, competitive pressures are pushing prices downward. This has been seen in the low-profit-margin grocery retailing industry where the buyer's ability to win extra allowances and favorable cash discounts may make the difference between profit and loss for the whole business.

Special promotion allowances might not be allowed

Some firms have violated the Robinson-Patman Act by providing *P.M.s (Push Money)*, demonstrations, *advertising allowances,* or other promotional aids to certain customers and not others. The act specifically prohibits such special allowances unless they are made available to all customers on "proportionately equal" terms. No proof of injury to competition is necessary, and the FTC has been fairly successful in prosecuting such cases.

The need for such a rule is clear, once price regulation begins. Allowances for promotional aid could be granted to retailers or wholesalers without expectation that any promotion would actually be undertaken. This plainly would be price discrimination in disguise.

The provision does work hardships, since it sometimes is difficult to provide allowances on "proportionately equal" terms to both large and small customers. The Robinson-Patman Act does not state clearly whether a small store should be allowed the same dollar advertising allowance as a large one or an allowance in proportion to sales. The latter probably would not buy the same promotional impact.

It may also be difficult to determine exactly who are competing customers. The FTC might define a relevant list of competitors much more broadly than either the seller or the competing buyers. Supermarket operators might only be concerned about other supermarkets and the new food discounters, while the FTC might feel small drugstores were competitors on health and beauty aids.[15]

In 1969, the FTC issued some new guidelines for advertising and promotional allowances, including more stringent requirements for informing all competitive customers that deals were available. As a result, we may see a trend away from cooperative advertising, and perhaps promotional allowances in general.[16]

How to avoid discriminating

One way to avoid discriminating is to avoid price differentials. Until this potentially powerful but confusing law is clarified, many business executives probably will continue to think it wise to de-emphasize price as a marketing variable. They have concluded that the safest course is to offer few or no quantity discounts, and to offer the same cost-based prices to *all* customers.

It would be unfortunate if all price competition were eliminated, ostensibly in the public interest but actually more to the benefit of individual competitors. Prices probably would rise, as would the total cost of distribution because of the restriction on the free operation of the economy.

A price structure is multidimensional

Price equals something

■ Prices are not only administered within our legal environment, but they are also multidimensional. As we saw in Chapter 4, the price which a consumer or channel member pays is the amount of money he exchanges for "Something." See Figures 4–6 and 4–7 for a review of the ideas introduced there. Clearly, in the Price area we are not interested only in the list price but also in any discounts or allowances or other important variations from this list price. Ultimately, the consumer is interested in what she pays for "something." Some of these possible variations are self-explanatory, while others will deserve some discussion in this chapter.

Prices start with a list price

■ Most price structures are built around *list prices*. How these list prices come to be determined is the subject of Chapters 24 and 25. For the moment, however, we must understand that there may be several list prices. Then, we will go on to see the many possible variations from list.

Basic list prices

Basic list prices are the prices that final consumers (or industrial customers) normally are asked to pay for goods. Unless otherwise specified, the term "list price" here will refer to "basic list price."

Unchanging list prices – an administrative convenience

For administrative convenience, some published list prices remain the same for long periods of time, perhaps years, but the actual price paid by the customer changes as these unchanging list prices are adjusted upward or downward by add-ons or discounts from the unchanging list prices. This method of changing prices is often used in industries where frequent price changes are necessary, since it avoids constant catalog price revisions. Rather than printing a complete new catalog, the firm can simply publish a new list of add-ons or discounts.

Phony list prices for bargain hunters

Sometimes, especially at the final consumer level, what might be called *phony list prices* are published so that customers can be shown that the price they are to pay has been discounted from "list." Some customers, in fact, seem more interested in the size of the purported discount than the list price itself, and they can wind up paying more than the competitive market price.

Most businessmen, Better Business Bureaus, and government agencies frown upon obviously phony prices. And the FTC has sought to control such deceptive pricing under the Wheeler-Lea Amendment of 1938, which prohibits "unfair or deceptive acts in commerce."

The FTC has issued "Guides against Deceptive Pricing." They say that manufacturers, distributors, and retailers "must in every case act honestly and in good faith on advertising a list price, and not with the intention of establishing a basis . . . for a deceptive comparison in any local . . . trade area." This was designed to reduce collusion on pricing along the channel. At the retail level, it is expected that the retailer will have a good grasp of competitive prices and not advertise so as to create a false impression of the value being offered.[17]

The FTC has had some court success, but deception is sometimes difficult to define. Sometimes the "two-for-one" and 1-cent sales are bona fide promotional offers which do appear to be appealing to the price conscious on the market grid.

Moreover, there is some question whether customers are really deceived by "high" list prices from which they bargain. Are the list prices from which discounts are offered on automobiles deceptive? The FTC thinks so, but auto industry executives feel that consumers understand the nature of the sticker price as a ceiling price or a starting point from which to begin bargaining.

Some customers get discounts off list

■ Discounts are reductions from the list price that are granted by a seller to a buyer who either *foregoes some marketing function* or *provides the function for himself.* Discounts can be highly useful tools in marketing strategy planning.

In the following discussion, consider what function the buyer is foregoing or providing for himself when he obtains each of these discounts.

Quantity discounts encourage volume buying

■ Sellers offer quantity discounts to *induce customers to purchase in larger quantities.* This enables the seller to get more of a buyer's business or shift some of the storing function to the buyer or reduce shipping and selling costs, or all of these. These discounts are of two kinds: cumulative and noncumulative.

Cumulative discounts apply to purchases over a given period — such as a year — and normally increase as the quantity purchased increases. Cumulative discounts are intended to encourage buying from a single company by reducing the price for additional purchases.

Noncumulative discounts are quantity discounts that apply to individual shipments or orders only. Such discounts encourage larger orders but do not tie a buyer to the seller beyond that one purchase.

Quantity discounts may be based on the dollar value of the entire order, on the number of units purchased, or on the size of the package purchased. While quantity discounts are usually given in the form of a price reduction, sometimes they are given as free or bonus goods — customers receive one or more units "free" with the purchase of a specified quantity.

Quantity discounts can be a very useful variable for the marketing manager. Some customers are eager to get them. But marketing managers must use quantity discounts, and especially cumulative quantity discounts, with care to avoid price discrimination.

Seasonal discounts — buy sooner or more

■ Seasonal discounts are especially important within channels. They induce buyers to stock earlier than immediate demand would necessitate. This discount tends to shift the storing function farther along in the channel. It also tends to smooth out sales during the year and, therefore, permit year-round operation. If seasonal discounts are substantial, channel members may pass them along to their customers. In coal sales, seasonal discounts are given in the spring and summer all the way through the channel to final consumers and users.

Cash discounts should encourage prompt payment

■ Most sales to channel members and final users are made on credit. The seller issues an invoice, and the buyer sends it through his accounting department for payment. Many channel members come to depend on other members for temporary working capital, and therefore it is extremely important for both sides to clearly specify the terms of payment, including the availability of cash discounts. The following terms of payment frequently are used:

Net means that payment for the face value of the invoice is due immediately. These terms are sometimes altered to "net 10" or "net 30," which mean payment is due within 10 or 30 days of the date of the invoice.

1/10 net 30 means that 1 percent discount off the face value of the invoice is permitted if the invoice is paid within 10 days. Otherwise, the full face value is due within 30 days. And it usually is implied that an interest charge will be made after the expiration of that 30-day free credit period.

The due date for payment usually is based on the date of the invoice. This often is the date the goods are shipped, but a convenient alternate way for the seller to offer additional credit without changing his basic terms is to *advance* the date of the invoice. This practice is called *forward dating* and is sometimes used in extremely competitive situations.

Why cash discounts are given and should be taken

Cash discounts are used chiefly to encourage buyers to pay their bills promptly, and smart buyers take advantage of them. A discount of 2/10, net 30 may not look like very much, but any company that passes it up is missing a good financial opportunity. It would be money ahead to borrow at a bank to pay such invoices on time.

The 2 percent discount is earned for paying the invoice just 20 days sooner than it would have to be paid anyway. And if it is not taken, the company in effect is borrowing at an annual rate of 36 percent. That is, assuming a 360-day year and dividing by 20 days, there are 18 periods during which the firm could earn 2 percent— and 18 times 2 equals 36 percent a year.

While the marketing manager can use the cash discount as a marketing variable, a specific cash discount may be so firmly established in his industry that he cannot change or use it to suit his needs. He must grant the customary terms, even if he has no need for cash. Purchasing agents are aware of the attractiveness of cash discounts and will insist that the marketing manager offer the same terms normally offered by his competitors. In fact, some buyers automatically will deduct the accepted cash discount from their invoices regardless of the seller's invoice terms.

Trade or functional discounts make channels work

■ A trade or functional discount is a list price reduction given to channel members in anticipation of a job they are going to perform.

A manufacturer, for example, might allow his retailers a 30 percent trade discount from the suggested retail list price to cover the cost of their retailing function and their profit. Similarly, the manufacturer might allow wholesalers a *chain discount* of 30 percent and 10 percent off the retail price. In this case, the wholesalers would be expected to pass the 30 percent discount on to retailers.

Trade discounts might seem to offer a manufacturer or wholesaler's marketing manager great flexibility in varying his marketing mix, but in fact they may limit him greatly. The customary trade discount can be so well established that he has to accept it in setting his prices. More will be said about this in the next chapter.

Some customers get allowances off list

■ Allowances are similar to discounts. They are given to final consumers or users for accepting less of "something," or adjusting for variations. Or they are given to channel members for providing a service, perhaps additional selling effort.

Bring in the old, ring up the new — with trade-ins

■ Trade-ins give the marketing manager a convenient way to reduce his price to the customer without reducing list price. Proper handling of trade-ins is especially important when selling durable goods, both to final consumers and intermediate customers. Customers buying machinery or buildings, for example, buy long-term satisfaction in terms of more manufacturing capacity. If the list price less the trade-in discount does not offer greater satisfaction or value — as the customer sees it — then no sales will be made.

Many firms replace machinery slowly, perhaps too slowly, because they value their old equipment more highly than the firm selling the new equipment. This same situation seems to apply to new cars. Customers want higher trade-ins for their old cars than their current market valuation. This prompts the use of high, perhaps "phony," list prices so that high trade-in allowances can be given.

Advertising allowances — something for something

■ Manufacturers frequently give price reductions to firms farther along in a channel to encourage them to advertise, display, or otherwise promote goods locally. Channel system thinking is involved here. General Electric has given a 1.5 percent allowance to its distributors of housewares and radios who, in return, are expected to provide something — in this case, local advertising.

P.M.s — push for cash

■ Push Money or Prize Money allowances are similar to advertising allowances. They are given to retailers by manufacturers or wholesalers to pass on to the retailers' salesmen in return for aggressively selling particular items or lines. The P.M. allowances usually are reserved for new merchandise, slower moving items, or higher margin items, and are especially common in the furniture and clothing industries. A salesman, for example, might earn an additional $5 for each mattress of a new type sold.

Some customers get extra somethings — trading stamps

■ Some retailers offer trading stamps to their customers in an effort to differentiate their "something." Some customers seem to be attracted by trading stamps because they feel they are getting something for nothing. In fact, they sometimes are, if competitive pressures do not permit the retailers to pass the cost of the stamps — 2 to 3 percent of sales — along to consumers. Also, the increased cost of the stamps may be offset by reduced promotional expenditures or by a substantial increase in sales.[18]

Retailers can buy trading stamps from trading-stamp companies or set up their own plans. In either case, customers can redeem stamps for merchandise premiums or cash or goods at the merchant's own store or at stamp redemption centers.

The early users of stamps in a community seem to gain a competitive advantage, but when competitors also start offering stamps, the advantage can be canceled. This is similar to competition in the product life cycle where innovators are copied and profits are squeezed.

There was much interest in trading stamps in the 1950s and 1960s but it now appears that the rapid growth in the use of stamps is over, especially in grocery retailing. There, food discounters cut into the attractiveness of seemingly "higher cost" stamp givers. Now that some of the initial enthusiasm for stamp plans is subsiding, perhaps they can be seen in perspective as a potential addition to a marketing mix, perhaps in lieu of a price reduction. Still, in some situations, stamp plans may be very effective, especially if half of the "mass market" would like stamps.[19]

List price may depend on who pays transportation costs

■ Retail list prices often include free delivery. Or free delivery may be offered to some customers as an aid to closing the sale. In short, what is included (or not included) in the retail list price may not be formally published. This helps the retailer adjust his marketing mix, depending on the needs and preferences (and interest or bargaining ability) of each customer.

Deciding who is going to pay the freight is more important on sales to intermediate customers than to final consumers, because more money may be involved. Usually purchase orders specify place, time, method of delivery, freight costs, insurance, handling, and other incidental charges. There are many possible variations here for an imaginative marketing manager, and a number of specialized terms have developed. A few are discussed in the following paragraphs:

F.O.B. the customer's doorstep

■ F.O.B. is a commonly used term regarding transportation. It means "free on board" some vehicle at some place, and typically is used in conjunction with *some named point*, that is, the location of the seller's factory or warehouse, as in "F.O.B. Detroit," "F.O.B. Chicago," or "F.O.B. mill." It means that the seller pays the cost of loading the merchandise onto some vehicle, usually a common carrier such as a truck, railroad car, or ship. At the point of loading, title to the goods passes to the buyer, who pays the freight and assumes responsibility for damage in transit, except as covered by the transportation agency.

Variations are made easily, however, by changing the *some named point* part of the terms. If the marketing manager wanted to pay the freight for the convenience of his customer, he could use: "F.O.B. delivered" or "F.O.B. buyer's factory" (or warehouse). In this case, title would not pass until the goods were delivered. If he did want title to pass immediately – but still wanted to pay the freight bill (and then include it in the invoice) – he could use: "F.O.B. seller's factory – freight prepaid."

F.O.B. shipping point pricing simplifies the seller's pricing but may unduly narrow his market. Since the delivered cost of his goods will vary depending on the buyer's location, a customer located at a greater distance from the seller must pay more for his goods and might be inclined to buy from nearby suppliers.

Zone pricing smoothes delivered prices

■ Zone pricing is designed to reduce the wide variation in delivered prices which result from an F.O.B. shipping point pricing policy. It also simplifies the charging for transportation.

Under zone pricing, an average freight charge is made to all buyers within certain geographical areas. The seller pays the actual freight charges and then bills the customer for an average charge. The United States might be divided into five zones, for example, and all buyers within each zone would pay the same freight charge.

The zone approach often is used by manufacturers of hardware and food items, both to minimize the possibility of price competition in the channels and to simplify the computation of transportation charges for the thousands of wholesalers and retailers they serve.

Uniform delivered pricing – one price to all

■ Uniform delivered pricing – sometimes called "postage stamp pricing" – is simply an extension of zone pricing. An entire country may be considered one zone, and the average cost of delivery is included in the price. It is most often used when transportation costs are relatively low and the seller wishes to sell his product in all geographic areas at one price, perhaps one which is nationally advertised.

Freight absorption pricing – competing on equal ground in another territory

■ When all the firms in an industry use F.O.B. shipping point pricing, a firm tends to do well near its plant or shipping point but not so well farther away. As salesmen solicit business at greater distances, delivered prices rise, and they find themselves priced out of the market.

Freight-absorption pricing enables manufacturers and wholesalers to compete in larger territories – which on the whole increases competition. When a marketing manager decides to penetrate a new territory, he generally absorbs freight cost so that his delivered price will meet the nearest competitor's. This amounts to cutting his price to appeal to new market grid segments.

With freight absorption pricing, the only limit on the size of his marketing territory is the amount of freight cost a marketing manager is willing to absorb. These absorbed costs cut net return on each sale, but the new business may raise total profit.

Basing-point pricing

■ Basing-point pricing policies benefit a company uniquely by reducing or eliminating the need for freight absorption. Here, competitors recognize the same shipping points—basing-points—as places from which to figure the cost of transportation, regardless of the actual shipping point. Basing-point pricing grows out of the competition in a dynamic marketplace.

To understand how basing-point pricing might develop, assume that all plants in a new industry are located together and have the same production costs. Each producer might start out selling F.O.B. his plant. Delivered prices in distant markets would be considerably higher than near the home market, and these higher prices would encourage competitive plants to develop in outlying markets. When they did, how would you determine what prices would be charged in these markets?

Single-basing-point system

This was precisely the situation during the early days of the steel industry. Most of the steel was produced in the Pittsburgh area and sold F.O.B. Pittsburgh. As additional plants developed in Cleveland and Chicago, there was a question of what price to set. If the Chicago producer had identical production costs and set his price F.O.B. Chicago, then he might eliminate Pittsburgh sellers from the Chicago market. Pittsburgh sellers could absorb freight costs, but this would reduce their profits. To solve this problem, the steel industry leaders decided that all steel in the country would be sold, regardless of where it had been produced, *as if it had come from Pittsburgh*—the single-basing-point for prices.

The advantage to the Pittsburgh sellers of a single-basing-point was obvious, but why did the Chicago area sellers agree? The answer is simple: it was extremely profitable for them. The system permitted them to charge their Chicago customers freight from Pittsburgh—what was called *phantom freight* (see Figure 23–2).

Basing-point pricing systems have been found in basic industries—such as steel, cement, and building materials—that are characterized by oligopoly, high fixed costs relative to variable costs, and high transportation costs relative to the goods' price. In such situations, it is desirable to expand sales volume, yet inelastic demand has made this difficult. A basing-point plan was an industry's reaction to a difficult market situation.

Basing-point pricing, however, was so obviously at variance with the consumer interest that the Federal Trade Commission, as early as 1921, took action against the U.S. Steel Corporation and other steel companies. As a result of this action, the steel industry, beginning in 1924 shifted to a multiple-basing-point system. The FTC opposed this multiple-basing-point system too, and finally, in 1945 and 1948, the U.S. Supreme Court ruled against *any* industrywide system involving phantom freight.[20]

Multiple-basing points

Something resembling basing-point pricing is still used in some industries. Now, however, all the major producing points usually are considered basing points. The practical result is that all competitors set their prices to compete with the nearest producing point, absorbing whatever freight cost is necessary.

Under these conditions, alert purchasing agents continually look

Figure 23–2
A single-basing-point system with Pittsburgh as the base gives Chicago
producers $10 in phantom freight in the Chicago market

for new or closer producers. When they find one, they exert pressure on their suppliers to treat this new source as a basing point, too, and so there is little likelihood of phantom freight charges lasting for long.

Present legal status of geographical pricing

■ There are two points of view on what constitutes geographical price discrimination under the Robinson-Patman Act. According to one view, the delivered price should be the same to all buyers. According to the other, the factory price should be the same to all buyers.

The first view would permit a considerable amount of freight cost absorption to enable the seller to broaden his territory, perhaps allowing him to expand his factory and operate at a more efficient level—assuming that economies of scale are possible.

The second view, by contrast, insists on F.O.B. pricing, on the assumption that it is improper for outlying customers to pay less than the "full cost." But without freight absorption, sellers might not be able to obtain this additional business, and their basic costs and prices could actually rise. In addition, strict F.O.B. pricing might encourage the development of monopoly areas around each firm's plant or warehouse.

This view is a logical extension of antitrust legislation designed to block price discrimination which would force some customers to pay more than others. This second view has long been favored by the FTC and is gaining acceptance in the courts. Currently, however, although basing-point systems involving phantom freight are illegal, freight absorption systems which are designed to enable firms to reach more distant markets are not considered illegal unless the members of an industry arrive at a common method through conspiracy.

Conclusion

■ The price variable has many facets and offers an alert marketing manager many possibilities for varying his marketing mixes. What pricing policies he will follow depends on his pricing objectives. We examined profit-oriented, sales-oriented, and status quo-oriented objectives. Ideally, objectives should be clearly stated and *written*, because they provide direction for subsequent pricing policies and price determination.

A marketing manager must set policies with respect to price flexibility, price level, who will pay the freight, and who will get how much in the way of discounts and allowances. Also, he should be aware of the pricing legislation that pertains to these policies.

In most cases, a marketing manager must set his own prices—that is, he must administer his prices. Starting with a list price, he may offer a variety of discounts and allowances to adjust for the variation in the "something" being offered in his marketing mix.

Throughout this chapter, we have assumed that a list price had already been established. We have placed primary emphasis on what may be included (or specifically excluded) in the "something" and what objectives a firm might have to guide its pricing policies. The critical matter of price determination itself was not discussed. We will cover this in the next two chapters, showing ways of implementing the various pricing objectives.

questions and problems

1 How should the acceptance of a profit-oriented, a sales-oriented, or a status quo-oriented pricing objective affect the development of a company's marketing strategy? Illustrate for each.

2 Distinguish between one-price and flexible-price policies. Which would be most appropriate for a supermarket? Why?

3 Cite two examples of continuously selling above the market price. Describe the situations.

4 Explain the types of market situations which might lead to a "meeting competition" pricing policy.

5 What pricing objective(s) would a skimming pricing policy most likely be implementing? Could the same be true for a penetration pricing policy? Which policy would probably be most appropriate for each of the following products: (a) a new type of home lawn-sprinkling system, (b) a new low-cost meat substitute, (c) a new type of children's toy, (d) a faster computer.

6 Discuss unfair trade practices acts. To whom are they "unfair"?

7 How would our marketing structure be changed if manufacturers were required to specify fair trade prices on *all* products sold at retail and *all* retailers were required to use these prices? Would this place greater or lesser importance on the development of the manufacturer's marketing mix? What kind of an operation would retailing be in this situation? Would consumers receive more or less service?

8 Would price discrimination be involved if a large oil company sold gasoline to taxicab associations for resale to individual taxi cab operators for $2\frac{1}{2}$ cents a gallon less than charged to retail service stations? What happens if the cab associations resell gasoline not only to taxicab operators, but to the general public as well?

9 Indicate what the final consumer really obtains when paying the list price for the following "products": (a) an automobile, (b) a portable radio, (c) a package of frozen peas, and (d) a lipstick in a jeweled case.

10 Are seasonal discounts appropriate in agricultural businesses (which are certainly seasonal)?

11 What are the "effective" annual interest rates for the following cash discount terms: (a) 1/10 net 60, (b) 1/5 net 10, (c) net 30.

12 Explain how a marketing manager might change his F.O.B. terms to make his otherwise competitive marketing mix more attractive.

13 What type of geographic pricing policy would seem most appropriate for the following products (specify any assumptions necessary to obtain a definite answer)? (a) a chemical by-product (no fixed costs charged to it), (b) nationally advertised candy bars, (c) rebuilt auto parts, (d) tricycles.

14 Explain how the prohibition of freight absorption (that is, requiring F.O.B. factory pricing) might affect a producer with substantial economies of scale in production.

notes

[1] W. Warren Haynes, *Pricing Decisions in Small Business* (Lexington: University of Kentucky Press, 1962).

[2] For more discussion of the behavior of satisficers, see Herbert A. Simon, *Administrative Behavior* (2d ed.; New York: Macmillan Co., 1961).

[3] "Squeeze on product lines," *Business Week,* January 5, 1974; p. 50 f and "Pricing Strategy in an Inflation Economy," *Business Week,* April 6, 1974, pp. 43–49.

[4] Joseph W. McGuire, John S. Y. Chiu, and Alvar O. Elving, "Executive Incomes, Sales and Profits," *American Economic Review,* September 1962, pp. 753–61; "For the Chief, Sales Sets the .Pay," *Business Week,* September 30, 1967, p. 174.

[5] *Wall Street Journal,* April 18, 1962, p. 1.

[6] For an interesting discussion of the many variations from a one-price system in retailing, see Stanley C. Hollander, "The 'One-Price' System—Fact or Fiction?" *Journal of Retailing,* Fall 1955, pp. 127–44.

[7] See, for example, "The Airline that Thrives on Discounting," *Business Week,* July 24, 1971, pp. 68–70; see also Zarrel V. Lambert, "Product Perception: An Important Variable in Pricing Strategy," *Journal of Marketing,* October 1970, pp. 68–76, and "Price and Choice Behavior," *Journal of Marketing Research,* February 1972, pp. 35–40.

[8] For more discussion on price dealing, see Charles L. Hinkle, "The Strategy of Price Deals," *Harvard Business Review,* July–August 1965, pp. 75–85.

[9] For discussion concerning European countries, see *Market Power and the Law* (Washington, D.C.: Organization for Economic Cooperation and Development Publication Center, 1970), 206 pp.

[10] Morris L. Mayer, Joseph B. Mason, and E. A. Orbeck, "The Borden Case—A Legal Basis for Private Brand Price Discrimination," *MSU Business Topics,* Winter 1970, pp. 56–63; Jacky Knopp, Jr., "What Are 'Commodities of Like Grade and Quality'?" *Journal of Marketing,* July 1963, p. 63.

[11] T. F. Schutte, V. J. Cook, Jr., and R. Hemsley, "What Management Can Learn from the Borden Case," *Business Horizons,* Winter 1966, pp. 23–30.

[12] Peter G. Peterson, "Quantity Discounts in the Morton Salt Case," *Journal of Business of the University of Chicago,* April 1952, pp. 109–20; "Is the Cost Defense Workable," *Journal of Marketing,* January 1965, pp. 37–42; and B. J. Linder and Allan H. Savage, "Price Discrimination and Cost Defense—Change Ahead?" *MSU Business Topics,* Summer 1971, pp. 21–26.

[13] *Business Week,* February 1, 1958, p. 53.

[14] *FTC* v. *The Mennen Company,* and *National Biscuit Company* v. *FTC.*

[15] Lawrence X. Tarpey, Sr., "Who Is a Competing Customer?" *Journal of Retailing,* Spring 1969, pp. 46–58; and John R. Davidson, "FTC, Robinson-Patman and Cooperative Promotion Activities," *Journal of Marketing,* January 1968, pp. 14–18.

[16] "The FTC Gets Tough on 'Promo' Payments," *Business Week,* November 24, 1973, p. 30; and L. X. Tarpey, Sr., "Buyer Liability under the Robinson-Patman Act: A Current Appraisal," *Journal of Marketing,* January 1972, pp. 38–42.

[17] "Guides Against Deceptive Pricing," Federal Trade Commission, October 10, 1958, and January 8, 1964.

[18] A. Haring and W. O. Yoder (eds.), *Trading Stamps Practice and Pricing Policy* (Indiana Business Report No. 27, Bureau of Business Research, Bloomington, Indiana University, 1958), p. 301.

[19] "Buyer's Choice: Stamps or Savings," *Business Week,* February 7, 1970, p. 106; and "Sharp Drop in Gas-Station Business Brings Trading-Stamp Industry More Profit Woes," *The Wall Street Journal,* March 1, 1974, p. 26.

[20] In cases against Corn Products Refining Co. and A. E. Staley Co. in 1945 and against the Cement Institute in 1948.

24

Pricing in the real world is cost-oriented

■ In the previous chapter, we accepted the concept of a list price and went on to discuss variations from this list price. Now, we will go on to see how the basic list price might be set in the first place. Although, in practice, there are many ways of arriving at a price, these can be reduced, for simplicity, to two basic methods: (1) cost-oriented and (2) demand-oriented price determination. We will emphasize the cost-oriented approaches in this chapter and demand-oriented approaches in Chapter 25.

Cost-oriented pricing is typically used in the real world. Accounting systems can estimate or accumulate the costs of doing particular tasks, and profit-and-loss statements show very clearly that all costs should be covered. Costs provide a floor below which prices cannot go (for long, anyway), and it is only logical that prices should be built on seemingly precise cost data.

As we shall see, however, cost-oriented pricing is not as simple or foolproof as it might seem at first glance. The analytical tools presented in Chapter 25 can improve cost-oriented price determination, but management judgment is still required. Price determination is a serious matter and deserves careful study. We will begin our discussion by examining how most firms, including retailers and wholesalers, set cost-oriented prices.

Pricing by wholesalers and retailers

A case can be made for using traditional markups

■ Most retail and wholesale prices are determined by using the traditional markups taken in those trades. The markup is normally the trade or functional discount allowed by the previous channel members. Using this method, the retailer or wholesaler adds a markup to the delivered cost of his goods.

Generally, the trade discounts or traditional markups are applied rather mechanically. Some retailers or wholesalers, in fact, use the same markup for all of their goods — which, if nothing else, certainly simplifies their pricing procedure. Other retailers (and sometimes wholesalers) may take a higher markup on some items because of their apparent quality or their slow turnover. Or they may take a lower markup to meet competitive prices or because they feel consumers will not accept the price set by using the traditional markups.

Considering the large number of items the average retailer and wholesaler carries and the small sales volume of any one item, this cost-oriented markup approach to pricing seems both reasonable and practical. Spending the time and effort to determine the best price to charge on every item in stock, day to day or week to week, probably would not pay for itself.

There are two kinds of markups: On cost and on selling price

■ Suppose that a retailer buys an article for $1. To make a profit the retailer obviously must sell this article for more than its cost. If the retailer adds 50 cents to the selling price of the article to cover his operating costs and provide a profit, we say that he is marking up the item 50 cents.

Markups, however, generally are expressed as percentages rather than dollar amounts. And this is where the difficulty begins. Is a markup of 50 cents on a cost of $1 a markup of 50 percent? Or should the markup be computed as a percentage of the selling price — $1.50 — and therefore be $33\frac{1}{3}$ percent? A clear definition is necessary.

We will use the following definition: Unless otherwise specified, *markup means "percentage of selling price."* By this definition, the 50-cent markup on the $1.50 selling price is a markup of $33\frac{1}{3}$ percent.

Markups are related to selling price for convenience. For one thing, the markup on selling price is roughly equivalent to the gross margin, which is computed in relation to total sales. Most businessmen have a full appreciation of the concept of gross margin because they continually see gross margin data on their profit-and-loss statements. (See the Appendix on Marketing Arithmetic if you are unfamiliar with these concepts.) They know that unless there is an adequate gross margin, there will not be any profits left at the end of the period. For this reason, businessmen readily accept traditional markups that are close to their gross margins.

Relating markups to the selling price also is consistent with our emphasis on the consumer. There is nothing wrong, however, with the concept of markup on cost. The essential thing is to clearly indicate which markup we are using, to avoid confusion. Some retailers use the term *mark-on* to indicate a markup based on cost, but this is by no means common. In the everyday world, the terms are often interchanged rather haphazardly.

Some retailers frequently need to convert a markup on cost to one based on selling price, or vice versa. Conversion tables have

Figure 24–1
Example of a markup chain and channel pricing

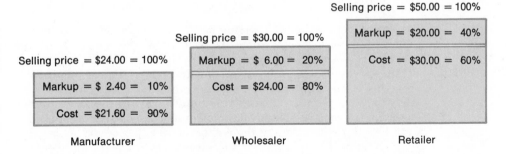

| Manufacturer | Wholesaler | Retailer |

been developed for this purpose, but they are not essential because the calculations are simple. (See "Markup Conversion," in Appendix: Marketing Arithmetic.)

Markup chain may be used in channel pricing

■ A chain of markups can set the price structure in a whole channel. A markup is figured on the selling price at each level of the channel. The producer's selling price becomes the wholesaler's cost; the wholesaler's selling price becomes the retailer's cost; and his marked up cost becomes the retail selling price. Each markup is expected to cover the expenses of selling and administration and to leave a profit. Figure 24–1 shows how a markup might be used at each level of a channel system.

This illustration starts with a production cost (factory cost) of $21.60. In this case, the producer is taking a 10 percent markup and sells the goods for $24. The markup is 10 percent of $24 or $2.40. The producer's selling price now becomes the wholesaler's cost —$24. If the wholesaler is accustomed to taking a 20 percent markup on selling price, his markup is $6, and his selling price becomes $30. The wholesaler's selling price of $30 now becomes the retailer's cost. And if the retailer is accustomed to a 40 percent markup, he adds $20 and the retail selling price becomes $50.

Fallacy of high markups —slow turnover

■ Some people, including some retailers, have associated high markups with high profits, but this is often in error. Some lines of business just have high operating costs and need high markups. In other cases, high markups may discourage sales and lead to low profits, or actually losses. Full appreciation of these ideas helps account for the spectacular success of the discounters. Why?

The fallacy of seeking high profits through high markups can be seen by an extreme example. A 90 percent markup on selling price may not be nearly as profitable as a 10 percent markup on selling price! This apparent paradox is easy to understand if we assume an extreme condition in which no units are sold at the high markup, but a very large number are sold at the low one. The key is *turnover*. You cannot earn much if you don't sell much, regardless of the size of the markup. Nevertheless, many retailers and wholesalers seem more concerned with the size of their markup than with their total profit.

Lower markups can speed the stockturn rate

■ Not *all* retailers and wholesalers, however, are enamored with the traditional markups. Some are concerned with speeding turnover to increase profit, even if this means reducing the markup. They see themselves running an ongoing system that is incurring costs as a function of time and the volume of goods handled. If they can sell a much greater volume of goods in the same time period, they may be able to take a lower markup on such items and still have a higher profit at the end of the time period.

An important concept here is the *stockturn rate* – the number of times the average inventory is sold in a given time period, such as a year. Various methods of computing a stockturn rate are used, but they are all involved with how many times the average inventory is sold. (See "Computing the Stockturn Rate," in the Appendix on Marketing Arithmetic.) If the stockturn rate is low, this may be bad for profits.

At the very least, a slow stockturn will increase cost by tying up working capital. If the stockturn were 1 (once per year) rather than 5, selling goods costing $100,000 would require $100,000 rather than $20,000 in working capital just to carry the necessary inventory.

What constitutes high or low stockturn depends on the industry. For instance, an annual rate of 1 or 2 might be expected in the retail jewelry industry, while 40 to 50 would be typical for fresh fruits and vegetables.

Living too high on the markup hurts the image

■ The use of high, inflexible markups can have a damaging impact on the image and subsequently on the profits in an industry. Hardware retailers, for example, have been especially inflexible about markups and this has led to real difficulties.

Many hardware retailers have traditionally marked up all items 50 percent *on cost* and received a high price image as a result. And consumers, feeling that hardware stores were high priced, have traded there only to get items unobtainable elsewhere. This has meant relatively low total profits for hardware retailers because, for thousands of their items, the turnover is so low that even the normal 50 percent markup yields no profit.

A study by the National Retail Hardware Association, a trade association of hardware retailers, found that fewer than 100 items in the average hardware store were bought on the basis of price. These were the items which were available in other kinds of stores and on which prices were generally cut. To remedy the unfortunate situation, the association has developed a *Turnover Handbook* which strongly urges the abandonment of the practice of marking up all goods by 50 percent of cost. Instead, it suggests classifying about 5,000 different items into six categories, on the basis of demand sensitivity.

In the "A" category are goods that should be sold competitively. The markup for these items vary from a 45 percent markup in a small town to only 10 percent in a large city where there is greater competition. The "A" category includes only a relatively small number of items but involves the store image; it is important that the store be competitive on these items.

The *Handbook* suggests that goods in the other five categories be marked up progressively, the last group to more than 100 percent of cost. The items for which the highest markups are suggested are (1) those carried as a community service—low-priced items with a low turnover—and (2) high-priced items that require extensive product knowledge to sell.[1]

Grocers run a fast company

■ Grocery supermarket operators have shown that they understand the importance of turnover. The big grocers put only small markups on fast-selling items such as sugar, shortening, soaps, and detergents, canned milk, soups, desserts, beverages, baby foods, pet foods, bleaches, flour, and canned vegetables. Sugar, for example, may carry a margin of 8 percent; shortening, 9 to 10 percent; soaps and detergents, 10 or 11 percent.

Since supermarket expenses run 12–18 percent of sales, some people feel that many of these items are carried at a loss. But since such figures are storewide averages, this need not be true.

Fast-moving goods generally are less expensive to stock and sell. They occupy valuable space for shorter periods, are damaged less, and tie up less working capital. Lower markups will cover the costs of these items and make a profit too. With lower markups, the goods may turn even faster, and a small profit per unit will be earned more frequently.

These fast-moving goods may be more profitable per item, in spite of the low margins, because of the higher turnover. The average turnover in the grocery department in one study was 14 times a year. Yet sugar turned over 31 times, beverages 28 times, shortening 23 times, and soups 21 times.

It should be noted here that the high-margin items were not necessarily unprofitable. They simply were not as profitable *per item* as some of the low-margin items.[2]

Discounters are running faster

■ The modern food discounters and mass merchandisers carry the fast-turnover concept of the supermarket even further. By pricing even lower and attracting customers from wider areas who purchase in substantial quantities, they are able to operate profitably on even smaller margins.

Pricing by producers

It's up to the captain to set the list price

■ Some markups eventually become customary in a particular trade whether retailers and wholesalers use a common markup for all items or whether they vary their markups. Most of the channel members will tend to follow a similar markup process, adding a certain percentage to the previous price. Who determines price in the first place?

The basic list price usually is determined by the channel captain —a large retailer, a large wholesaler, or most often the producer. From here on, we are concerned with the pricing approach of such firms, and for convenience we will call them "producers."

Customary formulas are common

■ Producers commonly use some cost-oriented approach. They may start with a dollar-cost-per-unit figure and add a markup, perhaps a customary percentage, to obtain the selling price. They may be guided by a rule-of-thumb formula such as: *Production cost × 3 = Selling price.* In the electronics industry, a customary formula is: *Price = Material cost + Direct labor cost + 100 percent of direct labor for overhead + 120 to 180 percent of direct labor for all other costs.*[3]

Each producer usually develops his own rules and markups in the light of his own costs and objectives. Yet even the single step of selecting the appropriate cost per unit to build on is no simple matter. So we must discuss several approaches to see how cost-oriented price determination really works.

The naïve cost-plus method is common and dangerous

■ One simple and common approach to price determination—the naïve cost-plus method—consists of adding a "reasonable" markup to the cost per unit. The cost per unit is found by assuming that all the inventory has been sold during a specific period, such as the past month, then taking the total cost for that period and dividing this figure by the number of units produced and sold in the same period.

If the total cost of the latest month were $5,000 for labor and materials and $5,000 for fixed overhead expenses (such as selling expenses, rent, and executive salaries), then total cost would be $10,000. If the company produced 10,000 items in the previous month, the average cost was $1 a unit. To get the price, the producer decides how much profit markup per unit seems "reasonable," then adds this figure to the cost per unit. If 10 cents were considered a reasonable profit for each unit (perhaps they had a target return of $1,000 a month), the new price would be set at $1.10.

It does not make allowances for cost variations as output changes

■ The chief merit of this approach is its simplicity. This is also its weakness. To see why, we will observe this firm further.

If, in the next month, only 5,000 units are produced and sold, the firm may be in trouble. Five thousand units sold at $1.10 each would yield a total revenue of $5,500. The overhead would still be fixed at $5,000 and variable material and labor costs would drop in half to $2,500, for a total of $7,500. This would mean a loss of $2,000 or 40 cents a unit. The method that seemed to allow for a profit of 10 cents a unit, instead would cause a loss of 40 cents a unit.

It is apparent that this naïve cost-plus method does not adjust for cost variations at different levels of output. Since all costs do not behave the same way as sales expand or contract, the average cost per unit may change considerably as output rises or falls. The following paragraphs explain these variations.

Cost-oriented pricing must consider various kinds of costs

■ One reason the naïve cost-plus approach fails is that total cost includes a variety of costs, and each of these changes in a different way as output changes. Any method that uses costs as the basis for determining prices must make allowances for these variations. The more realistic approach described below does so.

To fully understand this method, however, it will be desirable first to define and illustrate six types of cost. An understanding of the differences among these costs is important because these differences are at the root of the problems many companies have with pricing.

There are three kinds of total cost

■ *Total fixed cost* is the sum of those costs that are fixed in total regardless of output level. Among these fixed costs are rent, depreciation, executive salaries, property taxes, and insurance. Such costs must be paid even if production stops temporarily. Over a period of years, fixed costs can change—the factory may be expanded or sold; new executives may be hired or fired. But in the short run, total fixed cost is set.

Total variable cost, on the other hand, is the sum of those variable expenses that are closely related to output level—expenses for components, wages paid to workers, packaging materials, outgoing freight, and sales commissions.

At zero output, total variable cost is zero. As output increases, so do variable costs. If a dress manufacturer doubles his output of dresses in a year, his *total* cost of cloth would also roughly double (ignoring quantity discounts), although the cost of cloth *per dress* would remain about the same.

Total cost is the sum of total fixed and total variable costs. The rate of growth of total cost depends upon the increase in total variable cost, since total fixed cost, by definition, is already set.

There are three kinds of average cost

■ The pricing executive usually is more interested in cost per unit than total cost because prices in the marketplace usually are quoted per unit. Costs per unit are called "average" costs, and there are several types.

Average cost per unit is obtained by dividing total cost by the related quantity (i.e., the total quantity produced which led to the total costs).

Average fixed cost is obtained by dividing total fixed cost by the related quantity.

Average variable cost is obtained by dividing total variable cost by the related quantity. We commonly assume that average variable

Table 24–1
Cost structure of a firm

Quantity	Total fixed costs (TFC)	Average fixed costs (AFC)	Average variable costs (AVC)	Total variable costs (TVC)	Total cost (TC)	Average cost (AC)
0	$30,000	$	$ 0	$ 0	$ 30,000	$
10,000	30,000	3.00	0.80	8,000	38,000	3.80
20,000	30,000	1.50	0.80	16,000	46,000	2.30
30,000	30,000	1.00	0.80	24,000	54,000	1.80
40,000	30,000	0.75	0.80	32,000	62,000	1.51
50,000	30,000	0.60	0.80	40,000	70,000	1.40
60,000	30,000	0.50	0.80	48,000	78,000	1.30
70,000	30,000	0.43	0.80	56,000	86,000	1.23
80,000	30,000	0.38	0.80	64,000	94,000	1.18
90,000	30,000	0.33	0.80	72,000	102,000	1.13
100,000	30,000	0.30	0.80	80,000	110,000	1.10

cost is *constant per unit* over a short production range. Actually, average variable cost usually decreases as a firm gains some economies of scale, levels out for a while, and then it begins to rise again at still higher levels of output.

The assumption that average variable cost is constant for short ranges is reasonable only in certain cases – but when appropriate, it simplifies analysis. This assumption is used in the following example.

A cost structure example illustrates relations

■ In Table 24–1, typical cost data is presented for one firm; it is based on the assumption that average variable cost is constant for each unit. Notice how average fixed cost decreases steadily as the quantity increases, and how, although the average variable cost remains constant, total variable cost increases when quantity increases. Average cost decreases continually. This is because average variable cost is constant and average fixed cost is decreasing. Figure 24–2 graphs the behavior of the three average-cost curves.

The average-cost method watches how costs change

Average-cost-curve pricing commonly used

■ The pricing executive could set prices using a graph such as that in Figure 24–2. Assuming that the average-cost curve includes a provision for profit (either a fixed total amount included in total fixed cost or a fixed amount per unit included in average variable cost), then all he has to do is decide how many units the firm is going to sell. If he expects to sell 50,000 units, then by referring to

Figure 24–2
Typical shape of cost (per unit) curves when *AVC* is assumed
constant per unit

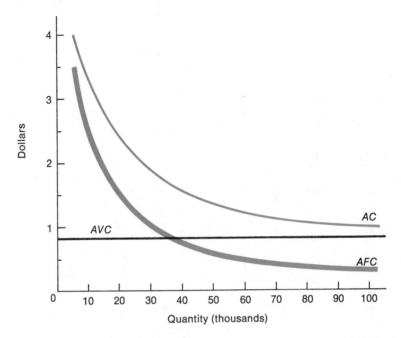

the average-cost curve shown here, the price could be determined.
It would be $1.40. If he plans to sell 80,000 units, the price sug-
gested by the average-cost curve would be $1.18.

Those using this approach often estimate the quantity to be sold
by assuming that next period's sales will approximate the volume
of the last period.

Assuming that the firm will sell a quantity similar to past sales,
the average-cost method works easily. The "average-cost" price is
found along the *AC* curve at that previous quantity. This seems to
assure that all the fixed costs will be covered. The fixed costs
covered by each unit are easily calculated. And it is an easy next
step to develop pricing formulas to ensure that on each item that
amount of fixed cost is covered.

Various cost-oriented pricing formulas might be invented but
the intent would be the same – to cover all the costs. The formulas
suggested earlier in the chapter illustrate the possibilities.

**Ignoring
demand is
its major
deficiency**

■ As long as actual sales do not vary too much from the previous
period, the average-cost approach will produce fairly good results.
As with the naïve approach, however, losses may result if actual
sales are much *lower* than in the previous period. On the other
hand, if sales are much higher than expected – if the demand curve
has shifted substantially – then profits may be good, but by accident.

Figure 24-3
Evaluation of various prices along a firm's demand curve

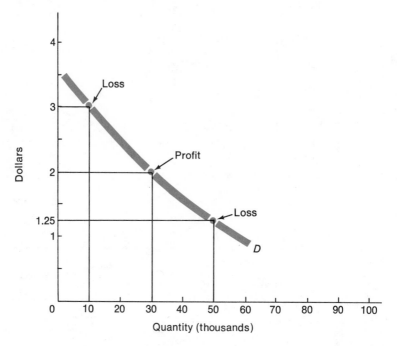

If a manager is to base his pricing on cost, he must be able to make some estimate of the quantity to be sold in the coming period. But unless this estimated quantity is related to price—that is, unless demand is considered—the pricing executive may set a price that either does not maximize profits or, worse, does not even cover total costs. Such a possible predicament can be seen in a simple illustration for a firm with the cost curves shown in Figure 24-2. This firm's demand curve is shown in Figure 24-3. It is important to recognize that customers' demands (and their demand curves) are still relevant, whether management takes time to analyze the demand curve or not.

In this example, whether management sets the price at a high $3 or a low $1.25, it will incur a loss. At $3, only 10,000 units will be sold for a total revenue of $30,000. But total costs will be $38,000, for a loss of $8,000. At the $1.25 price, 50,000 units will be sold, but a loss of $7,500 will result. If management made some attempt to estimate the demand curve, however crudely, the price probably would be set in an intermediate range, say at $2, where a profit of $6,000 would result.

In short, the average cost approach is simple in theory, but often very crude in practice. In static situations, prices set in this manner may yield profits—but not necessarily maximum profits. And interestingly, such prices might be higher than a price which would

Table 24-2
Results of target return pricing

	10,000 units sold		20,000 units sold	
Total revenue		$ 925,000		$1,850,000
Total cost				
Total fixed cost	$600,000		$600,000	
Total variable cost	400,000		800,000	
		1,000,000		1,400,000
Profit (loss)		($75,000)		$ 450,000
Return on investment	$\left(\dfrac{-75,000}{300,000}\right) = -25\%$		$\left(\dfrac{450,000}{300,000}\right) = 150\%$	

be better for the firm, as shown in Figure 24-3. When demand conditions are changing, the average-cost approach may be even less effective.

The target return method

Target return pricing scores ... sometimes

■ Target return pricing, seeking a target return objective, has become popular in recent years. With this approach, the price setter seeks to obtain (1) a percentage return (say 10 percent per year) on his investment or (2) a specific total dollar return.

The method is basically the same as the average-cost method described previously, since the desired target return is added into total cost. An example illustrates the method: 12,000 units were sold last year, and it is hoped the same quantity will be sold this year. Executive salaries, general administrative overhead, and other fixed expenses total $600,000. Total investment is $300,000. Target return is a 10 percent return on investment.

Therefore ... *total fixed cost*—including the 10 percent target return—is $630,000.

This total, divided by 12,000 units, yields a fixed cost and target return per unit figure of $52.50. If the variable cost per unit is $40, the price that apparently should be set to bring a 10 percent return on investment is $92.50.

This approach suffers from the same deficiency as the average-cost approach. If the quantity that actually is sold in a given period is less than the quantity used in setting the price, then the target return is not achieved, even though it seems to be an integral part of the price structure. To see more clearly how this happens, look at the results when either 10,000 or 20,000 units are sold (see Table 24-2).

If only 10,000 units are sold, there is a 25 percent *loss* on investment instead of a 10 percent return. If 20,000 units are sold, there is a 150 percent return on investment instead of only a 10 percent target return. Target return pricing clearly does not guarantee that the target objective will be achieved.

The long-run target return method

Hitting the target in the long run

■ Executives in some larger firms, wanting to achieve long-run target return objectives, have adopted another cost-oriented approach. Instead of estimating the quantity they expect to produce in any one year, they assume that during several years' time their plants will produce at, say, 80 percent of capacity. They use that quantity in their pricing.

No reference at all is made to current demand when setting current prices. Demand was estimated when the plant was built. Some demand and cost factors had to be considered at that time, and in reality it was the decision to build a plant of a certain size that determined subsequent prices.

Companies taking this longer run view assume that there will be recession years when sales drop below 80 percent of capacity, and the target return won't be earned, but also there will be other years when the plant operates at a higher level and betters the target return. Over the long run, the target return will be achieved.

This long-run approach to target return pricing sounds simple. But like pricing in general, it cannot be approached mechanically. For example, "capacity" is a rather flexible concept, perhaps referring to a five-day, single-shift operation or to a seven-day, three-shift operation.

Long-run target return pricing, consequently, need not lead to a unique price or a stable price. Typically, however, companies using long-run target return pricing tend to have more stable prices.

Bid pricing relies on costs

■ Many firms must set prices for each particular job, rather than developing a price structure which applies for all potential customers. Contractors, for example, must bid on possible building projects and architects and engineers must submit bids for jobs they would like to have.

The major task in bid pricing is assembling all the costs, including the variable costs and the fixed costs that should apply to each job. This may sound relatively straightforward, but in actual practice, thousands of cost components may have to go into a complicated bid. Further, management must include an overhead charge and a charge for profit. This is where competition must be considered. Typically, the customer will obtain several bids and accept the lowest one. So mechanical addition of overhead charges and profit rates should be avoided. Some bidders use the same overhead and profit rates on all jobs, regardless of competition, and then are surprised when they do not obtain some jobs.

Bidding can be an expensive process and a firm might want to be selective about which jobs it will bid on—presumably selecting those where they feel they have the greatest chance of success.[5] Thousands or even millions of dollars have been spent just developing cost-oriented bids for large industrial or government orders. To assure that all costs are included, computers often are used to help accumulate the costs. Great care is essential in developing such bid prices. The omission of an important cost item might make the firm the low bidder—but cause it to lose money on the contract.

Sometimes the bids are negotiated

■ Some buying situations, including much government buying, call for bids and the purchasing officer is obligated to take the lowest bid. In other cases, however, bids may be called for and then the company submitting the most attractive bid (perhaps not the lowest) will be singled out for further negotiation. This negotiation may include price adjustments, but it also may be concerned with: how additions to the job will be priced, what guarantees will be provided and the caliber of men and supervisors who will do the job. Some projects, such as construction projects, are hard to define exactly and it is important that the buyer be satisfied about the whole marketing mix, not just the price.

Some businessmen adjust for demand

■ Cost-oriented pricing is relatively simple and practical. But it is also clear that most cost-oriented approaches require some estimate of the likely quantity demanded. And as we have seen, a formal estimate of a demand curve might help avoid mistakes in pricing.

Explicit use of demand curves is not very common in the real world. Yet we do find businessmen setting prices as though they believe certain types of demand curves are present. And pricing research indicates they are. It is clear that some prestige, odd-even, and psychological pricing efforts do consider demand. And some retailers do adjust their markups in the light of their feelings about demand.

The following sections discuss various examples of demand-related pricing. Some efforts may be only intuitive adjustments of cost-based prices, but it is clear that demand is being considered.

Prestige pricing— make it high and not too low

■ To some target customers, relatively high prices seem to mean high quality or high status. If prices are dropped a little bit, these customers may see a bargain. But if the prices begin to appear cheap, they start worrying about quality and may stop buying.[6]

Such target customers present the marketing manager with an unusual demand curve. Instead of a normal downslope, the curve

Figure 24–4
Demand curve showing a prestige price situation

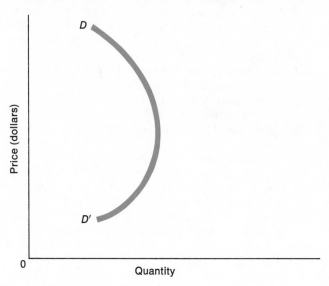

slopes down for a while, and then bends back to the left again (see Figure 24–4).

Marketing managers dealing with this kind of demand – such as jewelry and fur retailers and nightclub owners – typically set high prices, sometimes called "prestige prices."

Leader pricing – make it low to boost sales

■ At the other extreme from prestige pricing is leader pricing. Leader pricing is commonly used to get customers into retail stores. Certain products are picked for their promotional value and priced low, but above cost. In food stores, the leader prices are the "specials" that are advertised regularly to communicate an image of low prices. Large stocks of these low-priced items are sold.

The leader-priced items are bona fide bargains priced very low for the sole purpose of getting customers into the store. Leader pricing usually is restricted to well-known, widely used, items which customers don't stock heavily, such as milk, butter, eggs, and coffee, but on which customers will recognize a bona fide price cut. The idea is to attract customers, not sell large quantities of the leaders. And to avoid hurting the firm's own profits, it may be desirable to use items that are not directly competitive with major lines, as in the sale of bargain-priced cigarettes at a gasoline station.

Bait pricing – offer for a pittance, but sell under protest

■ Bait pricing, like leader pricing, is used to attract business. But unlike leader pricing, the seller *does not* plan to sell much merchandise at the low price.

This procedure is commonly used in the retail furniture trade. To attract customers, an extremely low price is offered on an item

Figure 24–5
Demand curve when odd-even pricing
is appropriate

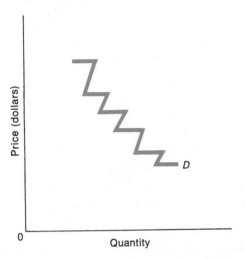

Figure 24–6
Demand curve when psychological pricing
is appropriate

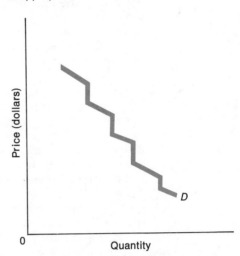

which the trade considers "nailed down." Then, once customers are in the store, the salesmen are expected to point out the disadvantages of the lower-quality item and to switch customers to higher-quality and more expensive products. Customers can buy the bait item, but only with great difficulty.

This policy attempts to attract bargain hunters, or customers on the very low end of the demand curve who are not normally part of the market. If bait pricing is successful, customers may be traded up, and the demand for higher-quality products will expand. But extremely aggressive and sometimes deceptive bait-pricing advertising has brought this method into disrepute. The Federal Trade Commission considers bait pricing a deceptive act and has prohibited its use in interstate commerce. Still, some retailers who operate solely within one state continue to advertise bait prices.

Odd-even pricing— it's $5.95. . .   ■ Some marketing men feel that consumers will react more favorably to prices ending in certain numbers, usually the odd numbers. Retail studies show that merchants *do use* certain prices more frequently than others.

For merchandise selling under $50, prices ending with 95— such as $5.95, $6.95, and so on—are common. In general, prices ending in nine are most popular followed by prices ending in five and three. For merchandise selling over $50, prices that are $1 or $2 below the even-dollar figure are the most popular.[7]

Marketing men using these prices seem to assume that they have a rather jagged demand curve; that consumers will buy less for a while as prices are lowered and then more as each "magic" price is reached. This kind of demand curve is shown in Figure 24–5.

It is debatable whether these odd prices are effective. They apparently were adopted by some retailers to force their clerks to make change. Then they would have to record the sale, and could not pocket the money. Today, however, it is not always clear why these odd prices are used and whether they are effective. Perhaps consumers have been conditioned to expect more favorable offers at certain prices and they do work. Or perhaps it is done simply because "everyone else does it."

Psychological pricing— some prices just seem right

■ Some businessmen simply feel that certain prices for some products are psychologically appealing. Between these prices are whole ranges where customers perceive prices as roughly equivalent. Price cuts in these ranges would not increase the quantity sold. Below such a range, customers would buy more for a while, and then the quantity demanded would remain constant.

The kind of demand curve that seems appropriate in this case is shown in Figure 24–6. Vertical drops mark the price ranges which customers see as equivalent. Some pricing research indicates that there do seem to be such demand curves.[8]

Pricing neckties at various levels—say, $2.50, $5, and $10— may be an attempt to price as nearly as possible to the top of such ranges. This conception of demand underlies the price-lining policy we will discuss later in the chapter.

Pricing a full line or total product

■ Our emphasis has been—and will continue to be—on the problems of pricing a single item, mainly because this simplifies our discussion. But most marketing managers actually are responsible for more than one product. In fact, their product may be the whole company line.

Full-line pricing— market or firm oriented?

■ Many companies offer a complete line (or assortment) of products and have to price this full line. But the correct pricing approach depends on which of two basically different strategies the firm follows. In one case, all products in the company's line may be aimed at the same general target market, which makes it important for all prices to be somewhat related to one another.

In other cases, the different products in the line might be aimed at entirely different target markets. Here, there doesn't have to be any relation between the various prices. A chemical manufacturer of a wide variety of organic compounds with a variety of target markets, for example, probably should price each product separately, in light of the needs and preferences in each market segment. To use a full-line pricing approach here (as some production-oriented firms might do) could lead needlessly to under-pricing some products and over-pricing others.

Examples of a full line being offered to the same target market are a TV manufacturer selling an entire line to retailers, or a fork-lift truck producer offering various sizes to large manufacturers, or a grocery retailer with his thousands of items. Here the firm *must* consider the customers' reaction to its full line of prices.

Usually the marketing manager attempts to price products in the line so that the prices will appear logically related and make sense to potential customers. Most customers, especially industrial customers, feel that prices should be related to cost, and this must be considered in developing prices. Customers usually realize that small production runs or handling small quantities is likely to cost more, and they may be willing to pay higher prices for items which they know have a small market.

Cost not much help in full-line pricing

■ The marketing manager must try to recover all of his costs on the whole line, perhaps by pricing quite low on competitive items and much higher on less competitive items. But costs are not much help to the marketing manager in full-line pricing. There is no single correct way to allocate a company's total fixed costs to each of the products. Many methods are tried in practice, but all are arbitrary. And if a certain method is carried through without regard to demand, it may lead to extremely unrealistic prices. The marketing manager has to be able to judge demand for the whole line as well as demand for each individual product in each target market in order to avoid mistakes.

As an aid to full-line pricing, the marketing manager can assemble directly variable costs on the many items in his line for calculating a floor under which he won't lower his price. To this he can add a "reasonable" markup based on his assessment of the quality of the product, the strength of the demand for the product, and the degree of competition he faces. But finally, the image projected by the entire line must be evaluated.

Price lining — a few prices cover the field

■ Price lining is similar to full-line pricing in that prices are developed for more than one product at a time. But here the focus is on prices at the retail level.

Price lining is the policy of setting a few price levels for given classes or lines of merchandise and then marking all items at one of these established prices. There are no prices at the intermediate points. Exactly how does price lining work?

It would be reasonable to assume that most men will pay between $2.50 and $10 for a necktie. In price lining, there will *not* be many prices in this range; there will be only a few. Ties will *not* be priced at $2.50, $2.65, $2.70, and so on. They will be priced in perhaps three levels at $2.50, $5, and $10.

The main advantage of price lining is that for both clerks and customers it lessens the confusion caused by a multiplicity of prices. Some customers may consider goods in only one price category. The major decision then becomes *which* item to choose at that price. Price no longer is a question unless the goods at that price are unsatisfactory. Then, perhaps the salesclerk can trade the customer up to the next price level.

For the retailer, price lining has several advantages. Sales may increase because he can offer a larger assortment in each price line and because it is easier to get customers to make decisions within one price line. Stock planning is simpler because demand is larger at the relatively few prices. Price lining also can reduce expenses because total stock requirements are lessened even though ample stocks are carried in each line. Price lining results in greater turnover rates, fewer markdowns, quicker sales, and simplified buying procedures.

Demand-backward pricing facilitates price lining

■ Demand-backward pricing is commonly used by producers of final consumer goods, especially shopping goods, such as women's and children's clothing and shoes, and other things like toys or gifts for which the customer will spend a specific amount because he is seeking "a two-dollar or a five-dollar gift." Here, a sort of reverse cost-plus pricing process is used, inspired by the availability of demand at various price levels. This process has been called "market-minus" pricing.

The producer starts with the retail price for a particular price line and then works backward, subtracting the typical margins which channel members expect. This gives him the approximate price he should charge. Then, he deducts from this price his average or planned marketing expenses to determine the allocation for the production cost of each item. The kind of a product he can offer at this price depends on the nature of his cost structure and the expected sales volume.

Obviously, demand estimates are necessary if demand-backward pricing is to be done effectively. Also, since competitors can be expected to make the best product possible, it is important to understand customer needs to determine the optimum amount to be spent on manufacturing costs. By increasing costs slightly, the product might be so improved in consumers' eyes that the firm would sell many more units. But if consumers are not quality conscious, but only seeking novelty, additional quality might not increase the quantity demanded and therefore should not be offered.

Conclusion

■ In this chapter, we considered various methods of cost-oriented price determination. Generally, retailers and wholesalers use traditional markups that they feel will yield a reasonable rate of profit. Some retailers and wholesalers use the same markup on all of their items; others have found that varying their markups may increase turnover and profit. And demand may enter here implicitly!

Cost-oriented pricing seems to make sense for retailers and wholesalers because they handle small quantities of many items. Perhaps they are not maximizing profit on each item, but the extra cost of more analysis might actually reduce total profit.

We found that it is less desirable for a producer or channel captain to use traditional markups. A common alternative, the naïve cost-plus approach, ignores demand completely and is not the answer. A more realistic cost-plus approach using average-cost curves requires some forecast of sales. Such a forecast often amounts to assuming that sales in the next period will be roughly the same as in the last period.

Given such an assumption, the average-cost pricing method enables the pricing executive to determine a price. But this price *may or may not* cover all costs and yield the desired rate of profit. It depends on how closely previous sales are to actual sales. If sales decline, profits may take a nosedive.

Cost-oriented pricing frequently yields a price that is "too high." This causes slow turnover and low profit, or even losses. The first concern of too many businessmen is an "adequate" margin. They do not like to take the risk of lowering prices in anticipation of increased sales and possibly greater profits. Their reluctance results both from their cost orientation and an absence of demand analysis.

It has become almost axiomatic in this book that the *customer must be considered before anything is done*. This certainly applies to pricing. It means that when management is setting the price, it must consider the price customers will be willing to pay. In fact, it appears that some businessmen do consider demand, if only intuitively. We saw this with respect to prestige pricing, leader pricing, bait pricing, odd-even pricing, psychological pricing, and full-line pricing.

In the next chapter, we will discuss methods of estimating demand curves and more explicitly including demand in pricing.

questions and problems

1 Why do department stores seek a markup of about 40 percent when some discount houses operate on a 20 percent markup?

2 A manufacturer of household appliances distributed its products through wholesalers and retailers. The retail selling price was $250, and the manufacturing cost to the company was $100. The retail markup was 40 percent and the wholesale markup 25 percent.
a. What was the cost to the wholesaler? Retailer?
b. What percentage markup did the manufacturer take?

3 Relate the concept of stock turnover to the rise of discounters. Use a simple example in your answer.

4 If total fixed costs are $100,000 and total variable costs are $200,000 at an output of 10,000 units, what are the probable total fixed costs and total variable costs at an output of 20,000 units? What are the average fixed costs, average variable costs, and average costs at these two output levels? Determine the price which should be charged. (Make any simplifying assumptions necessary to obtain a definite answer.)

5 Explain how target return pricing differs from average cost pricing.

6 Construct an example showing that mechanical use of a very large or very small markup might still lead to unprofitable operation while some intermediate price would be profitable. Draw a graph and show the break-even point(s).

7 How would a prestige pricing policy fit into a marketing mix? Would exclusive distribution be necessary?

8 Cite a local example of the use of odd-even pricing and then evaluate whether you feel it makes sense.

9 Cite a local example of the use of psychological pricing and then evaluate whether you feel it makes sense.

10 Distinguish between leader pricing and bait pricing. What do they have in common? How can their use affect a marketing mix?

11 Is a full-line pricing policy available only to producers? Cite local examples of full-line pricing. Why is full-line pricing important?

notes

[1] "Handbook Teaches Dealers How to Sell," *Printers' Ink*, March 27, 1959, pp. 65–69.

[2] *Super-Valu Study* (New York: *Progressive Grocer*, 1957), p. S-4-7.

[3] "Management Problems in the Electronics Industry," *Management Research Summary*, Small Business Administration, November 1962, p. 3.

[4] Some expenditures have both fixed and variable components and are called semifixed or semivariable costs. To simplify this discussion we will omit this refinement. For more discussion on the nature of costs, see Robert N. Anthony, "What Should 'Cost' Mean?" *Harvard Business Review*, May–June 1970, pp. 121–31; and F. E. Brown and A. R. Oxenfeldt, "Should Prices Depend on Cost?" *MSU Business Topics*, Autumn 1968, pp. 73–78.

[5] Stephen Paranka, "Competitive Bidding Strategy," *Business Horizons*, June 1971, pp. 39–43.

[6] Arthur G. Bedeian, "Consumer Perception of Price as an Indicator of Product Quality," *MSU Business Topics*, Summer 1971, pp. 59–65; David M. Gardner, "An Experimental Investigation of the Price/Quality Relationship," *Journal of Retailing*, Fall 1970, pp. 25–41; Kent B. Monroe, "Buyers' Subjective Perceptions of Price," *Journal of Marketing Research*, February 1973, pp. 70–80; and N. D. French, J. J. Williams, and W. A. Chance, "A Shopping Experiment on Price-Quality Relationships," *Journal of Retailing*, Fall 1972, pp. 3–16 f.

[7] Dik W. Twedt, "Does the '9 Fixation' in Retailing Really Promote Sales?" *Journal of Marketing*, October 1965, pp. 54–55; and H. J. Rudolph, "Pricing and Today's Market," *Printers' Ink*, May 29, 1954, pp. 22–24.

[8] E. R. Hawkins, "Price Policies and Theory," *Journal of Marketing*, January 1954, p. 236; see also, B. P. Shapiro, "The Psychology of Pricing," *Harvard Business Review*, July–August 1968, pp. 14–25.

25

Demand-oriented approaches to price determination

■ The last chapter showed the difficulty of trying to set prices without recognizing potential customer demand. In this chapter, we will bring demand explicitly into the analysis, using the economist's tools of marginal analysis. We will also discuss break-even analysis — a tool which is both understandable to cost-oriented businessmen and can be used to bring demand into the analysis. This chapter is more analytical than the first two pricing chapters, and the tools are not as commonly used. Yet, there are progressive companies making use of these approaches because they provide explicit ways of bringing management's judgment into the pricing decision.

Break-even analysis can evaluate possible prices

■ Some businessmen use break-even analysis in an attempt to bring prospective revenue (and perhaps demand) into pricing. They already know their costs fairly well, and are now concerned with what price to set. Perhaps they are trying to decide between several prices which are somewhere close to competition.

Break-even analysis focuses on the break-even point — the output where the firm's costs will just equal the incoming revenue — rather than profit or likely sales volume. The focus is on whether the firm would even be able to break even with a particular price. This is not a trivial matter, because a businessman must cover all of his costs in the long run or there is not much point in offering a product.

Break-even analysis usually uses break-even charts, with straight-line total cost and total revenue curves. A break-even chart has a total revenue curve which shows the total revenue which would be received at various levels of operation when selling *at an assumed price.* This total revenue curve can then be related to the total cost curve (usually shown as a straight line) to find where the company would break even. This intersection is called the break-even point *(BEP).* At this point, total revenue and total cost are equal; beyond it, at a greater output level, the company will begin to make a profit on each unit; and below it, the company incurs a loss. Figure 25–1, a break-even chart, shows these profit-and-loss areas.

Each price has its own break-even chart

■ Each assumed price will have its own break-even chart and break-even point, so it is possible to consider several alternative prices and break-even points at the same time. Here is where management's judgment must come in. If the break-even point for a particular assumed price is obviously high, then that price possibility may be dismissed. Note each price possibility must be evaluated for reasonableness. These are assumed prices which *might* be acceptable to some customers. Likely demand must be introduced by the managers when considering whether they are likely to reach or exceed each break-even point.

Break-even analysis can be very useful, but it must be used properly. The big question is: will break-even analysis help find the right price? Before answering this question, let us look at the details of break-even analysis.

How to compute a break-even point

■ In most break-even analysis, we make a few simplifying assumptions in order to facilitate the analysis. First, we assume that any quantity can be sold at the same price. For a graphical solution, this permits us to draw a straight-line total revenue curve. Similarly, we assume that average variable cost is constant per unit. This also permits the use of a straight-line total variable cost curve. Graphing the total revenue and total cost *(TFC* plus *TVC)* lines will yield the *BEP.* Or, the same result can be obtained by solving equations.

Finding the break-even point in units

The *BEP* may be computed in terms of units or dollar value of units. In units, the *BEP* can be found by using the following formula:

$$BEP \text{ (in units)} = \frac{TFC}{FC \text{ contribution per unit}}$$

The *fixed-cost contribution per unit* is a new term. It is the assumed selling price per unit minus the variable cost per unit. This number is used here because if we are to break even, then total fixed costs must be covered. Therefore, this break-even calculation determines the contribution which each unit will make to covering the total fixed costs (after paying for the variable costs which must

Figure 25–1
Break-even chart for a particular situation

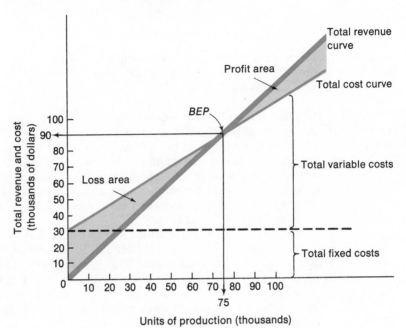

Units of production (thousands)

be covered or there is no point in producing the item), and then divide that per unit contribution into the total that has to be covered. The result is the *BEP* (in units).

To illustrate the formula, let us use the following cost data and assume a selling price per unit of $1.20. Using the following values:

Total fixed cost   = $30,000
Variable cost per unit   = $0.80
FC contribution ($1.20 − $.80) = $0.40

and substituting in the formula:

$$BEP = \frac{30,000}{.40} = 75,000 \text{ units}$$

From this it is evident that if this firm sells 75,000 units, it will cover exactly all its fixed and variable costs. If even one more unit is sold, then it will begin to show a profit—in this case, 40 cents. Note that once the fixed costs are covered, the portion of revenue formerly going to cover fixed costs now goes completely to profits.

Finding the break-even point in dollars

The *BEP* can also be figured in terms of dollar value:

$$BEP \text{ (in dollars)} = \frac{TFC}{1 - \dfrac{VC/\text{Unit}}{\text{Selling price/Unit}}}$$

Using the figures above, we obtain:

$$\frac{\$30,000}{1 - \dfrac{\$\ .80}{\$1.20}} = \$90,000$$

To check our result, we can multiply the selling price ($1.20) times the BEP in units (75,000): $1.20 times 75,000 equals $90,000, the BEP in dollars.*

Break-even analysis is helpful — but not a pricing solution

■ The results of the foregoing analyses can be graphed as shown in Figure 25–1. The definiteness of this graph and the ease with which it is understood by cost-oriented businessmen has made it popular. But it is too often misunderstood. The fact that the prices are assumed is often neglected. And the "Alice in Wonderland" quality of the ever-widening profit area is ignored – it is just too enticing to production-oriented men who think of economies of scale and like to increase output.

Although the graph, with its straight-line total revenue curve, makes it appear that any quantity might be sold at the assumed price, this usually is unrealistic. This is equivalent to assuming the existence of a perfectly horizontal demand curve at that price; but if demand is perfectly elastic, there is no need for pricing analysis because the pricing executive would have no pricing decision to make.

Break-even analysis can be useful for comparing pricing alternatives – providing the manager with alternative break-even points which he must consider in relation to market reality. Break-even analysis is especially useful for quickly eliminating obviously ridiculous pricing alternatives. But for really zeroing in on the most profitable price, he would be better off trying to estimate the demand curve more explicitly and then using marginal analysis, which is discussed next.

Traditional demand and supply analysis shows how to maximize profits

■ In Chapter 3, we saw that most demand curves are downsloping and most supply curves are upsloping. The intersection of these demand and supply curves would seem to determine price and, therefore, take care of demand-oriented pricing for the firm. Unfortunately, reality is not quite that simple.

Although such analysis may be appropriate for whole indus-

---

* Students familiar with algebra may find the following approach more meaningful. Where x equals BEP in quantity, and we solve for the intersection of the TR and TC lines.

$$\text{(Price)}(x) = TFC + VC(x)$$
$$1.20x = 30,000 + .80x$$
$$.40x = 30,000$$
$$x = 75,000 \text{ units}$$

and $1.20 (75,000) = $90,000 i.e. BEP in dollars.

tries, some refinements are necessary in applying it to the individual firm seeking to maximize profits.

■ In the following pages, we will discuss these refinements, concentrating on price determination in the large majority of situations in which demand curves are downsloping – that is, monopolistic competition situations. In these situations, the firm has carved out a little market for itself and does have a pricing decision to make. By contrast, in the pure or nearly pure competition situation, the marketing manager has little difficulty with the pricing decision. He simply uses the market price. The special case of oligopoly will be treated later in the chapter.

Our discussion will focus on how to maximize profits, not just seek some profits. This has been the traditional approach of economic analysis, and it is a reasonable one. If you know how to make the biggest profit, you can always adjust to pursue other objectives while knowing how much profit you are giving up!

■ In monopolistic competition, the marketing manager faces a downsloping demand curve. He must pick a price on that curve, and generally must offer that price to all potential buyers (to avoid price discrimination under the Robinson-Patman Act.) Therefore, he should consider the effect on total revenue of the alternative prices he is considering.

If he chooses a lower price, the demand curve shows that he will sell additional units, but *all* his customers would be offered this lower price, and he should calculate the impact on total revenue. Or, if he chooses a higher price, he must expect to sell less. What will be the impact on revenue, both total and marginal? The important point to see here is that the marketing manager usually does *not* have the option of selling individual items at different prices, but instead must make one decision about price and quantity, and then live with it for the length of the plan, or until a new plan is set.

Marginal analysis can help him make the best pricing decision. *Marginal analysis focuses on the last unit which would be sold and equates marginal revenue and marginal cost to find the most profitable price and quantity.* This is a very useful, but technical topic and is treated more fully in the next several pages. Be sure to study the tables and figures.

■ *Marginal revenue is the change in total revenue which results from the sale of one additional unit of product.* Since the firm's demand curve is downsloping, this extra unit can be sold only by reducing the price of all items. The total revenue that would be obtained if price were cut might still be positive, but the marginal revenue – that is, the extra revenue gained – might be negative.

Table 25–1 indicates the relationship between price, quantity, total revenue, and marginal revenue in a hypothetical situation with roughly a straight-line downsloping demand curve.

If four units could be sold for a total revenue of $420 and five

Table 25–1
Marginal revenue and price

Quantity q (1)	Price p (2)	Total revenue (1)× (2) = TR (3)	Marginal revenue MR (4)
0	$150	$ 0	
1	140	140	$140
2	130	260	120
3	117	351	91
4	105	420	69
5	92	460	40
6	79	474	14
7	66	462	−12
8	53	424	−38
9	42	378	−46
10	31	310	−68

units for $460, then marginal revenue for the fifth unit is $40. Considering only revenue, it would be desirable to sell this extra unit. But would this continue on if more units were sold at lower prices? No! Table 25–1 shows that negative marginal revenues occur at lower price levels. Obviously, this is relevant to pricing.

Marginal revenue curve and demand curve are different

The marginal revenue curve is always below a downsloping demand curve, as can be seen in Figure 25–3 where the data in Table 25–1 is plotted. The fact that the demand curve and the marginal revenue curve are different in monopolistic competition is quite significant. We will use both of them when finding the best price and quantity.*

Marginal cost is needed too

■ As we have already seen, various kinds of costs behave differently and there is an important kind of cost which is similar to marginal revenue: marginal cost. This cost is vital to marginal analysis.

---

* The data for drawing a marginal revenue curve always can be derived by calculating changes in the total revenue curve, but a simple graphical shortcut is available if straight-line demand curves are being used. Although the demand curve within the relevant range normally may not extend all the way to the horizontal and vertical axes, it can be extended to these axes. The marginal revenue curve is then obtained by drawing a line running from the intersection of the demand curve with the vertical (price) axis down to the point on the quantity axis bisecting the segment from 0 to the point where the demand curve extension intersects that axis. This marginal revenue curve also can be extended below the quantity axis to obtain the negative marginal revenue values. The only relevant part of the marginal revenue curve is that part directly below the relevant range of the demand curve.

When working with curved demand curves, tangents to the curve can be drawn at several places to obtain the general shape of the MR curve. Readers familiar with calculus probably will recognize that the marginal revenue curve is simply the derivative of the total revenue curve, and they can use this approach in finding the marginal revenue curve.

Table 25–2
Cost structure for individual firm

Quantity Q (1)	Total fixed cost TFC (2)	Average fixed cost AFC (3)	Total variable cost TVC (4)	Average variable cost AVC (5)	Total cost (TFC + TVC = TC) TC (6)	Average cost (AC = TC ÷ Q) AC (7)	Marginal cost (per unit) MC (8)
0	$200	$ 0	$ 0	$ 0	$200	Infinity	
1	200	200	96	96	296	$296	$96
2	200	100	116	58	316		20
3	200				331	110.33	
4	200	50			344		
5	200	40	155	31		71	11
6	200		168			61.33	13
7			183				15
8			223				
9			307		507	56.33	
10		20	510	51	710	71	203

Marginal cost is the change in total cost that results from producing an extra unit. According to the marginal cost concept, if it costs $275 to produce nine units of a product and $280 to produce ten units, then marginal cost is $5 for the tenth unit. In other words, marginal cost contrasted to average cost per unit is the additional cost of producing one more *specific unit,* while average cost is the average for *all units.*

An illustrative cost structure

Table 25–2 indicates how these costs could vary for a typical firm. You should fill in the missing numbers on this table. Notice that variable cost no longer is assumed constant per unit in Table 25–2. Here, we use the more realistic assumption that variable costs will decline for a while and then rise.

In Table 25–2 several important points should be noted. *First,* total fixed costs do not change over the entire range of output, but total variable costs increase continually as more and more units are produced. It is obvious, then, that total costs—the sum of total fixed costs and total variable costs—will increase as total quantity increases.

Second, average costs will decrease over most of the range of production, since average costs are the sum of average fixed costs and average variable costs, and total fixed costs are divided by more and more units as output mounts. For example, given a total fixed cost of $200, at a production level of four units, the average fixed cost is $50; at a production level of five units, the average fixed cost is $40.

Third, average costs in this table start rising for the last two units because average variable costs have been increasing faster than

Figure 25–2
Per unit cost curves (for data in Table 25–2)

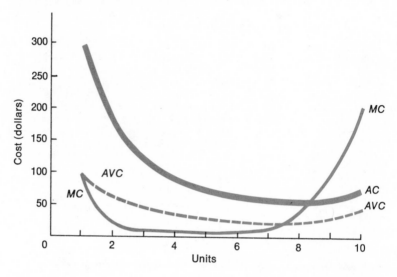

average fixed costs have been decreasing. The firm may have been forced to use less efficient facilities and workers, go into overtime work or pay higher prices for the materials it needed. This turn-up of the average cost curve happens frequently.

The marginal cost of just one more is important

■ The *marginal cost* column in Table 25–2 is the most important column for our purposes. It shows specifically what each extra unit costs, and suggests the minimum extra revenue we should get for each additional unit. Like average cost, marginal cost drops, but it begins to rise again at a lower level of output than average cost.

Total fixed costs do *not* affect marginal cost computations. Although average cost per unit is going down over most of the quantity range, marginal cost *starts up earlier* at five units. Figure 25–2 shows the behavior of the *average cost, average variable cost,* and *marginal cost* curves. Note that the marginal cost curve intersects the average variable cost and average cost curves from below *at their low points,* and then rises rapidly thereafter. This is how this curve typically behaves.

The marginal cost curve shows the *extra* cost of producing and selling each extra unit. This cost curve can be extremely important to a marketing manager who is trying to find a way to keep operating in depressed times and still not lose money out-of-pocket. A wholesaler or retailer, for example, would certainly not want to offer goods or services below their marginal cost. Similarly, a producer would not want to produce additional goods if he could not cover the direct out-of-pocket cost. (Note: If the goods have already been produced or purchased, however, then he might want to think of these as fixed costs and be willing to sell them even below their original cost if the alternative is not to sell them at all!)

Table 25-3
Revenue, cost, and profit for individual firm

Quan-tity q (1)	Price p (2)	Total revenue TR (3)	Total cost TC (4)	Profit (TR−TC) (5)	Marginal revenue MR (6)	Marginal cost MC (7)	Marginal profit (MR−MC) (8)
0	$150	$ 0	$200	$−200			
1	140	140	296	−156	$140	$ 96	$+ 44
2	130	260	316	− 56	120	20	+100
3	117	351	331	+ 20	91	15	+ 76
4	105	420	344	+ 76	69	13	+ 56
5	92	460	355	+105	40	11	+ 29
6	79	474	368	+106	14	13	+ 1
7	66	462	383	+ 79	− 12	15	− 27
8	53	424	423	+ 1	− 38	40	− 78
9	42	378	507	−129	− 46	84	−130
10	31	310	710	−400	− 68	203	−271

How to find the most profitable price and the quantity to produce

■ Given that a manager must choose only *one* price (for a time period), his problem is which one to choose. His price, of course, will determine the quantity he sells. If he is interested in maximizing profit, we now see that he should be willing to supply more units if he can obtain at least a marginal revenue equal to the marginal cost of extra units. From this we can derive the following *rule for maximizing profit: The firm should produce that output where marginal cost is just less than or equal to marginal revenue.*[*]

The selling price for this optimum quantity is determined by referring to the demand curve, which shows what price customers are willing to pay for the optimum quantity. The optimum price is *not* found on the marginal revenue curve.

This method of finding the most profitable price and quantity is a useful tool for the marketing manager. To assure full understanding of the approach, we will illustrate its application. To make doubly sure that this approach is fully explained, we will calculate the most profitable price and quantity using total revenue and total cost curves first, and then show that the same answer is obtained with marginal curves. This will give us a check of the method as well as perspective on how the marginal revenue – marginal cost method works.

Profit maximization with total revenue and total cost curves

Table 25-3 provides illustrative data on total revenue, total cost, and total profit for this firm. Figure 25-4 simply graphs the total revenue, total cost, and total profit relationships. It is clear from the

---

[*] This rule applies in the typical situations where the curves are shaped similarly to those discussed here. Technically, however, we should add the following to the rule for maximizing profit: *The marginal cost must be increasing at a greater rate or decreasing at a lesser rate than marginal revenue.*

498

Figure 25–3
A plotting of the demand and marginal revenue data in Table 25–1

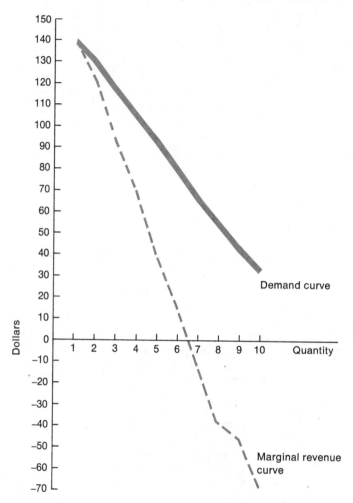

graph of the total profit curve that the most profitable quantity is six – this is the quantity where we find the greatest vertical distance between the TR curve and the TC curve. Table 25–3 shows that the most profitable price is $79 and a quantity of six will be sold.

It is clear that beyond a quantity of six, the total profit curve declines; the marketing manager would not be interested in selling more than this number.

Profit maximization using marginal curves

Now we can apply the rule we developed earlier for maximizing profit using marginal curves. The same best quantity and price are

Figure 25-4
Graphic determination of output giving greatest total profit for a firm

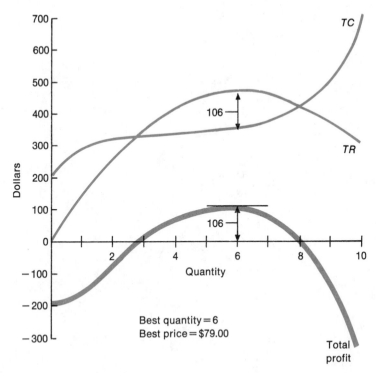

Best quantity = 6
Best price = $79.00

obtained, as is shown in Figure 25-4 based on the data for marginal revenue and marginal cost in Table 25-3.

In Figure 25-5, the intersection of the marginal cost and marginal revenue curves occurs at a quantity of six. This is the most profitable quantity. But the best price must be obtained by going up to the demand curve. It is *not* at the $MR-MC$ intersection. Again, the best price is $79.

The graphic interpretation is supported by the data in Table 25-3. At a quantity of six, marginal revenue equals $14 and marginal cost is $13. There is a marginal profit of $1, and this suggests that it might be profitable to offer seven rather than six units. This is not the case, however. The marginal cost of the seventh unit is $15 while its marginal revenue is actually negative. Offering to sell seven units (instead of only six) will reduce total profit by $27.

It is important to realize that marginal revenue can actually become negative. This simply means that the *total* revenue curve is declining, as shown in Figure 25-4.

It also is important to realize that *total* profit is *not* near zero when MR equals MC. *Marginal profit* (the extra profit on the last unit) is near zero, but that is exactly why the quantity obtained at the $MR-MC$ intersection is the most profitable. Marginal analysis

Figure 25–5
Alternate determination of most profitable output and price for a firm

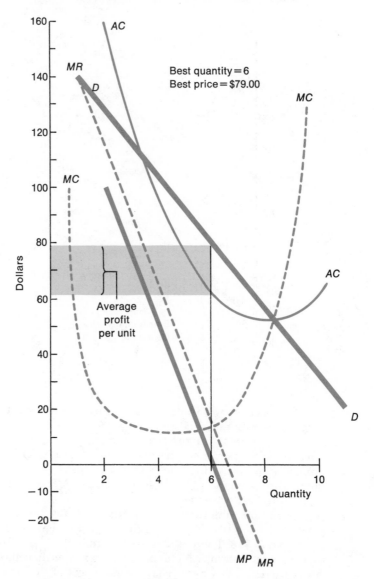

Best quantity = 6
Best price = $79.00

indicates that when the firm is determining the best price to charge, it should be willing to increase the quantity it will sell as long as the last unit it considers offering will yield *extra* profits.

Again, the marketing manager finally will choose only *one* price. Marginal analysis is useful in helping him to determine the best price to charge for all that he will sell. It might help to think of the demand curve as an "iffy" curve—*if* a price is selected, *then* a related quantity will be sold. Before the price is set, all these *if-then* combinations can be evaluated for profitability. But once a particular price is set, the results follow.

How to lose less, if you must

■ The marginal approach to determining the most profitable output also will determine that output which will be least unprofitable when market conditions are so poor that the firm must operate at a loss.

If sales are slow, the marketing manager may even have to consider suspending operation. When making this decision, he should ignore fixed costs, since these will continue regardless. Some fixed costs may even involve items that are so "sunk" in the business that they cannot be sold for anything near the cost shown on the company's records. The special-purpose buildings and machines of an unsuccessful company might be next to worthless to anyone else.

Marginal costs are another matter. If the firm cannot recover the marginal cost of the last unit (or more generally the variable cost of the units being considered), it should suspend operations temporarily or go out of business. The only exceptions are mitigating social or humanitarian considerations, or the fact that the marginal costs of closing temporarily are high and stronger demand is expected *soon*. But if marginal costs can be covered in the short run, even though fixed costs are not, the firm should remain in operation.

Marginal analysis helps get the most in pure competition

■ The marketing manager caught in a pure-competition situation also can apply the methods just discussed. He does not have a price decision, but he does have an output decision. The demand curve facing him is flat, and this means that the marginal revenue curve is also flat at the same level. He could equate that marginal revenue curve, therefore, with his own unique marginal cost curve to determine his most profitable (or least unprofitable) output level. A little experimentation will show that the marginal cost approach might lead to a different output decision than the average-cost approach. In general, a marginal approach is the most dependable if you are seeking to maximize profits or, if it is necessary, to minimize losses.

A profit range is reassuring

■ We have been seeking the most profitable price and quantity, but in a dynamic world this is an elusive goal. Fortunately, this optimum is surrounded by a profitable range.

Note that in Figure 25–4 there are *two* break-even points rather than a single point, which was the case when we were discussing break-even analysis. The second break-even point falls farther out because total costs turn up and total revenue is turning down.

These two break-even points are important to note because they define the range of profitable operations. Although we are seeking to find the point of maximum profit, we know that this point is an ideal goal rather than a realistic possibility. What is essential is that the marketing manager knows there is a range of profit around the optimum—it is not just a lone point. This should provide greater assurance that pursuing the optimum is a wise policy.

Marginal analysis applies in oligopoly, too

■ Marginal analysis can be used whenever a firm can estimate its demand and cost curves. The special kinked nature of the oligopoly demand curve is no obstacle.

When demand goes kinky marginal revenue drops fast

■ As we saw in Chapter 3, individual competitors in an oligopoly situation face a *kinked demand curve*. We said then that the tendency in such situations is to avoid the use of Price to avoid disastrous price cutting. Marginal analysis now helps us understand this situation more fully.

The dashed marginal revenue line in Figure 25–6 shows that marginal revenue drops precipitously at the kinked point. This is a technical but important matter, and helps explain why prices are relatively sticky at the kinked point. Even if costs change and, therefore, each firm's supply curve were to move up or down, it still might cross the *MR* curve someplace along its vertical drop. In this case, even though costs are changing and there might seem to be justification for changing the price, each firm may hold its price at the kinked price level.

A price leader usually sets the price

■ Most of the firms in an oligopoly situation are aware of the economics of the situation, at least intuitively. A price leader usually sets a price, perhaps to maximize profits or to get a certain target return on investment. Then, without any collusion, other members of the industry follow, and the price may be maintained for a long period or at least as long as all members of the industry continue making a reasonable profit.

The price leader must take his responsibility seriously. If the followers are not able to make a reasonable profit at the market price, then they may try secret price cuts to expand sales without incurring retaliation. If very much of this activity takes place, the price leader will lose a considerable volume of business, and the situation may degenerate into a violent price war. Or there may be a temptation to collude, which is illegal but done. Lacking an effective leader, the market may be unstable, and severe or retaliatory price cutting can be a continual threat.

The price leader might try to lead others to higher levels if basic industry conditions seem to warrant, perhaps if labor costs have increased. Or the leader might try to get the market price back up to former levels after an extended period of price cutting. But this must be done carefully. The competitors may not play the game, and the leader may lose substantially before being forced to retreat. The National Gypsum Co., for example, recently tried to return industry prices to list price levels and was "chopped up" during its two-month effort. As a result, the firm vowed not to try to lead the industry in price actions again. Its executives said that in the future, they were "going to be absolutely convinced in the marketplace by the actions of our competitors before doing anything."

Figure 25–6
Marginal revenue drops fast in oligopoly

Furthermore, "If they demonstrate statesmanship, our participation will go with them. But if we see them being cute, we will react differently."[1]

A price leader should have a good understanding of its own and its competitors' cost structures as well as an estimate of the industry demand curve. Setting too high a price may look attractive in the short run, but it may attract additional competitors to the market and lead to trouble later when capacity has expanded. Setting too low a price, on the other hand, can lead to action from antitrust officials who become concerned about the plight of small competitors. An optimal price may be one which is just high enough to support the marginal firm – the least efficient company whose production would be needed to meet peak long-run demands.[2]

If the price leader chooses a price that others can accept profitably, they may follow without any necessity for agreement. As we noted earlier, this is called "conscious parallel action." It is a situation that the FTC and the Justice Department deplore, but it still has not been declared illegal. Indeed, it is hard to see how it could be, because each firm must administer its prices and it certainly is legal to meet competition. In fact, essentially the same behavior is observed in pure competition. As long as conspiracy is avoided, meeting competition in any market situation probably will continue to be acceptable.

How to estimate demand curves

■ Businessmen obviously have some knowledge of the demand in their target markets and often seem to behave accordingly. Sometimes they may make only rough judgments, but even these may be better than nothing. As we saw earlier, even rough estimates of the elasticity of demand may be helpful in estimating the nature of the market situation and sometimes even the direction that price changes should take.

Ideally, we would like to have a quantitative estimate of the demand curve because this would enable us to use marginal analysis. Let's consider some of the ways we can derive demand curves.[3]

Asking-curve approach estimates whole demand curves

■ It is possible to "guesstimate" where a whole demand curve is with the asking-curve approach. The marketing manager (or other executives knowledgeable about the probable reaction of the market to price changes) can answer questions using his educated judgment. And these answers can lead to rough-and-ready, yet quantitative, demand curve estimates.

Here we want a whole demand curve, not just the small portion above and below the current price level. When we are seeking the most profitable price, substantial price shifts may be necessary, and focusing only on current prices is not suitable. Concern with small changes may be very useful in fairly static situations, but it also can be misleading because it often gives the impression that demand is inelastic around current prices – probably because of the inertia of customers' attitudes and habits. The asking-curve approach, which attempts to estimate a whole demand curve, gets around this difficulty.

Ask for just a simple Yes or No

In the asking-curve approach, managers are asked questions about whether they expect they would be able to sell more than certain quantities at specific prices. They are *not* asked to make specific numerical estimates. Only Yes or No responses are required. For most people, it is easier to say Yes or No to a suggested price than to conceive their own numbers.

The approach is to ask experienced executives: "Could you sell more than (a specific quantity) at (a specific price)?" The specific quantities and prices that are asked about are along a cost-per-unit asking curve that serves as a floor below which the firm probably would not want to sell anyway. By asking the executives several questions, eventually some Yes and No points are found in succession along the cost curve, and this suggests that the demand curve crosses this cost curve somewhere nearby. By connecting two such crossing points, it is possible to determine a workable approximation to the relevant demand curve. (See Figure 25–7, where a straight line is used to connect the crossing points.) More questions can be asked along this line to be sure it fits with management judgment.

Figure 25-7
Estimating location of a demand curve with "Yes" and "No" questions
along an asking curve

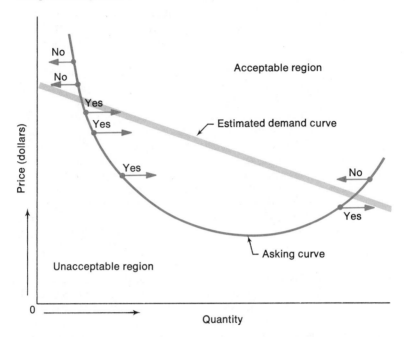

This subjective approach to quantifying management's feelings about demand appears to get the pricing executives within striking distance of the best price and quantity. It gives them a quantitative summarization of their attitudes – a demand curve – and if the price obtained through marginal analysis differs from their intuitive feel of the price they should charge, it may force them to recheck their thinking and subsequently to change their pricing decision.

One application stopped a planned price cut

In one case, for example, after the marketing manager's own feelings were converted to a demand curve, marginal analysis indicated that he should raise his retail price to 42 cents, not lower it as planned. The current level was 39 cents and he was seriously considering a price cut in reaction to price dealing and free goods being given away by his competitors.

Given that his own cost data and his own best estimates regarding demand were in the analysis, the manager finally decided to hold his general price level constant, while meeting the price cutting in extremely competitive areas. And further marginal analysis showed that selective price cuts in some areas would actually help cover overhead rather than lose money – as his accountants had figured with average cost analysis! This led to the development of different strategies for different target markets.[4]

Surveys and market experiments can aid demand estimation

■ Various research methods can be used for estimating demand. Surveys, for example, can be used, but with care. Questions such as: "What would you pay if . . . ?" must be interpreted cautiously. But if survey results suggest little interest in price—perhaps because of strong brand loyalty or simple indifference—it may be reasonable to conclude that demand is inelastic. Then, perhaps, prices can be raised substantially.

Industrial goods buyers may be more aware of prices and the impact costs have on their firms' operations. Their answers about possible reactions to price changes may be quite meaningful.

Market tests also may be useful, either in trial areas or as general experiments. Two classic cases of market tests are worth noting.

The long-play phonograph record industry long resisted price reductions. At last, one price cut was tried, and demand was found to be quite elastic. This brought about greatly increased sales and profits for all members of the industry.

Henry Ford's Model T was another famous experiment. He cut prices dramatically because he anticipated a much larger consumer demand, and in so doing, established the basis for great expansion of the automobile industry.

Historical analysis and its dangers

■ Historical sales data can be and has been subjected to statistical techniques to estimate demand. This approach is less valuable to us, however, because historical records are available only for essentially homogeneous commodities, such as farm, mine, and forest products, and these usually are sold in almost purely competitive or oligopolistic markets anyway. A potential price leader in oligopoly might find this approach useful, however.

The real need for demand estimates is in markets where conditions are shifting and products are continually changing. As seen in our discussion of product life cycles, changing conditions are inevitable. Analysis of historical data not only may be difficult but dangerous in these situations. Entirely different market situations may exist at different points in time, while statistical analysis of historical data must work with homogeneous data—and mechanical misuse of these methods may lead to invalid estimates.[5]

Conclusion

■ While most price determination is cost-oriented, demand can and does enter in, both implicitly and explicitly. In this chapter we have discussed some analytical tools which may facilitate price determination and, in particular, finding the most profitable price and quantity to produce.

Break-even analysis can be a useful tool for evaluating alternative prices. Management judgment must be used to evaluate the likelihood of reaching alternative break-even points. It does provide a rough and ready tool for eliminating obviously unworkable prices.

The economist's traditional demand and supply analysis can be a useful tool for maximizing profits. The most profitable quantity is found graphically at the intersection of the marginal revenue and marginal cost curves. To determine the *most profitable price,* the pricing executive takes his most profitable quantity to the firm's demand curve to determine what price target customers will be willing to pay for this quantity.

The major difficulty with marginal analysis is determining a demand curve. Several ways of estimating demand were presented and it was emphasized that some estimate of demand is better than ignoring it. The asking-curve approach asks Yes or No questions to estimate a complete demand curve. These questions should be asked of someone who is intimately familiar with the market and can predict probable reactions to the planned marketing mix. Market tests or other marketing research techniques also can be used to estimate demand.

Deriving demand curves is not easy nor will estimated curves be perfectly accurate. Nevertheless, experienced executives—aided perhaps by marketing research—can make estimates of the nature of demand for their products. Such estimates, even if they are inexact, are useful, since prices are usually changed in discrete steps anyway, and an estimated demand curve would probably get one in the right "ball park." Sometimes, when all that is needed is a decision about raising or lowering a price, demand estimates can be very revealing.

It is important to see that the firm's demand curve does not cease to exist simply because it is ignored. Some information is better than none at all.

questions and problems

1 The Brown Company's fixed costs for the year are estimated at $100,000. The variable costs are usually about 70 percent of sales. Sales for the coming year are expected to reach $380,000. What is the break-even point? Expected profit? If sales were forecast at only $200,000, should the Brown Company shut down operations? Why?

2 Distinguish among marginal revenue, average revenue, and price.

3 Draw a graph showing a demand and supply situation where marginal analysis would correctly indicate that the firm should continue producing even though the profit and loss statement shows a loss.

4 What are the basic assumptions which must be met in order to make the asking curve approach to demand curve estimation sensible?

5 Discuss the idea of drawing separate demand curves for different market segments. It seems logical because each target market should have its own marketing mix. But won't this lead to a considerable number of demand curves and possibly prices? And what will this mean with respect to functional discounts and varying prices in the marketplace? Would this be legal? Would it be practical?

6 Evergreen Pea Co. has been enjoying a profitable year. Their product sells to wholesalers for 20 cents a can. After careful study, it has been decided that a 60 percent gross margin should be maintained. Their manufacturing costs are divided in this manner: material, 50 percent of cost; labor, 40 percent of cost; and 10 percent of cost goes for overhead. Both material and labor costs experienced a 10 percent increase. Determine the

new price per can based on their present pricing methods. Is it wise to hold fast to a 60 percent margin, if *a price increase* would mean lost customers? Answer using graphs and *MC-MR* analysis. Show a situation where it would be most profitable to (1) raise price, (2) leave price alone, (3) reduce price.

notes

[1] "National Gypsum Vows Not to Lead Industry Again in Price Actions," *Wall Street Journal*, July 17, 1970, p. 11; and "Gypsum Makers Move to Stop Sharp Discounts," *Wall Street Journal*, December 3, 1969, p. 6. See also (re. cigarette industry) Marvin A. Jolson and Noel B. Zabriskie, "Nonprice Parallelism in Oligopolistic Industries," *MSU Business Topics*, Autumn 1971, pp. 33–41.

[2] See J. Howard Westing and Jon G. Udel, "Pricing and the Antitrust Laws," *Michigan Business Review*, November 1962, pp. 6–11.

[3] For additional discussion, see Edward R. Hawkins, "Methods of Estimating Demand," *Journal of Marketing*, April 1957, pp. 428–38; and Kent B. Monroe, "Measuring Price Thresholds by Psychophysics and Latitudes of Acceptance," *Journal of Marketing Research*, November 1971, pp. 460–64 and "Buyers' Subjective Perceptions of Price," *Journal of Marketing Research*, February 1973, pp. 70–80.

[4] For further discussion on this method, see "Determining a Subjective Demand Curve," in E. J. McCarthy, *Basic Marketing: A Managerial Approach*, rev. ed. (Homewood, Ill.: Richard D. Irwin, Inc., 1964), pp. 799–804.

[5] For further discussion on experiments, see Ray G. Stout, "Developing Data to Estimate Price-Quantity Relationships," *Journal of Marketing*, April 1969, pp. 34–36; E. A. Pessemier, "An Experimental Method for Estimating Demand," *Journal of Business*, October 1960, pp. 373–83; and William D. Barclay, "Factorial Design in a Pricing Experiment," *Journal of Marketing Research*, November 1969, pp. 427–29.

[6] For more details on estimating with this approach—basically a "least squares" approach—see Richard S. Watt, *A Method of Analyzing Demand for General Commodities, A Case Study of Salt* (U.S. Department of the Interior, Bureau of Mines, Information Circular 8057, 1962), p. 35.

Marketing management in action

Effective marketing strategies require creative planning—

Strategic plans and marketing
programs . . . research as
a management tool . . . controls
through sales and cost analysis

developing whole marketing mixes—and careful control of these plans

26

Strategic planning

■ In recent years, an increasing number of producers, wholesalers, and retailers have accepted the marketing concept and realize the importance of viewing a business as a total system of action. These companies have traveled a long, evolutionary road from the days when the overwhelming consideration of manufacturers and middlemen was producing or stocking products.

In this chapter we will round out our discussion of strategy planning and emphasize *why* an individual firm should see each of its internal activities as part of a whole – why it must plan whole marketing mixes to satisfy target markets, rather than focusing on only one or another of the four Ps.

Strategic planning is more than assembling four Ps

■ Strategic planning involves much more than assembling the four parts of a marketing mix. The four Ps must be blended together in a creative way so that the "best" mix is developed for the firm's target market. This may mean that the proposed plans of some specialists – the product manager, sales manager, physical distribution manager, and so on – may have to be adjusted to make the whole mix better.

Throughout the text we have given the job of integrating the four Ps to the marketing manager, but now it is critical that we formally recognize the need for this integrating role. It is all too easy for specialists to focus on their own area and expect the rest of the company to work for or around them. This is especially true in larger firms where specialists are needed just because the size of the whole marketing job is too much for one person.

It it vital here, therefore, for us to return to a consideration of planning whole marketing mixes and whole strategies. The primary emphasis in this chapter will be on marketing mixes. And then, in Chapter 27, we will discuss the planning of and selection among alternative strategies.

Blending the four Ps to satisfy target markets

■ The marketing concept emphasizes that all of a firm's activities should be focused on its target markets. It logically follows, therefore, that if one fully understands the needs and preferences of his target markets, then combining the four Ps should be "easy." There are three gaps in this line of reasoning, however: (1) we do not always know as much as we would like to about the needs and preferences of our target markets; (2) competitors are also attempting to satisfy these or similar needs and their efforts may force modification of a firm's marketing mix; and (3) the other uncontrollable variables may be changing and require other modifications in marketing mixes.

Even given these potential difficulties, if the needs of one's target market are "relatively" well understood, then developing a unique and profitable marketing mix may be "relatively" easy. Kodak, for example, has had continued success in the consumer film market even though it has had some competition. It has prospered by following George Eastman's original philosophy: "You press the button, we do the rest." Kodak offers good film, makes it conveniently available, and insures the availability of high quality, rapid processing. In recent years, however, it has faced a new kind of competition from Polaroid. Polaroid offers quite a different marketing mix—its major attraction is that pictures are delivered almost immediately. They may not be as good as a production-oriented chemical engineer would like to deliver, but they are delivered fast (providing time utility). And this speed apparently makes up for the lower quality and higher price, at least for some target markets. Polaroid's marketing mix has been extremely profitable for them, and Kodak is working on a system which will be directly competitive.[1]

Superior mixes make selection easier

When a marketing mix planner fully understands the needs and preferences of some target market, he may be able to develop a mix which is obviously superior to "competitive" mixes. Such understanding may provide a "breakthrough opportunity" until his direct competitors reach the same understanding of the market and are able to adjust their offering. Using Kodak as an example again, let us focus on the X-ray film market. Until a few years ago, the usual conception of this market was that radiologists wanted faster

X-ray pictures at cheaper prices, and the primary emphasis in marketing mixes was to satisfy these needs. But a more careful look at this market indicated that the real need in hospitals and health-care units was saving the radiologist's time. Time was precious and just giving the radiologist a faster picture was not enough. Something more was needed to enable him to do his total job faster. Kodak came to see that its business was not just supplying X-ray pictures, but really helping to improve the health care supplied to patients. As a result, Kodak came up with two new timesavers for the radiologist: a handy cassette film pack and a special identification camera that records all vital patient data directly on the X-ray at the time that the X-ray is made. Previously, this tagging had to be done in the darkroom during developing, which took more time and created the possibility of error. Clearly, this was a different marketing mix aimed at satisfying a different need.[2]

It is the continual development of superior new offerings such as this which has enabled Kodak to continue its sales and profit growth. And this is why we have continually stressed the importance of looking for breakthrough opportunities rather than merely trying to patch up or improve present mixes.

Inferior mixes are easy to reject

Just as some mixes are clearly superior, similarly, some mixes are clearly inferior or inappropriate. For example, a national TV advertising campaign might make sense for a large company while being completely out of the question for a small manufacturer who is offering a new product on the East Coast.

In-between mixes are harder to evaluate

Where competitors are hitting each other more or less "head on," it is even more necessary to understand the target market's needs and preferences and how it is likely to respond to alternative marketing mixes. Here, we have more need for estimating response functions.

Estimating response functions helps find better mixes

■ Developing good marketing mixes, especially in competitive situations, will be greatly aided by trying to estimate and make explicit the relevant response functions. A response function shows how the target customers will react to changes in marketing variables. Typically, we focus on how sales will vary with marketing expenditures, but it is also possible to consider changes in sales if prices were changed, if different promotion blends are used at a fixed budget level, or other variations. Such a function usually is plotted as a curve showing how sales (or profits) would respond (that is, increase or decrease) due to varying expenditures on one of the four Ps or for the whole marketing effort. Estimating response functions is not an easy task. They are probably changing all the time. Further, there will be different response functions for each target market. Here we will focus on response functions for each of the four Ps. The response function for the whole marketing mix will be discussed in the next section.

Response functions can be graphed as shown in Figure 26–1,

Figure 26–1
Four "illustrative only" response functions

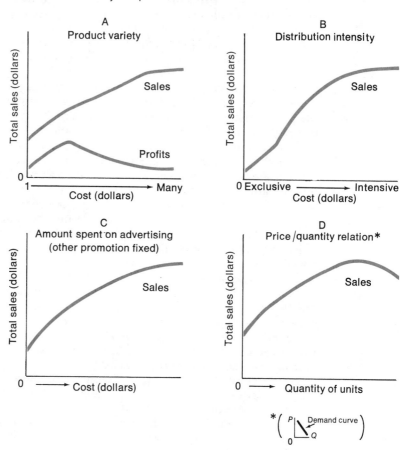

where possible response functions for each of the four Ps are illustrated. A response function with respect to product variety, for example, might indicate that adding more sizes and colors would increase sales (perhaps even continuously up to a point), but it may also increase costs and, therefore, result in a profit response function which reaches a high point and then declines. This "maximum point" may indicate the "best" level for product variety (depending upon the firm's objectives, of course!). (See Figure 26–1A.)

A Place-related response function which focuses on degree of market exposure desired (ranging from exclusive to intensive) might look like the response function shown in Figure 26-1B. The reason sales level off near the extreme of intensive distribution might be explained by the fact that when most outlets already carry the product, little increase in sales can be expected from the last few, perhaps marginal, outlets.

Figure 26–1C illustrates a possible response function for advertising. This figure suggests that even with no advertising, the personal salesmen (and other promotion efforts) would obtain some sales results, but sales would be higher with some advertising. On the extreme right of the response function, the curve starts to level off, showing diminishing results from extra advertising expenditures. (Although picking the best level is beyond the scope of this text, it is important to note that the best point may not be at the highest sales level. Marginal analysis can be used here to show that as the response function begins to flatten out, the marginal return of sales to advertising dollar begins to decline.)

The Price-oriented response function shown in Figure 26–1D illustrates the impact on sales and quantity sold of price level variations. This figure is simply another way of illustrating the down-sloping demand curve which we have discussed in various parts of the text. Note that a downsloping demand curve does mean that total sales will start declining at some quantity (recall that marginal revenue can go negative and this means that total revenue is declining). Therefore, it is not possible to expand total sales indefinitely!

It is important to note that each of the response functions shown above is simply illustrative of the general shape of the curve which *might* be found in the real world. A particular company aiming at a particular target market and facing a particular group of competitors might encounter quite different response functions. And these functions might lead a marketing manager to select very different mixes than his competitors or than similar companies operating in other product-markets. Again, the response functions illustrated here should be seen as illustrative functions only, *not* as typical ones.

The shape of such response functions is obviously critical to the evaluation and selection of the "best" blend for each particular P and for a whole marketing mix. Yet, we do not know much about the precise shapes of the functions. Worse, there is no published source of empirically verified response functions for varying situations. The manager usually must develop his own response functions. As difficult as such estimating may be, it is still necessary if a careful evaluation of alternatives is desired. Response functions do not "go away" if they are ignored, and decisions made without them may be just crude guesses.

Estimating general marketing effort response functions

■ Going beyond trying to estimate response functions for each of the four Ps, it would be desirable to estimate the general-response function for all the marketing effort within one marketing mix. Then alternative response functions for alternative mixes could be compared when seeking the "best" mix. Such a generalized marketing response function is presented in Figure 26–2, showing the relation between marketing effort (in dollars) and sales (or profits) for one marketing mix. The shape of this response function is important to consider because it probably is typical of the al-

Figure 26–2
A marketing effort response function for one marketing mix

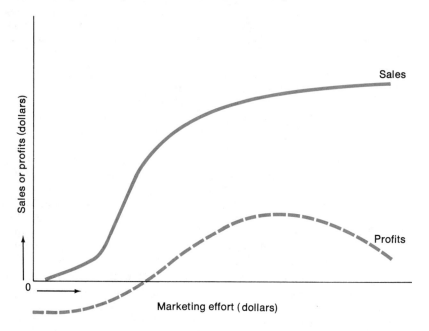

ternatives facing marketing managers. This response function shows that a higher level of marketing expenditures *may* yield a higher level of sales (or profits). But just spending more and more money for marketing will not necessarily guarantee better profits. Further, there is not a straight-line relationship between marketing expenditures and sales (or profits). Instead, some expenditure may be necessary to get any sales at all. This is sometimes called the *threshold level* of expenditure in that a certain minimal expenditure is needed just to be in a market. After this level, some increases in expenditures may result in substantial rises in sales (as the curve rises rapidly), after which additional expenditures may lead to little or no increase in sales (where the sales curve flattens out) but a decline in profits.

A response function for a whole marketing mix would be the result of the interaction of all the mix ingredients on the target customers. When one is trying to estimate the best amount to spend on one P — while holding everything else in the mix constant — then the highest sales or profit point might be the "best." But here we want to develop response functions for when everything is variable. There are technical ways for doing this, if we really know the shape of all the mix ingredient functions. But this topic is beyond our scope.[3] Besides, typically we will not have good enough estimates of all the necessary response functions to use the techniques.

For our purposes, we'll have to be satisfied with the knowledge that it is possible to "roughly" estimate response functions for al-

Figure 26-3
Response functions for three different marketing mixes for coming year

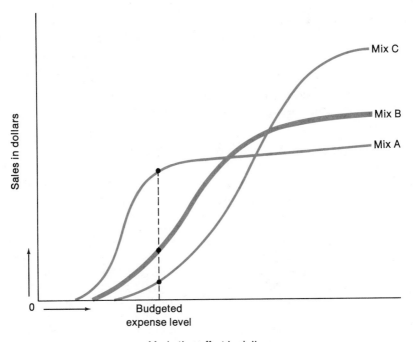

ternative mixes and that, therefore, it would be possible to select the best one, given the firm's resources and objectives. Figure 26–3 illustrates three different response functions for three different mixes. If the marketing manager's budget were fixed at the level shown in Figure 26–3 and he wanted to maximize sales in the short run, then mix A is best clearly.

Typical mixes are a good starting point ■ Typical mixes are a good starting point for developing alternative marketing mixes and estimating their response functions. What others have done in similar situations must have satisfied someone and, therefore, can serve as a guide. And, if actual sales and cost data are available or can be estimated, then at least a few points on response functions can be estimated. Beyond this, judgment or some marketing research will have to be used to develop the shapes of these functions. In this way, one can make the maximum use of past experience while not relying blindly on it.

We will discuss typical marketing mixes in the next section. They will serve as a good starting point for developing unique marketing mixes in the light of the firm's own target market and given its own objectives, resources, and the competition it faces.

During this discussion, try to develop a feel for what mix ingredients seem most "important." These will probably be the ones which have the most steeply rising response functions over reasonable expenditure levels (that's why they are typically used). For example, if personal selling is very important in a particular mix, this probably means that the personal selling response function is more attractive than some alternative mix ingredients. Even so, a marketing manager would want to evaluate how good personal selling is (over a range of expenditures) before naively spending all his promotion money on personal selling or (maybe worse) all his marketing money on this one ingredient.

Typical marketing mixes related to goods classes

■ Ideally, the ingredients of a good marketing mix will flow logically from all of the relevant dimensions of a target market. Usually, however, we just do not or cannot know all we would like to know about a potential target market. We may know enough, however, to specify whether the product would be considered a consumer good or an industrial good and, more, which particular goods class seems to be most relevant. The relevant goods classifications have a direct bearing on marketing mix planning because they are based on how potential customers view and buy the product, not characteristics of the products themselves. In the absence of knowing all about potential customers' needs and preferences, knowing how they would classify the company's product can give one a big headstart when developing a marketing mix.

A first step, then, would be to put each product into an appropriate goods class. This will simplify the selection of Place and Promotion since goods classes suggest how and why various products are typically distributed and promoted.

Now, we will tie what we know about goods classes together in a description of how and why various products typically are distributed and promoted. The major emphasis will be on how Place and Promotion are typically handled, although packaging and branding will be referred to when especially relevant.

Price will be more or less neglected in this discussion of typical behavior because, generally, Price is badly handled and also because goods classes are not as relevant for pricing (except when they suggest inelasticity of demand; e.g., as with impulse, emergency, specialty, and repair goods). After a manager has considered a mix that he might develop based on goods classes, he probably should spend a good deal more time considering what would be the best price, in the light of the firm's objectives. This matter has already been discussed in Chapters 23–25.

In the following discussion we will describe the typical methods of Place and Promotion which are used. Try to see the "why" of typical channels and typical promotion blends rather than memorizing "right" answers. Although these are typical, they are not necessarily right for all situations. Some very profitable marketing mixes have departed from the typical to satisfy some target markets better.

Typical mixes for consumer goods

Convenience goods – get them where the customers are

■ Most convenience goods, especially staples, are relatively uncomplicated items, seldom requiring installation, service, or even much personal selling.

The wide dispersion of target customers and the typically small size of each purchase encourage the use of several middlemen, especially merchant wholesalers and retailers. Setting up their own retail outlets would be impractical for the manufacturer.

Staples

Since staples are often in the market maturity stage with large potential target markets, a manufacturer's promotion blend usually emphasizes mass selling. If a producer promotes his product adequately, the merchant wholesalers and retailers may not have to do much more except handle, break bulk and store the appropriate assortment until needed.

Retailers usually will not voluntarily provide displays or special promotion aids except for their own dealer brands. Consequently, producers and wholesalers' salesmen have to promote each product to wholesalers and retailers and provide any store displays and point-of-purchase aids which are required.

Impulse goods

With impulse goods, the need for intensive distribution at retail is obvious. Basically, promotion of impulse goods is aggressively aimed at the channels, relying mainly on personal selling to the retailer. Although merchant wholesalers may stock the goods, the manufacturer usually has to go directly to retailers with his own salesmen, to assure well-placed displays. This usually requires highly persuasive personal selling to the retailer. Consumer advertising may not be essential unless several similar goods are competing in the channels. Then, a producer may have to promote his product to final consumers to impress retailers and wholesalers that his product is the best impulse item available.

Emergency goods

Since emergency goods are regarded as necessities for special circumstances, they must have wide distribution and must be available at times when regular distribution channels might not be open for business. A variety of outlets cater to emergency business – all-night service stations, open-till-midnight grocers, and vending machines. Intensive distribution to these outlets is indicated, and this could require intensive distribution to wholesalers to reach these outlets.

Little consumer promotion is needed, except that which is necessary to remind buyers of its availability when an emergency occurs. Mass selling to consumers could be used if a producer wanted to move a product from the emergency goods category – where brands are less important – to another category. Antifreeze manufacturers, for example, advertise to try to get motorists to install *their* brand early in the fall to avoid the last-minute rush. But despite their efforts, many drivers still wait until the first freeze warning and then pour anything that's available into the radiator. At this point, having widespread distribution is all-important to the producer and wholesalers.

The main promotion job, then, for these goods is in the channels – to obtain distribution. An especially persuasive personal selling job may be needed if competitive products are available. As with impulse goods, mass selling can be used to impress channel members with the firm's offering.

Shopping goods – the direct route if necessary

■ Target customers for shopping goods, like the customers for convenience goods, are widely dispersed, but shopping-goods customers are willing to make more of an effort to satisfy their needs. The producer needs fewer outlets, and direct-to-retail distribution is feasible. Producer-to-consumer selling is unlikely, however, because consumers generally want to compare shopping goods. Retailers play a key role here.

Homogeneous shopping goods

Homogeneous shopping goods do not require attractive surroundings or knowledgeable sales personnel. For well-known manufacturers' brands of appliances, for instance, price is important to some consumers on the market grid, and they are willing to patronize back-alley discount houses, if necessary, to buy them. Unbranded soft goods, such as towels and children's clothing, may be dumped into bins and customers will sort through them for the lowest-priced items.

A manufacturer of homogeneous shopping goods might decide that it is too difficult or even impossible to upgrade the consumer image of his product, especially if it is in the last stages of the product life cycle. He may then abandon selective distribution efforts and attempt to gain intensive distribution through as many wholesale and retail outlets as possible.

Some retailers use personal selling to try to get potential customers to see that they offer more than just low price. Others, such as the mass merchandisers, have gone to self-service and checkout counters for such goods. They still advertise products, however – emphasizing low prices – to project a low-price image for *all* their goods. Here the objective is to sell the store, not just particular items.

Heterogeneous shopping goods

Heterogeneous shopping goods are compared by consumers on more than price alone. For this reason they require more retail display and often more personal selling both to final consumers and to middlemen.

Producers frequently bypass wholesalers, because, in any case, they *must* tell the sales story to retailers, sometimes including technical information that must be explained directly to the retail clerks. And, since they must make the sales calls anyway, they feel they might as well take the orders and deliver the goods themselves. Fairly direct channels are also encouraged by the willingness of retail buyers to make regular trips to central markets, say, for furniture and clothing. Resident buyers also facilitate the direct movement of these goods especially in the style and fashion goods markets.

Mass selling may be used by manufacturers or retailers to inform customers about the different characteristics of these heterogeneous goods. Copies of national advertisements may be distributed to retailers and displayed by them to show customers that they offer nationally advertised products.

Generally, brand promotion is less important for these goods. Some manufacturers do little or no advertising for clothing and housefurnishings because consumers want to compare products in the store. Manufacturers may rely more heavily on informed retail clerks. Retail sales personnel may be paid financial incentives, such as a $5 bonus for each new mattress sold. Personal contacts in the channels, stressing economic arguments and demonstrating effective selling techniques, are essential here.

Specialty goods — hold a favored position with consumers

■ Specialty goods are normally distributed through the same channels as those convenience or shopping goods they most nearly resemble. The favored status of these products makes it relatively easy to promote them to wholesalers and retailers on the basis of profit potential.

Retailers advertising these products may use mass media such as billboards and newspaper advertisements simply to remind customers where they are for sale.

However, specialty goods might require continued mass selling by the manufacturer. Consumers are notoriously fickle. If similar products are being promoted aggressively, the manufacturer would not want to risk losing his customer franchise. New customers are continually entering the market and must be convinced that the product is a specialty good. This mass selling by producers also helps assure middlemen of continued customer acceptance.

Unsought goods — need some extra push

■ Unsought goods are in the introductory stage of their life cycle. All potential customers must be fully informed about them. Mass selling may be used by the manufacturer to reach final consumers, but order getters may be needed to convince wholesalers and retailers of the profit potential of these goods. If they are not convinced, the goods might not even reach the retail level.

A large, established firm just introducing an unsought good (but one similar to the firm's other products) may be able to use the rest of its line and its customer franchise to obtain distribution for the new product. The producer may still have to pay for or supply all promotion, but it *is* able to get distribution.

A smaller producer, or a larger one going into a new line might not be so fortunate. It may have to resort to the use of less efficient middlemen, mail-order selling, or house-to-house selling.

Aggressive and persuasive personal selling are needed to put these products across, especially in the channels. But to impress the channel members, it may have to be supported by mass selling — and even a pulling policy. Manufacturer's or wholesaler's salesmen may be needed to give demonstrations and set up displays and point-of-purchase materials. Perhaps the company will need to offer promotional pricing deals. Personal salesmen may have to adapt a company's marketing mix to each individual situation.

Typical mixes for industrial goods

For the industrial buyer, personal persuasion is important

■ Unlike final consumers, industrial buyers usually do not seek out the goods they will need. By accepted practice, they wait for the seller to present products or ideas. If a technical story must be told, direct distribution may be desirable or even necessary.

The promotion blends of both producers and middlemen tend to emphasize personal selling because the market is relatively limited and concentrated, and the selling job is often technical. The specific marketing mix, however, varies with the product.

Installations — president may turn salesman

■ Some installations — specific buildings or pieces of property, or custom-made machines — are unique and have special technical characteristics. Promotion must inform target customers about these products and persuade them of the advantages. Usually, personal selling is the most effective method.

New installations are normally sold directly by the contractor's or manufacturer's own salesman since (1) customers are relatively few and geographically concentrated, (2) the potential sales volume is large, and (3) there is a need for design, technical assistance and service of a kind that middlemen don't normally provide. Even smaller companies may sell directly, and the president or executive officers often serve as the sales personnel.

Brokers frequently handle sales of used buildings and land rights since buyers and sellers are only in the market irregularly. These specialized middlemen have a knowledge of the market and can provide a useful service.

Accessory equipment — middlemen often needed

■ With some accessory equipment, direct personal selling by the producer is common and paramount (1) to convince users of the merits of buying one company's product rather than another's and (2) to impart technical assistance when necessary. For other accessories, however, potential customers are widespread and need frequent contact by experienced sales personnel. For such products, large firms use manufacturers' agents or brokers in less populous areas, and smaller firms use them throughout the country. These agents provide continuous contact, and there is no cost to the producer except when a sale is completed. Since the cost of the agents' regular sales calls is spread over a number of products, the producer can obtain sales coverage without the high overhead sales cost he would incur doing this job for himself for only one line.

If good agents or brokers are not available, then merchant wholesalers—such as mill supply houses or oil field supply houses—may be used. Relatively little sales effort, however, can be expected from them. They may simply list the items in a catalog and sell them if customers ask about them. Typically, the salesmen are not specialists and cannot be expected to provide a technical sales job or service.

Farm product raw materials— many small farmers

■ The large number of small farmers creates a real discrepancy of quantity and perhaps of assortment. It also makes practical the development of many specialized middlemen. Assemblers are used to gather farm products in rural areas, and commission merchants and merchant wholesalers handle these products in the terminal markets as the products are brought closer to users.

Promotion for farm products is typically nonexistent, except for the routine order taking which would be needed to complete a sale. Usually, farm products are homogeneous commodities sold in almost pure competition, and the distribution systems have been set up to routinely bring buyers and sellers together.

Some farmers' cooperatives and trade associations have attempted to differentiate their offering, even to the extent of branding their products and spending fairly large sums on advertising. These mass selling efforts are not done by the individual firms, however.

Natural product raw materials— a few big producers

■ These are being produced by fewer and larger firms. There is little or no need for assemblers. Users are not numerous, at least not compared to final consumers. The result is that many of these producers handle distribution themselves, although smaller producers may use brokers or drop-shippers. The smaller firms need practically the same market coverage as the larger firms but have less to sell and, consequently, a smaller sales volume to cover selling costs.

Most of these products have reached the market maturity or even sales decline stages and tend to be standardized. Prices, which usually are widely disseminated, are competitive. Promotion is not unimportant, however. Buyers still must decide from whom they will buy. There are opportunities for considerable persuasive personal selling by order getters. The personality of the particular salesman and the company image which he conveys can, in fact, be the deciding factors.

Component parts and materials — personal contact may be vital

■ Most components producers are specialized and cater to a relatively small, concentrated group of users. Since technical and design assistance may be required, these producers normally deal directly with their target customers. If potential customers are numerous and widespread, however, agents may help locate and service new business. And they may be granted exclusive territories to encourage selling effort.

Promotion for these products must inform the prospective buyer about technical details as well as price, quality, and delivery dependability.

Personal selling is the chief means of promoting component parts and materials. Some components are custom-made for specific applications, and salesmen are vital to assure that both buyer and seller are aware of each other's needs and capabilities. Salesmen also are important because many competitors can offer the same technical service or even identical products, and much personal persuasion is needed. As with raw materials, again, given essentially homogeneous products and price, the competence and personality of the salesman play an important role.

Supplies — middlemen rank high for maintenance items

■ Maintenance items are used widely and are similar in many respects to convenience goods. Customers are fairly widely dispersed, purchases of each item are relatively small, and little technical assistance or service is required. Since this is an ideal situation for middlemen, merchant wholesalers are common in this field. Mill supply houses and office and stationery supply stores often serve as middlemen for maintenance items. They are contacted directly by the larger producers in the more populous areas and by manufacturers' agents in other areas. The smaller producer may use manufacturers' agents exclusively for his contacts with these merchant wholesalers.

For these goods, the producer's main promotion job is personal selling in the channel in order to get distribution. Some mass selling might be desirable to encourage wholesalers to stock his products, but personal selling is vital to actually get the business. The merchant wholesalers, then, provide an order-taking role.

Repair items

Repair items are used widely and, with some exceptions, may be distributed in the same way as maintenance items. Large customers might have complete repair facilities and prefer to buy repair parts directly; smaller manufacturers and contractors more often prefer to have wholesalers carry the parts inventory and perhaps handle the repair service, too.

Since most repair parts come directly from the original manufacturer, the main promotional task is to inform buyers of their availability. These products have a "captive market," and persuasion is not necessary.

However, if the market is large enough to attract competitors, as in the automotive and electrical goods fields, then persuasion must be used, too. The main promotional appeals are faster, more dependable service. Mass selling might be adequate to tell this story, but personal selling may have to be used anyway, to meet competition.

Operating supply items

Operating supply items, with few exceptions, are similar to maintenance items and are distributed in the same way. The exceptions are some bulky items, such as coal, lubricants, and fuel oil. Direct distribution of these supplies by the producer may be advisable because of technical service considerations (as for lubricants) or the large volume of sales (fuel oil). Drop-shippers commonly act as middlemen for the many small coal producers.

Services — usually are sold directly
■ Most services do not involve physical products and, therefore, there is nothing tangible to move through a distribution system. As a result, the producers typically sell directly to their customers. Where the potential customers are widespread, however, agents may enter to provide the initial contacts. Then, the producer's own salesmen can follow up.

Since most service businesses have relatively undifferentiated products, their promotional task usually is persuasive in nature. The emphasis is on personal selling.

When a service is new, information about price, availability, and dependability is important. But competitors usually enter a profitable field quickly, and personal persuasion is then needed to hold customers.

Special factors may affect the typical marketing mix

■ Each marketing manager must reconcile his own objectives and resources with the kind of marketing mix he might like to offer his target customers. He must consider various market realities, including peculiarities of the target market, special characteristics of the product, the market structure, and his own firm's special capabilities and limitations. Often, the marketing manager must settle for a marketing mix that is less than ideal and, sometimes, his company may even have to join a channel system that is controlled by another firm.

Not all targets look the same
■ It will be useful to see how some of these market realities might affect marketing mix decisions.

Size and geographic dispersion affect sales contacts needed

If the sales potential of the target market selected by the marketing manager is large enough, it may be possible for him to go directly to retailers, consumers, or users. This is especially true if the potential target customers are highly concentrated, as are the customers for many industrial goods. For final consumer goods, however, potential customers usually are numerous and widely dispersed, and buy in small quantities. Although the total market may be relatively large, it might be split up into small geographical segments, with too little demand in each market grid box to support a direct approach.

Geographical dispersion is a decisive factor in international marketing. Here, middlemen become almost indispensable. Even if world demand is great, direct distribution to individual markets is seldom feasible because of the distance between the producer and the many separate markets.

Value of item and frequency and regularity of purchases

Even low-priced items such as groceries may be handled directly if they are purchased frequently and the cumulative volume is large—as in the case of home-delivered milk and bread. But for products purchased seldom and irregularly—even though purchases are substantial—specialized agencies such as commission merchants, agents, brokers, and other middlemen may be useful. A critical factor is the cost of regularly providing the needed marketing functions in relation to the sales obtained over several months or a year's time.

Customer preferences for personal contacts

Customer preferences vary even within the same goods classification. Some target customers, especially some industrial customers, have a bias against dealing with middlemen, and even though they may want only small quantities, they may prefer to buy directly from manufacturers. This may be a nuisance to the manufacturer, but he may tolerate it because the customers occasionally may buy larger quantities.

Other buyers, however, may prefer the convenience of buying through a middleman because they can telephone orders and get immediate action from a local source. Two quite different marketing mixes handled through two channel systems, therefore, could be needed to fully satisfy both types of customers.

Not all products are the same

■ Some goods, because of their technical nature, perishability, or bulkiness, require more direct distribution than is implied by their goods classification.

Technical products

Complicated products, such as conveyor systems and electronic data processing equipment, call for a high degree of technical selling knowledge and expert installation and servicing. Wholesalers usually do not wish, nor are they equipped, to provide all these required services.

Perishability

Perishable items, such as cut flowers, milk, and fresh seafood, may have to be handled directly if produced on a small scale, perhaps in an isolated town or in a less developed economic environment. But if many small producers are clustered together, specialists may develop to handle transportation, refrigeration, and storage. Complicated terminal markets, such as those dealing in fresh produce, may develop, along with a host of specialized commission merchants, brokers, merchant wholesalers, and truck wholesalers.

High-fashion items also are perishable, and more direct distribution may be sensible to speed the flow to retailers. Sometimes retailers and final consumers even go directly to the producers to see the latest fashion showings, say in New York and Paris.

Bulkiness

Transportation, handling, and storage costs mount when bulky products are moved about, making it difficult for middlemen to operate. If a producer is unable to make an adequate number of sales contacts when selling bulky items direct, he may decide to use brokers, manufacturers' agents, and especially drop-shippers, to make sales contacts and then ship the goods himself directly to the customer. This is another example of function shifting and sharing in a channel system, required in this case because of the nature of the product.

Not all channel structures are the same

■ The marketing manager's "ideal" channel system may not be available or even possible, due to various uncontrollable variables discussed below.

Availability of suitable and cooperative middlemen

The kinds of specialists the marketing manager would like to use may not even be available or willing to cooperate, especially if the company is a late entrant in the field and his competitors already have tied up the best middlemen, perhaps as part of a selective or exclusive distribution policy. It is important to realize that *aggressive* market-oriented middlemen usually are not readily available and waiting for someone to pick them up. They *may be* receptive to good proposals, but just another "me too" mix may have trouble.

The specific customers already being reached by each proposed specialist are extremely important. If these do not include the marketing manager's target markets, then that middleman doesn't have much to offer. A wholesaler specializing in groceries would have a valuable customer list for the food business, but it would not be of much value in distributing electronic machinery.

Strength of traditional arrangements

The market structure may be dominated by traditional arrangements. There may be long-established, highly successful "home-owned" retailers or wholesaler-retailer links based on family or nationality ties. This kind of traditional arrangement is seen in its extreme in tropical Africa, where channels are divided by race and target markets. Large European-owned firms import goods and export domestic production. These Europeans sell to some smaller wholesalers and retailers, but generally Levantines in West Africa and Indians in East Africa serve as middlemen to small retailers who typically are Africans.

There are exceptions to these generalizations, and breakthroughs can happen for those who deviate from the traditional arrangements. But in international markets, the traditional roles of the various groups are long standing and firmly rooted.[4]

The rather freewheeling competition we see in the United States is not typical of international markets. Because of this, the traditional channels of distribution may be the only practicable ones for a newcomer. Innovators may be punished by social sanctions or even legislative restraints aimed specifically at them.

Uniformity of market coverage of available specialists

The middlemen available in large metropolitan centers may be highly effective there, but may not cover outlying areas. This may require two channels to reach both areas. But it may also lead to a dual distribution problem because the middlemen who might be suitable for outlying areas may also cover the large metropolitan areas, but not as well. Everyone likes to work where sales are plentiful and easy to make.

Nor does distribution through national or international companies guarantee uniform coverage. For example, A&P has a much larger share of the retail grocery market in the East than in the Middle West; Sears, Roebuck has been relatively stronger in the Middle West and West than in other sections. This uneven coverage of marketing specialists simply means that, in practice, every channel for every target market must be tailor-made. In this context, geographic dimensions may greatly expand the number of market grid boxes which must be treated separately.

Financing required in channel system

Adequate credit may be critical in smoothing the flow through a channel system. Some wholesalers enter a channel mainly because they can give financial assistance to the members.

We already have mentioned the role of factors, but some merchant wholesalers also hold a secure position in a channel because of their strong financial condition and ability to meet the financial needs of other channel members. This is especially true in international markets.

In some African markets, the credit cycle from sale to final payment may extend over three years. Since few African businessmen have this much working capital, well-financed European and Chinese importing and exporting firms have been attracted to Africa.[5]

Political and legal environment

Each geographical target market must be studied carefully for special legal or tax requirements. We already have mentioned the controls on exclusive distribution and the anti-merger legislation in the United States. Outside of the United States there are fewer controls of this type, but there are important tax considerations.

In Europe, a major portion of the tax income is collected from sales or "turnover" taxes that are assessed every time title passes from one level of distribution to the next. Partly because of turnover taxes — which may run as high as 25 percent — many European manufacturers sell directly to retailers or users. When they cannot or do not wish to sell directly, they use commission merchants, who make the contacts and sales but avoid taking title. This avoids the turnover tax, but using commission merchants who are intended for other purposes may reduce the effectiveness of the whole channel system.

Nature of
company
itself—is it
big, rich,
and un-
prejudiced?

■ In deciding what kind of mix to offer and how to work within a distribution system, each marketing manager—be he manufacturer, wholesaler, or retailer—must evaluate his own company's capabilities, needs, and potential contributions to a channel. If he is realistic, he may find that his best course is to join a strong system rather than try to play the role of channel captain himself.

Size of company and width of product line

A company's own size has an important bearing on its place in a channel system because it affects discrepancies of quantity and assortment. A large firm already handling a wide line of food or soap products, for example, may be in a good position to take on an additional product of the same type and handle it the same way, perhaps directly. In contrast, a smaller company or one with narrower lines might suffer from a discrepancy of quantity or discrepancy of assortment or both, and would probably find middlemen more practical. Similarly, a large company going into a completely unrelated line would lose its size advantage, since it would be functioning as the small producer of a new line.

Some industrial goods producers sell enough to overcome the discrepancy-of-quantity problem in *some* of their major markets. There they can use their own branches and warehouses. But the same producer may find middlemen more attractive where markets are smaller or scattered.

Financial strength

A company's financial strength can also be important if its customers need financial assistance. Firms not in a position to provide this financing may find specialized middlemen useful. Selling agents, factors, merchant wholesalers, or large retailers, may be in a position to finance a producer or channel members, including users or final consumers. In fact, a channel captain's dominance may depend heavily on his financing capacity.

Executive prejudices

Although the prejudices of company executives should not be a dominant factor, executives are a company resource, and their attitudes may influence marketing mix selection or even be incorporated into company objectives. Some "old-time" sales managers, for example, have strong anti-chain store attitudes which color their thinking about who to sell to and through. Likewise, some sales managers prefer to control their own sales force rather than work with independent manufacturers' agents who may resist strict direction.

Conclusion

■ This chapter has shown the importance of developing whole marketing mixes, not just policies for the individual four Ps which *hopefully* will fit together into some logical whole. The marketing manager is responsible for developing a workable blend—integrating all of his firm's efforts into a coordinated whole which makes effective use of its resources and guides it toward its objectives.

This requires consideration of response functions; i.e., how the four Ps should be combined in the light of varying sales responsiveness to alternative marketing variables. Ultimately, however, the manager must be concerned with the market's responsiveness to alternative marketing mixes. Ideally, he would know the exact shape of the alternative response functions but, in practice, he will have to rely on past experience (to some extent), marketing research if he has the time, and a substantial amount of judgment. He also can study typical marketing mixes and their apparent effectiveness in the marketplace for clues about what works and how well.

As a starting place for developing new marketing mixes, he can make use of the goods classifications which have served as a thread through this text. Even though he may not be able to fully describe the needs and preferences of his target markets, he may be able to make reasonable judgments about the appropriate goods class for a particular product and this, in turn, will have direct relevance for selecting the appropriate Place and Promotion.

This chapter has been a review, focusing on the development of a good or the "best" marketing mix for a particular target market. Developing and selecting among alternative strategies and strategic plans is a logical extension of the discussion in this chapter and is taken up in Chapter 27.

questions and problems

1 Distinguish between a general marketing effort response function and a response function for one of the four Ps.

2 Explain how the use of response functions, even if they must be crudely estimated, could be helpful in developing a marketing strategy.

3 Would a direct or some type of indirect channel of distribution be most appropriate for the following products? (Utilize the general factors discussed in this chapter and make any assumptions necessary to obtain a definite answer.) (a) Hedge clippers, (b) fly swatters, (c) earth moving machinery, (d) fingernail clippers, (e) motor scooters, (f) grass seed, (g) picture frames, (h) trucks, (i) fresh apple cider.

4 For those products in the previous question where indirect distribution was the answer (in the light of the assumptions), indicate specifically the kinds of channels and the rest of the producer's marketing mix which might develop.

5 Explain what marketing mix might be most appropriate for manufacturers of the following established products (assume average- to large-sized firms in each case and support your answer): (a) a completely new home permanent wave concept, packaged in a convenient kit, (b) a contracting service, capable of bidding on projects up to large dams, (c) lumber, (d) production tools for finishing furniture, (e) glass for window repair.

notes

[1] "How Kodak Will Exploit Its New Instamatic," *Business Week*, March 18, 1972, pp. 46–48.

[2] Ibid. p. 47.

[3] David B. Montgomery and Charles B. Weinberg, "Modeling Marketing Phenomena: A Managerial Perspective," *The Journal of Contemporary Business*,

Autumn 1973, pp. 17–43; J. Lambin, "A Computer On-line Marketing Model," *Journal of Marketing Research,* May 1972, pp. 119–26; Michael L. Ray, "A Decision Sequence Analysis of Developments in Marketing Communication," *Journal of Marketing,* January 1973, pp. 29–38; and Leonard M. Lodish, "'Vaguely Right' Approach to Sales Force Allocations," *Harvard Business Review,* January–February 1974, pp. 119–24.

[4] Edward Marcus, "Selling the Tropical African Market," *Journal of Marketing,* July 1961, pp. 27–28; and Alice G. Dewey, *Peasant Marketing in Java* (New York: Free Press 1962).

[5] Marcus, "Selling the African Market," p. 31.

Planning and implementing marketing programs

■ Our major stress so far has been on developing parts of, and whole, marketing strategies. This is an extremely important and creative aspect of the marketing manager's job. But now, we will see that a marketing manager must go beyond just developing strategies. He must develop strategic *plans* and then a whole marketing program—a set of strategic plans which, typically, seek to reach the firm's goals by making the most effective use of the firm's resources. Then, the marketing manager must go on to implement this program, perhaps with the aid of some flowcharting procedures which are discussed at the end of the chapter.

Strategic plans must be developed and evaluated

■ In our previous discussions of strategic planning, we have considered how one might put together alternative marketing mixes and strategies. In the last chapter, we reviewed some of the principles we have been discussing throughout the text with respect to strategic planning. Hopefully, by now you should have some "marketing feel"; i.e., an ability to develop or at least identify "good" strategies.

Now we must go one step further—to developing strategic *plans*—because it is strategic plans, not strategies, which we must develop and evaluate in the real world.

What is a strategic plan?

■ A strategy is a "grand design" for what a firm will do in some product-market area, while a strategic plan includes the time-related details for that strategy. Each strategy which gets implemented will be carried out over a period of time, and some time schedule is implicit in any strategy. A strategic plan simply makes this time period and the time-related details explicit. Usually, we think in terms of some reasonable length of time such as six months, a year, or a few years. But it might be only a month or two in some cases, especially when style and fashion are important factors. Or, a strategy might be implemented over several years, perhaps the length of a product life cycle or at least the early stages of the life of the product.

Basically, the strategic plan should spell out the following in detail: (1) What marketing mix is going to be offered to whom (i.e., the target market), and for how long; (2) what company resources (shown as costs) will be required, at what rate (month by month perhaps); and (3) what results are expected (sales and profits, perhaps month by month). It might also be desirable to include some control procedures so that whoever is to implement the plan will know when things are not going according to plan. This might be something as simple as comparing actual sales against expected sales with a "warning flag" to be raised whenever cumulative sales fall below some predetermined level.

Forms for each strategy can make planning easier

■ To facilitate the planning process and the communication of its results to others, including top management who may review the plans, it may be helpful to use forms, such as the set shown in Figure 27–1. In this case, there are separate blanks for descriptions of the target market as well as room for spelling out the dimensions of that target market. Further, there are blanks for describing the nature of competition, the stage of the product life cycle, and important aspects of the proposed four Ps.

Figure 27–1 also provides a place for the time-related details, including sales, direct costs, and contribution to profit by month. Coupled with a place for dollar estimates are the specific tasks which would have to be accomplished each month and which would contribute directly to the costs, and, hopefully, sales. Notice, also, that there are blanks for control purposes. Actual sales and costs would be inserted on the same planning form and actual and cumulative differences could be calculated with a view to determining when either changes in the plan or a wholly new plan might be needed.

What period of time should the strategic plan cover?

■ Company planning for marketing, production, finance, and other functions may be done on a monthly or quarterly basis, but most commonly it is on an annual basis. While there is nothing inherently superior about an annual period, accounting statements usually are prepared at least annually; the monies budgeted for the various marketing functions usually are related to time periods such as a year; and since seasons affect production and/or sales in most companies, the yearly period makes sense. As a result, in the absence of good reasons to the contrary, marketing plans usually cover a year, or a year as part of a longer period.

Figure 27–1

Forms to plan and control each of a firm's market-oriented strategic plans
—with illustrative comments and numbers for first two pages (one set of
forms for each plan, number of time periods depending on length of plan)

Product identification ___McCarthy, BASIC MARKETING, 5th ed.___

Target market title ___Instructors of first marketing course.___

Dimensions of target market ___All college and university level instructors interested in an integrated, analytical,___

___management-oriented approach to marketing—i.e. logical, organized, pragmatic instructors.___

Competition ___Several authors trying to satisfy the same market and/or everyone (actual names___

___used in real situations).___

Nature of competition ___Monopolistic.___

Product life cycle ___Market maturity.___

Marketing mix

Product characteristics

Type ___New (revised) component part and specialty good to students.___

Total product ___Package of teaching materials and aids.___

Branch familiarty ___Recognition to preference.___

Place policies

Type of channel members ___Direct to retailers.___

Degree of market exposure ___Exclusive OK.___

Pulling or pushing ___Push to instructors, contact retailers.___

Physical distribution service level ___Immediate delivery to bookstores.___

Promotion thrust

Blend type ___Heavy on personal selling.___

Type of salesmen ___Order getting and taking.___

Message emphasis ___Integrated analytical, etc., Package.___

Media emphasis ___Direct mail and professional journals.___

Price policies

Flexibility ___One price.___

Level ___Meet competition.___

Geographic ___F.O.B. shipping point.___

Discounts and allowances ___20 percent of selling price, restricted returns.___

1

Figure 27–1 (Continued)

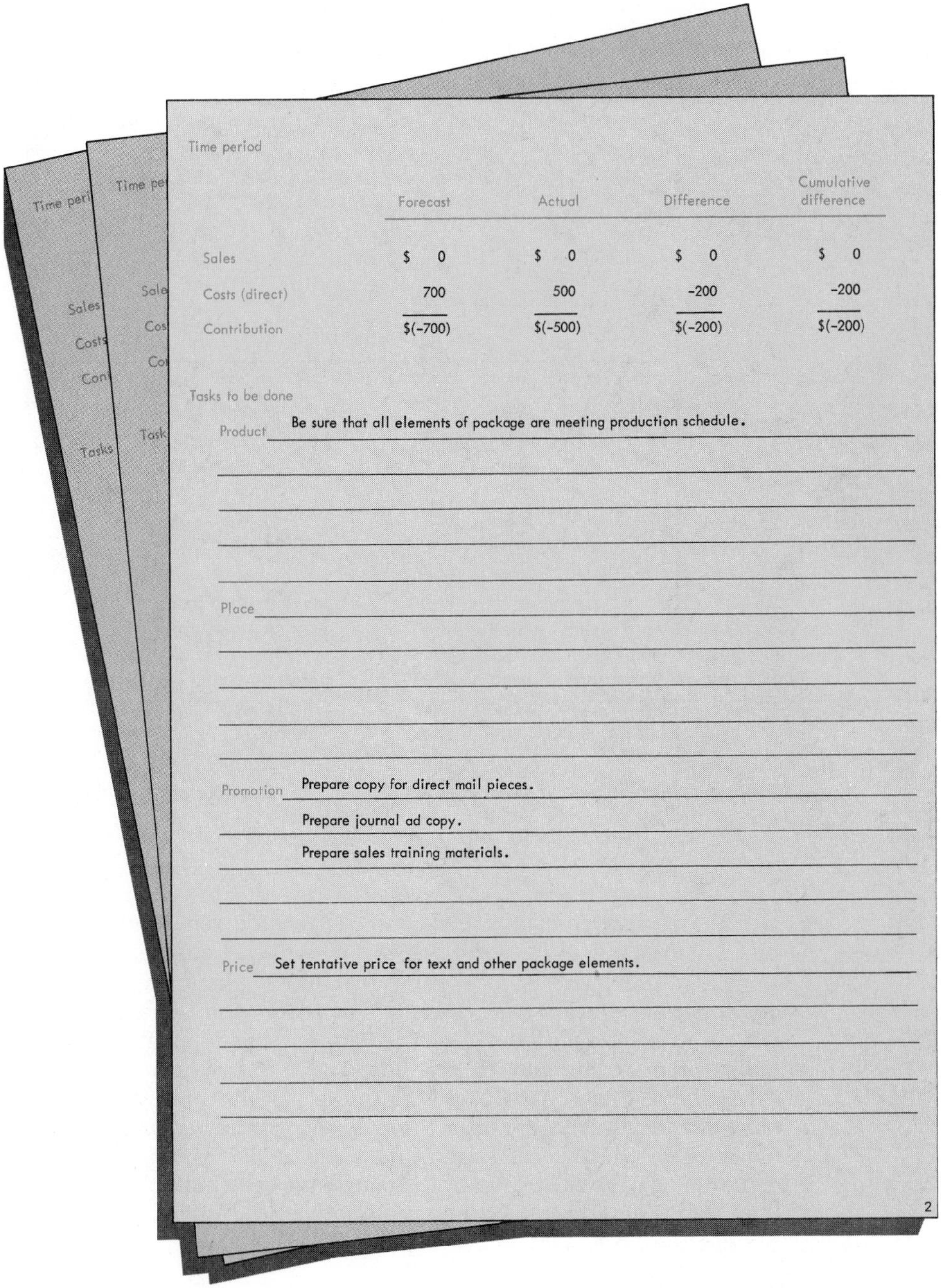

Time period

	Forecast	Actual	Difference	Cumulative difference
Sales	$ 0	$ 0	$ 0	$ 0
Costs (direct)	700	500	−200	−200
Contribution	$(−700)	$(−500)	$(−200)	$(−200)

Tasks to be done

Product   Be sure that all elements of package are meeting production schedule.

Place

Promotion   Prepare copy for direct mail pieces.
Prepare journal ad copy.
Prepare sales training materials.

Price   Set tentative price for text and other package elements.

2

Figure 27–2
Typical changes in marketing variables over the course of the product life cycle

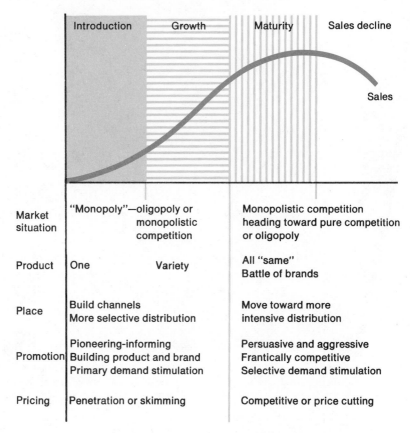

The use of such established time cycles is current practice, and our discussion will be within the framework of current practice. Logically, however, a marketing manager's plans might better cover periods shorter than, or more frequently, considerably longer than, a year. This period will vary in length depending on the nature of the product, the market situation, and the current product life-cycle stage. The 20- to 40-year planning periods, however, which have been traditional for evaluating new investments, probably are too long in the face of shortening product life cycles. In a less dynamic age, 20- to 40-year cycles may have been suitable, but now they seem more to reflect the regulations of the Internal Revenue Service than the realities of the marketplace.

Planning must use the product life cycle

■ So far we have been emphasizing the development of a good or the "best" marketing strategy for some target market. This can be risky, however, if too static a view of strategy planning is taken. In fact, as we have emphasized throughout the text, markets are continually changing, and this means that we must plan strategies which will adjust to likely changing conditions or be prepared to change strategies frequently. Some changes in the environment are completely uncontrollable and even unpredictable. But there are other changes which *are* more predictable and which should be taken into consideration explicitly when developing a plan. In particular, the product life cycle should be given serious attention because, typically, marketing variables should change throughout the product's life cycle.[1]

Figure 27–2 indicates some of the typical changes in marketing variables which might logically be made over the course of a product life cycle. This figure should be an instructive review. For example, you will see that as the product life cycle moves on, the marketing manager should *expect* to find more products entering "his" market and pushing the market situation closer to pure competition or oligopoly. This would suggest that as the cycle moves along he might want to shift from a selective to an intensive distribution policy *and* move from a skimming to a penetration pricing policy. His original strategic plan might include these likely adjustments and the probable timing involved. If it is likely that the cycle will move very quickly, then he may have to select a less-than-optimal approach early in the product life cycle, knowing that he will not be able to adjust fast enough later. Regarding his distribution structure, for example, he might choose intensive rather than selective distribution because he knows this will be necessary within a year's time.

It is not necessary to make plans which will last for the full length of a product life cycle. A firm can drop out of a market. But it must recognize that the cycle will move on, and should make its own plans accordingly.

Whole plans should be evaluated and compared

■ A highly detailed strategic plan can be developed for one year, perhaps to conform to company planning practices. But when it comes to *evaluating* alternative plans, it may make more sense to project their economic potential over a more logical planning period. If a product's life-span (before withdrawal from the market) is likely to be three years, for example, then a good strategy may not produce profitable results during the first six months to a year. But examine the plan over the projected three-year life-span, and it might look like a winner. When evaluating the potential of alternative strategic plans, it is important to evaluate like things — i.e., *whole* strategic plans.

Total profit approach can help evaluate alternative plans

■ The total profit approach to evaluating strategic plans requires forecasts of potential revenues during the life-span of the plan as well as cost projections for implementing the marketing mix associated with the plan. This is basically an extension of the response function discussion in the last chapter.

The prospects for each plan might be evaluated over a five-year

Figure 27–3
Expected sales and cost curves of two strategies over five-year planning periods

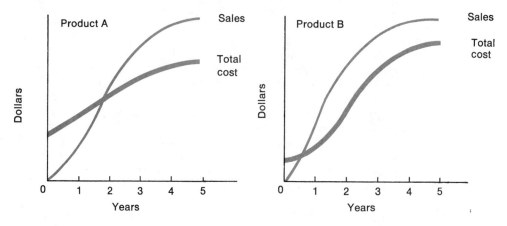

planning period, with monthly and/or annual estimates of sales and costs. This is illustrated graphically in Figure 27–3. Note that the product life cycle can be incorporated in this analysis through the shape of the sales and cost curves. There is nothing sacred, however, about the five-year period.

Note that, as shown in Figure 27–3, quite different strategic plans can be evaluated at the same time. In this case, a substantially improved product and product concept (product A) is being compared with a "me-too" product which is being considered for the same target market. In the short run, the "me-too" product would break even sooner and might look like the better choice if one were considering only one year's results. The new product, on the other hand, will take a good deal of pioneering but, over the five-year time span, will be much more profitable.

Return on investment (ROI) approach can help evaluate alternative plans, too

■ Besides evaluating the profit potential of alternative plans, it may also be desirable to calculate the return on investment of resources which are required to implement a plan. One plan might require a heavy investment in advertising and channel development, for example, while another relied primarily on lower price to move goods.

ROI analyses can be extremely useful for discriminating among alternative plans because equally profitable plans may require vastly different resources and offer different rates of return on investment. Some firms are very much concerned with ROI because often they must borrow money for working capital and there is little point in borrowing to implement strategies which will not even return enough to meet the cost of borrowing.[2]

Table 27-1
Evaluation of various alternatives with expected value approach

Alternatives	Payoff (in dollars of profit)	Probability of occurrence	Expected profit
1	$ 100,000 or 0	.50 .50	$ 50,000
2	25,000 or 0	.90 .10	22,500
3	1,000,000 or 0	.20 .80	200,000
4	500,000 or 0	.30 .70	150,000

Expected value approach may be useful where there is uncertainty

■ The total profit approach (and the ROI approach) require estimates of sales and profits. If fairly definite estimates can be made for alternative strategies, then these can be compared and the "best" one selected.

Where there is uncertainty about the likely outcome of individual plans, however, one might wonder which profit figures to use. If one can assess the likelihood of success of alternative plans, however, then it is possible to compute the expected profit and compare these expected profits for alternative plans.

See Table 27-1 for an illustration of how expected profit could be calculated for four alternatives. Assuming that the marketing manager is willing to accept expected profit as his criterion, then the strategy that is likely to produce the highest expected profit can be chosen. For example, in Table 27-1, strategy 3 would be chosen. An extremely conservative decision maker, however, might select strategy 2 because of its seeming certainty. In other words, even though profit were one of the objectives of management, the risk associated with alternative plans might lead different managers to select different plans.

Decision trees may help us see alternatives more clearly

■ When many alternative plans must be evaluated, putting them in graphic terms may be helpful. The tree diagram in Figure 27-4 shows several alternatives clearly. At the end of each branch, a measure of effectiveness, such as total profit and/or return on investment, can be shown for comparison. And, if success of any of the plans is uncertain, the expected values can be calculated and compared, as illustrated in Table 27-1. As a further aid, it might be useful to show the resources required for each alternative alongside the total profit and return on investment. Most firms are at-

Figure 27–4

Decision tree for evaluation of alternative one-year plans, given that target market and product have already been selected and one-year plans are realistic

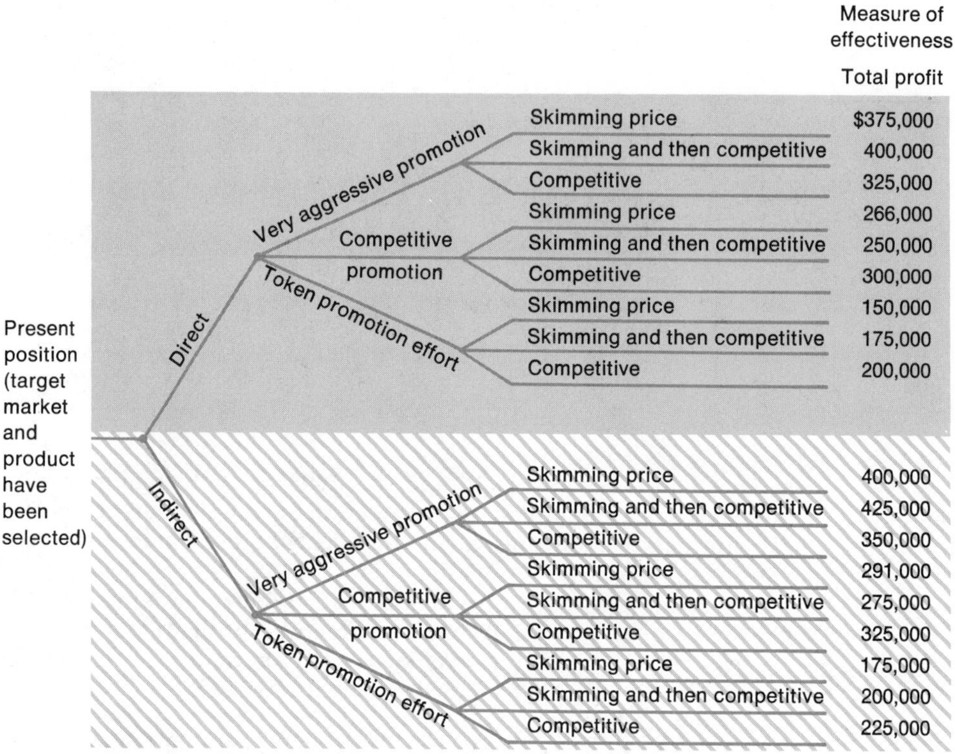

Measure of effectiveness

Total profit

Present position (target market and product have been selected)

Direct

Very aggressive promotion
- Skimming price — $375,000
- Skimming and then competitive — 400,000
- Competitive — 325,000

Competitive promotion
- Skimming price — 266,000
- Skimming and then competitive — 250,000
- Competitive — 300,000

Token promotion effort
- Skimming price — 150,000
- Skimming and then competitive — 175,000
- Competitive — 200,000

Indirect

Very aggressive promotion
- Skimming price — 400,000
- Skimming and then competitive — 425,000
- Competitive — 350,000

Competitive promotion
- Skimming price — 291,000
- Skimming and then competitive — 275,000
- Competitive — 325,000

Token promotion effort
- Skimming price — 175,000
- Skimming and then competitive — 200,000
- Competitive — 225,000

tempting to make a profit while using their resources effectively, but sometimes these are conflicting goals and it helps to have all of the relevant information conveniently displayed when management attempts to apply its judgment to choosing the best plan.

Companies plan and implement marketing programs

Several plans make a program

■ Most companies implement more than one strategic plan at the same time. Typically, they aim at several target markets and prepare different marketing mixes for each one of them. Each of these plans, therefore, must be merged into a total *marketing program*, which then becomes the responsibility of the entire company, working as a total system of action.

When the various plans which are part of the company's program are quite different, then there may be less concern with how well they fit together, except as they vie for the firm's usually limited resources.

When the plans are more similar, however, then the same sales force may be expected to implement several plans. Or, the firm's advertising department may be expected to develop the publicity and advertising for several plans. In such situations, product managers may be made responsible for championing their own plan and attempting to obtain enough of the common resources, say, salesmen's time, for their own plan.

In such situations, it may be desirable for the marketing manager, who is responsible for implementing the whole program, to graphically merge the several plans together to help guide the allocation of resources. To be more specific, he might merge several graphical plans of the type shown in Figure 27–1. This might show quite clearly that each product manager was expecting to make almost full use of the existing sales force. If this heavy use of salesmen were clearly a good idea for each of the plans, then it might be desirable to expand the sales force. Alternately, some trimming of the proposed plans will be necessary, given the available resources.

These kinds of potential problems would be spotted quickly while planning marketing programs, and this helps point out why such planning efforts are so vital. Almost always, a company's resources are limited, so the marketing manager must make hard choices. He cannot launch a plan to pursue every promising opportunity he sees. Instead, limited resources always force him to choose among alternative plans while developing his program.

Long-range planning can be helpful

Our primary emphasis has been on planning marketing programs with relatively short-time horizons; i.e., one to five years. This jibes with the reality of the fast-changing marketplace. At the same time, however, a wise marketing manager should be trying to think beyond this time frame.

Forecasting market opportunities far into the future is certainly risky, but not doing it can also be risky. Important changes in the uncontrollable environment, including competitors' actions, may signal opportunities which should not be neglected in favor of the pursuit of short-run profits.

By trying to think of markets in terms of changing life-styles and shifting needs and preferences, it may be possible to isolate "breakthrough opportunities" which can be capitalized on with relatively small changes in the firm's plans.

Taking such a long-run view of evolving market needs does not necessarily mean that a long-term commitment of resources is involved. The firm's present channels of distribution and production facilities may be quite adequate to meet these new needs *if* they are seen soon enough. A major requirement for long-range planning is looking outward toward the marketplace rather than inward toward the firm's own internal problems and the use of resources. This obviously is one of the responsibilities of a marketing manager and should be continually in his mind as he is developing marketing programs.

Find the best
program by
trial and
error

■ How do you find the best program? There is no one best way of comparing various plans. A great deal of reliance must be placed on management judgment. Yet some calculations are helpful, too. If a five-year planning horizon seems to be realistic for the firm's product markets, then expected profits over the five-year period can be compared for each plan.

Assuming that the company had a profit-oriented objective, the more profitable plans could be looked at first, both in terms of potential profit and resources required. Also, the impact on the entire program should be evaluated. One profitable-looking alternative might be a poor first choice because it will eat up all the company's resources and side-track several plans which together would be more profitable.

Some juggling among the various plans in relation to profitability versus resources needed and available tends to move the company toward the *most profitable* program.

This trial-and-error approach can be aided with a computer program if a great number of alternatives have to be evaluated. Actually, however, the computer would merely perform the same function—trying to match potential revenues and profits against available resources.[3]

Allocating budgets for marketing programs

■ Once the overall marketing program and five-year (or whatever) plans have been set, shorter-term plans also must be worked out. Typically, companies use annual budgets both to plan what they are going to do and to provide control over various functions. Each department may be allowed to spend its budgeted amount, perhaps by months, for each of their departmental functions. As long as departments stay within their budgets, they are allowed considerable (or complete) autonomy. But spending over the budget is considered a deviation from the general plan and requires a lot of discussion and clearance at a higher level.

Budgeting
for market-
ing?—
50%, 30%,
or 10% is
better than
nothing

■ The most common method of budgeting for marketing expenditures is to compute them as a percentage of either past or forcasted sales. The virtue of this method is its simplicity. A similar percentage can be used rather automatically each year, eliminating the need to repeatedly evaluate the kind and amount of marketing effort that is needed and its probable cost. It enables those executives who are not too tuned into the marketing concept to "write off" a certain percentage or numbers of dollars, and at the same time control the amount spent. When a company's top executives have this attitude, they often get what they expect from their marketing activities—something less than the best results.

Some marketing executives find this percentage-of-sales approach convenient. It assures them of a reasonable budget. It should be clear, however, that the believers in this approach do not fully understand the relation between effort and results.

Find the task, budget for it

■ Mechanically budgeting a certain percentage of past or forecasted sales leads, ironically, to expanding marketing expenditures when business is good and sales are rising, and contracting them when business is poor. It may, in fact, be desirable to increase marketing expenditures when business is good, though it is questionable whether this should be in a direct ratio. But when business is poor, the most sensible approach may be to be *more,* not less, aggressive!

There are other methods of budgeting for marketing expenditures. Some of these are as follows:

1. Match expenditures with competitors.
2. Set the budget as a certain number of cents or dollars per sales unit (by case, by thousand, or by ton), using the past year or estimated year ahead as a base for computation.
3. Set aside all uncommitted revenue, perhaps including budgeted profits. Companies willing to sacrifice some or all of current profits for future sales may use this approach, i.e., *invest* in marketing.
4. Base the budget on the number of new customers desired or the amount required to reach a predetermined sales goal, as when entering new territories, increasing volume, or seeking other objectives. This method is frequently called the "task method."

Task method can lead to budgeting without agony

■ In the light of our continuing discussion about planning marketing strategy to reach objectives, the most sensible approach to budgeting marketing expenditures would seem to be this last approach, the *task method.*

The amount budgeted, using this method, can be expressed ultimately as a percentage of sales, but developing this shorthand description would be much more involved than picking up a past percentage. It would require a careful review of the five-year plans discussed previously and the specific tasks to be accomplished this year as part of each of these five-year plans. The costs of these tasks, then, would be totaled to determine how much should be budgeted for marketing and the other business functions provided for in the one- and five-year plans. If a careful five-year planning procedure has been used and accepted by top management, it should be possible to assemble the budget directly from these detailed plans, rather than from historical patterns or ratios.

After the marketing department has received its budget for the year, it could, presumably, spend its money any way it saw fit. But if the previous planning-budgeting procedure has been followed, it would make sense to continue allocating expenditures within the marketing function according to the plans in the program.

Again, everyone in the marketing department and in the business should view the company as a system of action and plan accordingly. If this is done, it will be possible to eliminate some of the traditional planning-budgeting decisions which have been so agonizing because, in the nature of things, one executive often was pitted against another and one department against another.

Program implementation must be planned

■ Up to this chapter, we have been primarily concerned with planning strategies—i.e., the "big picture." Plans and programs bring this down to earth by adding the time-related details. Now we want to go a step further—illustrating graphical techniques which help marketing managers implement their plans and programs. First, we will discuss techniques which are helpful for introducing new products or controlling special projects. Then we will consider aids for ongoing programs.

New products or projects can use PERT flowcharts

■ Some marketing managers find it helpful to draw flowcharts or diagrams of all of the interrelated tasks that must be accomplished on schedule. In recent years, some firms have successfully applied such flowcharting techniques as CPM (critical path method) or PERT (program evaluation and review technique). These techniques were originally developed as part of the U.S. space program (NASA) to ensure that the various contractors and subcontractors' efforts would stay on schedule and reach their goals as planned.

The detailed flowcharts used in these approaches describe which marketing activities must be done in sequence and which can be done concurrently. These charts also show the time allotments needed for various activities. By totaling the time allotments along the various charts paths, the most critical (the longest) path, as well as the most desirable starting and ending dates for the various activities within the project will be shown.

How flowcharting helped Diamond Alkali

This flowchart approach is credited with helping Diamond Akali Co. avoid a difficult situation when introducing a new product. By spending a few days flowcharting their plans for this product, Diamond Alkali found that they would spend about 76 weeks introducing it—although their predetermined schedule had allotted only 36 weeks for the introduction. By rearranging their plans with the aid of the flowchart technique, they were able to squeeze the effort into 36 weeks. Now the use of flowcharts is mandatory for all Diamond Alkali new-product introductions.

Basically, a flowcharting effort follows a number of logical steps. First, a marketing strategy is needed. Then the various elements of the strategy which must be implemented over a period of time must be listed. Each of these elements, in turn, must be broken down into subelements or activities. A basic element such as sales promotion probably would include "Preparing a Sales Brochure." But this, in turn, would require detailed activities such as preparing performance charts and graphs, preparing rough copy, agency preparation of preliminary copy and layouts, and so on.

These activities are then flowcharted to pinpoint the bottle-necks.

The Diamond Alkali analysis isolated 105 activities, some of which could be done concurrently, but others which had to be done sequentially. Figure 27–5 shows the complete diagram drawn by Diamond Alkali analysts, with a heavier line drawn through the critical path which would have delayed the product introduction and very likely reduced its total profitability.

It should be noted that this charting is *not* unduly complicated. The Diamond Alkali chart took two men only about two days. Basically what it requires is that all of the activities which will have to be performed anyway be identified ahead of time and their probable duration and sequence shown on one diagram. (Nothing more than addition and subtraction is used.) Working with such information should be part of the planning function, anyway. Then the chart can be extremely useful for guiding implementation and control.

Regular plans call for monthly charts

■ Some marketing managers have found flowcharts helpful for diagramming all of the interrelated tasks in their ongoing plans. Each week or month in an ongoing 12-month plan, for example, can be graphed horizontally. How long each activity should take and when it should be started and completed can be seen. If it is clearly impossible to accomplish some of the tasks in the time allotted, this fact will become clear during the flowcharting process and adjustments can be made. This might be necessary, for example, when several product managers had included heavy responsibilities for salesmen during the same month.

Basically, this kind of flowcharting is similar to the scheduling done by production planners, where wall-size graphic aids are often used. Without such aids, it is easy to neglect some tasks or to just wishfully presume that there will be enough time to accomplish each of the necessary tasks. By planning ahead, aided by a visual approach, one has a greater chance of avoiding conflicts which can wreck the implementation of the company's plans and program.

Strategic planning extends the marketing concept

GE has a better idea — the strategic business unit

■ General Electric helped to pioneer the marketing concept and now it appears to be pioneering what might be seen as a logical extension of the marketing concept—the strategic business unit. They have reorganized their company into 43 "strategic business units." The objective of shifting emphasis to strategic business units is to shift the company's resources behind product lines that already have strong market positions and fast growth or at least the potential for fast growth. Product lines which are only in the middle in terms of profitability should be "harvested"—i.e., they should

Figure 27–5
How Diamond Alkali diagrams the critical path for new-product introduction

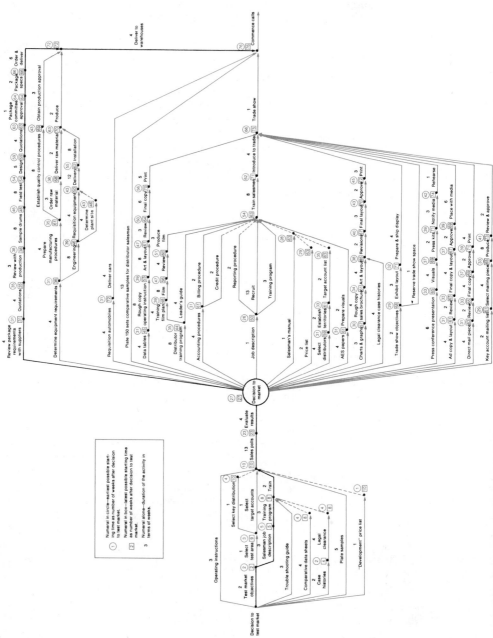

be allowed to generate cash for the businesses with more potential – while product lines with poor market position and low profits along with inadequate growth prospects are dropped or sold.

Perhaps the major differences between their previous approach to implementing the marketing concept and the current emphasis on strategic business planning is that managers are now rated in terms of their adherence to their strategic plans rather than short-term profits. Earlier, profits were emphasized, but the difference between long- and short-term profits was not always clearly realized. There was always a temptation for an eager manager to go for short-term results, while sacrificing long-term gains. Now the emphasis is on developing plans which, when accepted, are to be implemented aggressively. Under this concept, managers could be equally successful phasing out some product lines while others are moving ahead aggressively expanding sales in another market.

The point here is that each manager should be implementing a market-oriented plan which has been approved by management. The marketing concept is still important in this setup, but the importance of planning to do the job effectively has been superimposed to ensure that the company's resources are used effectively and that it accomplishes its own objectives also.[4]

Conclusion

◼ In this chapter, we have continued to emphasize the role of the marketing manager as an integrating force in company management. The marketing concept says that *all* the activities of a company should be directed toward satisfying target customers – at a profit. As we noted already, this may require eliminating the conflicting departmental "empires" often found within a company. We noted that General Electric, the pioneer of the marketing concept, has now placed greater emphasis on strategic planning in order to ensure effective implementation of the marketing concept.

Throughout the text we have emphasized the importance of marketing strategy planning. In this chapter, we have gone on to show that the marketing manager must develop a strategic plan for carrying out each strategy and then, in turn, coordinate a set of plans into a marketing program. Fortunately, if this planning has been effective, the allocation of budgets to particular functions should be relatively simple.

Evaluating alternative plans can make use of the total profit approach, the return on investment approach, and/or the expected value approach. Evaluation should not be limited to one year at a time, however, but should cover some reasonable time period, depending primarily upon the length of the product life cycle and the nature of competition in the firm's target markets. In some extremely competitive markets, a few months may be a reasonable planning cycle. In other markets, 5 to 20 years might be appropriate.

Finally, it is the marketing manager's job to coordinate the implementation of the whole marketing program. Two types of flowcharting techniques were discussed. Both may help him in this most difficult job of coordinating the activities within his firm so that they can better satisfy the firm's target customers.

questions and problems

1 Distinguish clearly between strategic plans and marketing programs.

2 Consider how the job of the marketing manager becomes more complex as he must develop and plan *several* strategies as part of his marketing program. Be sure to discuss how he might have to handle different strategies at different stages in the product life cycle. To make this more concrete, consider the job of a marketing manager for a sporting-goods manufacturer.

3 Explain the differences among the following approaches to evaluating alternative plans: total profit approach, return on investment approach, and expected value approach.

4 Briefly explain the task method of budgeting.

5 Discuss how a marketing manager could go about choosing among several possible marketing plans, given that he must because of limited resources. Do you feel that the job would be easier in the consumer goods or in the industrial goods areas? Why?

6 Explain why the budgeting procedure is typically such an agonizing procedure, usually consisting of extending past budgets, perhaps with small modifications for current plans. How would the budgeting procedure be changed if the marketing program planning procedure discussed in the chapter were implemented?

7 Explain how flowcharting might be helpful to a marketing manager in coordinating his implementation efforts. In particular, explain how flowcharts might be used to help him plan the implementation of his strategies on a week-by-week and month-by-month basis. Sketch what one such flowchart might look like.

8 The marketing concept seeks to satisfy customers, but does this mean that marketing management should seek to satisfy the customer in all respects if this entails a reduction in profit? What should guide the efforts of the marketing manager in this respect?

9 Distinguish between the operation of a strategic business unit and a firm which has only paid "lip service" to adopting the marketing concept.

notes

[1] John E. Smallwood, "The Product Life Cycle: A Key to Strategic Marketing Planning," *MSU Business Topics,* Winter 1973, pp. 29–35.

[2] J. Fred Weston, "ROI Planning and Control," *Business Horizons,* August 1972, pp. 35–42; Richard P. Hise and Robert H. Strawser, "Application of Capital Budgeting Techniques to Marketing Operations," *MSU Business Topics,* Summer 1970, pp. 69–76; and Louis V. Gerstner, "Can Strategic Planning Pay Off?" *Business Horizons,* December 1972, pp. 5–16.

[3] For further discussion on evaluating and selecting alternative plans see W. I. Little, "The Integrated Man-agement Approach to Marketing," *Journal of Marketing,* April 1967, pp. 32–36; Leon Winer, "A Profit-Oriented Decision System," *Journal of Marketing,* April 1966, pp. 38–44 (this article discusses discounting of cash flows for different lengths of time); see also S. M. Lee and R. E. Nicely, "Goal Programming for Marketing Decisions: A Case Study," *Journal of Marketing,* January 1974, pp. 24–32.

[4] "GE's New Strategy For Faster Growth," *Business Week,* July 8, 1972, pp. 52–58 and "Italy: A Big Overseas Turn-Around for GE," *Business Week,* September 23, 1972, p. 45.

28

Gathering information for marketing decision making

■ Successful planning of marketing strategies and programs obviously requires information – information about potential target markets and their likely responses to various marketing mixes, about competition and other uncontrollable factors.

It is the job of marketing research to help the marketing manager gather the information he needs to make wise decisions. This is not an easy job, because people and competitors are so unpredictable. It must be done, nevertheless. Without sound marketing information, the manager has to fly by the seat of his pants, and in our dynamic and highly competitive economy, this almost insures failure.

What is marketing research?

■ Marketing research is concerned with developing and analyzing the "facts" that help marketing managers do a better job of planning, executing, and controlling. Marketing research is much more than a bundle of techniques or a group of specialists in survey design or statistical techniques. Good marketing researchers must be both marketing- *and* management-oriented to assure that their research focuses on real problems on which action can be taken.

Research provides a bridge to consumers

■ Today, many marketing planners are isolated in company offices far from their potential customers. For this reason, they *must* rely on research to be sure they know what is going on. This point cannot be overemphasized because it is all too easy for management to lose touch with its markets. One of the critical tasks of the marketing researcher is to help management get the "facts" and understand them. The many potential markets in the United States *and* abroad are not necessarily like the markets lived in by the typical middle-class suburban managers.

Manager must know what re- searchers do

■ Marketing research details may come to be handled by staff or outside specialists, but the marketing manager must know how to plan and evaluate research projects. That is, he should be able to communicate with specialists in *their* language. He may only be a "consumer" of research, but he should be a knowledgeable consumer, perhaps regularly specifying what he wants to buy. For this reason, our treatment of marketing research will not focus on mechanics, but rather on how to plan and evaluate research. The marketing researcher must excel in these areas also, so in the following discussion we will take the marketing researcher's view, realizing that both of them should participate in the research process if the results are going to lead to action.

Researchers are improv- ing and inspiring more faith

■ Marketing research, as we know it today, began around 1900 and grew as more companies became interested in regional and then national markets. The development of sampling techniques in the 1930s, the use of the psychological interview, and other attitude and opinion measurement techniques have expanded the field markedly.

These and other refinements have increased the dependability of the findings. And this coupled with more decision-oriented researchers has prompted businessmen to put more money and faith in research. In some consumer goods companies, no major decisions are made without the support, and sometimes even the official approval, of the marketing research department. As a result, some marketing research directors rise to high levels in the organization. For example, at Pillsbury, this activity is headed by the Vice President of Growth and Technology.

Strategic planning framework can guide research

■ Marketing researchers often become involved with strategic as well as tactical planning. They also can be helpful in evaluating how strategies are working out – providing "feedback" and control which may lead to new plans. Thus, research is a continuing process. Some marketing researchers see themselves at the center of an information system which works to integrate all activities of the company.

With such a wide range of potential responsibilities, it is important that the marketing researcher see clearly what kinds of problems he is being asked to work on and what types of information are actually needed to solve the problems.

Deciding on the right problem level

■ The strategic planning framework introduced early in the text can be especially useful here—helping the researcher to see at what level the real problem lies. Do we really know enough about target markets? If so, do we know enough to work out all of the four P's? And so on down through tactical-level problems, such as how to motivate an older salesman or handle a price war in New York City or Tokyo.

The importance of understanding the nature of the problem and then trying to solve *that* problem can be seen more clearly in the following example of a manufacturer of a new easy-to-use baking mix. Top management had selected apartment dwellers, younger couples, and the too-busy-to-cook crowd as target markets—a logical market at first glance. Some modest research on the *size* of this market, *not* their interest in this product concept, indicated that if these consumers responded as expected, there were enough of them to create a profitable baking mix market. The company decided to cater to this market and developed a logical marketing mix.

During the first few months, sales results were disappointing. The manufacturer "guessed" that the product itself might be unacceptable, since the promotion seemed to be adequate. At this point, a consumer survey was undertaken—with surprising results. The product was apparently satisfactory, but the target consumers were just not interested—even simplified food preparation didn't particularly grab them. Instead, the best market turned out to be families who did their own cooking. They appreciated the convenience of the mix, especially when they needed a dish in a hurry.

In this case, the original strategy planning was done sloppily. The original choice of target markets was based on faulty executive guesswork. This led to an unsuitable strategy and wasted promotional expense. Preliminary research with a variety of consumers, about their needs and preferences, might have avoided this costly error. Both marketing research and management fumbled the ball by not studying the attitudes of the target market. Then, when sales results were poor, the company compounded the error by assuming that the product was at fault and overlooking consumers' real attitudes about the product. Fortunately, research finally uncovered the real problem, and the overall strategy was changed quickly.

The moral of this story is that our strategic planning framework can be useful for guiding marketing research efforts. If the marketing manager has the facts on his potential target markets, then he can focus his research efforts on required marketing mix ingredients, their sensitivity to change, and the effectiveness of various tactics. Without such a framework, marketing researchers can get sidetracked into working on the wrong problems.

Quick answers are needed

■ In our dynamic marketplace, marketing research often must try to provide answers to urgent questions—both strategic and tactical kinds. Sometimes answers are needed so urgently that quick-and-rough research work must be done. A little information may be better than total ignorance. Even though the most scientific approach is not feasible when time is short, researchers should attempt to use the best procedures possible. For this reason, we will begin our discussion of marketing research by using the scientific method to demonstrate that a logical approach to marketing problems is best. This scientific approach, combined with a strategic planning framework, can provide assured guidance in the typically chaotic and crisislike atmosphere of the business world.

The scientific method and marketing research

■ In seeking to relate the scientific method to marketing research, we are not trying to cloak marketing research with scientific respectability. Businessmen want to make the best decisions possible, and this cannot be done consistently other than on a logical basis.

The scientific method is such an approach. In marketing, this logical method forces the analyst to follow certain procedures that reduce the possibilities of slipshod work or reliance on intuition.

The scientific method consists, basically, of four stages:

1. Observation.
2. Formulation of hypotheses.
3. Prediction of the future.
4. Testing of the hypotheses.

With this method, we seek to develop *hypotheses* (such as "There is no significant difference between Brands A and B" or "There is no significant difference between response functions X and Y"), and then to test each hypothesis. The formulation of the hypothesis is extremely important. In fact, much exploratory research is aimed at getting information and suggesting testable hypotheses. But the research should always be decision-oriented, even if it is a question of whether to act or not.

Application of the scientific method helps the marketing manager develop and test the best hypotheses. It takes a commonsense but rigorous approach—formulation of hypotheses, testing, perhaps modifying, and testing again. The feedback principle is applied throughout the process.

The scientific approach to pain

■ To illustrate these stages in a simple nonmarketing case, consider a college student who develops a painful swollen ankle after a skiing accident. The ankle could be bruised, sprained, or broken. What should he do? If he goes to a doctor, he will probably find the doctor following the scientific method:

1. Observation: Pain seems to increase if foot is twisted, but pain is not unbearable.

2. Formulation of an hypothesis:	Since a sprain would be more painful than this, the ankle is broken.
3. Prediction of the future:	Pain and swelling will reduce, but bone may heal improperly if not set.
4. Testing the hypothesis:	X-ray the ankle; don't wait to see if hypothesis is correct in this case.

Let us now use the same framework to show how a businessman might use this method.

The scientific approach to offering shirt wrappers

■ A manufacturer of men's shirts had no major immediate problems, but wanted to develop new opportunities. The approach he took is shown below:

1. Observation:	Notices some competitors' sales increasing and many competitors shifting to a new plastic wrapping.
2. Formulation of hypotheses:	Assumes (a) that plastic wrapping is sole cause of competitors' sales increases and (b) that his products are similar.
3. Prediction of the future:	His sales ought to increase if he shifts to the new wrapping.
4. Testing the hypothesis:	Produce some shirts in new package and test them in the market.

The market test revealed that his prediction was correct — sales did increase. But what if they had not increased? In the answer to this question lies one important benefit of the scientific approach. Through careful control (making certain that the test was correctly designed and run) and evaluation of results, we should be able to isolate the reason why a given test failed and pinpoint where the hypotheses were in error.

In this case, either one of the hypotheses could have been wrong. Either increased sales by competitors were *not* caused by the new wrapping, or this manufacturer's products were *not* similar.

Assuming that the first hypothesis was wrong, further research might show that competitors' sales were up simply because their promotion had been more effective. Or, if the second hypothesis proved incorrect, it might be possible to identify ways the products differed and then to capitalize on these points, or modify the product.

Four-step approach to solving marketing problems

■ In marketing research, there is a four-step application of the scientific method: (1) definition of the problem, (2) situation analysis, (3) informal investigation, and (4) formal research project.

Observation, the first stage in the scientific method, is used during the first three marketing research steps. Once the problem is defined, *formulation of hypotheses* takes place, perhaps during the situation analysis or informal investigation. *Prediction of the future* occurs any time before a formal research project is planned. And *testing the hypotheses* is completed in the formal research project unless, as frequently happens, informal investigation solves the problem.

Actually, then, the scientific method is a vital part of marketing research. Table 28–1 may help us see the relationships. The precise meaning of these terms is explained in the following pages.

It should be emphasized again that this orderly procedure helps us keep clear what we are doing. Mastery of this approach will greatly improve your ability to plan marketing research projects and solve the right problems.

Definition of the problem

■ Defining the problem is the most important and often the most difficult job of the marketing analyst. It is slow work, requiring careful observation and sometimes taking up over half the time spent on a research project. But it is time well spent if the problem is precisely defined. The best research job on the wrong problem is wasted effort; it may even lead to more costly consequences, such as the introduction of a poor product or the use of an ineffective advertising approach.

Problems can occur at various levels but, basically, a problem arises when a firm is not able to reach one of its objectives. This may be a high level top-management objective of increasing sales for the company as a whole or in a particular geographic territory or for a particular product. Or, it might be as low level as finding a way to motivate one salesman to make more frequent sales calls on some less attractive customers.

Don't
confuse
problems
with
symptoms

■ Problem definition sounds simple, and therein lies the danger. Objectives are seldom stated clearly, if at all, and therefore, it is easy to fall into the trap of mistaking identification of symptoms for the definition of the problem. For example, suppose that the firm's continuing sales analysis shows that the company's sales are decreasing significantly in certain territories, while sales expenses remain constant, with a resulting decline in profits. Will it help to define the problem by asking the simple question: How can we stop the sales decline? Probably not. This would be the

Table 28-1
Relation of scientific method to marketing research

Scientific method stages	Used during the following marketing research steps
Observation	Definition of problem
	Situation analysis
	Informal investigation
	Formal research
Formulation of hypotheses	Situation analysis
	Informal investigation
	Formal research (Planning)
Prediction of the future (Action implications)	Situation analysis
	Informal investigation
	Formal research (Planning)
Testing hypotheses	Formal research (Unless management is satisfied with an earlier but more intuitive solution.)

equivalent of asking how to lower a patient's temperature instead of first trying to identify the cause of the fever.

We must discover *why* sales are declining (rather than increasing, which is the objective)—i.e., whether the cause is competitive activity, product deficiencies, inadequate support by company sales personnel, prices that are not competitive, inefficient advertising, or some other cause. If one or more of these factors can be isolated as the culprit, then the marketing executive is on the way to an effective solution. The basic overriding problem would be how to reach the objective of increasing sales. But the specific problem which he might focus on would be how to accomplish the objectives assigned to one or more of the four P areas. Perhaps advertising had been assigned the job of increasing awareness of the company's offerings in order to pave the way for the company's salesmen. If the advertising is ineffective, then the company's whole marketing plan may falter. The specific problem to be worked on in this case, then, might be how to improve the advertising or overall promotion effort.

The real problem may be very elusive. In the isolation of his office, the marketing manager may conceive of several likely problems he can investigate. He can start with the strategic planning framework, for example, and evaluate what he knows about the target market and the compatability of the marketing mix ingredients. If he has doubts about one or more of these factors, he can begin to focus on these likely problem areas. But without further investigation and evidence, he should not assume too quickly that he has defined the real problem. Instead, he should take his list of possible problems and then go on to the next step, trying to discover which is the fundamental cause of his trouble.

Situation analysis

■ When the marketing researcher feels that he has begun to focus on the problem, he can go on to this next step. He need not (and probably should not) commit himself completely to any particular problem as yet. Through this and the following steps, he should be prepared to revise or restate problems in the face of new facts. This reevaluation is continuous. Even after he has developed and tested an hypothesis by formal research, new factors can arise so that a new statement of the problem and a new hypothesis test may be necessary.

No talks with outsiders

■ In the situation analysis, the researcher first tries to size up the situation — but without talking to outsiders. He talks to informed executives within his own company, and studies and evaluates internal company records generated as part of the control function. He also searches libraries for all available published material.

This research is vital, since the analyst must be thoroughly familiar with the environment in which he must work. He analyzes information about his own company, its products, the industry, specific markets in which it is operating, dealers, its own promotion, and its competitors' activities. Libraries contain vast stores of information, but once the researcher has begun to narrow the scope of his problems, he can look for specific kinds of information.

Unless he knows what he is looking for, the researcher may be overwhelmed by the information available within his own company or in libraries. Let's take a closer look at the type of information we're talking about.

Secondary data sources can be valuable

■ The data we are concerned with here is called *secondary data.* This is information which is already published. *Primary data* is gathered specifically to solve the current problem. Gathering primary data is discussed later, but it must be emphasized that too often researchers rush out to gather primary data when there is already a plentiful supply of secondary information. And this data may be available immediately, at little or no cost!

One of the first places a researcher should look for secondary data, after looking at internal data, is a good library. Familiarity with the references in the library's card catalog and bibliographies enables the researcher to pursue secondary sources more knowledgeably. Frequently your local library has the answer you need to a question.

Government sources

The federal and state governments publish data on almost every conceivable subject. The federal government publishes a monthly guide to its current publications, but it is more practical to refer to federal government summary publications to obtain leads to more detailed documents.

Three useful summaries, available from the U.S. Department of Commerce for less than $10 a year and also found in most libraries, are the *Statistical Abstract of the United States*, the *County and City Data Book*, and the *Survey of Current Business*.

The most useful of these summaries, the *Statistical Abstract of the United States*, is similar to an almanac. It is issued each year and lists more than 1,000 summary tables from work being published by the federal government as well as other groups. References to world markets are included. Detailed footnotes can guide one to more specific detail on a topic. Each issue contains a "Bibliography of Sources and Statistics," about 40 pages in length, that lists all *Abstract* sources, classified by type of subject.

Every student should be familiar with the *Abstract* because it is probably the best starting point for locating statistical data. Marketing men must be experts on sources of information, and the time to start developing this expertise is *now*.

The *County and City Data Book*, published about once every three years, gives more local, geographical detail than the *Abstract*. It presents a selection of statistics for all counties and for cities of more than 25,000.

For more current data on a wide variety of subjects, monthly and quarterly statistics are published, without geographical detail, in the *Survey of Current Business*. Each issue of this monthly periodical also features articles on economic trends and other business subjects.

The U.S. Department of Commerce serves as a distribution agency for statistics compiled by all other federal departments. Commerce Department branch and field offices, located in major cities throughout the United States, are fertile sources of data. Staff members provide assistance and suggestions for locating specific data.

Some city and state governments have similar agencies that will provide leads for local data. University bureaus of business research may also prove helpful.

Private sources

Many private research organizations, advertising agencies, newspapers, and magazines regularly compile and publish data. A good business library is valuable here for sources such as *Sales Management: The Marketing Magazine, Industrial Marketing, Advertising Age*, and the publications of the National Industrial Conference Board. Some information is available inexpensively as a customer service to clients of advertising agencies or buyers of advertising space or time. For example, J. Walter Thompson Co., an advertising agency, and the *Chicago Tribune* maintain continuing panels of housewives for consumer research purposes. These panels enable researchers to spot trends, an extension of market awareness not easily obtained in one-time surveys.

Research by subscription

There are a number of research firms whose exclusive business is supplying, by subscription, research data that will aid the marketing manager in situation analysis. Two of the better-known organizations specializing in continuing research are the Market Research Corporation of America (MRCA) and A. C. Nielsen Co. MRCA makes available information on product movements through certain grocery chains, using data from a consumer panel of over 7,500 families located throughout the United States. These families record in diaries all food and drug items, plus other selected items, purchased each week. They list not only each item but its price and the store where it was purchased. This data is used by many large food and drug manufacturers to measure the rate of consumption of their products at the consumer level.

Similar reports are provided by A. C. Nielsen, which audits 2,350 retail food stores and drugstores to measure movement at the retail level. These two services ought to provide roughly the same measure of movement of products at the consumer level. Nielsen, however, provides additional information about competitors' use of retail displays, 2 for 1 sales, and other activities. For this reason, some large companies subscribe to both services. They often find out more about the activity and sales of their smaller competitors than some of these competitors know about themselves. Nielsen now offers similar services in other countries, including Canada, Mexico, Japan, and most Western European countries.

Trade associations can also be a good source of information about a particular industry. They not only compile data from and for their members but also publish magazines that focus on the problems and important topics in the industry. Some of these magazines will be found in good business libraries.

Problem solving during the situation analysis

■ If the problem is clear-cut, it can sometimes be solved at this point without additional expense. Perhaps someone else already has done a study that answers almost exactly the same question.

The fact that further research *may* be reduced or eliminated is important. Too often researchers rush out a questionnaire to 100 or even several thousand persons or firms. This gives the impression that the analyst is "really doing his job." An effective situation analysis, unfortunately, usually is less impressive. If a supervisor asks the analyst what he is doing, about all he can say is, "I'm sizing up the situation" or "I'm studying the problem."

The fact of the matter is that the situation analyst is really trying to determine the exact nature of the situation and the problem. The man who rushes out all the questionnaires may be doing this too— although this fact may surprise him! The point is that when the results of his questionnaire come in, he may finally see the problem, but he still won't have the answer. He will still have to proceed to the next step in analysis, just the same as the more "scientific" researcher.

Informal investigation

■ During the informal investigation, the analyst is still attempting to define his problem and formulate hypotheses. But now the idea is to get outside the company and the library, and to talk to informed people. By informed people, we mean intelligent and efficient retailers, wholesalers, customers, and other knowledgeable people in the industry. No formal questionnaire is developed, as the analyst is not yet *testing* hypotheses, except intuitively.

When considering the development of machine tool products, for example, it would make sense to talk to a few machine operators, plant superintendents in more efficient factories, design engineers at independent research organizations or universities, and perhaps a few good industrial distributors who have close contact with potential customers.

Fast, informative, inexpensive

■ While these talks would be informal, they should help the analyst pinpoint his problem and hypotheses. By this time, he should have the problem area narrowed down. This is important, because asking informed people to discuss *general* problems will not be productive. Only specific questions will elicit specific answers.

The virtues of the informal investigation are that it takes little time and can be very informative. Moreover, it is inexpensive compared with a large-scale survey.

On the basis of the information gathered in a situation analysis and informal investigation, the analyst should now be formulating some specific hypotheses. Or he may be able to refine his hypotheses at this point, developing an answer to his problem without further research. This is especially likely in the industrial goods area, where the number of customers is limited and buying behavior is fairly predictable. Here, the views of a few well-informed people may be representative of the industry.

If management has to make a decision quickly—if it cannot wait for a formal test—then well-considered hypotheses may have to serve as the basis for an intuitive solution. Occasionally, speed is more important than precision. In such cases, care in the preliminary steps may bear fruit far beyond the "extra" time and effort invested.

Planning the formal research project

■ If the analyst has failed to reach a solution to his problem by this time, his next step is to develop a formal research project to gather primary data. There are three basic methods that he can use: (1) the observation method, (2) the survey method, or (3) the experimental method.

Each method has its appropriate uses, and unless the problem is complex, only one method would be used in a single project. It is the analyst's responsibility to choose which method is best, according to problem characteristics as well as the time, funds, facilities, and personnel available to him.

The *observation method*, recognizing the possible pitfalls in direct questioning, avoids face-to-face interviews. Sometimes, however, asking questions cannot be sidestepped. Then, the *survey method* may be helpful. Telephone, mail, or personal interviews can be used for surveys. The *experimental method* may use either or both of the preceding methods. Its distinguishing characteristic is a more rigorous procedure, which usually includes establishing control groups and applying advanced statistical techniques.

Managers must be knowledgeable about research design to effectively evaluate it

■ The mechanics of the design of a research project are beyond the scope of this text but they are extremely important. Marketing managers and top managers ought to be familiar with some of the details of the research design so that they will be in a better position to evaluate the *quality* of the research which they may have to use to make important decisions.

Some researchers or survey groups may imply a great deal about the reliability of their data. But they may be using samples which are not very representative and try to pass off the information as reliable. The knowledgeable manager would not be persuaded by such sloppy work. He would understand that matters such as the research design and the size and representativeness of any samples used are technical topics which have relevance for the quality of the results.

Execution and interpretation of the research project

■ How to organize and conduct formal research projects is also beyond the scope of this text. This involves questionnaire and research design, training of field staff, tabulation, interpretation, and presentation of results, as well as the follow-through to make sure that results are utilized effectively. Such matters are explained in most *marketing research* texts and are specialized but highly important activities.[1]

Marketing manager and researcher should work in concert

■ The interpretation step is especially important for marketing management. While managers may not be research specialists, they have to evaluate the results of such research. The interpretation and presentation of the final results are a clue to the quality of the research and its planning.

If a report does not have action implications, for example, it may have little value to management and may suggest poor planning by the researcher.

If the research method and the reliability of the data are not presented, the marketing manager must use even greater judgment in evaluating the data. In fact, if the researcher does not explain his methods and then suggest specific action, he should not be surprised if the marketing manager chooses to ignore his work.

The desirability of close working relationships between the marketing manager and the marketing researcher should be obvious. Both should put all their efforts into making the best decisions.[2]

Real problem solving may require an integrated approach

■ Marketing analysts frequently must combine several steps to do an effective research job. These steps can be illustrated by an example of a company interested in expanding its market for interior decorating products.

The company wanted to increase its sales, but it did not know how many interior decorators there were in their market, or how much money consumers spent on the company's product type (*definition of the problem*). A review of U.S. *Census of Business* data indicated that there were approximately 1,300 interior decorators. According to their own sales records (*situation analysis*), this would not leave much room for expansion of sales volume with their present line. Management decided, tentatively, to branch out into other lines (*hypothesis* that business would improve in another market.)

Before taking off on this tangent, the company decided to do additional research in their present market area. They interviewed the company's salesmen, checked the circulation data of an interior decorators' magazine (more *situation analysis*), talked with informed credit people (*informal investigation*), and made a limited mail survey to check on the size of the market (a *formal research project* to test an hypothesis that there were more potential customers).

This research revealed that there were actually 9,700 interior decorators who spent some $75 million on the company's type of product alone. For some reason, probably their small size, the decorators had not all been included in the published census data. It was clear at this point that the company's biggest and best market was the one which they were already selling.

In this case, no research at all, or a too sketchy situation analysis would have led to incorrect results. But further analysis, along with an informal investigation and a limited survey, obtained results that proved very satisfactory.[3] This type of research is within the reach of even small firms, and the student should now be able to understand and participate in such an effort.

Cost and organization of marketing research

■ Relatively little, perhaps too little, is spent on the typical marketing research department. Often the research department's budget is about 0.2 percent of sales or $100,000 for a company with a $50 million annual sales volume.[4] This is in contrast to research and development budgets that frequently run to 5 or 10 percent of sales. Unfortunately, this situation sometimes leads to the development of products with little or no market potential.

Shortcuts cut cost, add risk

■ Even on modest budgets, however, good research work can be done.[5] When a problem is carefully defined, formal research projects may *not* be necessary. This is especially true in industrial marketing research because of the relatively small number of industrial customers. But taking shortcuts increases the risk.

More dependable research can become expensive. A large-scale survey could easily cost from $10,000 to $100,000, and the continuing research available from companies such as A. C. Nielsen or MRCA can cost a company from $25,000 to $100,000 or more a year. But companies that are willing or able to pay the cost of *marketing* research may learn more about their competitors and their market than the competitors know themselves.

Who does the work?

■ Most larger companies have a separate commercial or marketing research department to plan and conduct research projects. Even these departments, however, frequently use outside specialists, such as interviewing or tabulating services, to handle particular assignments. This points up, again, the importance of good research planning because when part of the research job is sent out, it is imperative that it be fully described. Further, specialized marketing consultants and marketing research organizations may be called in on more difficult problems or in "frontier" research areas.

Few companies with sales of less than $2.5 million have separate market research departments, relying instead on sales personnel or top executives for what research they do conduct.[6]

How much research should be done?

No firm can afford to do without marketing research

■ Most companies do some marketing research even if it is not called by that name. The majority of marketing executives would agree with the manager of marketing research for Dow Chemical Co. who states:

> I feel that it is impossible to run a company today without market research, whether it is done by the president, the sales manager, or a separate group set up specifically to perform the function. Few companies are small enough to afford the luxury of having their market research done by the president. No company can afford not to do market research at all.[7]

What is the value of information?

■ The high cost of good research must be balanced against its probable value to management. You never get all the information you would like to have. Very sophisticated surveys or experiments may be "too good" or "too expensive" or "too late" if all that is needed is a rough sampling of dealer attitudes toward a new pricing plan by *tomorrow*. Further, no matter how good the research effort was, the findings are always out of date in that past behavior was studied. It's the decision maker's job to evaluate beforehand whether the findings will still be relevant.

Marketing managers must take risks because of lack of complete information. That is part of their job and it always will be. They might like more data, but they must weigh the cost of getting it against its likely value. If the risk is not too great, then the cost of getting more or better information may be greater than the potential loss from a poor decision. A decision to expand into a new territory with the present marketing mix, for example, might be made with greater certainty of success after a $5,000 survey. But simply sending a salesman into the territory for a few weeks or a month to try to sell the potential customers would cost less than $5,000, and if he is successful, then the answer is in *and* so are some sales.

Faced with a continuous flow of risky decisions, the marketing manager should seek help from research only for problems where he feels the risk can be reduced substantially at reasonable cost.[8]

Some firms are building marketing information systems

■ In some companies, marketing researchers enjoy a high status and are deeply involved in major marketing decisions. In other companies, they have tended to be relegated (or relegated themselves) to data collectors. Sometimes they are involved in the analysis of the company's sales and sales call reports, or they may conduct special surveys to answer pressing problems. But they have not managed to sell the idea that good *information* (not just data) will improve decision making. As a result, marketing managers may make decisions based almost totally on their own judgment and very little hard information. And this is often the case even though data is or could be available.

Some companies are setting up marketing information systems (MIS) in an attempt to improve the quality and quantity of decision-related information which is available to their managers. Sometimes this means expanding the role assigned to the marketing research departments, turning them into marketing *information* centers. In other companies, this *information* function may be separated into a new department because management wants to make sure that it does not get buried in the ongoing activities of the marketing research department.

A *marketing information system* has been defined as follows: "A structured, interacting complex of persons, machines and procedures designed to generate an orderly flow of pertinent information collected from both intra- and extra-firm sources for use as the bases for decision-making in specific responsibility areas of marketing management."[9]

The need for a marketing information system (MIS) grows out of the recognition that most firms can or could generate more market-related data than they can possibly digest and turn into useful information. Computers can now print out over 1,000 lines per minute—much faster than any human can read. Some way must be found to convert raw data into information. Fortunately, one can build up to a MIS in stages. The sales and cost analysis techniques discussed in the next chapter are illustrations of rela-

Figure 28–1

A diagram of a marketing information system showing various inputs to a
computer and outputs to managers

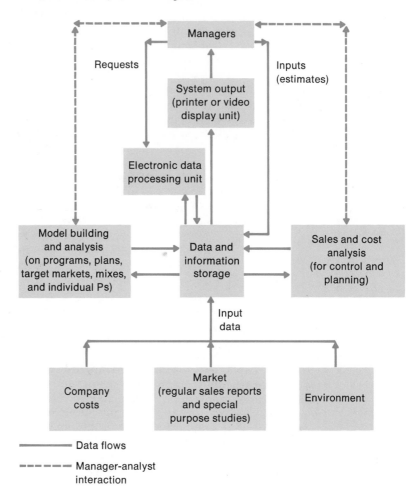

tively easy kinds of analysis that can be done. Going further, careful
analysis of this data and perhaps specially arranged experiments
can help the managers develop greater insights into the shape of
their various response functions, and this in turn will improve
subsequent planning.

Once marketing managers see how a functioning MIS can help
their decision making, they get almost greedy for more information.
They see that they can improve all aspects of their planning—
blending individual Ps, combining four Ps into mixes, and developing and selecting plans. Further, they can moniter the execution of ongoing plans, comparing results against plans and making
necessary changes more quickly. Figure 28–1 shows all the inter-

acting parts in a MIS, showing that it really is an information *system* intended to help managers make better decisions, not just to collect and massage data.

Encouraging the development of information systems is the growing realization that more sophisticated analysis of marketing data can yield good returns. And if one is really sure about the shape of his response functions, he may be able to take "daring" action. After a series of experiments and careful data analysis, for example, Anheuser-Busch felt that they understood the relation between sales and their advertising budgets and cut their advertising budget from \$14.8 million down to \$10 million a year. This is something that management probably would not have had the nerve to do without confidence in their knowledge of their response functions. While reducing advertising, sales continued to grow and their cost of advertising per barrel dropped in half. Obviously this had a good effect on profits.[10]

We probably will see continuing development and refinement of marketing information systems as researchers in this area become more experienced and computer costs continue to decline. The major obstacle may be the unwillingness of marketing managers to ask for more useful information and then to use it in their decision making. More will be said about this matter in the next chapter. There, we will discuss sales and cost analysis techniques which can be adopted more readily than a complete marketing information system, and yet even these techniques have not been fully utilized in most companies. As we have noted in various places in the text, there is still lots of room in marketing for able students who are willing to apply more sophisticated management techniques to solving real marketing problems.

Conclusion

■ In this chapter, we have shown that marketing research is not a mysterious cult practiced by statisticians. In the best sense, it is a management tool that helps the manager make better decisions based not on feel and intuition, but useful information. The manager should understand research procedures, and the researcher should understand management's problems of planning, executing and controlling marketing strategies. Without such a close working relationship, the output of a marketing research department may be sterile, and the department may be relegated to a mere collector of data.

Marketing research should try to apply the scientific method to the solution of marketing problems. Some organized approach is desirable because very often a researcher does not have the time or money to complete a full research project and if the early stages of his research effort have been effectively done, he may be able to "jump" to a solution early in the process. A scientific approach to solving marketing problems involves four steps: definition of the problem, a situation analysis, an informal investigation, and, if necessary, a formal research project.

Definition of the problem is obviously the most crucial step, because even good research on the wrong problem would be of no use. Then, a good situation analysis, using secondary data, may enable the researcher to solve the problem without going on to further steps in the analysis.

A good informal investigation, like a good situation analysis, may enable a researcher to solve his problem. This step requires informal interviewing of knowledgeable people. This progressive moving up on the problem should be stressed because there is more to marketing research than surveys. Yet surveys often are seen as the only activity of marketing research by outsiders. Surveys provide helpful information when they are needed, but there are many occasions when other methods provide better information at the same or lower cost.

As part of a formal research design, surveys might be needed, or the observation or experimental methods may be needed. Great care must be taken in research design and execution because these are technical subjects and it is very easy to make errors which will render the results useless.

The strategic planning framework which we have been using throughout the text can be of great aid in helping to identify the real problem. By focusing on the real problem, the researcher may be able to move quickly to a useful solution without the cost and pitfalls of a formal research project. If he has more time and adequate budget, he may be able to enjoy the luxury of more detailed and more sophisticated analysis. Some firms have even developed marketing information systems which enable them to make better estimates of the shape of their response functions and, therefore, better decisions. And others are making more effective use of sales and cost analysis techniques, which are discussed more fully in the next chapter.

questions and problems

1 Marketing research entails expense, sometimes a considerable expense. Why does the text recommend the use of marketing research even though a highly experienced marketing executive is available?

2 Explain the steps in the general scientific method and then show how the steps in marketing research are similar.

3 How is the situation analysis any different from the informal investigation? Could both these steps be done at the same time in order to obtain answers sooner? Is this wise?

4 Explain how you might use each of the research methods (observation, survey, and experimental) to forecast market reaction to a new kind of margarine which is to receive no promotion other than what the retailer will give it. Further, it should be assumed that the new margarine's name will not be associated with other known products. The product will be offered at competitive prices.

5 If a firm were interested in determining the distribution of income in the state of Ohio, how could it proceed? Be specific.

6 If a firm were interested in the sand and clay production in Georgia, how could it proceed? Be specific.

7 Go to the library and find (in some government publication) three marketing-oriented "facts" which you did not know existed or were available. Record on one page and show sources.

8 Discuss the concept that some information may be too expensive to obtain, in relation to its value. Illustrate.

9 Discuss the concept of a marketing information system and how its output would differ from the output of the typical marketing research department.

10 Discuss what will be needed before marketing information systems become common. Also, discuss the problem facing the marketer in a small firm which is not likely to be able to afford the development of a marketing information system.

notes

[1] Harper W. Boyd, Jr., and Ralph Westfall, *Marketing Research: Text and Cases,* 3rd ed. (Homewood, Ill.: Richard D. Irwin, Inc., 1972).

[2] J. G. Keane, "Some Observations on Marketing Research in Top Management Decision Making," *Journal of Marketing,* October 1969, pp. 10–15.

[3] Arthur P. Felton, "Conditions of Marketing Leadership," *Harvard Business Review,* March–April 1956, pp. 117–27.

[4] "Scouting the Trail for Marketers," *Business Week,* April 18, 1964, pp. 90–116.

[5] Donald F. Mulvihill, "Marketing Research for the Small Company," *Journal of Marketing,* October 1951, pp. 179–82.

[6] *The Role and Organization of Marketing Research,* (Experiences in Marketing Management, No. 20 [New York: National Industrial Conference Board, 1969]), 65 pp.

[7] William A. Marsteller, "Can You Afford a Market Research Department?" *Industrial Marketing,* March 1951, pp. 36–37.

[8] For more discussion, see P. E. Green and D. S. Tull, *Research for Marketing Decisions* 2d ed. (Englewood Cliffs, N.J.: Prentice-Hall, Inc., 1970), chap. 1).

[9] Richard H. Brien and James E. Stafford, "Marketing Information Systems: A New Dimension For Marketing Research," *Journal of Marketing,* July 1968, p. 21.

[10] David B. Montgomery, *Marketing Information and Decision Systems: Coming Of Age In The '70's* (Cambridge, Mass.: Marketing Science Institute, August 1973, pp. 29–30.); see also David B. Montgomery, "The Outlook for MIS," *Journal of Advertising Research,* June 1973, pp. 5–11; and L. D. Gibson, C. S. Mayer, C. E. Nugent, and T. E. Vollmann, "An Evolutionary Approach to Marketing Information Systems," *Journal of Marketing,* April 1973, pp. 2–6.

29

Controlling marketing programs

■ The basic management process consists of planning, execution, and control. Our primary emphasis thus far has been on planning.

Now, however, we must discuss *control* – the feedback process that helps the manager learn (1) how ongoing plans are working and (2) how to plan for the future.

A good manager wants to know: which products' sales are highest; why; whether the products are profitable; what is selling where; and how much the marketing process is costing. Unfortunately, the traditional accounting reports prepared for financial and production executives are typically of little help to the marketing manager. They are simply much too general. A particular company might be showing a profit, for example, while 80 percent of its business might be coming from only 20 percent of its products (or customers). The other 80 percent might actually be unprofitable, but without special analyses the managers would not know this. This 80/20 relationship, incidentally, is fairly common and is often referred to as the 80/20 rule.

Fortunately, it is possible for the marketing manager to obtain more detailed analysis of how his plans are progressing. This chapter discusses some of the kinds of information which can be available to the marketing manager, but also stresses that they will not be available unless the marketing manager asks for and helps develop the data he needs.

This is an important chapter, and the techniques are not unduly complicated – basically requiring only arithmetic and perhaps a computer if a large volume of adding and subtracting is required.[1]

Sales analysis shows what is going on

■ As indicated in Chapter 11, when we discussed sales analysis and sales forecasting, a detailed breakdown of a company's sales records can be very illuminating, especially the first time it is done. Detailed data can quickly update marketing executives who have been out of touch with what is happening in the field. In addition, routine sales analyses prepared each week, month, or year may show trends. These analyses also permit members of management to check their hypotheses, assumptions, and "gut feelings" about how, for example, various target markets respond to certain products, package sizes, and stores.[2]

Too much data can drown a manager

■ While some sales data is better than none or getting data too late for action, extremely detailed sales breakdowns can easily "drown" a manager in reports. Computers can now print out at over one thousand lines per minute, which is far faster than any manager can read. To avoid having to cope with mountains of data, much of which may be irrelevant, most managers move on to a slightly more sophisticated type of analysis, called *performance analysis*.

Performance analysis looks for differences

■ Performance analysis seeks exceptions or variations from planned performance. In simple sales analysis, the figures are merely listed, with no attempt to measure them against standards. In performance analysis, however, comparisons are made. One territory might be compared against another, against the same territory's performance last year, or against the expected performance based on a sales forecast in the marketing plan.

The purpose of performance analysis is to improve operations. The salesman, territory, or other factors showing poor performance can be identified and singled out for detailed analysis and remedial action. Or, especially outstanding performances can be analyzed to see whether the successes can be explained and made the general rule.

Performance analysis need not be limited to sales. Other data can be analyzed and compared, too. This data might include miles traveled, number of calls made, number of orders, or the cost of various tasks.

A performance analysis can be quite revealing of differences, as is evident in the following example.

Straight performance analysis — an illustration

■ A manufacturer of industrial products sold to wholesalers through five salesmen, each serving a separate territory. Total net sales for the year amounted to $1,193,000. Compensation and expenses of salesmen came to $99,000. This yielded a direct-selling expense ratio of 8.3 percent — that is, $99,000 divided by $1,193,000, times 100.

Table 29–1
Comparative performance of salesmen

Sales area	Total calls	Total orders	Sale–call ratio	Sales by salesman	Average salesman order	Total customers
A	1,900	1,140	60.0%	$ 456,000	$400	195
B	1,500	1,000	66.7	360,000	360	160
C	1,400	700	50.0	280,000	400	140
D	1,030	279	27.1	66,000	239	60
E	820	165	20.1	31,000	187	50
	6,650	3,284	49.3%	$1,193,000	$317	605

Source: Charles H. Sevin, "Analyzing Your Cost of Marketing," *Management Aids for Small Manufacturers (Washington, D.C.: Small Business Administration, June 1957), p. 2.*

This information, drawn from a profit and loss statement, was interesting but did not explain what was actually taking place from one territory to another. To obtain a clearer picture, the analyst segregated and compared the sales results with other data from each territory (see Tables 29–1 and 29–2).

The salesmen in sales areas D and E obviously were not doing well. Sales were low, and marketing costs were high. Perhaps salesmen with more "push" could have done a better job, but the number of customers suggests that the potential might be low. Perhaps the whole plan needs revision.

The figures themselves, of course do not provide the answers — but they do reveal the areas that need remedial action. This is the main value of performance analysis. It is up to management to provide the remedy — either to revise tactics or to change the strategic plan.

Performance indices simplify human analysis

■ With a straight performance analysis report, the marketing manager can personally evaluate the variations among salesmen in an effort to explain the "why." This is time-consuming, however, and sometimes the truth is that "poor" performances really are not so bad as the bare figures seem to indicate. There may be adverse uncontrollable factors in a particular territory which automatically lower the sales potential. Or, it may be found that a territory did not have good potential to begin with.

A better check on the effectiveness of performance is obtained using performance indices. With this approach, the marketing manager compares what "ought to have happened" with what did happen.

Table 29–2
Comparative cost of salesmen

Sales area	Annual compensation	Expense payments	Total salesman cost	Sales produced	Cost–sales ratio
A	$11,400	$ 5,600	$17,000	$ 456,000	3.7%
B	10,800	7,200	18,000	360,000	5.0
C	10,200	5,800	16,000	280,000	5.7
D	9,600	12,400	22,000	66,000	33.3
E	10,000	16,000	26,000	31,000	83.8
	$52,000	$47,000	$99,000	$1,193,000	8.3%

Source: Charles H. Sevin, "Analyzing Your Cost of Marketing," *Management Aids for Small Manufacturers* (Washington, D.C.: Small Business Administration, June 1957), p. 2.

What is a performance index?

■ When standards have been developed—that is, quantitative measures of what "ought to happen"—it is then a relatively simple matter to develop a *performance index*. This is merely a number, such as a baseball batting average, which shows the relation of one value to another.

Baseball batting averages are computed by dividing the actual number of hits by the number of times at bat (the possible number of times the batter could have had a hit). A sales performance index is computed by dividing actual sales by expected sales for an area (or salesman, product, etc.) and then multiplying this figure by 100 to eliminate decimal points. If a salesman is "batting" 82 percent, the index is 82.

A simple example shows where the problem is

The development of a performance index is illustrated in the following problem, which assumes that population provides an adequate measure of sales potential.

In Table 29-3, the population of the United States is broken down by regions as a percentage of the total population. The regions in this case are the Eastern, Southern, Midwestern, Mountain, and Western.

This firm already has achieved $1 million in sales and now wants to evaluate performance in each region. The actual sales of $1 million, broken down in proportion to the population in the five regions, are shown in column 2. This is how sales should have been distributed if population were a good measure of future performance. The third column in Table 29-3 shows the actual sales for the year for each region. The fourth column shows measures of performance (performance indices), which are column 3 divided by column 2, multiplied by 100.

Note that population in the Eastern region was 25 percent of

Table 29-3
Development of a measure of sales performance (by regions)

Regions	Popula-tion as percent of U.S. (Col. 1)	Expected distribution of sales based on population (Col. 2)	Actual sales (Col. 3)	Per-formance index (Col. 4)
Eastern	25	$ 250,000	$ 150,000	60
Southern	20	200,000	250,000	125
Midwestern	25	250,000	300,000	120
Mountain	10	100,000	100,000	100
Western	20	200,000	200,000	100
Total	100	$1,000,000	$1,000,000	

the population, and expected sales (based on population) were $250,000. Actual sales, however, were only $150,000. This means that the Eastern region's performance index was only 60—actual sales were much lower than would be expected on the basis of population.

If population is a sound basis for measuring expected sales (an important *if*), the explanation for poor sales performance will have to be traced further. Perhaps salesmen in the Eastern region are not doing as well as they should. Perhaps promotion there is not as effective as elsewhere. Or, competitive products may have entered the market in this region.

Whatever the cause, it should be understood that performance analysis does not solve problems. It pinpoints problems—and it does this well.

A series of performance analyses may find the real problem

■ Performance analysis enables a marketing manager to probe and discover whether the firm's marketing activities are working properly and, if not, to correct the problems. But this may require a series of performance analyses as shown in the following example.

To get an impression of the passage of time, follow this example carefully, one table at a time. Try to anticipate the marketing manager's decision.

The case of Stereo, Inc.

■ Stereo's sales manager found that sales for the Pacific Coast region were $130,000 below the quota of $14,500,000 (that is, actual sales were $14,370,000) for the January–June 1970 period. The quota was based on forecasted sales of the various types of

Table 29-4
Sales performance—Pacific Coast region, January–June 1970
(in thousands of dollars)

District	Quota	Actual	Plus or minus	Performance to quota
Los Angeles	$ 4,675	$ 4,765	Plus $ 90	102%
San Francisco	3,625	3,675	Plus 50	101
Portland	3,000	2,800	Minus 200	93
Seattle	3,200	3,130	Minus 70	98
	$14,500	$14,370	Minus $130	99%

stereophonic sound equipment which the company manufactures. Specifically, the quota was based on forecasts for each product type in each store in each salesman's territory.

The sales manager felt this discrepancy was not too large (1.52 percent) and was inclined to forget the matter, especially since forecasts usually err to some extent. He thought about sending a letter, however, to all salesmen and district supervisors in the region—a letter aimed at stimulating sales effort.

The overall story of what was happening to Stereo's sales on the Pacific Coast is shown in Table 29-4. What do you think the manager should do?

Portland district had the poorest performance, but it wasn't too bad. Before writing a "let's get with it, fellas" letter to Portland, and then relaxing, the sales manager decided to analyze the performance of the four salesmen in the Portland district. A breakdown of the Portland figures by salesmen is shown in Table 29-5. What conclusion or action is suggested now?

Since Smith previously had been the top salesman, the sales manager wondered if Smith were having trouble with some of his larger accounts. Before making a drastic move, he obtained an analysis of Smith's sales to five large accounts (see Table 29-6). What action could the sales manager take now? Should Smith be fired?

Smith's sales in all the large stores were down significantly, although his sales in many small stores were holding up well. It would seem that Smith's problem was general. Perhaps he was simply not working. One other aspect which the sales manager decided to investigate was Smith's sales of the four major products. The data in Table 29-7 was obtained. What action is indicated now?

Smith was having real trouble with portable phonographs. Was the problem Smith or the phonographs?

Further analysis by product for the whole region indicated that everyone on the Pacific Coast was having trouble with portable

Table 29–5
Sales performance—Portland district, January–June 1970
(in thousands of dollars)

Salesmen	Quota	Actual	Plus or minus	Perform-ance to quota
Johnson	$ 750	$ 780	Plus $ 30	104%
Smith	800	550	Minus 250	69
Jones	790	840	Plus 50	106
Carson	660	630	Minus 30	95
	$3,000	$2,800	Minus $200	93%

phonographs because a regional competitor was cutting prices. But higher sales on other products had obscured this fact. Since phonograph sales had been doing all right nationally, this problem was only now coming to light. Clearly, this is *the* major problem.

Since overall company sales were going fairly well, many sales executives would not have bothered with this analysis. They might or might not have traced the problem to Smith. But without detailed sales records and performance analysis, the natural human reaction of a Smith would be to blame business conditions or aggressive competition or to seek some other handy excuse.

Stay home and use the computer

This case shows that aggregate figures can be deceiving. Marketing managers should not jump on the first plane or reach for the telephone until they have all the facts. Even worse than rushing to the scene would be a rash judgment based on inadequate information. Some students have wanted to fire Smith after the store-by-store data (Table 29–6) was given to them.

The home office should have the records and facilities to isolate problem areas, then rely on the field staff for explanations and assistance in locating the precise problem. Continuing detailed analysis usually gives us better insights into problems, as this case shows. With electronic data processing equipment, this can be done routinely and in great detail, *provided marketing management requests it.*

The "iceberg" principle

■ One of the most interesting conclusions to be drawn out of the Stereo illustration is the iceberg principle.[3] Icebergs, as you probably know, show only about 10 percent of their mass above water level, with the other 90 percent below water level—and not directly below, either. The submerged portion almost seems to be searching out ships that come too near.

The same is true of much business and marketing data. Since sales volume may be large and overall company activities varied,

Table 29-6
Sales performance—selected stores of Mr. Smith in Portland district,
January–June 1970 (in thousands of dollars)

Stores	Quota	Actual	Plus or minus	Performance to quota
1	$140	$ 65	Minus $ 75	46%
2	110	70	Minus 40	69
3	105	60	Minus 45	57
4	130	65	Minus 65	50
5	205	150	Minus 55	73
Others	110	140	Plus 30	127
	$800	$550	Minus $250	69%

difficulties or problems in one area may be submerged below the
surface. All may appear to be calm and peaceful, yet a more careful
analysis may reveal jagged edges which can severely damage or
even "sink" the business. The 90:10 ratio or the 80:20 rule mentioned earlier must not be ignored. Averaging and summarizing
data can be helpful to the business executive, but he had better be
wary that his summaries do not hide more than they reveal.

Marketing-cost analysis

■ So far we have emphasized sales analysis. But sales cost money.
And costs can and should be analyzed and controlled.

Detailed cost analysis has been highly useful in the factory, but
much less has been done with marketing cost accounting.[4] Many
accountants, unfortunately, have shown little interest in the marketing process. Many think of salesmen as swingers who wine-and-
dine the customers, play golf all afternoon, and occasionally pick
up orders. In this situation, they feel it is impossible to tie the
wide-ranging costs of selling to particular products or customers.
Many accountants feel, too, that advertising is almost a complete
waste of money—that there is no way of relating it to particular
sales. They wind up treating it as a general overhead cost, then
forget about it.

Marketing costs have a purpose

■ Careful analysis of most marketing expenditures, however,
shows that the money is spent to accomplish a specific purpose—
either to prepare or promote a *particular product* or to serve
particular customers. It is reasonable, then, to seek ways to allocate costs to specific market segments, or customers, or to specific
products. In some situations it is practical to allocate costs directly
to the various market segments being served, especially when the

Table 29-7
Sales performance—Mr. Smith in Portland district,
January–June, 1970 (in thousands of dollars)

Product	Quota	Actual	Plus or minus	Performance to quota
Tape recorders	$ 70	$ 80	Plus $ 10	114%
Portable phonographs	430	160	Minus 270	37
Console phonographs	150	150	0	100
Speakers	100	110	Plus 10	110
Others	50	50	0	100
	$800	$550	Minus $250	69%

market grid has been broken up according to geographic area. This may permit direct analysis of the profitability of the firm's various target markets. In other cases, it may be desirable to allocate costs to specific customers or specific products and then aggregate these costs into market segments.

In either case, marketing cost analysis usually requires a new way of classifying accounting data. Rather than using the natural accounts which are typically used for financial analysis, we may want to use functional accounts, and go on to identify them as either fixed or variable costs. These distinctions will all have a bearing on how the costs are rearranged and analyzed later.[5]

Natural versus functional accounts

■ Natural accounts are the categories to which various costs are charged in the normal accounting cycle. These accounts include salaries, wages, social security, taxes, supplies, raw materials, auto, gas and oil expenses, advertising, and other such categories. These accounts are called "natural" because they bear the names of their expense categories.

This is not the approach to cost analysis used in factories, however, and it is not the one we will use. In the factory, functional accounts are set up to indicate the *purpose* for which the expenditures are made. Factory functional accounts include shearing, milling, grinding, floor cleaning, maintenance, and so on. Frequently, factory cost accounting records are so organized that the cost of particular products or jobs can be calculated from them.

Various marketing jobs are done for specific purposes, too. With some foresight and analysis, the costs of marketing also can be allocated to specific categories, such as customers and products. Then their profitability can be calculated.

First, get costs into functional accounts

■ The first step in marketing cost analysis is to reclassify all the dollar cost entries in the natural accounts into functional cost accounts. For example, the many cost items in the natural *salary* account might be allocated to functional accounts with the following

Table 29–8
Profit and loss statement

Sales		$17,000
Cost of goods sold		11,900
Gross Margin		5,100
Expenses		
Salaries	$2,500	
Rent	500	
Wrapping supplies	1,012	
Stationery and stamps	50	
Office equipment	100	
		4,162
Net Profit		$ 938

names: storage, inventory control, order assembly, packing and shipping, transportation, selling, advertising, order entry, billing, credit extension, and accounts receivable. The same would be true for rent, depreciation, heat, light, power, and other natural accounts.

The method of reallocating natural to functional accounts is not fixed. It depends on the method of operation of the particular firm. It might require time studies, space measurements, actual counts, and managerial estimates.

Then reallocate to evaluate profitability

■ The next step is to reallocate the functional costs to those items or customers or market segments for which the costs were incurred. The most common reallocation of functional costs is to products and to customers. After all of the appropriate costs are allocated, these detailed totals can be recombined in any way desired—for example, by product or customer class, region, and so on.

The costs allocated to the functional accounts would equal in total those in the natural accounts. They are merely organized in a different way. But instead of being used just to show total company profitability, they can now be arranged to show the profitability of territories, products, customers, salesmen, price classes, order sizes, methods of distribution, methods of sale, or any other breakdown desired. Each unit, in effect, can be treated as a profit center.

Cost analysis finds no-profit Jones—an illustrative example

■ These ideas can be seen more clearly in the following hypothetical example. In this case, the usual accounting approach—with natural accounts—showed that the company made a profit of $938 last month (Table 29–8). When a question is raised about the profitability of the company's three customers, the profit and loss statement is of no help. The marketing manager decides to use marketing cost analysis because he wants to know whether a change in marketing methods might improve profit.

First, the costs in the five natural accounts are distributed to

Table 29-9
Spreading natural accounts to functional accounts

		Functional accounts			
Natural accounts		Sales	Packaging	Adver-tising	Billing and collection
Salaries	$2,500	$1,000	$ 900	$300	$300
Rent	500		400	50	50
Wrapping supplies	1,012		1,012		
Stationery and stamps	50			25	25
Office equipment	100			50	50
	$4,162	$1,000	$2,312	$425	$425

four functional accounts — sales, packaging, advertising, and billing and collection (see Table 29-9) — according to the functional reason for incurring the expenses. Specifically, $1,000 of the total salary cost was for salesmen who seldom even come into the office, since their function is to call on customers; $900 of the salary cost was for packaging labor; and $600 was for office help. Assume that the office force split its time about evenly between addressing advertising material, and the billing and collection function. So the $600 is split evenly into these two functional accounts.

The $500 for rent was for the entire building, but 80 percent of the floor space was used for packaging and 20 percent for the office. Thus $400 is allocated to the packaging account. The remaining $100 is divided evenly between the advertising and billing accounts because these functions used the office space about equally. Stationery, stamps and office equipment charges are allocated equally to the latter two accounts for the same reason. Charges for wrapping supplies are allocated to the packaging account because these supplies were used in packaging. In another situation, different allocations and even different accounts might be appropriate, but these are workable here.

Calculating profitability of three customers

Now we are in a better position to calculate the profitability of the company's three customers. But we need additional information before we can allocate these functional accounts to customers or products. It is presented in tabular form in Table 29-10 for convenient reference.

Table 29-10 shows that the company's three products vary in cost, selling price, and sales volume. The products also have different "bulks," and so the packaging costs are unrelated to the selling price. For example, product C is six times bulkier than A. When packaging costs are allocated to products, this must be considered.

Table 29–10
Basic data for cost and profit analysis example

A. Products

Products	Cost/Unit	Selling price/Unit	No. units sold in period	Sales volume in period	Relative "bulk" per unit	Pack- aging "units"
A	$ 7	$ 10	1,000	$10,000	1	1,000
B	35	50	100	5,000	3	300
C	140	200	10	2,000	6	60
			1,110	$17,000		1,360

B. Customers

Customers	No. of sales calls in period	No. of orders placed in period	No. of each product ordered in period A	B	C
Smith	30	30	900	30	0
Jones	40	3	90	30	3
Brown	30	1	10	40	7
	100	34	1,000	100	10

This is accomplished by computing a new measure — a packaging unit — which is used to allocate the costs in the packaging account. Packaging units take into consideration relative bulk and the number of each type of product sold. While only 10 units of product C are sold, it is bulky and requires 10 times 6, or 60 packaging units. This will cause relatively more of the costs in the packaging account to be allocated to each unit of product C.

Table 29–10 also shows that the three customers require different amounts of sales effort, place different numbers of orders, and buy different product combinations.

Jones requires more sales calls. Smith places many orders which must be processed in the office, with increased billing expense. Brown seems to be a great customer, since he placed only one order — and that order accounted for 70 percent of the sales of high-valued product C.

The basic computations for allocating the functional amounts to the three customers are shown in Table 29–11. There were 100 sales calls in the period. Assuming that all calls took the same amount of time, it is logical to derive the average cost per call by dividing the $1,000 sales cost by 100 calls, giving an average cost of $10. Similar reasoning is used in breaking down the billing and packaging account totals. Advertising during this period was for the benefit of product C only, and this cost is split among the units of C sold.

Table 29–11
Functional cost account allocations

Sales calls =	$1,000/100 calls	= $10/call
Billing =	$425/34 orders	= $12.50/order
Packaging units costs =	$2,312/1,360 packaging units	= $1.70/packaging unit or
		$1.70 for product A
		$5.10 for product B
		$10.20 for product C
Advertising =	$425/10 units of C	= $42.50/unit of C

Calculating profit and loss for each customer

Now we can compute a profit and loss statement for each customer, combining his purchases and the cost of serving him. This is done in Table 29–12. A statement is developed for each customer, and of course the sum of each of the four major components (sales, cost of goods sold, expenses, and profit) is the same as on the original statement. We have merely rearranged and renamed the data, for analysis purposes.

The procedure is explained for customer Smith's statement in Table 29–12. Smith bought 900 units of A at $10 each and 30 units of B at $50 each for the respective sales totals ($9,000 and $1,500) shown in Table 29–12. Cost of goods sold is computed on the same basis. Thirty sales calls at an average of $10 each were made on Smith. Total sales calls cost $300. He placed 30 orders (at an average cost of $12.50 each) for a total ordering cost of $375. Total packaging costs amounted to $1,530 for A (900 units purchased times $1.70 per unit) and $153 for B (30 units purchased times $5.10 per unit). There were no packaging costs for C because Smith did not buy any of product C. Neither were any advertising costs charged to Smith, since all costs were spent promoting product C, which he did not buy.

Analyzing the results

We see now that Smith was the most profitable customer—yielding over 75 percent of the net profit.

This analysis shows that Brown was profitable, too, but not as profitable as Smith, because Smith bought three times as much. Jones was unprofitable because he didn't buy very much and received one third more sales calls.

It is clear the the "iceberg" principle is operating again here. Although the company as a whole is profitable, customer Jones is not profitable. Before dropping Jones, however, the marketing manager should study his figures and methods of operation very carefully. Perhaps Jones should be contacted less frequently, or maybe he will grow into a profitable account. Now, he is at least covering some fixed costs, and dropping him might only shift those

Table 29–12
Profit and loss statements for customers

	Smith	Jones	Brown	Whole company
Sales				
A	$9,000	$ 900	$ 100	
B	1,500	1,500	2,000	
C		600	1,400	
Total Sales	$10,500	$3,000	$3,500	$17,000
Cost of goods sold				
A	$6,300	$ 630	$ 70	
B	1,050	1,050	1,400	
C		420	980	
Total Cost of Goods Sold	$ 7,350	$2,100	$2,450	$11,900
Gross Margin	$ 3,150	$ 900	$1,050	$ 5,100
Expenses				
Sales calls ($10 each)	$ 300	$ 400.00	$ 300.00	
Order costs ($12.50 ea.)	375	37.50	12.50	
Packaging costs				
A	1,530	153.00	17.00	
B	153	153.00	204.00	
C		30.60	71.40	
Advertising		127.50	297.50	
	2,358	901.60	902.40	4,162
Net Profit (or Loss)	$ 792	$ (1.60)	$ 147.60	$ 938

fixed costs to the other two customers, making them look less attractive. (See the discussion on contribution margin later in this chapter.)

The marketing manager may also want to analyze his advertising costs against results, since this is a heavy advertising expense against each unit of product C. Perhaps his strategic plan should be revised.

Cost analysis is not performance analysis

■ Such an analysis is not performance analysis, of course. If the marketing manager had budgeted various costs to various tasks, it would be possible to extend the analysis to a performance analysis. This would be a logical and perhaps a desirable extension, but few companies have moved this far as yet.

As the cost of computer record keeping drops, we may see more companies accumulating detailed data on the cost of servicing customers. They could then compute fairly realistic profit and loss statements for individual customers, just as some factory cost accounting systems develop realistic cost estimates for products, and advertising agencies monitor the profitability of their clients.

Should all costs be allocated?

■ We have discussed the general principles, but the matter of allocating costs is a sticky one. Some costs are likely to be fixed for the near future, regardless of what decision is made. And some costs are likely to be *common* to several products or customers, making allocation difficult.

There are two basic approaches to handling this difficult problem — the full-cost approach and the contribution-margin approach.

Full-cost approach — everything costs something

■ In the full-cost approach, all functional costs are allocated to products, customers, or other categories. Even fixed costs (those that do not vary in the short run) are allocated in some way, as are common costs. Because all costs are allocated, it is possible to subtract costs from sales and calculate the profitability of various customers, and so on. This *is* of interest to some top managements.

The full-cost approach usually requires that some costs that are difficult to allocate be apportioned on some, perhaps arbitrary, basis such as dollars of sales or numbers of units.

The assumption here is that the services provided for those costs are equally beneficial to customers, to products, or to whatever group they are allocated. Sometimes this is done mechanically, but often logical reasoning can support the allocation if we accept the idea that marketing costs are incurred for a purpose. Advertising costs, for example, that are not directly related to specific customers or products, *might* be allocated to all customers on the basis of their purchases. The theory is that advertising has helped bring in the sales.

Contribution margin — ignores some costs to get results

■ When we use the contribution-margin approach, it is not necessary to consider all costs in *all* situations. Why?

When various alternatives are being compared, management may find it more meaningful to consider only the costs which are directly related to particular alternatives. Variable costs are particularly relevant here, as we saw when we discussed break-even analysis in Chapter 25.

The contribution-margin approach focuses management attention on variable costs rather than on total costs, which may include some fixed costs which do not change in the short run and can safely be ignored, or some common costs, which are more difficult to allocate.[6]

The distinction between the full-cost approach and the contribution-margin approach is *not* academic. Different decisions may be suggested by the two approaches. These are contrasted in the following example. Table 29–13 shows a profit and loss statement, using the full-cost approach, for a department store with three operating departments. (These could be market segments or customers or products.)

The administrative expenses, which represent the only fixed cost

Table 29-13
Profit and loss statement by department for the year 197X

	Totals	Depart-ment 1	Depart-ment 2	Depart-ment 3
Sales	$100,000	$50,000	$30,000	$20,000
Cost of goods sold	80,000	45,000	25,000	10,000
Gross margin	$ 20,000	$ 5,000	$ 5,000	$10,000
Other expenses				
Selling expenses	5,000	2,500	1,500	1,000
Administrative expenses	6,000	3,000	1,800	1,200
Total Other Expenses	$ 11,000	$ 5,500	$ 3,300	$ 2,200
Net Profit or (Loss)	$ 9,000	$ (500)	$ 1,700	$ 7,800

Source: Robert K. Jaedicke, "A Method for Making Product Combination Decisions," *Business News Notes* (Minneapolis: University of Minnesota, April 1958), pp. 1–2.

in this particular case, have been allocated to departments on the basis of percentage of sales volume of each department—a typical method of allocation. In this case, some executives argued that Department 1 was clearly unprofitable and should be eliminated because it showed a net loss of $500. Were they correct?

To find out, see Table 29–14 which shows what would happen if Department 1 were eliminated.

Several facts immediately become clear. The overall profit of the store would be reduced if Department 1 were dropped. Fixed costs amounting to $3,000, now being charged to Department 1, would have to be allocated to the other departments; this would reduce net profit $2,500, since Department 1 previously covered $2,500 of the $3,000 fixed costs charged. This shifting of costs would then make Department 2 unprofitable!

A contribution-margin income statement for the department store is shown in Table 29–15. Note that each department has a positive contribution margin. Here the Department 1 contribution of $2,500 is obvious. This actually is the amount that would be lost if Department 1 were dropped. (This example assumes that the fixed administrative expenses are *truly* fixed—that none of them would be eliminated if this department were eliminated.)

A contribution-margin income statement shows the contribution of each department more clearly, including its contribution to both fixed costs and profit. As long as a department or other unit has some contribution margin—and as long as there are no better alternative uses for the resources invested in it—the department or salesman or product or other variable in the particular analysis should be retained.

Table 29–14
Profit and loss statement by department for the year 197X if
Department 1 were eliminated

	Totals	Department 2	Department 3
Sales	$50,000	$30,000	$20,000
Cost of goods sold	35,000	25,000	10,000
Gross margin	$15,000	$ 5,000	$10,000
Other expenses			
Selling expenses	2,500	1,500	1,000
Administrative expenses	6,000	3,600	2,400
Total Other Expenses	$ 8,500	$ 5,100	$ 3,400
Net Profit or (Loss)	$ 6,500	$ (100)	$ 6,600

Contribution margin versus full cost—choose your side

■ The full-cost approach often leads to controversy within the company. Any one method of allocation tends to make some products or customers appear less profitable than another allocation method.

Assigning all common advertising costs to customers, based on their purchases, can be supported logically. But it also can be criticized on the grounds that it may make large-volume customers appear less profitable than they actually are, especially if the marketing mix which is aimed at the larger customers focuses more on price than on advertising.

Those in the company who want the smaller customers to look more profitable will argue for this allocation method on the grounds that general advertising helps "build" good customers because it affects the overall image of the company and its products.

In one sense, such arguments are futile, since the only goal of allocation is to clearly identify expenses and their sources and to give the firm a better picture of its operations.

The argument about allocation methods may be deadly serious, however, because the method used may reflect on the performance of various company executives and, subsequently, their salaries and bonuses. The product managers, for example, would be vitally interested in how the various fixed and common costs were allocated to products. Each, in turn, might like to have costs shifted to his colleagues' products.

Arbitrary allocation of costs also may have a direct impact on salesmen morale. If salesmen see their variable costs loaded with additional common or fixed costs over which they have no control, they may decide, "What's the use?"

To avoid this problem, the contribution-margin approach is frequently used. It avoids many of the problems of arbitrarily allocating fixed or common costs. It is especially useful for evaluating alternatives, and also for showing operating executives and salesmen how they are performing. The contribution-margin approach

Table 29–15
Contribution-margin statement by departments for the year 197X

	Totals	Dept. 1	Dept. 2	Dept. 3
Sales	$100,000	$50,000	$30,000	$20,000
Variable costs				
Cost of goods sold	80,000	45,000	25,000	10,000
Selling expenses	5,000	2,500	2,500	1,000
Total variable costs	$ 85,000	$47,500	$26,500	$11,000
Contribution margin	15,000	2,500	3,500	9,000
Fixed costs				
Administrative expenses	6,000			
Net Profit	$ 9,000			

Source: Robert K. Jaedicke, "A Method for Making Product-Combination Decisions," *Business News Notes* (Minneapolis: University of Minnesota, April 1958), pp. 1–2.

shows what they have actually contributed to general overhead and profit.

Top management, on the other hand, often finds full-cost analysis more useful. In the long run, some products, departments, or customers must bear the fixed costs. Full-cost analysis has its place here.

Planning and control combined

■ We have been treating sales and cost analyses separately up to this point. But management often will combine them to keep a running check on its activities—to be sure that the plans are materializing or to see when and where new strategies are needed.

**Sales +
Costs +
Everybody
helps =
$8,150**

■ Let's see how this works at the XYZ Hardware Co., a typical hardware retailer.

This firm netted $7,750 last year. Expecting no basic change in the competitive situation and slightly better local business conditions, the manager set this year's profit goal at $8,150, an increase of about 5 percent.

Next, he began developing tentative plans to show how this higher profit could be made. He estimated the sales volumes, gross margins, and expenses—broken down by months and by departments in his store—necessary to net $8,150.

Table 29–16 is a planning and control chart which the XYZ manager developed to show the contribution which each department should make each month. At the bottom of Table 29–16, the plan for the year is summarized. Notice that space is provided to insert the actual performance and a measure of variation, allowing both planning and control functions to be implemented with this table.

Table 29–16 shows that XYZ's manager is focusing on the

Table 29–16
XYZ Hardware Company planning and control chart

197X	Contribution to store				Total	Store ex-pense	Op-erating profit	Cumu-lative operat-ing profit
	Dept. A	Dept. B	Dept. C	Dept. D*				
January								
Planned	1,350	450	200	−50	1,950	1,200	750	750
Actual								
Variation								
February								
Planned	1,000	325	125	−50	1,400	1,200	200	950
Actual								
Variation								
November								
Planned	1,600	375	125	0	2,100	1,200	900	5,325
Actual								
Variation								
December								
Planned	3,150	625	200	450	4,425	1,200	2,825	8,150
Actual								
Variation								
197X								
Planned	15,800	3,500	3,450	−200	22,550	14,400	8,150	8,150
Actual								
Variation								

* The goal of minus $200 for this department was established on the same basis as the goals for the other departments, i.e., it represents the same percentage gain over 1959, when Department D's loss was $210. Plans call for discontinuance of the department unless it shows marked improvement by the end of the year.

monthly contribution by each department. The purpose of monthly estimates is to get more frequent feedback and to enable faster adjustment of plans. Generally, the shorter the planning and review period, the easier it is to correct problems before they become emergencies.

In this example, a modified contribution-margin approach is being used, since some of the fixed costs can be allocated logically to particular departments. On this chart, the balance left after direct fixed and variable costs are charged to departments is called "Contribution to Store." The idea is that each department will contribute to covering *general* store expenses, such as top-management salaries and Christmas decorations, and to net profits.

In Table 29–16, we see that the whole operation is brought together when the monthly operating profit is computed. The con-

Table 29–17
XYZ Hardware Company planning and control chart—Department B

| 197X | Sales | Gross profit | Direct expense | | | Contribution to store | Cumulative contribution to store |
			Total	Fixed	Variable		
January							
Planned	3,000	900	450	300	150	450	450
Actual	2,300	815	415	300	115	400	400
Variation	−700	−85	35	0	35	−50	−50
February							
Planned	2,500	750	425	300	125	325	775
Actual							
Variation							
November							
Planned	3,500	1,050	675	500	175	375	2,875
Actual							
Variation							
December							
Planned	4,500	1,350	725	500	225	625	3,500
Actual							
Variation							
197X							
Planned	30,000	9,000	5,500	4,000	1,500	3,500	3,500
Actual							
Variation							

Source: Wallace O. Yoder and Clarence E. Vincent, "Control Methods for Hardware Dealer," *Management Research Summary* (Washington, D.C.: Small Business Administration, May 1961), pp. 2–3.

tribution from each of the four departments is totaled, then general store expenses are subtracted to obtain the operating profit for each month.

Each department must plan and control, too

■ Table 29–17 shows a similar planning and control chart for a single XYZ department, Department B. In this table, actual results have been entered for the month of January. An unfavorable deviation is revealed between planned and actual sales performance (−$700), and gross profit (−$85).

Now, the marketing manager must determine why actual sales were less than projected, with a view to making new plans. Possible hypotheses are that: (1) Prices were too high; (2) promotion was ineffective; (3) the product selection was not satisfying the target customers; and (4) errors might have been made in marking the prices or in tallying sales.

Corrective action could take either of two courses; namely, improving tactics (or their implementation) or developing new, more realistic strategies.

Implementing the control process

■ All of this analysis can be implemented by manual methods, which may be best for small or nonrecurring jobs. But when the sales volume and complexity of the business have grown, mechanical methods not only may be faster and more accurate but may be the only way to handle the control procedure.

The marketing manager must take charge

■ Electronic data processing systems are commonly used for data analysis in larger companies. Increasingly, smaller companies have access to computing capabilities through time-sharing systems offered by computer manufacturers and service bureaus.

But this kind of analysis is not possible unless the sales and other performance data is in machine processible form, so it can be sorted and analyzed rapidly. At this point, the marketing manager can play a crucial role, by insisting that the data he wants is collected. If the data he wishes to analyze is not captured as it comes in, information will be difficult if not impossible to obtain later.

Practically, the only limitation on more effective and revealing data analysis is the imagination of the marketing manager, now that machines can handle the drudgery. But he must see the interrelation of the planning and control process, and be sure the data he wants to use will be available when needed. Then he can confidently ask the data processors to produce the reports he needs.[7]

The marketing audit

While crises pop, planning and control must go on

■ The analyses we have discussed so far are designed to help a marketing manager plan and control his own operations. They can help him do a better job. Often, however, the control process tends to focus on only a few critical elements — such as sales variations by product in different territories — and it misses such items as the appropriateness of various marketing strategies and the possible effectiveness of alternative mixes.

The marketing manager usually is responsible for the day-to-day execution function as well as planning and control functions, and he seldom has the leisure to casually contemplate the effectiveness of his efforts. Sometimes, crises are popping in several places at the same time, and a good deal of his concern must be focused on adjusting marketing mixes or shifting strategies in the short run.

To ensure that the whole marketing program is *regularly* evaluated — not just in times of crisis — marketing specialists have developed a new concept — the marketing audit. It is similar to the accounting audit or the personnel audit, both of which have been accepted by business for some time.

The *marketing audit* has been defined as "A systematic, critical, and unbiased review and appraisal of the basic objectives and policies of the marketing function and of the organization, methods, procedures, and personnel employed to implement the policies and achieve the objectives."[8]

**An audit
shouldn't be
necessary —
but, usually,
it is**

■ A marketing audit would take a big view of the business and evaluate the whole marketing program. It might be conducted by a separate department within the company, perhaps by a "marketing controller." Or to avoid bias, it might be desirable to have it conducted by an outside organization such as a management consulting firm.

Ideally, a marketing audit should not be necessary. A good manager does his very best in planning, executing, and controlling and should continually attempt to evaluate the effectiveness of his operation.

In practice, however, managers often become identified with certain strategies and pursue them persistently when alternate courses might be more effective. Since an outside view may give needed perspective, we may see greater use of the marketing audit in the future.

Conclusion

■ In this chapter, we have tried to show how sales and cost analysis can help a marketing manager control his marketing program, and that control procedures can be useful in his planning. Controls lead to feedback that can be incorporated into subsequent planning.

Simple sales analysis merely gives a picture of what has happened. But when sales forecasts or other data showing expected results are brought into the analysis, it is possible to evaluate performance, using performance indices.

Cost analysis also can be useful, providing "natural" accounting costs are allocated to market segments, customers, products or other appropriate categories, perhaps using functional cost breakdowns. There are two basic approaches to cost analysis — full cost and contribution margin. Using the full-cost approach, all costs are allocated in some way; using the contribution-margin approach, only the variable or direct costs are allocated. Both methods have their advantages and special uses.

Ideally, the marketing manager should arrange for a continual flow of data that can be analyzed routinely, preferably by machine, to enable him to control and subsequently plan new strategies. A marketing audit may assist him in this ongoing evaluation. Either a separate department within the company or an outside, objective organization might conduct this audit.

Whichever evaluation procedure is used, however, it is clear that a marketing program must be controlled. Good control helps the marketing manager locate and correct weak spots, while at the same time finding strengths which he may be able to turn to his own advantage and apply throughout his marketing program. Control works hand in hand with planning.

questions and problems

1 Various breakdowns of sales are suggested for sales analysis in certain situations, depending upon the nature of the company and its product. Describe a situation (one for each) where each of the following breakdowns would yield useful information. Explain why.
a. By geographical region.
b. By product.
c. By customer.
d. By size of order.
e. By size of salesman's commission allowed (on each product or product group.)

2 Explain carefully what the "iceberg principle" should mean to the marketing manager.

3 Explain the meaning of the comparative performance and comparative cost data in Tables 29–1 and 29–2. Why does it appear that eliminating sales areas D and E would be profitable?

4 Most sales forecasting is subject to some error (perhaps 5 to 10 percent). Is it proper to conclude then that variations in sales performance of 5 or 10 percent above or below quota are to be expected? If so, how should such variations be treated in evaluating performance?

5 Explain why there is a controversy between the advocates of the "net profit approach" and the "contribution margin" approach to cost analysis.

6 The profit and loss statement for June for the Brown Bag Co. is shown. If competitive conditions make price increases impossible, and management has cut costs as much as possible, should the Brown Bag Co. stop selling to hospitals and schools? Why?

	Retailers	Hos-pitals and schools	Total
Sales			
80,000 units			
at $0.70	$56,000		$56,000
20,000 units			
at $0.60		$12,000	12,000
Total	$56,000	$12,000	$68,000
Cost of goods			
sold	40,000	10,000	50,000
Gross margin	$16,000	$ 2,000	$18,000
Sales and			
adminis.			
expenses			
Variable	$ 6,000	$ 1,500	$ 7,500
Fixed	5,600	900	6,500
Total	$11,600	$ 2,400	$14,000
Net profit			
(loss)	$ 4,400	$ (400)	$ 4,000

7 Explain why it is so important for the marketing manager to be directly involved in the planning of control procedures.

8 Explain why a marketing audit might be desirable even in a well run company. Discuss who or what kind of an organization would be the best one to conduct a marketing audit. Would a marketing research firm be good? Would the present C.P.A. firms be most suitable?

notes

[1] Sam R. Goodman, *Techniques of Profitability Analysis* (New York: John Wiley and Sons, 1970), especially Chapter 1.

[2] R. I. Haley and R. Gatty, "Monitor Your Markets Continuously," *Harvard Business Review*, May–June 1968, pp. 65–69; and D. H. Robertson, "Sales Force Feedback on Competitors' Activities," *Journal of Marketing*, April 1974, pp. 69–71.

[3] Richard D. Crisp, *Marketing Research* (New York: McGraw-Hill Book Co., 1957), p. 144.

[4] Leland L. Beik and Stephen L. Buzby, "Profitability Analysis by Market Segments," *Journal of Marketing*, July 1973, pp. 48–53; D. R. Longman and M. Schiff, *Practical Distribution Cost Analysis* (Homewood, Ill.: Richard D. Irwin, Inc., 1955).

[5] Frank H. Mossman, Paul M. Fischer, and W. J. E. Crissy, "New Approaches to Analyzing Marketing Profitability," *Journal of Marketing*, April 1974, pp. 43–48, and "Segmental Analysis: Key to Marketing Profitability," *MSU Business Topics*, Spring 1973, pp. 42–49; and V. H. Kirpalani and Stanley J. Shapiro, "Financial Dimensions of Marketing Management," *Journal of Marketing*, July 1973, pp. 40–47.

[6] Technically, a distinction should be made between variable and direct costs, but we will use these terms interchangeably. Similarly, not all common costs are fixed costs and vice versa, but the important point here is to recognize that some costs are fairly easy to allocate, and other costs are not.

[7] For further discussion on the development of data processing systems, see E. J. McCarthy, J. A. McCarthy, and D. Humes, *Integrated Data Processing Systems* (New York: John Wiley & Sons, Inc., 1966).

[8] A. R. Oxenfeldt, "The Marketing Audit as a Total Evaluation Program," in *Analyzing and Improving Marketing Performance: Marketing Audits in Theory and Practice* (New York: American Management Association, 1959), p. 26; see also Frazer B. Wilde and Richard F. Vancil, "Performance Audits by Outside Directors," *Harvard Business Review*, July–August 1972, pp. 112–16; and Edward M. Mazze and John T. Thompson, Jr., "Organization Renewal: Case Study of a Marketing Department," *MSU Business Topics*, Summer 1973, pp. 39–44.

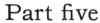

Part five

Marketing
reappraised

Can marketing people satisfy the critics and

an efficient and fair
system—the objectives of society . . .
direct the flow of goods
and services—the firm's objectives . . .
the primary purpose of the
marketing concept . . .

build a better marketing system—one that satisfies the customer?

30

Does marketing cost too much? An evaluation

■ Does marketing cost too much? Again, we return to this fundamental question.

Many people feel strongly that marketing costs too much – that it is a waste of resources which would be better used elsewhere. This may be partly because it is human to look for quick and easy solutions to pervasive problems, such as unemployment, rising prices, and unsatisfactory product quality. Marketing activities are especially vulnerable to public criticism. They are continuously exposed to the public, and people react emotionally when their pocketbooks are hurt.

In Chapter 1 and at various times throughout the text, we referred to criticisms of marketing and to the possible effects of business practices on consumer welfare. But we have *not* attempted to answer the underlying question of whether marketing costs too much – believing that you needed background information before developing your own answer.

We have attempted to provide this necessary background in this book. The focus has been primarily on the *micro* view of marketing – that is, marketing as seen through the eyes of the marketing manager. Now that you have a better appreciation of what the marketing manager does and how he can contribute to the *macro-* marketing process, you should be able to give thoughful consideration to whether marketing costs too much.

Your answer is extremely important. Your own business career and the economy in which you will live will be affected by your answer.

In this chapter, we will try to reach some conclusions regarding the effectiveness of marketing, particularly in the American economy.

What to measure and how?

Two measurements are necessary

■ As we saw in Chapter 1, it is useful to distinguish between two levels of marketing activity: the *macro* level and the *micro* level. Therefore, when evaluating the question of whether marketing costs too much, we must treat each of these levels separately.

Some complaints against marketing are aimed at only one of these levels at a time, while in other cases the criticism seems to be directed to one level but actually is aimed at the other. Some critics of specific advertisements, for example, probably would not be satisfied with *any* advertising.

To clarify our thinking, we gave two definitions of marketing.

The macro-level definition is: *Marketing is concerned with designing an efficient* (in terms of use of resources) *and fair* (in terms of distribution of output to all parties involved) *system which will direct an economy's flow of goods and services from producers to consumers and accomplish the objectives of the society.* This is clearly concerned with the whole economic system.

In contrast, the micro-level definition of marketing is: *Marketing is the performance of business activities which direct the flow of goods and services from producer to consumer or user in order to satisfy customers and accomplish the firm's objectives.*

Evaluating these two different levels of marketing requires different techniques. It also requires some agreement on the purpose of our economic system. Unless we agree on the purpose of our society, little can be accomplished through dialogue.

Satisfying the consumer is fundamental

■ We have emphasized the importance of the customer in planning marketing strategies because we have assumed that *the basic objective of our economic system is meeting consumers' needs as they, the consumers, see them.* Thus, the consumer is the focal point in both of our definitions of marketing. This is an acknowledgment in economic terms that in a free society, free men have a right to live as they choose.

This is no place for an extensive discussion of the merits of this objective. Philosophers, politicians, businessmen, and others are exploring this subject. Perhaps, eventually, such dialogue will lead to a change in our economic goals.

It is sufficient here to note that different economies have different objectives. Dictatorships, for example, may be concerned mainly with satisfying the needs of the society as seen by the political elite. In a socialist state, the objective might be to satisfy needs as defined by social planners—perhaps the equal division of output. In still other economies, the goal may be to build up the country militarily or economically, perhaps for the long-term benefit of all consumers (the people), but as seen by the state planners.

A marketing system would be required in *all of these economies*, but it might operate quite differently according to the various objectives.

In the following paragraphs, our basic concern will be evaluating the operation of marketing in the American economy where the present objective is to satisfy consumers' needs, *as consumers see them*. This is the essence of our system, and the business firm that ignores this fact does so at its own peril.

Measuring consumer satisfaction is difficult

■ Since consumer satisfaction is our goal, the efficiency of marketing must be measured by *the extent of this satisfaction*. Unfortunately, however, we cannot measure this satisfaction quantitatively and, therefore, provide a precise measure of marketing effectiveness. While there are a number of approaches to such measurement, none is fully satisfactory.

Measuring macro-marketing must be subjective

■ The macro-marketing definition refers to *efficiency* (in terms of use of resources) and *fairness* (in terms of distribution of output to all parties involved), as well as accomplishing the society's objectives.

Efficiency is concerned with the ratio of input to output. Given an economy's resources (and its state of technology), it would be possible to evaluate alternate ways of combining the inputs to increase the output, as measured, say, by GNP. For a particular year, the combination which yielded the highest GNP might be considered the most efficient.

The combination of resources which seems most efficient may not be considered "fair" by some people, however. The way resources are allocated in a society has a bearing on the fairness of the distribution of income and, therefore, output. Very efficient use of productive machinery, or richly endowed land, for example, together with low-cost labor might maximize the total GNP attainable but still seem unfair to some people because of low returns to labor and seemingly high returns to the machinery and land owners. But without these capital inputs, the labor might be less productive, or even unemployed, as we see in some less developed economies.

Further complicating the matter of evaluating a macro-marketing system is the fact that concern with efficient use of resources and fairness in allocating work roles (and therefore the distribution of income) are matters primarily related to "production" and *not* to how satisfied consumers are with the results of the production process. Input costs may be equated with output value—as is done with the value-added approach—but this does not really do the job because *cost* of production and distribution may have little relationship to consumer satisfaction.

The consumers' votes can be your guide

There is no quantitative way of measuring aggregate consumer satisfaction, so our evaluation of macro-marketing effectiveness will have to be subjective. The ultimate criterion, probably, is whether the macro-marketing system satisfies enough individual consumer/voters so that they vote—at the ballot box—to keep it running. They certainly have the right to (and regularly do) vote for modifications of the system. In some cases, this may lead to controversy because of the micro-macro dilemma discussed in Chapter 1. But when it comes to evaluating the whole macro-marketing system, let's remember that, in our economy, it is the consumers' votes in the marketplace, and in the ballot box, which finally decide whether the macro-marketing system costs too much. And it is important to note that each consumer's "dollar vote" counts in the marketplace, while in the ballot box only the majority rules. This may be one of the strongest arguments in favor of a market-directed system over a planned economy—the government (representing the majority of consumer/voters) can and does vote in constraints, but then the individual consumer gets to decide what will satisfy him uniquely.

Measuring micro-marketing must be subjective, too

■ Measuring micro-marketing effectiveness is also difficult, but here the relative cost or profitability of alternative ways of doing specific things could be used. The cost of alternative physical distribution plans or advertising campaigns designed to accomplish the same specific objective, for example, could be compared. Presumably the lowest-cost alternative would be "best." Care must be used when evaluating only costs, however, because using the lowest-cost method for one part of a system may not lead to lowest cost for the whole system. We saw this when we discussed physical distribution, and the same concept applies to a firm's complete effort.

Satisfaction can be loosely measured by company profits

In the final analysis, every company uses slightly different marketing strategies, and it is up to each customer to decide how effectively individual firms satisfy his needs. Generally speaking, customers are willing to pay higher prices or buy more of those goods which best satisfy them. Thus, efficient marketing plans can increase the profits needed to attract investment, provide jobs, and pay for research to develop new or better products. Profits are not only the goal of most businesses, but they can be used as a rough measure of a firm's efficiency in satisfying customers. In this sense, a firm's own interests and society's interests are not at odds.

Evaluating marketing effectiveness is difficult—but not impossible

■ In view of the difficulty of measuring consumer satisfaction and, therefore, the effectiveness of micro- and macro-marketing, it is easy to see why reasonable men might have different views on the subject. If the objective of the economy is clearly defined, however, and the argument is stripped of emotion, the broad question of marketing effectiveness and value probably can be answered.

In this chapter we will argue that micro-marketing (how individual firms and channels operate) *frequently does cost too much, but that macro-marketing* (how the whole marketing system operates), *does not cost too much, given the present objective of the American economy — consumer satisfaction.* These views should not be accepted as "gospel" but rather as arguments. In the end, you, the student of marketing, will have to make your own decision.[1]

Micro-marketing often *does* cost too much

The failure rate is high

■ Our focus throughout the text has been on what marketing managers should or could do to run a business more efficiently. But it must be acknowledged that the majority of firms are still production-oriented.

Many firms are not nearly as efficient as they might be. We have noted already that at least four out of five new products fail. New and old businesses fail regularly, too. The main reason for such failure is poor management or just plain managerial incompetence. One survey of 15,782 failures found that more than 90 percent were caused directly by incompetent or inexperienced management.[2]

Incompetence and bad management lead to higher costs of operation and tend to reduce the effectiveness of the business system in general. Generally speaking, business inefficiencies are due to one or more of three reasons:

1. Lack of interest in, or understanding of, the sometimes capricious customer.
2. Improper blending of the four Ps, caused in part by an over-emphasis on production and/or internal problems as contrasted with a customer orientation.
3. Lack of understanding of, or adjustment to, uncontrollable variables.

The company can get in the way of the customer

■ Serving the customer is plainly the function of business, yet some business managers seem to feel that customers avidly await any product they turn out. So they turn instead to internal problems. They do not understand a business as a "total system" responsible for satisfying customer needs.

The production manager, for example, may be primarily interested in designing products that are easy to make or can be made readily on the company's present machines. But he might be less worried about quality control. It is likely that way less than half of U.S. manufacturers have quality control procedures.[3] And this in turn may lead to consumer dissatisfaction, or injury. Furthermore, it is costly and annoying to retailers and wholesalers who must try to repair the goods or return them to the manufacturer.

Production people usually like long-production runs of standardized products since this helps to lower costs. Sometimes the production department emphasizes low-cost production mainly because it "sells" its products to the sales department at a fixed price, and, therefore, can make a good showing with sizable, low-cost runs. Yet this may create the need for costly promotion in an effort to move large quantities of less desirable goods.

Middlemen, too, often get tied up in their own internal problems. Goods may be stocked where it is convenient for the retailer to handle them, rather than for consumers to find them. And fast-moving, hard-to-handle goods may not be stocked at all because "They are too much trouble" or "We're always running out."

In the same fashion, accounting or financial departments in all kinds of businesses may try to cut costs by reducing raw material or finished-product inventory, even though this may not serve customers well. It may require more expensive hand-to-mouth buying, or cause loss of sales because of lack of stock.

The high cost of poor marketing mixes

■ Perhaps lack of concern for the customer is most noticeable in the ways the four Ps are combined – or sometimes are forced – into a marketing mix. This can happen in many ways, as the following discussion shows.

Product—forget the customer, full speed ahead!

Some production-oriented executives develop a company's product not to meet the needs of certain target customers but rather to satisfy some pet concept held by themselves or their friends. They sometimes produce products too high or too low in quality, or too complicated for many target markets. Then, to compound these errors, the packaging people frequently put this ill-conceived product in a container that is easy to make and fill but not really protective or appealing to the customer.

These poorly designed, poorly packaged products then are turned over to the sales department for unloading on the market. Sometimes these products cannot be moved off the counter or can be moved only with overly aggressive (or even fraudulent) promotion. Middlemen may participate in this aggressive selling if they are given high enough markups, or additional advertising or promotion allowances. This sort of promotion can be expensive and may become more common unless businesses become more customer-oriented.

Place—don't rock the boat, or sell to chains

Sales managers seldom make adjustments in channels as frequently as might be desirable, partly because of their personal relationships in their channel and partly because, being human, they prefer not to rock the boat. Yet such inflexibility can be extremely costly, especially in view of the "scrambling" we saw in the distribution structure.

Some old-timer salesmen are so tied to the idea of small independent wholesalers and retailers that they even refuse to sell to chain stores or large organizations. Their personal relationships with their old customers may make business more pleasant, but do not necessarily contribute to efficiency and profits. The continued use of obsolete and overly expensive channels may give substance to the charge of "too many" wholesalers and retailers.

Price—pick a price, any high price

Prices frequently are set on a cost-plus basis. This method of pricing may ignore customer demand and lead to unnecessarily high (and less profitable) prices. Many businessmen consider both margin and expected volume in pricing goods, but margins are definite, while volume is only predictable. These businessmen, therefore, choose high margins, which may lead to high prices and reduced volume.

Promotion—in spite of the advertising geniuses and star salesmen

If a product is poorly or improperly designed, or if inadequate channels are employed, or if cost-plus pricing is used, it is easy to see why promotion may be costly. Aggressive selling may be needed to overcome previous miscalculations or errors.

Even if a good job is done on the other three Ps, however, Promotion is sometimes inefficient and costly. As already noted, the sales manager and the advertising manager may not cooperate, each feeling that his own technique is most effective and does not need the support of the other. In some companies, the advertising manager and sales manager do not communicate at all.

Until recently, only lip service was paid to the value of customer research in some firms. Some advertising executives still feel that all a promotional campaign needs is their creative genius. And the difficulty of checking advertising results makes it hard to tell whether ad men are talking to the customers or to themselves.

Sales management also has its problems. There are many types of sales jobs. Recruiting the right person for each is difficult. Furthermore, the very nature of the sales job makes it difficult to measure sales performance.

Careful analysis and management are necessary to build a productive sales force at a reasonable cost. Unfortunately, many sales managers, although former "star" salesmen, are not up to this management task.

Company objectives may force higher cost operation

■ Top-management decisions on company objectives may unnecessarily increase the cost of marketing. A decision to pursue growth for growth's sake, for example, might mean excessive spending for promotion. Or diversification for diversification's sake could require development of costly new arrangements for Place. Or, if the established firms already had developed and protected basic ideas, perhaps through obtaining solid customer franchises, the firm might be forced to turn out second-rate products.

For these reasons, it is imperative that the marketing manager both be alert to the possibility of such pitfalls and participate fully in shaping the firm's objectives. Recognizing the importance of marketing, progressive firms have given marketing management a greater voice—and sometimes the dominant voice—in determining company objectives. Unfortunately, though, in many more firms, marketing is still looked upon as the department that "gets rid of" the product.

■ It appears that marketing does cost too much in many firms. However, the waste comes from misdirected effort, not some fallacy in the marketing concept. Despite much publicity, the marketing concept has not *really* been applied in many places. Where it was noticed at all, it was often given only "lip service." Sales managers may have been renamed marketing managers and vice presidents of sales were called vice presidents of marketing, but little else changed. Marketing mixes were still put together by production-oriented executives in the old ways. These firms clung to their "mass marketing" approach. The customer, in effect, was the last factor considered, rather than the first, as with target marketing.

But not all business firms and marketers should be criticized out of hand. An increasing number *are* becoming customer-oriented. And some (for example, General Electric) are paying increasing attention to strategic planning — in order to more effectively implement the marketing concept.

Further, various business organizations have developed programs which encourage emphasis on satisfying consumers. Among them are the Better Business Bureau, the Chamber of Commerce, the U.S. Department of Commerce, the American Marketing Association, the American Management Association, and various trade associations. And some organizations have developed "codes of ethics" to guide members' behavior with respect to customers. Some of these developments are responses to the consumerism movement, but others reflect long-established commitments. More industry groups might be willing to get together to discuss how to do a better job (with good intentions) but are inhibited from doing so because of possible criticism for collusion.[4]

And competition in our dynamic marketplace continues to press for the elimination of unnecessary costs *and* institutions. Distribution channels are continually shifting as new ways are found for doing the marketing job more effectively. Limited-function wholesalers have developed in many lines. Discount houses and mass merchandisers have eliminated many small, conventional retail stores which did not recognize changing customer demands. Wholesalers who have not adopted the new methods of storing and transporting have been bypassed.

One encouraging sign is the end of the notion that practically anybody can run a business successfully. This never was true, and today the growing complexity of business is drawing more and more professionals into business. This includes not only professional business managers but psychologists, sociologists, statisticians, and economists.

The professional business managers who adopt the marketing concept as a way of business life will do a better job. This concept provides that all the activities of the business will be integrated into one "total system of action" oriented toward the one objective of serving the customer, at a profit. If this is done effectively, both businesses and customers will benefit. Then *micro-marketing* will *not* cost too much.

Macro-marketing *does not* cost too much

■ Many criticisms of marketing take aim at the operation of the macro-marketing system. These criticisms suggest that advertising and promotion in general are socially undesirable; that the macro-marketing system causes an improper allocation of resources, restricts income and employment, and leads to an improper distribution of income. Most of these complaints imply that some micro-marketing activities should not be permitted; that because they are allowed, macro-marketing costs too much or yields poor results.

Much of this criticism is expressed by those who have their own version of the ideal way to run an economy. Some of the most severe critics of our marketing system are theoretical economists who use the pure-competition model as their ideal. They would give consumers free choice in the market but are critical of the way the present market operates. Other critics would take free choice away from consumers, or at least some of them, and substitute their own values for those of individual consumers. These divergent viewpoints should be kept in mind when evaluating criticism.

In the following discussion, the word *business* probably could be substituted for *marketing* in most instances. Marketing is the most exposed arm of business, but it is nearly impossible to separate this arm from the rest of the body. A criticism of marketing at the macro level usually implies a criticism of our entire market-directed economic system as it now exists and suggests that some modification or an entirely different system would be more effective. Let's look at some of these positions so we can evaluate whether or not our macro-marketing system does cost too much.

Is pure competition the welfare ideal?

■ A major criticism of our macro-marketing system is that it permits or even encourages the allocation of unduly large shares of resources for marketing activities and that this may actually reduce consumer "welfare." This argument is concerned with how the economy's resources (land, labor, and capital) are allocated for producing and distributing goods. These critics usually maintain that scarce resources could be better spent on producing goods than on marketing them. The foundation for this viewpoint is the assumption that marketing activities are unnecessary and do not create value, or more technically, that pure competition is the ideal for maximizing consumer welfare.

In pure competition, the assumption is that consumers are "economic men," i.e., that they are well informed about all available offerings and will choose rationally among the alternatives to maximize their own welfare. Therefore, these critics feel that emotional or persuasive advertising discourages the economic comparison required for their ideal pure-competition economy and further is wasteful because society does not need it.

Theoretical economic analysis can show convincingly that pure competition will provide greater consumer welfare than monopolistic competition—*provided* all of the conditions and assumptions of pure competition are met.

Different people want different things

At the outset, we can say that our present knowledge of the complexity of human behavior and peoples' desire for different products pretty well demolishes the economists' "economic man" assumption, and therefore the pure-competition ideal.[5] A pioneer in monopolistic competition analysis, E. H. Chamberlin, also argues logically against the pure-competition ideal. He observes that people, in fact, are different and that they do have different demands. He translates these differences into demands for different products. Given this type of demand (downsloping demand curves), monopoly elements naturally develop. He concludes that "monopoly is necessarily a part of the welfare deal. . . ."[6]

Once it is acknowledged that not all consumers know everything and that they have varied demands, the need for a variety of micro-marketing activities becomes clear.

It is certainly true that micro-marketing activities can lead to a different allocation of resources than would be found in a pure-competition economy. It takes more time and effort to satisfy varied demands. But this allocation of resources probably results in greater consumer welfare. People are getting what they want.

Advertising, for example, can make both the micro- and macro-marketing processes work better. It can cut promotion costs for a firm. And at the macro level, it can, says another economist, be a powerful influence in eliminating ignorance and disseminating price information, making the whole searching process more economical.[7]

Redirecting needs does not misallocate resources

■ It would seem, then, that simply satisfying customers' demands does not lead to a misallocation of resources. Giving individuals what they want, after all, is the purpose of our market-directed economic system. But there is still another issue that concerns certain critics. They ask, "Is it right to influence consumers' demands by creating new needs?"

We already have seen that psychologists view consumers as a bundle of needs and drives, some of which are innate, but most of which are learned. Some critics feel that promotion not only stimulates people's needs, or "wants," but often teaches entirely new ones—and that this violates, if only subtly, the individual's control of his own actions.

Behavioral scientists find that it *is* possible to change attitudes and behavior. But an important question is: How basic are the needs which might be created? If we think of promotion for a new recreational gadget as "creating new wants," there can be no argument. Promotion can do this job. But to state broadly that promotion can create a wish for (or pleasure in) recreation, distinctiveness, or emulation, is another matter. It is likely that the human being already has learned these needs in other ways or from other sources.

Take the midi, for example

It is difficult to think of any new product for which an entirely new set of basic needs or drives had to be created. Even the exaggerated, up-again-down-again styles of women's clothing meet some women's need to be distinctive, to be style leaders. Yet some new feminine styles do not sell well even with extensive publicity. Consider the "midi." In the 1960s fashion "leaders" tried to force this style on women and really put all their promotion resources behind it. The horrendous failure liberated many women from following the annual style changes and now we see more clothing variety than before the ill-fated midi.

Rather than seeking to create entirely new basic needs, which would be extremely difficult and expensive, business firms seek to stimulate or direct those needs or drives which already are held. They work with "wants." They find it is "easier to swim with the current than against it."[8] Marketing research is used to test the current.

Marketing research helps management discover what target customers want or would like, so that the four Ps can be tailored to their desires. Instead of just "guessing" what might be wanted, then working at expensive hit-or-miss development of new products, the modern marketing man seeks to assure maximum customer satisfaction by analyzing the customers' needs, wants, and likely behavior.

Once this data is known, marketing follows an intelligent course—not a selfish, pigheaded, or diabolical one. It gives the customer what he wants. In return, customers give the company what it wants: profits. This customer-oriented procedure reduces the need to rely on heavy promotion to differentiate a product or try to create basically new demands.

"False" standards according to whom?

■ Promotion also has been criticized for creating and serving "false" standards, and thereby leading to an improper allocation of resources. But this standard has never been precisely defined. What is "false" apparently depends on the critic's point of view.

Certain critics of "false" standards are either unwilling to accept the idea or are truly unaware that other people may prefer standards different from their own. They see judgment or taste measured on an absolute scale, ranging from "good" at the top—where they exist—to "bad" at the bottom, and they do not want the lower end of the scale served.

Regarding the serving of "false tastes," a well-known economist, George Stigler, said:

The marketplace responds to the tastes of consumers with the goods and services that are salable, whether the tastes are elevated or depraved. It is unfair to criticize the marketplace for fulfilling these desires, when clearly the defects lie in the popular tastes themselves. I consider it a cowardly concession to a false extension of the idea of democracy to make sub rosa attacks on public tastes by denouncing the people who serve them. It is like blaming the waiters in restaurants for obesity.[9]

Sometimes it's the little things that count

■ Criticism of promotion which focuses on minor product differences has been common, especially among the very "rational." Sociological and psychological research, however, indicates that promotion actually may create *new* values for these products—new psychological values that may be of greater value to the buyer than the physical product itself.

How does this value-creation process work? Consider an extreme example, the placebo or sugar pill that a doctor uses for his hypochondriac patients to give reassurance that, yes, they are being medicated. The doctor's advice (promotion) that the pill will do some good frequently gets very desirable results when, in fact, the only value of the pill is psychological, not medicinal.

In a similar way, promotion sometimes enables marketers to satisfy better the many varied demands of consumers without an expensive physical variation of the product. With a little help from an ad copywriter, women can imagine all sorts of desirable consequences of using a particular perfume or lipstick—and if they believe it, it may come true. (Value has been added!)

Micro-marketing efforts expand macro output through innovation

■ Some critics feel that marketing helps create monopoly, or at least monopolistic competition, and that this, in turn, leads to higher prices, restriction of output, and reduction in the national income and employment.

There is no arguing that firms in a market-directed economy make a real effort to carve out separate monopolistic markets for themselves. This approach may have the short-run effect of restricting output (depending upon the shape of the new demand and supply curves) and raising prices on *that particular new product.*

Customers are not taken advantage of in the short run, however. They do not have to buy the new product unless they feel it is a better value. The old products are still available. Ironically, the prices may even be lower on the old products to meet the new competition, and yet their sales may decline because customers shift to the new product.

Over several years, the profits of the innovator may rise—but the rising profits also act as a spur to further innovation by competitors. This leads to new investments, which contribute to economic growth, raising the level of national income and employment.

Here, the increasing profits attract competition. The profits then begin to drop as competitors enter and begin producing somewhat similar products. Recall the rise and fall of industry profit during the product life cycle.

Monopolistic competition, it is clear, provides a dynamic element in the economy and breeds its own competition. The innovators also pave the way for the coming of the *barnacle brands,* so called because they attach themselves to the successful market established by the innovators. They are offered at lower prices and for this reason are accepted in the latter stages of the product life cycle.[10]

Output pie not fixed in size

■ Some critics argue that there is only a certain amount of income to be spent and that higher prices, which sometimes accompany effective target marketing, could lead to a reduction in the level of income or employment. Most economists consider this a naïve view of the economy. The economic pie is not fixed in size. The levels of income and employment appear to be more directly related to the level of expenditures of consumers, business, and the government.

Advertising didn't concentrate them

■ Certain critics are concerned that promotion leads to greater concentration of industry – that is, a few large firms dominating each industry – and, as a result, a reduction in competition. This seems an illogical objection, since there was much concentration of industry before promotion became widespread in the 1920s and 1930s.

A recent analysis of the available statistical data shows that industrial concentration was not caused by advertising, but rather by the availability of economies through large-scale production and distribution and the potential for financial advantage in larger units. There appears to be no relationship between the intensity of advertising and the trend to concentration. Yet, despite the evidence, the FTC acts on this assumption – restricting large and successful advertisers from acquiring less dynamic firms. This could have the effect of reducing competition and be detrimental to the operation of our macro-marketing system.[11]

Large firms are vigorous, customers are benefiting

■ Another objection to micro-marketing activities is that supposedly they aid the growth of large organizations, thus further restricting market entry and reducing competition, output, and employment. In recent years, though, the reverse seems to be true. Many firms have grown quite large, but this growth has been primarily because of diversification into many different fields.

In many industries, competition (using all four Ps) is extremely vigorous among a number of large, well-diversified organizations. They have the money to undertake basic research, resulting in true innovation. These firms can afford the extensive market research and careful planning of marketing mixes needed to compete effectively with their large competitors. They can underwrite and carry a new product until volume permits economies of scale and lower prices.

These large firms may compete aggressively, true, but out of this may come better service to the public than is offered by small firms which take refuge in guildlike behavior, following the "accepted customs of the trade."

A well-known economist, John Maurice Clark, cites the home-building industry and small retailing as illustrations of areas in which the existence of many small firms has not led to especially good results. He concluded that consumer interests often are best served by companies that are strong and well financed.[12]

Marketing people get their fair share of income

■ The main concern about distribution of income is that a market-directed economic system may divert a large share of the national income to marketing people because of the greater profitability of firms which have successfully differentiated their products. Such criticism does not seem justified, however, if the purpose of a free economy is to satisfy consumers and if market-oriented firms do that job better. Logically, the marketing segment of the economy should then be entitled to its higher incomes and higher profits.

Incomes in marketing *are* high for certain types of jobs, especially order-getting salesmen and certain advertising and sales promotion people. But it also is true that many of the order takers, especially retail salespeople, have low incomes—even below the federal minimum wage. These salaries probably reflect fairly accurately the contribution of each to the economy.

Market system is automatic and effective

■ Our market-directed system provides for a fairly automatic operation of the economy. Many competitors in a relatively free market serve the needs of millions of consumers far better than central economic planning could serve them.

In the planned Soviet economy, it usually has been necessary to tolerate a gray or black market and free-economy-type brokers to make the economy work. Now the Soviets are coming to see that product differentiation, branding, and advertising actually may facilitate the operation of an economy. They find that when customers recognize products by advertised brand, this permits self-service, speeds selling, and cuts cost. Requiring that each plant succeed in the market with its own brand acts as an automatic control on quality. Bureaucratic control, using standards and inspectors, would be increasingly difficult or impossible to accomplish now that the economy of the U.S.S.R. is offering more heterogeneous products.[13]

Consumers ask for it, consumers pay for it

■ Certainly, we do not now have the economists' "ideal"—pure competition. But the monopolistic competition situation that is typical of our economy is the result of customer preferences, *not* manipulation of markets by businessmen. Monopolistic competition may seem costly at times—when we look at micro-level situations, but it seems to work fairly well at the macro level—in serving the welfare of consumers who have many and varied demands.

All of these demands add to the cost of satisfying consumers. Certainly, the total cost is larger than it would be if spartan, undifferentiated products were offered at the factory door on a take-it-or-leave-it basis to long lines of buyers.

But if the role of the marketing system is to serve the consumer, then the cost of whatever services he demands cannot be considered excessive. It is merely the cost of serving the consumer in the manner he wants to be served.

Should the consumer be king?

■ Some critics sincerely question the doctrine of *consumer sovereignty*, which allows each consumer to choose what he wants to buy for himself. They don't think that some consumers are able to make correct choices for themselves, or even if they can, that they should have this right, especially if it might use up valuable resources or add to our polluted environment.[14]

Those who take the consumer's side agree that some people do not use their income wisely by others' standards; but at the same time, they argue that we do not yet have (*a*) ways of measuring consumer satisfaction, or (*b*) mechanisms for allowing one person to impose his choice of "correct" purchases on another citizen, except through the ballot box.

Planners often make such choices in totalitarian or socialist states. But it is axiomatic in democracies with market-directed economies that individual consumers *are* the best judges of what will satisfy them most. This system has its deficiencies and some consumers make mistakes, but it is generally considered to be better than letting someone else decide for you. A college student might appreciate this idea better by reflecting on whether he would rather have someone else — his parents, for example — make all of his decisions for *him*.

Does marketing cost enough?

■ The question, "Does marketing cost too much?" has been answered by one well-known financial expert with another question, "Does distribution cost enough?"[15] His analysis demonstrated that marketing is an important and integral part of our economic system. And he suggested that perhaps even more should be spent on marketing, since "distribution is the delivery of a standard of living" — that is, the satisfaction of consumers' basic needs and wants.

The role of marketing and business in our market-directed economy is to satisfy consumers. Production cannot do this job alone, nor can marketing. It makes little sense to think of production and marketing as truly separate entities. They are different sides of the same coin.

Mass production requires mass distribution and our macro-marketing system helps make the whole market-directed economic system work well. In this sense, then, macro-marketing does not cost too much. Some of the activities of individual business firms may cost too much, and if these micro-level activities are improved, the performance of the macro system probably will improve. But regardless, our macro-marketing system performs a vital role in our economic system.

What is needed to satisfy critics and build a better marketing system?

■ We have suggested that our macro-marketing system does not cost too much, given the present objective of our economy, while acknowledging that the micro-level performance of many business firms leaves a lot to be desired. At this point, it should be worthwhile to suggest what may be needed to meet the rising tide of consumerism. Should anything be done in this area, and if so, what?

Would need better performance at micro level

■ Some businessmen seem to feel that in a market-directed economy they should be completely "free." They don't understand the idea that ours is a market-directed system and that—in the long-run anyway—the needs of consumer/citizens must be served. Instead, they focus on their own internal problems, without satisfying consumers very well.

May need real application of the marketing concept

Greater acceptance of the marketing concept may help here— that is, guiding firms to determining what consumers want and *then* satisfying *this* demand, rather than simply trying to persuade them that what the firm has *is* what they want. And having obviously "better" marketing mixes would certainly reduce the need for or temptation to resort to fraud, deception, collusion, and other unethical or illegal practices.

May need more social responsibility

A smart businessman would put himself in the consumer's position, even when making manufacturing or other seemingly internal decisions. A useful rule to follow might be: "Do unto others as you would have others do unto you." At the operational level, this would mean developing satisfying marketing mixes for specific target markets. Note, however, that this would not always mean producing the "highest quality" that could be produced or offered for sale. Low-quality, short-lived products might be quite suitable in certain circumstances, as long as the target market understood what it was getting. Recall our cost-conscious couple in the paint market in Chapter 4. Low-cost products, such as the paint in that example, might be seen as a "good value" by certain market segments. In other markets, an entirely different marketing mix might be required to offer "good value."

Production-oriented businessmen often neglect this market-oriented rule and thus provide ammunition for the critics. It often is difficult, or impossible, to determine what grade or quality is being offered at what prices. Labels, salesmen, and advertising may offer no help at all. Further, the producer himself may not even know, because no specific customer-related quality has been built into the product. He may feel it is better, because higher-cost components have been installed. And these higher-cost components may result in higher prices, but they may or may not contribute to consumer satisfaction. In such cases, it is understandable why some promotion men, faced with production-oriented bosses, would resort to extremely aggressive, or even deceptive and fraudulent, promotion to "get rid of the goods."

It seems doubtful that production-oriented approaches will work well in the future. Tougher competition and more watchful government agencies may force the typical production-oriented businessman to reorient his thinking if he wishes to survive and prosper. The "lip service" acceptance of the marketing concept in the past, or plain production-orientedness, will no longer do. It seems clear that a good share of the concerns of the consumerism movement are due to the failure of businessmen to put the marketing concept into practice, and this must change.

Then, would need internal company changes

A wholehearted endorsement of the marketing concept will require considerable change within some organizations, to assure acceptable marketing strategies. Research, product design, and promotion may have to work together more closely, because what consumers consider "acceptable" and "reasonable" in product quality may change with time. This, in turn, will affect future consumerism activity, along with court and out-of-court settlements.

And may need more communication with consumers

Business firms may also have to help educate consumers about the advantages and *disadvantages* of their own and competing products, because almost any product has potential disadvantages. Anything which uses power, for example, could be potentially dangerous. A manufacturer of gas and electrical appliances argues, "It's not feasible to design a product so that it's foolproof." Citing the case of an oven, he says: "If it were cool on all sides, it would be either too small inside to cook a turkey, or too big outside to fit in the kitchen."[16]

Clearly, more communication with consumers about the advantages and disadvantages of various alternatives is needed. And we will probably see much more because the advertising industry has now accepted the concept of using comparative advertising — i.e., making direct and open comparisons, including prices of competing products.[17]

Would need better perform-ance at macro level

■ One of the advantages of a market-directed economic system is that its operation is relatively automatic. But in our version of this system, consumer/citizens provide certain constraints (laws). And at any time, these constraints can be strengthened or modified.

Need tougher enforcement of present laws

Before piling on too many new or different constraints, however, it probably would be wise to apply and vigorously enforce the ones we have. The antitrust laws, for example, have often been applied to protect competitors from each other when in fact they were intended to protect competition. Refocusing present constraints could make a big difference. The FTC seems to be shifting to a consumer-oriented emphasis.[18] Congress and local authorities also are taking stronger stands, e.g., with respect to product safety, truth-in-lending, and deceptive advertising.

Laws should affect top management

The results of vigorous enforcement of present constraints could be far-reaching if more price fixers, fraudulent or deceptive advertisers, and others who are obviously violating existing legislation—and thereby affecting the performance of the macro-marketing system—were sent to jail or given heavy fines. A quick and basic change in attitudes might occur if members of the board of directors and top management, who plan business strategy, were prosecuted, rather than the salesman or advertisers who are required to "deliver" on weak or undifferentiated strategies "or else" (lose their jobs).

In other words, if the government made it clear that it was serious about improving the performance of our economic system, much could be achieved within the present system, *without* adding new constraints or trying to "patch up" the present ones.

Need better informed and politically active business leaders

Further, it probably would be desirable for business leaders to expand their understanding of, and efforts to improve, our macro system. That is, take the offensive, not the defensive. More dialogue with legislators, government administrators, and consumer advocates could increase awareness of each others' problems, perceptions, and even use of terminology. Confusion or differences regarding the meaning of words such as: competition, product, market, consumer needs, rationality, and information can be crucial.[19]

Need better informed consumers

And some changes may be desirable, to help potential customers choose among the bewildering array of goods and services on the market. Legislation to ensure that consumers do have grounds for comparing products (for example, life expectancy of light bulbs and appliances) would be useful. And consumer education programs designed to teach people how to buy more effectively could be helpful.

But great care must be exercised here, so that the consumer's free choice *really* is preserved. If only those characteristics which are easily measurable are used, consumers might be encouraged or even trained to use quantitative criteria, when qualitative characteristics (for example, style, taste, freshness, and fun in use) would be more important for many of them.

Moreover, arbitrarily restricting the kinds of offerings that can be made would be inadvisable, because this would restrict innovation. Besides, from a pragmatic viewpoint, it is difficult to draw other than minimum specifications for some products. As noted, the Soviets have discovered this fact the hard way.[20]

Need socially responsible consumers

We have been stressing the responsibility of producers to act responsibly, but consumers have some responsibilities too. Some consumers abuse returned goods policies, change price tags in

self-service stores, and expect attractive surroundings and courte-
ous sales and service personnel, but want discount prices. Others
are downright abusive of salespeople. And others think nothing of
"ripping off" businesses. Unfortunately, "U.S. consumerism has
emphasized consumer rights while ignoring consumer responsibilities."[21]

**We may
need a new
macro-
marketing
system**

■ How far should the marketing concept be allowed to go? Some
marketing critics are just not happy with the idea of the consumer
as king. In part, this is because they see the consumer becoming
too "materialistic" and deplore this trend. They would rather
limit personal consumption in some way—especially for the middle-
and upper-income groups—and redistribute resources to others,
either in this country or elsewhere.

Unbridled application of marketing concept may have to go

Some critics question whether continued growth of GNP really
is a desirable goal for the economy, given that we usually equate
more goods and services with more satisfaction for consumers.
These observers feel that greater satisfaction could be achieved
by a less aggressive pursuit of material growth or even redirecting
our goals. Greater support has been given to this position by the
"energy crisis," and the growing recognition that pollution comes
with economic growth and the production and consumption of
more material goods. They feel that a better balance must be found
between our needs as producers/consumers and our needs for a
more livable environment.

Should marketing manager limit consumers' freedom of choice?

Achieving a "better" macro-marketing system is certainly a
desirable goal, but an important question is what role should a
marketer play—in his role as a producer. As a consumer/citizen,
there is no doubt that he has the right and obligation to contribute
his view and vote to improving our system. But as a producer, what
should he do?

This is an extremely important matter, because some marketing
managers, especially those in very large corporations, might be
able to have an impact which is far larger than in their role as a
consumer/citizen. Should they, for example, deliberately refuse to
produce "energy-gobbling" appliances or cars which are in strong
demand. Or should they be expected to install safety devices which
inevitably will increase costs and which are very definitely *not*
desired by potential customers?

These are very difficult questions to answer, and are certainly
of a different order than whether quality control should be applied
to a firm's products or whether a higher level of protective packaging should be used in order to reduce excessive costs of breakage
and handling further in the channel.

Some things which marketing managers can do are clearly in
both the firm's and consumers' interests in that they lower costs
and/or improve the options available to consumers. Other choices,
however, might actually reduce consumer choice. And such

decisions would seem to be at odds with a desire to improve the effectiveness of our macro-marketing system.

Consumer/citizens should vote on the changes

It seems reasonable to suggest, therefore, that marketing managers should be expected to improve and expand the range of goods and services they make available to consumers—always seeking to more fully satisfy the needs and preferences of potential customers. This is the job which has been assigned to business. To the extent that aggressive pursuit of this objective makes "excessive" demands on scarce resources or causes an "intolerable" level of ecological damage, then consumer/citizens have every right and responsibility to vote for constraints to restrict the many individual firms which are attempting to satisfy consumers' needs. These firms cannot be expected to fully appreciate the cumulative impact of their actions; this is the role which we as consumers have assigned to the government—to ensure that the macro-marketing system works effectively.

It is important to recognize that some critics of marketing are really interested in basic changes in our macro-marketing system. And, some basic changes *might* be accomplished by *seemingly minor* modifications in our present system. Allowing some government agency (e.g., the FDA or Consumer Product Safety Commission) to prohibit the sale of products for seemingly good reasons may establish a precedent which could lead to severe restrictions on new or existing product offerings. (Bicycles, for example, are now the most hazardous consumer product and perhaps they should not be sold.) Clearly, such government actions could seriously reduce consumers' present "right" to freedom of choice, including "bad" choices.[22]

Therefore, consumer/citizens should be careful to distinguish between proposed changes designed simply to modify our system and those which are designed to change it, perhaps drastically. In either case, the consumer/citizen should have the opportunity of making the decision (through his elected representatives). This decision should not be left in the hands of a few well-placed producers' representatives (even if they are marketing managers!) or government planners.

Marketing people may be even more necessary in a new system

Regardless of the changes which might be voted by consumer/citizens, some kind of a marketing system would be needed. And market-oriented businessmen probably would be needed to help define and satisfy any "new needs." In fact, if satisfying more subtle needs, such as the "good life," becomes the goal, it could be even more vital to have market-oriented firms. And the market grid concept might be especially important. It may be necessary, for example, not only to define individual's needs, but also collective needs, for a "better neighborhood" or "more enriching social experiences," and so on. As one goes beyond tangible physical goods into more sophisticated need-satisfying blends of goods and services, the trial-and-error approach of the typical production-oriented businessman becomes even more inappropriate.

Macro-marketing system must keep satisfying customers, micro-marketers can help

■ Once again, macro-marketing does *not* cost too much. Business firms, in the aggregate, have been assigned the role, by consumers, of satisfying their needs. Customers find it satisfactory, and even desirable to permit businessmen to cater to them and even to stimulate wants. As long as consumers are satisfied, macro-marketing will not cost too much, and business firms will be permitted to continue as profit-making entities.

Market-oriented businesses can help make this system work better by pinpointing consumers' needs more accurately and then developing marketing mixes to satisfy them more effectively. In other words, aggressive, market-oriented businessmen can make a difference. They can provide a dynamic element to the macro-marketing system. They can ensure that new and evolving consumer needs will be satisfied.

Yet make no mistake. Business in a free economy enjoys no special privilege. Its role is neither God-given nor royally sanctioned nor bureaucratically protected. The right to do business is a right given by individuals in their capacities as consumers, through continued patronage, and as citizens, through their votes. At any time, the right to engage in business can be revoked by the consumer citizen. Many businesses fail for lack of customers. More drastically, consumers may revoke private business's right to operate, and turn the activity over to public authorities.

This has happened in the United States in such cases as power plants taken over by municipalities; establishment of the postal service, TVA, and school systems; and government operation of defense plants and the railroads. Outside of the United States, more governments have been expanding into the "private" sector, taking over airlines and railroads, steel mills, mines, and oil fields and refineries.

It must always be remembered that business exists at the consumers' discretion, and it is only by satisfying the consumer that a particular business firm and our private enterprise system can justify its existence and hope to perpetuate itself.[23]

Conclusion

■ Our macro-marketing system certainly *does not* cost too much. It provides a necessary function in our economy, which is keyed to serving the consumer. By the decisions of many consumers and businesses, rather than a few planners, the needs and desires of consumers are satisfied.

In carrying out this role granted by consumers, however, the activities of business firms are not always as effective as they might be.

Many businessmen do not understand the marketing concept nor the role that either marketing or business play in our way of life. Furthermore, many businessmen are not as competent as they should be. In this sense, micro-marketing does cost too much. This situation is being improved, however, as training for business expands and as more competent people are attracted to marketing and business generally.

The efficiency of business and marketing would be increased greatly if more business managers understood and accepted the marketing concept — that the primary purpose of the whole business operation is to satisfy the customer. Acceptance of this philosophy forces an integration of all the activities of a business into a total system of action. This integration and the direction of all activities toward a specific goal can only lead to more effective business management, and in aggregate to more effective operation of a macro marketing system — be it an advanced economy like the United States or an underdeveloped economy.

questions and problems

1 It appears that competition sometimes leads to inefficiency in the operation of the economic system in the short run. Many people argue for monopoly in order to eliminate this inefficiency. Discuss this solution to the problem of inefficiency.

2 How would officially granted monopolies affect the operation of our economic system? Specifically, consider the effect on allocation of resources, the level of income and employment, and the distribution of income? Is the effect any different than if a monopoly were obtained through winning out in a competitive market?

3 Discuss the merits of various economic system objectives. Is the objective of the American economic system sensible? Do you feel more consumer satisfaction might be achieved by permitting some sociologists or some public officials to determine how the needs of the lower-income or less-educated members of the society should be satisfied? If you approve of this latter suggestion, what educational or income level should be required before an individual is granted free choice by the social planners?

4 Discuss the conflict of interests among production, finance, accounting, and marketing executives. How does this conflict contribute to the operation of an individual business? Of the economic system? Why does this conflict exist?

5 Why does the text indicate that the adoption of the marketing concept will encourage more efficient operation of an individual business? Be specific about the impact of the marketing concept on the various departments of a firm.

6 Should the goal of our economy be maximum efficiency? If your answer is yes, efficiency in what? If not, what should the goal be?

7 Cite an example of a critic using his own value system when evaluating marketing.

8 Is there any possibility of a pure competition economy evolving naturally? Could legislation force a pure competition economy?

9 Comment on the following statement: "Ultimately, the high cost of marketing is due only to consumers."

10 Should the consumer be king? How should we decide this issue?

notes

[1] For an extensive discussion of the problems and mechanics of measuring the efficiency of marketing, see; Stanley C. Hollander, "Measuring the Cost and Value of Marketing," *Business Topics*, Summer 1961, pp. 17–26; and Reavis Cox, *Distribution in a High-Level Economy* (Englewood Cliffs, N.J.: Prentice-Hall, Inc., 1965).

[2] B. Charles Ames, "Trappings vs. Substance in Industrial Marketing, *Harvard Business Review*, July–August 1970, pp. 93–102; and Merchant's Service, National Cash Register Co., *Establishing a Retail Store*, p. 3.

[3] This is improving but only 20 percent had in 1968. See "Government Crackdown on Unsafe Goods," *Detroit Free Press*, October 7, 1968, p. 9–B.

[4] "AMA Code of Ethics Voted by Directors" (American Marketing Association), *Marketing News*, Mid July 1970, p. 3.

[5] F. M. Nicosia, *Consumer Decision Processes* (Englewood Cliffs, N.J.: Prentice-Hall, Inc., 1966), p. 39.

[6] E. H. Chamberlin, "Product Heterogeneity and Public Policy," *American Economic Review*, May 1950, p. 86.

[7] George J. Stigler, "The Economics of Information," *Journal of Political Economy*, June 1961, p. 213.

[8] Psychologist George Katona, in a seminar at the University of Notre Dame, 1962.

[9] "Intellectuals Should Re-Examine the Marketplace; It Supports Them, Helps Keep Them Free; Prof. Stigler," *Advertising Age*, January 28, 1963; see also, E. T. Grether, "Galbraith versus the Market: A Review Article," *Journal of Marketing*, January 1968, pp. 9–14; and E. T. Grether, "Marketing and Public Policy: A Contemporary View," *Journal of Marketing*, July 1974, pp. 2–7.

[10] Jules Backman, *Advertising and Competition* (New York: New York University Press, 1967), p. 44; and William T. Moran, "Why New Products Fail," *Journal of Advertising Research*, April 1973, pp. 5–13.

[11] Backman, *Advertising*, pp. 113–14; H. Paul Root, "Should Product Differentiation Be Restricted?" *Journal of Marketing*, July 1972, pp. 3–9; and Dean S. Ammer, "Our Antitrust Laws Are Anticompetitive," *Business Horizons*, October 1971, pp. 37–48.

[12] "How U.S. 'Giants' Compete," *Business Week*, February 3, 1962, pp. 104–5; and John Maurice Clark, *Competition as a Dynamic Process* (Washington, D.C.: Brookings Institution, 1961).

[13] "A New Perspective of Product Differentiation and Advertising: The Soviet View," *Business Review*, Boston University, Spring 1962, pp. 3–12.

[14] Philip Kotler, "What Consumerism Means for Marketers," *Harvard Business Review*, May–June 1972, pp. 48–57; Stephen A. Greyser, "Public Policy and the Marketing Practitioner—Toward Bridging the Gap,"

in Fred C. Allvine (ed.), *Public Policy in Marketing Practices* (Chicago: American Marketing Association, 1973), pp. 219–32.

[15] Paul M. Mazur, "Does Distribution Cost Enough?" *Fortune*, November 1947.

[16] "The Pressure Is On For Safer Products," *Business Week*, July 4, 1970, pp. 36–39.

[17] "Policy Statement and Guidelines for Comparative Advertising," American Association of Advertising Agencies, April 1974.

[18] R. E. Wilkes and J. B. Wilcox, "Recent FTC Actions: Implications for the Advertising Strategist," *Journal of Marketing*, January 1974, pp. 55–61; and "FTC Calls Autos 'Public Utility,' Urges Car Quality Control Law," *Advertising Age*, February 23, 1970, pp. 1 f.

[19] R. Bauer and S. Greyser, "The Dialogue that Never Happens," *Harvard Business Review*, November–December 1967, pp. 2–12 and 186–90; and T. Levitt, "Why Business Always Loses," *Harvard Business Review*, March–April 1968, pp. 81–89.

[20] Louis L. Stern, "Consumer Protection via Increased Information," *Journal of Marketing*, April 1967, pp. 48–52, and Louis L. Stern, "Consumer Protection via Self-Regulation," *Journal of Marketing*, July 1971, pp. 47–53.

[21] George Fisk, "Criteria for a Theory of Responsible Consumption," *Journal of Marketing*, April 1973, p. 25.

[22] "Dictating Product Safety," *Business Week*, May 18, 1974, pp. 56–62; and Y. Hugh Furuhashi and E. Jerome McCarthy, *Social Issues of Marketing in the American Economy* (Columbus, Ohio: Grid, Inc., 1971).

[23] Marketing men are paying much more attention to the issue of social responsibility in marketing and the performance of the macro-marketing system. See Milton L. Blum, John B. Stewart, and Edward W. Wheatley, "Consumer Affairs: Viability of the Corporate Response," *Journal of Marketing*, April 1974, pp. 13–19; William G. Nickels and Noel B. Zabriskie, "Corporate Responsiveness and the Marketing Correspondence Function," *MSU Business Topics*, Summer 1973, pp. 53–58; "How Business Faces a Hostile Climate," *Business Week*, September 16, 1962, pp. 70–72; "How Social Responsibility Became Institutionalized," *Business Week*, June 30, 1973, pp. 74–82; Robert W. Ackerman, "How Companies Respond to Social Demands," *Harvard Business Review*, July–August 1973, pp. 88–98; T. H. Spratlen, "Marketing: A Social Responsibility," in B. W. Becker and H. Becker (eds.), *Marketing Education and the Real World, Combined Proceedings of the 1972 Spring and Fall Conferences* (Chicago: American Marketing Association, 1973), pp. 65–75; and Albert Z. Carr, "Can An Executive Afford a Conscience?" *Harvard Business Review*, July–August 1970, pp. 58–64.

Appendix

Appendix

Marketing arithmetic

■ The beginning business student must become familiar with the essentials of the "language of business." Businessmen commonly use accounting terminology when discussing costs, prices, and profit. So it is essential for the student to have an understanding of this terminology if the use of accounting data is to become a practical tool in analyzing marketing problems.

The following discussion introduces the basic ideas underlying the operating statement, some commonly used ratios relating to the operating statement, markups, and the markdown ratio which is frequently used in retailing. Other analytical techniques are introduced at various parts in the text and so are not treated separately here.

The operating statement

■ An operating statement for a wholesale or retail business, commonly referred to as a profit and loss statement, is presented in Figure A–1. A complete and detailed statement is presented so you will see the framework throughout the discussion, but the amount of detail on an operating statement is by no means standardized. Many companies present financial statements in considerably less detail than that shown. Their emphasis is placed on clarity and readability, rather than detail. To understand an operating statement, however, one must be aware of the items of which it is composed.

The operating statement is, in fact, only a simple description—

Figure A–1

Operating Statement
for
XYZ Company
For the year ended
December 31, 197X

Gross sales			$54,000
Less: Returns and allowances			4,000
Net sales			$50,000
Cost of goods sold			
Beginning inventory at cost		$ 8,000	
Purchases at billed cost	$31,000		
Less: Purchase discounts	4,000		
Purchases at net cost	$27,000		
Plus freight-in	2,000		
Net cost of delivered purchases		29,000	
Cost of goods available for sale		$37,000	
Less: Ending inventory at cost		7,000	
Cost of goods sold			30,000
Gross margin (gross profit)			$20,000
Expenses			
Selling expenses			
Sales salaries	$ 6,000		
Advertising expense	2,000		
Delivery expense	2,000		
Total Selling Expense		$10,000	
Administrative expense			
Office salaries	$ 3,000		
Office supplies	1,000		
Miscellaneous administrative expense	500		
Total Administrative Expense		4,500	
General expense			
Rent expense	$ 1,000		
Miscellaneous general expenses	500		
Total General Expense		1,500	
Total Expenses			16,000
Net Profit from Operation			$ 4,000

or model – of the company's operations. It presents a summary of the financial results of the operations of the company over a specified period of time. Some beginning students may object that the operating statement is not simple in its description or summary of ordinary business operations, but as we shall see, this is not the case. *The primary purpose of the operating statement is the determination of the net profit figure, and presentation of data to support that figure.*

Only three basic components

■ The basic components of an operating statement are sales, which are derived from the sale of goods or services; the costs which are incurred in the making and selling process; and the balance (called profit or loss), which is merely the difference between sales and costs. So there are only three basic elements in the statement: *sales, costs, and profit.*

Time period covered may vary

■ There is no single length of time which an operating statement covers. Rather, statements are prepared to satisfy the needs of a particular business. This may be at the end of each day or at the end of each week. Usually, however, an operating statement summarizes results of transactions over a period of one month, three months, six months, or a full fiscal year. Since this time period does vary with the company preparing the statement, this information is included in the heading of the statement, as follows:

Operating Statement

for

XYZ Company

For the (period) ended (date)

Management uses of operating statements

■ Before proceeding to a more detailed discussion of the elements of our operating statement, note some of the uses for such a statement. A glance at Figure A–1 reveals that a wealth of information is presented in a clear and concise manner. With this information, management can readily determine the *percentage of its net sales* represented by the cost of goods sold, by the gross margin, by expenses, and by the net profit. *Opening and closing inventory figures* are available, as is the amount spent during the period for the *purchase of goods for resale.* The *total expenses* are classified for the purpose of comparison with previous statements and control of these expenses.

All of this information is of vital interest to the management of a company. Assume that a particular company prepares monthly operating statements. It should be obvious that a series of these statements represents a valuable tool for the direction and control of the business. By comparing results obtained from one month to the next, management can uncover adverse trends in the sales, expense, or profit areas of the business, and take corrective action.

A skeleton statement gets down to essential details

■ Let us refer to Figure A–1 and begin to analyze this seemingly detailed statement. The intention at this point is to acquire first-hand knowledge of the composition of the operating statement.

As a first step, suppose we take all the items that have dollar amounts extended to the third, or right-hand, column. Using these items only the operating statement looks as follows:

Gross sales	$54,000
Less: Returns and allowances	4,000
Net sales	$50,000
Less: Cost of goods sold	30,000
Gross margin	$20,000
Less: Total expenses	16,000
Net profit (loss)	$ 4,000

Is this a complete operating statement? Note that the skeleton statement differs from Figure A–1 only in the matter of supporting detail. It is obvious that we have a complete operating statement, because all of the basic elements are included. In fact, the only items we *must* list to have a *complete* operating statement are:

Net sales	$50,000
Less: Costs	46,000
Net profit (loss)	$ 4,000

These three items are the *essence* of an operating statement. All other subdivisions or details are merely useful refinements.

Meaning of "sales"

The next step is to define and explore the meaning of the terms that are used in the skeleton statement.

The first item is sales. But just what do we mean by sales? The term *gross sales*, as used in this discussion, is the total amount of original billing to all customers. It is inevitable, however, that there will be a certain amount of customer dissatisfaction, or just plain errors in ordering and shipping goods. This results in *returns and allowances.*

A *return* is the act of a customer bringing or sending back goods previously purchased. The company either refunds the purchase price or allows the customer an equal amount in credit or exchange goods.

An *allowance* occurs when a customer is not fully satisfied with the purchased goods for some reason, and the company grants a price reduction on the original invoice but the customer keeps the goods.

These refunds and reductions must be taken into account when the sales figure for the period is computed. We are only interested in the revenue which the company manages to retain—that is, the actual sales dollars received or which will be received. Therefore, all reductions, refunds, cancellations, and so forth—made because of returns and allowances—are deducted from the original total (gross sales) to give us the *net sales* figure. This may be illustrated as follows:

Gross sales	$54,000
Less: Returns and allowances	4,000
Net sales	$50,000

Meaning of "cost of goods sold"

■ The next item appearing in the operating statement, cost of goods sold, shows the total value (at cost) of all the goods sold during the period. We will discuss the computation of *cost of goods sold* later. Meanwhile, merely note that after the cost of goods sold figure is obtained, it is subtracted from the net sales figure to get the amount of gross margin.

Meaning of "gross margin" and "expenses"

■ *Gross margin*, or gross profit, may be defined as the funds available to cover the cost of selling the goods and managing the business (and hopefully, to provide a profit after these expenses have been met).

Selling expense commonly is the major expense below the gross margin. It should be noted that in Figure A-1 all expenses are deducted from the gross margin to arrive at the net profit figure. The expenses, in this case, are the selling, administrative, and general expenses. Notice that the cost of goods purchased and sold is not included in this total expense figure—it has been deducted previously from net sales to determine gross margin.

The net profit figure at the bottom of the statement shows what the company has earned through its operations during this particular period. It is the amount left after the cost of goods sold and the expenses have been deducted from net sales.

Detailed analysis of sections of operating statement

Cost of goods sold for a wholesale or retail concern ▪ The cost of goods sold section includes details which are used to determine the cost of goods sold ($30,000), which is placed in the third column. But just what do we mean when we say cost of goods sold? By this term we mean *the cost value of goods sold—that is, actually removed from the company's control—and not the cost value of goods on hand at any given time.*

In Figure A-1, it is obvious that beginning and ending inventory, purchases, purchase discounts, and freight-in are all necessary in the computation of cost of goods sold. If we pull the cost of goods sold section from the operating statement, it appears as follows:

Cost of goods sold		
Beginning inventory at cost		$ 8,000
Purchases at billed cost	$31,000	
Less: Purchase discounts	4,000	
Purchases at net cost	$27,000	
Plus: Freight-in	2,000	
Net cost of delivered purchases		29,000
Cost of goods available for sale		$37,000
Less: Ending inventory at cost		7,000
Cost of goods sold		$30,000

The inventory figures merely indicate the cost of merchandise on hand at the beginning of and at the end of the period the statement covers. These figures may be obtained by a physical count of the merchandise on hand on these dates, or they may be estimated through a system of perpetual inventory bookkeeping which would show the inventory balance at any given time. The methods used in determining the inventory should be as accurate as possible, since these figures have a decided effect upon the cost of goods sold during the period, and consequently upon the net profit realized.

The net cost of delivered purchases must take into account freight charges incurred and purchase discounts received, since these items affect the cash actually spent to procure the goods and bring them to the place of business. A purchase discount is merely a reduction of the original invoice amount agreed upon at the time the goods were purchased, or which is given in consideration of prompt cash payment of the amount due. The total of such discounts is subtracted from the original invoice cost of purchases to determine the *net* cost of purchases. To this figure we add the freight charges for bringing the goods to the place of business. This gives the net cost of *delivered* purchases. When the net cost of delivered purchases is added to the *beginning* inventory at cost, we have the total cost of goods available for sale during the period. If we now subtract the *ending* inventory at cost from the cost of the goods available for sale, we obtain the cost of goods sold.*

Cost of goods sold for a manufacturing concern

■ Figure A–1 illustrates the way the proprietor of a wholesale or retail business would arrive at his cost of goods sold. Such a business would *purchase* finished goods and resell them. In a manufacturing concern, the purchases section of this operating statement would be replaced by a section called "cost of goods manufactured." This section would then take into account purchases of raw materials and parts, direct and indirect labor costs, and factory overhead charges (such as heat, light, and power) necessary in the production of the finished goods. The cost of goods manufactured would be added to the beginning finished-goods inventory, just as the net cost of delivered purchases has been, to arrive at the cost of goods available for sale. Frequently, a separate cost of goods manufactured statement is prepared, and only the total cost of production is shown in the operating statement. See Figure A–2 for an illustration of the cost of goods sold section of an operating statement for a manufacturing concern.

Expenses

■ Expenses typically appear below the gross margin. They usually include the costs of selling, and administering the business. They do not include the cost of goods, either purchased or produced.

There is no specific method for classifying the expense accounts or for arranging them on the operating statement. They might just as easily have been arranged alphabetically, or according to amount, with the largest being placed at the top, and so on down the line. In a business of any size, though, it is desirable to group the expenses in some manner and to use subtotals by groups for analysis and control purposes. This was done in Figure A–1.

Summary on operating statements

■ The statement presented in Figure A–1 contains all of the major categories in an operating statement, together with a normal amount of supporting detail. Further detail could be added to the statement under any of the major categories without changing the nature of the statement. The amount of detail normally is determined by the use to which the statement will be put. A stockholder

---

* One important point should be noted in connection with cost of goods sold. Inventory valuation methods vary from one company to another, and these different methods may cause large relative differences in the operating statements of these companies. Consult any basic accounting textbook for descriptions of the various inventory valuation methods.

Figure A–2
Cost of goods sold section of an operating statement for a manufacturing firm

Cost of goods sold		
Finished goods inventory (beginning)	$ 20,000	
Cost of goods manufactured (Schedule 1)	100,000	
Total cost of finished goods available for sale	$120,000	
Less: Finished goods inventory (ending)	30,000	
Cost of goods sold		$ 90,000
Schedule 1. Schedule of Cost of Goods Manufactured		
Beginning work in process inventory		$ 15,000
Raw materials		
Beginning raw materials inventory	$ 10,000	
Net cost of delivered purchases	80,000	
Total cost of materials available for use	$ 90,000	
Less: Ending raw materials inventory	15,000	
Cost of materials placed in production	$ 75,000	
Direct labor	20,000	
Manufacturing expenses		
Indirect labor	$4,000	
Maintenance and repairs	3,000	
Factory supplies	1,000	
Heat, light, and power	2,000	
Total manufacturing expenses	10,000	
Total manufacturing costs		105,000
Total work in process during period		$120,000
Less: Ending work in process inventory		20,000
Cost of goods manufactured		$100,000

Note: Last item, cost of goods manufactured, is used in the operating statement to determine the cost of goods sold, as above.

may be presented with a sketchy operating statement, while the one prepared for internal company use may incorporate a great amount of detail.

We have already seen that the elimination of some of the detail in Figure A–1 did not affect the essential elements of the statement — net sales, costs, and net profit. Whatever further detail is added to the statement, its purpose is to help the reader to see how these three figures have been determined. A very detailed statement might easily run to several single-spaced pages, yet the nature of the operating statement would remain the same.

Computing the stockturn rate

■ A detailed operating statement can provide the data which is needed to compute the stockturn rate. This is a measure of the number of times the average inventory is sold during a year. Note, the stockturn rate is related to the turnover during the course of a *year, not* the length of time covered by a particular operating statement.

The stockturn rate is an especially important measure because it shows how rapidly the firm's inventory is moving. Some lines of trade typically have slower turnover than others, but a decrease in the rate of turnover in a particular business can be very alarming. For one thing, it may mean that the firm's assortment of goods is no longer as attractive as it was. Also, it may mean that more working capital will be needed to handle the same volume of sales. Most businessmen pay considerable attention to the stockturn rate, attempting to achieve more rapid turnover.

Three methods, all basically similar, can be used to compute the stockturn rate. Which method is used depends somewhat on the data which is available. These three methods are shown below and usually give approximately the same results.*

$$\frac{\text{Cost of goods sold}}{\text{Average inventory at cost}} \quad (1)$$

$$\frac{\text{Net sales}}{\text{Average inventory at selling price}} \quad (2)$$

$$\frac{\text{Sales in units}}{\text{Average inventory in units}} \quad (3)$$

The computation of the stockturn rate will be illustrated for formula (1), since all are similar. The only difference is that the cost figures used in formula (1) are changed to a selling price or numerical count basis in formulas (2) and (3). It is necessary, regardless of the method used, to express both the numerator and denominator of the formula in the same terms.

Using formula (1), the average inventory at cost is determined by adding the beginning and ending inventories at cost and dividing by 2. This average inventory figure is then divided *into* the cost of goods sold (expressed in cost terms) to obtain the stockturn rate.

For example, suppose that the cost of goods sold for one year was $100,000. Beginning inventory was $25,000 and ending inventory $15,000. Adding the two inventory figures and dividing by 2, we obtain an average inventory of $20,000. We next divide the cost of goods sold by the average inventory ($100,000 divided by $20,000) and get a stockturn rate of 5.

Further discussion of the application of the stockturn rate is found in Chapter 24.

Operating ratios help analyze the business

■ The operating statement data is also used for a number of other purposes. In particular, many businessmen calculate what are called "operating ratios" from their operating statements and com-

---

* Differences will occur because of varied markups and nonhomogeneous product assortments. In an assortment of tires, for example, those with high markups might have sold much better than those with small markups, but with formula (3) all tires would be treated equally.

pare these ratios from one accounting period to another, as well as comparing their own operating ratios with those of competitors. Such competitive data is often available through trade associations. Each firm may report its results to the trade association, and then summary results are tabulated and distributed to the members. These ratios help management to analyze their operations and also are often used for control purposes. If some expense ratios are rising, for example, those particular costs are singled out for special attention.

Operating ratios are calculated by dividing net sales into the various operating statement items which appear below the net sales level in the statement. Net sales is used as the denominator in the operating ratio, because it is this figure with which the businessman is most concerned – that is, the revenue actually received and retained in the business.

We can see the relation of operating ratios to the operating statement if we think of there being an additional column to the right of the dollar figures in an operating statement. This additional column would contain percentage figures, using net sales as 100 percent. This idea may be illustrated as follows:

Gross sales	$540.00	
Less: Returns and allowances	40.00	
Net sales	$500.00	100%
Cost of goods sold	350.00	70
Gross margin	$150.00	30%
Expenses	100.00	20
Net profit	$ 50.00	10%

The ratio of gross margin to net sales in the above illustration shows that 30 percent of the net sales dollar is available to cover sales expenses and the administration of the business, and to provide a profit. Note that the ratio of expenses to sales, plus the ratio of profit to sales, equals the 30 percent gross margin ratio. The net profit ratio of 10 percent indicates that 10 percent of the net sales dollar is left for profit.

The usefulness of percentage ratios should be obvious. The percentages are easily derived, and much easier to work with than large dollar figures. With net sales as the base figure, they provide a useful means of comparison and control.

It should be noted that because of the interrelationship of these various categories, only a few pieces of information are necessary and the others can be derived easily. In this case, for example, knowledge of gross margin percent and net profit percent would enable the derivation of expense and cost of goods sold percentages. Furthermore, the inclusion of a single dollar amount would enable the calculation of all other dollar amounts.

Markups

■ A markup is the amount a firm adds to its cost to obtain its selling price. The gross margin is similar to the markup, as it is the margin available to cover the costs of selling and the management of the business, as well as to provide a profit. Gross margin and the concept of markup are related because the amount added onto the unit cost of a product by a retailer or wholesaler is expected to cover the selling and administrative expenses, and to provide a profit.

The markup approach to pricing is discussed in Chapter 24, so it will not be discussed extensively here. A simple example will illustrate the idea, however. If a retailer bought an article which cost $1 when delivered to his store, then obviously he must sell it for more than this cost if he hopes to make a profit. He might add 50 cents onto the cost of the article in order to cover his selling and other costs and, hopefully, to provide a profit. The 50 cents would be the markup.

It would also be the gross margin or gross profit on that item *if* it is sold, but it should be emphasized that it is *not* the net profit. His selling expenses might amount to 35 cents, 45 cents, or even 55 cents. In other words, there is no assurance that the markup will cover his costs. Furthermore, there is no assurance that the customers will buy at his marked-up price. This may necessitate markdowns, which are discussed later.

Markup conversions

■ Sometimes it is convenient to talk in terms of *markups on cost,* while at other times *markups on selling price* are useful. In order to have some convention, *markup (without any clarifying comment) will mean percentage of selling price.* By this definition, the 50 cent markup on the $1.50 selling price is a markup of $33\frac{1}{3}$ percent.

Some retailers and wholesalers have developed markup conversion tables so they can readily convert from cost to selling price depending on the markup on selling price they desire. To see the interrelation, we present below two formulas which can be used to convert either type of markup to the other.

Percentage markup on selling price

$$= \frac{\text{Percentage markup on cost}}{100\% + \text{Percentage markup on cost}} \tag{4}$$

Percentage markup on cost

$$= \frac{\text{Percentage markup on selling price}}{100\% - \text{Percentage markup on selling price}} \tag{5}$$

In the previous example, we had a cost of $1, a markup of 50 cents, and a selling price of $1.50. We saw that the markup on selling price was $33\frac{1}{3}$ percent, and on cost, it was 50 percent. Let us substitute these percentage figures into formulas (4) and (5) to see the process of conversion of markup from one basis to another. Assume first of all that we only know the markup on selling price, and want to convert to markup on cost. Using formula (5) we obtain:

$$\text{Percentage markup on cost} = \frac{33\frac{1}{3}\%}{100\% - 33\frac{1}{3}\%} = \frac{33\frac{1}{3}\%}{66\frac{2}{3}\%} = 50\%$$

If we know, on the other hand, only the percentage markup on cost, we could convert to markup on selling price as follows:

$$\text{Percentage markup on selling price} = \frac{50\%}{100\% + 50\%} = \frac{50\%}{150\%} = 33\frac{1}{3}\%$$

These results can be proved and summarized as follows:

Markup $0.50 = 50% of cost or 33⅓% of selling price
Cost $1.00 = 100% of cost or 66⅔% of selling price
——————————————————————————————
Selling price $1.50 = 150% of cost or 100% of selling price

It is essential to see that only the percentage figures changed, while the monetary figures of cost, markup, and selling price remained the same. Notice, too, that when the selling price is used as the basis for the computation (100 percent), then the cost percentage plus the markup percentage equal 100 percent. But when the cost of the product is used as the base figure (100 percent), it is obvious that the selling price percentage must exceed 100 percent (by the markup on cost).

Markdown ratios help control retail operations

■ The ratios we discussed earlier were concerned with figures on the operating statement. Another important ratio, the markdown ratio, is an analytical tool which is used by many retail merchants to measure the efficiency of various departments and their whole business. But note, it is *not directly related to the operating statement*. It requires special calculations.

A *markdown* is simply a retail price reduction which is often required because the customers will not buy some items at the originally marked-up price. This refusal to buy may be due to a variety of reasons—soiling, style changes, fading, damage caused by handling, or an original markup which was too high. To dispose of these goods, the merchant offers the merchandise at a lower price.

Markdowns are generally considered to be due to "business errors," perhaps because of poor buying, too high original markups, and other reasons. Perhaps the goods were damaged or soiled on display, but this, too, may have been due to poor buying or display. Regardless of the cause, however, markdowns are reductions in the original price and are important to managers who want to obtain some measure of the effectiveness of their operations.

Markdowns are similar to allowances in that price reductions have been made. Thus, in computing a markdown ratio, markdowns and allowances are usually added together and then divided by net sales. This markdown ratio is computed as follows:

$$\text{Markdown } \% = \frac{\$ \text{ Markdowns} + \$ \text{ Allowance}}{\$ \text{ Net sales}} \times 100$$

The 100 is multiplied times the fraction to reduce the handling of decimal points.

Returns are *not* included in the calculation of the markdown ratio. Returns are considered as "consumer errors," not business errors, and therefore are *not* included in the computation of this measure of business efficiency.

Retailers who use markdown ratios maintain a record of the amount of markdowns and allowances in each department and then divide the total by the net sales in each department. Over a period of time, these ratios give management a measure of the efficiency of the buyers and salespersons in the various departments.

It should be stressed again that the markdown ratio has nothing to do with the operating statement. It is not calculated directly from data on the operating statement, since the markdowns take place before the goods are sold. In fact, some goods may be marked down and still not sold. Even if the marked down items are not sold, the markdowns–that is, the reevaluations of their value–are included in the calculations in the period when they are taken.

The markdown ratio would be calculated for a whole department (or profit center), and *not* individual items. What we are seeking is a measure of the effectiveness of a whole department, not how well the department did on individual items.

questions and problems

1 Distinguish between the following pairs of items which appear on operating statements:

a. Gross sales and net sales.
b. Purchases at billed cost and purchases at net cost.
c. Cost of goods available for sale and cost of goods sold.

2 How does gross margin differ from gross profit? From net profit?

3 Explain the similarity between markups and gross margin. What connection do markdowns have with the operating statement?

4 Compute the net profit for a company with the following data:

Beginning inventory (cost)	$ 15,000
Purchases at billed cost	33,000
Sales returns and allowances	25,000
Rent	6,000
Salaries	40,000
Heat and light	18,000
Ending inventory (cost)	25,000
Freight cost (inbound)	9,000
Gross sales	130,000

5 Construct an operating statement from the following data.

Returns and allowances	$ 15,000
Expenses	20%
Closing inventory at cost	60,000
Markdowns	2%
Inward transportation	3,000
Purchases	100,000
Net profit (5%)	30,000

6 Data given:

Markdowns	$ 10,000
Gross sales	100,000
Returns	8,000
Allowances	12,000

Compute net sales and percent of markdowns.

7 (a) What percentage markups on cost are equivalent to the following percentage markups on selling price: 20, $37\frac{1}{2}$, 50, and 66.67? (b) What percentage markups on selling price are equivalent to the following percentage markups on cost: $33\frac{1}{3}$, 20, 40, and 50?

8 What net sales volume is required to secure a stockturn rate of 20 times a year on an average inventory at cost of $100,000, with a gross margin of 30 percent?

9 Explain how the general manager of a department store might use the markdown ratios computed for his various departments? Would this be a fair measure? Of what?

Cases

Guide to the use of these cases

Cases can be used in many ways. And the same case may be fruitfully considered several times, for different purposes.

The following cases are organized under several headings to suggest when they might be used *for the first time*. The basic criterion for placement, however, was *not* whether the subject matter of the case fit best there, but rather whether any text principles or technical terminology to be covered later in the text were needed to read the case meaningfully. Some early cases might require some consideration of Price, for example, and might be used twice, say in regard to product planning and later pricing. But cases listed under Price can be treated more effectively *after* the Price chapters have been covered.

Introduction to marketing management

**1
Sweeley
Foods,
Incorporated**

■ Sweeley Foods, Inc., is a 105-year-old Chicago-based food processor. Its multiproduct lines have achieved widespread acceptance under the "Sweeley" brand name. The company and subsidiaries engage principally in the preparing, canning, packaging, and marketing of canned and frozen foods. Beginning with beef, the company expanded its operations to include pineapple from Hawaii and other fruits, vegetables, pickles and condiments, Alaskan salmon, and can manufacturing. Operating more than 27 processing plants in the United States, Sweeley has become one of the largest U.S. food processors, with annual sales in 1968 of $348,-065,000.

Until 1941, Sweeley was a subsidiary of a major midwestern meat-packing company, and many of the present executives came up through the meat-packing industry. Sweeley's president recently said: "Almeat's (the meat-packing firm) influence is still with us. Sweeley has always been run like a meat-packer. As long as new products indicate a potential for an increase in the company's sales volume, they are produced. Traditionally there has been little, if any, attention paid to margins. We are well aware that the profits will come through good products."

In full agreement with the multiproduct-line policy was Howard Keene, a 25-year Sweeley employee and now production manager. Mr. Keene volunteered, "Volume comes from satisfying needs. We at Sweeley will can, pack, or freeze any meat, vegetable, or fruit we think the consumer might want." He also acknowledged that much of the expansion in product lines was dictated by economics. The typical plant facilities in the industry are not fully utilized. By adding new products to use this excess capacity, costs are spread over greater volume. So the production department is regularly looking for new ways to make more effective use of its present facilities.

The wide expansion of product line coupled with Sweeley's line-forcing policy has resulted in 85 percent of Sweeley's sales coming from supermarket chain stores, such as Kroger and A&P. Smaller stores are generally not willing to accept the Sweeley policy which requires that any store desiring to carry the Sweeley brand name must be willing to carry the complete line of 68 varieties of fruits, vegetables, and meats. Mr. Keene explains, "We know that only large stores can afford to invest the amount of money in inventory that it would take to be adequately supplied with our products. But, the large stores are the volume! We give the consumer the choice of any Sweeley product she wants, and the result is maximum sales." Many small retailers have voiced complaints about Sweeley's policy, but they have been considered to be too small in potential sales volume per store to be of any significance.

In 1969, a stockholders' revolt concerning low profits (in 1968, they were only $5,769) resulted in Sweeley's president and two of its five directors being removed. Thomas Speh, a lawyer previously employed as staff assistant to the chairman of the board, was elected president. One of the first things Mr. Speh decided to focus on was the erratic and inadequate level of profits generated by Sweeley in the past several years. A comparison of Sweeley's results with those of the California Packing Corporation (Calpack) and some other large competitors supports Mr. Speh's concern. In the past five years, Calpack had an average profit return on shareholder's investment of 10.8 percent, H. J. Heinz averaged 9 percent, Hunt Food 6 percent, and Sweeley 3.8 percent. Further, Sweeley's sales volume, $348,065,000 in 1968, had not increased significantly from the 1956 level of $325 million, while operating costs have soared upwards. Profits for Sweeley were about $8 million in 1956. The closest they have come since then is about $6 million, in 1964.

In his last report to the Sweeley board of directors, the outgoing president blamed his failure on an inefficient marketing department. He wrote, "Our marketing department has deteriorated. I can't exactly put my finger on it, but the overall quality of marketing personnel has dropped and morale is bad. The team just didn't perform." When Mr. Speh confronted Jerry Brown, the vice-president of marketing, with the previous statement, his reply was, "It's not our fault. I think the company made a key mistake after World War II. It expanded horizontally—by increasing its number of product offerings—while competitors like Calpack were expanding vertically, growing their own raw materials and making all of their packing materials. They can control quality and make profits in manufacturing which can be used in marketing. I lost some of my best men from frustration. We just aren't competitive enough to reach the market to the extent we should with a comparable product the price."

In further conversation with Jerry Brown, Mr. Speh learned

more about the nature of Sweeley's market. Although all the firms in the food-processing industry advertise extensively to the consumer market, there has been no appreciable increase in the size of the market for processed foods. Further, consumers are not very selective. If they can't find the brand of food they are looking for, they will pick up another brand rather than go without a basic part of their diet. No firm in the industry has much effect on the price at which its products are sold. Chain store buyers are used to paying about the same case rate for any competitor's product and will not exceed it. They will, however, charge any price they wish on a given brand sold at retail, (i.e., a 48-can case of sweet peas might be purchased from any supplier for $5.83, no matter whose product it is. Generally, the shelf price for each is no more than a few pennies different, but chain stores occasionally attract customers by placing a well-known brand on "sale.")

At this point Mr. Speh is wondering why Sweeley is not as profitable as it once was. Also, he is puzzled as to why the competition is putting products on the market with low potential sales volumes. For example, one major competitor recently introduced a small line of dietary fruits and vegetables, with a potential sales volume so small that virtually every nationally known food processor had previously avoided such specialization.

Discuss Sweeley's policies and what it might do to improve its present situation.

2 Horn's Cleaners

■ Mike Horn is a 26-year-old ex-Navy frogman and lifelong resident of Traverse City, Michigan, a beautiful summer resort area situated on Grand Traverse Bay along the eastern shore of Lake Michigan. The permanent population is about 20,000, and this more than trebles in the summer months.

Mike spent seven years in the Navy after high school graduation, returning home in June 1971. Mike decided to go into business for himself, after he was unable to find other satisfactory work in the Traverse City area. He established Horn's Carpet and Furniture Cleaners. Mike felt that his accumulated savings would enable him to establish the business without borrowing any money. His estimate of required expenditures were: $2,900 for a used panel truck, $425 for a steam cleaning machine adaptable to carpets and furniture, $270 for a heavy-duty commercial vacuum cleaner, $50 for special brushes and attachments, $75 for the initial supply of cleaning fluids and compounds, and $200 for insurance and other incidental expenses. This total of $3,920 still left Mike with about $2,800 in savings to cover living expenses while getting started.

One of the reasons Mike chose this line of work is his previous work experience. From the time he was 16, Mike had worked part-time for Charles Balcom. Mr. Balcom operated the only other successful carpet-cleaning firm in Traverse City. (One other firm operated in Traverse City but was rumored to be near bankruptcy.)

Mr. Balcom prided himself on quality work and had gained a

loyal clientele. Specializing in residential carpet cleaning, Balcom had been able to build a strong customer franchise. For 35 years, Balcom's major source of new business has been retailer recommendations and satisfied customers who told friends about the quality service received from Mr. Balcom. He is so highly thought of that the leading carpet and furniture stores in Traverse City always recommend Balcom's as "preventive maintenance" in quality carpet and furniture care. Often Balcom is entrusted with the keys to Traverse City's finest homes for months at a time when owners are out of town and want Balcom's services. Balcom's customers are so loyal, in fact, that a Vita-Clean national household carpet-cleaning franchise found it next to impossible to compete with him. Even price cutting was not an effective weapon against Mr. Balcom.

Mike Horn felt that he knew the business as well as Mr. Balcom, having worked for him many years. Mike was anxious to reach his $20,000-per-year sales goal because he thought this would provide him with a comfortable living in Traverse City. While aware of opportunities for carpet cleaning in businesses, office buildings, motels, and so on, Mike felt that the sales volume available there was only about $7,000, because most businesses maintained their own cleaning staffs. As he saw it, his only opportunity was direct competition with Balcom.

To get started, he allocated $530 to advertise his business in the local newspaper. With this money he was able to purchase two half-page ads and have enough left over to buy daily three-line ads in the classified section, listed under Miscellaneous Residential Services, for 52 weeks. All that was left was to paint a sign on his truck and wait for business to "catch on."

Mike had occasional customers and was able to gross about $100 a week. He had, of course, expected much more. These customers were usually Balcom regulars who, for one reason or another (usually stains, spills, or house guests), weren't able to wait the two weeks required until Balcom could work them in. While these people did admit that Mike's work was of the same quality as Balcom's, they preferred Balcom's "quality care" image that had been built up over 35 years of established work. On several occasions Mike did get more work than he could handle. This happened during April and May, when resort owners were preparing for summer openings and owners of summer homes were ready to "open the cottage." The same rush repeated itself in September and October as resorts and homes were being closed for the winter. During these months, Mike was able to gross about $100–$120 a day, working 10 hours.

Toward the end of his first year in business, Mike Horn began to have thoughts about quitting. While he hated to think of the prospects of having to leave Traverse City, he couldn't see any way of making a living in the carpet and furniture cleaning business in Traverse. Mr. Balcom had the whole residential market sewed up, except in the rush seasons and for people who needed fast cleaning.

Why wasn't Mike able to reach his goal of $20,000? Is there any way Mike can stay in business?

**3
Polymers
Manufac-
turing
Company**

■ Polymers Manufacturing Co. is a large manufacturer of basic chemicals and polymer resins, located in Pennsylvania.

Bob Zicuti, a bright young engineer, has been working for Polymers as a research engineer in the polymer resins laboratory. His job is to do research on established resins to find new, more profitable applications for resin products.

During the last five years, Bob has been under intense pressure from top management to come up with an idea that would open up new markets for the company's foamed polystyrene.

Two years ago, Bob developed the "spiral dome concept," a method of using the foamed polystyrene to make dome-shaped roofs and other structures. He described the procedure for making domes as follows:

The construction of a spiral dome involves the use of a specially designed machine which bends, places, and bonds pieces of plastic foam together into a predetermined dome shape. In forming a dome, the machine head is mounted on a boom, which swings around a pivot like the hands of a clock, laying and bonding layer upon layer of foam board in a rising spherical form.

According to Bob, polystyrene foamed boards have several advantages:

1. Foam board is stiff, but capable of controlled deformation and can be bonded to itself by heat alone.
2. Foam board is extremely lightweight and easy to handle. It has good structural rigidity.
3. Foam board has excellent and permanent insulating characteristics. (In fact the major use for foamed board is as an insulator)
4. Foam board provides an "excellent" base on which to apply a variety of surface finishes.

With his fine speaking and reasoning abilities, Bob had little trouble convincing top management of the soundness of the idea.

According to a preliminary study carried out by the marketing department, the following were areas of construction that could be served by the domes:

1. Bulk storage.
2. Cold storage.
3. Educational construction.
4. Industrial tanks (covers for).
5. Light commercial construction.
6. Planetariums.
7. Recreational construction (such as a golf course starter house).

The study was based on uses for existing dome structures. Most of the existing domes are made out of concrete or some cement base material. It was estimated that considerable savings would be realized by using foam boards, due to the reduction of construction time.

Because of the new technology involved, the company decided to do its own contracting (at least for the first four to five years after starting the sales program). It felt this was necessary to make sure that no mistakes were made by inexperienced contractor crews. For example, if not applied properly, the plastic may burn.

After building a few domes to demonstrate the concept, the company contacted some leading architects across the country. Reactions were as follows:

It is very interesting, but you know that the Fire Marshal of Detroit will never give his OK.

Your tests show that foamed domes can be protected against fires, but there are no *good* tests for unconventional building materials as far as I am concerned.

I like the idea, but foam board does not have the impact resistance of cement.

We design a lot of recreational facilities and kids will find a way of sawing holes into the foam.

Building codes around L.A. are written for wood and cement structures. Maybe when the codes change.

After this unexpected reaction, management did not know what to do. Bob still thinks the company should go ahead. He feels that a few reports of well-constructed domes in leading newspapers would go a long way toward selling the idea.

What should Polymers do? Why did it get into the present situation?

Customer behavior

**4
Sloan,
Incorporated**

■ Mr. William Sloan is the president and only stockholder of Sloan, Inc., a small, successful enterprise engaged in the restaurant and recreation business in the small town of Jefferson, the site of the state university, (population 7,000 plus 20,000 students). Mr. Sloan attended the university in the 1930s, and during his college career paid most of his educational and living expenses by selling refreshments at all of the school's athletic events. In a truly enterprising fashion, he expanded his business by hiring local high school students to assist him. The business became so profitable that it was only natural that Mr. Sloan stay on in Jefferson after graduation, renting a small building adjacent to the campus and installing a restaurant.

Over the years, his restaurant business prospered and provided Mr. Sloan with a $36,000 profit on sales of $1,462,500 in 1972. The restaurant now consists of an attractive 40-table dining room, a large drive-in facility, and free delivery of orders to any point on the campus. The only thing that hasn't substantially changed is Mr. Sloan's clientele. He estimates that his restaurant business is still over 90 percent students, and that over three fourths of his sales are made between 6 P.M. and 1 A.M. There are several other restaurants with comparable facilities in the immediate vicinity of the campus, but none of these is as popular with the university students as his "Papa Bill's."

As a result of the restaurant's success with the student market, Mr. Sloan has aimed his entire promotional effort in that direction by advertising only through the campus newspaper and over the campus and local "rock" music radio stations. In an attempt to bolster his daytime business, from time to time Mr. Sloan has used such devices as coupon mealbooks priced at 85 percent of face value. And he features daily lunch "special" plates. Nevertheless, he concedes that he has been unable to compete with the university cafeterias for daytime business.

In 1969, when Mr. Sloan was seeking a new investment opportunity, he contacted a representative of a national manufacturer of bowling equipment and supplies about the feasibility of establishing a bowling lanes operation. Jefferson didn't have such a facility at the time, and Mr. Sloan felt that both the local and university communities would provide a receptive market. He already owned a large tract of land which would be suitable for construction of the bowling lanes. The land was next to the restaurant, and he felt that such proximity would result in each business stimulating the other.

The decision was made to go ahead with the venture, and to date the results have been nothing short of outstanding. Several local and university groups have formed bowling leagues. The university's men's and women's physical education departments schedule several bowling classes at Mr. Sloan's bowling lanes each term. And the casual bowling in the late afternoons and evenings is such that at least 12 of the 16 lanes are almost always in use. Some local radio advertising is done for the bowling lanes, but not much is considered necessary by Mr. Sloan. The success of the bowling lanes has prompted the developer of a small shopping center in the "residential" part of town to make tentative plans to include a similar facility in his new development. But, Mr. Sloan believes that competition won't hurt his business because he has more to offer in his recreation center—a restaurant and bowling.

Overjoyed by the profitability of his latest investment, Mr. Sloan decided to expand his recreational center operation even further. He noted the participation of both students and local citizens in his bowling lanes and concluded that the addition of an attractive, modern billiard parlor would also have a common appeal. There were already two "poolrooms" in Jefferson. One was modern, but about 2 miles from campus. The other one was considered to be a local "hangout" and was avoided by townspeople and students. Mr. Sloan decided that distance and atmosphere were the factors which resulted in both operations being only marginally successful. Further, he felt that by offering a billiard parlor operation, he would be able to supply yet another recreational demand of his market. He obtained a loan from a local bank and proceeded to build a third building on the rear portion of his tract of land. The billiard parlor was outfitted with 12 tables, a snack bar, wall-to-wall carpeting, and a soft-music background system.

Today, eight months later, Mr. Sloan is extremely disappointed with the billiard parlor operation. After the first two or three weeks, business steadily dropped off until at the present time only one or two tables are usually in use, even during the evening hours when business at the bowling lanes is at its peak. Promotion for the billiard parlor has been combined with promotions for the other facilities, which are still doing very well.

In an effort to discover what went wrong, Mr. Sloan interviewed several of his restaurant and bowling customers. Some typical responses were:

- a coed, "Bowling in a short skirt is tricky enough. There's just no way you can gracefully shoot pool in one!"
- a fraternity man, "My idea of a good date is dinner at Papa Bill's, then the movies or an evening of bowling. You just can't make a good impression by taking a girl to play pool."
- Jefferson citizen, "I've never allowed my children to enter the local pool halls. What's more, as a kid I wasn't allowed either, and thus have never learned the game. It's too late to teach an old dog new tricks!"

Mr. Sloan is considering selling the billiard equipment and installing some pinball machines.

Evaluate Mr. Sloan's overall position and suggest what should be done.

5
Inland Steel
Company

■ Inland Steel Co. is one of the two major producers of wide-flange beams in the Chicago area. The other major producer in the area is the U.S. Steel Corp. (USS), which is several times larger than Inland as far as production capacity on this particular product is concerned. Bethlehem Steel Co. and USS have eastern plants which produce this product. Also, there are some small competitors in the Chicago area, and foreign competition is sometimes a factor. Generally, however, U.S. Steel and Inland Steel are the major competitors in wide flange beams in the Chicago area, because typically the mill price charged by all producers is the same and the customer must pay freight from the mill. Therefore, the large eastern mills landed price would not be competitive in the Chicago area.

Wide-flange beams are one of the principal steel products used in construction. They are the "modern" version of what are commonly known as "I-beams." USS rolls a full range of wide flanges from 6 inches to 36 inches. Inland entered the field about 15 years ago when it converted an existing mill to the production of this product. This mill is limited to flanges up to 24 inches, however. At the time of the conversion, it was estimated that customer usage of sizes over 24 inches was likely to be small. In the past few years, however, there has been a very pronounced trend toward the larger and heavier sections.

The beams produced by the various competitors are almost

identical, since the customers buy according to standard dimensional and physical property specifications. In the smaller size range, there are a number of competitors, but above 14 inches only USS and Inland compete in the Chicago area. Above 24 inches, USS has not had any competition.

All the steel companies sell these beams through their own sales forces. The customer for these beams is called a structural fabricator. This fabricator typically buys unshaped beams and other steel products from the mills and shapes them according to the specifications of his customer. The fabricator's customer is the contractor or owner of a particular building or structure which is being built.

The structural fabricator typically sells his product and services on a competitive bid basis. The bidding is done on the basis of plans and specifications which are prepared by an architectural or structural engineering firm and forwarded to him by the contractor desiring the bid. Although several hundred structural fabricators compete in the Midwest, relatively few account for the majority of wide-flange tonnage. Since the price is the same from all producers, they typically buy beams on the basis of availability (i.e., availability to meet production schedules) and performance (reliability in meeting the promised delivery schedule).

Several years ago, Inland production schedulers saw that they were going to have an excess of hot-rolled plate capacity in the near future. At the same time, a new production technique was developed which would enable a steel company to weld three plates together into a section with the same dimensional and physical properties and almost the same cross section as a rolled wide-flange beam. This technical development appeared to offer two advantages to Inland: (1) it would enable Inland to use some of the excess plate capacity, and (2) larger sizes of wide-flange beams could be offered. Cost analysts showed that by using a fully depreciated plate mill and the new welding process it would be possible to produce and sell larger wide-flange beams at "competitive" prices, i.e., at the same price charged by USS.

Inland executives were excited about the possibilities because they thought customers would appreciate having a second source of supply. Also, the new approach would allow the production of up to a 60-inch depth of section and an almost 30-inch width of flange. With a little imagination, these larger sizes could offer a significant breakthrough for the construction industry.

Inland decided to go ahead with the new project. As the production capacity was being converted, the salesmen were kept well informed of the progress. They, in turn, promoted this new capability, emphasizing that soon they would be able to offer a full range of beam products. Several general information letters were sent to the trade, but no advertising was used. Moreover, the market development section of the sales department was very busy explaining the new possibilities of the process, particularly to fabricators at engineering trade associations and shows.

When the new line was finally ready to go, the reaction was disappointing. In general, the customers were wary of the new product. The structural fabricators felt they could not use it without the approval of their customers, because it would involve deviating from the specified rolled sections. And, as long as they could still get the rolled section, why make the extra effort for something unfamiliar, especially with no price advantage. The salesmen were also plagued with a very common question: "How can you take plate which you sell for about $121 per ton and make a product which you can sell for $122?" This question came up frequently and tended to divert the whole discussion to the cost of production rather than the way the new product might be used.

Evaluate Inland's situation. What should it do to gain greater acceptance for its new product?

6
Toni's
Restaurant

■ Toni's was a fairly large restaurant, covering about 20,000 square feet of floor space, located in the center of a small shopping center which was completed early in 1968. In addition to this restaurant, other businesses in the shopping center included a bakery, a beauty shop, a liquor store, and a meat market. There was room for several cars in front of each of the stores.

The shopping center was located in a residential section of a growing suburb in the East. The center was situated along a heavily travelled major traffic artery. The nearby population was composed largely of middle-income families, and although the ethnic background of the residents was fairly heterogeneous, a large proportion of Italians were represented in the neighborhood.

Toni's Restaurant, which deals primarily in full-course dinners (no bar), is operated by Anthony Rocco, a neat-appearing man who was born in the community in 1920, of Italian parentage. He graduated from a local high school and a nearby university and had been living in this town with his wife and two children for many years. He had been in the restaurant business (self-employed) since his graduation from college in 1945. His most recent venture, prior to opening this restaurant, was a large restaurant which he operated successfully with his brother, from 1961 to 1967, at which time he sold out because of illness. Following his recovery, he was anxious for something to do and opened the present restaurant in April, 1968.

Toni felt that his plans for the business and his opening were well thought out. He had even designed his very attractive sign three years before. When he was ready to go into this business, he inspected several possible locations before finally deciding on the present one. He said: "I looked everywhere, and this is one of the areas I inspected. I particularly noticed the heavy traffic when I first looked at it. This is the crossroads from north to south for practically every main artery statewise. So obviously the potential is here."

Having decided upon the location, Toni attacked the problem of the new building with vigor. He tiled the floor; put in walls of surf-wood; installed new plumbing and electrical fixtures, and an extra washroom; and purchased the necessary restaurant equipment, all brand new. All this cost him $32,000 – which came from his own cash savings. He then spent an additional $600 for glassware, $1,500 for his initial food stock, and $475 to advertise his opening in the local newspaper. The local newspaper covered quite a large area so the $475 purchased only three quarter-page ads. These expenditures also came from his own personal savings. Next, he hired five waitresses at $50 a week and one chef at $85 a week. Then, with $6,000 cash on hand, he was ready to do business. Reflecting his "sound business sense," Toni realized the necessity of having a substantial cash reserve to fall back on until the business had had time to get on its own feet. He expected this to take about one year. He did not have any expectations about "getting rich overnight."

The business opened in April and by August he had achieved a weekly gross revenue of only $900. Toni was a little discouraged with this, but he was still able to meet all his operating expenses without investing any "new money" in the business. However, he was concerned that he might have to do so if business did not pick up in the next couple of months. It had not by September, and Toni did have to invest an additional $900 in the business "for survival purposes."

Business had not improved in November and Toni was still insisting that it would take at least a year to build up a business of this nature. In view of the failure to "catch on rapidly," Toni indicated that he had intensified his advertising to see if this would help the business any. In the last few weeks, he had spent $170 of his own cash for radio advertising – ten late evening spots. Moreover, he was planning to spend even more during the next several weeks for some newspaper ads.

By February 1969, business had picked up very slightly – about a $20–$30 increase in the average weekly gross.

By April 1969, the situation had begun to improve and by June his weekly gross was up to between $1,300 and $1,400. By March in the following year, the weekly gross had risen to about $1,700. Toni increased the working hours of his staff 6 to 7 hours a week and added another man to handle the increasing number of customers. Toni was more optimistic for the future. He had not put any new money into the business since the summer of 1969 and expected business to continue to rise. He had not yet taken any salary for himself, but indicated that he was in a position to do so if he wished. Instead, he planned to put in an air-conditioning system at a cost of $5,000 and was also planning to use what salary he would have taken for himself to hire two new waitresses to handle his ever-increasing volume of business.

In explaining the successful survival and growth of his business, Toni said: "I had a lot of cash on hand, a well-planned program, and the patience to wait it out."

Evaluate Rocco's marketing strategy. How might he have improved his chances for success and achieved more rapid growth?

■ After several years as a partner responsible for sales in a medium-sized manufacturing concern, Alvin Wallis disposed of his interest in the concern quite profitably. Then, searching for an interesting opportunity that he felt would be less demanding, he spent considerable time researching alternatives. He decided to purchase a recently completed 60-room motel at the edge of a small town in a relatively exclusive but rapidly expanding resort area. He saw a strong market potential for public accommodations. The location was also within one-half mile of a new interstate highway which was just being completed. Fifteen miles away in the center of the tourist area were several nationally-franchised full-service resort hotels suitable for prolonged vacations.

He was able to hire the necessary staff, which initially consisted of four maids and a handyman to care for inside and outside maintenance. Mr. Wallis looked after registration and office duties, assisted by his wife. Since he had done a great deal of travel himself and had stayed at many different hotels and motels, he had some definite ideas about what vacationers wanted in the way of accommodations. He felt that a relatively plain but modern room with a comfortable bed, standard bath facilities, and complete air conditioning would appeal to most patrons.

He did not consider a swimming pool or any other non-revenue producing additions to be worthwhile, and considered a restaurant to be a greater management problem than the benefits that would accrue. However, after many customers commented, he arranged to serve a continental breakfast of coffee and rolls from a service counter in a room next to the registration desk.

During the first year after opening, occupancy began to stabilize around 50–60 percent of capacity. According to figures which Mr. Wallis obtained from the publication *Trends in the Hotel-Motel Business* published by the accounting firm of Harris, Kerr Forster & Company, his occupancy rate ranked considerably below the average of 78 percent for his classification — motels without restaurants.

Examination of these results after two years of operation began to disturb Mr. Wallis. He decided to evaluate his operation and search for means of increasing both occupancy rate and profitability. He did not want to sacrifice his independence and was trying not to compete directly with the resort areas offering much more complete services. For advertising and promotion, Mr. Wallis had stressed a price appeal in his signs and brochures. He was quite proud of the fact that he had been able to avoid all the "unnecessary" expenses of the resorts and was thus able to offer lodging at a very modest price, much below that of even the lowest-priced resort. He found that the customers who stayed at his motel found the accommodations quite acceptable, but was troubled by what seemed to be a large number of cars driving into his parking lot and looking around but not coming in to register.

Mr. Wallis was particularly interested in the results of a recent study conducted by the regional tourist bureau. This study revealed the following information with regard to area vacationers:

1. 68 percent of the visitors to the area are young couples and older couples without children.
2. 40 percent of the visitors plan their vacations and reserve rooms more than 60 days in advance.
3. 66 percent of the visitors stay more than three days in the area and at the same location.
4. 78 percent of the visitors indicated that recreational facilities were instrumental in their choice of accommodations.
5. 13 percent of the visitors had family incomes of less than $7,500 per year.
6. 38 percent of the visitors indicated that it was their first visit to the area.

Evaluate Mr. Wallis' strategy. What should he do to improve the profitability of ABC Motel, Inc.?

8
The American Bank of Meadville

■ The American Bank of Meadville, Missouri, was organized in 1898 and has been in continuous operation since that time. The bank is located in a community of about 6,500 people, which is situated 35 miles south of Kansas City. Being in Scott County, Meadville is considered to be part of the Greater Kansas City metropolitan area. The county has been experiencing rapid population growth, particularly in its northern sectors. The 1960 census gave Scott County a population of 60,000. The population in 1970 was about 145,000. Meadville's 1960 population was 5,400. The community has four local factories which employ about 700. All other local employment is in service businesses, such as clothing, grocery, drug, and hardware stores. A significant number of people commute to Kansas City to work. Four buses now shuttle workers to jobs at three Kansas City plants.

Meadville is the primary retail trade center for southern Scott County. Market studies have shown that it has an effective trade radius of about 8 miles. The American Bank has been the only bank serving the community since the early 1930s, when the Farmers and Merchants Bank was liquidated. American's footings in 1970 were about $10 million, a growth of about $1.5 million over 1968.

The largest bank in the county, with footings of $11 million, is located 10 miles northeast of Meadville in the town of Hempstead. Immediately adjacent to Hempstead is its twin city of Anderson. Both communities have a combined population of about 14,000 people. The Anderson State Bank's 1970 footings were about $7 million. The Bank of Scottsdale, located at the county seat six miles northwest of Meadville, has footings of about $3.5 million. The American Bank has no other banking competition for a distance of 25 miles to the southwest, south, and southeast.

The American Bank is controlled by a prominent local physician, Dr. Yokum. He also controls the local savings and loan association and owns much real estate in the community. He exerts considerable influence upon the operating policy of the American Bank and has seen to it that American has had a very conservative image. Likewise, he has not been a strong advocate for community growth.

As recently as 1964, he said, "I'm very happy with Meadville just the way it is."

The American Bank now employs about 23 people and has 5 operating officers. The executive vice president and cashier, Mr. Martin, is about 48 years old and came to American 10 years ago from The Commerce Bank of Kansas City. The assistant to the vice president is Sam Yokum, Dr. Yokum's son, a recent political science graduate of a small men's college. The three assistant cashiers are Mr. Smith (age 54), Mrs. Conti (age 60), and Mr. Sanders (age 26). Mr. Smith handles the consumer loan department and is noted in the community for his sour disposition. Mrs. Conti handles the real estate loan department and has been experiencing some health problems the past six months. In recent years an increasing proportion of Meadville's real estate financing has been handled by Piedmont Federal Savings and Loan, located 30 miles to the south in the town of Stapleton. Mr. Sanders supervises the bookkeeping department and is noted in the community for his enthusiasm and drive. He graduated from the local high school and went to work as a teller at American. Since that time, he has taken 60 hours of accounting and similar subjects in night school at the University of Missouri at Kansas City.

American occupies a large two-story building which was remodeled in 1966. In 1968, it opened a new drive-in-walk-up facility in a shopping center on North Main Street. This facility represented an investment of about $175,000, and many in the community were surprised that "old Doc Yokum" has been persuaded to go into this venture. Hours at the bank and drive-in are similar to those of other banks in the county. And the bank offers a full line of services common to banks in the area. Its interest rates and charges are now the same as other county banks.

The officers of American can always be found in the bank. No formal plan exists for its officers to make regular visits to businesses in the community. Mr. Martin tries to get out and about town, but he has found that he must spend considerable time instructing Sam Yokum in banking matters. Both Sam's and Mr. Martin's memberships in Rotary are paid by the bank, but only Mr. Martin belongs to any other community organizations. These include the local industrial development board and the Chamber of Commerce. All bank employees are encouraged to participate in church activities and Mrs. Conti is particularly active.

The American Bank advertises in two papers having concentrated circulation in the Meadville area. The bank also advertises in an "ad" paper printed at the county seat. This paper has free countywide distribution, and all of its costs are borne by its advertisers. American has no road signs of any type and does not advertise over the county's one radio station. Recent promotional efforts have included the distribution of American Bank calendars, telephone book covers, and sending congratulation messages to area high school and college graduates. In addition, a large meeting room on the bank's second floor is made available to various local organizations. No charge is made for the use of this room. This service has not been pushed, however, and only six meetings were held in this room in the past year.

Early in 1971, a group of local business and professional men were granted a state charter to establish and operate The First State Bank of Meadville. The new bank building will be $1\frac{1}{2}$ blocks north of the American Bank. The board of directors of First State have announced, through local news media, that they will aggressively pursue an energetic and progressive banking policy — to give the people of Meadville the outstanding financial services needed by a rapidly growing community.

Discuss American Bank's past strategy and what they should do now.

Product

9
B & B Floral-
Gift Shoppe

■ The B & B Floral-Gift Shoppe is owned and operated by Bruce and Betty Douglas (a husband and wife team). Offering hundreds of varieties and arrangements of flowers, B & B also carries small gift items intended to complement a floral arrangement. Mr. Douglas serves primarily as manager and salesclerk, while Mrs. Douglas' artistic talents lend themselves more to the selection and arrangement of appropriate flowers. Since opening in 1965, sales for B & B have been gratifying. Mr. Douglas, however, is concerned about the failure of a recent addition to his gift line.

The Douglases purchased the present operation in 1965 from Rick Allen, who had been in that location for 20 years. Called Allen's Florists, the shop was then generating about $100,000 a year in business. Bruce and Betty were confident that their previous 12 years' experience owning a smaller floral shop in a tiny (pop. 6,500) resort town less than 20 miles south would enable them to become a success in their new location.

Bruce Douglas feels their new store is in an excellent location. Situated in a residential area of a northeast Indiana community of 130,000 population, the new B & B Floral-Gift Shoppe is somewhat isolated from other neighborhood stores. It is 8 blocks to the nearest store, a drugstore, and $3\frac{1}{2}$ miles to the closest shopping center. But, it is near the intersection of the major north-south and east-west thoroughfares.

Mr. Douglas was keenly aware of his primary customers' characteristics. This perception enabled him to direct his efforts more efficiently. As a result, B & B's sales increased steadily from $150,000 at the end of 1965 to $300,000 in 1972. Most of his regular customers were women from medium- to high-income families living in the local middle-class residential areas. Also, Mr. Douglas was pleased to see that some of his "old customers" from the resort town come to B & B, probably because a strong customer acceptance had been built on friendly service and quality floral arrangements. Those customers who stopped in less frequently were assumed to be similar to the "regulars."

The largest part of the shop's business consists of weddings, funerals, parties, dances, and other big, one-time events which utilize flowers. However, about 25 percent of the purchases are by casual buyers who like to browse and chat with the Douglases. Approximately 60 percent of the sales are telephone orders, while the remaining 40 percent are made in the shop. Almost all of the telephone orders are for special, one-time events, while the walk-in traffic is divided equally between special events and spur-of-the-moment purchases. Virtually no one buys flowers on a daily or regular basis. There is some FTD (Florist Telegraph Delivery) business, but Mr. Douglas considers this to be an added service, and it constitutes only about 5 percent of his volume.

Mr. Douglas feels that flowers are fairly homogeneous, unbranded products. Therefore, he feels that he must charge competitive prices to meet those of his 14 competitors throughout the community.

The shop was remodeled in 1972, and space for all operations was doubled. To fill in the increased display area, it was decided to add several complementary gift items, such as a famous brand of candies, high-quality flowerpots and vases, a quality line of sheep- and lamb-skin rugs, pen-and-pencil sets, and candles. All the new lines, except the sheep- and lambskin rugs, have taken hold and have increased in sales each month since the items were added. Sales of rugs have been very disappointing. In fact, they haven't paid their way on the basis of display area allotted (about 1/50 of the total display area).

When the busiest store traffic occurs (during a three- to four-day period before traditional flower-giving days), additional help is used. When available, Lisa and Kevin Douglas, the high school-aged children of the proprietors, fill these jobs. (It was the children who suggested that the market for sheep- and lambskin rugs was growing in their high school during the last school year.) At other times, only one of the proprietors and a full-time salesclerk handle store traffic.

Samples of everything the shop has for sale are on display. The primary activity of the salesclerk is to show customers various selections which could be used for a particular occasion and then ring up the sale. Other than store display, advertising consists only of what is printed on the delivery truck, an ad in the yellow pages of the local telephone directory, and an occasional ad (five or six times per year) in the daily newspaper. None of the advertising mentions anything but flowers, because the proprietors wish to maintain their identity as florists.

Mr. Douglas is wondering if more display area, a lower price, or extra promotion by the salesclerks might increase the movement of the sheep- and lambskin rugs. Further, he is thinking of disposing of the rugs, but isn't sure what should replace them if he did.

Evaluate the B & B Floral-Gift Shoppe's present operation and why sheep- and lambskin rugs don't sell. What strategy should it follow?

■ The Block Pharmaceutical Company is a well-known manufacturer of high-quality cosmetics and ointments. A little over a year ago, Mr. Fine, the president of Block, was scanning the income statements for the last three quarters and did not like what he saw. At the next board meeting he stated that Block should be showing a larger profit. It was generally agreed that the reason for the profit decline was that the firm had not added any new products to its line during the last two years.

Management was directed to investigate this matter and remedy it if possible.

Mr. Fine immediately requested a report from the product-planning group and found that it had been working on a new formula for a toothpaste that might be put into production immediately if a new product were needed. Mr. Archer, the head of the research department, assured Mr. Fine that the new ingredients in this toothpaste had remarkable qualities. Clinical tests had consistently shown that the new, as yet unnamed, dentifrice cleaned teeth better and prevented decay significantly more efficiently than the many toothpastes furiously battling for prominence in the market. Based on these tests, Mr. Fine concluded that perhaps this product was what was needed and ordered work to proceed quickly to bring it to the market.

The marketing research department was asked to come up with a name that was pleasing, and a tube and carton design. The results were reported back within two months; the product was to be called "Smile" and the package would emphasize eye-pleasing pastels.

The marketing department decided to offer Smile along with its other "prestige" products in the drugstores which were carrying the rest of Block's better-quality, higher-priced products. Block's success had been built on moving quality products through these outlets, and management felt that quality-oriented customers would probably be willing to pay a bit more for a significantly better toothpaste. Block was already well established with the wholesalers selling to these retailers and experienced little difficulty obtaining distribution for Smile.

It is now six months after the introduction of Smile, and the sales results have not been good. The established wholesalers and retailers carried the product, but relatively little was purchased by final consumers. And now many retailers are requesting that Block accept returns on Smile because obviously it is not going to catch on with consumers, despite the extremely large (matching that of competitors) amounts of advertising which have supported Smile.

Mr. Fine has requested the marketing research department to analyze the situation and explain the disappointing results thus far. An outside survey agency interviewed several hundred consumers and has tabulated its results. These are pretty well summarized in the following quotes:

"The stuff I'm using now tastes good. Smile tastes terrible!"

"I never saw that brand at the supermarket I shop at."

"I like what I'm using . . . why change?"

"I'm not going to pay that much for any toothpaste . . . it couldn't be *that* much better!"

What recommendation would you make to Mr. Fine? Why?

11
Dow
Chemical
Company

■ Dow Chemical Company is one of the larger chemical companies in the United States, making a diversified line of organic and inorganic chemicals, plastics, bioproducts, and metals. Research has played a vital role in the company's growth.

Recently, Dow's research laboratories developed a new product in the antifreeze line – Dowtherm 209. Much research was devoted to the technical phase, involving various experiments concerned with the quality of the components in the new product.

The antifreeze commonly used now is ethylene glycol. If it leaks into the crankcase oil, it forms a thick pasty sludge that can produce bearing damage, cylinder scoring, or a dozen other costly and time-consuming troubles for both the operator and owner of heavy-duty equipment.

Dow Chemical believed that Dowtherm 209 would be very valuable to the owners of heavy-duty diesel and gasoline trucks as well as other heavy-equipment owners. Chemically, Dowtherm 209 consists of methoxy propanol, as distinguished from the conventional glycol and alcohol products. It cannot prevent leakage, but if it does get into the crankcase, it will not cause any problems.

Dowtherm 209 has been proven in the laboratory to prevent seizing of rod and main bearings, pistons, rings, and piston pins which are common with glycol leakage. The new product will not remain in the engine oil and will cut down on the sludge residue.

At first, Dow thought it had two attractive markets for this product: (1) the manufacturers of heavy-duty equipment, and (2) the users of heavy-duty equipment. Dow salesmen have made numerous calls and so far neither type of customer has been very interested. The manufacturers are reluctant to show interest in the product until it has been proven in actual use. The buyers for construction companies and other firms using heavy-duty equipment have also been hesitant. Some felt the price was far too high for the advantages offered. Others didn't understand what was wrong with the present antifreeze and dismissed the idea of paying extra for "just another" antifreeze.

The price of Dowtherm 209 is $12.98 per gallon, which is more than twice the price of regular antifreeze. The higher price is a result of higher costs in producing the product and an increment for making a better type of antifreeze.

Explain what has happened so far. What would you do if you were responsible for this product?

■ Two years ago Harry Ranebow purchased the inventory, supplies, equipment, and business of Washington Sport Sales, which was located in one of the suburbs of Spokane, Washington. The business was in an older building along a major highway leading out of town, but it was several miles from any body of water. The previous owner had achieved sales volumes of about $50,000 a year, just breaking even. For this reason, plus the desire to retire to southern California, the owner had been willing to sell to Harry for roughly the value of the inventory. Washington Sport Sales had been selling two well-known brands of small pleasure boats, a leading outboard motor, two brands of snowmobiles, and a complete line of trailer and pickup truck campers. The total inventory was valued at about $18,000 and Harry used all of his own savings and borrowed some from two friends to buy the inventory. At the same time, he took over the lease on the building so he was able to begin operations immediately.

Harry had never operated a business of his own before, but he was confident that he would be able to do well. He had worked in a variety of capacities as an auto repair man, service man, and generally a jack of all trades in the maintenance departments of several local businesses.

Soon after beginning operations, Harry hired a friend of his who had had a similar background. Together, they handled all selling and set-up work on new sales, and maintenance work as necessary. Sometimes they were extremely busy—at the peaks of each sport season. Then, both sales and maintenance kept them going up to 16 hours a day. At these times it was difficult to have both new and repaired equipment available as soon as desired by customers. At other times, however, Harry, and his friend Jim, had almost nothing to do.

Harry generally charged the prices suggested by the various manufacturers, except at the end of a weather season when he was willing to make deals in order to minimize his inventory. Harry was a little annoyed that some of his competitors sold principally on a price basis, generally offering 10 to 20 percent off of the manufacturer's suggested list prices. Harry did not feel he wanted to get into that kind of business, however, because he wanted to build a loyal following based on friendship and personal service. And he did not feel he really had to cut price, because all of the lines he carried were "exclusive" for him in the area. No dealers within a ten mile radius carried any of his brands.

To try to build a favorable image for his company, Harry occasionally placed advertisements in local papers and purchased some radio spots. The basic theme of this advertising was that Ranebow Sports Sales was a good place to purchase the equipment needed for that season of the year. Occasionally, he mentioned the brand names he carried, but generally he was attempting to build his own image. He decided in favor of trying to build his own image because, although he had exclusives on the brands he carried, there generally were 10 to 15 different manufacturers' goods being sold in each product category at any one time and most of the products were quite similar. Harry felt that this degree of similarity among competing products almost forced him to try to differentiate himself on the basis of himself and his own store's services.

The first year's operation was not profitable. In fact, after paying minimal salaries to Jim and himself, the business just about broke even. And this was without making any provision for return on his investment. In hopes of improving his profitability, Harry jumped at a chance to add a line of lawn tractors and attachments as he was starting into his second year in business. This line was offered by a well-known equipment manufacturer who was expanding into his market. The equipment was similar to that offered by other lawn equipment manufacturers, but had a number of unique features and specialized attachments. Harry was also attracted by the manufacturer's willingness to do some local advertising on his own and to provide some point-of-purchase displays. And he also liked the idea that customers probably would be wanting this equipment sometime earlier than they would become interested in boats and other summer items. Therefore, he would be able to handle this business without interfering with his other peak selling seasons.

Now it is two years after Harry started the Ranebow Sport Sales Company and he is still only breaking even. Sales have increased somewhat, but he has had to hire some part-time help. The lawn equipment line did help to expand sales as he had expected, but unfortunately it did not appear to increase profits. The part-time helpers were needed to service this business, in part because the manufacturer's advertising had generated a lot of sales inquiries. Relatively few of these resulted in sales, however, and so it is possible that Harry may have even lost money handling the new line. He is reluctant to give up this line, however, because he has no other attractive alternatives on the horizon and he does not want to give up that sales volume. Further, the manufacturer's salesman has been most encouraging, assuring Harry that things will get better and that they will be glad to continue their promotional support for Harry's business during the coming year.

Evaluate Harry's overall strategy. What should he do in the future, especially regarding the lawn tractor line?

13 Tober's Ice Cream Company

■ Tober's Ice Cream Company was first established in 1940 in a small but growing town of approximately 6,000 persons. At that time, there was almost no competition in the local ice cream market, and Tober's sales grew from about $5,000 the first year to slightly over $100,000 a year in the early 1960s. Sales efforts were concentrated primarily on the local grocery stores, restaurants, and drug stores. In addition, a soda fountain was operated in the front of the building used to manufacture the ice cream. A number of customers were served there and pints, quarts, and so on of ice cream were sold for take-out.

Tober's had a good reputation locally, based on the production of high quality ice cream and friendly service.

Due to a death in the family, Tober's was sold to Albert Evans in early 1967. Mr. Evans felt that the purchase of Tober's would be a good investment, certainly better than the gasoline service station he had been operating in the community with the assistance of his son, Dave. Tober's had been yielding a return on sales of about 5 percent a year, after salaries and wages of between $15,000 and $20,000 a year. Mr. Evans felt that this would provide an adequate return to his family and assure some retirement income for his wife and himself. It is now 1969, however, and Mr. Evans is gravely concerned. His annual sales volume has declined about $5,000 per year in the last two years and he is baffled because he has not made any major changes in the business since he bought it two years ago.

The ice cream making process at Tober's is quite easy and Mr. Evans found no difficulty in adapting to the daily routine. Generally, Tober's operates on an eight-hour day, five-day week. Milk is brought in by local farmers in ten-gallon cans. These farmers have been selling milk to Tober's for years and they receive the same price as they would at the local dairy. Samples are taken from each can to determine the cream content and to comply with health requirements. The cans are then stored in a large cooler until the supply of pasteurized milk is nearly depleted. Then the milk is poured into a large vat and pasteurized, and then transferred into another large chill vat for storage until needed. These processes require a minimum of effort and can be handled along with the normal ice cream making chores, which have been handled for years by one man who is now in his late 50s and extremely competent. In fact, Mr. Evans feels that he is quite fortunate to have such an employee, because he never has to worry about getting the ice cream made.

Only one mixing machine is used, and generally not more than 15 to 18 gallons are made at any one time. The most common flavors are vanilla, strawberry, and chocolate, and these are always kept on hand. Other flavors are made as sales warrant. Often, a special "flavor of the month" is made to be sold at a slightly reduced price. The two and one-half gallon containers for sale to drug store soda fountains are filled directly from the mixer. Other ice cream is transferred to a dispensing machine where cup, pint, quart, half-gallon, and gallon containers are filled. These smaller containers are all pre-printed, except for the flavor which is stamped onto each container with a rubber stamp at the time of filling.

In addition to the ice cream, Tober's makes a few novelty-type items—popsicles, fudgesicles, chocolate-covered ice cream on a stick, and ice cream cups with strawberries or chocolate on the top.

These items are also made by hand, since Tober's is not large enough for automated processing.

During the winter months when demand for ice cream is not too heavy, Mr. and Mrs. Evans often assist in filling the containers. In the summer, Mr. Evans hires a high-school boy to work full-time and finds it necessary to help out himself. He sometimes finds himself at the soda fountain. Customers entering the front door cause a bell to ring in the plant, and then someone goes to the soda fountain to wait on them.

Tober's has one delivery truck which is three years old and wearing out rapidly. Dave Evans, Mr. Evans' son, is the truck driver and also the only sales contact with outside customers. He has several daily routes which are routinely covered. On Mondays, Wednesdays, and Fridays he stays primarily in the local area, serving grocery stores, drug stores, and restaurants. On Tuesdays and Thursdays he goes to similar outlets at rural crossroads and in the small surrounding towns. In the last six months, the truck has broken down more frequently and Dave has had to miss some of the stops. But he feels that these stops can always be made up the next time around without any problem. Recently, however, he has noticed that several of the grocery stores which had previously handled only Tober's ice cream now have another brand—from a larger out-of-town company—sharing the freezer space.

The population has continued to grow in the area—about 75,000 now live in the city and "suburbs"—and this has attracted a large supermarket and two smaller ones. These stores have carried ice cream produced by out-of-town competitors, and often their prices are lower than Tober's price. These stores also carry Tober's ice cream because of its established local reputation, and Mr. Evans is confident that his reputation for good quality will keep sales up. And sales have been holding steady in these larger stores.

The local soda fountains appear to be losing business to the new drive-in type establishments which serve soft-serve ice cream, however. And Tober's soda fountain business has dropped off in the last two years. Further, hardly any customers now come to Tober's for cartons of ice cream.

Mr. Evans is becoming much more concerned about the situation, because if sales continue to drop at the present rate, all his plans for a comfortable living and the accumulation of a nest egg for retirement will come to nothing. In fact, if the present trends continue he will be forced to close the business and lose his investment. He is thinking seriously about advertising in the local newspaper but he is reluctant to incur any additional costs, especially when he realizes that the previous owner seemed to get along well without any advertising. Perhaps he could add additional ice cream flavors. Or maybe he should cut his price. He has been thinking about this for the last year, and does not know which way to move.

Evaluate Tober's strategy and explain what Mr. Evans should do and why.

Place

■ Major Camera Co. is located in a city of 250,000 near a major university. It sells high-quality still and movie cameras, accessories, and projection equipment, including 8 and 16MM movie projectors, 35MM slide projectors, opaque and overhead projectors, and a large assortment of projection screens. Most of the sales of this specialized equipment are made to area school boards for classroom use, to industry for use in research and sales, and to the university for use in research and instruction.

Major Camera offers a wide selection of film and a specialized film-processing service. Rather than processing film on a mass production basis, however, each roll of film is given individual attention to accentuate the particular features requested by the customer. This service is used extensively by local industries who need high-quality pictures of lab or manufacturing processes for analytical and sales work.

To encourage the school and industrial trade, Major Camera offers a graphics consultation service. If a customer wishes to construct a display, whether large or small, professional advice is readily available. Along with this free service, Major Camera carries a full line of graphic arts supplies.

Major Camera employs four full-time store clerks and two outside salesmen. These salesmen make calls on industry, attend trade shows, make presentations for schools, and assist both present and potential customers in their use and choice of visual aids.

The people who make most of the over-the-store-counter purchases are serious amateur photographers and some professional photographers who buy in small quantities. Price discounts of up to 25 percent of the suggested retail price are given to customers who purchase more than $500 worth of goods per year. Most regular customers qualify for the discount.

A few years ago, Eastman Kodak introduced the Kodak Instamatic Camera. This camera comes in several models, each offering selected features and ranging in price from $11.95 to $140. Kodak has had great success with this camera, especially in the low-price range. The features which are especially appealing are cartridge loading ("just drop it in and shoot"), no rewinding (this is done by a spring motor), and no adjustments (camera is completely automatic). The most popular film for the Instamatic is the 35MM, 2×2 slide film.

The camera's major appeal is to those people who typically have had difficulty with more complicated cameras, but still enjoy taking their own pictures. Kodak claims "You get a perfect picture every time."

Because the Instamatic camera is available in discount houses, drugstores, department stores, and nearly every other possible outlet, Major Camera does not carry it. However, it does sell the film cartridges, which come with a mail-in processing envelope.

Andrew Machey, the manager of Major Camera, felt that with so many people taking 35MM slide pictures there ought to be a good demand for some way of viewing them. Therefore, he planned a special pre-Christmas sale of inexpensive slide projectors, viewers, and home-sized projection screens. Hoping that most of these would be purchased as Christmas gifts, Machey selected some products which offered good value and discounted the prices to competitive levels, for example, projectors at $29.95, viewers at $3.95, and screens at $11.95. To promote the sale, large signs were posted in the store windows and ads were run in a Christmas gift suggestion edition of the local newspaper. This edition appeared each Wednesday during the four weeks preceding Christmas.

At these prices and with this promotion, Machey hoped to sell at least 150 projectors and screens, and 200 viewers. When the Christmas returns were in, total sales were 22 projectors, 15 screens, and 48 viewers. He was most disappointed with these results, especially because trade estimates suggested that sales of projection equipment in this price and quality range were up 300 percent over last year.

Evaluate what happened. What should Mr. Machey do in the future?

15
Hickey
Company

■ John Hickey graduated in business from a large midwestern university in 1971. After a year as a car salesman, he decided to go into business for himself. In an effort to locate new opportunities, John placed several advertisements in his local newspaper—in Toledo, Ohio—explaining that he was interested in becoming a sales representative in the local area. He was quite pleased to receive a number of responses. Eventually, he became the sales representative in the Toledo area for three local manufacturers: the Sampson Drill and Press Co., which manufactured portable drills; the J. C. Peterson Co., which manufactured portable sanding machines; and the Gilbert Lathe Co., which manufactured small lathes. All of these companies were relatively small and were represented in other areas by other sales representatives like John Hickey.

Hickey's main job was to call on industrial customers. Once he made a sale, he would send the order to the respective manufacturer, who would, in turn, ship the goods directly to the particular customer. The manufacturer would bill the customer, and Hickey would receive a commission varying from 5 percent to 10 percent of the dollar value of the sale. It was Hickey's responsibility to pay his own expenses.

Hickey called on anyone in the Toledo area who might use the products he was handling. At first, his job was relatively easy, and sales came quickly because there was little sales competition. There are many national companies making similar products, but at that time they were not well represented in the Toledo area.

In 1973, John Hickey sold $150,000 worth of drills, earning a 10 percent commission; $50,000 worth of sanding machines, also earning a 10 percent commission; and $75,000 worth of small lathes earning a 5 percent commission. He was most encouraged with his progress and was looking forward to expanding sales in the future. He was especially optimistic because he had achieved these sales volumes without overtaxing himself. In fact, he felt he was operating at about 70 percent of his capacity.

Early in 1974, however, a local manufacturer with a very good reputation—the Porter Electrical Equipment Company—started to manufacture a line of portable drills. It had a good reputation locally, and by April of 1974 Porter had captured approximately one half of Sampson's Toledo drill market by charging a substantially lower price. Porter was using its own sales force locally, and it was likely that it would continue to do so.

The Sampson Company assured Hickey that Porter could not afford to continue to sell at such a low price and that shortly Sampson's price would be competitive with Porter's. John Hickey was not nearly as optimistic about the near-term prospects, however. He began looking for other products he could handle in the Toledo area. A manufacturer of hand trucks had recently approached him, but he was not too enthusiastic about this offer because the commission was only 2 percent on potential annual sales of $150,000.

Now John Hickey is faced with another decision. The Howard Paint Company in Cleveland, Ohio, has made what appears to be an attractive offer. They heard what a fine job he was doing in the Toledo area and felt that maybe he could help them solve their present problem. Howard is having difficulty with its whole marketing effort and would like John Hickey to take over.

The Howard Paint Company has been selling primarily to industrial customers in the Cleveland area and is faced with many competitors selling essentially the same product and charging the same low prices. Howard Paint is a small manufacturer. Last year's sales were $80,000. They would like to increase this sales volume and could handle at least double this sales volume with ease. They have offered Hickey a 12 percent commission on sales if he will take charge of their pricing, advertising, and sales efforts in the Cleveland area. John was flattered by their offer, but he is a little concerned because there would be a great deal more travelling than he is doing at present. For one thing, he would have to spend a couple of days each week in the Cleveland area, which is 110 miles distant. Further, he realizes that he is being asked to do more than just sell. But he did have some marketing courses in college and thinks the new opportunity might be challenging.

What should John Hickey do? Why?

16
The Belmont
Tool
Company

■ The Belmont Tool Co. is a manufacturer of industrial cutting tools. These tools include such items as lathe blades, drill press bits, and various other cutting edges used in the operation of large metal cutting, boring, or stamping machines. The president of the company, Ray Gillespie, takes great pride in the fact that his company, whose $1,342,500 sales in 1968 is small by industry standards, is recognized as a producer of the highest-quality line of cutting tools to be found.

Competition in the cutting tool industry is intense. Belmont Tool must contend with competition not only from the original manufacturers of the machines, but also from many other relatively powerful companies offering cutting tools as one of many diverse product lines. This situation has had the effect, over the years, of standardizing the price, specifications, and in turn, the quality, of the competing products of all manufacturers.

Approximately one year ago, Mr. Gillespie was tiring of the tremendous financial pressure of competing with companies enjoying economies of scale. At the same time, he noted that more and more potential cutting tool customers were turning to small custom tool and die shops because of specialized needs that were not met by the mass production firms. Mr. Gillespie then considered a basic change in strategy. Although he was unwilling to become strictly a custom producer, Mr. Gillespie felt that quite possibly the recent trend toward buying customized cutting edges was a good indication of the development of new markets which would be too small for the large, multiproduct-line companies to serve profitably. He thought that the new markets might be large enough so that a flexible company of Belmont Tool's size could make a good profit.

An outside company, Brook Marketing Research Associates, was asked to study the feasibility of serving this potential new market. The initial results were encouraging. It was estimated that Belmont Tool could increase sales by 50 percent and double profits from servicing the emerging market.

The next step taken by Belmont Tool was to develop a team of technical specialists to maintain continuous contact with potential cutting tool customers. They were supposed to identify any present or future needs which might exist in enough cases to make it possible to profitably produce a specialized product. The technical specialists were not to take orders, nor to "sell" Belmont Tool to the potential customers. Mr. Gillespie felt that only through this policy could these men easily gain access to the persons in possession of the required information.

The initial feedback from the technical specialists was most encouraging. The company, therefore, decided to constantly adapt its high-quality products to the ever-changing, specialized needs of users of cutting tools and edges.

The potential customers of Belmont Tool's specialized tools are widely dispersed. The average sale per customer is not expected to exceed $200 at a time, but the sale will be repeated several times within a year. Because of the widely dispersed market and low sales volume per customer, Mr. Gillespie does not feel that selling the products direct, as would be done by small custom shops, is practical. At the present time, the Belmont Tool Company distributes 90 percent of its regular output through a large industrial supply wholesaler which serves the entire area east of the Mississippi River. This wholesaler, although very large and well known, is having trouble moving cutting tools. It is losing sales of cutting tools in some cities to newer wholesalers specializing in the cutting tool industry. The new wholesalers are able to give more technical assistance to potential customers and therefore better service. The Belmont Tool wholesaler's chief executive is convinced that the newer, less experienced concerns will either realize that a substantial profit margin cannot be maintained along with their aggressive tactics, or they will eventually go broke trying to "overspecialize."

From Mr. Gillespie's standpoint, the present wholesaler is an established landmark and has served Belmont Tool well in the past. The traditional wholesaler has been of great help to Belmont Tool in holding down Belmont Tool's inventory costs by increasing the amount of inventory maintained in the 34 branch wholesale locations operated by the wholesaler. Although he has received several complaints regarding the lack of technical assistance given by the wholesaler's salesmen, Mr. Gillespie feels that the present wholesaler is providing the best service it can, and he discounts the complaints as "the usual trouble you get into from just doing business."

Mr. Gillespie feels that there are more pressing problems than a few complaints—profits are declining. Sales of the new cutting tool line are not nearly so high as anticipated, even though all indications are that the company's new products should serve the intended market perfectly. The high costs involved in the high-quality product line and the technical specialist research team, in conjunction with less than expected sales, have significantly reduced the firm's profits. Mr. Gillespie is seriously wondering whether it is wise to continue catering to the needs of specific target markets when the results are this discouraging. He also is contemplating an increase in advertising expenditures in the hope that customers will "pull" the new products through the channel.

Evaluate Belmont's strategy. What should Mr. Gillespie do now?

17
Frank
James

■ Frank James, now 55 years old, has been a salesman for over 30 years. He started selling in a department store but gave it up after 10 years to work in a lumberyard because the future looked much better in the building materials industry. After drifting from one job to another, he finally settled down and worked his way up to be the manager of a large wholesale building materials distribution warehouse in Kansas City, Kansas. In 1959, he decided to go into business for himself, selling carload lots of lumber to large retail yards in the western Missouri, eastern Kansas area.

He made arrangements to work with five large lumber mills on the West Coast. They would notify him when a carload of lumber was available to be shipped, specifying the grade, condition, and number of each size board in the shipment. Frank was not the only man representing these mills, but he was the only one in his area. He was not obligated to take any particular number of carloads per month, but once he told the mill he wanted a particular shipment, title passed to him and he had to sell it to someone. Frank's main function was to buy the lumber from the mill as it was being shipped, find a buyer, and have the railroad divert the car to the buyer.

Frank has been in this business for 15 years, so he knows all of the lumberyard buyers in his area very well and is on good working terms with them. Most of his dealings are made over the telephone from his small office, but he tries to see each of them about once a month. He has been marking up the lumber between 4 to 6 percent, the standard markup, depending on the grade, and has been able to make a good living for himself and his family.

In the last two years, however, interest rates were raised for home loans and the building boom slowed down. Frank's profits did, too, but he decided to stick it out, figuring that people still needed housing, and business would pick up again.

Six months ago, a new, aggressive salesman, much younger than Frank, set up in the same business, covering approximately the same area but representing different mills. This new salesman charged about the same prices as Frank, but would undersell him once or twice a week in order to get the sale. Many lumber buyers, knowing that they were dealing with a homogeneous product, seemed to be willing to buy from the least expensive source. This has hurt Frank financially and personally, because even some of his "old friends" are willing to buy from the new man if the price is lower. The near-term outlook seems dark, as Frank doubts if there is enough business to support two businesses like his, especially if the markup gets shaved any more.

One week ago, Frank was contacted by a Mr. White, representing the Pope and Talbott particleboard manufacturing plant. Mr. White knew that Frank was well acquainted with the building supply dealers in the area and wanted to know if he would like to be the sole distributor for Pope and Talbott in that area, selling carload lots, just as he did lumber. Mr. White gave Frank several brochures on particleboard, a product introduced about 15 years ago, describing how it can be used as a cheaper and better subflooring than the standard lumber now being used. The particleboard is also made with a wood veneer so that it can be used as paneling in homes and offices. He told Frank that the lumberyards could specify the types and grades of particleboard they wanted. Therefore, they could get exactly what they needed, unlike lumber where they choose from carloads that are already made up. Frank knew that a carload of particleboard cost about 30 percent more than a carload of lumber and that sales would be less frequent. In fact, he knew that this product has not been as well accepted in his area as in many others, because no one has done much promotion in his area. But the 20 percent average markup looks very tempting, and the particleboard market is expanding.

Frank has three choices:

1. Take Mr. White's offer and sell both products.
2. Take the offer and drop lumber sales.

3.   Stay strictly with lumber and forget the offer.

Mr. White is expecting an answer within another week, so Frank has to decide soon.
Evaluate what Frank James has been doing. What should he do now? Why?

Promotion

18
The Staffer
Corporation

■ Foster Adams helped to found Staffer Corp. of Muncie, Indiana, in 1957. At that time, "hope chest items" were purchased directly from independent factories and then sold directly to single, working girls. Hope chest items are goods purchased in anticipation of marriage and consist mainly of cookware, cedar chests, china, silverware, crystal, and cutlery.

Staffer Corp. has a retail volume of just over $1 million per year and is consistently ranked in the top 10 companies in its field, based on sales volume. Adams owns 100 percent of the corporation's stock, and all management functions are entirely under his control. Due to his firm insistence on paying cash at all times, Staffer Corp. is financially secure; yearly profits rank with the best in the industry.

In 1961, Adams founded Key Associates, Inc., which has now grown to be the largest single-office finance company in Indiana, with accounts receivable of $750,000. Key offers easy financing and competitively low interest rates to its customers. Its stock is owned solely by Adams and the managers of the Staffer Corp. Key's primary function is financing the orders of Staffer and Staffer's subcompanies.

Staffer's primary source is Regal, Inc., the largest manufacturer of cookware in the world. The other primary source is the Lane Co., Inc., from which three lines of cedar chests are purchased. Staffer ranks 11th in the world in sales of Lane chests (for comparison, Sears, Roebuck ranks 12th), and first in sales among its direct competitors.

Staffer also deals with high-prestige lines of name-brand products of crystal, silverware, and cutlery. Every Staffer product is made to specification and not sold in any stores, making Staffer the exclusive distributor. All the products are priced somewhat higher than store merchandise (but close to the prices of competing direct sales companies). This is justified by Staffer because it feels that it is offering products of substantially superior quality. It feels that stores could not sell such high-quality lines, since the typical consumer would not be willing to pay a premium price because she cannot differentiate among such products.

Selling efforts are concentrated on the single working girl who has completed at least a high school education, because she can save money for such things at this time in her life. Further, most girls and their mothers have traditionally felt that it is logical to begin "investing in the future" at this time. Sales "contacts" are often made in and around office buildings, where appointments are made for demonstrations ("displays") in the girl's home or apartment. And leads to other girls are always requested after each display.

Of the many competing companies, only a very few carry as complete a line of items as Staffer. Further, due to the competition's smaller sales volumes, they often must pay higher prices for goods of comparable quality. Nevertheless, some competitors offer stiff competition.

A survey of salesmen's records shows that competition is beginning to affect Staffer's market by selling to girls who are still in high school. Therefore, by the time the girls begin working, they have already purchased many of their hope chest items. Further, although the general market is growing in size, a growing proportion of young girls attends college rather than working. And the trend is likely to continue. Staffer is worried about this trend and is researching ways to cope with it.

The firm does not advertise but relies exclusively on personal selling and community goodwill. Staffer considers itself to be a wholesaler that buys direct from the factory, warehouses the products, and then sells the products to distributors. There are two types of "self-employed" distributors: the distributor salesmen and the subcompany distributorships.

Distributor salesmen are hired directly by Staffer within the states of Michigan, Illinois, Indiana, Kentucky, and Ohio. For them, the company supplies delivery and bookkeeping. They have no required investment and are paid a commission based on the difference between the cost and selling price of products sold.

Outside of this five-state area, subcompany distributorships are used. With this arrangement, the distributorship takes title to the goods. In the usual case, a company inquires if it may buy from Staffer. Staffer agrees, but adds that no financing is available, and recommends Key. Key agrees to finance the distributorship only if it will deal exclusively in Staffer products and if a bond to cover financial responsibility can be arranged with an insurance company. These terms are common between wholesaler and finance company throughout this industry. Staffer subcompanies presently exist in 25 states and account for approximately $500,000 annually.

Six full-time managers are employed by Staffer to supervise Staffer salesmen. These managers are paid a salary plus a commission on what their salesmen sell.

Staffer feels that price is set by competition. All competitors have similar prices, which are closely related to factory prices. All its competitors use similar markups on merchandise cost, to cover promotion and operating costs. It appears that the consumer will see higher prices in the future, as factories are beginning to raise prices due to higher material costs, notably in stainless steel. Staffer feels that it will have to raise prices, since the "limited nature of their market offers no other alternative."

Salesmen are currently selling 50 percent of all displays at an average of $224 per sale. Little improvement is believed possible. The sales volume of July and August is about equal to that of the other 10 months of the year. This is the result of mass hiring of college students for summer jobs. These students are good salesmen for Staffer, as they have friends (girls) ready to begin jobs and get married.

It has been learned through experience that for every new man recruited as a distributor salesman, about $1,000 in volume is generated. The current philosophy takes this into account and states that sales growth will come through new people.

Staffer is now focusing on hiring more full-time managers. College student salesmen are being approached as future managers. The argument is that they are making too much money not to continue full time. Some exceptional students earn $9,000 a year working during the summer and part-time during the school year. Further, competitor's managers are being offered superior fringe benefits, profit-sharing options, and other plans designed to enhance financial security.

There are several reasons for expanding the manager force. More full-time managers should be able to recruit more college students to sell for Staffer. Also, they will have more time to sell directly to girls themselves, because they will have smaller territories to cover. Further, it is hoped that managers will come to have greater familiarity with their smaller territories and will be able to achieve a deeper penetration in all markets, but especially among girls who have gone on to college.

Evaluate Staffer Corp.'s general strategy planning and in particular its current effort to hire more sales managers.

19
Brownman
Company

■ The Brownman Co. produces wire rope and cable ranging from $1/_2$ inch to 4 inches in diameter. The Chicago-based company produces and sells on a national basis. Principal users of the products are manufacturing firms employing cranes and various other overhead lifts in their operations. Ski resorts have become customers, as cables are used in the various lifts. However, the principal customers are still cement plants, railroad and boat yards, heavy equipment manufacturers, mining operations, construction companies, and steel manufacturers.

Brownman employs its own sales specialists to call on the purchasing agents of potential users. All the men are qualified engineers who go through an extensive training program covering the different applications, strengths, and other technical details concerning rope and cable. Then they are assigned a region or district, the size depending on the number of customers.

Charles Roste went to work for Brownman in 1952, immediately after receiving a civil engineering degree from Purdue University.

After going through the training program, he was assigned, along with one other representative, to the Ohio, Indiana, and Michigan region. His job was to service and give technical assistance to present customers of rope and cable. He was expected to solicit new customers when the occasion arose. But his primary duties were to: (1) supply the technical assistance needed to use rope or cable in the most efficient and safe manner, (2) handle complaints, and (3) provide evaluation reports to customers' management regarding their use of cabling.

Charles Roste became one of Brownman's most successful representatives. His exceptional ability to handle customer complaints and provide technical assistance was noted by many of the firm's customers. He also brought in a considerable amount of new business, primarily from the automobile manufacturers and ski resorts in Michigan.

Roste's success established Michigan as Brownman's largest-volume state. As a result, Michigan was designated as a separate district, and Charles Roste was assigned as the representative for the district in 1959.

Although the company's sales in Michigan have not continued to grow in the past few years, the replacement market has been steady and profitable. This fact is primarily due to the ability and reputation of Charles Roste. As one of the purchasing agents for a large automobile manufacturer mentioned, "When Charles Roste makes a recommendation regarding use of our equipment and cabling, even if it is a competitor's cable we are using, we are sure it is for the best for our company. Last week, for example, a cable of one of his competitors broke and we were going to give him a contract. He told us it was not a defective cable that caused the break, but rather the way we were using it. He told us how it should be used and what we needed to do to correct our operation. We took his advice and gave him the contract as well!"

Four years ago, Brownman introduced an expensive wire sling device for holding cable groupings together. The sling makes operations around the cable much safer and its use could reduce hospital and lost-time costs due to accidents. The profit margin for the sling is high, and Brownman urged all its representatives to push the sling.

The only man to sell the sling with any success has been Charles Roste. Eighty percent of his customers are currently using the wire sling. In other areas, sling sales are negligible.

As a result of his success, Brownman is now considering forming a separate department for sling sales and putting Charles Roste in charge. His duties would include traveling to the various sales districts and training other representatives in how to sell the sling. The Michigan district would be represented by a new man.

The question confronting Brownman management is: Should they gamble on losing profitable customers in Michigan in hopes that sling sales will increase?

What would you advise? Why?

**20
Whiteside
Furniture
Company**

■ Mrs. Ann Alden has been operating the Whiteside Furniture Co. for ten years and has slowly built the sales to $300,000 a year. Her store is located in the downtown shopping area of a city of 150,000 population. This is basically a factory town, and she has deliberately selected "blue-collar" workers as her target market. She carries some higher-priced furniture lines, but places great emphasis on budget combinations and stresses easy credit terms.

Mrs. Alden is most concerned because she feels she has reached the limit of her sales potential; at least it would seem that way because sales have not been increasing during the last two years. Her newspaper advertising seems to attract her target customers, but many of these people come in, shop around, and then leave. Some of them come back, but the majority do not. She feels her product selections are very suitable for her target market and is concerned that her sales personnel do not close more sales with potential customers. She has discussed this matter several times with her sales personnel. They respond that they feel they ought to treat all customers alike, the way they personally would want to be treated—that is, they feel their role is merely to answer questions when asked, and not to make suggestions or help customers arrive at their selections. They feel that this would be too high-pressure.

Mrs. Alden feels her sales personnel's attitudes are interpreted

Table 1

In shopping for furniture I found (find) that:	Demographic groups				Marital status	
	Group A	Group B	Group C	Group D	Newlyweds	Married 3–10 Yrs.
I looked at furniture in many stores before I made a purchase	78%	57%	52%	50%	66%	71%
I went (am going) to only one store and bought (buy) what I found (find) there	2	9	10	11	9	12
To make my purchase I went (am going) back to one of the stores I shopped in previously	48	45	39	34	51	49
I looked (am looking) at furniture in no more than three stores and made (will make) my purchase in one of these	20	25	24	45	37	30
No answer	10	18	27	27	6	4

Source: *The New Consumer: Cautious or Confident?* Report #2, 1963, conducted for Kroehler Mfg. Co. by the Institute for Motivational Research.

Table 2
The sample design

Demographic status

Upper class (Group A) 13% of sample
This group consisted of managers, proprietors, or executives of large businesses. Professionals, including doctors, lawyers, engineers, college professors and school administrators, research personnel. Sales personnel, including managers, executives, and upper-income sales people above level of clerks.
Family income over $10,000
Middle class (Group B) 37% of sample
Group B consists of white-collar workers including clerical, secretarial, sales clerks, bookkeepers, etc.
It also includes school teachers, social workers, semiprofessionals, proprietors or managers of small businesses; industrial foremen and other supervisory personnel.
Family income between $5,000 and $10,000
Lower middle class (Group C) 36% of sample
Skilled workers and semiskilled technicians were in this category along with custodians, elevator operators, telephone linemen, factory operatives, construction workers, and some domestic and personal service employees.
Family income between $5,000 and $10,000
No one in this group had above a high school education
Lower class (Group D) 14% of sample
Nonskilled employees, day laborers. It also includes some factory operatives, domestic and service people.
Family income under $5,000
None had completed high school; some had only grade school education

as indifference by the customers who are attracted to the store by her advertising. She feels that customers must be treated on an individual basis—and that some customers need more encouragement and suggestion than others. Moreover, she feels that some customers will actually appreciate more help and suggestion than the salespeople themselves might. In support of her opinion, she showed her salesmen the data from a study about furniture store customers (Tables 1 and 2). She tried to explain to them about the differences in demographic groups and pointed out that her store was definitely trying to cater to specific groups. She argued that they (the salesmen) really had different attitudes than their target customers and that as a result, the salesmen ought to cater to the needs and desires of their customers and think less about how they would like to be treated.

Evaluate Mrs. Alden's thinking and suggest implications for her promotion.

Price

**21
Acme
Bending
Company**

■ Acme Bending Co., located in Minneapolis, Minnesota, is a custom producer of industrial wire products. The company had had a great deal of varied experience bending wire into many shapes, and also has the facilities to chrome- or gold-plate finished products.

The company was started 10 years ago, and has slowly built its sales volume to $1 million a year. Just one year ago, Robert Thomas was appointed sales manager of the consumer products division. It was his responsibility to develop this division as a producer and marketer of the company's own branded products, as distinguished from custom orders which the industrial division produces for others.

Mr. Thomas has been working on a number of different product ideas for almost a year now, and has developed several unique designs for letter holders, flowerpot holders, key and pencil holders, and other novelties. His most promising product is a letter holder in the shape of a dog. It is very similar to one which the industrial division produced for a number of years for another company. In fact, it was experience with the seemingly amazing sales volume of this product which interested the company in the consumer market and led to the development of the consumer products division.

Mr. Thomas has sold hundreds of units of his various products to local chain stores and wholesalers on a trial basis, but each time the price has been negotiated and no firm policy has been established. Now he is faced with the decision of what price to set on the dog-shaped letter holder which he plans to push aggressively wherever he can. Actually, he has not yet decided on exactly which channels of distribution he will use, but the trials in the local area have been encouraging, and, as noted above, the experience in the industrial division suggests that there is a large market for the product.

The manufacturing cost on this product is approximately 10 cents if it is painted black and 20 cents if it is chromed or gold-plated. Similar products have been selling at retail in the 75 cents to $2.50 range. The sales and administrative overhead to be charged to the division would amount to $25,000 a year. This would include Mr. Thomas' salary and some office expenses. It is expected that a number of other products will be developed in the near future, but for the coming year it is hoped that this letter holder will account for about half the consumer products division's sales volume.

Evaluate Mr. Thomas' marketing strategy. What price should he set?

22
Quik-Prints
Photo-
finishing
Corporation

■ Organized in 1948, the Quik-Prints Photofinishing Corp. soon became one of the four major Colorado-based photofinishers, each with annual sales of about $2.5 million.

Quik-Prints was established by three men who had had considerable experience in the photofinishing industry, working in Kodak's photofinishing division in Rochester, New York. Quik-Prints started in a small rented warehouse in Boulder, Colorado. Today it has seven company-owned plants in five cities in Colorado and western Kansas. The two color processing plants are located in Boulder and Hays, Kansas. Black-and-white processing plants are located in Boulder and Hays, as well as Pueblo, Denver, and Colorado Springs, Colorado.

Table 3

Type of business	Percent of dollar volume
Sales to retail outlets	80
Direct-mail sales	17
Retail walk-in sales	3
	100

Quik-Prints does all of its own processing of black-and-white films, slides, prints, and motion pictures. While they do own color processing capability, Quik-Prints has found it less costly to have most color film processed by the regional Kodak processing plant. The majority of color film sold today is Kodachrome, and Kodachrome processing is sufficiently complicated so that the cost of equipment to do the work is prohibitive for Quik-Prints. The color film processed by Quik-Prints is of the "off-brand" variety or is special work done for professional photographers. Despite this limitation in color finishing, Quik-Prints has always given its customers fast, quality service. All pictures, including those processed by Kodak, can be returned within three days of receipt by Quik-Prints.

Quik-Prints was established originally as a wholesale photofinisher, and later developed its own processing plants in an effort to achieve a greater profit margin. Its customers are drugstores, camera stores, department stores, photographic studios, and any other retail outlets where photofinishing is offered to consumers. These retailers insert film rolls, cartridges, negatives, and so on, into separate bags, marking on the outside the kind of work to be done. The customer is handed a receipt, but seldom sees the bag into which his film has been placed. The bag has the retailer's name on it, not Quik-Prints'.

Each processing plant is fronted by a small retail outlet for drop-in customers who live in the immediate vicinity of the plant. This is a minor part of Quik-Prints' business.

The company is also engaged in direct-mail photofinishing within the state of Colorado. Each processing plant in Colorado is capable of receiving direct-mail orders from consumers. All film received is handled in the same way as the other retail business.

A breakdown of the dollar volume by type of business is shown in Table 3.

All processing is priced at the level established by local competition. Quik-Prints establishes a retail list price, and each retailer then is offered a trade discount based on the volume of business he generates for Quik-Prints. The pricing schedule used by each of the major competitors in the Colorado-Kansas market is shown in Table 4. All direct-mail processing for final consumers is priced at the $33\frac{1}{3}$ percent discount off retail price, but this is done under a

Table 4

Monthly dollar volume (12-month average)	Discount (2/10 e.o.m.)
$ 0–$ 100	33⅓%
$ 101–$ 500	40 %
$ 501–$1000	45 %
$1,001–above	50 %

disguised name so that retailer customers are not antagonized. Retail walk-in accounts are charged the full list price for all services performed.

Retail stores offering photofinishing are served by Quik-Prints' own sales force. Each processing plant has at least three men servicing accounts. Primarily, their duties include daily visits to all accounts to pick up and deliver all photofinishing work. These salesmen also make daily trips to the Greyhound bus terminal nearby to pick up and drop off color film that is being processed by Kodak. Since the consumer does not come in contact with Quik-Prints, the firm has not found it necessary to advertise its retail business. To reach business firms, Quik-Prints has provided a listing in the Yellow Pages of all telephone books in cities and towns served by its seven plants. In addition, salesmen offer some photographic equipment to retail customers for resale. But, this business is seen only as a service and does not really generate much profit. There has been no attempt at making the consumer aware of Quik-Prints' service, since all consumers are served through retail stores.

The direct-mail portion of Quik-Prints' business is generated by regular advertisements in the Sunday pictorial sections of newspapers servicing Pueblo, Denver, Colorado Springs, and Boulder. These advertisements usually stress the low-price service, two-week turn-around, and fine quality. Quick-Prints does not use its own name for these markets. Mailers are provided for the consumer to send in to the plant being utilized. Some people in the company felt this part of the business might have great potential if pursued more aggressively.

Recently, the president of Quik-Prints, Mr. Humma, has become worried over the loss of several retail accounts in the $500–$1,000 discount range. He has been with the company since its beginning and has always stressed quality and rapid delivery of the finished product. Demanding that all plants produce the finest-quality reproductions, Mr. Humma personally conducts periodic quality tests of each plant through its direct-mail service. Plant managers are called on the carpet for any slips in quality. In order to find out what is causing the loss in retail accounts, Mr. Humma has been reviewing salesmen's reports and talking to various employees.

In their weekly reports, Quik-Prints' salesmen have reported a possible trend toward higher trade discounts being offered to retailer customers. Insty-Film, a competitor of equal size that offers the same services as Quik-Prints, is offering an additional 5 percent discount in each sales volume category. This price differential really makes a difference at some stores, because these retailers feel that all the major processors can do an equally good job. Further, they note, consumers apparently feel that the quality is acceptable, because there have been no complaints so far.

Quik-Prints has encountered price cutting before, but never by an equally well-established company. Mr. Humma cannot understand why these retailer customers would leave Quik-Prints, because it is offering higher quality and the price difference is not that large. He is considering a direct-mail and newspaper campaign to consumers to persuade them to demand Quik-Prints' quality service from their favorite retailer. Mr. Humma feels that consumers demanding quality will force retailers to stay with or return to Quik-Prints. He says: "If we can't get the business by convincing the retailer of our fine quality, we'll get it by convincing the consumer."

Evaluate Quik-Prints' strategies and Mr. Humma's present thinking. What would you do?

23
The Stran
Manu-
facturing
Company

■ The Stran Manufacturing Co. of Los Angeles, California, is a leading manufacturer in the wire machinery industry. It has patents covering over 200 machine variations, but it is rare for Stran's customers to buy more than 30 different types in a year. Its machines are sold to wire and small-tubing manufacturers when they are increasing production capacity or replacing outdated equipment.

Established in 1865, the company has enjoyed a steady growth to its present position with annual sales of $27 million.

About ten firms compete in the wire machinery market. Each is about the same size and manufactures basically similar machinery. Each of the competitors has tended to specialize in its own geographic area. Five of the competitors are in the East, three in the Midwest, and two, including Stran, on the West Coast. All of the competitors offer similar prices and sell F.O.B. their factories. Demand has been fairly strong in recent years, and as a result, all of the competitors have been satisfied to sell in their geographic areas and avoid price cutting. In fact, there is an adversion to price cutting because about 20 years ago one firm tried to win additional business and found that others immediately met the price cut but industry sales (in units) did not increase at all. Within a few years prices had returned to their earlier level, and since then, competition has tended to focus on promotion.

Stran's promotion has depended largely on company salesmen who cover the West Coast. These men usually are supported by sales engineers when the company is close to making a sale. Some advertising is run in trade journals, and direct mailings are used occasionally, but the primary promotion emphasis is on personal selling. Personal contact outside of the West Coast market, however, is through manufacturers' agents.

Andrew Lunter, president of Stran Manufacturing Co., is not satisfied with the present situation. Industry sales have begun to level off and so have Stran's sales, although Stran has continued to hold its share of the market. He would like to find a way to compete more effectively in the other regions, because he is coming to see that there is great potential outside of the West Coast if he can only find a better way of reaching it.

Stran has been acknowledged by competitors and buyers as one of the top-quality producers in the industry. Its machines have generally been somewhat superior to others in terms of reliability, durability, and productive capacity. The difference, however, has not been great enough to justify a higher price because the others are able to do the necessary job. In short, if a buyer had a choice between Stran's and another's machines at the same price, Stran would probably get the business. But it seems clear that Stran's price must be at least competitive.

The average wire machine sold by Stran (or any of the competitors) sells for about $115,000, F.O.B. shipping point. Shipping costs within any of the three major regions averages about $1,500, but then another $1,000 must be added on shipments from the West Coast to the Midwest (either way) and another $1,000 from the Midwest to the East.

Mr. Lunter is considering the possibility of expanding his market by being willing to absorb the extra freight costs which would be incurred if a midwestern or eastern customer were to buy from his West Coast location. In other words, he would absorb the additional $1,000–$2,000 in transportation costs. By so doing, he would not be cutting price in those markets, but rather reducing his net return. He felt that his competitors would not see this as price competition and therefore would not resort to cutting prices themselves. Further, he felt that such a move would be legal, because all the customers in each major region would be offered the same price.

The sales manager, Bernard Chelps, felt that the proposed freight absorption plan might actually stimulate price competition in the midwestern and eastern markets and perhaps on the West Coast. He proposed instead, that Stran hire some salesmen to work the midwestern and eastern markets, rather than relying on the manufacturers' agents. He felt that an additional three salesmen would not increase costs too much and could greatly increase the sales from these markets over that brought in by the agents. With this plan, there would be no need to absorb the freight, and therefore there would be no need to gamble on disrupting the status quo with respect to competitive methods. He felt this latter matter was especially important, because competition in the Midwest and East was somewhat "hotter" than on the West Coast because of the number of competitors in these regions. The situation had been rather quiet in the West, because only two firms were sharing this market.

Mr. Lunter agreed that Mr. Chelps had a point, but in view of the leveling off of industry sales, he felt that competitive situations might change drastically in the near future and that he would rather be a leader in anything that was likely to happen rather than a follower. He was impressed with Mr. Chelps's comments regarding the greater competitiveness in the other markets, however, and therefore was unsure about what should be done, if anything.

Evaluate Stran's strategy planning in the light of its market situation, and explain what it should do now.

Marketing management

■ The Waterside Canning Co. is a well-established manufacturer in the highly seasonal vegetable canning industry. It packs and sells canned beans, peas, carrots, corn, peas and carrots mixed, and kidney beans. Sales are made primarily through food brokers to merchant wholesalers, supermarket chains (such as Kroger, Safeway, A&P, Jewel, etc.), cooperatives, and other outlets, mostly in the Chicago area. Of secondary importance, by volume, are sales in the immediate local market to institutions, grocery stores, and supermarkets, and sales of dented canned goods to "walk-in" customers at low prices.

Waterside is the second largest vegetable canner in the Devil's River Valley area of Wisconsin, with sales in excess of $10 million annually (exact sales data is not published by the closely held corporation). Plants are located in Riverside, Portertown, and Williamston, Wisconsin, and Clearview, Minnesota, with main offices in Riverside. The Waterside brand is used only on canned goods sold in the immediate local market; in most other cases, the goods are sold and shipped under the retailer's label, or the broker's/wholesaler's label.

Operating since 1905, Waterside has established an excellent reputation over the years for the consistent quality of its total product offering. And it is always willing to offer competitive prices. Strong channel rapport was built by Waterside's chairman of the board and chief executive officer, H. E. Edwards. Mr. Edwards, who owns controlling interest in the firm, had "worked" the Chicago area as an aggressive company salesman in the firm's earlier years before he took over from his father as president in 1931. He was an ambitious and hardworking executive, active in community affairs, and the firm prospered under his direction. He became well known within the canned food processing industry for technical/product innovations, and during World War II was appointed to a position in Washington, D.C., on the Board which formulated wartime food rationing policies.

During the "off-canning" season, Mr. Edwards traveled extensively. In connection with his travels, he arranged several significant business deals. His 1968 and 1970 trips culminated in the following two events: (1) inexpensive pineapple was imported from Formosa and marketed in the central United States through the Waterside Canning Co., primarily to expand the product line; (2) a technically advanced continuous process cooker (65-feet high) was imported from England and installed at the Riverside plant in February/March 1972. It was the first of its kind in the United States and cut process time sharply.

Mr. Edwards retired in 1972 and named his son-in-law, the 35-year-old Mr. Evans, as his successor. Mr. Evans is intelligent and hard-working. As a member of the firm, he had been engaged primarily with financial matters, but more recently with marketing problems. During his seven-year tenure as financial director, the firm had received its highest credit rating ever and was able to borrow working capital ($3 million to meet seasonal seed, fertilizer, can stockage, and wage requirements) at the lowest rate ever received by the company.

The fact that the firm isn't unionized allows some competitive advantage. However, minimum wage law changes have increased costs. And these and other rising costs have caused profit margins to narrow. The narrowed profit margins prompted the recent closing of the Williamston plant and then the Portertown plant, as they became comparatively less efficient to operate. The remaining two plants were considerably expanded in capacity (especially warehouse facilities), so that they could operate more profitably due to maximum use of existing processing equipment.

Shortly after Mr. Edward's retirement, Mr. Evans reviewed the company's current situation with his executives. He pointed out narrowing profit margins, debts contracted for new plant and equipment, and an increasingly competitive environment. Even considering the temporary laborsaving competitive advantage of the new cooker system, there seemed to be no way to improve the "status quo" unless the firm could sell direct, as they do in the local market, absorbing the food brokers' 5 percent commission on sales. This was the plan of action decided upon, and Mr. Burns was directed to test the new method for six months.

Mr. Burns is the only full-time salesman of the firm. Other top executives do some selling, but not much. Being a relative of Mr. Edwards', Burns is also a member of the board of directors. He is especially competent in technical matters as he has a college degree in food chemistry. Although Mr. Burns formerly did call on some important customers with the brokers' salesmen, he is not well known in the industry or even by Waterside's usual customers.

Five months later, after Mr. Burns has made several selling trips and hundreds of telephone calls, he is unwilling to continue sales efforts on his own. He is insisting that a sales staff be formed if the current operation is to continue. Orders are falling off in comparison to both expectations and the previous year's operating results. And sales of the new pineapple products are practically nil. Even in normal channels, Mr. Burns sensed a reluctance to buy, though basic consumer demand had not changed. Further, some potential customers have demanded quantity guarantees considerably larger than the firm can supply. Expanding supply would be difficult in the short run because the firm typically must contract with farmers for production acreage, to assure supplies of the type and quality they normally offer. The only success the new plan has had is in a territory where Waterside's regular broker recently retired.

Mr. Edwards, still the controlling stockholder, has scheduled a meeting in two weeks to discuss the status of Waterside's current operations.

Evaluate Mr. Evans' strategy planning. What should he tell Mr. Edwards? What should be done next?

25
Jiffy Johns, Incorporated

■ Jiffy Johns, Inc., is a well-established family-owned and -operated company specializing in the rental of portable toilet facilities in the southern part of Florida. The portable toilets, called Jiffy Johns, are made of aluminum in the traditional outhouse design. They are made by an aluminum siding company in Tampa at a cost of $140 per unit. The toilet uses a chemical solvent to reduce odors and inhibit bacterial growth. This solvent must be changed regularly, and this is part of the service offered by Jiffy Johns, Inc.

The management of Jiffy Johns established the business 20 years ago, after an analysis of the service requirements of construction firms in southern Florida. In addition to portable toilets, Jiffy Johns soon discovered that some construction firms also required on-the-site construction offices, tool sheds, and minijohns which could be raised by cranes to upper levels of multistory buildings. These products were added to the line as needed, and are easily constructed in Jiffy Johns' own warehouse.

The company's facilities consist of the warehouse and an office, both in Pompano Beach. They also have three custom-equipped tank trucks and several smaller trucks and trailers for pickup and delivery. The tank trucks are used on regular service routes to pump dry and refill with fresh chemicals each portable toilet every two or three days. At the present time, they service about 600 Jiffy Johns. Further, about 50 portable offices and tool sheds have been placed at various sites in southern Florida. The toilets rent for $40 per month, and the portable offices for $55 per month. Since there are some savings when many units are serviced at one stop, price discounts are given depending on how many units are used at a particular site.

The business has grown rapidly in recent years because more local health ordinances are requiring toilet facilities on construction sites. Some further sales growth can probably be expected for this reason, although the business naturally fluctuates depending on the activity in the construction industry.

The majority of the firm's customers seem to be well pleased with its service, and management cannot think of any way to improve the service to its present customers. Naturally, the company is always willing to provide the same service to new customers, and it carries on a regular promotion effort to this end. This effort has been concentrated on building contractors through trade journals and direct mailing. In addition, all units have large signs on both sides with the name Jiffy Johns and the local phone number. Because of the appearance of Jiffy Johns on so many construction sites, the company regularly receives inquiries from contractors and construction companies. The name Jiffy Johns has become so common in contracting circles, that even competing firms' products have been referred to as "Jiffy Johns." In fact, when informed of the true nature of the business, one caller replied: "I thought you must be the largest contractor in Florida."

The company has one full-time salesman, and the general manager also spends a portion of his time generating new accounts. However, because Jiffy Johns, Inc., is so well known, much of the business is conducted over the phone with people who are using or have used Jiffy Johns.

The company has several small competitors, but they offer the old-fashioned wooden outhouses. One small company, however, has entered recently with fiberglass units. Each of these competitors is much smaller than Jiffy Johns, Inc., and regularly tries to offer lower prices to take some of the company's business. Jiffy Johns has never met this price competition and has seldom lost any accounts for this reason. Generally, the company is well known for its dependable service, and some contractors even seem to enjoy making humorous references to their Jiffy Johns.

The Jiffy Johns management is now considering expanding into northern Florida and perhaps later to the Bahamas. Entry into the northern Florida market would be with approximately similar plant and equipment. A proposed warehouse in Jacksonville is expected to be able to handle another 600 Jiffy Johns and 50 portable offices, and a similar fleet of tank and delivery trucks will be needed for the service work.

The company's long-run goal is to dominate the northern market with a quality product-service package as it has done in the south. Although the Jiffy Johns name is not known in northern Florida, management hopes to be able to establish its name fairly quickly because there are no well-recognized competitors in the north. There are many small competitors currently offering this service, however. Most offer portable wooden outhouses similar to some of Jiffy Johns' competitors in the south. The general price level is lower, by about $5 to $10 a month for the portable toilet. Portable offices are generally not available from the present competitors. The lower price level seems to have been due to several rounds of price cutting in recent years, as some firms have resorted to this competitive tool in order to stay in business. Some of these firms have not been able to meet costs when prices were cut to the $30-a-month level and have gone out of business. But there still seem to be many other small competitors willing to offer their current services at these lower prices. The primary emphasis has been on low price, rather than offering better quality toilets, such as Jiffy Johns.

On the whole, new construction has not grown as fast in northern Florida as in the southern part of the state, but Jiffy Johns management expects that the passage of many more local health ordinances will have the same affect on the market as it did in the southern part of the state. Therefore, they hope that with a transfer of their know-how to this new market they will come to dominate this northern market just as they have done in the south. And if all goes well, they will move on to the Bahamas in maybe a year or two.

Evaluate Jiffy Johns, Inc.'s strategic planning for the southern market and then discuss whether it is likely to be successful in the northern market.

26
Mack Plastics
Company

■ Bob McMahon is currently employed as a sales representative for a plastics goods manufacturer. He calls primarily on large industrial accounts, such as refrigerator manufacturers, who might need large quantities of custom-made products. He is on a straight salary of $12,000 per year, plus expenses and a company car. He expects some salary increases but does not see a great long-run opportunity with this company. As a result, he is seriously considering changing jobs and investing $10,000 in the Mack Plastics Co., an established midwestern thermoplastic molder and manufacturer. Harry Mack, the present owner is nearing retirement age and has not developed anyone to run the business for him. He has agreed to sell the business to John O'Gorman, a lawyer-entrepreneur, who has invited Bob McMahon to invest and become the sales manager. Mr. O'Gorman has agreed to give Bob McMahon his current salary plus expenses, plus a bonus of 1 percent of profits. However, Bob must invest to become part of the new company. He will obtain a 5 percent interest in the business for his $10,000 investment.

The Mack Plastics Co. is well established and last year had sales of $1.5 million, but no profits. In terms of sales, cost of materials was 46 percent; direct labor, 13 percent; indirect factory labor, 15 percent; factory overhead, 13 percent; and sales overhead and general expenses, 13 percent. The company has not been making any profit for several years but has been continually adding new machines to replace those made obsolete by technological developments. The machinery is well maintained and modern, but most of it is similar to that owned by competitors. Most of the machines of the industry are standard. Special products are then made by using dies in conjunction with these machines.

Sales historically have been approximately two thirds custom-molded products (that is, made to order for other producers or merchandising concerns) and the balance proprietary items, such as housewares, and game items, such as poker chips and cribbage sets. The housewares are copies of articles initiated by others and indicate neither originality nor style. Harry Mack is in charge of the proprietary items distributed through any available wholesale channels. The custom-molded products are sold through three full-time sales engineers who receive a 5 percent commission on sales up to $10,000 and then 3 percent above that level, as well as three independent representatives working part time on a similar commission plan.

Financially, the company seems to be in fairly good condition, at least as far as book value is concerned, as the $10,000 investment would buy approximately $30,000 in assets.

Mr. O'Gorman feels that, with new management, the company offers great opportunity for profit. He expects to make some economies in the production process and hold custom-molding sales to approximately the present $1 million level. The other major expectation is that he will be able to develop the proprietary line from a sales volume of about $500,000 to $2 million a year. Bob McMahon is expected to be a real asset here because of his sales experience. This will bring the firm up to about capacity level, but of course it will entail adding additional employees. The major advantage of expanding sales would be spreading overhead. Some of the products proposed by the lawyer for the expansion of the proprietary line are listed below.

New Products for Consideration

Women's tool kit — molded housewares
Six-bottle soft drink case
Laminating printed film on housewares — molded
Short legs for furniture — molded $0.5 million minimum market
Home storage box for milk bottles $0.5 million minimum market
Step-on garbage can without liner
Importing and distributing foreign housewares
Black-nylon-handled table utensils
Extruded and embossed or formed wall coverings
Extruded and formed wall decorations — nursery rhyme figures, etc.
Formed butyrate outside house shutters
Formed inside shutters in lieu of venetian blinds
School and toy blackboards
Translucent bird houses
Formed holder for vacuum cleaner attachments
Formed household door liners
Formed "train terrain" table topography for model trains
Formed skylights
Perforated extruded sheet for industrial sale as grilles
Formed drawers for housewares sale with supports for under-furniture
    storage
Formed drawers for industrial sales
Formed children's furniture, including chest of formed drawers and metal
    angles
Extruded corrugated butyrate sheet for outdoor patio and storage covers
Extruded corrugated translucent styrene sheet for indoor room dividers
Formed restaurant tray, with surface grain
Formed lap board for studying, serving
Formed washboard
Extruded and formed traffic and street signs

There is a great deal of competition in these markets, and most retailers expect a wide margin, sometimes 40 to 50 percent, but even so, manufacturing costs are such that there is some room for promotion while still keeping the price competitive. Apparently many customers are willing to pay for the novelty of new products.

How would you advise Bob McMahon? Explain your reasoning.

27
The Perlick
Company

■ The Perlick Co., of Milwaukee, Wisconsin, has been in business for 50 years, manufacturing a line of brass and copper fittings used in the production and dispensing of beer. The product line consists of valves, casings, and connectors used in breweries, as well as tapping equipment used in taverns and restaurants. Their products are sold by several of their own salesmen, who call directly on breweries, taverns, and restaurants.

Several years ago, the salesmen reported an opportunity to offer better-quality refrigeration equipment for chilling bottled and tap beer in restaurants and taverns. Following some preliminary market and engineering research, the company decided to expand its product line in this direction. It set up a "Cabinet Division" to manufacture a high-quality line of all-metal beer coolers and glass chillers. The company offered four different sizes of refrigerator cabinets, but all were basically the same style and color (black).

The same salesmen who were selling the other Perlick products had considerable success selling the new products to current customers. The salesmen had correctly seen that some of their customers' equipment had depreciated to the point where they would be very interested in new equipment. The salesmen also received some business from those setting up new establishments. But this business was more difficult to obtain because the salesmen traveled widely and were not always aware when and where new businesses were being organized. Some inquiries came to them from small ads which were placed in trade magazines appealing to restaurant and tavern operators. All such inquiries were followed up immediately by the salesmen, and the high quality of Perlick's product helped close many sales.

The cabinets were well designed from an engineering standpoint and technically superior to similar products available from competitors. (In particular, they were built more solidly. It was expected that they would outlast competitive products by four to six years. They also chilled beer faster, were more compact, and had a longer lasting finish). This higher quality enabled the cabinets to be sold for 10 to 15 percent more than competitors' products; prices ranged from $300 for the smallest size cooler to $2,400 for the largest unit.

Perlick enjoyed considerable prosperity for the first two years, since production was easily standardized on the four sizes it was producing. Further, Perlick was concentrating its sales effort in the upper Midwest to keep its selling costs low – 90 percent of sales were made in Wisconsin, Illinois, Indiana, and Michigan. This also had the effect of reducing customers' delivered costs, because typically customers paid transportation costs from the factory. Most of Perlick's competitors sold on a nationwide basis, and many were located in other parts of the country.

Some units were sold by Perlick outside its normal selling area. These orders came in response to the small ads which were placed in leading trade magazines. The salesmen did not follow up these inquiries personally, but occasionally the telephone was used to handle closing details.

Two years after Perlick entered this business, its sales began to slip. Competitors began offering a wider variety of styles, colors, and sizes to suit the tavern and restaurant owners. Competitors' cabinets became available in black, white, blue, grey, and brown. Up to 15 different sizes were offered to meet customers' space limitations. Formica and plastic finishes were offered to supplement the metal exteriors already available. Perlick countered these offerings by extending a 10-year guarantee on the refrigeration unit, in addition to the free installation and service already provided. Sales failed to increase, however, and the sales manager recommended that the company meet the demands of customers.

The production manager maintained, however, that increasing variety in the product line would greatly increase cost. Perlick was currently producing 15 cabinets per working day, after reaching a high of 20 cabinets a day before the sales decline. The production manager estimated that if the product line were expanded as the sales manager recommended, the company would have to produce and sell an average of 45 cabinets per day to hold down its costs, while keeping quality constant.

The production manager felt that the sales manager should expand his market coverage, and perhaps also should find distributors in the present territories who could provide continuing representation, thereby supplementing the efforts of the salesmen. Basically, he felt that Perlick had developed an efficient production system, and a relatively small increase in sales would enable the company to continue profitably with its present operation. He estimated that a doubling in capital investment would be required to expand to the higher volume. This was risky, and he felt that more attention should be paid to expanding sales of the present line rather than investing in more plant and equipment to offer a wider line and greater variety.

The sales manager, on the other hand, claimed that Perlick had to remain competitive in the marketplace or the sales decline would continue. He felt that simply expanding the territory would only add to cost and not result in a significant improvement in sales. Further, he noted that the company's financial condition was good. It had the resources to increase production as he recommended, and he felt that now was the time to take action. He wanted to go on the offensive rather than wait to see what happened. Specifically, he wanted permission to expand the sales force to develop a nationwide selling program and generate the sales which would keep the expanded production facilities going. To begin with, he wanted the addition of three more salesmen and the company's commitment to expand the product line. Otherwise, he felt the morale of the salesmen would continue to decline and conditions would continue to deteriorate.

Evaluate the present situation and explain what Perlick should do.

Indexes

Index
of
names

Index of names

Index
of
subjects

This book has been set in 9 point and 8 point Primer leaded 1 point. Part numbers are set in 18 point and titles in 24 point Bookman; chapter numbers are set in 11 point and titles in 24 point Bookman. The size of the type page is 31 x 49²/₃ picas.

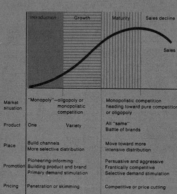

	Introduction	Growth	Maturity	Sales decline
Market situation	"Monopoly"—oligopoly or monopolistic competition		Monopolistic competition heading toward pure competition or oligopoly	
Product	One	Variety	All "same" Battle of brands	
Place	Build channels More selective distribution		Move toward more intensive distribution	
Promotion	Pioneering-informing Building product and brand Primary demand stimulation		Persuasive and aggressive Frantically competitive Selective demand stimulation	
Pricing	Penetration or skimming		Competitive or price cutting	

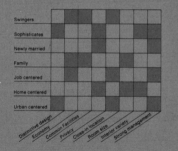

Good marketing strategy pla **may call for a promotion bler** **of personal selling and adver** **(see page 398).**